CHECKLIST FOR ESSAY REVISION

1. *Content (ideas)* Does the essay have a main idea? Are all the ideas sound and fully thought out?

2. *Purposes (primary, secondary, etc.)* Does the essay have a clear primary purpose? What other purposes does it achieve?

3. *Structure (organization and form)* Is there a conscious structure to the essay? What is the organizational pattern? Would an alternative pattern be stronger?

4. *Correctness (grammar and mechanics)* Do all sentences have subjects and verbs and express complete thoughts? Has the essay been proofread for items such as word endings and punctuation?

5. *Effect (style and voice)* Are sentences clear? Forceful when necessary? Is the level of language appropriate?

OTHER CHECKLISTS

Writing Invention Form and Style

LEONARD A. PODIS
Oberlin College
JOANNE M. PODIS
Dyke College

Scott, Foresman and Company
Glenview, Illinois
Dallas, Tex.   Oakland, N.J.   Palo Alto, Calif.
Tucker, Ga.   London, England

Library of Congress Cataloging in Publication Data

Podis, Leonard A.
    Writing : invention, form, and style.

    Includes index.
    1. English language—Rhetoric.   I. Podis, JoAnne M.
II. Title.
PE1408.P62   1983   808'.042   83–16470
ISBN 0–673–15525–0

Credits:
p. xvi: Lionel Delevingne/Picture Group
p. 14: Herb Levart/Photo Researchers
p. 36: Peter Menzel/Stock, Boston
p. 58: Nicholas Sapieha/Stock, Boston
p. 104: Tom Hollyman/Photo Researchers
p. 143: © 1982, Los Angeles Times Syndicate. Reprinted with permission.
p. 152: Scott, Foresman
p. 194: Jean-Claude Lejeune
p. 226: David A. Krathwohl/Stock, Boston
p. 262: Scott, Foresman
p. 282: Courtesy of Volkswagen of America
p. 283: Courtesy of Alfa Romeo
p. 284: Clemens Kalischer/Image Photos
p. 322: © Joel Gordon
p. 346: Clemens Kalischer/Image Photos
p. 396: Scott, Foresman
p. 432: Stuart Rosner/Stock, Boston

Literary acknowledgments begin on page 553.

PREFACE

In the last decade, a renaissance of interest and innovation in the teaching of composition has taken place. Various reasons for this renewal have been suggested, among them the literacy crisis, the call for "back-to-basics," and the diversification of the student population to include large numbers of nontraditional students.

Whatever the reasons, the result has been a major shift in approach to the teaching of writing. The traditional emphasis on the study of finished pieces of writing has given way to an exploration of the process of composing. This increased emphasis on the teaching of writing as a process has expanded the teacher's role. Composition teachers now see themselves as more than leaders of class discussions of professional writing and graders of student papers. They are coaches and guides, leading their students through the process of inventing, drafting, and revising.

Writing: Invention, Form, and Style is designed to reflect this change in approach to the teaching of writing while still retaining the best features of the product-centered approach. We believe that a sound knowledge of the qualities of effective composition undergirds and, to an extent, directs the process of writing. Thus, in this text we combine attention to the written product with attention to the writing process.

Emphasis on the Composing Process

This book reflects some of the most recent theories about the composing process. The emphasis on process is strongest in the Introduction, which gives an overview of the writing process; in Chapter 1, which treats purpose, audience, and the rhetorical situation; and in Chapter 2, which discusses how to find and generate ideas. The process approach is also evident elsewhere in the book—for example, in the treatment of revision as a form of invention (Chapter 3), the discussion of the jotted outline as a flexible tool in planning (Chapter 5), and the numerous rhetorically based, problem-solving suggestions for writing (throughout).

Emphasis on the Written Product

At the same time, *Writing: Invention, Form, and Style* retains the strongest aspects of the product-centered approach. Chapters 3 through 6 offer a close study of the forms of writing—sentence, paragraph, and essay— and Chapter 4 also explores the traditional patterns of exposition. An emphasis on the qualities of logical argument is woven into Chapters 1 and 4; the Appendix focuses on argumentative fallacies. Finally, the product-centered approach is reflected in the numerous, annotated prose models throughout the text.

Emphasis on Student Writing

Not only does *Writing: Invention, Form, and Style* present professional articles and essays to illustrate the various forms of writing, it also includes numerous examples of good student writing—far more than textbooks traditionally do. We have found that using student essays as models builds confidence in the beginning writer. The student pieces in this book can be emulated by most college writers—they are good, but not so sophisticated that they will intimidate the learner.

Key Features

We have found that students profit most from reading and discussing the materials in this text while they are in the process of drafting and redrafting their own papers. For this reason we include abundant suggestions for writing in all chapters—more assignments than most instructors will assign.

Writing: Invention, Form, and Style also devotes five chapters to special assignments: the essay exam, the research paper, business writing, the literary essay, and essays and reports for other disciplines.

Finally, we include a Handbook of Grammar and Usage which reviews the parts of speech, sentence structure, common usage errors, and punctuation and mechanics, and includes a glossary of usage. A partial Answer Key to the exercises in the Handbook is provided so that students may identify immediately those areas in which they need more practice.

Acknowledgments

We are grateful to many people for their help. Our sincere thanks go to Robert Rudolph of the University of Toledo, who has produced a solid and accessible Handbook to complement our text. He was also a helpful reviewer of other sections of the book. For suggestions and inspiration early in the writing of this text, we are indebted to Lawrence Buell of Oberlin College. Darwyn Batway, of Dyke College, provided consultation on using the library. Edward Brown, of Dyke College, offered advice on the revision of the Introduction. Special thanks go to Jane Bennett of Oberlin College, who allowed us to reproduce her guidelines for the lab report in Chapter 12, and to Peter McInerney, David Stevensen, and Michael Zimmerman, all of Oberlin, who made helpful comments on our early drafts of that chapter.

We would also like to thank these colleagues from other schools who reviewed our manuscript at various stages: Thomas Adler, Purdue University; Marilyn Cooper, University of Southern California; Patrick G. Hogan, Jr., University of Houston; David Martin, Monmouth College; John Mellon, University of Illinois at Chicago; Robert Perrin, Indiana State University; James C. Raymond, University of Alabama; Martha Reid, Moravian College; John J. Ruszkiewicz, University of Texas at Austin; Jack Selzer, Pennsylvania State University; David Skwire, Cuyahoga Community College; and Leonora Woodman, Purdue University.

We are grateful to the editorial staff at Scott, Foresman. Thanks especially go to Harriett Prentiss, who encouraged us to begin the book; to Amanda Clark and Jane Steinmann, who monitored its development during the early and middle stages; and to Kathy Lorden, who edited it with unrelenting energy, good sense, and consummate skill.

Equally diligent were our typists: Karen Barnes, Patt Clarkson, Bobbie Lynch, and April Paramore, whose efforts we greatly appreciate.

Finally, we want to thank our many students; whether their work actually appears in the book or whether they contributed by participating in our classes over the years, they have made this book possible.

Leonard A. Podis
JoAnne M. Podis

CONTENTS

HANDBOOK
OF GRAMMAR AND USAGE   433

WRITING
INVENTION
FORM
AND
STYLE

Introduction

THE COMPOSING
PROCESS

Imagine that you've enrolled in a course in portrait painting. You can't paint very well, but you figure this course will teach you how. During the first week your instructor talks about the qualities of a good portrait: color, composition, texture, and so forth. At the end of the week she brings in a reproduction of Leonardo Da Vinci's *Mona Lisa* and asks the class to discuss it. Then you get your first painting assignment: Now that you can appreciate the qualities of the *Mona Lisa*, paint a picture of similar quality.

Could you do it? Could anyone?

For years many composition textbooks and instructors taught writing in a manner similar to this. They would lead the class in examining effective pieces of writing and then urge students to produce similar material of their own. More recently, teachers of composition have come to believe that students should learn more about the *process* of writing, and that courses should teach them how to compose papers successfully, rather than merely how to recognize good writing.

In this introduction, we will discuss the composing process as described by contemporary researchers. We hope that you will become more aware of how you actually create a piece of writing. Knowing more about the composing process will not, of itself, guarantee that you will become a better writer. You must, after all, practice writing in order to improve. Still, you will greatly increase your chances of success if you follow steps that good writers agree are important parts of the process.

A MODEL OF THE WRITING PROCESS

Composition courses and textbooks have often treated the writing process as a straightforward matter of putting one's thoughts into written language, as shown in Figure 1. In reality, however, the process is seldom that clear-cut or direct. Most writers find that their first try at writing a given paper is actually an exercise in *discovery*. That is, they start with some definite ideas and intentions, but the actual process of choosing words and putting them on the page stimulates their

1	2	3
The writer has clearly defined thoughts ready to be expressed.	The writing process translates the clearly defined thoughts into words.	The result is finished, polished language in need of little further change.

Figure 1
A linear model of the writing process

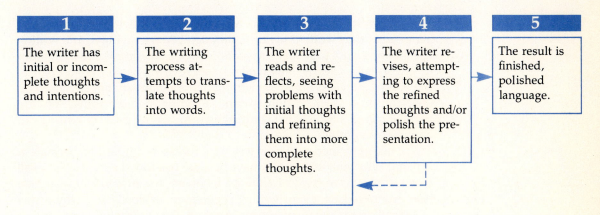

Figure 2 A five-step model of the writing process

thinking further and actually clarifies or even changes their thoughts and their understanding of their purpose. Then they have to go back and rewrite so that the paper communicates their newly found meaning.

A more accurate model of the writing process for most people is shown in Figure 2. The dotted arrow shows that, after completing step 4, the writer may move backward to repeat step 3. In fact, the writer may need to do so an unlimited number of times, forming a kind of loop. Writers exit from this loop and proceed to step 5 only when they are satisfied that the writing clearly expresses their final word on the topic.

Although this five-step model applies to the writing of a whole composition (letter, essay, paragraph), writers may go through the five steps many times while composing a paper. In other words, the five steps also describe what a writer might do in composing just one sentence, or even a clause or phrase within a sentence. The steps likewise can apply to two- or three-sentence "chunks" of writing within a paragraph. Depending upon the circumstances and the writer's inclination, the writer may or may not decide to go back from step 4 to step 3 at any given point during the composing process. When applying the model to a small unit of writing, such as a sentence, a successful writer knows that arrival at step 5, "finished, polished language," may be only temporary. Perhaps the writer has revised a sentence to the point of step 5 and, after writing two more sentences, goes back to reread all three sentences as a chunk. If the writer decides that changes are now needed in that first sentence, what had been a finished bit of writing from the earlier point of view is now moved back to step 4.

According to this model, writers aren't always completely sure about what they want to say until they actually try saying it, and writing itself involves not only forward motion but also *backward* motion in order to go forward. Clearly, this model treats revising as an integral part of the writing process, not as something that may or may not be tacked on once the process of writing is done. Reading and rereading, too, are parts of composing, so that composing even a brief piece of writing can be time consuming.

This new model of the writing process is important because it explains why you, as a writer, have become frustrated at times (as we all have). If you have tried to write by following the first model, you may have wondered why your writing progressed so slowly and why it was so difficult to say what you meant. After all, the first model suggests that it's a straightforward matter to take what you mean and express those thoughts in language. But most experts now view that model as unrealistic.

Of course, composing occasionally *is* straightforward. For instance, when you have thought for a long time about a topic before starting to write, and you know the material completely, your composing process may approximate the three-step model. At other times, you may compose without any real "initial thoughts" to speak of—an approach called *freewriting*. This would eliminate step 1. Different people compose differently, and even the same person may compose differently under different circumstances. But generally, the five-step model is the most useful.

AN EXAMPLE OF THE WRITING PROCESS

We've arrived at this model after reading in the theory of composing, questioning others about the processes they use, and analyzing our own methods. To illustrate the model, let's examine the way in which a friend of ours, who is a professional writer, composed an article that appeared in the October 1982 issue of *McCall's*. What she did matches well with our model. Here is the entire article in its final form:

WHY I'M STILL LIVING AT HOME

[1]Recently I was accused of getting along with my father. It was in a still-darkened movie theater, at the close of a very popular and very sentimental family movie. Two of my oldest friends sat on either side of me, crying silently as the credits rolled onto the screen. I was taken aback—*I* have always been the sap of this trio, yet I wasn't moved to tears.

[2]"Maybe it's because you have a good relationship with your

father," suggested one friend, who has never gotten along with hers. She's absolutely right; I do get along well with my father. I get along with my mother, too. That's why we live together. And I want, here and now, to stop apologizing for it.

³There is a certain stigma attached to living at home. Once you've finished school and landed yourself a real job, you're supposed to move out on your own. If you don't, you risk being labeled lazy or selfish—or worse, you may be revealing an inability to cope with the outside world. And so I have found myself making excuses for living at home, saying, "It's only till I can afford to move out." It has always seemed like a situation that had to be apologized for, or at least explained.

⁴At 23, I readily confess an inability to cope with astronomical rents and a tight housing market. Yet, while the extenuating circumstances are real, they aren't the only reason I'm living at home. I'm there because I want to be. I enjoy living with my parents. It's an odd choice to have to justify—after all, what better place to live than at home? Isn't that what the word means?

⁵Yes, I live at home, and I like it. By "home," I mean the same six rooms in which I grew up, with two of the three people I grew up with. My brother's gone, and the cat is different, but in many ways—*good* ways, for I had a happy childhood—things are very much the same as they were when I was growing up. My father and I are still the wisecracking early risers, cheerfully teasing my mother out of her pre-coffee morning stupor. And, on the occasional evening when we're all home for dinner, my mother still perches on the kitchen stool to hear the latest updates on my social and working life while I chop vegetables for the salad. We all play Scrabble, and my mother and I wear the same size clothes. In short, it's a felicitous living arrangement, so if my parents think it's okay for me to stay at home for a while as long as I do the dishes, so do I. It's more than okay—I'm delighted.

⁶Not everyone is so lucky. I'll never forget the day my best friend told me she couldn't stand her father. I had grown up with this family, and he had always seemed like a perfectly decent man to me. The very idea of not loving a member of your own family, a parent, was horrifying. But family harmony is not automatic, no matter how badly we want it to be. My own brother and my parents were constantly at war as long as they lived in the same apartment.

⁷I'm lucky and I know it. I number my parents among my closest friends. I'm lucky because my parents and I have always loved each other and because we can live peacefully under the same roof. Certainly I sometimes wish for the privacy of my own apartment: I would probably invite people over more often, and I might keep even

stranger hours than I do now. But I know that, when I do have a place of my own, I will be losing something, too.

[8]Don't get me wrong: Ours is no domestic paradise. My mother's clothes come out wrinkled when I do the laundry, and she doesn't like the way I dust. When my father does the laundry, black and navy blue are the same color and all the socks end up mismatched in the wrong drawers. In the morning, when I pack my lunch, my mother "helps" me by reciting the inventory of the entire refrigerator. I write all over my father's desk blotter when I use his phone, and we both forget to put grapefruit on the shopping list when we eat the last one. He clips articles from the morning paper before anyone else has even seen it—but, after all, it is his subscription.

[9]I cherish this time to live with my parents. I don't want to live at home forever, but I'm as grateful for this time there as I am for the roof over my head. And I realize now that my teary-eyed friends in the movie theater (who, unlike me, did move out on their own as soon as they saved enough money) were reacting as much to what they brought to the movie as they were to the movie itself. Because I *am* a champion weeper, and I have parents at home to thank for keeping me dry-eyed this time. (Ellen Darion)

Keeping in mind what this writer finally produced, let's retrace the steps she took in composing the piece.

Step 1   The writer has initial or incomplete thoughts and intentions.

A staff writer for *McCall's*, Darion decided that her own experience of living at home would be of interest to the magazine's readers. So she knew from the start that she wanted to discuss the general subject of living at home. She also knew that she wanted to emphasize the benefits of such a living arrangement. Initially, she felt these points should be made: that she gets along well with her parents, that it's okay to do so, and that she is fortunate to be in such a position. She wasn't sure exactly how to develop and organize her essay at this point, but she knew she was ready to start putting her ideas in writing, for she had thought quite a bit about the subject.

Step 2   The writing process attempts to translate thoughts into words.

In this case, the actual composing process began with Darion's attempts to draft a suitable opening sentence. She tinkered with the opening sentence for a while:

(1)   I'm fortunate my parents and I get along beautifully.

~~I'm fortunate my~~ *My* parents and I get along beautifully.

(2)   My parents and I get along beautifully.

My parents and I get along, ~~beautifully.~~

(3)   My parents and I get along.

~~My parents and~~ I get along, *with my parents.*

(4)   I get along with my parents.

Note how, from the very beginning, the writer's attempts to translate thoughts into words involved not only *writing*, but *rewriting*. This opening sentence went through four different versions before Darion was satisfied with it. And she didn't stay satisfied with it for long. (It is not the opening sentence of the final version.)

This, then, begins to illustrate the sentence-by-sentence process of composing. Since we are mainly concerned here with step 2 of the overall composition of a piece, let's examine the completed opening paragraph of the first draft that resulted from Darion's attempts to put her initial thoughts into words:

> I get along with my parents. That's why we live together. I'm lucky that we can live peacefully under the same roof. I'm lucky because we have always loved each other and been able to express that love. For many people, such warmth doesn't come easily.

To complete her first draft, she then followed up on the ideas expressed in this opening paragraph. The first draft contained some material which actually appears in the final draft (for instance, the details of her happy home life). But it also contained two paragraphs elaborating on the idea that "warmth doesn't come easily" for many people who feel that it's not fashionable to show one's emotions.

Step 3 The writer reads and reflects, mentally refining what has been written.

At this point our writer reread her draft and decided that what she had written was not exactly what she meant. She did want to emphasize the positive aspects of living with her parents. However, she realized that she was not interested in pursuing the point about people's difficulty in expressing their emotions. While it was a good point—and a point somewhat related to her subject—it wasn't exactly the point she wanted to make in *this* piece. Conferring with an editor about her project, she decided to drop that point and save it for another day. In its place the editor suggested discussing the stigma that many young people feel in living at home. Considering the editor's advice, Darion began to recognize that counteracting that stigma had been one of her strongest motivations for undertaking the piece. She saw that unless she called attention to the stigma and discussed it in some detail, the point would be lost.

Step 4 The writer revises, attempting to express the refined thoughts and/or polish the presentation.

The next day Darion composed another draft, this time stressing the new and refined points she had developed. In particular, she deleted the two paragraphs about people's inability to express their emotions, and composed the following paragraph, which was to appear in the final version as paragraph 3:

> There is a certain stigma attached to living at home. Once you've finished school and landed yourself a real job, you're supposed to move out on your own. If you don't, you risk being labeled lazy or selfish—or worse, you may be revealing an inability to cope with the outside world. And so I have found myself making excuses for living at home, saying, "It's only till I can afford to move out." It has always seemed like a situation that had to be apologized for, or at least explained.

She then took the option again of moving backward to step 3—to read, reflect, and refine further. This time, besides seeing the need for ongoing revisions in language, she was struck with an idea for a more effective introduction. The opening paragraph of the first draft had given her a good footing from which to write the first draft, but it now seemed too businesslike and unimaginative. Recalling a recent experience, she came up with a scene which could serve as a point of departure for her article. The new introduction would focus on her sitting in a movie theater with friends who were crying over a reconciliation between a father and daughter. Moving forward again to step 4, she rewrote the introduction. It now read this way, as it does in the final version:

> Recently I was accused of getting along with my father. It was in a still-darkened movie theater, at the close of a very popular and very sentimental family movie. Two of my oldest friends sat on either side of me, crying silently as the credits rolled onto the screen. I was taken aback—*I* have always been the sap of this trio, yet I wasn't moved to tears.
> "Maybe it's because you have a good relationship with your father," suggested one friend, who has never gotten along with hers. She's absolutely right; I do get along well with my father. I get along with my mother, too. That's why we live together. And I want, here and now, to stop apologizing for it.

A quick reading convinced her that she had arrived at step 5, at least until some later rereading suggested still further changes.

In fact, when the first galley proof came back, the editor suggested that Darion might strengthen the article by acknowledging some of the disadvantages of living at home and admitting to occasional desires to live on her own. Darion agreed that this would improve the article, and composed and included the material in paragraph 7 and paragraph 8 of the final version.

Step 5   The result is finished, polished language.

The article as it appeared in the magazine constitutes step 5.

By following the writer's path through the steps of the composing process, we see that both the meaning and the language of her article evolved as a result of considerable work over a period of time. We see how significantly the content of the essay changed during the process of composing. Numerous small-scale changes were made along the way, too. For instance, here is the next-to-last version of the concluding paragraph with the final changes written in:

```
    I cherish this time to live with my parents.  I don't want to live

at home forever, but I'm as grateful for this  opportunity to spend time
      there
    with them as I am for the roof over my head.  And I realize now that
                                        (who, unlike me, did move out on their
                                          own as soon as they saved enough money)
my teary-eyed friends in the movie theater were reacting as much to

what they brought to the movie as they were to the movie itself.
            I am
Because, I'm a champion weeper, and I have my parents at home to thank
        keeping
for  making me dry-eyed this time.
```

The change from "for this opportunity to spend time with them" to simply "for this time there" reduces wordiness. Adding the parenthetical statement emphasizes the writer's difference from her friends. The third change, from "I'm" to I *am*," allows the writer to be more emphatic, underscoring the point that she has nothing to cry about. Finally, changing "making" to "keeping" results in a clearer expression.

Obviously, the final version was not the result of a simple, straightforward exercise in translating pre-existing ideas into finished language. If we read only the finished product, we might think the writer was always moving forward confidently; but our behind-the-scenes look shows that this was not the case.

For most writers, the best approach to good writing combines a knowledge of the writing process with an awareness of the qualities of effective papers. Throughout this book we will present what to aim for as well as how to achieve those aims.

Suggestion for Writing

Write a short paper on one of the following topics:

My first impressions of the campus
My least/most likable classmate, past or present
My first job

Exercise

After you have written the paper for the above exercise, describe in as much detail as possible the process you went through in writing it. List the steps you went through and number each item. Make sure that the final version of your list shows the time frame or chronology of your writing process. For example, your list might begin like this:

1. Jan. 24, 8:45 a.m.: Instructor asked me to write on one of the suggested topics.
2. Jan. 24, 12:30 p.m.: Thought over the suggestions; liked the second one; wasn't sure whether to write about least likable or most likable classmate, high school or college?
3. Jan. 24, 8:00 p.m.: Made lists of friends & "enemies."

When you have completed your list, divide the process you went through into several definite stages and label those stages. To what extent do the stages match up with the composing models presented on pages 2–3?

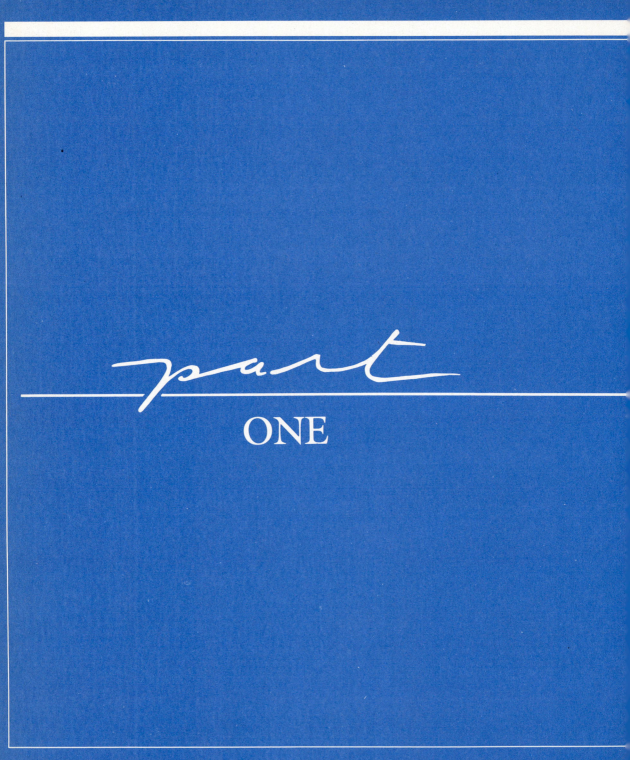

part

ONE

INVENTION

14

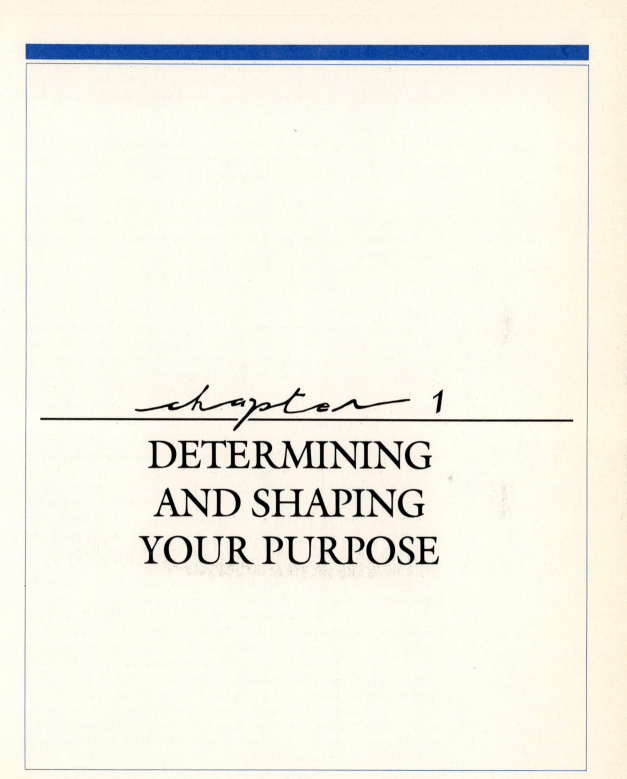

chapter 1

DETERMINING
AND SHAPING
YOUR PURPOSE

Most writing is a response to a particular need. For example, the writer of the article discussed in the introduction began by deciding that she wanted to write something for publication in *McCall's*. In other words, she had a *purpose* for writing. One writing teacher puts it this way:

> I see a problem and write to solve it; . . . I read something and write a response; I love someone and therefore I write a letter; my boss wants a report, so I write one; I like a movie, so I write a review. . . .

The first section of this book explores *invention*, the process of discovering what to write and how to write it. Since writers usually begin invention by considering their purpose, we too will begin with a look at purpose.

THE WRITER HAS A PURPOSE

Suppose your composition instructor asks you to write a paper stating your career interests and detailing your work experience and education. After some thought, you conclude that your major interest is computer science. You've done some data processing and simple programming during your summer jobs at a hospital and a bank. You're majoring in math, and you've taken several courses in computer languages and circuitry design. Thinking that you have a basic idea of what you want to say, you begin the paper.

What might you hope to achieve by writing such a paper? You would be exploring and explaining your career plans. You would also be practicing your composition skills.

Now suppose that you decide to answer a classified advertisement placed by a local computer design consultant who is looking for a part-time assistant. Examine the ad, shown in Figure 1.1. This situation also calls for you to write about your career goals, experience, and education. But what would you hope to achieve by writing an answer to this ad? Getting yourself a job, of course.

Although what you have to say in each of these cases would be quite similar, your purpose for writing would be different. In composition, *purpose* is defined as the practical aim of your writing. By writing, you hope to accomplish a goal—whether to inform, to persuade, to explain, to recommend, to motivate, to warn, to inspire, and so on.

Here's another example of how saying the same thing can achieve different purposes under different circumstances. Seeing your friend fumbling for her watch, you say to her, "It's ten o'clock." Clearly your purpose is to inform her. Saying the sentence is a way of accomplishing your purpose, no less than if you had moved your wrist in front of your friend's eyes so that she could read your watch herself. But let's change the situation. Suppose your friend arranged to meet you at nine o'clock to borrow some desperately needed money. You had another engage-

Figure 1.1
A classified ad

> **COMPUTER DESIGN ASSISTANT.** To work part-time for successful consulting firm. Experience with machine languages and available hardware and software. Minimum two years college completed. Send letter stating career goals and detailing experience and education. $9.50/hour. Box A–252.

ment, but canceled it because your friend's request sounded so urgent. At the appointed time you arrive, but she's not there. You wait and wait, getting angrier all the while. Finally she shows up an hour late. "It's ten o'clock," you say.

What is your purpose for making such a statement this time? Probably not to inform; rather, you would most likely intend the sentence to show your annoyance with your friend.

Whether you are speaking or writing, your purpose for communicating depends on the situation in which you find yourself. Different situations require different kinds of responses. You know this to be true from everyday experience. But as a writer you must consciously devote some time to analyzing and describing each writing situation for yourself. Once you understand the nature of a situation, you will be better able to balance your ideas and intentions against the requirements of that situation.

Exercise

Look at each topic listed below. If you were asked simply to write about each one, how would you decide on your purpose(s) in each case? Now consider the specific writing situations suggested for each topic. What would the purpose(s) be if the topic were to be used in the situation(s) given?

TOPIC	WRITING SITUATION
1. Someone nagging or teasing you at home	Letter to a friend
2. Inconvenient change in bus or train schedule	Letter to the editor of the local newspaper
3. Unreasonable assignment made at school or work	Complaint to the school board Letter of resignation to boss
4. A boastful acquaintance	Character reference for a job the person has applied for
5. A sticking typewriter at work	Memo to supervisor Requisition to service/maintenance department

Suggestion for Writing

Choosing one of the topics in the exercise above and one of the suggested situations accompanying it, compose the actual piece. Be certain to consider which purpose, among those you identified, you would like to pursue (for example, in **1,** to entertain your friend, to complain about your life, or to do a little of both).

Levels of Purpose

Any writing task involves multiple levels of purpose, and you must decide how actively you will pursue those various levels. For instance, consider the case of a business executive writing a memorandum to his supervisor. The executive has helped interview a pool of candidates for an accounting position. The supervisor also was present at the interviews, and so has only suggested, not required, that the interviewers submit written responses to her. When the executive writes his memo, he is apparently doing so to recommend the hiring of a particular candidate. This is his primary purpose. However, in presenting a clear and detailed rationale for the candidate of his choice, he is also attempting to establish himself as a shrewd judge of character and as a sophisticated writer. This is his secondary purpose. Moreover, he is also hoping to impress the boss by demonstrating that he takes his job seriously in submitting a memo where none was actually required. This last aim is an incidental purpose.

Generally, the *primary purpose* is the major goal of your writing, and it is usually explicit or obvious in the paper. For instance, the business executive is above all concerned with presenting his recommendation on hiring an accountant. The *secondary purpose* is also important, but it is not generally the main reason for writing. Often it is an unstated goal that the writer is trying to achieve. If, for example, the executive presents a particularly effective or shrewd argument, he may succeed not only in supporting his recommendation, but also in presenting himself favorably as a thinker, adviser, and writer. *Incidental purposes* are those which the writer achieves more or less automatically in the act of satisfactorily completing the writing task. Whereas the business executive probably devoted much thought to ways of fulfilling the primary and secondary purposes, his incidental purpose (impressing the boss with his initiative) was achieved in the course of achieving the other two.

Let's take another look at the hypothetical situation in which you were asked to write a paper on your career interests. Earlier, we noted two purposes:

1. To explore and explain my career plans

2. To practice my writing skills

If we think a while, we can add others:

3. To fulfill one of the requirements for the composition course

4. To earn an *A* in the course

5. To express myself

6. To heighten my self-image

You might also have a purpose like this one:

7. To show my instructor that I'm a serious student with definite career plans (computer science)

Perhaps you're also a good guitar player and have been thinking seriously about dropping out of school to join a rock band. But because you have purpose 7 in mind, you reject this career option when deciding what to say in the paper.

How would these seven purposes fit under the three categories of primary, secondary, and incidental? Perhaps like this:

PRIMARY	SECONDARY	INCIDENTAL
Purpose 1	Purpose 7	Purposes 2 through 6

Does this classification of the seven purposes match your own?

We say "perhaps" about our classification because different writers can put different values on certain purposes. What most people would call "incidental" might loom so large in some writers' minds that it becomes a secondary or even a primary purpose. A premed student who is very concerned about grades might elevate "To earn an *A*" out of the incidental category, for instance. And a business report writer interested in establishing a positive image might elevate what would ordinarily be a secondary concern for writing style to the level of primary purpose. In the process, the more apparent purpose of the communication would be overshadowed.

Every time you are faced with a writing task, identify at least one purpose at each of the three levels. If you can determine the nature and requirements of a writing situation and use this knowledge in developing a list of three purposes (one primary, one secondary, and one incidental), you will be doing consciously what most accomplished writers do more or less intuitively.

Exercise

1. Read the following letters to the editor and list at least one primary purpose, one secondary purpose, and one incidental purpose for each.

Dear Editor:

I was greatly displeased with the material concerning Galena in your June story *Illinois Time Trip*, by Lawrence Rand. Had your reporter been willing to dig a little harder, he would have had different impressions of the community. The article reads as though your reporter gave up on the story because two restaurants were closed during what is our slow time of the year. Galena is a unique community blessed with many talented people who care about the historic nature of the city as well as the positive benefits of a small-town lifestyle. Moreover, there is a great tolerance for individual lifestyles.

> P. Carter Newton, President
> Galena/Jo Daviess County
> Chamber of Commerce,
> Galena
> (*Chicago*)

Dear Editor:

Thank you for Virl Osmond's story on coping with his hearing loss. When we were first told our 2½-year-old son Jason was hearing handicapped, we felt helpless. But our feelings didn't compare to the frustrations Jason himself was experiencing because he couldn't communicate with us. However, with help, our son, who is now 4, is communicating well with sign language and can hear somewhat with the assistance of a hearing aid. We are trying to let Jason grow and be himself but sometimes it is hard because, as parents, we feel the need to protect him. Virl's article has given me a new reassurance that Jason too will find his own special place in life.

> Niceta Cover
> Dixon, Illinois
> (*People*)

Dear Editor:

In his May column, Bob Greene wrote, "There are no such things as vampires. There just aren't." He is wrong.

As I am considered the world's foremost authority on vampires, I can assure Bob Greene, as well as the young girl with whom he spoke (who did finally make contact with us), that we are interested only in legitimate cases of those who have seen vampires, those who have been attacked by vampires, and those who enjoy the real subject. We do not believe in the supernatural, but we believe that almost every myth and legend may have a basis of truth.

> Stephen Kaplan, Ph.D.
> Vampire Research Center
> Elmhurst, N.Y.
> (*Esquire*)

Dear Editor:

Perhaps that was Bob Greene menacing "A Red-Blooded American Girl" in May's American Beat photograph, but it was certainly no vampire. Any vampire hunter worth his garlic knows that those nasty old undead cast no shadows.

Ty Hillman
Rockford, Illinois
(*Esquire*)

2. Choose two pieces (perhaps a paper and a letter) you have written recently and identify at least one purpose at each level—primary, secondary, incidental. Thinking back to the thoughts you had as you composed may be more helpful than simply rereading the finished piece. Once you have your lists of purposes, compare them. Are the purposes in each case similar or different? Why? Are there any other purposes you might have tried to achieve?

Suggestion for Writing

Write a letter to the editor of your campus newspaper, the local newspaper, or a national magazine. Be sure to think about your purpose or purposes before you compose. In a letter like this, a typical primary purpose would be to complain about a problem, correct an inaccuracy or a misconception, or express thanks. A typical secondary purpose would be to convey a sense of your objectivity or outrage, or to portray yourself as witty or clever. A typical incidental purpose might be to gain some experience in taking a stand in public.

PURPOSE AND AUDIENCE

In most writing situations, you can achieve your purposes only by communicating effectively with your reader, or *audience*. You must give special attention to meeting the audiences' needs and expectations in order to write successfully. Unfortunately, beginning writers often assume that a piece of writing will be viewed the same way no matter who reads it.

But audiences differ, and experienced speakers and writers take the differences into account in designing their messages. For example, a major league baseball player hired to speak on the value of our national pastime wouldn't give the same speech to a group of little leaguers that he would to a group of seasoned sportswriters. If he gave the sportswriters' speech to the little leaguers, he would allude to players and specific plays they probably don't know about. If he gave the little leaguers' speech to the sportswriters, he would bore them with simple examples and insult their intelligence. Obviously, these are not the purposes he wants to achieve.

In everyday situations, we all gear our responses to the needs of an audience. For instance, if you dropped an armload of heavy books on your foot, you would probably not utter the same expression in the company of your grandmother that you would in front of a close friend. Or, suppose you have just been griping to a coworker about your broken calculator. Suddenly the president of the company strolls through your department, smiling and saying, "How are you? How is everything going?" You would probably smile back and say, "Fine," and make no mention of the calculator. You know that in a casual walk through the building the president doesn't really want to hear about your problems.

In the first example, you are adjusting your language to fit the expectations of your audience. Whether in the presence of your grandmother or your friend, you are crying out in pain and disgust. But you would probably use a milder term ("darn" or "ouch") in front of your grandmother. In the second example, you are adjusting the message itself. Instead of complaining about your calculator, you are stating that all goes well. In each case, you are making some adjustment in order to achieve one or more purposes which you had in mind. What might your actual purposes be in these situations?

Writers use an awareness of audience to help shape and achieve their purpose or purposes by adjusting their work in three areas: content, form, and style. Let's look at each in detail.

Consider again the example of writing a paper on career goals versus answering a classified ad. You would be writing about your own experiences in each case, but because of the requirements of each audience, the specific *content* of the paper would differ from that of the letter. For instance, you might decide that your chances of getting the job are better if you present yourself as experienced. So the unpaid, three-hour-a-week position as a computer lab assistant (required as part of a course) that you call "educational background" in your paper version becomes "work experience" in your job application.

Similarly, *form* is dictated by the expectations of your audience. Your instructor asks you to write an essay; the Personnel Director expects to receive a letter of application in response to the classified ad. Sometimes, the situation is not quite so cut-and-dried. On the job, for instance, you might have the option of writing a memo or a letter. Knowing that the recipient of the message prefers one or the other could influence you to choose the preferred form. In that way you can increase the likelihood of a favorable response from your reader, thereby increasing the chances of achieving your purposes.

Understanding your audience's expectations about form is particularly crucial in test-taking. If the instructions are to "identify the major types of irony and the chief characteristics of each," for example, you would determine the form of your answer according to the instructor's preferences. If your instructor wants an essay response, you would construct your answer as a series of paragraphs, as shown in Figure 1.2.

In each paragraph of the body, you would probably discuss one type of irony and its characteristics. If, on the other hand, you know that

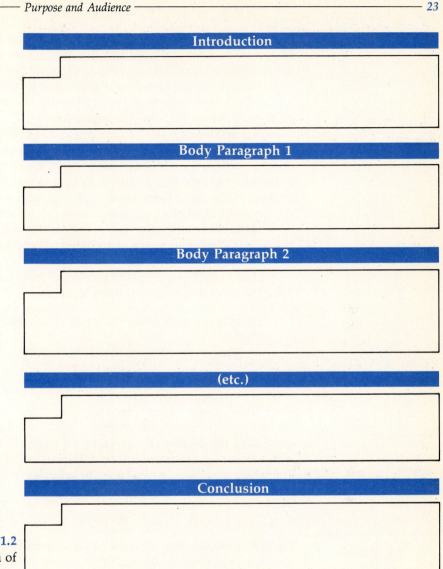

Figure 1.2
The construction of
an essay response

the instructor does not expect an essay response, you can present the
information in a simple list or an outline:

Type 1. Character Irony
    A.   Characteristic 1
    B.   Characteristic 2
       (and so on)
Type 2. Irony of Situation
    A.   Characteristic 1
    B.   Characteristic 2
       (and so on)

If you fail to use the essay form when the instructor expects an essay, you could lose all credit for the question. And although writing an essay where a simple list was expected might not be perceived quite as negatively, it would cause your instructor to question your ability to follow directions. Moreover, it would cost you time, decreasing your chances of completing the test successfully.

In considering *style*, you must also think of the reader and choose the appropriate level of language. The style you would use for the paper on your career interests would probably be similar to that you would use in the letter of response to an ad. In both cases, you want your level of language to be fairly formal—after all, you wish to appear an educated, serious individual. But in many cases, style will vary considerably, depending upon audience. For instance, the major league ball player would use simpler language in speaking to little leaguers than he would in addressing sportswriters.

Here's another example of varying style to suit different audiences. Read the following versions of the same idea:

I think there must be something to all this stuff about men from other planets.
It's likely that intelligent life exists elsewhere in the universe.

The first sentence would be appropriately used in everyday conversations or perhaps in writing to a friend. The second uses a slightly higher level of language: "Men" becomes "intelligent life," "other planets" becomes "elsewhere in the universe," and the informal "all this stuff" is eliminated completely. This second sentence could appear in a magazine article popularizing recent findings in biophysics and astronomy. The writer must decide what level of language is appropriate, given the intended audience.

Exercise

Each item in the first column below contains a writing assignment directed to a given audience. The second column lists one or more alternative audiences for the assignment. For each entry in the first column, decide what changes in content, form, or style might be necessary if the piece were being written for each audience listed in the second column. In every case, how might the writer's purposes be affected in addressing the new audience?

1. Describe the first week of your new summer job in an informal letter to a close friend.

—To a distant relative who "pulled strings" to help you get the job
—To a foreign exchange student who will soon be arriving to stay with your family for the coming year

2. Write an advertisement designed to sell your $3,000 stereo system to the readers of the local newspaper's classified ads.

—To the readers of *High Fidelity* magazine

3. Describe your successful science fair project to your physics instructor in a scientific report.

—To your English instructor
—To the head of an organization that grants scholarships to promising science students

4. Narrate your experiences rafting down the treacherous Tuscarawas River to yourself for your diary.

—To the editor and readers of *Outdoor Adventure* magazine

5. Detail your reasons for wanting to attend a certain college in an informal letter to a close friend who is attending the same college.

—To the admissions officers of the college to which you are applying
—To another close friend attending a different college

Sizing Up the Audience: The Demands of College Readers

Since much of the writing you will be doing for the next few years will be aimed at your instructors and your fellow students (as well as yourself), it is important to spend some time thinking specifically about the requirements of the college audience.* To achieve your various purposes for writing, you will have to understand the needs and expectations of your audience in the areas of content, form, and style. Before you determine those specific needs, however, you should consider the nature and motivations of the audience.

In analyzing any audience, a good first step is to consider how your readers differ from yourself. In general, the more similar two individuals are in such characteristics as age, race, education, sex, and attitudes, the easier it is for them to communicate. Therefore, determining how your audience differs from yourself can help you spot those characteristics which are potential obstacles to effective communication.

In considering your instructors as an audience, keep in mind that their educational backgrounds are broader than your own. Particularly when compared to students, they are experts in their fields. They are also almost certainly older than you. Depending on how much older they are, their interests and tastes may be quite different from your own. In addition, there may be a status barrier between professor and student. Looking at all these factors, you may feel as though none of

---

*The techniques for analyzing the college audience are fundamentally the same as those used to analyze any other audience. Thus much of what we will discuss here also applies to any writing addressed to those other audiences.

your ideas can possibly be interesting to your professor. But you should realize that this is not always the case. Most instructors are ready to learn from their students, as well as teach them.

Also, keep in mind some of the positive features of the educational setting. Your instructors strive to maintain objectivity as they read what you write, perhaps more so than do readers in the "real world." After all, college instructors seek to encourage critical thinking and try to remain open-minded about divergent points of view. Moreover, even when they are acting as readers, your instructors are still concerned mainly with teaching you. They point out faults so that you will learn through trial and error.

At times you may also be sharing your writing with your fellow students. In this situation, there may be fewer differences to consider. You are likely to be about the same age. Chances are, you share similar tastes in such areas as music and fashion, as well as similar educational concerns. Because little or no status barrier exists, your peers may be more open and direct with you. They aren't as likely to worry about the results of their comments as your instructors are. Knowing that they are outspoken may motivate you to do your best work, just as knowing the instructor will give you a grade can be a powerful motivator.

Although you write primarily for others to read, you should also consider yourself as part of your audience. Obviously, analyzing yourself as an audience to uncover differences is not useful. However, considering yourself as part of your audience is a helpful way of refining your incidental purposes. That is, although your primary purpose in writing is probably not to bolster your self-image or to maintain your own interest in your paper, creating satisfaction with what you write is important. A feeling of pride and accomplishment is essential to good writing, and reading your own well-written paper can provide just that. As you write, then, keep in mind that you must please yourself, not just others, with the result.

Demands of Instructor-Audience   What do these various audiences demand in terms of content, form, and style? Your instructors will have the most to say about all three areas, and so their demands will probably influence your writing the most.

For most instructors, content is the single most important element in a paper. It is so important, in fact, that in much college writing your content and your purpose become nearly identical. Your primary purpose often amounts to explaining and supporting your main idea. Thus, if your main idea were "Far from being a complete waste of six months, my bout with mononucleosis was in many ways beneficial," your primary purpose would be to explain and support this idea. Demonstrating the truth of a sound main idea is the most reliable route to achieving your purpose in writing for a college instructor.

Additionally, your instructors, like most real-world readers, are looking for accuracy, completeness, and appropriateness. If they assign a general topic, then the content of your paper must fit that topic. Further, because they are knowledgeable in their fields, they may already know at least some of what you're telling them in your paper. Rather than seeking to learn new information from your work, the college instructor primarily seeks to discover whether you are learning the course material and methodologies. Thus, as you think about what you are going to say in your writing, a secondary (or perhaps primary) purpose must be to demonstrate knowledge or mastery of the concepts being discussed. Instructors expect to find evidence of that mastery in the content of your writing more than they expect to be introduced to new ideas—although if you do produce fresh insights, they will probably be even happier with your work.

Composition instructors may have different expectations on content than other instructors do. For one thing, the content of your writing is likely unfamiliar to them, since they frequently assign topics based on personal experiences. And if you should write on a specialized or technical topic for your composition instructor, you must remember that your audience will need a slower and more careful explanation than an audience of specialists or experts would.

Instructors often specify the form your work is to take. The essay is the basic form demanded in college writing, both in examinations and out-of-class assignments. Very often, too, a length is suggested. Thus, as you compose, consider the form required, whether it be a five-page essay, a twenty-page term paper, or a 250-word paragraph. Your instructor's explicit demands will probably make the decision for you.

Composition instructors in particular will tend to value the way in which you express your ideas. It is, after all, their business to encourage the improvement and sophistication of your writing skills. This does not mean that the composition teacher will ignore content in favor of expression, or that instructors for your other courses will not also value how you convey your message—far from it. But it does mean that the nature of the composition course itself demands that much attention be paid to the technical aspects of your communication, including form.

Audience expectations on style are not always as clear-cut. Obviously, in writing for English professors, you need to pay significant attention to your style. Especially in composition courses, style is as important as content, and your instructors will evaluate your writing on the basis of its stylistic features as much as its content. In courses in other disciplines, however, style may play a less prominent role. All readers expect clear and readable prose, but instructors whose primary concern does not lie in the teaching of writing may be more likely to overlook misspelled words or sentence fragments, provided these errors do not affect the clarity of expression.

On the other hand, certain instructors in any field can be very demanding on matters of style and usage. Even though they are not "teaching English," they still consider style as important as content. It is to your advantage to learn early if your instructor feels this way. Still, even instructors who profess not to care much about your "English" on a paper cannot help but be more favorably impressed with sound, careful writing.

Any instructor grading an essay exam will probably be more lenient on stylistic errors. Careful proofreading is not always possible in the exam situation, and most instructors make allowances for that. However, if the writing on an examination is unclear, ambiguous, or disorganized, the content obviously can easily be misunderstood. Using a clear style can enhance your content. When you write essay exams, you should balance the need for clarity against the constraints of the exam situation.

Exactly what kind of style will best help you achieve your purposes in writing for the college instructor? This question requires a careful answer, and Chapters 6 and 7 discuss it in detail. Generally, your instructors are looking for a clear, direct, middle-of-the-road approach. They want you to stay away from the extremes of being too informal and casual or too formal and pompous.

Recall these two sentences discussed earlier in this chapter:

I think there must be something to all the stuff about men from other planets.
It is likely that intelligent life exists elsewhere in the universe.

Let's add a third sentence:

The inspiring likelihood that beings of superior intellect are flourishing on celestial bodies other than earth has been made gloriously manifest to this author.

This new version is too pretentious and wordy to suit anyone's tastes. The language is inappropriate and at too high a level—and, near the end of the sentence, it approaches the ridiculous. Note, too, that this sentence takes more time than the others to express the same basic idea. The writer apparently is trying to impress the reader with his mastery of the language. He is also trying to show that "this author" is quite a deep thinker. But instead, the sentence ends up being overdone.

Unfortunately, some students think this is the kind of writing they should strive to write when they enter college. Knowing that college writers sound intelligent and scholarly, they aim for a fancy vocabulary and pretentious phrasing. But the second sample sentence illustrates the style of writing most instructors expect and want from students: clear, concise, and uncluttered.

Demands of the Peer Audience

When writing for your peers, you primarily need to consider their expectations on content. They may be unfamiliar with the information contained in your paper, and you may have to provide more explanation and more background for them than for your instructor. They may expect simply to enjoy reading your paper, or be interested, as well as informed, by your writing. They will usually have little to say about the form your work takes, and are probably not accustomed to analyzing writing for style. In a composition class, however, the instructor will be helping all students become more discriminating readers. In that case, when your peers read what you write, they will be more sophisticated on matters of form and style, and so writing for them will be much like writing for your instructor.

When you write for your fellow students, you may be tempted to use a less formal style. Whether or not you should do this depends on the situation. If you are unsure, you should probably use the same level of style that you would for the instructor. Your peers know that you and they are all operating within a college setting, and they may want you to keep things somewhat more formal, just as your instructors would. Using slang or casual language to win them over may backfire; they may be insulted by your failure to treat them as a mature college audience.

Demands of Yourself as Audience

Considering yourself as part of your audience is a lot like considering your peers. You, too, should be interested by the content of your work. You'll probably be learning something from it, either about a certain topic or about yourself. If you find yourself getting bored as you think over your ideas and purposes, modify them to recapture your interest. As your knowledge of form and style increases, you can—and should—become more demanding of your own work.

Finally, in sizing up the college audience, remember that sometimes audience analysis can be carried too far, particularly if you completely subordinate your personal views and values to those of your intended readers. In that case, your writing may be stripped of its personal quality and seem artificial and contrived. In the college setting, where so often a student writes only for an instructor—and, unfortunately, mainly for a grade—it is easy to slip into overanalysis. Don't determine the content, form, and style of your papers solely by trying to answer the question, "To what kind of work will my instructor give an A?"

In fact, what most college readers want to hear is what you have to say, not what is already in their own heads. Particularly when you are writing about your ideas or beliefs, it is generally useless, and may even be harmful, to spend time trying to figure out where your instructor's prejudices might lie. Considering the audience's needs and expectations should not translate into sacrificing the integrity of your own ideas. A college audience usually approaches your ideas in an unbiased frame of mind, evaluating them not by how closely they coincide with their own, but by how well you support and develop what you say.

Exercise

Think about the different audiences for whom you have been writing, or for whom you will write, while in college. List at least three instructors in different subject areas and two peers who represent different circles of your friends or acquaintances. How closely do these audiences fit with the categories of *instructor, peer,* or *self* that we have discussed? What characteristics differentiate them? What similarities do they have? How do their expectations influence the content, style, or form of the messages you communicate to them?

Sizing Up the Audience: The Demands of "Real-World" Readers

Learning to write well for a college audience can prepare you to write well for most situations you will encounter outside of school. The basic techniques of audience analysis are the same regardless of whom you are writing for. Yet while there are definite similarities, "real-world" audiences can differ from college audiences in several ways.

For one thing, the range of audiences you address is likely much broader. If you work for a large organization, for instance, you may write to managers, accountants, or marketing researchers of varying ages and backgrounds. Some of these people may be your supervisors, others your subordinates, and still others your peers. Some may be clients with whom you correspond and whom you have never met.

In addition, your real-world readers generally do not already have much of the information you're communicating to them. While some memos and letters are written to confirm decisions and otherwise document events known to the reader, many more are written to convey new information. A stove manufacturer, for example, would know nothing of the problem with your oven's thermostat until your letter arrives.

We've seen that, in many cases, demonstrating the truth of a main idea is your primary purpose in college writing. But in writing for readers outside the college setting, you may find that your main idea and your primary purpose are not so closely related. In the case of your letter to the stove manufacturer, your main idea is that there is a serious problem with your stove, which the local service people have been unable to correct. However, your primary purpose is to influence the manufacturer to do something to solve that problem. Similarly, in a letter to a potential client, your main idea may be that your firm offers a whole range of useful services, while your primary purpose is to persuade the client to use those services. Thus you must not only establish the truth of an idea, but also do it in such a way that it has the desired impact on your reader, thereby enabling you to achieve your purpose.

These are some significant differences between audiences inside and outside of the college setting. In both cases, however, you need to take into account the expectations of your audience as you decide the proper content, style, and form for your writing.

As you think about your potential readers, consider these questions:

1. How much of my message will be familiar to my readers?

2. What form and style do my readers prefer?

3. How receptive are my readers likely to be to my message?

   a. Do my readers have any prejudices or biases about the subject?

   b. Are there any specific objections I can anticipate and handle?

Let's discuss each of these questions.

Knowing whether your audience is familiar with the information you are relating can influence your handling of both content and style. If you are presenting information unknown to your readers, you will probably want to include more thorough explanations, more details, and perhaps more background information. You may also want to use a less specialized vocabulary in explaining new information.

Knowing what form and style your readers prefer will also aid you in achieving your purposes. For instance, if you wanted your letter to the editor of *Time* magazine to be published, you would greatly increase your chances of success by using the form and style the editors seem to favor. You would study several issues to become familiar with the type of letters they publish. Then you would try to use that form and style, and compose a letter of one paragraph, written in terse, emphatic language.

Determining how receptive your audience is and making the proper adjustments for that audience can be difficult. But you must do so if you are to become a successful writer. Obviously, you wouldn't say the same things to a suspicious or hostile audience that you would to a receptive one. For instance, suppose you are a respected law-enforcement official and have served for many years as a homicide investigator. You have been asked to write an article for a magazine published by a national group that opposes gun control. You and the editors have agreed that you will write an article expressing your view that handguns must be more closely monitored. Your primary purpose is to convince your audience that some form of gun control is necessary.

Clearly you can't write about this topic in the same way you would for a group that favors gun control or even for a neutral audience. You would consider your readers' generalized prejudices and try to dispel whatever misconceptions or myths they may have. You would also want to consider some of their specific objections and diplomatically try to counter these in your article. Indeed, the knowledge that your audience is unreceptive would guide you in shaping content, form and style to help you achieve your purpose. Content would have to be carefully chosen: You would want to select only the most compelling cases of irresponsible handgun ownership as examples. Form, too, would need careful handling. Rather than opening with a strong statement on the value of gun control, you might start with a story of a tragic shooting that you had investigated. Then you could more gently state your views. Finally, you would choose words carefully, avoiding language that might demean your readers' beliefs.

In analyzing the demands of your audience, think over their personal and professional characteristics:

1. *Role* What features of my readers' roles (or positions) might influence their reaction to my writing?

2. *Status* Is the status (social, political, professional, and so on) of my readers the same as or different from my own? Does their status affect their needs and expectations?

3. *Educational Background* What is my audience's level of education? Should it affect my strategy for presenting my message?

4. *Age* What is the age (or range of ages) of my audience? Does this affect their expectations?

5. *Cultural or Ideological Background* Does my audience have a perspective different from my own which might affect their needs and receptivity?

Because real-world audiences tend to be diverse, the answers you derive from these questions, and the ones on page 31, won't always be clear-cut. For instance, consider the question, "How much of my message will be familiar to my readers?" A lawyer writing a brief in a suit against a public utility company might answer this way: "A small but important segment of my audience—judges and lawyers—already knows the subject very well, but a larger and perhaps more important group—the public—knows only what has appeared in the newspapers." In this case, the writer has to juggle the demands of differing audiences simultaneously. This is a tricky business, because a strategy that reaches one audience may alienate another.

Let's consider a more detailed example of how writers juggle the demands of real-world audiences to achieve their purposes. Suppose you are an investigator who has been hired by the state to report on the cause of a structural failure in the new wing of a state office building. The collapse resulted in several serious injuries and one death. Your expertise in architecture and structural engineering enables you to pinpoint the cause of the failure: undersized steel girders in the ceilings. Your first impulse is to explain the failure for yourself and an audience of your colleagues. In doing so, you would explain the collapse in the terms of physics and math. But you remember that you have been hired by the state to write an investigative report, not simply a mathematical or scientific explanation of the structural failure. Your audience is not only your colleagues but also the members of the state board of inquiry. Therefore you will have to include *in plain English* the reasons behind the failure: in this case, a design error that was allowed to pass because of an outdated building code.

Once you start thinking about your obligations and purposes in writing the report, you realize that it will be read and used by other audiences as well. Lawyers and judges will rely on it when injury and wrongful death suits come to trial. So you decide to supply even more documentation in support of your findings so that they will clearly stand up in court.

It then occurs to you that your report can have some extremely important effects. First, you can inform architects of the design error and perhaps help them avoid making similar mistakes in the future. Second, you can help bring about a change in the building code. To achieve both purposes you will have to juggle. You must explain the design error not only to architects and structural engineers but also to the department of building codes and inspection. In other words, the language will have to be technical enough to be of use to design experts, but not so technical as to confuse those in charge of changing and enforcing the building codes.

A final problem arises when you realize that a certain powerful group of people on the state board of inquiry and in the department of building codes will be extremely unreceptive to your message. They were strong opponents of the last attempt to reform the building codes, and do not want public criticism of their decision. If you are to succeed in your purpose of initiating reform, you must avoid the temptation to attack directly the old codes they had defended. Rather, you will stress the need to avoid similar structural failures in the buildings now being designed. You realize that this group may decide to fight reform anyway, but if you can structure your report so that it does not emphasize their involvement, they may be won over by the strong evidence you offer.

In both this example and that of the law-enforcement official writing for the gun owners' magazine, the writers calculated the changes they would like to bring about in the minds of their readers. One of the writers' aims was to introduce items unpopular with the audience (or part of it), and to present these items in such a way that the readers would change their perceptions. In the one case, the readers should come to agree that the old building codes are outdated and inadequate; in the other, they should accept that gun control might be necessary under certain circumstances.

One more point: Even the most skilled writers cannot always succeed in juggling the demands of all their readers. Likewise, they are not always able to learn as much about their readers as they would like. When you write, try to meet the demands of your audience as much as possible. Know as much about your audience as you can, and use that knowledge to help you compose a message that will be received as you intend, thus increasing the chances that you will achieve your various purposes in writing.

Exercise

1. Look back to the exercise on pages 24–25. Most of the audiences listed there belong to the "real world." Go through that exercise again, providing fuller answers by using the techniques suggested in this section.

2. Choose a record album or novel that's among your favorites. Now assume that you are an advertising writer for a record or book club. Your task is to design promotional materials for that novel or album to be sent in the club's monthly mailings to members. Define one type of audience to whom you would appeal in promoting the product of your choice. Explain how the personal or professional characteristics of that audience would influence the content or style of a promotional letter to them. How might the characteristics of a different audience change the flyer?

Suggestion for Writing

Compose the promotional letter outlined in Exercise 2.

SPECIAL CONSIDERATIONS FOR ARGUMENT AND PERSUASION

We've discussed the importance of understanding your purpose and knowing your audience in all types of writing. This same awareness of your practical aim and the nature of your readers is even more crucial for successful argumentative and persuasive writing. To argue or persuade effectively, you must have a clear sense of your goals. Likewise, you must know your audience well in order to gauge what you need to say (or omit) to bring them around to your point of view.

Much of the writing we do is persuasive. A popular dictionary defines *to persuade* as "to move by argument, entreaty, or expostulation to a belief, position, or course of action.''[1] In this sense, the article on gun control that we discussed earlier is persuasive, for the author hoped to move his readers to a new position, and perhaps even to get them to take action. As we noted, his success depended totally on his ability to tailor his comments so as to win over an unreceptive audience.

Although argument and persuasion are often seen as identical, there is a fine distinction between the two. *Argument* is defined as ''a coherent series of reasons offered,'' generally ''given in proof or rebuttal.''[2] In other words, argument is a more limited and logical activity than persuasion, although it is often part of persuasion. All arguments attempt to be persuasive, but all persuasion does not consist of argument only. Writers may, for example, attempt to persuade their readers by making emotional appeals rather than offering logical reasons or evidence. Or, as in the essays on gun-control and the building failure discussed earlier, they may suppress certain arguments and emphasize others as a part of their persuasive strategy.

Keep the distinction between argument and persuasion in mind when assessing your audience. Emotional appeals, clever manipulation of facts and statistics, or testimonials by famous people may succeed in persuading the average reader, but the college audience is generally best persuaded by the logic and soundness of the arguments you can offer. When writing for a college audience, then, you should emphasize facts, rational reasons, and objectively verifiable evidence. You should also show open-mindedness in considering arguments that might oppose your own argument, and explain why you reject them.

One problem you will confront in writing arguments is that objectivity itself is sometimes variable. That is, what may appear to be objective evidence to one person may seem mere speculation to another. For instance, we could compose today an irrefutable argument to prove that the earth is round, but several hundred years ago many people would have regarded an astronomer's scientific evidence in support of such a claim as speculation. Thus a discussion that would be recognized today as pure argument would have been seen as unsound argument in an earlier period.

Similarly, many issues that require a great deal of judgment are difficult to argue because people may disagree on what is valid and what is not. Thus, whenever you construct an argumentative essay for a college audience, take care to present as much careful reasoning and factual evidence as you possibly can. In the next chapter, we will discuss a number of thinking patterns that are helpful in generating specific arguments.

---

[1] *Webster's New Collegiate Dictionary* (Springfield, Mass.: G. & C. Merriam Co., 1976), p. 856.

[2] *Webster's*, p. 60.

chapter 2

DECIDING
WHAT TO SAY

During invention, writers try to discover what to say not only by assessing their purposes but also by generating recollections, ideas, and mental images. From this pool of basic materials they attempt to arrive at *a main idea* to complement their purposes. They also look to this pool for materials for *subordinate ideas* with which to support the main idea.

In the first chapter, we considered purpose as the important first step in invention—important because an understanding of why you are writing is essential in determining what you will say. In this chapter, we will explore specific techniques for generating your ideas, both main and subordinate. After all, the reason people read your writing is to learn your ideas, to hear what you have to say.

THE WRITER HAS SOMETHING TO SAY

All writing attempts to communicate some aspect of the writer's view of the world. We write to tell our readers how we see things, what we think, what we have observed or experienced, what we feel is the truth. Of course, the task of communicating our view of the world is carried out at different levels. Elementary school children may write about a class trip to the local theater to see a Walt Disney movie. High school students may write a term paper summarizing what they have read about the history of the German cinema. College students may analyze the post-World War I expressionist movement in cinema, or do a critique of a movie by Von Stroheim. But all three pieces are the result of the writer's *having something to say* about the general topic of film.

In all three instances it would be useless (if not impossible) for the students to attempt to write about something they did not know about or something they did not want to tell someone. As a writer, you must learn to stimulate your thinking processes and thereby discover what you want to express. Later in this chapter we will suggest numerous ways of stimulating your thinking. For now, keep in mind that recognizing what *in particular* you mean to say can solve a lot of problems.

For example, the elementary school children could describe specifics from their experience: the trip to the theater, the popcorn that needed more salt, the front-row seats, and, perhaps, what happened on screen. For their term paper, the high school students would read a number of books on the history of the German cinema, take notes, and put together an orderly and logical account using their own words. The college students may summarize some readings, too, but will narrow the scope more and will provide not only their own words but their own judgments and ideas about the subject. In particular, the college writer may try to answer questions about the nature, purpose, or function of expressionist cinema, or questions about the theme, structure, or imagery of a specific expressionist movie.

It is no coincidence that as we move from grade school to college in these examples, the writing tasks become both more difficult intellectually and narrower and more intense in their focus or approach. Grade schoolers are permitted quite a range of choice in talking about the visit to the movies and probably will write a little bit of everything. They do not yet have the discipline and ability to focus narrowly or to go into depth on a subject. The high schoolers have less freedom to roam, though still quite a bit of choice as to which periods of history to talk about and what to include in each period. Though far more disciplined than the grade schoolers, they are generally not ready to think very deeply about their subject. College students, however, are obligated to concentrate on making known, in depth, their particular ideas about the topic chosen or assigned—in this case, the expressionist movement. The college student's writing is the most strictly controlled because that student has the intellectual maturity needed to deal thoroughly with a limited subject. In-depth analysis and observation require a kind of complex thinking not required for looser, wide-ranging discussions. The college student who devotes a whole paragraph to a single expressionist camera technique will have to do more research and analysis than the high school student who devotes only one paragraph to the whole expressionist movement in a paper on the history of the German cinema.

The process of invention occurs at all three levels, but in the case of the elementary school students, it is fairly spontaneous. These students will think a little about what they should write—but probably not much. And their invention will be a straightforward matter of remembering what happened on their trip to the movies. For the high school students, invention will be more complex. They will decide what to say after a lot of rather difficult reading about the history of the cinema. But since they will be only summarizing what they have read, their invention process will not be very sophisticated. College students writing about the expressionist movement, on the other hand, will have to employ more rigorous forms of invention because they are striving to come up with complex ideas of their own.

Of course, college students (and adult writers in general) sometimes simply summarize like the high school students, and sometimes they write about their experiences like the grade schoolers. In fact, many of the writing assignments in this book are based on your personal experience, because such assignments do not require any research, and they draw on familiar, accessible material. Unlike grade school students, however, as an adult writer you will be expected to take a thoughtful approach to your everyday experiences. Rather than just telling what happened to you, you might point out the significance of what happened or explain why it happened. Given their more mature thought processes, it is natural that adults should be concerned with the meaning of their experiences. Moreover, as discussed in Chapter 1, adult readers have expectations that adult writers need to recognize and satisfy. To come up with these more complex kinds of observations requires a careful process of invention, involving not only audience analysis but also attempts to generate significant ideas.

As we noted earlier in this chapter, having something to say usually means being able to generate a pool of materials from which to draw a main idea and subordinate ideas to support it. The following opening paragraph from a student essay illustrates the concept of a *main idea*. In this case, the main idea for the whole essay is stated in the next-to-last sentence.

THE CHAOS ON WALL STREET

A month before the end of my freshman year, I received a phone call from my father concerning my summer job in New York City. He told me that I had been given a job to work on the floor of the New York Stock Exchange for a well-known brokerage firm. Immediately I had grand visions of working in a very prestigious position where I would be taught about the market. I thought I would be working in a booth doing a dignified job on the floor, where I had heard that things ran very smoothly. During my brief tenure there, *I came to realize that Wall Street in general and the firm I worked for, specifically, were very unorganized.* This disorganization led to a chaotic state of work which resulted in more people having to be hired to correct other workers' mistakes.

In the remainder of the essay, the student supports his main idea with a number of subordinate ideas: that the chaos was at least partly caused by the papers which constantly flew about in the air, that the brokers' attitude toward women furthered the disorganization, that the chaos persisted even when the writer was transferred to a new department, that in fact it got worse, and so on. (The entire essay is found in Chapter 4, pp. 119–21.)

Note that the essay is not simply about "My Experience on Wall Street," but "The Chaos on Wall Street." As an adult writer, the student wished to interpret in a selective way what he had experienced, rather than to describe everything that happened to him on his summer job. Thus his process of invention involved more than simply recalling the daily events of the summer. He needed to think in ways that a simple, unfocused description would not require.

Exercise

Choose two pieces you have recently written, whether school papers, on-the-job memos, personal letters, letters to the editor, and so on. In each case, think back to how you created the piece. Where did you get the ideas expressed? Were they with you a long time? Did they just come to you? Were they suggested to you by the circumstances of the particular situation or the needs of your audience? Did you devote much time—consciously or unconsciously—to invention?

Are your answers to these questions similar or different for each piece of writing? ✒︎

GENERATING IDEAS

> I have written one page. Just one page. I went about thinking and forgetting—sitting down before the blank page to find that I could not put one sentence together. . . . I am frightened when I remember that I have to drag it all out of myself. . . . Other writers have some starting point. Something to catch hold of . . . they know something to begin with—while I don't. I have some impressions . . . and it's all faded. . . . I am exceedingly miserable.

We've all felt this way at times. But this quotation comes from a letter written by Joseph Conrad, one of the best English authors of all time. If he wasn't ashamed to admit to a lack of ideas, neither should you. Of course, Conrad had plenty of ideas—and so do we all. The problem is remembering them when we need them.

In Chapter 1, we looked at one approach to generating ideas: analyzing your purpose(s) and your audience. Think back to the example in which you were writing an article for the anti-gun control magazine. You realized that your audience required certain information if they were to change their views, and so decided to include specific examples of the misuse of handguns. In this way, your awareness of your purpose and audience led you to generate ideas for the article. Let's explore some other techniques for invention.

Using Personal Experience

Perhaps the most natural type of invention involves using personal experience to give you ideas for writing. Personal writing is often the easiest path to interesting expression. Consider the following student paragraph:

> My fear of the devil began in childhood. I was always told in school that the devil could take any form and could be any person, and to this day certain ways that people look at me or talk to me convince me that they are Satan themselves. I've imagined my mother really being the devil in disguise just waiting for a chance to trap me. I've had similar fears about most people I've been involved with, even those who are the least likely to ever do me any harm. Seeing the movie *The Exorcist* didn't help much, either. Now there are certain noises and laughs that bring the devil to mind. When I tell people not to give me a certain look because it reminds me of the devil, they only laugh and make more obvious the look they were giving me before. Perhaps this is

their way of showing me how ridiculous a statement I have just made, but it only makes me think more of how they must be Satan.

Reaching into her own life, this student draws on personal experience for her ideas. We may shake our heads at the silliness of her predicament, but at the same time we recognize that her fears are no more ridiculous than some of our own. Personal experience writing often does just this: It works both on a specific level, in expressing the experiences of the individual writer, and on a general level, in which the writer becomes all of us.

If you think about it for a moment, you will realize that *all* writing is based on some form of personal experience. The elementary school child writing about a trip to the movies drew heavily on personal experience. But so did the high school and college students we discussed. The high school student based the history-of-cinema paper on the personal experience of reading books on that history. The college student derived the paper on the expressionist cinema from the personal experience of reading books, watching and discussing movies, and responding to and thinking about all these stimuli along the way.

We are actually talking about two kinds of personal experience: everyday experience (the trip to the movies) and intellectual experience (readings on the history of film or lectures on expressionist cinema). Both types can be used in generating ideas for writing. The kind of everyday experience examined in the student paragraph about the fear of the devil can be especially useful in personal writing assignments for composition courses, for instance. And even though many writing tasks have no place for such direct use of everyday experience, these experiences can often be the basis for more thoughtful or intellectual writing. Consider the difficulty in writing about a complex and controversial issue, such as mandatory jail sentences for repeat offenders. Without any everyday experience or intellectual experience related to this topic to draw on, you will resort to using every cliché that you have heard (note, again, the reliance on some form of personal experience—in this case, the clichés you have heard). A useful strategy of invention would be to sift through your memory for an everyday personal experience that is somehow related to the topic. For example, the issue of mandatory sentencing involves people—the offender and also the victims—whose lives have been affected by crime. You may have had some experience with crime yourself: your apartment may have been burglarized, perhaps, or a relative or friend may have been mugged. This experience caused you to think about the problem of deterring crime at some point in your past. Thus you may actually have a pool of thoughts from which you can generate ideas about one or more aspects of the mandatory sentencing issue.

Here's a more specific example. A student was assigned to write about either the advantages or the disadvantages of some aspect of modern technology. At first she decided to write about the disadvantages of nuclear power, but she found that she could not get very far with the topic. Everything she said seemed to repeat what everybody else was always saying; she didn't know enough about nuclear power to get beyond superficial comments.

In rethinking the assignment, she suddenly realized that she had had some experience herself with modern technology. Having grown up on a farm, she had spent the past two summers working on a modern farm and had been somewhat disappointed in what she saw there. She believed that recent advancements in technology had changed the farmer's work and outlook for the worse. By seeing the assignment in terms of a topic that was clearly related to her personal experience, she was able to write her paper. This is how she began her essay on the disadvantages of agribusiness:

> Agricultural experts today love to extoll the virtues of modern technology, often citing the fact that five percent of our population feeds the other ninety-five percent. In the world of agribusiness, productivity is the priority. The more output per acre, the better. This increased output is accomplished through the use of high technology equipment which aids in virtually every aspect of farming: preparing, planting, cultivating, controlling pests, harvesting.
>
> Increased mechanization and massive output, however, have had negative side effects. Technology has put a distance between the farmer and his land. Since he can view his fields from the comfort of an air-conditioned cab, contact with the crops and the soil is lost. Alienation from his product leads to a lack of concern for its quality. Pride in the product and reverence for the ritual soon disappear when the demand is for high yield. Rather than laboring hard for ten perfect bushels of corn, the modern agribusinessman cranks out ten hundred bushels, satisfied merely that they meet governmental standards.

Francis Bacon, the seventeenth-century philosopher, recognized that previous experience with a topic is necessary before a writer or speaker can generate ideas. He felt that what we are calling *invention* is not so much invention as *remembrance*. For Bacon, the process of generating ideas was "to recover or resummon that which we already know" in order to apply it to a writing task. This is precisely what the student did with her summer farming experience.

Remembering your personal experience with a topic is the place to start the invention process. "Resummoning" what you have experienced will enable you to use ideas, thoughts, opinions, and examples you already have stored in your head. And unless you consciously try to draw on these, you will often overlook them.

You can also tap a previous intellectual experience and use it to invent ideas about a topic. Suppose that in your first college English course you are assigned to write on *Henry V*, one of Shakespeare's history plays. The instructor has not given very specific instructions; she has asked only for a paper of two to three pages. You know very little about literature in general and even less about drama. However, you did find certain sections of the play interesting. Particularly intriguing was the scene in which Henry, disguised as a common soldier, debates with a group of soldiers the question of responsibility for killing during wartime: Are the soldiers responsible for the lives they have taken, or does their action in the name of the King absolve them of personal guilt and place the blame on the King? As you begin the invention process, you sift your personal experience and attempt to cross-match ideas. After some false starts and dead-end ideas, you recall that in your sophomore year in high school you gave an oral report on the subject of the "good Germans" who carried out Adolf Hitler's orders for mass murder of European Jews. Although the report was done for a history class rather than a literature class, what you learned forms a pool of material from which to draw ideas about *Henry V*. You now know that you have something worthwhile to say about the play. Your essay is far from written at this point, of course—certainly you cannot simply transfer what you remember from your sophomore report about Hitler's Germany directly to your college paper about *Henry V*. However, you have a basis of experience—reading and thinking—to work from. You have "invented" what you will write about. Your essay will not be about Shakespeare's use of figurative language or his techniques as a playwright because you know very little about such subjects. But you will write an interesting and convincing paper on Shakespeare's views on obedience and responsibility in *Henry V*.

Searching your personal experience doesn't guarantee that you will discover a sound line of approach to a particular topic you have been assigned. But your personal experience is a rich storehouse of ideas which should never be ignored as you think about what you will write.

© 1980 United Feature Syndicate, Inc.

Exercise

1. Read the cartoon on page 44. Why does Charlie Brown advise Sally that she'll need to do "hard research" to write about Ulysses Grant? How much previous experience do you think Sally has had with her topic?

2. Writing based on personal experience should be thoughtful, not merely descriptive. That is, it should raise arguments or suggest points of view, convey insights, and make or imply judgments about the topic of the paper. Read the following paragraphs which conclude an essay about the revival of interest in Hitler and the feelings of young Germans about Hitler and the "ugly Germany." In the section leading up to this excerpt, the author has described a visit with some German high school students to see a film, *Hitler, A Career*, and to tour Dachau, a World War II concentration camp.

[1]Ten days later, a class of sixteen-year-olds in Hamburg who, like most other people, had never associated Hitler with anything except the lost war and the murder of the Jews were aghast to hear of his euthanasia program, in the course of which around 80,000 physically and mentally handicapped German and Austrian hospital patients, about a third, I told them, children, were gassed. Some of them, as a matter of fact, I said, were killed in one of the special children's sections in a hospital in their own city, Hamburg.

[2]"You mean *Germans*?" a boy said in a tone of utter disbelief. "*Children*? *German Children*?" said another. "Here? In Hamburg?" They came back to it, time and again. Jews were unreal to them: in that class of thirty-six children (and in nine of the eleven young groups with whom I met), no one had ever met a Jew. And figures such as 6 million Jews, or 11 million Russian civilians—or, for that matter, 50 million dead altogether by 1945—are as impossible to absorb or visualize as is, in fact, the word "extermination." But the thought that sick *children* had been deliberately killed, in a *hospital*, in their own city, Hamburg . . . that struck a chord. One young teacher, Christa, said later, "This was worth weeks of lessons; they'll never forget it." But another teacher, elsewhere, disapproved of children being given such information . . . which may be as good an explanation as any why no German children are given it. "You shouldn't have told them things like that," she said. "They won't sleep tonight."

[3]Her reaction was significant. But I found it even more important that a shy and obviously inarticulate boy who, throughout the two hours I had spent with the Hamburg class, had not said a word, *did* say something in the end, long after we had left the subject of "mercy killing."

[4]"I've been thinking about what you said, that they killed all those people," he said, "Jews and Russians and Poles, and people who were handicapped and mentally ill. I've been thinking," he repeated, the class deathly still. "It is wrong," he said in his ponderous way. "Every human being is of value."

[5]At Dachau that day, walking his group past the "whipping post" in the square, the priest told the boys about the punishments the SS meted out every day. "They didn't say anything for quite a while," he told me, "and then one of them said, 'If one sees that . . . that thing, one has to feel ashamed of being German.' And another said, 'But were they human beings at all if they did such things?' And then finally a third, after a long pause, 'But not *all* SS were bad like those who were here,' and then he added after a moment, 'My grandpa was in the SS.'" I think that shook Father Blöckl; he couldn't think of an answer for this boy. Who can?

[6]When I saw *Hitler, A Career* I remembered something from my own childhood that I had pushed away. It was 1936. I was thirteen, traveling to Vienna from my boarding school in England. The train stopped in Nuremberg—it was the day of the rally and we were told we would be held up for several hours. "Why don't you go and see it?" said the guard to me and another little girl. "It's exciting." We went. We stood way back on the very edge of what looked like a million people, all standing in perfect symmetry and brilliant light and darkness. It was the most beautiful thing I had ever seen. And when this man suddenly appeared, seemingly out of nowhere, and all alone, the sound of his steps echoing in the huge arena, walked the long distance to the platform, I felt and shared the vibrant silence of that mass of people. And then, when he arrived and the shout began: "*Sieg Heil, Sieg Heil*" . . . I suddenly felt myself shouting with them—and so did my English friend, who spoke no German.

[7]I knew, at thirteen, what Hitler was. I had listened to clever people, and I knew that dreadful things were going to happen in our lives. I never told anyone about my hour at the Nuremberg rally: it was then, and remains, a thing of shame. But sitting in the Fest Film, I knew what these young people were feeling; and I knew and know the danger.

[8]Perhaps the time has come, outside even more than inside Germany, to exercise much sharper self-censorship, to avoid printing, publishing, and screening what is inflammatory, tendentious, or merely titillating. Above all, young Germans must come to understand that thoughtful people in other countries do not consider the children responsible for the parents' sins. (Gitta Sereny, "Germany: The 'Rediscovery' of Hitler")

a. What is the relationship between the two incidents recounted here? How does the author use the second incident to comment upon the first?

b. Do you think that the incident surrounding the Nuremberg rally is included mainly to give insight into the author's character, to shed light on human character in general, or to do both?

c. What sort of devices (for example, dialogue, detailed description) help make the piece effective?

*Suggestions
for Writing*

1. Like the author of the article on Hitler, we have all done things of which we are ashamed and which we do not like to talk about. Choose such an incident from memory and think about how you could write it up. Then write a short paper describing the incident and explaining why you acted as you did.

2. A friend has written you about an embarrassing incident she was involved in, and she is clearly depressed over the incident. To cheer her up, you have decided to write her a letter in which you humorously describe an event from your own past which you found embarrassing at the time, but which you now can laugh at. Remembering that your primary purpose is to entertain your friend, search your memory for an appropriate incident and then compose the letter. ✍

Thinking It Over Most writers spend a certain period of time before the actual writing in carefully considering what they will say in their work. We suggest a four-step approach to guide this thinking:

1. Search your memory, looking for connections with the general topic and jotting down what comes to mind.

2. Expand on as many of these items as you can by including more details.

3. Look for a main idea and subordinate ideas.

4. Allow your thoughts to simmer over a period of time—from several hours to a few days.

Let's assume that you're writing a paper on the general topic of *holidays*. Here's how the four-step approach might work:

Step 1 Taking the term *holidays*, you think back on related experiences. At first only some general images and thoughts come to mind: happy faces around Christmas trees, people stuffing themselves at picnics. Gradually you remember particular events and experiences: the tension of last-minute Christmas shopping last year, the relief you always feel when Memorial Day finally comes and you can take a weekend trip, the argument you had with your Uncle Joe last Thanksgiving. Your initial list might look something like this:

> Little brother's excitement the night before Christmas
> Easter egg hunts
> The July 4 weekend when we rented a sailboat at Tappan Lake
> Thanksgiving dinners at Aunt Florence's

Argument with Uncle Joe last Thanksgiving
Last-second shopping for Jane's Christmas present at the mall
Household always crazy before Christmas and New Year's parties
Running short of food when Abernathys stopped by last New Year's Day
Never have enough clothes for holidays
Never have enough money for holidays

Step 2 You proceed from one item in the list to another, trying to expand each one by adding more details and related ideas to it. For example, you reconsider the item "last-second shopping for Jane's Christmas present at the mall" and add to it the following:

Tense atmosphere
No spaces in parking lot
Packed aisles—bare shelves
Fight with clerk at Smiley's
Woman beat me to last bottle of Shalimar cologne

As you expand the items on your list, you find that one entry often leads to another: Thinking about the fight with the clerk may remind you about losing the bottle of cologne.

Again, consider how you might expand "Argument with Uncle Joe last Thanksgiving":

Uncle Joe yelled at Aunt Florence about late dinner
Uncle Joe in rare form—bossier than ever
20 years old, but he made me sit at the card table with the children
Humiliated my little brother for wanting potato salad at Thanksgiving dinner
Couldn't get him to shut up
Finally walked out

Step 3 After expanding the items on your list, you have a sizable pool of material from which to draw both a main idea and subordinate ideas. In this case, let's say that your attempts to expand your jottings went much easier for certain items than for others. You've had more experiences with the negative aspects of holidays—or at least the negatives were more vivid and more firmly stamped in your memory. Reviewing your jottings, you note that under "Easter egg hunts" all you could add was "Used to like to go out with Mom." But under headings like "Never enough money for clothes," "Argument with Uncle Joe," and "Last-second shopping," you had plenty to add.

The items that best reflect your experiences and recollections lead you to form a main idea. You decide that it will have something to do with the negative side of holidays. For your subordinate ideas you will use the more detailed items—such as the last-second shopping trip—to back up the main idea.

Step 4   After you have generated a main idea and some subordinate ideas, you take a break and let your thoughts simmer. Mulling over the various ideas you've generated, you decide to change some, to consolidate others, or to add new ones as they occur to you. (You can mull over your ideas during the time you spend waiting in lines, riding on the bus or subway, jogging, weeding the garden, or doing other tasks which demand little mental exertion.) During this stage, you reexamine the ideas that form the content of your paper, since you will likely come up with new ones and may begin to see problems with some you had planned to use. At this point you may also rehearse in your head or jot on paper various refined versions of your main idea.

During the simmering stage you decide that your main idea will be that you dread the aspects of holidays which most people find so rewarding: family gatherings, gift-giving, and preparing for parties. For your subordinate ideas you will talk about the dinners at Aunt Florence's that turn into fights with Uncle Joe, about the joyous thoughts of gift-giving that turn into nightmarish last-second shopping trips to the mall, and about the festive preparations for holiday parties that leave you broke, frazzled, and upset about an empty clothes closet and an empty refrigerator.

Obviously, at the end of this four-step process, you still have a lot of work ahead of you. You still need to put your ideas into some type of logical sequence. And, since the steps tend to overlap (as do the stages of the composing process), you may find yourself going backward and forward and repeating earlier steps to generate additional subordinate ideas. In generating and formulating ideas before you begin organizing or writing, however, you are giving yourself an edge. There is little worse, as our students have often told us, than facing an empty sheet of paper on which is "magically" to appear an essay of the proper length, discussing the proper topic, and deserving at least a C+. "Thinking it over" before beginning to write is not an optional part of the overall writing process—it is essential.

Exercise

Giving yourself a time limit of twenty minutes, jot down all the ideas that come to mind when you think about holidays. Return to the list later in the day and spend another twenty minutes expanding the items on your list. At this point, review the list, looking for likely main and subordinate ideas. Then put the list aside and let the ideas simmer for two or three days. If your thoughts have changed in any way during the simmering stage, explain how.

After completing the Exercise above, write a short paper on some aspect of a holiday. ⚬—

Using Common
Patterns of
Thinking in
Invention

So far we have suggested that you begin the process of invention by searching your personal experience and by carefully thinking over your preliminary ideas. With these techniques you can generate a main idea as well as a number of subordinate ideas with which to develop the paper.

In this section we will focus on another aspect of invention: how to use a knowledge of common thought patterns to generate your material. Rational thinking and writing follow one or more of several well-established patterns; among these patterns are illustration, cause and effect, comparison/contrast, process, and classification. In Chapter 4, we will discuss these patterns as ways to structure an essay. For now we will examine how some of these patterns can be used to assist you in formulating ideas.

We will conduct a two-part discussion for each pattern, first briefly explaining or defining the pattern and then showing how a knowledge of the pattern's existence can lead you to generate ideas on a given topic. We will use the same general topic as the basis for invention in the case of all the patterns.

Rather than discuss how to use all possible patterns for invention, we will demonstrate the technique by selecting three: illustration, cause and effect, and appearances/reality. Note, however, that the additional patterns which are treated as structural devices in Chapter 4 could also be used for invention.

Illustration   *Illustration* is the use of concrete examples to support a statement. In this excerpt, note how the statement made in the first two sentences is illustrated in the rest of the passage:

> As elderly people began to lose their social status, the world developed a more elaborate vocabulary with which to abuse them. The result was the invention of a new language to express contempt for old people. If we consult the *Oxford English Dictionary*, we discover that most of the pejorative terms for old men appeared for the first time in the late eighteenth and early nineteenth centuries. Some were old words which had earlier carried an honorific meaning—*gaffer*, for example. *Gaffer* had been a title of respect, even a term of endearment, in seventeenth- and eighteenth-century England. It probably arose as a contraction of godfather. But by 1820 *gaffer* (usually *old gaffer*) had been converted from a praise word into a pejorative expressing general

contempt for old men. Another such word is *fogy*, which before 1780 meant a wounded military veteran. By 1830 *fogy* had become a "disrespectful appellation for a man advanced in life." The term was put to heavy use in American politics during the 1850's, at the tide of the "Young American" movement: the rhetoric of the movement reviled *fogyism* (the characteristic thought of fogies), *fogydom* (the genus of fogies), and *fogyish* behavior in all its forms. (David Hackett Fischer, *Growing Old in America*)

You can use illustration to help you come up with an approach to your topic. Here's how one student did it. Jane was to write a paper based on a recent experience that strongly influenced her life. After searching her memory and thinking her ideas over, she chooses to focus on a bout with mononucleosis that curtailed her activities for a six-month period. This is her general topic, but what will she say about it?

Jane decides to use illustration to provide her with an approach. She first thinks of important facts, events, or incidents surrounding her illness and then works backward toward a statement of what they might mean. She makes a list of her activities immediately preceding the illness:

> Studying for midterms
> Rehearsing for a community theater production
> Tutoring at the teen center
> Planning surprise party for Dad

Looking over her jottings, she is struck by how active she had been and how the illness had made her so suddenly and totally inactive. She remembers how much she missed her theater friends, and how she lost a role for which she had been preparing hard. She notes how she had always been in good health before, and how restricting her activities for medical reasons was completely foreign to her. Recalling how depressed she was over the loss of the active and free way of life she had taken for granted, she decides on this for her main idea: "my experience with mononucleosis proved the old saying, 'You don't appreciate what you have until you've lost it.'" For her subordinate ideas, she will present the series of concrete illustrations that she used to invent the main idea.

Exercise

Each of the following student paragraphs illustrates a main idea, but neither one specifically states the idea. For instance, the first paragraph, written by a cafeteria server, presents a particular student's "attitude and eating habits" as being typical, but never says explicitly what that attitude is. Read both paragraphs and formulate an appropriate general statement of the main idea for each.

1.   The typical attitude and eating habits of students on campus can be seen in the behavior of a student named Steve. Steve comes up to the counter frowning and grunting as he examines the day's meal. No sooner has he turned up his nose than he has put his hand down on a plate of week-old beef Stroganoff about which he comments, "It looks more like dog food." The ambitious Steve proceeds to scrutinize the many hundreds of green peas with shells as protective as armored tanks. He then eases two greasy pork sandwiches onto his plate. But we have not seen the last of that young man; he reappears ten minutes later, grumbling about bad food—trying to poison him and such—but his hand eases up to the counter and removes another grease sandwich.

2.   Student A sits up straight in his chair, leaning very slightly to his right. His head, shoulders, and body are facing forward, but his eyes are focused on the exam paper on his neighbor's desk. He quickly jots down a few of the answers he has just found. Earlier, right before class, he had finished his homework assignment by copying another's paper. In another class, student B sits obediently watching the instructor who is discussing the subject, symbolism in *Hedda Gabler*. This student has already completed her assignment for today, and will be sure to study for her exam tomorrow. She is now concentrating on absorbing the information her teacher is relating. When the results are calculated at the semester's end, both students will receive the same final grade in their course—an *A*.

Cause and Effect   We are often concerned with causes and effects in our thinking, our speaking, and our writing. A *cause* is an agent (person, object, event) or an action responsible for something's happening. An *effect* is the thing that happens as a result of the cause. The following paragraph uses cause and effect to structure its main idea:

> The rise of Southeast Asian piracy is an indirect outgrowth of the war in Indochina. The end of the conflict provided a bonanza of cheap surplus weaponry. At the same time, Thailand's fishing industry, which expanded to replace Viet Nam's war-torn fleet, had to sail farther and farther to meet demand. As seafood prices tripled, a number of fishermen discovered that it was easier and more profitable to hijack fish than to catch them. Since then, piracy has spread and diversified. . . . ("The Jolly Roger Still Flies," *Time*)

Here the effect is "the rise of Southeast Asian Piracy," mentioned in the first sentence. The overall cause is "the war in Indochina." More specific and detailed causes are given in the remainder of the paragraph.

When you use cause and effect as a technique for invention, ask these questions:

1. Why does (did) this happen?

2. What happens (happened) next?

Any given effect not only *is caused* by something, but may itself *cause* a further effect. For instance, imagine that during an attempt at a transatlantic crossing, a helium-filled balloon bursts. The cause was a bird's sharp beak piercing the balloon:

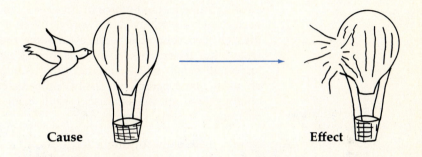

Cause　　　　　　　　　　　　　　　　　　**Effect**

And the *effect* (balloon bursting) in turn becomes a *cause* of the balloon's falling into the ocean:

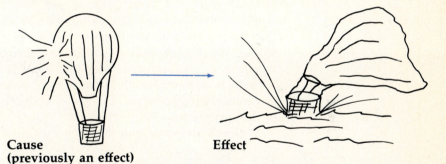

Cause　　　　　　　　　　**Effect**
(previously an effect)

During invention, then, you can usually start with any given event and work either backward to find its causes or forward to find its consequences or effects. For instance, Jane could take her experience with mononucleosis and ask herself the two cause-and-effect questions. Trying to answer "Why did this happen?" could lead her to this idea: "My bout with mononucleosis was in part caused by a growing carelessness about my body's needs for proper diet, rest, and relaxation." Answering "What happened next?" could lead her to this approach: "My experience with mononucleosis cost me not only time and money, but also an opportunity to get started in my acting career."

Notice how different these two approaches are. Starting with the same body of preliminary ideas, you can generate radically different ideas by using the two cause-and-effect questions.

Exercise

Read this student paragraph, which presents causes for the author's basic problems with writing:

> Not until I took this composition course did I begin to understand the reasons for my writing problems. Now I know that it is difficult for me to write a well-planned and well-organized composition because I have not known about the tools a writer needs to express herself. Before I begin to write my thoughts on paper, I do not make the message clear to myself, and therefore do not focus attention on creating sentences to enforce it. As a result, my thoughts are disconnected and my phrasing is wordy. Often I am not aware of the disconnected sentences because I assume the reader knows exactly what I am trying to say. In making that assumption, I omit very important details that would make the main point clear. Composing an elementary paragraph, essay, or research paper has been an onerous task for me because I have been unaware of the basic techniques for expository writing.

Apparently, in working through her ideas, this student has answered only the first cause-and-effect question, "Why does this happen?" What main idea could be developed from answering the second question, "What happens next?"

Appearances/Reality   The pattern of appearances/reality is based on the idea that the reality or deeper truth of a subject is not the same as the surface appearance. Perhaps you know someone who smiles constantly, makes jokes at all opportunities, and is always surrounded by people. He appears to be happy. But from years of observation you know that he is inwardly sad and lonely. The reality is different—in fact, the opposite of the appearance.

Here's an example of the appearances/reality pattern:

What appears to be true   The proposition that we are entering an age of scarce natural resources is constantly recited, with little more evidence than that "everyone knows" it is true. Behind the proposition is the notion that a reservoir of some necessary material—copper, for example—exists in the earth in lodes that become successively harder to mine and that bear ever lower grades of ore as mining continues. According to this reasoning, the price of copper must rise as copper becomes more difficult, and therefore more expensive, to mine. But here is a peculiar *What is really true* fact: Over the course of history, up to this very moment, copper and other minerals have been becoming not more scarce but rather more abundant. In this respect, copper follows the same historical trend as radios, undershirts, and other consumer goods, and with even greater force. (Julian L. Simon, "The Scarcity of Raw Materials")

In applying the appearances/reality idea during invention, look for aspects of your topic which contradict what seems true at first glance. In considering the negative aspects of her six-month illness, the student with mononucleosis overlooked some benefits. After thinking for a while about this new approach, she might come up with this main idea: "Far from being a complete waste of six months of my life, my experience with mononucleosis taught me greater patience, gave me better concentration and more efficient study habits, and made me more knowledgeable about my nutritional needs." The appearance is that the illness was "a complete waste . . . ." But the reality is that there were definite benefits. In an essay using this main idea, the subordinate ideas would be the particular benefits derived.

Exercise

1. Which of the following topics could be developed using an appearances/reality approach? Why? What might be the appearances in each case? The reality?

   Descriptions of food on a menu
   An attractive piece of resort property for sale
   Your relationship with a close friend or relative
   A new miracle cancer treatment
   Your reasons for wanting to pursue a certain career

2. In discussing invention, we've examined three of the common thinking patterns: illustration, cause and effect, and appearances/reality. Several more patterns are discussed in Chapter 4, which focuses on using the patterns as structural and organizational devices (pp. 116–47). Read those pages and become familiar with the additional patterns. Then try to discover a likely main idea and some subordinate ideas for *one* of the following topics by using each pattern.

   My (a friend's, a relative's) fear of air travel
   Family quarrels
   Fad diets
   Job hunting

Suggestions for Writing

1. Choose one of the five topics from Exercise **1** and write a short paper, using the appearances/reality pattern to help you invent your ideas.

2. Select a paper you have written for this course. Using the same topic as a point of departure, develop a new main idea and some subordinate ideas by applying one of the common thinking patterns to the material. You may employ one of the three patterns discussed in this chapter or one of the additional patterns presented in Chapter 4. Write a short paper, making use of the new ideas you have invented.

part

TWO

FORM AND ARRANGEMENT

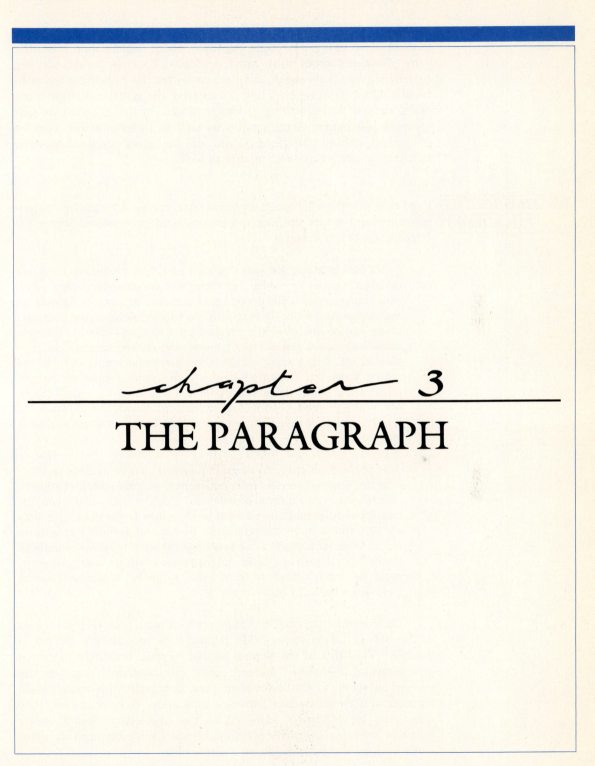

chapter 3

THE PARAGRAPH

Looking at the structure of a paragraph, you can see that it is a miniature version of an essay. The same questions about organization arise; the same decisions about form must be made. Because paragraphs are usually shorter than essays, they are easier for the beginning writer to handle. Once paragraph writing is mastered, the writer can transfer the skills learned to the writing of longer pieces. In this chapter, we will examine the nature of paragraphs as well as techniques for effective paragraph writing. At the end, you will be better prepared to write paragraphs and essays and reports as well.

WRITING UNIFIED PARAGRAPHS

Read carefully the following successful paragraphs. A freshman composition student wrote the first; an experienced professional writer for *Interiors* wrote the second.

> *It's hard to believe that such a valuable part of the anatomy as the mouth could get someone in trouble, but throughout my elementary school years, mine always seemed to find a way.* I got C's in conduct, not for fighting on the playground or for dipping girls' pigtails in ink wells, but because I made use of one of God's greatest gifts to man—speech. I simply talked too much, and obviously the teachers never blamed God; they blamed me. I had an amazing ability to say the wrong thing at the wrong time, but I couldn't help myself. Some people are natural athletes and some are natural students; I was always a natural talker. My mouth seemed to work of its own accord. Words would pop out of it at the most inconvenient times and lead to the most embarrassing situations.

> *In public architecture, the symbolic is essential.* While modern architecture does not allow the frills and follies of gold-gilded chambers, nevertheless, the county courthouse, the city hall, and even the municipal office building all must be somehow larger than life if they are to impress upon the public the power and authority of government. Minimal budgets often work against such maximal intentions; thus every element in a design no matter how mundane or "ordinary" must be manipulated to contribute symbolic content. (Daralice Donkevoet Boles, "Court Curves")

Each of these paragraphs has an obvious main idea. The main idea of the first could be stated, "My talking in school always got me in trouble." The idea of the second is that "Public buildings represent governmental authority." In each case, all statements made in the paragraph relate to the main idea. (You can verify this easily: Read through and consider each sentence separately. Note that every one comments on the main idea—either the problem of being overly talkative or the symbolism of public buildings. Each paragraph is *unified*, controlled from start to finish by a single idea.

These paragraphs also have other desirable features. Both have a clearly worded *topic sentence* (italicized) which expresses the main idea and prepares the reader for what is to come. Furthermore, the main idea in each paragraph is fully developed. As readers, we feel that the writer has given us enough information to support the idea of the paragraph. This is particularly important because, in both paragraphs, supporting the main idea is the writers' primary purpose. Because these paragraphs are so unified, accomplishing the primary purpose is easier. All the sentences serve to convince the reader of the truth of a single statement.

Exercise

Read the following paragraphs and determine the main idea of each. If the paragraph has a topic sentence, underline it.

1.   The raccoon's intelligence is nearly matched by its strength and ferocity. One raccoon with a good foothold in its tree suspended in midair a 200-pound Yale professor who had grabbed it by the tail. A cornered raccoon backs up against a wall, rock or tree trunk to avoid being attacked from behind; and with its slashing claws and needle-sharp teeth it can disembowel or cut the jugulars of two or three dogs its size or larger. (A.B.C. Whipple, "The Raccoon Life in Darkest Suburbia")

2.   Most people think that being a department store salesperson is not a difficult job, but from my experience I know that it takes time, effort, and patience to be successful. Once you have helped the customers, you have to ring up and bag the merchandise, then be sure to thank them. You also have to help with displaying the merchandise attractively, with putting out new lines, with taking inventory, with keeping stock organized, and with keeping the counter area clean and tidy. You have to know what is in stock and what needs to be put out. Then, too, a salesperson must be courteous when a customer is unreasonable and demanding. As you can see, a salesperson does more than just stand around and ring up orders.

3.   Unlike the white high school, Lafayette County Training School distinguished itself by having neither lawn, nor hedges, nor tennis court, nor climbing ivy. Its two buildings (main classrooms, the grade school and home economics) were set on a dirt hill with no fence to limit either its boundaries or those of bordering farms. There was a large expanse to the left of the school which was used alternately as a baseball diamond or a basketball court. Rusty hoops on the swaying poles represented the permanent recreation equipment, although bats and balls could be borrowed from the P.E. teacher if the borrower was qualified and the diamond wasn't occupied. (Maya Angelou, *I Know Why the Caged Bird Sings*)

4.   Several years ago, a trip to Washington, D.C., cost me $12.50 in gasoline and $24.00 a night in a hotel. This spring the gasoline was over $50 and the hotel was $108 a night. Similarly, a local news columnist recently reported being charged $6.00 for a Coke at a New York hotel while covering the Democratic Convention. A friend who visited Europe this summer reported that things are even worse there for Americans—a gin and tonic in France went for $12.50.

USING THE TOPIC SENTENCE

As we have seen, the *topic sentence* states a paragraph's main idea, capturing the focus of the whole piece in one sentence. The topic sentence is probably the single most important device for helping writers guide their paragraphs. It provides the reader with a sense of direction and the writer with a feeling of control. The topic sentence often—but not always—comes at the beginning of a paragraph. The following student paragraph illustrates the function of a topic sentence:

> *Being responsible for a car of my own has shown me that car ownership shouldn't be taken lightly.* Before I owned a car, I would use my friends' cars frequently and thought that all there was to having a car was putting gas in it and driving away. Now, however, I know about car notes and insurance premiums, which you have to pay if you want to keep driving. I am more concerned about checking things like tires, the battery, and the brakes because if I don't do this, no one else will. I am also more careful about my driving habits since I could have an accident otherwise, causing my insurance rates to increase. And if I were to dent my car, I would get less money for it if I wanted to sell it.

Note that the writer states her main idea—that owning an automobile increased her sense of responsibility—in the first sentence. All other sentences comment on or support this idea. Although the writer probably had more information about car ownership (the convenience and prestige her car affords her, its reliability, and so on), her topic sentence indicates that she was concerned only with showing the reader how she gained a sense of responsibility when she bought a car. As she completed the actual writing of the paragraph, she used the topic sentence as a guide in deciding whether any given sentence belonged in her paragraph. If the paragraph included sentences about the car's many options or its comfortable ride, we would feel that something was wrong; our expectations would be violated by the inclusion of sentences which do not relate to the idea clearly expressed in the topic sentence.

A topic sentence, then, is a convenience for writer and reader alike. Like most conveniences, it is not a necessity—every paragraph need not have one. However, a well-constructed topic sentence simplifies the writing task and is a reliable tool in the composition of effective paragraphs.

Exercise Choose any three paragraphs from a paper or papers you have written for this course. Underline the topic sentence—if there is one—of each paragraph. If there is no topic sentence, compose a sentence which expresses the paragraph's main idea. As you look back at your writing, try to get a feeling for your own habits as a paragraph writer. Do most of your paragraphs have topic sentences? Do you recall being aware of your paragraphs' main ideas at the time you wrote them, or did you write the paragraphs chiefly by intuition?

Invention and the Topic Sentence

A main idea should be a natural outgrowth of your invention process. So, in shaping a topic sentence, avoid hastily thinking up a statement like, "I enjoy reading detective fiction for several reasons," and then struggling to come up with the "several reasons." You may, in fact, enjoy detective fiction for only one or two reasons. A better approach is to go through a careful process of invention, such as we discussed in Chapters 1 and 2. The subordinate ideas that you generate to support the main idea of a whole essay can, in turn, be main ideas of paragraphs. Expand those subordinate ideas by adding related, more detailed thoughts, and you will produce a paragraph. The topic sentence will express the main idea. Not only will that sentence introduce the topic or subject, but it likely will also state or imply the perspective from which you view your subject matter. The example discussed in the section on invention (pp. 47–49), for instance, focused on generating ideas relating to *negative* experiences with holidays.

The following is an introductory paragraph for an essay on that topic. The main idea for both the paragraph and the whole essay is expressed in the opening topic sentence:

> *Tell me, can you think of anything more nauseating than holiday preparations*? To me, they are a series of events I suffer through. I think that the holidays involve too many decisions. I have to figure out what to cook, what to buy for everyone, and what decorations to use. My family and I rush from store to store trying to decide what the younger children will wear. After those decisions have been made, I spend quite a bit of time thinking over my own holiday wardrobe. If the preparations led to anything enjoyable, perhaps I would not mind them, but after all the work is done, what's waiting for me is a large group of loud and cantankerous relatives!

Note that the topic sentence introduces the subject ("holiday preparations") and the perspective ("nauseating" causes the reader to expect to read about what's undesirable about holiday preparations). In this case, because the paragraph launches an entire essay, each subordinate idea within the paragraph (too many decisions about food, clothes, and parties; bad experiences with relatives) will become the main idea of a paragraph in the body of the essay. Thus each subordinate idea in this opening paragraph helps the writer invent the topic sentence for each paragraph of the body.

Even the most careful attempts at inventing may not always result in your knowing exactly what you will say in a paragraph before you start writing. The act of writing itself will often help you refine the main idea, resulting in a more meaningful topic sentence. Refining your topic sentence through the act of writing may occur when you are writing a single, self-contained, free-standing paragraph, and is even more likely to occur as you compose paragraphs that are parts of lengthier essays.

Suggestion for Writing

Write a single paragraph based on one of the following topics. Using the approaches to invention suggested in Chapters 1 and 2, generate a main idea and then compose a topic sentence that reflects your thinking. Proceed to write a draft of the paragraph, remembering that the inventive process may continue into the actual writing.

A hobby or special interest
My most forgettable night out
Saturday morning cartoon shows
Choosing a career

Making the Topic Sentence Appropriately General

Keep the topic sentence appropriately general; that is, abstract enough to include the ideas, attitudes, or feelings that form the paragraph, but specific enough to include *only* those ideas, attitudes, or feelings. Check that your topic sentence is appropriately general, and you will discover whether the sentence is an effective one.

Many beginning writers compose topic sentences that are too general and, consequently, too vague. For example, a student who was to write a paragraph explaining why she liked or disliked a certain person wrote this topic sentence:

My paragraph is about a friend of mine, Carol Phillips.

The problem with the sentence is that it does not tell, specifically, what the writer will discuss about her friend. The paragraph following such a sentence could discuss any number of things—the friend's hobbies, her educational background, her unfortunate accident last summer; virtually anything could be included, so long as it related in some way to Carol Phillips.

Looking at the rest of the first draft of her paragraph, the writer found the key to revising the topic sentence:

. . . Carol is someone you can tell your problems to without worrying that she will repeat them to others. For instance, if I were to tell her about an argument I had with my boyfriend, I know she would never tell anyone the details. I also like Carol because I can count on her for a favor. I know if I ever need some money, if she has it, she will lend it to me. And whenever I need help making a decision, Carol is one of the few people I'll go to for advice.

The paragraph explains the reasons for the writer's closeness to her friend—particularly her trust in and admiration for her. She altered the topic sentence to reflect this fact:

Carol Phillips is my best friend because she is trustworthy and dependable, one of the few close friends I have.

Instead of stating the very general idea that the paragraph will be "about Carol Phillips," the writer indicates she will be discussing particular qualities Carol has.

Exercise

Assume that your assignment is to write a paragraph of approximately 150 words. Read through the following sentences, commenting on the level of generality of each. Which are the stronger possibilities as topic sentences for a paragraph? Rewrite the sentences that are not appropriately general. You may wish to consider each sentence from the standpoint of the number of topics it will permit you to discuss. The more general the idea, the more items to which it can refer, and the less suitable it is as a topic sentence.)

1. There are many ways to spend free time efficiently.
2. Psychology is a practical course to take because it can help you better understand your relationships with other people.
3. Academic reputation, cost, and social opportunities are three things I considered before choosing a college.
4. Academic reputation is something I considered in choosing a college.
5. Two qualities I value in others are honesty and generosity.
6. Some things about people annoy me.
7. Playing racquetball is fun.
8. I like to help people.
9. For several reasons, the Pittsburgh Steelers are a fine team.
10. Many years of education have shown me the way to success.

Even though a topic sentence expresses an idea that is more general than any other in the paragraph, keep your wording of that idea as specific as possible. For example, if your paragraph discusses four important considerations to keep in mind while serving a tennis ball, you should say just that in the topic sentence: "When you are serving a tennis ball, keep these four important considerations in mind." Avoid using *several* or *a few*. You know there will be four, no more and no less, and so you should inform your reader of that fact. If your paragraph describes four tips on arm movements while serving a tennis ball, your topic sentence could be this specific: "There are four important points to remember about arm movements during the serving of a tennis ball." The rest of the paragraph would explain the individual tips, and the topic sentence, referring as it does to all four items, would still be the most general statement in the passage.

Exercise

1. In each of these student paragraphs, the topic sentence is italicized. What words could be changed to make each topic sentence reflect more precisely the information contained in the paragraph?

   Basketball is a good hobby not only for me but for anyone else. It's fun and it's a valuable exercise that helps me stay in shape. It has made me a more competitive person. It strengthens the mind, because you're always thinking while you're on the court. It also quickens your reflexes. And if you're afraid of crowds, basketball helps you overcome this because you play in front of small and large crowds. Basketball is exciting, competitive, and healthful.

   It's surprising to see what some of the residents of Georgetown do. Many times pieces of furniture are, for no obvious reason, left out on the street to be destroyed. I can recall once walking down 35th Street and seeing a wooden rocking chair that, though slightly damaged, could have been easily repaired. I remember thinking how my grandmother had often talked about having a rocking chair, and I wanted to take it home to her. Instead, the city collection truck came by, swept up the chair, and threw it onto the load of metal scraps and old tires. I couldn't help feeling that it would have been better suited to my grandmother's living room.

2. Reconsider the paragraph you drafted for the assignment on page 64. Is the topic sentence of that paragraph appropriately general? Why or why not? If it is not, try making it more general or more specific, as needed, and then rewrite the paragraph accordingly.

In addition to making a topic sentence appropriately general, you should consider that its wording, especially if it is the first sentence in the paragraph, will be a signpost for your reader. Its positive or negative phrasing will set up the reader's assumptions about what follows.

Recall the topic sentence of the paragraph on page 63: "Tell me, can you think of anything more nauseating than holiday preparations?" The most important single word in this sentence is *nauseating*; the highly negative associations of that word manipulate the reader's response right from the start. As another example, note again this topic sentence: "Carol Phillips is my best friend because she is trustworthy and dependable, one of the few close friends I have." The words *trustworthy*, *dependable*, *best friends*, and *close* all help shape the reader's awareness of what will follow in the paragraph.

Exercise

1. Parts of the topic sentences in the following paragraphs have been deleted. Read the paragraphs carefully, and then complete the topic sentences. Work on filling the blanks with words that reflect accurately what the paragraphs are about. Choose words that are as precise as possible, words that will capture the meaning as well as the tone or attitude of the whole paragraph.

By no means are all teenagers _____. Indeed, across the nation, youngsters are working hard in schools and jobs. They are making pragmatic decisions at an earlier age and are more involved in community affairs. The high school dropout rate has even declined: In 1977 it was 25 percent as opposed to 31 percent in 1960. Of those who graduate, 45 percent go on to attend college, up from 33 percent. ("How Tough Should Parents Be?" *Ladies Home Journal*)

My first thoughts about the writing class _____. I told myself that the course was probably a waste of time and effort. The professor would probably teach the course in a dry, theoretical fashion. In other words, first he would have the students work at using good vocabulary, then writing sentences, then paragraphs, and finally full papers, all of which seemed wasteful to me. Following the acceleration to a full paper, the instructor would assign topics for papers that were very long and the students probably wouldn't have any idea of what the topics really meant. These beliefs reinforced my other reasons for not wanting to enroll in English Composition.

The town _____; not much is there except the cotton mill, the two-room houses where the workers live, a few peach trees, a church with two colored windows, and a miserable main street only a hundred yards long. On Saturdays the tenants from the near-by farms come in for a day of talk and trade. Otherwise the town is lonesome, sad, and like a place that is far off and estranged from all other places in the world. The nearest train stop is Society City, and the Greyhound and White Bus Lines use the Forks Falls Road which is three miles away. The winters here are short and raw, the summers white with glare and fiery hot. (Carson McCullers, *The Ballad of the Sad Café*)

Oscar Wilde's academic career at Trinity [College]_____
_____. He was twice placed in the First Class in
the university examinations, he won a Composition Prize for Greek
Verse, he was elected to a Foundation Scholarship in Classics in
addition to the two entrance scholarships which he already held, and
in February 1874, when in his third year, he carried off the coveted
Berkeley Gold Medal for Greek. This last distinction gave his father
particular pleasure, and the elder Wilde wrote to Sir John Gilbert, the
president of the Royal Irish Academy, inviting him to celebrate the
event in Merrion Square: "We are asking a few old friends upon
Moytura cheer [i.e., to drink whiskey or poteen] on Thursday, and
also to cheer dear old Oscar on having obtained the Berkeley Gold
Medal last week with great honour. You were always a favourite of his,
and he hopes you will come." (H. Montgomery Hyde, *Oscar Wilde*)

2. Choose one of the topics below and follow invention techniques to
   generate ideas on it. Using those ideas, compose a topic sentence
   appropriate for a paragraph, concentrating not only on shaping the
   main idea, but also on making the sentence appropriately general
   and accurate in its expression of your attitudes toward your
   subject.

   A favorite pet
   A musical group or singer
   A humorous childhood experience
   An exciting sporting event you attended
   A treasured possession

Structuring the Topic Sentence

To be sure your topic sentence both introduces your topic and pinpoints
your perspective on it, consider the grammatical subject of the sentence
to be equal to the paragraph's topic; the predicate then establishes your
perspective. For example, this topic sentence is much too general for a
successful paragraph to be based on it:

Sports | are healthful exercise.

subject | predicate

The sentence refers to any and every sport, and the paragraph that
would follow could discuss all types of exercise derived from sports. We
could easily make the subject, "sports," less general by specifying one
sport—"skiing," perhaps—or type of sport—"water sports." And we
could make the predicate, "are healthful exercise," more specific by
defining precise types of exercise, depending on the sport chosen. For
instance, assume we choose "racquetball" as the subject. The topic
sentence could read, "Racquetball improves stamina, quickens reflexes,

and builds stronger leg muscles." The predicate now states exactly what kind of "healthful exercise" can be gained from the sport.

Exercise

The following potential topic sentences need revision. Revise each by making the subject, the predicate, or both less abstract.

1. Hard work develops good character traits in most people.
2. My reaction to my father's serious illness has taught me some things I never knew about myself.
3. Janet and her best friend have begun to drift apart because of their differing attitudes.
4. My recent success can be attributed to my approach to life.
5. Travel offers many opportunities, but it also exposes the traveler to certain dangers.

Placement of the Topic Sentence

It is generally helpful to put the topic sentence first and then follow through with a series of sentences supporting it. Both student and professional writers often use this strategy successfully. Note, for example, the placement of the topic sentence in the following paragraph on Afghanistan:

> *Health conditions are appalling.* In the countryside, almost anywhere you look, you are likely to see people squatting and spreading their robes. Excrement may make good fertilizer, but it also gets into the drinking water. Everywhere, people of all ages are wheezing and coughing up phlegm. Noses drip. Much of the year it is too cold to bathe regularly, and few people do. Half the children of Afghanistan die before they reach the age of five. (Jonathan Kwitny, "Afghanistan: Crossroads of Conflict")

Similarly, this student paragraph, written for a final essay examination in a marketing course, uses the topic-sentence-first technique:

> *Institutional advertising and product advertising are two different marketing approaches open to manufacturers.* Institutional advertising promotes the company's organizational image, ideas, prestige, and possibly political position. Product advertising, on the other hand, focuses directly on the product or service for sale by the company. Unlike institutional advertising, which almost always broadly stresses the whole company image, product advertising can focus on the product as a whole or on one aspect of the product.

The writer first states the main idea. He then explains and supports his first sentence throughout the rest of the paragraph. Of course, the topic sentence of this paragraph could, with slight alteration, have been placed at the end of the passage: "Thus, institutional advertising and product advertising are two clearly different marketing approaches open to manufacturers." Placing the topic sentence last would not have significantly changed the meaning of the paragraph. But since this paragraph was written as a direct answer to an examination question, the writer chose to place the topic sentence first to establish immediately, for his instructor, an understanding of what the paragraph would be about and, for himself, a sense of control over its contents.

Take a look at the paragraphs we have used as examples so far in this chapter and you will see that nearly all of them begin with a topic sentence. But research has shown (and a quick glance through any magazine or book will verify) that a large percentage of paragraphs do not feature an opening topic sentence. There are, in fact, numerous reasons why certain paragraphs do not begin with a topic sentence. Although the paragraph on Afghanistan quoted above does begin with a topic sentence, most of the paragraphs in the article from which it was taken do not. In the following paragraph, for example, the topic sentence is the second in the paragraph:

> Poverty and ill health are at the roots of the upheaval that has been going on in Afghanistan for the past two years. *Yet the Communists don't seem to have addressed these problems directly.* I asked Shanawaz Shanwany, the governor of Kandahar province, one of the largest in the country, what he thought his government's number one problem was. "No problems," he replied. "We are all happy." Then he reconsidered, and acknowledged that he does have a problem— resisting the imperialists who occasionally cross the border from Pakistan. (Shanawaz, thirty-eight, a former army officer and party stalwart, had just become governor of his third province in the past year. He confessed to me that he had no idea of its population, its principal exports, or how many of its people were affected by the country's tumultuous land reform program last year. His appointment, like all important decisions in the country, came from the party's revolutionary committee in Kabul, a tightly knit, little known group.)

All sentences after sentence two expand on the idea that the Communists have not addressed the country's problems (and aren't even aware of them). The paragraph does not elaborate on the idea of sentence one—that poverty and ill health are the problems responsible for upheaval. But we can easily see why the opening sentence is needed if we look at what comes *before*. It sums up a major point of several preceding paragraphs and leads into the purpose of the paragraph quoted, functioning, therefore, as a *transition*.

Other paragraphs in this same article do not have a topic sentence at all. Consider this one:

The literacy rate is estimated at 10 percent, perhaps the world's lowest, and that means the ability to read a simple signboard, not the works of Kierkegaard. At a conservative minimum, 80 percent of the people live off the food they grow and the animals they raise.

Each sentence focuses on a different subject (sentence one, literacy; sentence two, agriculture). And although no single sentence directly expresses the main idea, such an idea is clearly implied. The paragraph works by giving two specific examples which support an implied topic sentence. If a topic sentence were included, the paragraph might read like this:

> *Afghanistan does not enjoy even an adequate standard of living, by modern guidelines*. The literacy rate is estimated at 10 percent, perhaps the world's lowest, and that means the ability to read a simple signboard, not the works of Kierkegaard. At a conservative minimum, 80 percent of the people live off the food they grow and the animals they raise.

Although the use of a topic sentence in writing paragraphs is wise (particularly in writing paragraphs for college papers), the notion of the main idea itself, which is embodied by the topic sentence, is ultimately the most important matter. You should make use of the topic sentence most of the time, and when you write a paragraph without an actual topic sentence, you should make sure that all sentences are obviously related to some broader, central idea.

The following paragraph also raises questions about the placement of the topic sentence. Note how the paragraph seems, at first, to have a typical opening topic sentence:

> Our American enthusiasm for competing in sports has overflowed into many other areas of our lives. We use the vernacular of sport as the metaphor to describe our feelings about people and events. Phrases such as a whole new ballgame, a winning streak, Monday morning quarterback, he's a winner, she's a great competitor, they're a bunch of losers, have become everyday catchalls, used in politics, business, and even in the arts. Vince Lombardi's famous maxim that winning isn't everything, it's the only thing, sometimes seems to have become our new golden rule. (Maeve Slavin, "Winning Is Everything . . . Or Is It?")

On finishing this paragraph, you probably are unsure of whether the first or the last sentence is the topic sentence. Both are certainly strong contenders. This paragraph is fairly typical of the kinds of paragraphs we come across in everyday reading, and yet it seems to defy much of what we have said about the topic sentence. But notice that the paragraph is controlled by a central idea and that its compound topic sentence has been split into its two clauses, each treated as a separate sentence—one of them placed at the beginning to focus our attention initially, and the other placed at the end to sum up. The first and last sentences could be combined into a single topic sentence:

> Our American enthusiasm for competing in sports has overflowed into so many other areas of our lives that Vince Lombardi's famous maxim, "Winning isn't everything, it's the only thing," sometimes seems to have become our new golden rule."

The split topic sentence is not all that rare. Consider this paragraph:

> *Before last week's culmination of Voyager's odyssey, a two-day close encounter of the most extraordinary kind, Saturn was relatively unknown.* It is a gigantic swirling gaseous ball, mostly hydrogen and helium that could encompass 815 earths, but even with the best telescopes and the most settled atmospheric conditions, it had never been seen as much more than a fuzzy yellow ringed sphere. *Now, in a flash of binary bits across space, it had become a clearly recognizable place under the sun, with its own wonders, surprises and mysteries.* (Time)

Here, too, the split topic sentence was used to express a two-part main idea. We could express the main idea in this condensed form:

> Before last week, Saturn was relatively unknown, but now it had become clearly recognizable.

In actual practice, a topic sentence can appear anywhere in a paragraph. Let's look at another paragraph from *Time* magazine:

> On the eve of Independence Day, which falls on September 15, the President of Costa Rica traditionally lights a "Liberty Torch" in the old capital city of Cartago and the next day addresses schoolchildren in the present capital of San Jose. *This year things did not work out too well.* At Cartago, President Rodrigo Carazo Odio, 54, was shouted down when he tried to speak, and later discovered that the air had been let out of his tires. At San Jose he did not even bother with the customary oration. He quickly paraphrased the first verse of the country's national anthem ("Costa Ricans, remember that beneath the limpid blue of your skies, there will always be work and peace") and just as quickly sat down.

As you can see, either a split topic sentence pattern or a topic sentence in the middle of a paragraph is quite acceptable. But when you are unsure about how to write a given paragraph, you should rely on the more dependable topic-sentence-first pattern.

Exercise

1. Compose an appropriate topic sentence for each of the following student paragraphs and then decide where in the paragraph it ought to be placed—or whether it should be included at all.

    a.   Now that he is retired, my grandfather enjoys gardening and spends much of his time during the summer with his strawberry plants and melon vines. During the winter, he spends his time inventing all sorts of things that he feels will make life easier for us around the house. If he isn't inventing, he is reading. He loves to read anything he can get his hands on. He also has a great love for children and plays with them constantly when relatives come over during the holidays.

    b.   My sisters and I received a Tinkertoy set one rainy Christmas. Miniature donut-shaped things with holes in the sides and cylindrical sticks of various colors and lengths were the building blocks. The kit also came with a booklet revealing some of the things that could be achieved, though the possibilities really seemed endless. We could grab a handful of Tinkertoys and build virtually anything! A zoo with over a dozen animals ranging from a giraffe to a turtle was created. A three-story house was erected in just a few hours. We all had our masterpieces; mine was a movie camera. It had three legs and a lens which turned, and was nearly as tall as I was. For a whole week I roamed around "shooting" everything in sight. When, by chance, a leg would fall off, I'd merely stick it back on and the camera was as good as new. Finally I got tired of it and, as most frustrated artists do, threw it in a corner. An hour later, though, I was building the "greatest windmill ever!" The toy had its faults, of course; it broke too easily and the pieces disappeared. But it did keep our attention for a couple of months, much longer than most toys.

2. One virtue of using an opening topic sentence is that, in the event you do stray from your main idea, the strong and clear presence of the topic sentence provides a means for spotting the difficulty and correcting the problem. By systematically checking each sentence against the opening topic sentence, you can determine whether the paragraph goes off the topic and, if so, exactly where. Check the sentences in each of the following paragraphs against the opening topic sentence to determine whether any do not belong:

    a.   *My explanation of terrorism is that people feel they need a way to express their feelings toward a situation involving them, over which they have no immediate control.* Some of the people in the Middle

East can be seen in these terms. An article in *U.S. News and World Report* reported a Palestinian terrorist offense costing the lives of 21 school children. The terrorists were pictured as frustrated and angry men in the article, which was titled, "Terrorists' Goal: Sabotage Peace at All Costs!" "It was a familiar pattern confronting Henry Kissinger: a Palestinian outrage, Israeli retaliation." There were no hostages involved in this offense. One high ranking official said "There are no easy problems anywhere. Mr. Kissinger overcomes one difficulty only to find himself up against another, equally frustrating and hard to solve."

b.   *For Japanese people, smiling is a part of language.* Through a smile, we are able to understand each other's thoughts and desires. For instance, when someone asks a girl to go to a movie with him, and she responds "Well . . ." and gives him a smile, he understands that she doesn't want to go. Or when I ask my friend how he did on a tough examination and he says "Let's see . . ." and gives me a smile, I will immediately realize that he did poorly. Most Westerners don't understand the Japanese smile, but it is very important that they learn to recognize it. To them, the smile seems mysterious. Japanese people need smiling to express feelings they could not convey through language alone.

As you grow more confident in your use of the topic sentence, you may want to experiment with placing it in different positions in the paragraph or with omitting it altogether. Begin your experiments with the topic-sentence-last pattern. Unlike paragraphs with an opening topic sentence, those with a closing topic sentence start out with *uninterpreted* facts, details, or observations, and then lead up to a topic sentence that explains the meaning or importance of what has gone before it. The freshman who wrote the following paragraph was consciously experimenting with placement of the topic sentence. She could have placed the last sentence (or a slight variation of it) at the beginning of the paragraph, but instead tried for a different effect:

I had been going to school for ten years before I ever had to worry about a class. My grades were always good even though I spent a minimal amount of time studying. And if I ever did have trouble grasping a concept, I had only to try a little harder, expend a little more energy, and eventually I could understand it. I had no sympathy for students who had problems with their studies because I assumed that they were just being lazy. That attitude changed abruptly when I enrolled in chemistry. Every day I went to class, listened attentively to the lecture, took careful notes and thought I understood what was going on. But every night when I went home and tried to do the assignments, it all seemed like gibberish. I simply did not have the intelligence, the capacity for knowledge and understanding, that I needed for that subject. With the help of some friends and my father, I passed the course, although I never did learn much chemistry. *Instead, I learned that diligence is only partly responsible for academic success; you also need intelligence.*

In this case, the topic sentence at the end provides the necessary conclusion for the reader.

Exercise

The student who wrote the following paragraph felt that a concluding topic sentence was effective. Do you agree? Why or why not?

Recently my music teacher and I were discussing how to achieve the best tone quality on my instrument, the marimba. As I played, he asked me to look at where I was striking the sharp and flat keys with my mallets. He explained that the string that holds the bars on the instrument creates a nodal point having very little resonance. Striking the bar just forward of this string produces a pretty good sound, but if the bar is struck at the very edge, it will resonate much more. As I had been playing just ahead of the string, I was getting a *good* sound, but because of this I had never looked for a *better* one. His idea made sense, but it was difficult for my mind and my hands to grasp this new way of playing because the old way had become habit. With practice, however, I have finally begun playing on the edge of the bars. To develop a new approach to playing my instrument took patience, time, and retraining, but it has produced a better sound.

Suggestion for Writing

Choose one of the situations outlined below and write the appropriate paragraph.

1. In your new position as an editorial writer for the college newspaper, you have been assigned to write a one-paragraph editorial containing a humorous observation about a school event you have attended (perhaps a dull pep rally or a disorganized political forum). The editor has asked you to write the piece in order to bolster sagging interest in the paper.

   Aim for 150 to 200 words. Using the invention techniques, work on developing a main idea and a topic sentence to express it. Then use the topic sentence as a guide in deciding which details to include in the paragraph. Remember that you are trying to take a humorous perspective on the event you select.

2.   The college planning committee has announced a public hearing on the parking problems on and around campus. You cannot attend the meeting, and so decide to make your views known in writing.

Compose a paragraph of about 200 words that you will send to the committee. Develop your main idea and topic sentence by using the invention techniques. Then use the topic sentence as a guide in deciding which details to include in the paragraph. Remember that your purpose is to persuade the committee that more parking facilities are (or are not) needed.   ✍

DEVELOPING THE PARAGRAPH FULLY

Besides striving to give your paragraphs unity of idea, you should give them depth by fully explaining or supporting the main idea. In writing a paragraph you must not only state your central idea and stick to it throughout the paragraph, but also say enough about it to convince the reader of its truth and to demonstrate your command of the subject. After all, these are usually your primary and secondary purposes in writing a paragraph. Notice how this student paragraph thoroughly develops and supports the idea stated in the opening topic sentence:

> *Supertankers transporting oil from Alaska should not be allowed in Puget Sound because any accident involving a huge tanker could devastate the many natural resources and recreational facilities that the sound provides.* The absence of shellfish due to an oil slick could wipe out industries which profit in clams, oysters, shrimp, crab, and mussels. Many people would be left jobless. Moreover, animals that thrive solely on shellfish, like certain types of waterfowl, would slowly disappear, thus disrupting the delicate ecological balance. Fish would suffer, too, hurting industry and, again, disrupting the natural balance. Recreation, which makes the Puget Sound area so popular, would cease to be. Beaches would be ruined, swimming areas no longer clean, and pleasure boats damaged. The beauty of the area would soon be destroyed. Even though the Sound is the most logical place to unload the oil, economically and geographically, and even though the tankers must abide by strict safeguards, the safeguards are not flawless, and it would take but one mistake to destroy a valuable natural asset.

Whether or not you agree with the point of view expressed in the paragraph, it would be hard to deny that the writer seems to know what she is talking about. Consider how much less effective the paragraph would be if she had failed to develop it fully:

> Supertankers transporting oil from Alaska should not be allowed in Puget Sound. There is too much danger of an accident, and this could upset the delicate balance of nature. We would all suffer: industry,

wildlife, and all the people who live in the area would be dealt a devastating blow.

This version merely states ideas; it does not attempt to support them.

The best approach to developing a paragraph fully is to have something genuine to say about its topic. Doing a careful job of invention is as valuable for achieving development as it is for achieving unity. The student who wrote the paragraph on Puget Sound was, in fact, from the state of Washington and knew her subject well. The best writing techniques available could not have helped her fill in the details of her paragraph if she did not have the facts.

In considering invention as part of achieving full development of ideas, you may wish to refer to the patterns of thinking discussed on pages 50–55 in Chapter 2 and on pages 116–46 in Chapter 4. The patterns and devices discussed there are useful not only for generating ideas, but also for helping you follow through on the content of a paragraph once you have determined your central point.

For example, the paragraph on Puget Sound is developed through a combination of *illustration* and *analysis*, and the paragraph on institutional advertising and product advertising (p. 69) is developed through *comparison/contrast*. This student paragraph makes significant use of *process analysis* in order to arrive at a *definition:*

> A "push" policy is one type of promotional effort often used in marketing. Through such a policy manufacturers attempt, by advertising to wholesalers, by sales promotion, and through personal selling techniques, to get the wholesaler to carry a product. The wholesaler then attempts to get the retailer to carry the product through the use of similar techniques. Each channel advertises to the channel directly below it. In this way the product is pushed down to the final consumer. This is a policy used by manufacturers of high-priced products, by industrial manufacturers, and by those whose products are selectively distributed.

Keep in mind, too, that writers can construct sound paragraphs, whose sentences all advance the main idea, in two ways: (1) All sentences may relate directly to the topic sentence or implied topic sentence, or, (2) Some sentences may relate to the ones immediately preceding them, and thus relate indirectly to the topic sentence. In the following paragraph, the topic sentence is italicized. Sentences 2 through 4 directly support it; each contributes a reason why writing biographies is "demanding." Sentences 5 through 7, however, elaborate on the idea that sentence 4 expresses. Each of the three sentences provides a concrete example of a person who went to "considerable trouble" to thwart would-be biographers. Obviously these examples strengthen the main idea stated in sentence 1, but they refer *directly* to sentence 4.

(1) *Biography has always been a demanding discipline.* (2) "It is perhaps as difficult to write a good life as to live one," said Strachey. (3) A good biographer should combine the skills of the novelist and the detective, and add to them the patience and compassion of the priest. (4) Few people want their shortcomings exposed (biography has added a new terror to death, complained one 18th century writer), and they, or their heirs, often go to considerable trouble to hide them. (5) Somerset Maugham asked his friends to destroy his letters; both Willa Cather and Ernest Hemingway inveighed against posthumous publication of theirs. (6) Charles Dickens burned thousands of letters while his sons roasted onions in their ashes, and Henry James destroyed 40 years of correspondence. (7) Walt Whitman carefully tore pages out of his notebooks, altered the sequence of his love poems so that no one could figure out to whom they were addressed, and wrote in code the initials of his lovers. (*Time*)

In order to write thorough and thoughtful paragraphs, consider expanding sub-ideas by adding more specific statements whenever possible. Take another look at the less-developed version of the Puget Sound paragraph:

(1) *Supertankers transporting oil from Alaska should not be allowed in Puget Sound.* (2) There is too much danger of an accident, and this could upset the delicate balance of nature. (3) We would all suffer: industry, wildlife, and all the people who live in the area would be dealt a devastating blow.

There are perhaps sufficient generalities here, but few specifics. The paragraph does not so much lack support for sentence 1 as it lacks support for sentences 2 and 3. It needs additional sentences relating directly to the statement that an accident would "upset the delicate balance of nature" as well as to the statement that "we would all suffer . . . a devastating blow." Such additional supporting sentences would give concrete details supporting or explaining further the ideas expressed in sentences 2 and 3. The more fully developed student paragraph on Puget Sound (p. 76) shows what form the supporting sentences could take. In your own writing, check all your paragraphs to see if you can say more about the topic sentence and also about the sentences that support it.

If, after following these procedures, you suspect that a paragraph is still too thin or too short, use this brief checklist to get some ideas about how to finish the paragraph:

1. Why do I feel that what I say in the topic sentence (or any of its supporting sentences) is correct?

2. What do I mean by saying what I do?

3. How do I know that what I say is true? Can I point to any evidence to strengthen my case?

4. Are there other ways of looking at this matter? If so, what are they, and why have I chosen to reject them?

Look once more at the student paragraph on Puget Sound:

(1) Supertankers transporting oil from Alaska should not be allowed in Puget Sound because any accident involving a huge tanker could devastate the many natural resources and recreational facilities that the sound provides. (2) The absence of shellfish due to an oil slick could wipe out industries which profit in clams, oysters, shrimp, crab, and mussels. (3) Many people would be left jobless. (4) Moreover, animals that thrive solely on shellfish, like certain types of waterfowl, would slowly disappear, thus disrupting the delicate ecological balance. (5) Fish would suffer, too, hurting industry and, again, disrupting the natural balance. (6) Recreation, which makes the Puget Sound area so popular, would cease to be. (7) Beaches would be ruined, swimming areas no longer clean, and pleasure boats damaged. (8) The beauty of the area would soon be destroyed. (9) Even though the Sound is the most logical place to unload the oil, economically and geographically, and even though the tankers must abide by strict safeguards, the safeguards are not flawless, and it would take but one mistake to destroy a valuable natural asset.

You can see that many of the sentences in this paragraph are direct responses to the checklist questions. In particular, the first question is answered in the second half of sentence 1. Sentences 2 through 7 all answer question 3 on the checklist, for they point to specific evidence (though hypothetical in this case because no oil spill has occurred) in support of the main idea. Finally, the last sentence of the paragraph serves as a response to question 4. It looks briefly at other views of the situation (Puget Sound is, after all, the most logical place to unload the oil, and there are strict safeguards) and then explains why these other views are to be rejected (the safeguards aren't foolproof, the gains wouldn't justify the enormous risk). In a paragraph like this, a careful response to the questions helps ensure full development.

Refer to this checklist to give yourself a little push to complete a paragraph you have already started, or to add to a paragraph you have finished but with which you are not satisfied. Before giving in to despair and insisting that you can't add anything to your two-sentence paragraph, consult the checklist. You might be able to supply answers to one or more of the four questions and thereby achieve more satisfactory development.

Finally, remember that adequate paragraph development is important because your readers are demanding. They will not automatically accept what you say at face value, but will instead look for evidence that what you say is true. They will, furthermore, expect you to be logical and thorough. Thus, if you can answer the questions in this checklist, your writing will probably satisfy your readers' demands.

Exercise

1. Read the following paragraphs and decide whether each is fully developed. The paragraphs were written for someone unfamiliar with the concepts discussed. Therefore, if you do not understand something, you may assume that the writer is to blame for not having developed the idea fully enough. If you decide that a paragraph is not fully developed, specify which points you feel need more elaboration.

   a. Imagery is a valuable tool for a poet. By appealing to the reader's senses, the poet may say more in less space and fewer words. He or she is also able to convey attitudes along with information. The appeal may be to any one of the senses; the poet is not confined to using only visual images.

   b. One of the most important techniques in photography is to draw the eye of the viewer to the main focal point of the photograph. It is not crucial that this main focal point be in any specific place. However, in a well-composed photograph this main point should not be placed in dead center. Such a photograph rarely holds the interest of an audience.

2. Read the following paragraph carefully and decide which sentence is the topic sentence. Then, assign the number *1* to the topic sentence, *2* to a sentence which directly supports the topic sentence, and *3* to a sentence which directly supports the sentence you labeled *2*.

   I thought I really knew and liked a friend with whom I went to school until she spent an entire week with me in my home. During this week I learned that she had the hottest temper of any person I knew. She also did many little things that I just couldn't bear, like rolling the tube of toothpaste at the bottom after using it and sleeping past noon every day, only to wake up grouchy. I found that we disliked more of the same things than we liked. She didn't care much for my mother's cooking, which I simply adore. She enjoyed listening to types of music different from what we listened to and discussed at school. Moreover, she kept my room very messy. I had told her to make herself at home, but little did I know that meant she would leave clothes and other items all over the floor, beds, dressers, and any other object in sight.

*Suggestions
for Writing*

1. In the paragraph in Exercise 2, the writer discusses the qualities that she very much dislikes in her friend. Select *one* quality of a friend or relative and examine it as fully as you can in one paragraph. It can be a quality you admire or one you dislike intensely. A logical topic sentence that begins (or ends) the paragraph could state what quality amuses or aggravates you: "The selfishness of my cousin Phil really disturbs me."

2. Write a letter to a prospective employer, trying to convince him or her that you are qualified for a particular summer job. Ideally, the entire situation (including the job opening, the employer, and your qualifications) should be real—write this letter for a job you really do want and that you have some hope of getting. Do some research to find the right company or organization and the right contact person. You may, however, fabricate as much of the situation as is necessary to complete the assignment. After considering the types of invention mentioned in Chapters 1 and 2, structure the body of your letter as a series of three or four paragraphs, each of which points out one of your qualifications and elaborates on it.

3. The following essay examines the pros and cons of bicycles as a serious means of transportation in the United States. Read the article carefully and then write a paragraph summarizing the views for or against the use of bicycles in cities. In your paragraph, be sure to include a general topic sentence and less general supporting sentences to enumerate the views, as well as specific sentences to support each of the less general sentences. As you read the article, pay attention to the author's use of topic sentences (for example, the opening sentence of paragraph 6: "The poor urban cyclist inhabits a hostile world").

THE GREAT BICYCLE WARS

[1]When New York Mayor Edward Koch visited China last winter, he was beguiled by the sight of a million Chinese gliding harmoniously through their streets on bicycles. "I was swept away," Koch said later, "by the thought of what could be." Traffic back home, of course, is a lot denser and meaner than in Peking, but for a time Koch thought that the vision might translate at least partly to New York. A transit strike there last spring swelled the ranks of the city's commuting bicyclists to nearly Chinese proportions. Like Toad of Toad Hall discovering the motorcar, Koch seemed to conceive a passion for the bike. As an expression of his enthusiasm, he spent $300,000 from the city's depleted treasury to install 6-ft.-wide bike lanes along two avenues in Manhattan.

[2]But Koch's passions are sometimes ephemeral; last week, after the lanes had been open for only three months, the transportation

department sent crews out to tear them up—at a cost of $100,000 more—while bikers disconsolately demonstrated and tied up traffic. The lanes did not work, the mayor said, because bikers did not use them—his own bureaucrats' statistics contradicted him, but never mind—and everyone else thought they hopelessly slowed motor traffic that even at the best times inches along in a fuming stream of steel through midtown. Koch's decision was both premature (the lanes should have been tried for at least a year) and a bit scatterbrained, but it was also calculatedly political. In the street wars among cyclists, motorists and pedestrians, the mayor judged that he had been backing a loser.

[3]The bicycle, formerly a Christmas-tree item or a Sunday diversion, has become a serious vehicle of transport in some American cities. But when bikes move into heavy traffic, problems of incompatibility arise. The circulatory system of the metropolitan U.S. is designed for cars and trucks, with pedestrians granted their margin on the sidewalks. In the culture of freeway or gridlock, the bicycle is a fragile but aggressive intruder. Today around the nation the shaken fist and flourished finger are exchanged between bikers and cabbies and bus drivers and commuting motorists—and, above all, pedestrians who chance to step in the path of a kamikaze ten-speed scorching silently up on the blind side. Bicycles, those sweet chariots of the old Consciousness III, now flourishing under the flag of narcissofitness, are becoming a distinct source of urban tension.

[4]More and more bikers are demanding their share of the American street and road. In 1972, bicycles outsold cars in the U.S. for the first time. Five years ago, an average of 470,000 Americans commuted to work on bicycles on any given day, and Washington hopes that by 1985 as many as 2.5 million will be on the streets, saving as many as 77,000 bbl. of oil a day. OPEC and the huge American self-regard coincided to persuade millions of Americans that the bike makes both financial and cardiovascular sense.

[5]But its virtue has not made the bicycle welcome in many U.S. cities. New York is a serious cyclists' town—but also one of the most dangerous. Still, if it now lacks bike lanes, Manhattan at least has the advantages of being both comparatively flat and geographically compact. Terrain must be right. The sheer distances of Los Angeles rule out anything but neighborhood cycling; San Francisco's hills discourage all but the most muscular. The Federal Government is firmly and officially on the side of the bicycle (healthy, energy-saving and the most efficient means of transportation for millions with short commutes, said the 1978 Energy Conservation Policy Act), but Washington, D.C., itself belongs pretty much to the fuming motorcar. Only a few smaller communities in the U.S., like Davis, Calif., and Eugene, Ore., have welcomed bicyclists with special lanes and bicycle parking areas.

[6]The poor urban cyclist inhabits a hostile world. He regards the car as incomparably more homicidal than the bicycle and more profoundly antisocial—rocketing down the avenues like a bobsled, excreting carcinogens. Yet bicycling is dangerous—905 cyclists died last year in the U.S.—and the unhelmeted are always merely a tumble away from disasters to the brain. The urban cyclist steers among the potholes with a fierce concentration. People have a way of abruptly opening car doors in his face. Cabbies are spitters of high caliber and range. Drivers flick hot cigar and cigarette butts at him. Some truck drivers with a pathological sense of fun like to see how closely they can blast by a cyclist. Pedestrians jaywalk; their eyes, programmed to see cars, are eerily oblivious to bikes. A man throwing his arm up abruptly to hail a cab can coldcock a passing cyclist. And when the bike is finally parked, thieves as dense and dispassionately professional as cockroaches descend with heavyduty bolt-cutters that can bite through anything but expensive U-shaped metal alloy locks.

[7]The noncycling creature, of course, sees the world with different eyes. Drivers who are not necessarily hostile to bicyclists are often simply terrified of hitting them and think that fragile frame with a person perched on it has no business trying to navigate such savage waters. The bike seems a sort of prissy intrusion, about as welcome as a rosy-cheeked second lieutenant from Princeton being sent in to command a filthy, unshaved squad that has been in combat for a year. The veterans at the wheels figure that the biker is either going to get himself killed or maybe bring down mayhem on everyone else. Pedestrians see bikers as a silent menace—and with good reason. In New York just before Koch's bicyclical mood, bikers killed three people trying to cross the street.

[8]Governments around the world have proved to be extraordinarily stupid about trying to reconcile bicycles and cars; they behave as if bikes merely contributed to the squalor of traffic instead of being a way to dissolve it—an anticoagulant. But reconciliations become harder and harder to finance; cities with their treasuries already bleeding away seldom have money to spare for anything as frivolous and unpopular as bicycle lanes.

[9]Bicycles still zip around with an aura of childishness, of unseriousness. They still await the mass discovery that they are in fact splendidly functional. They will never replace cars, but they can provide quick, superior transportation for great numbers of people daily over short distances, at tremendous savings in fossil fuels and breathable air. The bike rider also knows that riding one as the day begins is a brief pure *aubade* of exertion and contemplation. Why else would cyclists risk it? Then, too, subconsciously, the bicyclist may be engaged in a long-term Darwinian wager: In 100 years, which mechanism will still be at work—the bicycle or the automobile? (Lance Morrow)

ORGANIZING THE PARAGRAPH

Organizing the ideas in a paragraph (sometimes called the *arrangement* of a paragraph) is a task that you, the writer, perform primarily for the convenience of the reader. Sometimes writing can be a process of discovery for you—by articulating ideas, you may learn something about your feelings or attitudes. But most often, especially if you are diligent during invention, you know what your ideas are and how they are related, even though your thoughts have come to you in a fairly disorganized way. Imposing order on your ideas, therefore, is necessary so that your reader can follow your thinking. A well-marked, orderly route is always easier to follow than a tangled path.

In ordering your thoughts, you are making your writing logical. The various types of organizations, like chronological or spatial, are logical orders, and using them makes your writing clearer. And once you choose a certain order, you can follow through with confidence—providing you have firmly in mind what that order entails.

Grouping Likes with Likes

As you start to organize what you have to say, keep in mind that your message will be clearest if you group like ideas together. All sentences relating to a given point or sub-point should come together, rather than being intermixed with sentences on other points. Such grouping can happen quite naturally, because we use this principle of organization not only in writing, but in everyday communication, too. For instance, suppose you were placing a single order for yourself and two friends at a fast-food restaurant. You would probably not say, "One hamburger, one order of french fries, another hamburger, one chocolate milkshake, another order of french fries, another hamburger, another chocolate milkshake," and so on. Rather, you would say, "Three hamburgers, three orders of french fries, and three chocolate shakes." Grouping like items together insures the most efficient communication. Using the random approach in giving your order would only confuse and irritate the person behind the counter.

To see how grouping likes with likes can help you organize a paragraph more effectively, study this student paragraph that has some problems with organization:

(1) Frank Frazetta emerged as my favorite artist and won my respect during my high school years. (2) Frazetta's imagination and creativity show in the exaggerated physiques his subjects display. (3) During high school I became more familiar with the work of Frazetta. (4) The imagination and fantasy of Frazetta's work compel you to look at his work in awe. (5) Some of my friends, who idolized Frazetta, introduced me to the imaginative, wild world of Frazetta art. (6) Frazetta art depicts a fantasy world, the type of world many people would see as barbaric: a swamp monster commanded by a large-bottomed, bald woman; an extremely muscular swordsman ready to terminate an

adversary; a wild man fighting for his life against a creature half-man, half-ape. (7) Never before has an artist influenced my visions of the boundaries of art like Frank Frazetta.

This paragraph seems to have two main groupings: those sentences dealing with the writer's introduction to the artist's work, and those focusing on the nature of the art itself. Yet the writer has failed to cluster like sentences together. The ideas of sentences 1, 3, and 5 belong to the first grouping, and so these sentences should be grouped together (actually, sentence 3 can be dropped entirely in the reorganization). The ideas of sentences 2, 4, and 6 belong to the second grouping and should therefore be grouped together, without interruption from sentences in the first group. Both groupings are related to the topic sentence (7), which emphasizes both the nature of the art and the writer's introduction and response to it. Revising the paragraph by grouping likes with likes results in this version:

> (1) Frank Frazetta emerged as my favorite artist and won my respect during my high school years. (5) Some of my friends, who idolized Frazetta, introduced me to the imaginative, wild world of Frazetta art. (4) The imagination and fantasy of Frazetta's work show in the exaggerated physiques his subjects display. (6) Frazetta art depicts a fantasy world, the type of world many people would see as barbaric: a swamp monster commanded by a large-bottomed, bald woman; an extremely muscular swordsman ready to terminate an adversary; a wild man fighting for his life against a creature half-man, half-ape. (7) Never before has an artist influenced my visions of the boundaries of art like Frank Frazetta.

Notice how much more clearly and smoothly this version of the paragraph reads. The new arrangement can therefore be termed much stronger than the original, weaker version. The terms *stronger* and *weaker* are more helpful in discussing organization of your paragraphs than the terms *right* and *wrong*. That is, the organization of the first version of the Frank Frazetta paragraph is not *wrong*—after all, the paragraph still makes a good deal of sense. But it is a weak paragraph because of its faulty organization. When organizing a paragraph, you should not be searching for any single, magical, *right* organization. Rather, you should be flexibly experimenting, looking for a plan that will make a possibly weak arrangement stronger and more effective.

Exercise

1. Read the following paragraphs carefully. Would you consider them well organized? Why or why not? Has the writer in each case grouped likes with likes?

I always felt like a stranger in my high school. Somehow, I never fit in walking down the dimly lit corridors, clutching my books in front of me like a shield. I couldn't take the other students seriously, and I told myself that I didn't like the school. The classes were boring. The student population cared for nothing but play. I told myself that I was too good to be in that school. The students were, I thought, too childish and lacking in self-discipline. Once I went as far as to suggest that I should be paid for listening to my teachers' uninspired lectures. At other times, I felt old. I had forgotten how to play and to laugh at jokes. A strong wall of isolation and loneliness surrounded me. I had smothered myself with hatred. I was all alone and knew for certain that nobody would ever love me. It's strange, but in college I feel as if I have traveled many miles and finally come to a place that I can call home.

Senior year was when I finally grew up and learned to be responsible for myself. In addition to working to bring up my poor grade point average, I had to find a college that could offer me what I needed. In order to raise my *C−* grade average I had to start taking my studies seriously. I cut out all extra-curricular activities and all weekday socializing. I quit working every night after school and got a job working Saturdays only. I also took a crash course in study skills. At the same time, I was busy searching for that ideal college. Because of my weak record I had to rule out the best institutions. I also looked for a school which was strong in liberal arts but which was located not far from where I lived, and which was not too expensive, either. Finding all these things was easier said than done. If I was to get into the school of my choice, I would have to do solid work my senior year, so I talked to each of my teachers about extra help. They recommended me for special tutorial programs which my school was starting to offer. Finally, some of my friends helped me form weekly study groups in my most difficult classes.

The Florida night was hot and close, filled with the noise of the last members of an undisciplined teenage army turned loose by the band they had come to worship, AC/DC. The desolate lot around the shabby arena was littered with cans, bottles and other artifacts of a desperate good time. Occasionally, an energized soul would throw a beer bottle, provoke a fistfight or punish the engine of his father's car. (Peter Bodo, "Guillermo Vilas")

2. Consider the paragraph that you wrote for assignment 1 on page 81. In that paragraph, you paid particular attention to full development of your ideas. Looking now at the paragraph's organization, decide how well you succeeded in grouping like ideas together. If possible, revise your paragraph to strengthen your grouping of likes with likes.

Moving from General to Specific, Specific to General

The most typical order in paragraph writing involves moving from the general to the specific. Such a paragraph begins with a topic sentence that makes a general observation and proceeds to a series of specific statements that back up or explain the general statement. Consider the following example:

General observation   Among manufactured goods, electronic products probably have the
Specific support best track record on prices. Four years ago, Hewlett-Packard sold its popular HP3000 business computer for an average price of $300,000. Today, the same model is four times as powerful but sells for only half as much. On a smaller scale, National Semiconductor's four-function
Specific support Model NS835 calculator still sells for the $9.95 it fetched three years ago. (From "How to Beat the Spiral" in *Newsweek*, March 3, 1980. Copyright © 1980 by Newsweek Inc. All rights reserved. Reprinted by permission.)

Note that the general-to-specific pattern fulfills most readers' expectations and demands for clarity in writing. The generalization stated at the start of a paragraph usually occurs to the writer after some study of the specific information. But in presenting the findings, the writer almost always reverses the original order of thinking and puts the conclusion first, because this order will best allow the reader to follow the overall direction of the discussion. For instance, during invention, the writer of this paragraph most likely observed the specifics first and then drew the conclusion which ultimately appeared as the opening sentence of the paragraph:

(1) Specifics —Four years ago, Hewlitt Packard HP3000 cost $300,000. Today, 4 times as powerful but costs only $150,000.
—National Semiconductor's NS835 calculator cost the same ($9.95) for the last 3 years.
(2) Generalization Electronic products probably have best record on prices among
(conclusion) manufactured goods.

The general-to-specific order in the paragraph often reverses the order of the thought process that originally took place.

Most paragraphs written in general-to-specific order can, with some modification, also be written in the reverse order, from specific to general. For instance, the information on the prices of electronic products could have been presented this way (the italicized words have been added):

Four years ago, Hewlett-Packard sold its popular HP3000 business computer for an average price of $300,000. Today, the same model is four times as powerful but sells for only half as much. On a smaller scale, National Semiconductor's four-function Model NS835 calculator still sells for the $9.95 it fetched three years ago. *It is clear from examples such as these that*, among manufactured goods, electronic products probably have the best track record on prices.

This specific-to-general version is just as acceptable as the original general-to-specific version. However, it creates a somewhat different effect than the original. Rather than presenting the writer's conclusion at the outset, this version encourages the reader to follow the same discovery pattern that the writer went through during prewriting.

To make the specific-to-general and general-to-specific patterns work to your best advantage, use them consciously; don't leave your organization to chance. Notice how the following writer states the general observation first to avoid confusing the reader about the exact point of a rather lengthy discussion (the generalization is in italics):

> *Of all the movie-created American archetypes, none is so prominent or so influential as the western hero*. He is the American knight-errant, a paladin of the plains motivated by only one credo—to do right. The Hollywood cowboy didn't get entangled in the cactus patch of moral ambiguities. Like the nation that created him, he had little capacity for self-doubt. His code was generally an admirable one, and only rarely was he led astray. He was, on the whole, above reproach. He didn't cotton to rough language. He revered womenfolk. He often fought for Indian rights. And he usually stood up for the oppressed. He was a myth on horseback. From the advent of the movies until the mid-1950s, when the arrival of television nearly obliterated his cinematic incarnation, he embodied America's shining dream of itself. The image of the Hollywood cowboy should be questioned only at the risk of misjudging the national psyche. After all, it was no less a real-life buckaroo than former secretary of state Henry Kissinger who told Italian journalist Oriana Fallaci, "I've always acted alone. Americans admire the cowboy leading the caravan alone, the cowboy entering a village alone on his horse . . . a Wild West tale, if you like." (Steve Oney, "The Last Roundup")

In this case, it would not have been wise to use specific-to-general order. The reader's attention might easily have gone in the wrong direction by the time the conclusion was reached; it would have seemed like the paragraph was about Henry Kissinger and not about the cowboy as an American hero.

Exercise

Which of the following paragraphs make use of general-to-specific order? The specific-to-general order? For the paragraphs that employ general-to-specific order, mentally change the order to specific-to-general and then decide whether any significant changes in the paragraph's effect result.

1.　　My own feeling is that a grade ought to represent a degree of mastery of a subject in terms of what students—now and in the past—have been able to do in a particular course. I like to take the top score for each graded activity—quiz, examination, paper, recitation—and add them up. Allowance can be made for an unusual genius by looking at the second-highest scores, and for a mediocre class by looking at scores from previous years. Still, by relying on scores that some student or students actually made, one corrects in a way for inaccurate or unfair examinations, for example, and avoids basing grades on an unrealistic or arbitrary standard. (James A. Huston, "The Meaningless Mean")

2.　　After eleven o'clock, when the library closes, I can often be found with friends at the Tap House. It isn't necessarily the 3.2 beer that brings me there, but the escape that the place offers me. After a day of continuous "college" work and "college" thought, the Tap House is a great place to go and relax, have some good food, and get back to the real world. Although it is rather small and a bit earthy, there is a world inside which is far removed from the classroom. The people, the pinball, and the roadside-diner decor remove it from the educational commotion two blocks away. Sitting there and discussing whatever comes to mind, instead of academic subjects, gives my mind a chance to open up. Visiting the Tap House makes the next day with its hectic schedule an easier pill to swallow.

3.　　What particularly angers South African blacks is the whites, official and semi-official, who profess to speak for them and presume to know them and talk about what is good for them. On no issue is this more clear than on the question of investment or disinvestment by American companies in their South African holdings. Though a burning question on American campuses, it is hardly a question at all in South Africa. Blacks think American corporations are like all other large companies, corrupt and cynical and socially amoral. Disinvestment, they declare, would not change anything. But what infuriates them is not just that they are forbidden by law to talk on this issue (they have to ask me to put away my pen, because if they are quoted they are subject to arrest under the terrorism statutes); worse, some whites, always sincere, who speak in their name, say they are for investment because it helps *blacks*, blacks need the jobs. Most urban blacks want to scream at this. Their anger is fierce, almost shrill. One black speaks for many: "They do not want us to suffer now, they want us to have jobs. Well, we are talking about 90,000 jobs and we already have 2 million urban unemployed, so we are already suffering. Let there be no more investment since we are already suffering: let them suffer too. How dare they say they know what we want when they do not know us, when they do not talk to us, when they have never been in our homes and we have never been in theirs and they do not know the schools that our children go to? When I hear the white man say that he knows the soul of the black man, and they are always saying it, I want to freeze. They do not know our souls and I am not sure they know their own.'' (David Halberstam, *The Atlantic*)

An easy and natural way to arrange a paragraph is to follow *spatial order*, that is, to describe the relationship in space of objects to each other. For instance, in describing a room according to spatial order, you can simply write what you see, adopting a spatial order of left-to-right, right-to-left, top-to-bottom, or the like:

> The room was disgusting. Over by the far window was a trash can piled high with crumpled papers. In the middle of the room was a gaudy, round king-size bed littered with rotting fruit peels. The path between the bed and the doorway, where I was standing, was choked off by heaps of dirty clothes and old newspapers.

This order follows a movement of far-to-near, helping the reader envision the room (shown in Figure 3.1) more easily.

Sometimes, however, even when working with spatial details, you will want to use a different scheme of order—arrangement according to *order of importance*. For instance, another writer might describe this room by noting the details in their order of importance:

> The room was disgusting. Right in the center was a gaudy, round king-size bed littered with rotting fruit peels. The path between the bed and the door where I was standing was choked off by heaps of soiled clothes and old newspapers. Over by the far window was a trash can piled high with crumpled papers.

In this case, the writer begins by describing what first catches the eye—the gaudy bed, right in the center of the room. This object is the most striking and so the writer wishes the reader to picture it immediately, to notice it first. Thus the detail about the bed is placed in the important initial position. The next most striking detail is the littered pathway, and the least noteworthy object is the trash can, which one might even expect to look a bit messy. For this writer, most-important-to-least-important order takes precedence over spatial order because the primary purpose of the paragraph is to give emphasis to certain details of the room, rather than to enable the reader to picture the room's overall set-up.

A third scheme of order is *chronological*. Almost anytime you tell a story you use chronological order. Consider this student paragraph:

> Rick and I were best friends for two and a half years. Then, when we were in the middle of the seventh grade, Rick's family moved to

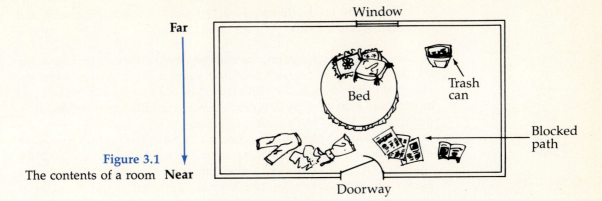

Far

Window

Bed

Trash
can

Blocked
path

Figure 3.1
The contents of a room **Near**

Doorway

the other side of town. Even though we still went to the same junior high school, we slowly drifted apart. He began to make friends on his side of the town, and I on mine. I became more studious, setting high expectations for myself; Rick barely made it through the seventh and eighth grades. I began working the summers as a lifeguard, and he still cut grass. Rick began to get in lots of trouble. As time progressed he seemed to get into more and more scrapes, not just in school where he was constantly skipping and disrupting classes, but with the police, too.

Notice how this paragraph follows the decline of the writer's friendship with Rick over the passage of time. The writer simply tells what happened as he and Rick drifted apart.

But writing a good chronologically ordered paragraph is not as simple as it might appear. The writer who uses chronological order must be careful to avoid using needless details. For instance, the student who wrote the above paragraph does not tell everything that happened. Rather, he limits himself by choosing the most important details that support the purpose of the paragraph. If, after noting that Rick "still cut the grass," the writer had added, "He used a rotary-type mower," he would have included an unneeded—and confusing—detail.

Another type of paragraph order is arrangement by *topic* or idea. Topical order is extremely useful in writing paragraphs for college coursework. It usually involves listing in an opening topic sentence a series of two or three points that will be covered in the paragraph. Let's consider how the chronological paragraph about Rick might read if the author had used topical order instead. The opening topic sentence would probably read something like this:

About the middle of seventh grade, my best friend, Rick, and I drifted apart because we lived on different sides of town and because we began to develop different attitudes toward schoolwork and after-school activities.

In completing the paragraph, the student would elaborate on how living on different sides of town led each to develop different circles of friends. He would then discuss the "different attitudes toward schoolwork and after-school activities" by describing his own studiousness and industriousness and Rick's lack of these qualities.

The value of topical order would also be apparent in a paragraph that discusses, for example, the character traits of a movie or book character. At first, a student writer might be tempted to treat such a paragraph chronologically—to tell what happened to the character as the book or movie plot progressed. But it would be more efficient to single out two or three characteristics, list them in the topic sentence, and then discuss each characteristic in turn. In such a paragraph, the characteristics or topics would be discussed without considering when in the book or movie they were noticeable. A typical topic sentence for a paragraph of this type might read: "In the movie *Desperate Minutes*, Robert Reed was basically naive, selfish, and inconsiderate."

Exercise

1. Read the following student paragraph, which makes use of chronological order. Could the material in the paragraph be organized topically? Spatially? (Note that a different order might change the emphasis and the contents and meaning of the paragraph.)

One day after school, I was riding home at a leisurely pace on my brand new Sting-Ray bicycle when I was suddenly challenged to a race by another fourth grader. My new bike was extremely fast, so I accepted the challenge and the race began. But, unknown to me, there was a sharp bend in the road that we were racing on. Just as we came upon this bend, a car was coming in the opposite direction. The car appeared as though it was going to hit me, so I panicked and grabbed the front brake a split second before I grabbed the back brake. This caused my bike to do a flip, sending me flying through the air. I landed in the street on my stomach, but I had hit the ground first with my mouth. I was so dazed that I didn't realize that the car had stopped and taken me home. My mother rushed me to the emergency room where the damage proved to be extensive: I had cracked three teeth and broken my palate; the 1300 dollars and three years my parents and I had spent on my braces were down the drain. I had also cut my forehead in two places so badly that each wound needed four stitches, and I had received a minor concussion. Two days later when I went back to school, every kid in that school knew what had happened to me. Fourth graders can be the meanest people in the world; I was mocked for the rest of the year about the accident.

2. Write a short paragraph describing a room or a building with which you are familiar. Use a simple spatial order. When you have finished, set the paragraph aside and write another paragraph of similar length, describing the same room or building, but using topical order. You may leave out some details from the first paragraph and add new details, but try to make it recognizably the same room or building.

GAINING COHERENCE IN THE PARAGRAPH

If you follow the suggestions made in this chapter, your paragraphs will probably have the quality known as *coherence*—everything you say will hold together and flow smoothly. But sometimes you will want to make an extra effort to achieve coherence. Sometimes, even though all the sentences of a paragraph belong together, their exact connection or relationship to each other may be unclear—and thus confusing—to the reader. Your most reliable tool in achieving coherence in such a case is the *transition*.

Coherence Through Transitions

A transition can be any word, phrase, sentence, or paragraph that clearly shows the reader how an idea relates to the one or ones which precede it. When writing individual paragraphs, you are likely to use transitional words and phrases that fall into these three categories:

1. Transitions to ideas that add to, or amplify, what you have just said:

also	similarly
in addition	then
moreover	in other words
furthermore	

If the idea is a specific instance used to support the previous, more general thought, you can employ the following:

for example
for instance
to illustrate

Or, you may wish to use numbers or sequence markers when presenting a list of more specific ideas:

first	finally
second	last
next	

Note how the authors of this paragraph use *in addition* to add another detail to their list:

What did we do with nearly $10,000? We purchased photography equipment, rented communications equipment, covered food costs for nine for approximately 30 days, rented a mobile home, provided for extra winter clothing, film and developing, and secured first aid supplies and professional instruction. *In addition*, we allowed for those essential incidentals such as telephone, transportation, and printing costs, before and after the actual interstate trek. All in all, after some additional funding by the college, our final budget was approximately $13,000. (Herman Beavers and Richard Littlejohn, *The Black Collegian*)

2. Transitions to ideas that contrast with what you have just said:

but	none the less
by contrast	despite
however	on the contrary
nevertheless	yet

The word *yet* in this paragraph signals a shift in thought:

Six years ago inflation forced Marcia Dimick, mother of two, to find a way to earn money. With a three-year-old at home and a six-year-old in school, she was faced with a problem familiar to many of today's mothers. Working outside her home meant she would have to arrange and pay for child care, a choice she was reluctant to make. *Yet* how could she remain at home and still earn enough money to ease the family's financial burden? Her solution—providing care in her home for the children of other working parents—is one that more and more mothers are finding profitable and enjoyable. (Leah Yarrow, *Parents*)

3. Transitions to ideas that conclude, summarize, or otherwise add a sense of finality to what you have written:

in conclusion	consequently
to conclude	in summary
therefore	as a result
thus	accordingly

In the following paragraph, the transitions of all types are italicized:

In their haste to get practical preparation for a career, students often overlook the liberal arts college. *Yet* there are good reasons why they should consider a liberal arts school, even if getting a job is their main concern. *For one thing*, learning itself may be more exciting in a liberal arts college due to a broader and more flexible curriculum than one might find at a technical school. *Thus* students may do better in their courses and earn a higher grade point average, which will certainly make them more attractive to employers. *More important*, a liberal arts education is the most likely to develop one's ability to think, speak, read, and write—all critical skills that business and industry are coming to value more and more. *Finally*, students should realize that a liberal arts education has always been the preferred path for entry into the top professions: law, medicine, government, and education.

If you reread this paragraph and skip over the italicized transitions, you will notice that the paragraph still makes sense with the transitions omitted, but that it reads much more smoothly and clearly with them. In a way, transitions are like highway signs. Even though we *might* be able to find our way from one city to the next without the signs, we will take fewer wrong turns if we have them. Similarly, we might be able to figure out the relationship of these two sentences without a transition:

You upset me very much last night. I still want to go out with you.

But the direction is much clearer when a transition is provided:

You upset me very much last night. *However*, I still want to go out with you.

Because transitions indicate precisely how the writer's thoughts are interrelated, they are indispensable in paragraph writing.

Exercise

Supply any transitions needed in the following sentences. You may combine the sentences if you wish.

1. The car wouldn't start because we were out of gas. We had a flat tire.
2. The three terrorists were convicted of murder. They were set free.
3. The clock was five minutes slow. The painter was late for work.
4. It was pouring when I arrived. I got soaked.
5. The majority of Americans have much leisure time to fill. More than thirty million people now play racquet sports.
6. My daughter hates school lunches. She takes her own yogurt to eat.
7. Five more banks have gone into receivership. The Federal Reserve Board has taken no steps to ease interest rates and increase consumer confidence.
8. Microcomputers promise to revolutionize our whole way of life. I plan to take a course in programming as soon as I can.
9. All morning the phone was ringing. The receptionist never answered it.
10. The waves were steadily rising and the wind was nearing gale force. Night was fast approaching and he knew that his boat's lights didn't work. He decided to take the boat out "for a short ride."

Coherence Through Repetition and Parallel Structure

Writers should usually avoid repetition, especially in matters of style and organization. But one form of repetition is desirable: the repetition of key words to achieve coherence within a paragraph. This first paragraph of a student essay illustrates the principle well:

> *Keeping a journal*, though time consuming and perhaps thought of as a burden, can prove valuable to your psychological growth. Like any form of expressive art, *a journal* can say anything. *Keeping a journal* should not be thought of as an everyday commitment in which you simply describe the events of the day, thereby making it a laborious chore; rather, it should be thought of as a time for yourself. With *a journal*, you are your own audience. Nobody else has to see what you write. There is no teacher looking over your shoulder ready to pounce on any grammatical errors. You are free to write however you wish.

The student created a very tight and coherent paragraph by continually coming back to the term she started out with: *"Keeping a journal . . . a journal . . . Keeping a journal . . . a journal."* Note how such repetition improves the paragraph rather than detracts from it. Looking closer at the paragraph, we see more repetition for coherence: The phrase *thought of* is used three times—in sentence one ("perhaps *thought of* as a burden") and twice in sentence three ("*thought of* as an everyday commitment . . . *thought of* as a time for yourself"). And note how the writer maintains a consistent point of view through repeated use of *you-your*: "*your* . . . growth," "*you* . . . describe," "for *yourself*," "*you* are," "*you* write," "*your* shoulder," "*you* are," "*you* wish."

Repetition is thus a useful device for increasing the coherence of a paragraph. Of course, you should not overuse this tool. The student writer did not use repetition wherever possible; she gave the idea of communicating or expressing oneself through a journal a different verb each time: "a journal can *say* anything," "you simply *describe*," "what you *write*."

Exercise

Read the following student paragraph carefully. Then go back and underline or highlight any words or phrases that are repeated.

> In Erich Fromm's essay, "Is Love an Art," from the book, *The Art of Loving*, Fromm contends that love is an "art" to be mastered just like medicine. However, this view makes love sound cold and unfeeling. To me, love is above all forms of art, for we can do without most forms of art, but we cannot do without love. It is the one thing that holds humanity together. There are so many unexplained factors about love. Here lies the mystery, the overwhelming factor that draws one person toward another person even though we have been struck down or rejected before. The fact that we do not know everything about love

and that we place it above all other art forms is what draws us to seek love. By saying that love is an art form to be mastered like medicine, we are degrading it. I am talking not only about the love between a man and a woman but the love of humanity. We can only try to achieve love in our lifetime; we will never come to master it like we master an art.

Which terms did you highlight? Are all the repeated terms used effectively to achieve coherence? Is some of the repetition needless?

A second means of ensuring the internal coherence of a paragraph is to use parallel structure. This technique is closely related to the use of repetition in that it often makes use of repeated words and phrases, too. But parallelism creates a *regular pattern*. Note how effectively Martin Luther King used parallel structure to give coherence to his writing and emphasis to his statements:

. . . Perhaps it is easy for those who have never felt the stinging darts of segregation to say, "Wait." *But when you have seen* vicious mobs lynch your mothers and fathers at will and drown your sisters and brothers at whim; *when you have seen* hate-filled policemen curse, kick, and even kill your black brothers and sisters; *when you see* the vast majority of your twenty million Negro brothers smothering in an airtight cage of poverty in the midst of an affluent society; *when you suddenly find* your tongue twisted and your speech stammering as you seek to explain to your six-year-old daughter why she can't go to the public amusement park that has just been advertised on television, *and see* tears welling up in her eyes when she is told that Funtown is closed to colored children, *and see* ominous clouds of inferiority beginning to form in her little mental sky, *and see* her beginning to distort her personality by developing an unconscious bitterness toward white people; *when you have to concoct* an answer for a five-year-old son who is asking, "Daddy, why do white people treat colored people so mean?"; *when you take* a cross-country drive and find it necessary to sleep night after night in the uncomfortable corners of your automobile because no motel will accept you; *when you are humiliated* day in and day out by nagging signs reading "white" and "colored"; *when your first name becomes* "nigger," your middle name becomes "boy" (however old you are) and your last name becomes "John," and your wife and mother are never given the respected title "Mrs."; *when you are harried* by day and haunted by night by the fact that you are a Negro, living constantly at tiptoe stance, never quite knowing what to expect next, and are plagued with inner fears and outer resentments; *when you are* forever fighting a degenerating sense of "nobodiness"— *then you will understand* why we find it difficult to wait. ("Letter from Birmingham Jail")

Here the same *structure* (and some of the same words) is being repeated. King uses a lengthy series of subordinate clauses ("when you . . .") that finally culminates in the main clause, "then you will understand why we find it difficult to wait." In fact, he uses ten subordinate clauses in a row here. Because these clauses follow each other in direct sequence, they are said to be parallel to each other. This parallel repetition of a structural element holds the material of the paragraph tightly together.

Exercise

Read the following paragraph taken from an article about the barrier separating East Germany from West Germany. Does the writer use parallelism to achieve coherence? Point out as many specific instances as you can. Are any other devices used (repetition of key words or transitions)?

At Grüsselbach the wire fence is 9 ft. high and anchored 3 ft. deep in the ground to prevent tunneling. It is topped with specially sharpened mesh so fine that a fingerhold is impossible. It is hung with powerful fragmentation mines at head, chest and knee level that can be triggered automatically by trip wires or detonated from nearby guard towers. For 547 yds. back into East Germany, all vegetation has been cleared, and the ground is raked regularly so telltale footprints will show. Farther back runs a deep trench that prevents vehicles from reaching the fence. Nearly a mile inside the border is a second fence, equipped with detection devices and automatically triggered shot-guns. ("Life Along the Death Strip," *Time*)

REVISING THE PARAGRAPH

Much of the material we have already discussed in this chapter applies to revising paragraphs as well as to writing them. So as you revise a paragraph, you may want to look back at, say, the section on placement of the topic sentence or the section on grouping likes with likes.

Rewriting and Invention

Rewriting is generally considered the final stage of composing a paragraph. But, in the actual process of composing, invention, writing, and rewriting often overlap. If everything goes smoothly (and it seldom does), you will first generate your ideas for a paragraph, then write the actual paragraph, and finish up by rewriting it to achieve more fully the qualities of unity, development, coherence, and polished style. But more often you'll find that the writing stage turns into an extension of invention. That is, choosing words to express your ideas on paper may lead you to discover exactly what it is that you want to say, so that by the time you are finished with a first draft you may have changed the idea itself. If this happens, you will need to do more than make minor changes and corrections during revision; you will need to redefine your main idea and rewrite your topic sentence. For example, Tom, the student who wrote the following rough draft, had initially decided that he wanted to write about the demands of playing professional football:

> Professional football is demanding and emotional. The spectator can not conceive the preparation that is put into every game, or for that matter every practice, until he actually visits a professional team in training. Usually, coaches work long hours watching films, planning strategies, and discussing player performance. Besides carrying out the normal duties of successful coaching, the coaches must instill a positive mental attitude in the players' mind. The player must believe in himself, and believe he is superior to his opponent. The player must also be in excellent physical condition. He must be able to withstand rigorous and draining endurance tests in order to be successful. The player can never hesitate at any moment; all actions must be aggressive and spontaneous. He who hesitates is lost, since mind and body must be totally involved. This is true especially for the offensive lineman, who has one of the toughest jobs in the game.

By the time Tom reached the end of his draft, however, he had decided he was more interested in the subject of the offensive lineman than in the general demands of professional football. He had written his way into a new and, for him, more interesting idea. After further thought, he rewrote the paragraph:

> In the game of football, offensive linemen can never hesitate at any moment; all actions must be aggressive and spontaneous. The offensive line must coordinate its efforts to the split second in order to have a successful attack. If an offensive lineman falters, especially when his team is nearing the goal line, the particular play that is being executed could be a failure. Some people believe that plays that are run from the interior of the line, such as trap plays, must have a higher degree of aggression and animal instinct. Yet, plays such as passes require the same aggressive blocking by the offensive line. The team that does not hesitate on the line and that performs its duties with authority will win.

Once Tom felt more comfortable with his topic, he was able to settle down and focus in depth on a single idea. The paragraph about the skills of offensive linesmen does not much resemble his rough draft; it is a stronger paragraph, largely because it is more narrowly focused and more coherent. When you revise, then, remember that just because you think you have completed the writing stage of the composing process, you are not necessarily going to need only cosmetic changes in your work. The actual writing of the paragraph may turn out to be an extension of invention; scrutinize what you have written with that idea in mind.

Exercise

Read the following paragraphs at least twice. What do the main ideas seem to be? What are the topic sentences? Can you make any suggestions for revision?

1. Our country's defense budget interferes with the government's moral obligation to provide a decent standard of living and needed domestic services for its citizens. While countless megatons of nuclear explosives lie stockpiled and ready to destroy the world's population many times over, children throughout America go hungry; yet government officials talk in the same breath about "trimming the fat" from our welfare system and increasing our "defense preparedness." While the United States maintains large and costly bases around the world, many students are deprived of a decent education. The Vietnam War is a perfect example of this moral irresponsibility. Our involvement in Vietnam cost us dearly. We wasted 50,000 American lives and hundreds of billions of dollars. The Vietnam War damaged our reputation as the leading power in the free world. Our interference in the affairs of Vietnam lost us not only the respect of the rest of the world, but our self-respect as well. We defoliated and destroyed the landscape and decimated the population of a country whose affairs were not ours to interfere with. We lost the support of many trusted allies. The war dragged on for years and divided our country, leading to such tragedies as the Kent State shootings.

2. College is very much different from high school, and then again in some ways the two are quite the same. When I was in high school the sports activities were very exciting because I participated in them. It didn't matter whether we won or lost (although most of the time we lost), but it was all the spirit we had. Our school had two kinds of groups that would perform at the games, the majorettes and the flyerettes. Maybe everyone was just looking forward to seeing their friends, but they did show up to support their teams. In college, the team loses just like our team did at home, but the spirit is down. Most of the students do not even come to the games. Maybe it seems this way to me because I have only seen the football season. I realize that some people prefer basketball to football, but we will see.

3.   TV violence has been proven to have a negative influence on the behavior of children exposed to it frequently. One recent study, for example, indicates that children who watched a series of cartoons featuring aggressive, violent behavior tended to exhibit more aggressive behavior themselves after watching the shows. The children also enjoyed the spectacle of talking ducks, cows, and rabbits in one of the cartoons. In general, it seems that young children prefer programs featuring animal characters. Another research study demonstrated that young children often justified their actions by referring to similar acts performed by their TV heroes. One child, for example, insisted he was justified in kicking his sister because she took his toy, since he had just seen Sylvester the cat receive similar treatment at the hands of an angry bull dog. A third study notes that children become extremely passive while doing the actual viewing of the programs and suggests that activities which involve the youngsters in more creative outlets are better for them to participate in. Continued exposure to violent acts, particularly when the observer is youthful, tends to foster a casual attitude toward human life, and for this reason preschoolers and other young children should not be allowed to watch too much TV.

Revising the Paragraph to Achieve Detail and Specificity

Many beginning college writers have a tendency to be too vague and general. Instead of including details that the reader can picture and absorb, the writer uses a general phrase and does not elaborate or clarify it. For instance, consider these two versions of the same sentence from a student paragraph:

General   Since I arrived on campus I have noticed a wide range of women's clothing styles.

Specific and detailed   Since I arrived on campus I have seen women wearing a wide range of styles, from lacy gowns and high heels to combat fatigues and steel-toed boots.

Note that the addition of details adds clarity to the sentence—it is hard to *picture* a term like "a wide range of styles," even though we know what it means. The details also give more personality to the writing, for each writer will choose different details to illustrate a term.

A first step in revising to achieve detail is to check your focus. That is, make sure your paragraph is based on a limited, single main idea. If your paragraph is too broadly focused, you will not have the time or opportunity to develop or support any single point because you will be busy moving on to a new point. Such was the case with this first version of a student paper:

The television production of Alex Haley's masterpiece, *Roots*, was without doubt one of the greatest stories I have ever viewed. The actions and the people portrayed combined to form one of the most realistic fictionalized television programs every broadcast. The realism apparent in the show made it clear how difficult the task of surviving was for my ancestors. Though there were previous shows on the struggle of oppressed people, *Roots* was unique in its depiction of one family's struggle to freedom and its undying dream. *Roots* opened the eyes of all people from various backgrounds to some of the positive sides of the Negro family.

After discussing this first draft with his instructor, the student decided to narrow the focus of the paragraph to only one idea—the topic of realism in *Roots*. He rewrote his topic sentence and proceeded to explain in detail what was realistic in the show:

> The realism of Alex Haley's television production, *Roots*, made the show an educational experience. The horrid nature of slavery was depicted honestly, leaving little to the imagination. From the very opening show, in which Kunta Kinte, the major character, was taken from his homeland in chains, until the final episode, when Kunta's grandchild and great-grandchildren were set free, the savagery of slavery was omnipresent. The brutal beatings of slaves seemed so real that all who watched could feel every lashing. Entire limbs of slaves were cut off so that they would never be able to run again. The portrayal of these and many other tortures left me in awe of how brutally realistic this program was for something made for television.

In this revised version our attention is immediately drawn to the *realistic* aspect of *Roots*, and what follows allows us to understand in more detail what the writer means by this term. Notice that when realism was mentioned in the first draft, we had to guess what the writer had in mind.

Sometimes vagueness is not the result of too broad a focus but of a failure to back up what you have to say with concrete details. In other words, it is a form of underdevelopment. Most of the sentences in this paragraph would profit from an additional sentence or two giving some specific details:

> (1) Dormitory living has provided me with unusual glimpses into the lives of fellow students. (2) These glimpses were unusual at first perhaps because I was simply not accustomed to the living arrangement. (3) I was overwhelmed by the number of people I met and was surprised to find so many different types of people. (4) Now that I'm a veteran of dormitory living, however, I'm not so quick to call something unusual.

In revising this paragraph, the writer would want to describe in detail some of the "unusual glimpses." What were they? Messy housekeeping? Strange bathroom habits? Unorthodox study schedules? Similarly, after sentence three, the writer would need to clarify the term "different types of people" by adding some specific details. Even the last sentence could be improved by giving a quick example of the kind of behavior that no longer would seem unusual.

Exercise

1. The following paragraph was written by a new student on her first day of class. How would you suggest that she revise it? Does she need to add details? Should she narrow the focus before doing anything else?

    I am totally impressed with the wide variety of people that I have met since my arrival on campus. With the friendly atmosphere here, I have found it quite easy to meet new people and learn about the differences and similarities we each possess. Because I came from a parochial school, it has been an enlightening experience for me to associate more closely with people with widely differing backgrounds. In the short week that I have been here I have met many people different from myself and some almost the same. I realize that meeting a variety of people isn't always a successful experience but it is a worthwhile one.

2. This paragraph is from a student essay written to show that old clichés usually hold true. What advice could you offer the writer for revising the paragraph?

    The observation that "there's nothing new under the sun" can be related to the area of song writing. A music composer is strictly limited with the number of notes and chords available on a particular instrument when writing a song. Thus the composer is technically limited in what she has to work with and has to rely on personal interpretation to bring originality to her music.

Suggestion for Writing

Review all the writing you have done so far in this course and choose the one piece which still needs the most revision. Consider the advice on revision discussed in this chapter and develop a plan for making significant improvements in the piece. Submit the original version and a brief description of your plan to your instructor for comment and approval. After considering your instructor's remarks, rewrite the piece.

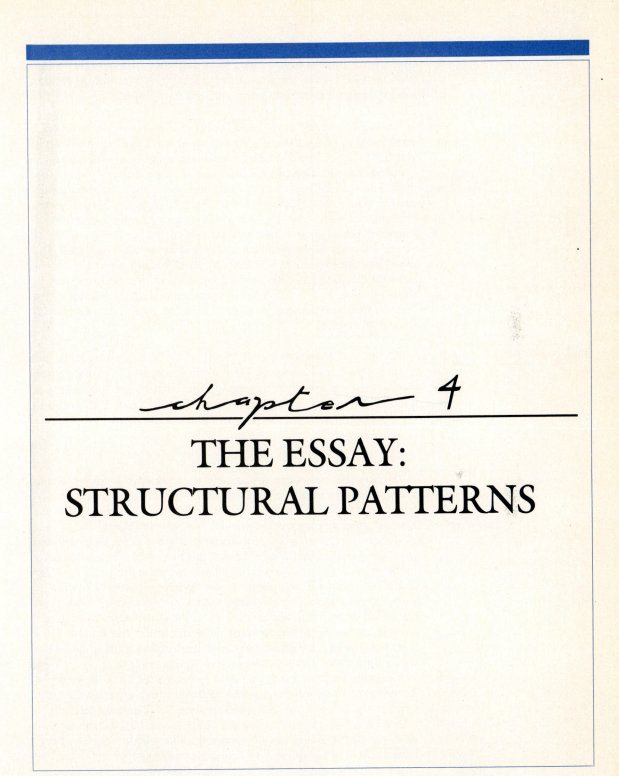

chapter 4

THE ESSAY:
STRUCTURAL PATTERNS

THE FORM OF In order to understand the structure of an essay, we can study the essay
THE ESSAY as an expanded version of the basic topic-sentence-first paragraph (see
Chapter 3, p. 62). That is, we'll see the paragraph as a miniature version
of the essay. Examine the following student paragraph:

Topic   I recently learned a valuable lesson that many students of voice
sentence have failed to realize: There is a methodical way to get the most out of
practice time and avoid wasting precious minutes in a rehearsal room.
First point Focused concentration on only one point at a time is the important first
of development step. The student must forget about the basics and concentrate fully
on the particular objective of the rehearsal session. Secondly, the
Second point student can save time by being self-critical. Listening carefully to
oneself is not as good as having a singing coach, but it will enable the
singer to catch some mistakes and avoid repeating them over and
Third point over. Equally important is the ability to sight-sing a piece from the
score. If this skill has been learned beforehand, the rehearsal will be
Fourth point more efficient. A last helpful step involves studying the lyrics to the
song in advance to ensure good pronunciation when it comes time for
the actual singing.

Paragraph into Essay By amplifying and expanding each point made in this paragraph, the
writer, Patty, produced an essay. The topic sentence of the paragraph
became the *thesis statement* of the essay, and each major subpoint was
translated, more or less, into the topic sentence of its own paragraph in
the essay. As you read, observe how much more detail and explanation
the essay form permits:

[1]During this past term, I was able to study with a voice teacher.
Sentence 2 is *Through this experience I learned a valuable lesson that many student vocalists*
the essay's *have failed to realize: There is a methodical way to get the most out of practice*
thesis statement. *time and avoid wasting precious minutes in a rehearsal room.*
[2]*Focused concentration on only one point at a time is the important first*
step. Some singers find it difficult to single out and approach a specific
problem because there are so many basic technical problems to worry
about. For example, a student singer trying to devote a session to
working on a particular problem with vowel placement often gets
distracted by thinking about controlling the diaphragm, tone, pitch,
and air intake. However, to learn most efficiently, the student must
trust that the basics have already been learned and must forget about
them, thus concentrating only on vowel placement.
The first [3]*Secondly, the student can save time by being self-critical.* It would be
sentences great if every student singer could rehearse with a coach in the room
of paragraphs to act as the singer's ears. But not every one can. Listening carefully to
2, 3, 4, and 5 oneself is not as good as having a singing coach, but, if done right, it
are the topic does enable the singer to catch some mistakes. Unfortunately, being
sentences of self-critical is not easy. One of a singer's biggest problems is the fact
each paragraph. that the instrument is part of the singer's body.

Not only does the vocalist have to produce the sound, he or she must be able to listen to that sound and understand why the sound was or was not produced correctly. A singer should concentrate on how the vocal apparatus feels when the correct sound is being produced. Then, in the future, the student will be able to recall the same sounds and sensations and judge his or her own performance more knowledgeably.

[4]*Equally important in making rehearsals efficient is having some ability to sight-sing a piece from the score.* At every level of vocal accomplishment, sight-singing will reduce the amount of time spent pounding out notes at a keyboard. Study of a piece can't seriously begin unless the singer has a sure grip of the notes. Learning this skill may require some special help in ear training, but once the rudiments of sight-singing are learned, the student can apply them profitably in practice sessions.

[5]*The last helpful step doesn't take place in a practice room at all; it involves studying the lyrics to the aria or art song one plans to rehearse in order to practice proper pronunciation of the foreign words.* It's difficult to work on something like vowel placement when you don't know what vowel you're placing. Studying the lyrics takes only a few minutes of spare time before the practice session. The only things needed are the music, some brain power, a dictionary, and a pencil. This is a guaranteed way to save pain and time when it comes to the actual singing in the practice room.

Conclusion emphasizes the value of method. [6]Since January I have been using these steps in my own practicing and have found the results to be worthwhile. It may be only a coincidence, but I received my first professional audition shortly after I started following the method.

Although Patty's essay and the paragraph upon which it is based both cover the same material, the essay explores the material in depth. Structurally, the similarities between paragraph and essay versions could be diagrammed as shown in Figure 4.1 (see p. 108).

Besides having a structural relationship to the paragraph, the successful essay, like the successful paragraph, must have both unity and a limited scope. Just as the writer of a paragraph achieves unity by making certain that all sentences are closely related to the paragraph's main idea, so the essay writer achieves unity by closely relating each paragraph to the essay's overall focus. We can see this kind of unity in Patty's essay on vocal rehearsals.

Limiting the scope of an essay is also necessary. An essay whose paragraphs all work to create coherence could still be too broad in its overall scope. For instance, if Patty had written on "methods for conducting efficient rehearsals *and performing successful auditions*," her essay would have then required three or four more paragraphs to discuss successful auditions. Even though all the paragraphs would technically be related to the essay's main idea (effective methods), that idea would be too broad for a short composition.

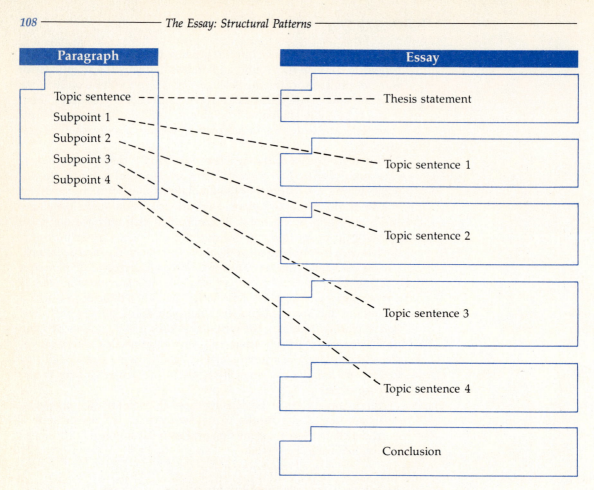

Figure 4.1 Structural similarities between paragraph and essay

Exercise

1. Examine the following student paragraphs and consider the possibilities for expanding them into essays. Neither example is as systematically structured as was the student paragraph on voice lessons. Therefore, you may have to consider restructuring the ideas and deleting some material, as well as predicting what kinds of additional information would be needed to complete an essay version. If you decide that either or both pieces would not be suitable for expansion into essays, explain why in some detail.

   a. The working hours of every Wednesday seem to drag on forever, and I'm always ready to cut loose and dance hard at night. The day begins with all those irritating errands: "Go to bank," "Pay treasurer," "Put in application for Winter Term," "Wash," "Cram last-minute statistics," etc. etc. Then, at 11:00, I'm sitting in Statistics, which at times has surprised me by being genuinely interesting, yet most of the time I feel like a moron who is fated to be stupid, air-headed, unable to understand one of the easiest math courses the college offers. Lunch could be fun, a nice break, but I greet lunch with an anxious smile, a growling and angry stomach, and a hysterical fear of being fat. So by the afternoon I'm feeling the hint of misery and self-hatred and if I'm lucky I get some statistics done—if not I'll waste time, drink coffee, or sleep until 3:00 when Band rolls around. 4:30 brings the end to band and I trudge off to work at the dining hall, cleaning floors and picking up all the garbage my fellow classmates have left. At 6:30 I should be glad for the half-hour break before my 7:00 seminar—but again I'm hungry, I'm tired, and my fat phobia is gripping. 9:00 p.m.! The day's classes are all over, finally. The pressure in my body, in my mind, feels unbearable, and the disco doesn't have to advertise for me. I'm there, dancing, getting totally engrossed in the sound, the lights, my muscles freely moving every which way they can.

b. During the fall break, I visited Canada with two Japanese boys who live in Asia House. It was a pleasant and exciting trip, although we spent most of the time in the car. But this wasn't the only problem. To cut down the cost, we cooked for ourselves most of the time, and I was in charge of cooking. This was not surprising, as it is very natural in Japanese society that a woman does all the cooking and a man watches TV and relaxes. Those two boys expected me to do it. I always cooked lunch and dinner all by myself. I did not mind it at all, either. So I cooked and cooked, every night dinner and the next day's lunch at the same time. After the trip, however, I could not get up from bed because of a backache and weariness. Some of my American friends came to see me, and when I told them about our trip to Canada and about my cooking the first thing they said was, "That's ridiculous!" They emphasized the equal rights of men and women. To my surprise, an American boyfriend of mine invited me for dinner the next day. He said that he would cook fish for me. What a difference! I became aware of the equal role women have in the U.S. I think that's wonderful. They say that Japanese society is getting Americanized, but in reality, most women do all the cooking, washing dishes and clothes, cleaning house, and bringing up children. I wish Japanese men would help us a little. The American boy told me, "Be more liberal. You are not living up to men's expectations. You don't have to obey what they say." I sensed the spirit of America in his words.

2. Choose one paragraph you have written this term or semester and study it to see whether it could be the basis for an essay. Explain why or why not. If so directed by your instructor, expand one of your previously written paragraphs into an essay.

The Standard
Essay Pattern
In the student essay on voice rehearsals, we saw an example of the standard essay pattern:

> Introduction
> Body
> Conclusion

This pattern has become standard because it helps both writers and readers. Writers can use it to organize nearly any topic, while readers appreciate its inherent logic. For example, the reader may be oriented to the topic in the introduction, progress through specific ideas about the topic in the body, and be reminded of its significance in the conclusion. Read the following student essay and note how it is structured:

THE PROVERBIAL UNCLE GEORGE

Introduction *Sentences 1–5 introduce the topic. Sentences 6–8 state the ideas to be covered in the rest of the essay.*

[1](1) Everybody has an Uncle George. (2) He's the one we all like to talk about. (3) Everyone in the family wants to know what he did the last time he visited. (4) Any mention of his name begets "What did he do this time?" (5) And there is always plenty to talk about, because my Uncle George, my father's uncle, has many eccentricities. (6) He has a habit of constantly complaining; in fact, there is nothing on earth that he will not complain about. (7) Also, he is very particular: everything must be just so or he cannot function. (8) Yet despite all of these eccentricities, we all love him very much and love to be with him, for there is not a more kind, generous, or sweet person to be found.

Body *Develops idea mentioned in sentence 6 of par. 1*

[2]The subjects of Uncle George's complaints range from the very important to the ridiculously trivial. He has many of the same complaints that we all do concerning things such as the cost of living, politics, and the New York Giants, but he also complains about incredibly unimportant things. He once asked me why our dog ate fast. Though I told him that all dogs eat fast, he thought that I should "get that dog to slow down before he chokes to death." Another incident led me to discover a very important fact about my uncle's complaining. One day several years ago, he and my father were watching a football game on television. Since the game was going smoothly, there was nothing to complain about. Or so we thought. To my astonishment, Uncle George began to complain about the goalposts! It was then that I realized that he is not happy unless he has something to complain about.

Body *Develops idea mentioned in sentence 7 of par. 1*

[3]Uncle George is very particular about almost everything. For example, his surroundings must be meticulously clean. Everyone in the family at one time or another has caught him inspecting their home when he comes to visit. He tries not to be noticed, but we all know from experience that he is looking for those infamous dust particles. As soon as he finds them, he begins to cough. However, if

he is really sensitive to dust, can he live in New York City? Also, his food must be prepared in a certain way or he is dissatisfied. For instance, he believes he is allergic to pepper. Whenever he smells or sees it, or even if he just knows it is there, he sneezes. Yet he has had dinner with us several times when there has been pepper in the food, and he did not know it was there.

Body Develops idea mentioned in sentence 8 of par. 1

⁴Although they can, at times, be exasperating, none of these eccentricities could ever keep my family and me from loving our Uncle George. He is very kind and would go out of his way to help someone, which many believe is a rare trait in a New Yorker. When he comes for a visit, he feels that he must do some chore around the house or buy a bag of groceries to show his appreciation, even though we always let him know that we would rather see him relaxing and enjoying himself. Uncle George's generosity is unlimited. When we visit him, we are often greeted with "I thought you might be able to use this." Everyone in the family comes home with a carload of things which he thought we might be able to use. We have often wondered how he manages to have so many things in such a small, meticulously clean apartment.

Conclusion Reiterates ideas expressed and stresses Uncle George's good points

⁵You might say that Uncle George is a very lovable person who happens to have a few odd habits. But these habits can make sense if one uses simple reasoning. His environment must be just so or he is unhappy. If he is unhappy about something, he will complain, which makes him very happy. He is a very colorful character, and just like everyone else's family, mine would not be the same without our Uncle George.

Here the writer's primary purpose is to support the idea that her uncle is not only eccentric but also is kind and is loved by his family. She does this by providing examples of his idiosyncracies and also of his generosity, all within the framework of a basic "beginning-middle-end" structure.

There are no set limits on the lengths of the introduction, the body, or the conclusion, although common sense dictates that neither the opening nor the closing should dwarf the middle. An essay might feature a very short introduction (perhaps one sentence), followed by three paragraphs in the body, and a long, two-paragraph conclusion. A longer essay may have a whole page of introduction and a body of a dozen or more paragraphs. Consider the following example:

Sentence 1 is the thesis statement. The rest of the sentences in paragraphs 1 and 2 support that idea.

¹The trained seamstress is not always the one who produces the most attractive finished product. One of my friends, Lois, spent four years in a tailoring and design school and learned to do work of excellent quality: Her seams are straight, buttonholes perfectly executed, and zippers always smartly inset. In spite of these skills, Lois does not have a feel for color, design, and balance. She seldom makes a wise match between fabric and pattern. Frequently she will choose a

very plain housedress pattern for an exquisite designer wool. And, at the other extreme, she once completed a beautiful designer business suit in a cotton gingham fabric. Buttons, belts, and other accessories such as contrasting collars and cuffs are rarely well chosen by Lois. Her penchant for selecting large glittering buttons for a very tailored suit invariably ruins the suit's appearance. Her collars of white linen make a pastel summer dress look like a uniform.

²Just the opposite is Melvina who, at 16, was turning out spectacular-looking clothes with no sewing training whatsoever. She once made a belt for a dress without having any idea how to apply the belt backing to the fabric. She simply tacked a strip of fabric onto an old belt she found around the house. Melvina hardly ever makes buttonholes because she simply doesn't know how and is not willing to slow down her projects while she learns. So she just sews snaps to the underside of her buttons. Mel has the amazing ability to team a pretty but cheap 99-cents-a-yard piece of fabric with a smartly designed pattern and come up with a smashing party dress. Sometimes by lunging right in with a pair of dull scissors, without a pattern or training in pattern drafting, she will come up with a suit that looks like a Paris original. Her most notable example of this is the white wool Chanel-type jacket and skirt she whipped up last year.

Conclusion restates the thesis statement ³Watching these two seamstresses at work has taught me a valuable lesson: The most expert sewing instruction does not guarantee the ability to produce a great-looking garment.

Most readers would agree that this piece is an acceptable, even effective, college essay. It states a main idea and then supports it; it has full development and good coherence; and it is interesting and lively. In place of a separate introductory paragraph, it uses a single opening sentence that is a part of the first paragraph of the body. This single opening sentence serves as an introduction and, at the same time, as a topic sentence for the first paragraph. The body of the essay has only two paragraphs, but each is well developed. The concluding paragraph contains only one sentence.

Exercise

Read the following student essays carefully. Examine the structure of each, identifying, where appropriate, the following:

Thesis statement (and/or main idea)
Topic sentences
Introduction
Body
Conclusion

1. *A FOOL AND HIS MONEY*

[1]Have you ever paid for something and then found out that the item purchased was cheap and not really worth anything? Have you purchased something like "Wrinkles Away" and found that, after using the product, you had more wrinkles than you started off with? If so, you are not the only one that the old cliché "A fool and his money are soon parted" applied to. Everyone has been ripped off at least once, and I am no exception.

[2]When I was a child, full of curiosity and the desire to spend money on my own, I found that not everyone was honest. I remember looking through a comic book and spying an ad for Extra Sensory X-Ray Glasses, which supposedly allowed you to see through people and view their biological make-up and functions. I was so impressed and enthusiastic that I cracked open my piggybank and sent $2.85 (which was a lot of money to a child back in those days) to the address in the ad. I remember running home from school every day, hoping that a package would be there, only to find that nothing had come. Weeks passed and finally I gave up hope, and then one day I came in the house and sighted a package on the living room table. I pounced on it like a lion would on a defenseless lamb, tore it open, and put the glasses on my face. I ran into the kitchen and looked at my mother, only to see that she was still whole! There was no skeleton, no blood flowing—nothing. No one to this day knows how disappointed I was.

[3]You would think that after such a disappointing experience I would have learned my lesson, but once again I was taken for a fool. This time I was reading through *Vogue* magazine and saw an ad for some low-priced designer jeans. Well, like a fool, hoping to get something for practically nothing, I sent out for a pair of size nine Gloria Vanderbilt jeans. Fortunately this time I didn't wait endless weeks for my package, only 14 days. When I got the package, I ripped it open, pulled out the jeans and once again stood aghast in disbelief. The so-called designer jeans were made of light-weight denim, had bright red stitching, and when I tried them on, or shall I say attempted to try them on, I couldn't get them past my knees. A tear trickled down my face and rolled off the point of my chin. I took the jeans off from around my knees, threw them on the floor and swore never again to send away for anything.

[4]Now my days of foolish buying are over, and I have decided that I will not purchase anything unless it is guaranteed, it fits right, or it is worth the money. As for all the other people, including innocent young children, who have yet to experience dissatisfaction, disappointment, and malcontent, I have these words of advice: Spend your hard-earned money wisely and never buy anything unless you can feel it, test it, or try it on, or you will find that you will be taken for a fool and parted from your money.

2.   *A USE FOR MATHEMATICS*

[1]After receiving a C on my first calculus test, I contemplated giving up mathematics completely. Math class had gotten so complicated and abstract that sometimes a whole week would pass without a single number being used! Finally, last week, my professor taught a practical, useful application of the numerous complex symbols and letters that I had slaved to master since the start of school. The problem is in story form and is solved by using complicated calculus principles such as increments, differentials, and formulas like $C=2\pi r$. However, I will illustrate these principles in a form that can be pictured.

[2]Once upon a time, in a city far away, there lived a very rich man named Harry. Harry had done or tried everything; he owned almost everything that could be owned and was willing to pay for most anything else; in short, money was no obstacle for Harry. There was one thing Harry wanted to do before he died; he wanted to have a rope made that would reach completely around the earth. He went to a rope maker and ordered a rope 25,486.27 miles long (the exact circumference of the earth at the equator). Two weeks later, the rope was delivered to his house and Harry was off to fulfill his dream. He crossed deserts, sailed oceans and climbed mountains with his rope only to find that when he finished, his rope was one foot too long!

[3]Harry felt like shooting the rope maker who had measured the rope incorrectly. The easy solution would have been to cut the last foot of rope off, making a perfect fit, but he felt as though that was cheating. Instead Harry decided to hire the best mathematicians and physicists to figure out the exact distance that the rope should be elevated (at every point on the course) to make its ends meet. After months of calculating, the committee of scholars decided that the rope must be raised 1.9098 inches off the earth (at all points). Harry did so, the ends met, and he lived happily ever after.

[4]I feel this is an almost unbelievable concept, especially taking into account this next example. Suppose you have a regulation size basketball and for some reason you wanted to tie a rope around the "equator" of the ball. Now imagine that the rope was exactly one foot too long, therefore keeping the ends from meeting. If instead of cutting the rope, you decided to prop it off the ball a certain distance, what would the distance be? To allow the ends to match up exactly, you would have to elevate the rope precisely 1.9098 inches from the ball at all points, the same amount as in the previous problem!

[5]I'm still contemplating giving up mathematics completely, but if Professor Mittleman comes up with any more of these fascinating applications of calculus, I may be forced to hang around mathematics a foot or so longer!

3.   *JUST RATIONALIZATION*

[1]It is common knowledge that for hundreds of years whites have discriminated against blacks. However, many people do not realize

the extent to which whites have developed rationalizations for their poor treatment of blacks. There are many such concepts whites originated that I was totally unaware of until recently when I took a course called Black Nationalism. What amazed me was how these concepts were twisted even after they had been formulated to meet their original needs.

²One of the first theories formulated was the Curse of Ham. This theory was based on a passage in the Bible. It dealt with a curse Noah put on his son and all his descendants for committing a sinful act. The curse states that Ham and his descendants will be the servants to all mankind. During the period of the slave trade it was believed that the Hamites, who were black, were the descendants of Ham and thus there was justification for putting them in bondage.

³The Curse of Ham was also used as a rationalization by America's founding fathers. During the American Revolution, Americans were fighting for freedom of speech and equality. The Constitution's Preamble states that "all men are created equal regardless of race, creed, or color. . . ." Blacks fought side by side with whites for this freedom and emancipation from Great Britain. Yet when this was obtained, white Americans who cried and fought so desperately for their freedom turned around and put blacks into bondage. In so doing, the whites used the Bible as justification for this enslavement. This rationale continued to be used until something happened that challenged the belief.

⁴In 1896 the Italians were unsuccessful in holding off resistance of the Ethiopians, who were supposedly the sons of Ham. The Ethiopians had defeated the Italians, but this was impossible if one believed in the Curse of Ham. Whites were faced with the question of how this resistance could be proven biblically. Their justification was that the Ethiopians were actually not black but a "brown extension of the Caucasoid race." In order to patch up their theory, the whites washed the Ethiopians white. Other European civilizations had imposed their culture on the Ethiopians and this is why they were able to defeat the Italians. Yet, despite their rationalizations about Ethiopia, whites now saw that the Curse of Ham would not always hold up. Therefore, they had to search for something else.

⁵In 1858 Charles Darwin published a book in which he stated his theory of evolution, which included "survival of the fittest." Although this was a biological theory, it would make a perfect rationalization if it were applied socially to blacks. The idea was referred to as Social Darwinism and it explained that blacks could not adapt to social change; therefore, they were inferior. Yet this is another concept that is difficult to understand. When Charles Darwin formulated his theory he was referring to natural selection of animals and plants, an area which does not have anything to do with the social structure among humans.

⁶Even today, Nobel Prize winner Schockley has written a book "scientifically proving" that blacks are inherently inferior. Through

analyzing the results of standardized testing, he believes he has proven this. It is a shame that one race must continually try to prove its superiority over another. Peaceful coexistence without chauvinistic ideologies seems virtually impossible.

4.   *HONESTY IS NOT ALWAYS THE BEST POLICY*

[1]An honest person is said to be truthful and sincere. Many times, though, total honesty can hurt others unnecessarily. The following will show that honesty is not the best policy if it hurts someone for no good reason or if it gets one into needless trouble.

[2]When a friend asks you to tell her the truth about her appearance in a certain dress, she is not necessarily looking for the real truth, but she wants her confidence to be built up. If you tell her that she looks terrible in the dress, her confidence will be shattered and she is liable to be deeply offended by your remark. If, on the other hand you tell her the dress "does something for her," her confidence is built up and everyone remains happy.

[3]Also, being honest can make saying "no" to a date more painful than necessary. A person who likes you will certainly take a "no" answer badly, and he will want to know why he has been turned down. You can tell him that you cannot stand him or you can be a little less than honest and tell him that you already have a boyfriend (even if you do not); he will immediately understand. Feelings will be saved on both sides and he will probably think of you as a very loyal person.

[4]Finally, honesty may not be the best policy if it gets one into needless trouble. For example, if you drop your mother's cake on the floor, why tell her? It would save the nervous system just to tell her that it fell while in the oven. Your nerves are much more important than a cake.

[5]Therefore, honesty is not always the best policy. If a person's feelings are at stake, or if it causes needless trouble for yourself, a little dishonesty may prove to be best.

CHOOSING A PATTERN OF DEVELOPMENT

In Chapter 2, we discussed three common patterns of discourse and emphasized the use of those patterns to stimulate thinking during invention. Besides working to stimulate thought, these patterns can aid you in structuring and developing your essays effectively. In the pages that follow we will discuss illustration, comparison/contrast, process, classification, definition, and analysis. We will stress their value as tools for organizing and developing essays and comment on ways to use them efficiently.

Although we must treat these patterns one by one, keep in mind that frequently you will use more than one at a time. You might use contrast, for instance, in an essay that is largely organized through the use of illustration. Or perhaps definition might be a necessary component of a largely analytic paper. Once you understand the basic

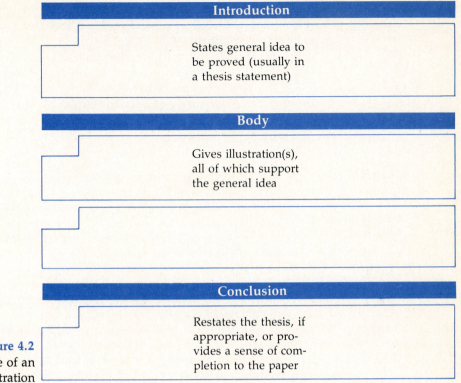

Introduction

States general idea to be proved (usually in a thesis statement)

Body

Gives illustration(s), all of which support the general idea

Conclusion

Restates the thesis, if appropriate, or provides a sense of completion to the paper

Figure 4.2
The basic structure of an essay using illustration

principles of using these patterns of development, you will find it easier to combine them when appropriate.

In addition, the use of any of these patterns must be closely related to your purposes in writing and should never be an end in itself. Your writing should make some point; it should not be simply a "comparison/ contrast" essay or a "definition" essay. For example, if you contrast two films, you must say more than "they are different." The point you make may be evaluative—that the acting in one is superior to that in the other. Then the contrasts you pinpoint serve to reveal that superiority. Or you might demonstrate that the differences between them arise from the different historical circumstances of the times in which the films were made. The contrast would be a means to an end, not an end in itself.

Illustration A specific illustration, or extended example, can support and clarify a general idea. Making use of illustrations is thus an effective way to organize an essay in which you are attempting to prove some general point. A good illustration is generally developed through a paragraph or two, not just through a single phrase or a few sentences. An essay using illustration is generally structured as shown in Figure 4.2. A variation of that pattern is to omit the initial thesis statement, begin with the illustration(s) directly, and end with a general statement which follows logically from what has gone before.

Obviously, you must choose your illustrations with care. Make certain that each supports your main idea in a direct and obvious way.

The student essay that follows shows how to use illustration (in this case, one extended example) to support a main idea. Note especially its structure and the way in which the central illustration develops the point fully.

Paragraph 1 establishes the direction of the essay: The writer must show how she regretted giving in to peer pressures. Paragraph 2 gives essential background information.

[1]Peer pressure exerts its greatest force on a young teen. Looking back, I can remember several occasions when I disobeyed my parents because of the pressure exerted on me by my peers. I lived to regret each of those occasions.

[2]One such occasion involved smoking cigarettes. I have always been raised with a strong understanding of right and wrong. And I knew that for a child my age cigarette smoking was wrong. My parents smoked when I was younger, and had allowed me a puff now and then, but had since kicked the habit and resorted to lecturing me on the hazards of smoking.

Paragraphs 3 and 4 recount the actual occurrence.

[3]One day, at a party at a friend's house, I decided to ignore all the lectures I had received at home about smoking. At first the party was going well; everyone was dancing and enjoying themselves. Then Ralph brought out a pack of cigarettes and everyone became "instant smokers." Those who did not become instant smokers were strongly urged to try it. And those who continuously refused were told they were not cool or hip. They were called scaredy-cats; the guys were told they were just plain stuck-up. After all the pressure exerted by the "cool" kids, everyone at the party had at least one puff.

[4]Then tragedy struck—at least tragedy for all of us at the party. Gwen's parents, smelling all the smoke, came down the stairs. Their first thought was that something was on fire. But when they discovered what the real problem was, it would have been better for each of us if *we* had been what was burning. Her father hit the ceiling and a couple of the kids also. Her parents' first thought was to make each of us smoke a whole pack, but luckily for us they thought again. They then took each of us, one by one, and called our parents, telling them of our misbehavior and asking them to come and get their child.

Paragraph 5 details the results.

[5]My parents were furious. Not only did I receive another lecture about the hazards of smoking, but I also heard for a week about how embarrassed they were because I had acted as if I had received no training at home. Lectures were by no means the extent of my punishment. I also lost use of the phone for two weeks, which by itself was punishment enough in my eyes. However, my parents also thought it appropriate that I should not be allowed to attend any parties for a whole month.

The concluding
sentence states the
impact on the writer
and reiterates the
idea of regret.

[6]Needless to say, I did not smoke any more after this incident. And I was also not so quick to go along with whatever the gang was doing.

The essay is successful because the illustration supports and amplifies the writer's thesis. In addition, the narrative gives a liveliness and vividness to the writing that mere statements could not.

This essay is also effective because the paragraphs providing the illustration flow smoothly. Note the transitions with which paragraphs two, three, and four begin: "One such occasion . . ."; "One day, . . ."; "Then . . . ." Paragraph six also begins with a transitional expression, "Needless to say," and provides the reader with a sense of finality by stating how the experience influenced the writer's future behavior.

In organizing a longer paper or in attempting to prove a complex point, you may have to coordinate a series of illustrations. In such cases, you will need to arrange the illustrations in a logical manner, perhaps chronologically or most-important-to-least-important (see pp. 90–92). Any time you employ illustration, you will be presenting your argument more concretely.

Exercise

Compose a concluding paragraph for the following student essay that uses a series of illustrations. Be certain that the paragraph restates the thesis statement.

THE CHAOS ON WALL STREET

[1]A month before the end of my freshman year, I received a phone call from my father concerning my summer job in New York City. He told me that I had been given a job on the floor of the New York Stock Exchange by a well-known brokerage firm. Immediately I had grand visions of working in a very prestigious position where I would be taught about the market. I thought I would be working in a booth doing a dignified job on the floor, where I had heard that things ran very smoothly. During my brief tenure there, however, I came to realize that both Wall Street in general and the specific firm I worked for were very unorganized. This disorganization led to such chaos that people had to be hired to correct others' mistakes.

[2]The first place I worked was on the floor of the New York Stock Exchange in a booth located right next to the entrance of the floor. My job as a clerk was to organize all order tickets, filing the completed ones in one cabinet and the uncompleted ones in their own separate file. I was also in charge of collecting all ticket stubs each day from the four booths run by my firm. Finally, I also had to make sure that our

two teletype machines were working and that all orders coming through the machine were distributed to the appropriate brokers so that they could fill them.

[3]Although my own duties were well organized, the entire area in which I worked was chaotic. First of all, there were always incredible quantities of paper flying around. Papers would fly around and hit you in the head and chest, and, if you were very unlucky, you might get a ball or two of paper in your mouth. The paper problem got really bad when trading was up or when one stock was doing unusually well—so bad that you could not see people through all the flying paper. So the area looked quite sloppy and disorganized. Also, the brokers and other clerks would take so many coffee and cigarette breaks that I was never sure who was on the floor and who was on a break. Sometimes I was left alone to work the entire booth for a few minutes. Within this short period of time we would almost always get a large amount of orders, resulting in a backlog and an overflow of paperwork.

[4]One of the biggest problems that led to chaos on the market floor was the brokers' unliberated attitudes toward women. Women caused a lot of trouble because they were considered distractions to the men on the floor, especially if the women wore unusual or tight-fitting clothes. Whenever these women came onto the floor, everything would stop. Brokers would actually stop their trading to whistle and hoot at most of them. Clerks and stock exchange employees would howl, throw paper in the air, and stop working, causing a chaotic state in general. A few times, because of all the distractions and paper flying around, I misfiled order tickets or, even worse, lost them and then had to dig through the mounds of paper on the floor to find them.

[5]After two weeks on the chaotic floor, I was moved to the Stock Records Department of the same company, only a few blocks away from the New York Stock Exchange. My first job there was transferring customer stock accounts from one set of records to another. This was done by transferring certain information by hand from a computer sheet to a pad showing the customer's account number, the number of shares, and the price of the stock. In a sense, this was a waste of time because it could have been done by a computer, avoiding the human errors of adding or copying numbers incorrectly. On a big account, it would take me two days to find the error that might have thrown me off by a few dollars (an average account had about three to five million dollars worth of stock, with individual shares being worth anywhere from one penny to hundreds of thousands of dollars). For example, one time I made a three-dollar error on a sixteen-million-dollar account. It took me over two days to find my error, but the company would rather pay me two days' salary than put three dollars into the account. This is a perfect example of disorganization and waste.

[6]After doing that boring work for six weeks, I was moved into another department called Stock over the Wire. The chaos and disorganization in this department were too widespread to believe. First of all, my job was to track down lost stock (that became lost due to

a mistake made by the company) and credit or debit the customer. Finding lost stock was extremely difficult—I had to go back to records of the day it was actually sent over the wire and start tracking it down. Stocks could be put into another customer's account, sent to the wrong department, have wrong account or identification numbers, or just disappear and end up in another branch office. Half the time, the record books that were needed to find the stock were lost or were missing the crucial page. If I were using microfiche to find the stock, I had to find a working viewer and find the piece of microfiche that I needed. If I were using microfilm, I would have to wait in line to use a machine because we had only one working machine for over one hundred people.

[7]Working in Stock over the Wire, I had to solve problems that stemmed back to 1978. And besides having the computer tell us we were missing stocks, we received about 75 calls a day from clerks wanting to know where their stock was. Of course, all of them wanted their problems to be solved immediately. We would also receive calls about missing bonds and certificates—actually another department's responsibility, but that department was so busy that they had given the clerk the run-around.

[8]Our area was in such a state of confusion and so far behind that we sometimes would not pick up the phone, or we would file requests away until we would receive a fourth or fifth request. It became so hectic on one day that when I picked up the phone and responded to a customer's request by telling him what my boss told me, the man went into a tirade and threatened to tell the head of the company about me. To top things off, our head boss was always on vacation, our desk boss was never at his desk, and two of the four workers would not show up or would come in an hour late, causing what was already a disorganized mess to become pure chaos.

Suggestion for Writing

Write an essay demonstrating the truth of a general observation about life. You might choose an old saying or proverb and illustrate it with your own experiences. Here is a partial list of proverbs; you can probably think of many more:

A bird in the hand is worth two in the bush.
Absence makes the heart grow fonder.
Crime does not pay.
He who hesitates is lost.
Look before you leap.
Out of sight, out of mind.
Nothing ventured, nothing gained.
When it rains, it pours.

As a model for the paper you can use the essay "A Fool and His Money" (p. 113) or "Honesty Is Not Always the Best Policy" (p. 116).

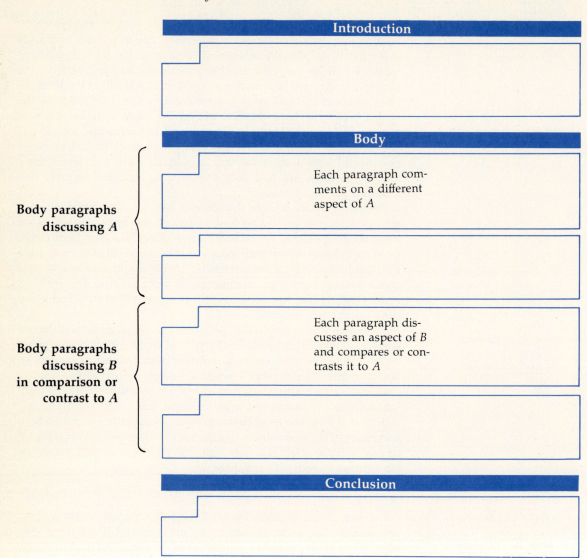

Introduction

Body

Body paragraphs
discussing *A*

Each paragraph comments on a different aspect of *A*

Body paragraphs
discussing *B*
in comparison or
contrast to *A*

Each paragraph discusses an aspect of *B* and compares or contrasts it to *A*

Conclusion

Figure 4.3 The "*A*, then *B*" pattern of a comparison/contrast essay

Your general observation does not have to be an established saying or proverb; it can be an observation of your own. Note that the writers of the essays on peer pressure (pp. 118–19) and the trained seamstress (pp. 111–12) came up with their own sayings. You might also think about new twists to an old saying, such as "He who hesitates gets bossed," or "When it rains, it drizzles."

In choosing or formulating your general observation, don't forget to make use of the invention techniques. Try using the idea of illustration in reverse (see pp. 50–51). That is, rather than choosing a general observation and then attempting to find an example to support it, recall

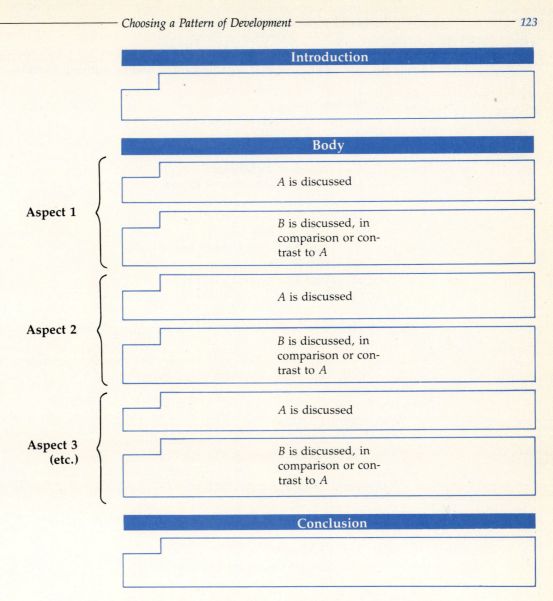

Figure 4.4 The "*A, B, A, B*" pattern of a comparison/contrast essay

an important or interesting incident from your recent experience and work backward to generate an observation explaining it. Then, when you write the paper, structure it with the generalization first.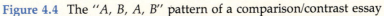

Comparison/Contrast Commenting on similarities or differences between objects, persons, situations, or ideas is a common goal of communication. Organizing and developing comparisons and contrasts effectively is an important skill, both in college work and beyond.

There are two basic approaches to organizing a comparison/ contrast essay, as shown in Figures 4.3 and 4.4. Let's assume that two objects are being considered and that four points are being compared. An essay using the first organization would be outlined like this:

Introduction
I. Discuss Object *A*—Chevrolet Citation
   A. Point 1—Price
   B. Point 2—Options Available
   C. Point 3—Gas Mileage
   D. Point 4—Frequency of Repair

II. Discuss Object *B*—Toyota Corona
   A. Point 1—Price
   B. Point 2—Options Available
   C. Point 3—Gas Mileage
   D. Point 4—Frequency of Repair
Conclusion

The writer would cover all points regarding Object *A* and then move on to Object *B*.

The same essay could employ the second organization, however, and would then use this outline:

Introduction
I. Point 1—Price
   A. Discuss Object *A*—Chevrolet Citation
   B. Discuss Object *B*—Toyota Corona

II. Point 2—Options Available
   A. Discuss Chevrolet Citation
   B. Discuss Toyota Corona

III. Point 3—Gas Mileage
   A. Discuss Chevrolet Citation
   B. Discuss Toyota Corona

IV. Point 4—Frequency of Repair
   A. Discuss Chevrolet Citation
   B. Discuss Toyota Corona
Conclusion

In this essay the writer moves from point to point, discussing Object *A*, then Object *B*. Either organizational structure can lead to an effective essay.

In writing a comparison/contrast essay, it is important to avoid falling into the "descriptive trap," which involves merely *describing* each item rather than actually *comparing* the two. The descriptive trap results when the writer fails to recognize and establish a common point or points for comparison. Notice that the outlines above concentrate on the same qualities for each car, thus establishing common points for comparison. It would be illogical to try to compare, say, the Chevrolet's roominess with the Toyota's ease of handling. In the course of a long essay, it is easy to lose sight of the need for common points of comparison, resulting in simply a description of each item. If the writer mentioned under "Frequency of Repair" that the Chevrolet has reliable brakes and electrical components and a long-lasting exhaust system, and later mentioned that the Toyota has a remarkably durable engine and transmission, no real comparison or contrast has been made; rather, two loosely related descriptions have been written. To transform such descriptive writing into a true comparison, you would have to add commentary on the meaning of the facts described. For example, you might observe that the Toyota is more reliable in the area of major components, while the Chevy is more reliable in smaller but nonetheless crucial components related to safety of operation.

Besides common points of comparison organized in one of two patterns, a successful comparison/contrast essay requires a purpose to guide it. Without a purpose it will amount to little more than a description of similarities and differences. The comparison or contrast you make must contribute to some larger insight you have or support some general concept you're trying to prove. In our example, contrasting the two automobiles may lead to a decision to purchase one or the other, or to the belief that little real difference exists. Saying only that the two cars are "alike" or "different" will likely lead your reader to ask, "So what?"

The following student essay contrasts two instructors using the "*A*, then *B*" approach:

Par. 1 presents the main idea of the paper (sentence 2). The writer makes it clear from the start that the contrast will support this insight.

[1]In many subjects, such as mathematics and science, the teacher has few opportunities to inject his or her own personality and background into the subject matter. Yet in presenting something where one's own interpretation plays a major role, as in history, the teacher's ethnic, social, political, and educational background has much to do with the perspective from which the course is taught. The points of view of two recent Modern European history teachers I have had were as different as the two poles, because of the teachers' respective backgrounds.

Par. 2 and 3 describe the background and teaching perspective of A.

[2]My first teacher, Joseph Calmon, was a Frenchman and schooled entirely in France, receiving his Ph.D. at a French university. Being European, Calmon knew more about the subject matter than many other historians and gave obscure, but very interesting, pieces of information not readily available to the average American or non-European historian. For example, his detailed descriptions of

Napoleon's influence on the French people provided me with a great insight into Napoleon and his motivations.

[3]Unfortunately, his perspective of European history was not in the least bit unbiased, nor did he attempt to separate his obvious French favoritism from his presentation of a thorough and overall history. This was the case when Calmon proudly gave full credit for the entire European Enlightenment to the various French philosophers of that time. The class really should have been retitled, "The French Impression of European History." Calmon was indeed a very patriotic and conservative Frenchman who would let it be known just how the French saw other European countries and nations in other parts of the world.

Par. 4 and 5 describe those of B. [4]My second teacher, Kenneth Stringer, was a United States citizen, completing his doctoral dissertation at the American University in Washington, D.C. As more of an outside observer of European history, Stringer could not provide first-hand tidbits as Calmon did, but he was able to evaluate equally all interpretations of history—whether French, Russian, German, English, and so on—and form them all into one congruent picture. Thus Stringer's account of history was far more neutral than Calmon's was. He was also able to parallel certain European developments (for example, the Enlightenment) with the development of the United States.

[5]Yet even Stringer was not totally unbiased. He was a relatively young teacher, had served in Vietnam, and was an old sixties radical. Hence, his opinions on most topics were extremely liberal, and it showed in what trends and factions he chose to emphasize and sympathize with. More often than not, Stringer examined the development of the political Left or extreme Left rather than the Right, and he spent a great deal of time teaching the rise of Marxism.

Par. 6 reiterates the writer's main point. [6]In history and other disciplines like it, two people with the same amount of education and basic factual information, like the two teachers, can view the past differently, emphasizing different interpretations to fit the way they view the world.

In this essay, the contrast exists for the purpose of supporting the writer's assertion that the instructors' backgrounds influence their approaches to their subject matter. The paper does not exist for the sole purpose of pointing out the differences between two teachers.

In contrast, read this essay:

The student comments that her grandparents are "different." [1]Not every family has even one set of grandparents living. But God has blessed me with two sets of healthy, but different, grandparents.

She uses the "A, then B" approach, devoting par. 2 to one set of grandparents and par. 3 to the other. [2]My grandmother and grandfather on my father's side are unique people. They live in a two-story apartment in a small town in New York. My grandmother for many years worked as a secretary for a local firm. Now she is just content to be a homemaker. My grandfather for many years worked as a diamond setter. Now he is retired, and finds great pleasure in taking a careful inventory of all the items he has collected in his home. Their basement is just amazing. Everything is in its place, and everything has a date on it. My grandparents are two people that love to watch old Laurel and Hardy movies and eat fresh rolls from the nearby bakery.

[3]My grandmother and grandfather on my mother's side are also unique. They live in a mobile home in Florida. My grandmother has always been a homemaker. When my grandfather came home from work she would always have his meal waiting for him. My grandfather's profession was that of professional house painter. Now he is content to sit on his beautiful patio, which is surrounded by flowers. He reads the Bible and whistles to the birds. My grandparents love to play cards with their close friends, and place bets at the dog races.

Par. 4 restates that [4]My two sets of grandparents are very different, but they are very
her relatives are different. special. They have taught me a great deal about life, and I thank God I have them.

Notice that this essay does not go beyond being a description, nor does it make an overall point. The writer presents many concrete details about her relatives, but because common points were not carefully established, many of the details are not comparable. No insight or idea ties the details together.

When this student thought about how she could revise her essay, she decided that the most significant difference between her sets of grandparents lay in their contrasting attitudes toward life: One set prefers being as independent as possible, while the other grandparents enjoy as much contact with their families as possible. The writer then revised her paper to emphasize this idea:

The writer maintains the "A, [1]Not every family has even one set of grandparents living. Howev-
then B" structure, but er, God has blessed me with two sets of healthy, although different,
focuses on the differing grandparents.
attitudes of her grandparents.

The first sentence in [2]My grandmother and grandfather on my father's side are very
par. 2 emphasizes independent people, and are content just being around each other. For
the independence of one many years they have lived in a two-story apartment in a small town in
set of grandparents. New York. My parents are continually asking them to come spend a few weeks with them. But they always say, "There are too many things to do here, and we really don't want to put you to any trouble." My grandparents don't have many close friends, but that doesn't matter to them because they are content just being together. They do get involved with their own activities. My grandmother enjoys making her great German dishes, and my grandfather is content with taking inventory of all his possessions. The most important thing to both of them is just to relax with each other, and perhaps watch an old Laurel and Hardy movie in peace.

Here the contrasting [3]My grandmother and grandfather on my mother's side are two
attitude of the second people who need their loved ones around them and who need to do
set is pointed out. things with other people. For many years my grandparents lived in

New Jersey near my uncle and his family, so they always spent much of their time with the family. Now that my grandparents live in Florida, being so far away from their son and daughter makes them very unhappy. They continually ask to see my mother and my uncle. Since they are unable to visit with family, my grandparents are always looking for friends. Though they don't especially care to, they, too, do things on their own. My grandmother tends to her garden, and my grandfather sits on the patio and whistles to the birds. Their biggest enjoyment is finding another couple and spending the day with them at the dog races.

The writer concludes by emphasizing the different degrees of independence her grandparents have; that particular aspect of their lives was her main concern in this essay.

[4]My two sets of grandparents are very different, particularly in their need for other people, but they are both very special. They have taught me a great deal about life, and I am grateful I have them.

As you compose papers of this type, keep in mind that the comparison or contrast you establish should support some central idea. In general, avoid writing papers that only describe items or note the existence of some unlabeled similarity or difference.

Exercise

Read this student paper, which contrasts the various schools the writer has attended. Preserving the information contained in it, how could you reorganize it to achieve a tighter structure?

[1]One thing I have found through going to different elementary schools is that there is a deep gulf between predominantly black public schools and predominantly white schools, at least the ones that I've been to. Now that I think about it, I'm amazed at the differences I encountered.

[2]I've attended many schools in my hometown in upstate New York. The first school I went to was Montgomery Street Elementary School, which was pretty much all black. I had been there a little over two and a half years when my family moved across town to an integrated neighborhood and, for me, a new school.

[3]As I think back, it was when I went to West Street Elementary School, which was predominantly white, that I first felt a big difference. A feeling of strangeness hit me as soon as I walked through the big school door. I noticed much less noise, fooling around, and running in the hallways. This school was much older than the one I had previously attended, and as such, it had established, rigid rules and guidelines that had been passed down through the years. For example, there was no eating and especially no gum chewing in class or in the hallway, and no talking without raising your hand and being called on by the teacher. Montgomery Street School was completely different. There was constant and open eating in the classrooms, not

to mention in the hallways; and spontaneous outbursts were the rule, not the exception. I had to go through a few scoldings at the new school and also a few visits to the principal's office before things sank in.

[4]When I transferred to West I had to get over some feelings of inadequacy. I felt like I had been put in too high a grade. They were using some books in my new class, which was second grade, that I wouldn't have seen until the end of the third grade in my old school, Montgomery. In the books that were familiar to me from Montgomery, my new class was chapters ahead of where I left off, and it took me the rest of the year even to begin to catch up.

[5]Approximately two years later I was bussed to another school that was even whiter. My change of schools was the result of citywide desegregation in my hometown. This school, Temple Hill Middle School, was in the suburbs, and was even more accelerated than West Street School. Surprisingly, I had little problem adjusting to it.

[6]As I reflect back now, it seems the better the educational system, the better the grades I was receiving. In my earliest years, I was a C student. After that my grades started creeping up, until about the eighth grade when I was a B+ student. I had a feeling of being able to achieve something, and that's something I don't think I would have gotten had I gone to a predominantly black school in my area. Though I would have felt much more at ease in an all-black environment, the teachers would not have pushed me nearly as hard, nor made me feel as good about myself had they done so.

[7]It can't be just a coincidence that white children overall get a better education than black children. Though the standards the schools set is one of the reasons for students' achieving well, it's not the only one. And though there are economic and other factors involved, it does seem to be true that the color of your skin, or rather the racial make-up of the school you go to, has a lot to do with the quality of education you will get.

Suggestion for Writing

As a member of your college's student activities board, you have been involved in selecting a performer or performing group to come to campus for the homecoming concert. The board has narrowed the choice to two possibilities and the chairperson has now asked each member to submit a written report indicating his or her choice and providing supporting reasons. The board has decided that the main criterion in the final phase of selection should be the performer's (or group's) attractiveness to the audience, which will be composed of middle-aged people from the town as well as students from the campus. Thus you are to support your recommendation by comparing the two performers or groups in terms of their appeal to such a mixed audience. (For this assignment, choose any two performers or groups with whom you are familiar.)

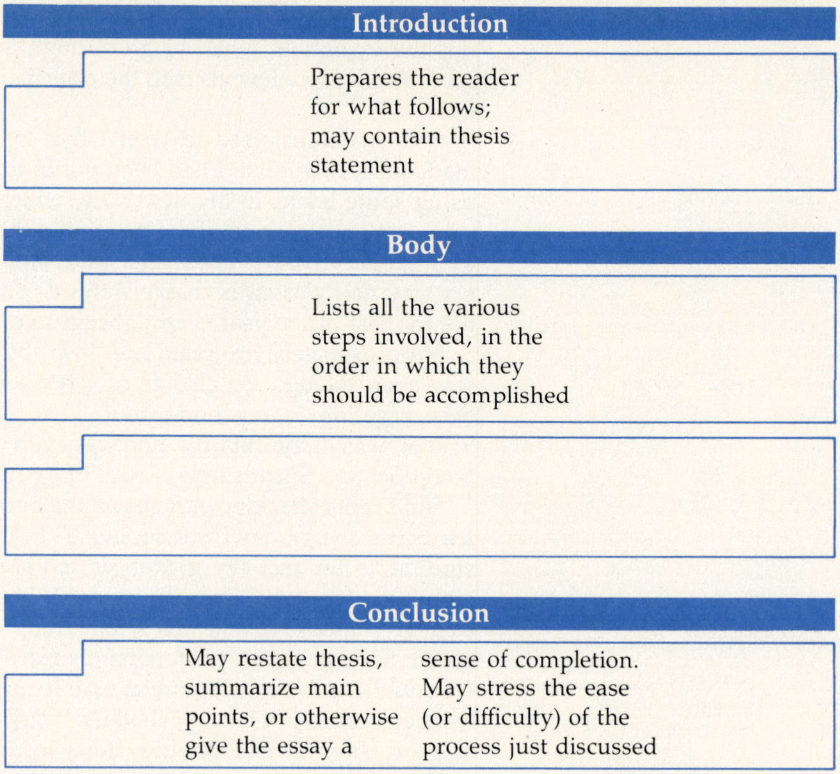

Introduction

Prepares the reader
for what follows;
may contain thesis
statement

Body

Lists all the various
steps involved, in the
order in which they
should be accomplished

Conclusion

May restate thesis,   sense of completion.
summarize main   May stress the ease
points, or otherwise   (or difficulty) of the
give the essay a   process just discussed

Figure 4.5
The basic structure of a
process essay

Process   Writing an essay that explains process—how to do something—is, from a structural point of view, one of the easier writing tasks. If the process you discuss has, for instance, seven steps, you must describe them in the order in which they are performed: step one, step two, and so on. Thus, chronological order is the basic structure of a process paper, which can be diagrammed as shown in Figure 4.5.

Process papers can achieve a variety of purposes. They may be written to instruct the reader. For instance, owners' manuals contain "how-to" sections geared toward readers who will need to carry out the described procedures. On the other hand, your purpose in writing may be to convince the reader that a certain process is simpler (or more difficult) than one might assume. In that case you are being informative, but you are not expecting your reader actually to undertake the process.

In any case, process papers should contain precise language that makes it easy for readers to visualize the various steps. Particularly in technical pieces, writers may need to use visual aids to achieve yet greater precision. Unusual or specialized terminology may need defining if the context does not provide the meaning. In addition, if your purpose is to enable readers to duplicate the process, then giving a rationale for doing a step in a certain way helps ensure that they will remember to do it as you suggest.

The following paragraphs are from an essay on how to graft fruit trees. In the first paragraph the writer establishes his primary purpose, in this case a very practical one (the thesis statement is italicized):

> There are about 10,000 named varieties of apple, but only a few are available as trees. To a lesser but similar extent, the same situation exists with other fruits and nuts. Some lesser-known varieties, to use the apple for an example, have excellent flavor and tender, melting flesh, but either because they do not color well, or ripen over a long period, or are too tender to ship, these varieties aren't of interest to commercial growers and so are not generally offered by nurseries. Scions of forgotten varieties are, however, often available—if not from nurseries, from private growers. *If you can graft, you can establish them in your orchard.* (Robert Kurle, "The Whip-and-Tongue Craft")

In the next several paragraphs the writer describes the various tools needed for grafting, cites reference books available, and asserts that the grafting method he advocates is among the easiest. Then he explains the method itself:

Note that the writer describes the steps precisely, since he's aiming at readers who will try to duplicate them.

. . . You are now ready to make a whip-and-tongue graft. The time is early spring. The scion is a length of vigorous stem with at least two buds on it from last year's growth (for best results). The thickness of the wood should be about the diameter of a pencil. Scions of smaller diameter don't carry enough food and are more difficult to graft. Match the scion to the tree (stock) at a point where they both have the same diameter. Cut the scion as shown in the first diagram. Match the

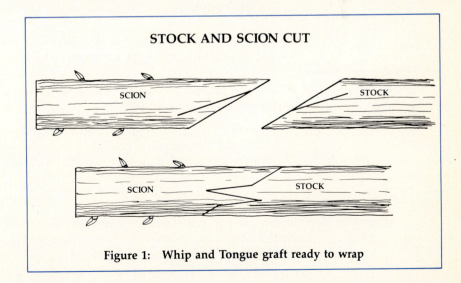

STOCK AND SCION CUT

SCION   STOCK

SCION   STOCK

Figure 1: Whip and Tongue graft ready to wrap

slant of the scion cut in the stock and work it together until both the scion cut and the stock slant fit as closely as possible. Sometimes because of the irregularity in shape, the two pieces may not want to fit perfectly together all around, but make sure most of the two cambium layers are touching each other.

He gives reasons for what he says whenever possible, thereby stressing the value of following his method exactly.

Now cut the "tongue" into the stock near the top (see figure 1 again). Don't cut too deeply, but let it follow almost parallel to the splice cut. Next, hold the scion up to the stock and estimate where to cut the scion tongue so that when they're pressed in place, the two pieces will fit together perfectly or nearly so. The tongues have to slip into each other far enough so the two pieces meet snugly at top and bottom. Make a few practice grafts on discarded wood before you do the real thing, and you will quickly learn how far up the slant of the scion to make the tongue cut so the two pieces will slide together closely.

Now wrap the union with a rubber band or budding tape, tucking the band end under at the last wrap so no knot is needed. Then cover with plastic. (Or, if you can make a perfect splice union, you may just wrap the graft with freezer tape only.) Be careful to graft back to a main branch; if you're too far out on a limb, there's no place for the new stock to grow.

In addition to presenting the grafting techniques, he answers questions that he guesses may remain in the readers' minds. Note again that he offers rationales for what he advises.

If you want to test a bunch of varieties in a hurry you can make from ten to 30 grafts on a six- to seven-foot fruit tree in your orchard. Often this method will give you fruit the second year after grafting. However, when testing this way, I recommend doing only one tree a year. Then if there is a virus or other disease in any of these varieties, only one tree is infected. You should not add more grafts to that multiple variety tree the next year. That way, if virus or disease were to show up from new grafts, you'd lose only one year's grafting. Be cautious about taking scions off the test tree, too. Wait two or three years, since some viruses may not show symptoms the first year.

Besides using precise language and careful explanations, this writer used a visual aid to make his descriptions clearer.

Suggestion for Writing

Choosing a process you know well, write an essay based on it. Assume one of the following contexts:

1. You're trying to persuade your reader that the procedure is simple (or difficult). Your reader is basically unfamiliar with it.
2. You're trying to demonstrate that the process is easier (or harder) than it looks.

Classification

In composing classification essays, writers attempt to show the major types, categories, or divisions into which their material breaks down. Drama, for example, may be classified into various categories such as comedy/tragedy, or musical/nonmusical. Words may be classified into

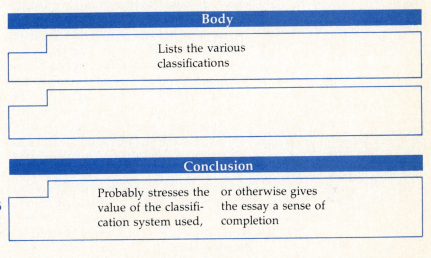

Figure 4.6
The basic structure of a
classification essay

parts of speech based on their functions in sentences: nouns, verbs, pronouns, adverbs, and so on. Any time your topic is a general one consisting of various specific types or kinds, using classification can make it clear to your reader. Making the general subject matter clearer or more precise for both you and your reader is usually the purpose of writing a paper based on classification, and in this way it is related to *definition* (which will be discussed next). Also, classifications may reveal unexpected complexities or show trends over periods of time.

Structuring the classification essay presents no special problems, since it will take the form of a list of the categories under discussion (see Figure 4.6). Within the body, the classifications may be listed in any logical order—chronological and most-important-to-least are two possibilities.

In deciding how to classify the aspects of your topic, you will be looking for categories that are *similar* in that they all share some general characteristic(s), but *different* enough to be seen as separate types. For instance, certain music can be labelled *rock*, but within that group are many varieties: *rockabilly, soft rock, punk rock, rhythm and blues*, and *heavy metal*, to name a few. By classifying the major types within the topic "rock music," you could write a paper to inform a reader what the term *rock* involves.

The following student essay classifies into various types the image of Mary in religious writings and art in order to give the reader an overall view of how Mary has been perceived through the centuries.

Introduction sets the stage by noting that the image of Mary has changed. Reader expects a discussion of the various images.

[1]An interesting concept found in the study of religion is the phenomenon of how Mother Mary is depicted differently during different time periods. As people's thoughts about the world and religion changed, so did their image of Mary.

Par. 2 establishes the two major classifications of Mary's image; discusses the change from one to the other.

[2]Mary has been seen at times as a part of the profane or human world and at other times as sacred or holy. The earliest books of the New Testament were probably written thirty years after the death of Jesus. It is in these books that Mary is shown as a shepherd who is tired and weary and gives birth to a baby boy in a stable. Here Mary is pictured as a person as she goes through the very human act of giving birth. Approximately one century A.D., when the Gospel of Luke was written, the idea of Mary's being a virgin becomes a much more important idea in the story of the birth of Jesus. It is during this period that Mary is elevated to the stature of a more central and sacred figure in the Church.

Par. 3 explains two subtypes of Mary's "divine" image.

[3]Between the second century and the beginning of the Renaissance, Mary's image goes through two phases. First she begins to be thought of as almost equivalent to God, since He is termed as the father of Jesus and Mary as the mother. She is thus further heightened to the status of a divine being. Next Mary seems to be a link from the profane world to the sacred world as she is the one who has brought the divine into the profane world. She is thought to be one who can bring gods into the world.

Par. 4 tells how Mary's image returned to a more human one, stresses human aspects that differ from the original "weary shepherd" image in par. 2.

[4]Moving closer to the Renaissance, when people were becoming more humanistic, Mary's image takes on a personality. The personality she represents is that of a loving, caring mother. Mary begins to be viewed not as almost a god but more as a mother that will always forgive you. She is shown as one who cares for a person in need. In particular the "Loving Mother" image of Mary is common at the beginning of the Renaissance. Later, around the fourteenth century, Mary is seen as the "Weeping Mother." She is pictured crying as she holds the dead body of Jesus in her arms, and is thought of primarily as a mother who is devastated by the death of her son.

Par. 5 sums up relationship between changing modes of thought and changing images of Mary.

[5]One can see, then, how the image of Mary changed though time from that of a tired, weary shepherd to that of a divine being and back to a kind and very human person. In the process, as Mary was given more divinity, she lost her personality. Conversely, as Mary's personality grew, her divinity became less important.

Note that the discussion proceeds chronologically, one of the possible approaches to organizing a classification paper. The material in this essay could also be structured according to the two major classifications of human and divine—that is, by first discussing the various images of Mary that portray her in a humanistic manner and then discussing the various divine images, without giving much consideration to when the images were current. Another alternative, if the writer had enough detailed information, would be to subdivide the categories human and divine images yet further and write an essay focussing on one particular time period, such as the early Renaissance.

Exercise

1. Following are some facts, in random order, about tennis racquets. The information covers three basic areas of concern to anyone shopping for a racquet: frame composition, head size, and stringing. If you were writing a paper to advise readers on the choice of a proper racquet, how would you classify these statements? Use the three basic areas as your major guidelines for classification.

   a. Racquets with oversized heads are usually strung at very high tension (70–80 pounds).
   b. Metal frame racquets give maximum power.
   c. Gut strings are the most expensive and offer the best control, but they are the least durable.
   d. Wood racquets give a good balance between power and control.
   e. Graphite racquets, the latest innovation, combine the best characteristics of metal and wood.
   f. Midsized racquets offer a larger string area than standard racquets, but without the diminished control common to oversized racquets.
   g. The newer oversized racquets are usually strung with oil-filled nylon strings.
   h. One company recently introduced a racquet with an elongated head, resembling a snowshoe.
   i. Tournament nylon, the longest-lasting type of stringing, delivers more power than oil-filled nylon, but less control.

2. Choose one of the following topics and explain how you would develop an essay using classification on that topic.

   Career goals
   TV programs
   Diets
   Political parties
   Strategies for winning in ———— (any sport or game)

Suggestion for Writing

You are a free-lance writer, and you have just heard that a new magazine, *Pop Culture*, is interested in buying a series of pieces on current trends in popular art forms. For their first issue, the editors want basic introductory articles describing the contemporary scene in American films, rock music, and popular dances.

Choose the area with which you are most familiar and write an article (approximately three or four typed pages) covering trends and types as you see them during the past two or three years. You know that one major aspect of your project will be to *classify* your subject according to its major types, because the editors have indicated that classification is essential to informing their audience. However, you are not limited to classification. For instance, if you write about current dances, you might also want to describe the *process* of doing some of the less familiar dance steps. If you choose to construct a classification of current films, you will almost certainly bring up particular films as *illustrations* of the types. In discussing rock music, you might find *comparison/contrast* a useful tool in differentiating between the types of rock music you have identified.

Definition

Essays built around definition tend to define complex or abstract concepts, such as *education, success,* or *love*. Because the concepts are complicated, they consist of many aspects and are thus open to *extended definition* (that is, to be defined at length). Often the definition may include illustrations to amplify what is intended, or comparison/contrast ("Happiness is a warm puppy") to define further what is meant by a certain concept.

Structuring an essay that defines should be handled through a topical arrangement. Group ideas dealing with similar aspects together under one topic or subpoint, and move from one consideration of the overall concept to another (see Figure 4.7 opposite).

Examine the following essay, which defines the term *competition*:

Paragraph 1 gives the major distinction: positive and negative definitions of competition.

[1]Anyone who has felt the thrill of winning a hard-fought game knows that competition can be stimulating and valuable. On the other hand, anyone who has lost a friend by competing with that person for good grades, a summer job, or a boyfriend or girlfriend knows that competition can be dangerous to one's mental health. Competition is a complex concept which can be defined from many perspectives, positive and negative.

The body examines different aspects of competition (economic, academic, and athletic), thus defining the activity. Within each discussion both positive and negative views are presented, giving the reader a better, fuller understanding of what competition can mean. Note also the use of classification:

[2]To a capitalist, competition is a necessary, desirable state of affairs to be encouraged at all times and cultivated actively. It makes progress possible by stimulating production and encouraging efficiency. To a communist, competition is a counterproductive, useless activity to be eliminated for the good of the state. It hampers progress by getting people involved in their own petty self-interests.

[3]In academics, competition may be a motivating force, encouraging capable students to try harder to win anything from a grammar school gold star to a college scholarship to a graduate fellowship. For less prepared students, such competition may be psychologically destructive, forcing them to enter a contest in which they know they must fail.

[4]Likewise, athletic competition can be defined as a positive or negative activity. At its best, athletic competition offers the individual an exhilarating experience, an excitement that can be among the best

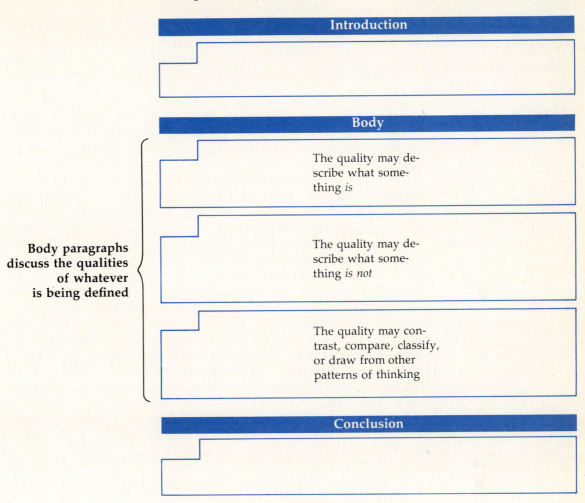

Introduction

Body

Body paragraphs discuss the qualities of whatever is being defined

The quality may describe what something *is*

The quality may describe what something *is not*

The quality may contrast, compare, classify, or draw from other patterns of thinking

Conclusion

Figure 4.7 The basic structure of an essay that defines

The writer subdivides competition *into "positive" and "negative."*

that life has to offer. At its worst, competition produces many undesirable side effects, such as meddling parents, unethical behavior, and humiliation for the losers. Too often when people talk about the "benefits of healthy competition," they really mean the "need to win or else."

The next-to-last paragraph looks at competition from the standpoint of those who find it neither healthy nor unhealthy, but simply unwise.

[5]And yet opinion seems increasingly divided on the value of winning the competition one has entered. Indeed, in our modern society, for every story we hear about someone striving to win, we hear a tale about those who feel it is better to drop out of competition altogether. In professional football, for instance, where the team with the worst record gets the first pick in the college draft, there has been speculation that the weaker teams hope to lose as the season draws to a close. And we're all familiar with the logic of unemployment

compensation, which sometimes dictates that it's in a job seeker's best interest *not* to compete for a job.

The one-sentence conclusion draws the reader's attention to the main point.

[6]Competition is definitely a two-sided coin, and any attempt to deal with it should always take that fact into account.

Here the student uses definition to achieve the primary purpose, which is to show that competition can be a valuable experience or a detrimental one. Note that definition is therefore a means to an end, not an end in itself.

A writer attempting to define something may also use the "type/special characteristic" approach. This involves first establishing the general type or class of an object, then further defining the topic according to the special characteristics it possesses and that others of the same general type do not. For instance, a *battalion* is a military unit (type); it is also a unit having more than two-hundred but fewer than eight-hundred men (special characteristic). A complete type/special characteristic definition of the term would read "A *battalion* is a military unit which contains more than two-hundred but fewer than eight-hundred men." Similarly, an *overture* is a musical composition (type) performed by a full orchestra and serving as the introduction to an opera, musical, or similar long work (special characteristics). A type/special characteristic definition would read "An *overture* is an orchestral composition that serves as the introduction to an opera, musical, or similar long work."

Another useful technique is defining a concept or entity according to what it is *not* as well as according to what it is. Consider these examples:

A true friend is not someone who will abandon you when you most need help.
Genuine faith is not something that can be forced on a person.

One caution: A great many negative definitions are possible for any term and, although most will be accurate, they will be of no help to the reader. For example, such definitions as "*Friendship* is not a banana peel" and "*Faith* is not a mosquito" provide no useful information.

Exercise

Provide a one-sentence definition for each of the following terms. Use either the type/special characteristic(s) or the negative technique, whichever you feel is more appropriate.

1. pentameter
2. gazebo

3. incense
4. liberal education
5. archipelago
6. justice
7. fascism
8. anarchist
9. slavery
10. conscience

Suggestions for Writing

Choose a particular term or concept and write a paper defining it. Here are some suggested contexts:

1. A close friend of yours from high school writes you that he/she has been betrayed by people in his/her new circle of friends and expresses strong doubts about the nature of friendship. You decide to write back a letter defining friendship as you understand it, hoping to restore your friend's belief in friendship.

2. Someone you have been dating on and off for some time calls you and says that he/she is ready to make a commitment to you and to a long-term relationship. You decide to write him/her a letter defining such a commitment as you see it.

3. Pressures at school had become unbearable and your grades had dropped dramatically for two consecutive terms. Your parents are fed up with paying the huge tuition bills and they want you to withdraw and go to work for a year. You know you can turn things around if you have another chance. You need your parents' support, but they think you are making empty promises. You decide to write them a letter defining the faith and trust you hope they will have in you.

4. You have written a series of letters to a pen pal about your favorite hobby (or sport). In this installment, define an important (and perhaps complex) term used in the activity.

Analysis

Many college writing assignments require a substantial amount of analysis. Students are often expected, in their written work, to demonstrate that they are capable of closely examining a topic from as many perspectives as possible. This type of detailed examination forms the core of an analytical essay.

Structuring an analytic essay is less cut and dried than using such organizing patterns as comparison/contrast or illustration. For one thing, there is an element of analysis present whenever substantial thinking takes place, and thus essays primarily using another mode (for instance, comparison/contrast) may also be analytic.

Generally, however, an analytic paper is organized topically—that is, according to the main points the writer is trying to make. The body of the essay is therefore a series of paragraphs developing, one by one, those main ideas (see Figure 4.8 opposite).

Any analysis you attempt will probably arise from close observation of your subject matter and from questioning yourself regarding that observation. Your analysis may provide reasons for the occurrence of an event or the development of a situation. It may explain how something (for instance, a magazine advertisement) is put together or how it achieves its intended purpose. It may evaluate the success or failure of a project or method. In every case, the analytic papers you write should contain ideas that go beyond or beneath the surface meanings of the subject matter.

Read carefully the following student essay. The writer analyzes the purpose and the appeals of folk music, using a song by Woody Guthrie as support. Notice that the paper, although using the song lyrics as evidence, does not merely paraphrase those lyrics. Instead, the writer discusses such things as the *impact* of Guthrie's words on his listeners, a task which obviously calls for thinking of a substantial sort.

The opening paragraph establishes the type of analysis the writer intends to do.

[1]Many kinds of art are created for many different purposes. Folk music is one art form that affects me very strongly in an emotional way. To create strong emotional responses is one of its purposes. It also tries to use its emotional power to increase people's awareness of and sensitivity to social and moral issues, decrease apathy, and give hope to struggling people.

Par. 2 summarizes the event on which the song is based. Note that this paragraph is introductory and descriptive, not analytic. It provides necessary background for the reader.

[2]Woody Guthrie was a great inspiration for many of the famous folk singers active in the past 20 years. His song, "1913 Massacre," is a good example of the power of folk music when it addresses social issues. "1913 Massacre," is about a community of copper miners celebrating Christmas. The incident took place before unions had been successful, and so the miners were pretty much on their own in their strike. The whole mining community was having a party and ball in a large hall, when the "scabs" decided to play a joke. They yelled that there was a fire, and though the majority of the people didn't believe them, and told each other not to pay any attention, some people got nervous.

[3]"A few people rushed and 'twas only a few. It's just the scabs and the thugs fooling you. A man grabbed his daughter and carried her down. And the thugs held the door and he couldn't get out." Unfortunately, 73 children were smothered when 100 other people rushed to the door, and the people outside "just laughed at their spree."

Pars. 4 and 5, in contrast, are examples of analysis. In them, the writer considers not the literal or surface meanings

[4]There are many reasons why this song is so effective. It is sung in the first person, so the listener is totally absorbed in a man telling his personal experience. The words are simple, direct, and descriptive, as spoken stories describing true incidents usually are. The singer makes no judgments; he just tells what happened. Also the description of the

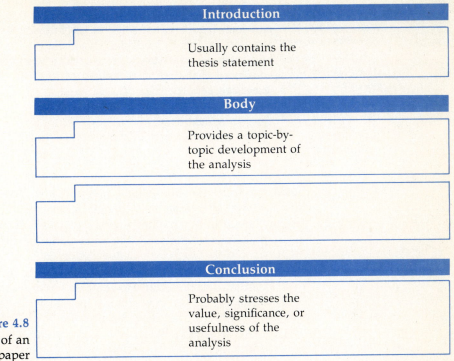

Introduction

Usually contains the thesis statement

Body

Provides a topic-by-topic development of the analysis

Conclusion

Probably stresses the value, significance, or usefulness of the analysis

Figure 4.8
The basic structure of an analytic paper

of the song's lyrics, but instead closely examines the effects on the listener of the words and music.

celebrating before the tragedy gives strong images of the suffering, love, and simpleness in the miners' lives. However, if the lyrics were just by themselves, they still wouldn't have nearly the effect they have with the music. The hoarse, melancholy voice, simple melody, and plain background consisting of one folk guitar combine with the lyrics to bring most listeners to tears.

[5]As many other folk songs do, this song brings a listener's perspective out of the narrow confines of his own experience and into the souls of people different from him. It shows one things he would rather not know, but in a way so powerful he can't block them out. So a positive effect of this song is that it raises people's sympathy and understanding of the plights of poor workers, and moves them enough to make them want to do something about it. It also frightens the listener by its story of incredible cruelty.

To add validity to the analysis, par. 6 provides information drawn from Guthrie's own life.

[6]I know that this was Woody Guthrie's purpose because he suffered greatly in this life in order to sing his songs and tell his stories. He started his singing career by singing to migrant workers to help them escape their problems for a short while, and to give them the spirit to unionize. He wrote for or about them and was beaten up or had his life threatened for singing his songs. He even took the risk of singing them on the radio in order to make more people aware of the conditions and plight of these workers.

The final paragraph comments on Guthrie's influence on more contemporary artists and thus adds to the significance of the thesis.

[7]These are some functions of folk music. Bob Dylan, Arlo Guthrie, and Joan Baez are just some of the folk singers who say they were inspired by Woody Guthrie. These singers have also written songs addressing social issues such as racism, war, and poverty. And I am convinced that they have helped to raise the consciousness of the American people.
"The parents they cried and the miners
    they moaned
See what your greed for money has done."

Exercise

Read carefully the following student essay. The writer attempts to discuss what she views as a change in her attitude toward her mother and a change in her mother's feelings as well. In what ways does this essay make use of analysis? Are other patterns used? Which ones?

[1]When I was much younger, I thought of my mother as my guardian and protector. However, as I have grown I have also learned to see her as an individual, a person with her own needs, joys, sorrows, and, ultimately, her own life.

[2]At the age of five, I was hit by a car. I remember my mother holding me in her arms while I was being driven to the hospital. She quieted me and reassured me. While I was in the hospital, she visited me daily, though she had worked all day and had other children to care for when she returned home each evening. And she gave me this type of love and devotion throughout my childhood.

[3]Though she worked as an elementary school teacher, she was never too tired to care for her three children. I can remember her playing hide-and-seek and jacks with us; she always took time to play a game with us or just spend time with us so that we would grow up really knowing her. She taught us morals and emphasized to us the importance of a good education. I recall that finishing our homework was a must before any "fun" activities took place. She demanded our respect and did not believe in sparing the rod. Every Sunday morning she got up early to provide us with a big breakfast before we all went to church. She was a God-fearing woman and taught us also to trust God.

[4]She was a quiet woman, with few acquaintances or friends outside her own sisters and our family. She devoted so much of her energies to caring for her husband and children that she had little time left for outside interests. I never once remember her complaining about all the time and energy it took to care for us. She was as close to the perfect mother as one might hope to come.

[5]Today, I am able to see my mother as an individual. She is still the loving, caring woman that she was in my younger days. Yet, she has changed, as all people do, as time has progressed. She no longer has three babies to devote all her time to; her youngest child has recently

turned sixteen. Therefore, she has the need and time to pursue outside interests. And I must say that she has pursued those interests in such a way that anyone would be proud of her.

⁶One of her main interests centers around the Sunday School class she teaches at church. She spends hours planning lessons and activities; the class' latest trip was a visit to the zoo. She also spends a lot of time with her sister's children, Inger and Hal. She truly enjoys taking them to plays and concerts in the park, as she did with her own children. She also has acquired a few more close friends. They often go to plays together or take their husbands along for a nice evening out.

⁷Though she spends less time in family-oriented activities, my mother still lets us know that her love is present. And she is still a very beautiful person who has devoted the better part of her life to the ones she loves.

Suggestions for Writing

1. Write an essay in which you first explain the message of the following cartoon and then analyze how it makes its point.

2. Write an essay in which you analyze the one important aspect of your own character—your personality and behavior—that you consider your greatest strength or greatest weakness. For instance, you might be unusually determined, or particularly enthusiastic, or hopelessly naive, or sensible and businesslike. Part of your invention process for this assignment may involve consulting with others—friends and relatives—who know you well, for often we are too close to ourselves to be able to analyze our own behavior. When someone mentions an important trait you hadn't thought about, you'll probably be able to find numerous incidents to support it. Although your instructor (and perhaps your classmates) will be reading your paper, consider *yourself* as the most important audience for this paper.

Three types of analysis are especially useful because they can be applied to a wide variety of situations. These are appearances/reality, cause/effect and problem/solution. We discussed briefly the first two in our section on invention (pp. 52–55) in Chapter 2. Structurally, these three patterns of development are analogous, as shown in Figure 4.9.

The following paragraphs form a section of a longer essay on the advantages and disadvantages of experimental medical treatments. The section is structured along the lines given in Figure 4.9 and develops an appearances/reality approach:

Paragraph 1 describes how many patients perceive that doctors have an appearance of objectivity and scientific precision, a perception sometimes shared by doctors themselves.

[1]While for many illnesses there is one best treatment, for a large number of others (including treatment for breast cancer, coronary artery disease, gall bladder disease, hypertension, etc.) a wide range of potential treatments is available, each with its advantages and disadvantages. The patient who believes in the myth of medical objectivity, however, expects that since medicine is a science there will be one best treatment for his condition; moreover, he assumes that the doctor, as an objective scientist, will recommend it. He cannot believe that his doctor would recommend an overly dangerous treatment, or that a researcher would subject him to a risky procedure. And the doctor, too, often believes this myth; his training in emotional detachment from patients, his paternalistic habits, and his immersion in medical literature may lead him to extend his scientific authority beyond reasonable limits.

The long second paragraph refutes this perception by describing potential conflicting interests of doctors

[2]Yet the physician may want to do risky procedures in order to make a diagnosis that will not improve treatment. Or, since success in medicine is generally measured by longevity, he may recommend painful, debilitating therapy. Several recent studies using the techniques of utility theory and decision analysis have shown that patients

Introduction
Same for all 3 types; includes thesis statement or other introductory material

Body Paragraph 1

- For problem/solution papers: describes a particular problem

- For appearances/reality papers: describes what apparently exists

- For cause/effect papers: discusses the causes or reasons for the existence of a given situation. (You may wish to put the effects—the existing situation—here and look at the causes in Body Paragraph 2.)

Body Paragraph 2

The results of your analysis

- For appearance/reality papers: discusses what actually exists, the underlying reality

- For cause/effect papers: discusses the effects produced by the causes or reasons explained above

- For problem/solution papers: describes the proposed solution to the problem detailed above

Conclusion

Figure 4.9
The basic structures of three patterns of development

Same for all 3 types; generally stresses the *value* of the analysis *and patients. (Iatrogenic means a disease caused by the treatment.)* may choose less painful or disfiguring treatments than what doctors would recommend, even if they will not live as long. These preferences are not necessarily irrational or unscientific; they merely reflect different values or a willingness to take fewer risks. Doctors may be willing to accept higher rates of iatrogenic disease than many of their patients; they may take more risks for a higher chance of cure—or for a "definitive diagnosis." At times the interests of M.D.'s and patients *may* be the same, or—in terms of decision-analysis—the two groups may have similar utility curves, but there is no reason to assume this must be always be true. And we will see below that the difference in interests between the patient and the medical researcher in the situation of therapeutic research is even greater.

Par. 3 presents what the writer feels is the "correct" approach for a patient, given that the patient understands the reality the writer has described. [3]While it may be to the advantage of all concerned for the doctor to guide patients past irrational and childish fears, it is important for patients to continually remind their doctors that longevity is not everything, that dignity and subjective feelings of wellness can be as important as extra years. The patient who says, "Do what you think is right," and thereby throws himself on the mercy of his doctor, may be abdicating the territory of his own preferences, which might be the decisive factor in a treatment. (David Hellerstein, "Cures That Kill")

Suggestion for Writing

Choose what you consider the most pressing problem facing students at your institution (for instance, the lack of social and recreational activities, the difficulty of getting into required courses because too few sections are offered, an overemphasis on sports to the detriment of scholarship). Write an essay in which you clearly describe the problem and then suggest a solution. Make sure that the problem section explains the issues in enough detail and that the solution section explains how and why the solution would work.

You will find that, in practice, the various patterns of development will often overlap. By knowing what the frequently used patterns are and how to structure essays based on each one, you will be able to blend the forms more readily and effectively.

Exercise

Read the following student essay carefully. How many patterns of development are used? How would you evaluate the organization?

THE CLONING CONTROVERSY

[1]"The science fiction of today is the science fact of tomorrow." That well-known adage is coming into play now, and bringing with it many

debates over moral and social rights. One area in which the debates are especially controversial is the issue of cloning.

[2]Cloning is the exact duplication, by biological means, of somebody. The clone and the original would be exact twins, closer than any normal biological twins could ever be. Theoretically, to clone a person, all that has to be done is to remove the nucleus of any cell in the body. Then that nucleus is exchanged with the nucleus from a female egg. At that moment the egg should start to divide, duplicating the process that goes on in the normal fertilization of an egg. At the time when the egg reaches seventy or eighty cells, it is surgically placed in the womb of a female volunteer, for the rest of gestation and a normal childbirth.

[3]There have been many articles and discussions about cloning, but most people say that it is impossible. They say that the microsurgery required to exchange nuclei is too complex, and that it will never work. However it has been done, at least to a point. According to an interview in *Omni* magazine, a Dr. Landrum Shettles, a gynecologist who has been researching this field for some time, has come close to actually cloning a person. He has, with homemade equipment, implanted a male nucleus into a female egg. He watched the cell divide until it was ready to be implanted into a womb. But he has not gone any further.

[4]Now that cloning is so close at hand, we must face some interesting problems. Do people have the right to be cloned? Shettles says yes. In *Omni* magazine, Shettles says, "If I want to be buried or cremated, that's my choice, too, isn't it? Some people would rather be cloned than clubbed." But is that really so? A middle-aged president of some big company could decide to have himself cloned. The clone would then have the same type of personality and, presuming that it was brought up under the same environment as the president was, the clone could turn out to be an exact emotional duplicate, as well as a physical duplicate. Then by the time the president wanted to retire, his clone would be old enough to take over the business. Imagine the dynasties that could form, with the leadership of major businesses, or even whole countries, being passed down from clone to clone.

[5]But a bigger problem may arise. Imagine what would happen if you gathered the most skilled workers from every occupation and cloned them. Each occupation would then have a work force of superskilled people, fantastically increasing the production as well as the quality of the products. But what would be the legal rights of the clones? All they are being bred for is work. Indeed, would this new "working class" be turned into nothing but slaves? And what about all the other people that would be put out of work? Is a clone a legitimate person, or just a xerox of somebody, subjected to the whim of the "master copy"? Could a clone be given constitutional status? These questions are going to have to be answered before we start playing around with clones.

STRATEGIES FOR STRUCTURING ARGUMENTATIVE ESSAYS

Many of the essay patterns discussed in this chapter can be used to structure extended arguments. For instance, an essay arguing that a new trend in our criminal justice system is potentially harmful or dangerous might make use of cause-effect structure. Let's say that the writer has grown alarmed at the increase in the use of plea bargaining—reducing charges against lawbreakers in exchange for their testimony against someone else or as a "reward" for their pleading guilty. In setting up his argument, the writer will likely use the cause/effect structure in two ways. For his main argument, he will explore a number of undesirable *effects* that he believes may result from plea bargaining (the *cause*), as shown in Figure 4.10 below.

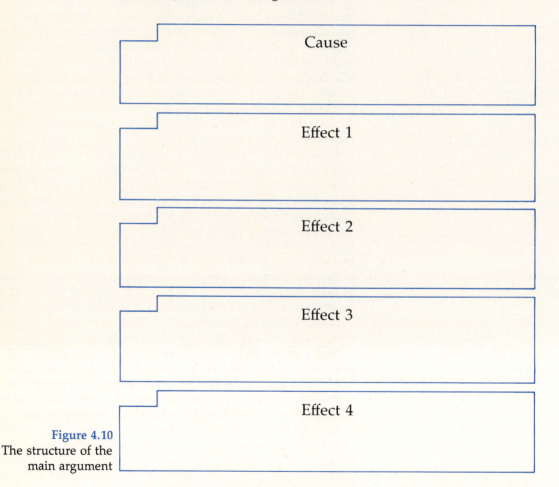

Cause

Effect 1

Effect 2

Effect 3

Effect 4

Figure 4.10
The structure of the main argument

In this case, the central argumentative strategy is to demonstrate that harmful effects will result from plea bargaining. But before presenting the main argument, the writer may want to provide some background by exploring evidence of the trend toward plea bargaining and then examining the causes of the trend (see Figure 4.11, opposite).

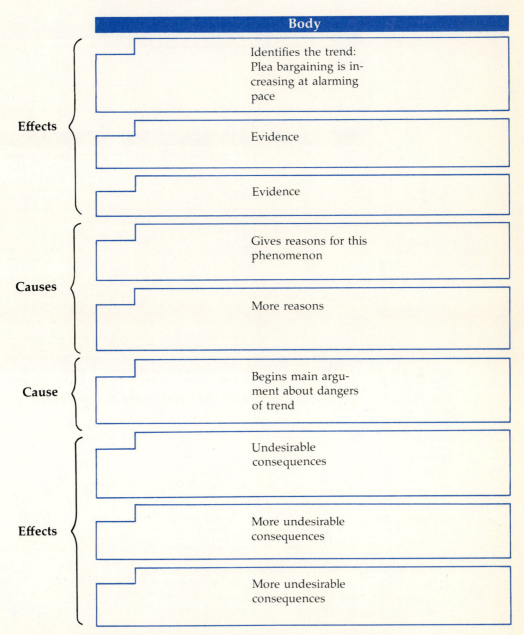

Introduction

Provides a brief overview

Body

Effects
- Identifies the trend: Plea bargaining is increasing at alarming pace
- Evidence
- Evidence

Causes
- Gives reasons for this phenomenon
- More reasons

Cause
- Begins main argument about dangers of trend

Effects
- Undesirable consequences
- More undesirable consequences
- More undesirable consequences

Figure 4.11 The background information and the main argument

The writer could add one last section to the paper: a suggested solution to the problem. Thus the introduction and body of the essay state a problem, and the conclusion constitutes the solution, as shown in Figure 4.12 below.

An argument such as this one thus simultaneously embodies two types of essay patterns to give it an effective structure. It makes

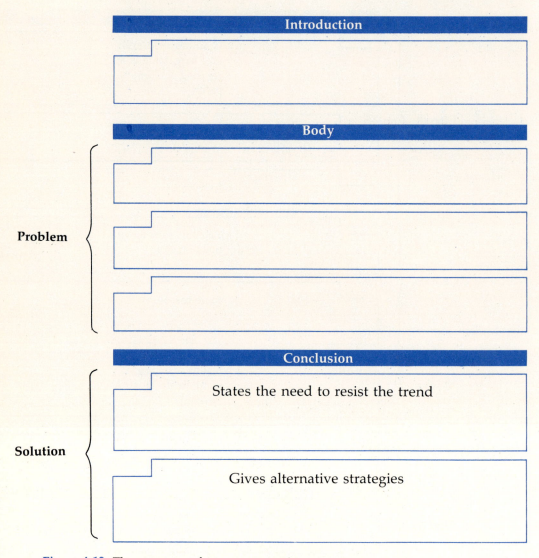

Figure 4.12 The structure of an argumentative essay

considerable use of cause/effect patterning, and embeds that structure within an overall problem/solution framework.

This example illustrates not only that essay patterns may be used to structure arguments, but that a combination of patterns, rather than one single pattern, may be used. Other patterns discussed in this chapter can also structure arguments. For instance, the comparison/contrast pattern could be used to present the argument that one of two competing theories is superior.

chapter 5

PLANNING
AND WRITING
THE ESSAY

PLANNING THE ESSAY

In Chapter 4 we discussed basic essay structures and patterns. No matter which ones you choose, you will still have to devote time to more detailed planning and organization before beginning the actual writing. In this section we will consider specific approaches to planning and organizing the essay.

An Informal Approach to Planning: The Jotted Outline

As writers proceed with the process of invention, they gain an awareness of their purposes and ideas, and they may construct a tentative thesis statement as well. They also generate a lot of other, related ideas during invention. An outline is a conventional form many writers find helpful in organizing these ideas into what will be the overall structure of the finished essay. The outline can be quite formal and detailed (we will discuss this type of outline in the next section), or it can be an informal guide, designed for the writer's eyes only.

Bear in mind that any outline is merely a *means* to an end: a way of aiding a writer in creating a well-organized and logical paper. It should be *your* plan for manipulating *your* ideas. The outline's main purpose is to serve as your guide, making at least two aspects of the composing process easier. First, having an outline means you needn't trust your memory alone to preserve your main ideas, the ways of developing them, and their approximate order. Second, having a good outline also means that you know what you will be putting into your essay, thus making the actual writing less anxiety-ridden and altogether easier than writing without an outline would be. Of course, an outline, useful though it may be, should not be viewed as a fixed, unchangeable plan. Often you will develop new ideas after you have written your outline. But even when the outline is totally altered during the actual composing, it has served you by helping you to get where you're going.

An outline is thus one of the most practical of writing aids. Unfortunately, sometimes student writers get caught up with the form of the outline and forget its purpose and function. They worry (needlessly) over whether their outline will have the prescribed formal configuration:

I.
- A.
- B.
    - 1.
    - 2.

II.
- A.
- B.
- C.
    - 1.
    - 2.
    - 3.

In a formal outline, every *I* postulates a *II*, every *A* a *B*, and so forth. But a writer who is organizing ideas should, above all, be concentrating on those ideas and on their logical development, not on counting the *A*s and *B*s. Adding an idea so that the outline will "look right" makes it an artificial device rather than the practical tool it should be.

If you're writing the outline for someone else's eyes (usually the instructor's) besides your own, then you do need to be concerned with the conventions of outlining—that's one reason why we discuss those conventions in the next section. But in the more usual situation, all you will be turning in is the completed essay. In this case, a "jotted" outline may be all you need. Written solely for you, the jotted outline need not even preserve the traditional Roman and Arabic numbering system. Your major criterion for determining which aspects of the outlining convention you use should be the ideas you are organizing. And the overall organization should arise from your thesis statement or tentative thesis statement.

As a specific case, let's reconsider Jane, the student who is writing a paper based on her experience with mononucleosis. Her invention leads her to this thesis statement: "Far from being a complete waste of six months of my life, my experience with mononucleosis taught me greater patience, better concentration, and more efficient study habits, and made me more knowledgeable about my nutritional needs." This sentence, however, is not all Jane has to work with. She also has the various ideas she jotted down in mulling over her topic. From these two sources—the thesis statement (or a tentative thesis statement) and one's ideas in rough form—a writer can create an outline for an essay.

In this case, Jane's strategy will be to work from her thesis (which contains the main ideas her essay will develop) to her group of ideas, fitting them under the categories the thesis sets up. First, she examines her thesis statement. It breaks down into five major sections:

1. Far from being a complete waste of six months of my life . . .
2. my experience with mononucleosis taught me greater patience . . .
3. better concentration . . .
4. and more efficient study habits . . .
5. and made me more knowledgeable about my nutritional needs.

Each of these sections is a category under which some of her rough ideas will fall, and each will be a major subpoint of the main idea in the completed essay.

Next, Jane checks her list of ideas to see which idea is related to which part of the thesis statement. In effect, she will group likes with likes (one of the basic organizational principles we discussed in Chapter 3). She does this to ensure that she will thoroughly discuss each major heading before going on to the next. Here is the list of her ideas. How would you fit them into the five categories listed above?

Realized I had to watch what I eat—less "junk" food
Got sick in June, end of spring term
Long illness—six months in hospital and at home
Had to budget time better in studying—got tired easily
Doctor wouldn't let me resume college classes until January
Learned diet is important
Found out about essential vitamins
For first time had to slow down significantly
Made greater use of previewing textbooks
Had nothing better to do but study!—fewer distractions
Didn't get impatient as easily—too tired!
Learned to take my time getting things done
Hospital stay made me more tolerant of other people (roommates, staff, family)
Got accustomed to greater self-discipline

In the process of categorizing her ideas, Jane begins to create an informal outline, using the outlining convention of indentation. She decides to position the more general ideas (the main categories) to the left. As she adds her rough ideas, she indents; the more specific the idea, the farther to the right she indents it. She groups her ideas as follows:

Far from being a complete waste of six months of my life . . .
  Got sick in June, end of spring term
  Doctor wouldn't let me resume classes until January
  Six months' illness, including time in hospital and at home
My experience with mononucleosis taught me greater patience . . .
  For first time, had to slow down significantly
    Didn't get impatient as easily—too tired!
    Learned to take my time getting things done
  Hospital stay made me more tolerant of other people
  (Roommates, staff, family)
Better concentration . . .
  Fewer distractions
    Had nothing better to do but study!
And more efficient study habits . . .
  Made greater use of previewing texts
  Learned to budget time more wisely in studying
And made me more knowledgeable about my nutritional needs
  Learned diet is important
  Realized I had to watch what I eat
    Less "junk food"
    Learned about essential vitamins

There are several things you should note about this informal outline. First, Jane doesn't bother to use complete sentences. She writes down enough information so that she doesn't forget what she wants to say, but since the outline is an aid to her alone, she isn't formal about usage. Also, she chooses to jot the ideas down using no numbering system. (You might wish to number the major headings, or not, as *you* decide. Keep in mind the jotted outline must be clear to you and if numbering helps, do it.) And Jane will probably modify her jotted outline a bit as she writes the essay. For example, she will probably have to expand the "better concentration" and "more efficient study habits" sections. Jane also realizes that the first section will be an effective introduction; it serves the purpose of setting the stage for her reader. Further, her outline, as it stands, has no conclusion in the traditional sense. Because the essay looks like it will be fairly lengthy, she may wish to add a few sentences or a short paragraph to the end to give the essay a sense of completion and to reiterate her purpose in writing.

Jane will probably not modify the outline so much that she also has to change her thesis statement. But such modification can easily occur. For example, as Jane actually writes her essay, she could find that she has a good deal more to say about certain aspects of her topic than she realized when she wrote the outline, and so decide that she should concentrate only on those. Or, were she to exceed the recommended length for her essay after covering only the points about patience, concentration, and study habits, she might decide to drop the last section on nutrition, thus necessitating a change in her original thesis statement. Since the outline is not a public contract but a personal plan representing what she thinks she will write, it could easily be changed later on.

Regardless of possible changes, the jotted outline provides Jane with a clearly defined strategy for writing her essay, a strategy which has grown naturally out of her ideas rather than being artificially imposed on them. Working from her outline, she can write her essay with the confidence of knowing what to say next.

___

Exercise

1. Categorization, which groups items according to similarities they share, is useful for organizing ideas. As we have noted, outlining involves establishing categories or classes of ideas.

   Think of and write down a dozen personality traits you find admirable. Then jot down the names of ten of your friends. Using the traits you have chosen as categories, assign each of your friends to as many of the categories as are appropriate. How would you categorize yourself?

2. Below are the initial notes a student jotted during invention for a paper about her grandmother. The thesis she subsequently decided to pursue was this: "My grandmother is an exception to the American stereotype of the elderly as feeble and disabled; she is one of the most active and energetic women I know." When she

began her invention process, she did not know what her thesis would be, and so the categories she set up at this time don't closely match up with the thesis statement. Yet many of the ideas would be useful in supporting the eventual thesis.

Reread the thesis statement, read the notes below, and then, using both, set up an informal outline of the type Jane developed. Which ideas in the notes serve no purpose and so should be discarded? Does any aspect of the thesis need ideas that are *not* mentioned in the notes? If so, indicate this by leaving space for them in the informal outline you devise.

CHARACTER: GRAMMY

What she looks like	*What she does*	*Things that remind me of her*
Me	Owned a carpet	Smells
Blonde-white hair	store; she now	Expressions
always up in a bun	works in it	Other old women
Always dress, never	Theater, ballet,	Magazines
pants	concerts	Grape juice
Recently skirts	Shopping	spritzers
Jewelry	Out to dinner	
Plump	Travels	*How she acts*
Practical clothing	Writes letters	Hides emotions
Coat, hat, gloves,	when away	from grampa
shoes	Visits	Money
	Shopping bags to	"Her city"
When I see her	balance	Guilt infliction
With family	Not so good a cook	Proud (of us)
Alone for shopping,	(good marmalade)	
theater		
At her place		
Holidays at our		
house		

A Formal Approach: The Conventional Outline

What we have stressed about the value of a jotted outline applies as well to a more formal approach to planning. A conventional outline provides the same boost to your memory about your ideas and the order in which you will write them down, and likewise contributes to greater confidence as you begin the actual writing of the essay.

The formal outline differs from the jotted outline, however, in that the formal outline is generally written to satisfy the needs of a reader (usually an instructor) as well as those of the writer. An instructor may have a number of reasons for making an outline part of the assignment. One of the most common is to check on the progress of a project: If a student can put together an outline, then a good deal of work has already been done—and the instructor may wish to verify that this is the case.

In any event, conventional outlines must be clear not only to the writer but also to a potential reader. They follow a prescribed numbering system and may use words, or phrases, or whole sentences, or even paragraphs. This is the usual format:

I. Uppercase Roman numerals are used to indicate major divisions or headings.
   A. Uppercase Arabic letters show major ideas within divisions.
      1. Arabic numerals indicate more specific ideas supporting the
      2. Major ideas within divisions.
         a. Lowercase Arabic letters indicate
         b. Further, more specific development.
            (1) Use numbers within parentheses
            (2) To indicate yet more specific ideas.

In practice, outlines seldom get beyond the first three levels.

A *topic outline* follows the above format and uses words and phrases to indicate the ideas that will be discussed. A *sentence outline* expresses the ideas in full sentences, rather than in abbreviated form.

Let's take another look at the jotted outline from the previous section:

Far from being a complete waste of six months of my life . . .
   Got sick in June, end of spring term
   Doctor wouldn't let me resume classes until January
   Six months' illness, including time in hospital and at home
My experience with mononucleosis taught me greater patience . . .
   For first time, had to slow down significantly
      Didn't get impatient as easily—too tired!
      Learned to take my time getting things done
   Hospital stay made me more tolerant of other people
      (Roommates, staff, family)
Better concentration . . .
   Fewer distractions
      Had nothing better to do but study!
And more efficient study habits . . .
   Made greater use of previewing texts
   Learned to budget time more wisely in studying
And made me more knowledgeable about my nutritional needs
   Learned diet is important
   Realized I had to watch what I eat
      Less "junk food"
      Learned about essential vitamins

These ideas can be outlined more formally like this:

   I.   Introduction (Thesis statement)
  II.   One Result: Greater Patience
      A.   Enforced slowing down
      B.   Too tired to be impatient
      C.   Had to take my time
      D.   Became more tolerant
 III.   Second Result: Better Concentration
      A.   Nothing to do but study
      B.   Learned more efficient habits
         1.   Text previewing
         2.   Time management
 IV.   Third Result: More Knowledge of Nutrition
      A.   Importance of diet
      B.   Monitoring of diet
      C.   Essential nature of vitamins

The same outline could easily be expanded into a sentence outline:

   I.   The introduction will explain the length of my illness, in the hospital and at home. It will include my thesis statement.
  II.   One result of my illness was that I learned greater patience.
      A.   For the first time, I had to slow down significantly.
      B.   I was too tired to muster the energy to be anything but patient.
      C.   I learned to take my time getting things done.
      D.   I became more patient with other people, as I was in constant, close contact with family, hospital staff, and roommates.
 III.   A second result was I gained better powers of concentration
      A.   I had nothing else to do but study, with few distractions.
      B.   I learned more efficient study habits.
         1.   I began to preview texts.
         2.   I began to budget time more carefully.
 IV.   A third result was that I became more knowledgeable about nutrition.
      A.   I learned that proper diet is important.
      B.   I learned to watch what I eat and to avoid "junk" food.
      C.   I learned that vitamins are essential to good health.

Remember that these outlines are written with a reader in mind. They are no longer jotted down just to help the writer. Consequently, the outlines must be clear enough so that someone other than the writer can understand the ideas they contain.

In our discussion of informal outlining, we commented that sometimes writers worry over the convention that an *A* means there must be a *B*, or that a *1* demands a *2* to follow. But following that convention usually presents no problem. Logically, if you have decided on a major concept to be discussed—a *I*—you will likely have more than one sub-idea because of the complexity of your thought. Similarly, if you're working with a second-level concept—*A*, *B*, and so on—and you can only think of one sub-idea—*(1)*—you may not need to list that sub-idea at all. It may be easier to include that idea in your description of *A* itself.

Whether using a jotted or formal outline, be sure to remain flexible. Study your outline carefully before writing to make sure it is the best approach to your topic. If it's not, take a minute to make some changes. Changing the order of ideas in outline form is a very simple matter, indeed. But waiting until you've written out the essay to switch the order of your thoughts can be costly in both time and effort.

Exercise

Two student essays from Chapter 4 are reprinted here. Reread them carefully and outline each, following the conventional numbering arrangement we discussed above. Find the thesis statement of each essay and place it before the outline. Example:

Thesis Statement: Far from being a complete waste of six months of my life, my experience with mononucleosis taught me greater patience, better concentration, and more efficient study habits, and made me more knowledgeable about my nutritional needs.

I. One Result: Greater Patience
  A. Enforced slowing down
  B. Too tired to be impatient (and so on)

A. ¹Peer pressure exerts its greatest force on a young teen. Looking back, I can remember several occasions when I disobeyed my parents because of the pressure exerted on me by my peers. I lived to regret each of those occasions.

²One such occasion involved smoking cigarettes. I have always been raised with a strong understanding of right and wrong. And I knew that for a child my age cigarette smoking was wrong. My parents smoked when I was younger, and had allowed me a puff now and then, but had since kicked the habit and resorted to lecturing me on the hazards of smoking.

³One day, at a party at a friend's house, I decided to ignore all the lectures I had received at home about smoking. At first the party was going well; everyone was dancing and enjoying themselves. Then Ralph brought out a pack of cigarettes and everyone became "instant smokers." Those who did not become instant smokers were strongly urged to try it. And those who continuously refused were told they were not cool or hip. They were called scaredy-cats; the guys were told

they were just plain stuck-up. After all the pressure exerted by the "cool" kids, everyone at the party had at least one puff.

[4]Then tragedy struck—at least tragedy for all of us at the party. Gwen's parents, smelling all the smoke, came down the stairs. Their first thought was that something was on fire. But when they discovered what the real problem was, it would have been better for each of us if *we* had been what was burning. Her father hit the ceiling, and a couple of the kids also. Her parents' first thought was to make each of us smoke a whole pack, but luckily for us, they thought again. They then took each of us, one by one, and called our parents, telling them of our misbehavior and asking them to come and get their child.

[5]My parents were furious. Not only did I receive another lecture about the hazards of smoking, but I also heard for a week about how embarrassed they were because I had acted as if I had received no training at home. Lectures were by no means the extent of my punishment. I also lost use of the phone for two weeks, which by itself was punishment enough in my eyes. However, my parents also thought it appropriate that I should not be allowed to attend any parties for a whole month.

[6]Needless to say, I did not smoke any more after this incident. And I was also not so quick to go along with whatever the gang was doing.

B.   [1]An interesting concept found in the study of religion is the phenomenon of how Mother Mary is depicted differently during different time periods. As people's thoughts about the world and religion changed, so did their image of Mary.

[2]Mary has been seen at times as a part of the profane or human world and at other times as sacred or holy. The earliest books of the New Testament were probably written thirty years after the death of Jesus. It is in these books that Mary is shown as a shepherd who is tired and weary and gives birth to a baby boy in a stable. Here Mary is pictured as a person as she goes through the very human act of giving birth. Approximately one century A.D., when the Gospel of Luke was written, the idea of Mary's being a virgin becomes a much more important idea in the story of the birth of Jesus. It is during this period that Mary is elevated to the stature of a more central and sacred figure in the Church.

[3]Between the second century and the beginning of the Renaissance, Mary's image goes through two phases. First she begins to be thought of as almost equivalent to God, since He is termed as the father of Jesus and Mary as the mother. She is thus further heightened to the status of a divine being. Next Mary seems to be a link from the profane world to the sacred world as she is the one who has brought the divine into the profane world. She is thought to be one who can bring gods into the world.

[4]Moving closer to the Renaissance when people were becoming more humanistic, Mary's image takes on a personality. The personali-

ty she represents is that of a loving, caring mother. Mary begins to be viewed not as almost a god but more as a mother that will always forgive you. She is shown as one who cares for a person in need. In particular, the "Loving Mother" image of Mary is common at the beginning of the Renaissance. Later, around the fourteenth century, Mary is seen as the "Weeping Mother." She is pictured crying as she holds the dead body of Jesus in her arms, and is thought of primarily as a mother who is devastated by the death of her son.

[5]One can see, then, how the image of Mary changed through time from that of a tired, weary shepherd to that of a divine being and back to a kind and very human person. In the process, as Mary was given more divinity, she lost her personality. Conversely, as Mary's personality grew, her divinity became less important.

Arrangement of Ideas Within the Essay

Once you have shaped the essay structure and decided on one or more of the patterns, you still have to determine how to arrange the various ideas within the essay structure. If you have decided to use the illustration pattern and have come up with three illustrations to develop your thesis statement, for instance, in what order should you place the three? Which comes first? Which next? Why?

In connection with this discussion of arrangement, you may wish to reread the discussion of arrangement within the paragraph (Chapter 3, pp. 84–93), which covers such approaches as grouping likes with likes and organizing from general to specific and from most important to least important. In fact, most of the organizational principles that apply to the paragraph also apply to the essay. But certain principles of arrangement are of particular relevance to essay writing. Let's consider those.

In attempting to organize your ideas logically within an essay structure, remember this three-part principle of arrangement:

1. Every essay ought to have a consciously crafted scheme of arrangement.

2. There is no single correct organizational scheme for any given essay, nor is there any totally wrong organization. Rather, there are _stronger_ and _weaker_ alternative arrangements; you should first discover these alternative arrangements and then choose from among them.

3. The best arrangement is the one which best highlights the main ideas of your essay.

The first statement suggests that making a deliberate attempt to organize your ideas in the first place is essential. Even if the organization you come up with is not the best one, any consciously planned order is better than no order at all. By analogy, it is better to have library cards neatly arranged in rows of drawers rather than heaped in a large pile on the floor. Of course, it would be even more helpful to have the cards arranged alphabetically within the drawers—and this observation leads to the second part of the principle.

The basic idea of statement two is that there is no ultimately *right* order—only better or worse alternative arrangements. No one has an answer key listing the right organizational scheme to use for any given essay topic. To determine what order to use, you must decide on some possibilities and then reason out what makes one arrangement better or stronger than another. Again, an analogy from everyday life is helpful. A radio announcer reads the day's baseball scores: "Detroit 6, Baltimore 4; Cleveland 7, Chicago 5; Boston 1, New York 2." Obviously, the final score is the odd one. Most listeners are jarred by hearing "New York 2," because they probably expected to hear "New York 0." But is the order used by this newscaster *wrong*? It isn't really wrong, for we can still make sense of the score. Still, "New York 2, Boston 1" is a *better* order. We expect to hear the winning team's score first because scores are traditionally given with the winning team mentioned first. And it is appropriate to *mention* the winning team ahead of the losing team because, in fact, the winning team *finishes* ahead of the losing team.

The idea that the winning team's score should be given first leads us into statement three. This part of the principle, probably the most important of the list, states that the better or stronger arrangement is the one that best highlights the main ideas of the essay. That is, an organization that works well for one paper will not necessarily work well for another paper. Imagine, for instance, that you are going to write an essay about how you gradually developed a greater sense of responsibility by working at summer jobs during your high school years. Probably the most natural organization for the body of this essay would be to start with incidents from the job you held during the summer following your freshman year and proceed chronologically to your senior year. A chronological organization would be effective because you would be trying to show how your sense of responsibility grew as time passed. In other words, the organization would highlight your main idea that you *developed* responsibility *over the years*. Now imagine that you want to write a paper in which you will demonstrate that your high school calculus teacher was an entertaining and effective, although sometimes incoherent, lecturer. You have chosen several specific instances to illustrate your point. But, in this case, chronological order will probably not be helpful. Most likely, the entertaining instance you will want to present first did not occur before all the other instances; perhaps it even happened last. So a more effective approach would be to arrange the examples in the body of the essay according to their types or topics (for example, jokes in lectures, effective teaching techniques, fits of incoherence). Although using chronological order in this essay might still allow your main idea to emerge, it would tend to dull the force of the idea rather than to highlight it. Thus topical order is the preferable, or stronger, alternative.

The following rough draft and revised version of a student essay show the three-part principle of arrangement in practice. Notice that, in the rough draft, the student-writer, Chris, made little conscious effort to organize the material. What little organization the draft does have is weak and is not geared toward highlighting the essay's ideas. In fact, the organization is so weak that the reader is uncertain of what Chris is trying to say.

[1]Abraham was a good, strong man, and he was favored by the Lord. The Lord chose to make Abraham the father of a great nation ". . . I will make of you a great nation, and I will bless you, and make your name great, so that you will be a blessing" (Genesis 12:2). Abraham was the father of the Jews, and his great nation was Canaan, commonly known as Israel. Abraham was not perfect, but his belief in God was strong. God made his covenant with Abraham; "Behold my covenant is with you, and you shall be the father of a multitude of nations." (Genesis 17:4) Being the first man to receive the covenant, Abraham was the first Jew. The Lord promised Abraham a great number of descendants, but Sarah, Abraham's wife, had not borne any children. Abraham questioned God, and the Lord replied, "Is anything too hard for the Lord?" (Genesis 18:14) With the birth of Isaac to Abraham and Sarah came proof that nothing was beyond the Lord's power. It showed Abraham that God was good and was dependable; all of his questions and doubts were erased with that one act. Even later when Abraham was told to sacrifice his only son he had no question. Abraham feared God so much that he almost sacrificed Isaac, but he was stopped by an angel and told ". . . I know that you fear God, seeing you have not withheld your son, your only son, from me" (Genesis 22:12). Because Abraham did as God told him, he was rewarded. Thus his descendants were multiplied.

[2]All of the events already stated show how Abraham came to be the "ideal Hebrew." All throughout his life Abraham was a good man, and a believer in God, but when he was chosen to lead the Jews he became a model for other Jews. God used Abraham as an example of what a Jew should be. Abraham was the first person God would use to convey his message. Now Abraham was not an angel; he made his mistakes and was human, but when God needed to show his power, Abraham could be his medium. I don't mean Abraham made miracles, but miracles were made for Abraham. Abraham was ninety-nine years old when his wife bore their only son. Because Abraham made the covenant with God, and because he trusted God, he was awarded with his only son. To fear God was to love God and that is just what Abraham did. He followed God's order because he loved God, but also

because he feared punishment if he didn't. That was symbolic of what all Hebrews were to do.

³The life of Abraham started the Hebrew movement to the promised land, Canaan. Before the appearance of the ten commandments, Abraham's lifestyle, attitudes, and practices toward God were the guidelines other Jews were to follow.

In conference with his instructor, Chris said that the main idea was supposed to be that Abraham represented the ideal Hebrew—but most of the material in the draft is not arranged to support this notion.

In his revision, Chris expressed his main idea immediately in the essay's title and, in the first paragraph, explicitly stated the three major qualities his essay would discuss:

HOW THE CHARACTER OF ABRAHAM SYMBOLIZED THE IDEAL HEBREW BELIEVER

¹The Hebrew people had a strong belief in God, and because God chose them to share his covenant, they became special people. The major qualities of the Hebrew believer were: (1) to believe in a convenant with God, (2) to trust God and not to doubt his goodness, and (3) to fear God and follow his rules. In the story of Genesis, Abraham embodied all of those qualities, and symbolized the ideal Hebrew believer.

²Abraham was a good, strong man; he was favored by the Lord. The Lord said to him ". . . I will make you a great nation, and I will bless you, and make your name great so that you will be a blessing" (Genesis 12:2). The great land referred to was the land of Canaan, commonly known as Israel. Abraham was to be the father of the Hebrews. To prove his unity with God Abraham was circumcised, and the Lord said, "Behold my covenant is with you, and you shall be the father of a multitude of nations." (Genesis 17:14) If a Jew did not keep the covenant, he was cut off from the group. To be cut off from the group was to be excluded from God's special plan for the Jews. They had been given " . . . the land of Canaan for everlasting possession . . ." (Genesis 17:8). The covenant with God was an important part of Abraham's life.

³The Lord promised Abraham a great number of descendants, but Sarah, Abraham's wife, had never borne children. Sarah was ninety when the promise was made. Abraham, being ninety-nine, had some doubts that he would ever have an heir. The Lord knew of his doubts and asked him, "Is anything too hard for the Lord?" (Genesis 18:14). When Isaac, Abraham's son, was born, the Lord proved that nothing was beyond his power. The Lord's fulfilling of his promise helped to secure Abraham's trust. Overall, trust in God was a valuable quality in the Hebrews. Many times, trust in God was all the Hebrews could rely on to bear them up in tough situations. The birth of Isaac was a miracle

that other Jews could see as a way of God blessing Abraham. Also, it could be seen as a way of God showing the Jews that to trust God was an inroad to blessings.

[4]Later in Genesis, Abraham was told to sacrifice his son, Isaac. Without question, Abraham went to give his son. As he began the ceremony he was stopped by one of God's angels who said, ". . . I know that you fear God, seeing you have not withheld your son, your only son, from me" (Genesis 22:12). Abraham's near sacrifice of his son symbolized a fear of God, and disobeying God could only lead to punishment. A good Jew would follow God's rules, and trust God enough not to worry about misfortune.

[5]Abraham's personality was symbolic of the qualities a Jew was to embody. He was the first leader of the Jews, and all the Jews saw him as a symbol of faith. All three qualities of the Hebrew believer—the covenant with God, the trust in God, and the fear of God—involved faith. Abraham showed his faith by demonstrating those three qualities. Abraham's undying faith was an inspiration to his descendants.

By being more aware of the need to arrange his material and by understanding the connection between ideas and arrangement, Chris was able to use organization to highlight the point of the essay. Notice, for instance, how the mention of Abraham's age is moved from near the end of the first version to the second paragraph in the body of the final draft. There it supports the writer's point about trust in God. Notice also that in reorganizing his material to fit his ideas, the writer deleted certain material (like the observation that Abraham was not "an angel") because it served no clear purpose.

COMPOSING THE ESSAY

You've shaped the structure of your essay, decided which pattern (or patterns) of development you will use, and determined how you will arrange the ideas within the essay structure. All of these are parts of the process of composing your essay. But to complete the essay, to ensure that it fulfills its purpose, you will write an introduction and a conclusion, and will employ transitions within the essay. Let's examine each of these elements of the effective essay in turn.

Writing Introductions

An introduction leads your reader into your essay by employing one of several techniques. For instance, you can begin an essay by describing some shocking or extraordinary event or by quoting an unusual fact or statistic and in that manner capture the reader's attention:

I am about to make some statements that may surprise many of you who read this magazine—intelligent, health-conscious people who keep up with the latest, most authoritative information on fitness, nutrition, and preventive medicine:

• There is no scientific reason for the American public at large to cut down on dietary salt.
• It follows that there is no good reason for food processors to lower the amount of salt in their products. (John H. Laragh, M.D., "Giving Salt a Fair Shake")

Here the writer attracts the reader's attention by challenging a much-publicized theory, hoping thereby to motivate the reader into reading the rest of the article.

Other alternatives are to build suspense at the start of your essay, to ask a question and suggest some answers, and to tell a story that leads into your thesis. Indeed, there are almost an unlimited number of ways to open an essay.

A conventional introduction, one that presents an overview of the paper, establishes a contract between you and your reader. In it, you commit yourself to delivering certain ideas in certain ways; you set up readers' expectations that you are then obligated to fulfill. Keep this in mind as you compose introductory paragraphs. But no matter what type of introduction you write, the contractual quality of the opening paragraph remains. The reader forms impressions immediately and (in most cases) wants some notion of what you'll be considering in the essay.

Here is an example of a conventional introduction, taken from an essay discussed earlier:

In many subjects, such as mathematics and science, the teacher has few opportunities to inject his or her own personality and background into the subect matter. Yet in presenting something where one's own interpretation plays a major role, as in history, the teacher's ethnic, social, political, and educational background has much to do with the perspective from which the course is taught. The points of view of two recent Modern European history teachers I have had were as different as the two poles, because of the teachers' respective backgrounds.

Note that the student introduces her topic by making two statements about teaching. The second, signalled by *yet*, is her thesis statement. The third sentence further prepares the reader by explaining how she intends to support her point. What the reader logically expects to follow in the rest of the essay is development of the contrast between the two professors; the reader can predict this with some certainty because of the explicit wording of the introduction.

An introduction need not be limited to one paragraph. Note the following:

Communication—like friendship—is a two-way street. If you want to be able to talk to animals, you must first listen to what they have to say to you.

Pets have several modes of communication. Sometimes they will use one, sometimes another. If you are not hearing them, they will snow you with all systems at once. Both dogs and cats are past masters of the art. (From "What is Your Pet Telling You?" by Jean Burden in *Woman's Day*, July 8, 1980. Copyright © 1980 by CBS Publications, the Consumer Publishing Division of CBS Inc. Reprinted by permission of Woman's Day Magazine.)

In these two paragraphs, the writer effectively prepares the reader for what is to follow—an explanation of the body language used by cats and dogs—and also establishes the reader's need for the information ("If you want to be able to talk to animals, . . .").

How long should an introduction be? Generally, as brief as possible. For a paragraph, the topic sentence, placed first, can effectively introduce to your reader what you wish to say. For a short essay, a sentence or two may likewise be adequate; for a longer paper, you may need a paragraph or more. Keep in mind, however, that an introduction that is too long can distract from the essay as a whole.

Exercise

Read the following introductions carefully. Then compare and contrast them, evaluating them on the basis of (1) their length and (2) their function in establishing an appropriate contract with the reader.

1. (*Note*: This introduction is from a two-and-one-half page student essay that focuses on the trials of an elderly nursing home patient, Anna, for whom the writer felt particular sympathy.)

   Aging is the process in which the mind and the body deteriorate. Some of the visible signs of aging are the loss of hair and hair color, the loss of skin and muscle tone, the loss of mental acuity, and the loss of vigor.

   The process of growing old is looked down upon in the present American society. Society's pressures urge us to diet, medicate, stay physically fit, look young, and have vigor. Millions of dollars are spent every year on beautifying aids that supposedly make a person appear younger. In our society, the elderly are affected greatly by these pressures. They are pushed aside and forgotten. We have taken away their role in life and have neglected their personal needs and feelings.

2. (This paragraph introduces an eight-page student research essay examining the history of political control and reform in large urban police departments.)

While it is more or less accepted that old-time police departments were controlled by political bosses, not everybody argues that police forces today are run by politicians. Lawrence W. Sherman, in *Police Corruption Control: Environmental Context Versus Organizational Policy*, feels that the political hierarchy strongly influences police action, and that where system-wide police corruption exists, it cannot be controlled. On the other hand, James Q. Wilson, in *Politics and the Police*, questions the existence of such influence. Wilson believes that the police are keenly sensitive to their political environment without in all cases being governed by it. Though I do not intend to argue the question of political control over the police department of today, I will in this paper examine the history of political control and reform in the police departments. Though the reformers generally approached their task with the best of motives, they were as guilty as the political machine of trying to control the police.

Writing Conclusions

An essay's conclusion should provide a sense of completion. In reading it, the reader should feel that the writer has ended the discussion and has accomplished the purpose behind writing—rather than merely run out of time or ink. Conclusions, like introductions, should be brief. Papers that are complex may demand more substantial conclusions, but in general a short paragraph will serve you adequately.

For most of the types of essays we have discussed (illustration, comparison/contrast, analysis, and so on), the conventional method of concluding is to summarize the main ideas. Very often, readers remember most what they read last, and so the conclusion is an excellent place to remind your readers of the concepts you wish them to retain. You should avoid verbatim repetition from the introduction or elsewhere; you can, however, reiterate certain key terms or phrases for emphasis.

The two essays whose introductions we examined on pages 168–69 conclude in this manner:

> In history and other disciplines like it, two people with the same amount of education and basic factual information, like the two teachers, can view the past differently, emphasizing different interpretations to fit the way they view the world.

> If you want to communicate with your pet, first make sure you understand what it is trying to say to *you*. This is an ongoing process, not something you learn in a week. Don't just talk baby talk to your pet. Sure, it is partly your child, but not wholly. It is also an individual spirit with a life of its own and a language to match. Talk to it on a horizontal level, not from your lofty perch. You'll be surprised how much you'll learn. (Jean Burden, "What Is Your Pet Telling You?")

In the first example, the writer reiterates her main idea without repeating word-for-word what appeared in her introduction or in the body of her essay. She does use certain key terms and synonyms: *One's own interpretation, perspective*, and *different* in the introduction appear in the conclusion as *different interpretation* and *the way they view the world*. In this way, she stresses her thesis without boring or insulting her reader with verbatim repetition.

In the second example, the writer likewise emphasizes the main idea—here that you must listen to what your pets say in order to communicate with them. The writer adds another idea that has been important in the article—the notion that communicating with animals must be done in a respectful, not condescending, way. Taken together, these two ideas form the core of what the writer wishes the reader to remember from the essay.

A conclusion, then, should relate in some way to whatever the writer has stressed in the essay as a whole. It may include a summary of main ideas or a reiteration of the value of the concepts the writer presents. Or, it may give a more general or philosophical parting view of your subject; that is, it may look at the larger importance of what the paper has achieved. Having supported your main ideas in the body of the paper, you may want to answer one of these questions in the conclusion: "So what?" "Where do we go from here?" "Are there any further implications, now that we accept the main idea?" In any case, the conclusion should complete the thoughts explored in the paper.

Exercise

Look through writings you have done recently and through several professionally written articles. Choose one example of a conclusion that you feel is done well and one that could be improved. Be prepared to give specific reasons to support your choices.

Transitions in Essay Writing

In Chapter 3, we discussed briefly the concept of transitions (pp. 93–95). What we noted there is even more important to successful essay writing. Because essays generally discuss ideas in greater detail and contain more complicated concepts than do paragraphs, using transitions to make explicit the relationships among ideas is important, indeed. Transitions guide the reader from one thought to another and aid the writer in determining exactly what to say next.

The same types of transitional words and phrases used in paragraph writing are also used in essays. Additionally, an entire paragraph of an essay may serve as a transition from one thought to another. But whether the transition used consists of a word, a phrase, or a series of sentences, the purpose of guiding the reader through a thought process remains.

To use transitions effectively, you must have carefully thought out what you wish to write, to the point that you are well aware of the ways in which your ideas are related. Transitions then become signposts for your reader in understanding what you have written. Too often, writers assume that their ideas are "obviously" related, so obviously that transitional expressions are unnecessary. But you are better off leaving nothing to chance. Adding "for example" to indicate an upcoming illustration, or "consequently" to introduce an effect of what you've just discussed, or "more important" to highlight a major thought can only make the logic of what you write more apparent to your reader. As you reread what you've written, get into the habit of checking for places where transitions may be needed. Putting yourself in the place of a reader, ask whether you can move easily from one idea to another. If you can't, then a transition may be needed.

In this essay, the student writer has used transitions both within paragraphs and between them:

The phrase more specifically *informs the reader that the general idea expressed in sentence 1 will be narrowed in sentence 2.*

[1]The fourth century B.C. in Greek art was not only a period of flowering creativity but also one of innovation. *More specifically*, in the field of sculpture, one sees a change in both style and approach from the Classical era. An example of this is the Pothos by Skopas.

In pars. 2–5 the writer presents a detailed description of the statue. Several times the relationship among the ideas is one of either similarity or contrast. Accordingly, the writer uses these transitions (italicized) to cue the reader that the next feature will be either similar to or different from the previous one. The sentences would still be clear without the transitions; with them, however, the writer makes the reader's job easier.

[2]This torso, about fourteen inches high, is a Roman copy of the Greek original. Unfortunately, it is poorly preserved. The once whitish marble has turned a light yellowish color with occasional brown spots throughout. *Similarly*, the surface is scarred and therefore roughened by chips, also an indication of bad exposure. The hips are worn, minimizing somewhat the fuller natural curve, and at the same time exposing the original color.

[3]The torso is all that is left of the once fully-sculpted male figure. His head, now lost, would have been bent slightly toward his right, accompanied by a corresponding drop of the right shoulders. The left shoulder, *however*, tilts upward because of the raised left arm, which is almost completely broken. *Likewise*, only the upper right arm is left to show us a slight bend, extending across the abdominal area.

[4]The tilt of the shoulders, along with the positions of the arms, inevitably affects the posture of the rest of the body. The trunk doesn't remain straight and rigid anymore but takes on a slight curve, bending the torso's left side. We feel the whole weight of the body resting on its right leg.

The description concludes with a statement (end of par. 5) that summarizes the effect of the statue as a whole; appropriately, it opens with a transition to signal that such a statement follows.

[5]Even though both legs are broken, the left one at the knee and the right one above the knee, they still indicate their positions clearly. Because it has to support the body, the right leg takes a firm and fixed position, allowing no bend at the knee. The right foot would have been flat on the ground. *On the other hand*, the left leg is completely relaxed, crossing the right leg and touching the ground with only the front part

In par. 6, the writer moves to his major point, a discussion of the characteristics of post-Classical sculpture. The first sentence is a transition that explicitly links what has come before with what is to follow. As a consequence, one expects to read next about post-Classical sculpture—and this is what happens. Thus the reader moves smoothly from one concept to another.

Par. 7 explains another feature of post-Classical sculpture. Its first sentence, too, serves as a transition, the initial words indicating what will be discussed next. Further on, the writer stresses the difference between Pothos and classical sculpture by again using on the other hand.

As the writer swings into his concluding paragraphs, he has one more major idea to present, an idea that qualifies what he has said thus far. He makes use of a suitable transition. The whole sentence prepares the reader for a modification of what the writer has been saying.

Pars. 8–9 give two specific examples of idealized features of Pothos—the S-shape and the smooth muscles. Tying the two together is likewise (9). Again, the examples would be clear even without the transition, but likewise removes any possibility of misunderstanding. Finally, to make explicit to the reader that he is presenting his concluding and thesis statement, the writer uses another transitional word. Using then lends an air of finality to his thought.

of its foot. These positions force the right hip to be pushed slightly above the left one. _In general_, we have a body realistically presented, standing in a completely relaxed pose.

⁶_Through the realistic style of Pothos, one is introduced to the characteristics of the post-Classical sculptures._ Predominant here is the S-shape used so often by sculptors of that period to determine their forms. With the head bending toward the right, we see a clear frontal presentation of the S-shape. Perhaps even more apparent is the S-shape when looked at from the torso's back. The curving of the spine toward the right and the change of direction at the hips, plus the whole body contour, clearly represent this S-shape.

⁷_Another departure from the Classical period exemplified in Pothos is a new style of presentation._ Pothos is meant to be viewed from any angle. One sees a statue that has dimension and depth unlike those in the Classical style. The Discobolis of the Classical period was meant to be seen only in front and back. If one were to view it at an angle, the thinness of the figure would be absurd. Pothos, _on the other hand_, looks real from all angles.

⁸_But to say without qualification that Pothos gives us the "real" man is not correct._ The S-shape should be seen as an aesthetically pleasing conceptualization rather than as a wholly realistic portrayal of man.

⁹The effects of the smoothened muscles on Pothos's body are _likewise_ aesthetically pleasing if not completely realistic. The artist here clearly emphasizes style and visual presentation. He uses realistic details only to combine them into a more idealized whole. To him, form is that which determines essence.

¹⁰Pothos, _then_, is still an embodiment of the symbolic and idealistic concepts of man, although the sculptor's style differs markedly from that of his classical precedessors.

Transitions help ensure that your reader will understand your thoughts better by making the relationships among them more obvious.

Use transitions wherever appropriate, and especially as you move from one part of your paper to another.

Exercise

Read carefully the following essay. Find as many examples of transitions as you can, and tell how they reveal relationships among the ideas discussed.

BASEBALL'S $20 MILLION MAN

[1]The scouts came to the University of Minnesota in 1973 with high hopes and open wallets. The man from the Minnesota Vikings had his eye on a prospect for tight end, a graduating senior big enough (6 ft. 6 in., 220 lbs.) and fast enough to make it in the N.F.L. despite the fact that he had not played football since high school. The scout from the Atlanta Hawks sought to sign up a power forward who had averaged 15.3 points and 7.4 rebounds a game during his college basketball career. And the fellow from the San Diego Padres was ecstatic over a pitcher-outfielder with a fine arm and a better bat (.379 with nine homers in his senior year).

[2]Each of the teams made its designated player an early-round draft choice. The only problem was that the three selections were all the same man: Dave Winfield. An athlete for all seasons, Winfield thus became one of the few players ever drafted by professional teams in three sports.

[3]He opted for baseball, and last week the decision paid off handsomely. After languishing for eight years with the flaccid Padres, Winfield, 29, signed a contract with the New York Yankees that will reportedly bring him as much as $20 million over the next ten years. His agreement with the Yankees, by far the richest contract since baseball's free-agent era began in 1976, makes him the highest-paid American athlete. Houston Astro Pitcher Nolan Ryan's $1 million a year and fellow Yankee Outfielder Reggie Jackson's $500,000-plus a year pale in comparison with Winfield's estimated $1.3 million annual stipend. Included in the deal is a $1 million signing bonus, as well as complicated provisions tying extra compensation to the inflation rate and the price of Yankees tickets.

[4]Some baseball observers were aghast at the huge sum laid out for a player who had hit over .300 only twice in his eight-year major league career. Is Winfield worth it? Says Baltimore Oriole General Manager Hank Peters: "Not in my judgment. I don't think any athlete in any team sport can be important enough to command that kind of money." But Winfield had a ready retort: "Everything has a market value. How do you set a price on a precious gem?"

[5]To be sure, Winfield was perhaps the brightest diamond among a rather lusterless crop of free agents this year, the 48 veterans who played out their options after at least six years in the majors. Yet some

of those players won astronomical contracts, considering their limited skills. Former New York Met Outfielder Claudell Washington reportedly received $2.5 million over five years from the Atlanta Braves, despite a lifetime average of .279 and a seven-year home run total of 47. Texas Rangers Utility Infielder Dave Roberts received a new contract for more than $200,000 a year from the Astros, even though Houston officials admit that he will not be in the starting lineup.

[6]On the other hand, quite a few major leaguers boast more impressive statistics than Winfield's, except for the salary figure. Baltimore Oriole First Baseman Eddie Murray, 24, has played in the majors only four years, but he has already hit 111 home runs, driven in 398 runs and averaged .291, yet he earned just $150,000 last season. He will be eligible to declare himself a free agent after the 1982 season. If Winfield's price is $20 million, Murray's value is almost incalculable.

[7]Yet Winfield is no slouch. A respectable hitter (major league average .279, with 154 home runs and 626 RBIs), he is a sure-handed outfielder whose speed and accurate arm keep base runners back on their heels. Last season he was something of a disappointment, batting only .276 with 20 homers. At least some of his problems at the plate can be blamed on the Padres' weak-hitting lineup. American League pitchers will not have the luxury of pitching around Winfield in a Yankee batting order that also includes such sluggers as Jackson (41 homers last season), Graig Nettles (16 home runs despite missing 65 games because of hepatitis) and Bob Watson (.307 season's average).

[8]Perhaps the biggest benefactors of Winfield's windfall will be the other denizens of Owner George Steinbrenner's Bronx zoo. Jackson's contract expires at the end of the 1981 season, and as he is the only major leaguer to hit 25 or more home runs each year for the past ten consecutive years, his asking price will probably be even higher than Winfield's. Pitcher Ron Guidry, a 1978 Cy Young Award winner with one year left on his estimated $250,000-a-year contract, will be after a bigger slice of the Yankee pie too—unless Steinbrenner deals him first to the Boston Red Sox as part of a trade that would bring hard-hitting Centerfielder Fred Lynn to New York.

[9]Steinbrenner feels Winfield's contract is justified because the Yankees desperately need to fill a gap in their lineup that has yawned since Catcher Thurman Munson's death last year in the crash of his private plane. Winfield brings righthanded power to a roster overloaded with lefthanders. His speed should also help the Yankees' sluggish base running, a weakness painfully exposed by the Kansas City Royals during the playoffs last fall. Says Pittsburgh Pirates Executive Vice President Harding Peterson: "A player's worth depends on what the market will bear, the needs of a given club and its policy on salaries. So things fit together for Winfield and the Yankees. Still, that's a lot of money for a .276 hitter. That's a lot of money for a .400 hitter."

[10]Nonetheless, ten teams entered the sweepstakes for Winfield. Three—the Mets and the Cleveland Indians as well as the Yankees—

made firm, eight-figure offers. But Winfield had had enough of second-division teams and wanted to play for a club with genuine pennant hopes. "I chose the Yankees to find out how good I am and to contribute to a winning cause," said Winfield. "Winning a World Series is one of my aspirations, and now I have a chance." Jackson warned Winfield that the megabucks Yankees endure a special scrutiny, from both fans and George Steinbrenner. Said Jackson: "It's either a lion's den or it's Disney World." Winfield took a long look at his $20 million deal and concurred: "There will be a tremendous spotlight on me. There is no easy money here." (B.J. Phillips)

REVISING THE ESSAY

In most cases, essay revising should involve more than simply smoothing out the rough spots in language or proofreading the rough draft; it should be a process of reading, rereading, redefining, and rewriting what you have written. Countless professional writers have attested to the absolute necessity for revision and also to the fact that true revision does not come easily or cheaply. The message should be clear: If you hope to write successful essays, you must make serious revising a regular part of your approach.

An Approach to Revision

Effective revision* requires that you give attention to each of these five qualities in every essay you write:

1. *Content (ideas)*   Does the essay have a main idea? Are all the ideas sound and fully thought out?

2. *Purposes (primary, secondary, and so on)*   Does the essay have a clear primary purpose? What other purposes does it achieve?

3. *Structure (organization and form)*   Is there a conscious structure to the essay? What is the organizational pattern? Would an alternative pattern be stronger?

4. *Correctness (grammar and mechanics)*   Do all sentences have subjects and verbs and express complete thoughts? Has the essay been proofread for items such as word endings and punctuation?

5. *Effect (style and voice)*   Are sentences clear? Forceful when necessary? Is the level of language appropriate?

To answer these questions, you must understand what constitutes effective and purposeful writing. That is, knowing the qualities you

---

*In Chapter 3, pp. 98–103, we discussed revising paragraphs, and in Chapter 6, pp. 220–25, we will discuss revising sentences. Everything included in those sections is also directly applicable to revising essays, because the essay contains both sentences and paragraphs. Be sure to review that material as you revise your essays.

need to *build into* your writing also enables you to *check for* these qualities and thus successfully revise your work.

There is another technique you should incorporate into the rewriting stage: You must be able to read your own material objectively, as though you were someone else picking up an unfamiliar essay and trying to make sense of it.

However, pretending that you are someone else as you read your own writing is often easier said than done. You may tend to assume that your writing is clear and sound because *you* know what you were trying to say, and it seems natural that everyone else would, too. Also, your draft may seem good as you reread it because you are so strongly hoping that it is good—you become a kind of cheerleader for your own side, unwilling to admit the possibility of faults with the essay. But good writers do manage to see their own material as a stranger would, and this enables them to spot weaknesses and correct them. To help you in revising your essays, here is a list of questions that approximates the process most readers go through in responding to and judging college writing. You can put yourself in the place of another person by pretending that you are "the reader," the "I" in the following list. When you read over your work you are *not* "the writer," even though you actually wrote the draft. In fact, assume that you are a little skeptical by nature, and that you need to be convinced that "this writer" actually has something to say.

First Reading: The Reader Reacts

1. What are the purposes of the paper? What central point does the writer try to make?

2. Which sections seem particularly effective or particularly weak?

3. What is my first reaction to this paper and its subject? Is it positive or negative? Does the paper hold my interest?

Second Reading: The Reader Analyzes

1. What is this writer attempting to do? Is a primary purpose evident? How do I know? Is the purpose worth pursuing? Why or why not?

2. What is the writer trying to say? How do I know? Is it worth saying? Why or why not?

3. Is a main idea stated explicitly? If so, can I pinpoint the sentence(s)? If not, can I formulate a topic or thesis sentence myself as reader? Could the writer have provided one for me?

4. If there is no main idea, then what are the minor ideas? How many are there and why don't they add up to a main idea? Does the writer need them all?

5. Can I trace the flow of the main idea? If so, how has the writer carried it through? Through logical explanation, through illustration (specific examples), through chronological process, through comparison/ contrast?

6. If I cannot follow the flow, where does the progression break down? Do any sentences or groups of sentences seem irrelevant?

7. Do any points need more elaboration? Should the writer explain anything in greater detail or supply a specific example to illustrate and clarify the point?

8. Are all sentences clear and grammatical? Why did certain sentences or words strike me as effective (or weak) when I first reacted to the paper? Can I explain why these usages are effective (or weak)?

9. Are the various points in the paper organized in the best way possible? What would be the effect of rearranging the ideas?

10. Does the writer make smooth transitions between ideas?

11. If the paper holds my interest, is it because I find the topic inherently interesting, or because the writer has created the interest for me through his/her particular approach or use of language?

This list reflects the kinds of questions an experienced reader will ask in responding to your papers. The more comfortable you can become with the role of "the reader" when rereading your work, the more likely you will revise your essays successfully. As you become better skilled at reading your work as another would read it, you will find that what is called the revising *stage* of the overall composing process will begin to blend in with the other stages of the process; it will no longer be a separate stage that is necessarily done last. In fact, most good writers actually do a good bit of revising as they compose. They have developed the ability to shift quickly into the role of the reader while they are writing a sentence or developing a paragraph within their essay. Such shifting back and forth becomes a natural and efficient way of shaping and reshaping what they have to say, eliminating the wait until a rough draft is completed before revising.

Exercise

Using the list of questions on pages 177–78, evaluate the student essay that follows. Be thorough and specific in your responses.

    [1]The reality of starting college and leaving home has not actually dawned on me yet. At times I can hardly believe that I am a freshman in college. I anticipated college to be perfect, but in reality I have come

to realize all the things that I have taken for granted over the years. When we grow up we become attached to certain people and things without realizing it and before we know it we have to let go. What I expected college life to be and what it has turned out to be are two different things.

[2]This summer I was really excited about starting college, but when it came to the actual process of leaving home, I felt a little apprehensive. The thought of leaving my family for such a long period of time made me very sad. I would especially miss my little sister. We have grown so close that we each know what the other is thinking about. I can say this about my whole family. This closeness made me feel very secure. My brother, sister, and I went to the same school. So we were constantly together and we could share what we experienced at the end of the day. Leaving home also meant giving up my room. I had done a lot of growing up and thinking in that room. When I saw my room, I saw myself. I would have to give up many other comforts and conveniences, but most importantly I would have to give up a lot of time with my family.

[3]On the other hand, I anticipated college to be perfect. I thought to myself that I would finally be on my own. I expected everything from the room to the food to be perfect, but it was far from it. The one thing that really did turn out to be perfect was my classes. I got into the classes that I wanted and the work load is not too steep, which has really been an advantage.

[4]In some ways, college life has been a little harder than I expected it to be. There are a few minor inconveniences in that I have to rely more on myself. But a lot of my expectations have come true as far as the setting and atmosphere. The campus is beautiful and the people are very relaxed.

[5]The reality of starting college and my anticipation of it has not put an end to my life at home. At first I thought that this would be the case. Now I feel that my living away from home will let me grow as a person. In doing so, I will have more to share with my family and they will have more to share with me. We will not end up going in opposite directions.

Suggestion for Writing

Choose an essay you have written this term or semester and evaluate it according to the questions on pages 177–78. Using the responses that you, as the reader, have made, thoroughly revise the essay.

Revising to Solve Specific Problems

Covering all the particular strategies and techniques one could use in revising a weak draft into a strong essay is impossible. And even if it were possible, memorizing all the revision strategies would probably not be worthwhile. A much more useful approach involves learning to spot problem areas for yourself and to figure out ways of handling them. Let's examine two student essays that were in need of revision when they were first handed in, and see how, in each case, the student chose to revise.

Dave, the student who wrote the first essay, wanted to praise his favorite high school teacher by focusing on his positive characteristics. But, because of Dave's approach, you may wonder whether you actually have a coherent picture of Mr. Donovan by the end of the essay.

[1]Mr. James Donovan is the subject of this paper. I learned to respect him as my history teacher and high school football coach. Through many associations with him socially I began to trust him as I do a friend. Most of this respect that I have for Mr. Donovan was derived from his sincere and concerned actions.

[2]In all the years that I have known Mr. Donovan, I have never known him to be anything but honest, friendly and fair. I feel confident that any advice he gives to me will be completely honest, sensible, and well thought out. No matter what the occasion is, I can always count on Mr. Donovan to be supportive, cooperative and involved. Although all of these traits are beneficial, I feel his greatest attribute is that he is fair. As a teacher, he didn't accomplish his duties by testing us on trivial facts, but on basic concepts and understanding of the material. Of all my teachers in high school I felt that he best utilized the facilities which the community had to offer. Because of his practices I feel that I learned more in his class than I learned in any other.

[3]Mr. Donovan's spirit and interest in youth are evident at all times around the school and community. No matter how useless and expensive a fund-raiser item was, a student could be assured that he would purchase many. If an adult advisor or volunteer was needed, Mr. Donovan rarely turned down the opportunity to help. Throughout my period of poor health he was anxious to listen when I was down, and this characteristic has become the most important element throughout many of our associations.

[4]Because of doctor's orders I was forced to stay out of athletics until halfway through my junior year of high school. Having always been a devout football fan I decided to start playing during my senior year. It was only through the confidence and opportunity which Mr. Donovan bestowed upon me that I was able to have a successful football career. His full use of my abilities, as well as those of my teammates, produced an excellent season for our team and myself. His philosophy, centering around player-coach respect, was a positive aspect of our team. His main concern was for his players' well-being.

[5]I respect Mr. Donovan as a teacher because I agreed with his teaching method, and because he was eager to help out when I was in need.

⁶People like Jim Donovan are few and far between. I am honored that I am still able to call him a friend.

Unfortunately, Dave had not decided on a clear central idea—all he knew was that he would talk about Mr. Donovan's good qualities. Thus the essay is a fairly loose collection of points about Mr. Donovan and even about Dave himself (his illness, his football prowess, and so on). Moreover, we seldom see Mr. Donovan in action. We are only told that he did admirable things and that he is therefore admirable. But what exactly did he do?

By working on two specific areas—the need to have a clear main idea and the need to illustrate Mr. Donovan's qualities instead of just talking about them abstractly—Dave produced this revision:

¹Mr. James Donovan, a high school teacher of mine, is the subject of this essay. I chose Mr. Donovan on account of his many years as a teacher, football coach, and responsible member of the community. The guidance, leadership, training, and help that Mr. Donovan has given me and other students for the past decade have had a great impact on us all. I will discuss some of the qualities which make Mr. Donovan a concerned adviser, a skillful teacher, and a successful football coach.

²In my four years of high school I became aware of numerous activities that Mr. Donovan participates in after the 2:30 bell rings. In the fourteen years he has been at Oberlin High, he has held offices of acting principal, acting athletic director and self-proclaimed adviser and guidance counselor. Serving as the head of the History department and as president of numerous teachers' clubs, he has shown leadership ability and judgment that are respected by all. With Mr. Donovan as its faculty adviser, the city's high school booster club has become one of the top organizations in the community. Their financial and manpower assistance made possible the construction of the new athletic complex and concession stands, as well as the acquisition of equipment and supplies for all varsity sports.

³Not only is Mr. Donovan active in adult organizations, but he is also willing to advise most any student organization. He has served as class adviser four times in his years at OHS. He and his wife have attended all but one formal dance as chaperones in the past six years. In attendance at last weekend's Jog-a-thon for athletic uniforms, he earned $50 for the account.

⁴In class Mr. Donovan is one of the best. His philosophy of teaching is very sound. I remember a test we once had on the Civil War era. There was so much information to master in the chapter that I knew that I could never remember the specific dates of specific battles or the number of lives lost in each. Instead of questions of this nature, the test consisted of essays on the reasons for and characteristics of these

battles—much more useful information in the long run. In lectures, Mr. Donovan never becomes too abstract or removed from the class. In general when teachers lecture, there are times when hypothetical situations must be given to clarify points. Instead of providing all of these for us himself, Mr. Donovan uses people in class to construct these situations and make them more meaningful.

⁵Lastly, I would like to comment on Mr. Donovan as football coach. Although I could write many pages on his career, I will pick the basic highlights. The average size of the Oberlin High football team is 32 people. Out of the 32 about ten have the ability to play good football. With this lack of depth, the team is forced to double platoon every game, thus becoming exhausted by the close of the third quarter. Five teams on the schedule are from schools with more than 1800 students, whereas OHS has only 500 students. Even though fiercely outnumbered, the Indians have been one of the best teams in the conference. Under Coach Donovan's direction, the team has had five conference titles and only two losing seasons in the past fifteen years. In addition, last year's team was regarded as the most exciting team in the area because of its explosive, record-breaking offense.

⁶Probably the biggest compliment is the fine athletes from Coach Donovan's past teams who have made it in to the NFL or the CFL. So few high school football players ever succeed in professional sports that this achievement is a tribute to the coach.

⁷These are a few of the basic reasons why I admire Mr. Donovan. I could list more, but all would have the same thing in common; they all would be examples of Jim Donovan's care and concern for youth. I'm glad that I made his acquaintance and hope to call him a friend for a long time.

Notice how this second version has been fully revised, not merely patched up. Dave provides a new and more precise statement of his main idea: "I will discuss some of the qualities which make Mr. Donovan a concerned adviser, a skillful teacher, and a successful football coach." His primary purpose is to demonstrate the validity of this thesis, and each section of the paper examines one of the three roles. Instead of relying only on general and vague statements as he did in the first draft (such as "this respect that I have for Mr. Donovan was derived from his sincere and concerned actions," or "because of his practices I feel that I learned more in his class than I learned in any other"), Dave here supplies concrete illustrations of Mr. Donovan in action. As readers, we feel that we are getting a sense of the man's character and that we can concur with the writer's judgment.

The second essay we'll examine centers around the matter of effective organization. Writing about a concept she learned of in a course titled *Sociology of Police*, Amy was quite certain about her primary purpose. She wanted to prove that the positive image of Japanese police was directly attributable to two factors. Her paper would be a blend of two patterns, comparison/contrast and cause/effect. She would contrast the Japanese police with the American police while analyzing the causes for their differing images. All these were good choices. But, in writing the essay, Amy also made a questionable decision—to use the "*A*, then *B*" organization (*A* = Japanese police, *B* = American police). Because she had so many points to make and so much information to include, it became difficult to keep everything straight using this organization. Here is the first version:

[1]An extremely interesting concept is that of comparing various police institutions. It has been found that Japanese police behavior appears to differ significantly from that found in the United States. Two important aspects that produce the differences are the various police contacts with the people and their attitudes toward them.

[2]In Japan, the police see masses of utterly ordinary people on friendly terms. They do not wish to frighten people. The policemen do not carry guns. Swearing and crude language are not common among Japanese police. When they become suspicious of people who arouse their attention, the police are able to conduct discreet interrogations rather than making a scene. The Koban, a place where many police operations take place, is very crucial. One of its major functions is to provide information to the people. It is also a place to provide community services and emergency help. Often people come in just to talk, to seek help for their problems, or to get basic counseling. In Japan a biannual residential survey requires the officer to meet everyone who lives and works on the patrol route. In addition to this there exist very few patrol cars; therefore police officers are seen commonly walking amongst the crowds. Their appearance is very informal. Through these various situations the police come into contact with all sorts of people, not just criminals. They are rewarded handsomely by the happiness they give others through the Koban. The Japanese police are, as a result, proud of their job.

[3]American police, on the other hand, do not play a visible role in ordinary social affairs. The police through their size and their intimidating attitudes make a threatening visual presence. The ones on patrol are more dependent on their appearance. It is never self-effacing. They rely on technology rather than knowledge of self-defense. Automobiles and guns have shaped police procedure. The police are more official than Japanese police. The American police are official and self-conscious. Often a street cop draws challenging stares from criminals and is easily provoked. Such occasions are conducive to verbal abuse. They engage in one-upmanship, a game to maintain respect of their colleagues. Rarely do United States police officers come in contact with people other than criminals. Due to this distance the American police see themselves as enforcement technicians, not members of the society.

[4]In conclusion, the manner in which the police in Japan and the United States act varies tremendously. Perhaps a change in police technique to bring about a closer relationship with the common person can make the job a more respected position in the United States. However, under the present conditions it has been found that the Japanese police are proud rather than defensive. The American police have not yet developed the kind of pride and self-discipline found in Japan.

Actually, not much is wrong with this essay. Its general purpose is clear. However, after discussing the paper in conference, both Amy and her instructor felt that it could be made even stronger. By using $A_1/B_1–A_2/B_2$ organization (A_1 = police contacts, Japanese; B_1 = police contacts, American; A_2 = police attitudes, Japanese; B_2 = police attitudes, American), Amy decided she could maintain a stronger control over the "two important aspects" while still contrasting Japanese and American police. In the first version, the "two important aspects" got lost among the details, but in the revised version they stand out clearly:

[1]It has been found that Japanese police behavior differs significantly from that found in the United States. Two important aspects that produce the differences are the various police contacts with the people and the attitudes of the police toward the public.

[2]In Japan, police contacts with people are frequent; they see masses of utterly ordinary people on friendly terms. Police officers are seen commonly walking amongst the crowds. Their appearance is very informal. In addition to this the Japanese police have very few patrol cars. The Koban, a place where many police operations take place, is very crucial. One of its major functions is to provide information to the people. It is also a place to provide community services and emergency help. Often people come in just to talk, to seek help for their problems, or to get basic counseling. In Japan there is also the biannual residential survey, which requires the officer to meet everyone who lives and works on the patrol route. Through these various situations the police come in contact with all sorts of people, not just criminals.

[3]American police, on the other hand, do not play a visible role in ordinary social affairs. The police, by their mere physical size (there are minimum height and weight requirements), make a threatening appearance. They rely on technology rather than knowledge of self defense. Automobiles and guns have shaped police procedure. Police operations are organized in terms of patrol cars. Police in the States seldom come in contact with the public unless these people are criminals or victims of crimes.

[4]Police attitudes are also important in shaping the overall image of the police. In Japan, the basic element of community among the police

is pride. They realize high public expectations are a mark of respect. The Japanese police do not wish to frighten people. They do not even carry guns. Swearing and crude language are not common among Japanese police. When they become suspicious of people who arouse their attention, they conduct discreet interrogations rather than make a scene. They are rewarded handsomely by the happiness they give others through the Koban. The Japanese police are, as a result, proud of their job and enjoy helping others.

[5]In the United States, by contrast, public respect for police is low and, as a result, their attitudes are poor. Their sense of group solidarity or community is based on feelings of rejection; consequently their attitude is vindictive. Often a street cop draws challenging stares from criminals and is easily provoked. Such occasions are conducive to verbal abuse. The police engage in one-upmanship, a game to maintain respect of their colleagues. The ones on patrol not only depend on their intimidation but are also ready to back it up with aggressive behavior. In public they are official and self-conscious so as not to be challenged. Unlike the Japanese, American police lack the sense of pride needed to achieve a better interaction between themselves and the people, and thereby to improve their image.

[6]In conclusion, the manner in which the police in Japan and the United States act varies tremendously. The Japanese police are proud rather than defensive, and American police have not yet developed the kind of pride and self-discipline found in Japan. But if the American police are to improve, it will require that the environment around them change. Perhaps a change in police technique to bring about a closer relationship with the common person can make the job a more respected position and change police decorum in the United States.

Note that Amy's essay required less revision than Dave's. Although Amy added some new discussion, the content of her revision is fundamentally the same as that of the original version; she modified only the structure to improve clarity. Yet Amy, like Dave, approached the task of revision seriously and energetically. As a result, she produced a more successful essay.

Exercise

To test your comprehension of all the material presented on the essay (both in this chapter and the preceding one) reread "Baseball's $20 Million Man" (pp. 174–76). This time, instead of concentrating only on its use of transitions, write a brief analysis in which you comment on all aspects of the essay—its basic structure, its use of the patterns of development, its arrangement of ideas, its introduction and conclusion, and so on.

1. Read the following article by Roger Simon and then write an essay about a memorable work experience of your own. (It may be about either paid or unpaid work you have done.) Conclude your essay like Simon does: by stating something you learned from the experience.

WORKERS AND BUMS

[1]We would go out on the beach just before dawn when it was still cool enough to work. The sharp smell of the lake would be strong then and there would be no sound except for the lapping of the waves.

[2]We dressed disreputably. Ripped sneakers, blue jeans, sweatshirts with the sleeves torn off. We carried three-foot sticks tipped with sharpened nails. Over our shoulders were canvas sacks, stained an indeterminate color by years of trash.

[3]As the sun struggled up through the purple haze of steel mill smoke that lay on the horizon the beach's banquet of garbage would be revealed to us. It spread for nearly a mile.

[4]We were hired to impale the garbage on the ends of our sticks and place it in our bags. Except for my current one, it was the best job I ever had.

[5]I once referred to the job in front of my foreman as unskilled labor. I meant no insult. I had completed my freshman year of college and, therefore, knew everything. For me this was a summer job to earn enough money for my sophomore year.

[6]My foreman was insulted by my characterization. He led me over to the low concrete wall that separated the beach from the park.

[7]At that hour of the morning you could just hear the snoring of the bums who were sleeping off the previous night's wine binge under a grove of trees.

[8]He pointed in their direction. "That," he said, "is unskilled labor. You are semi-skilled."

[9]Four or five of us would spread out along the beach in a line and march forward, picking up trash as we went. There was a wide variety. Not just food and paper and bottles but every possible article of clothing. I never did figure out how people could possibly walk home lacking some of the things they had left behind.

[10]Beer cans we liked. They were still made out of steel then and they would yield to our nailed sticks with a satisfying crunch. We had contests to see from how far away we could spear them.

[11]It was a point of pride to pick up everything on the beach. The great sin was to kick sand over a piece of garbage that was too difficult or too disgusting to handle. Hot dog buns, soaked by the morning dew, fell into this category.

[12]The lifeguards, clean-shaven, muscled, athletic, were the heroes of the beach. But we were the anti-heroes. Sweating, filthy, wearing

our work gloves as a badge of honor, we scowled professionally whenever our friends waved to us as we rode by on the tractor that dragged the wire trash baskets up the beach for collection.

[13]I came from a family where physical labor was neither romanticized nor degraded. My father was a truck driver. And I remember the mornings when the beach was particularly filthy—the Fifth of July was always the worst—and halfway through the job looking back and seeing only the bare golden sand where before there had been a half-ton of garbage.

[14]I learned that summer the palpable satisfaction of doing a job well, even if that job is picking up garbage.

[15]I got the job the way a lot of people get summer jobs: unfairly. The father of a friend knew a politician and the politician wrote a letter for me.

[16]I brought the letter to the park district headquarters and waited in a long line of job applicants. A passing clerk saw the envelope in my hand and took me by the sleeve to the head of the line and into an office.

[17]"Why dincha say something?" he asked, writing out my job assignment. "You had a letter. You don't have to wait if you have a letter."

[18]And so I began learning about the ways things worked.

[19]Years later, when I was not only reformed but a reformer, I interviewed the politician when he retired. He did not, of course, remember the letter he had written for me. But I reminded him of it.

[20]"I controlled maybe 100 to 200 jobs a year," he said with pride. "Over the years, I placed thousands of people. Thousands."

[21]But it wasn't really fair, was it? I asked. Giving out jobs that way?

[22]"Tell me something," he said with a weary smile. "You did the job? You picked up the garbage?"

[23]Sure, I said. I did the job. I did a good job.

[24]"So what wasn't fair?" he said. "As long as the job got done, what wasn't fair?"

[25]I recall all this every time I hear complaints about public workers not doing their job. "It's politics," people say. "That's what's wrong with this country."

[26]Maybe. But maybe it is something a little more basic. Maybe it is what my foreman was trying to tell me that morning: That the difference between doing a job and not doing it is the difference between a worker and a bum.

2. Read the following piece by X.J. Kennedy, paying special attention to Kennedy's focus on King Kong's frustration and his feeling of being out of his true element. Then write an essay in which you discuss a source of frustration in your own life or a situation in which you feel out of your element. You might develop the essay

by analyzing the cause of your feeling and discussing how you reduce your frustration or how you find a way of living with the uncomfortable situation.

WHO KILLED KING KONG?

[1]The ordeal and spectacular death of King Kong, the giant ape, undoubtedly have been witnessed by more Americans than have ever seen a performance of *Hamlet, Iphigenia at Aulis,* or even *Tobacco Road.* Since RKO-Radio Pictures first released *King Kong,* a half-century has gone by; yet year after year, from prints that grow more rain-beaten, from sound tracks that grow more tinny, ticket-buyers by thousands still pursue Kong's luckless fight against the forces of technology, tabloid journalism, and the DAR. They see him chloroformed to sleep, see him whisked from his jungle isle to New York and placed on show, see him burst his chains to roam the city (lugging a frightened blonde), at last to plunge from the spire of the Empire State Building, machine-gunned by model airplanes.

[2]Though Kong may die, one begins to think his legend unkillable. No clearer proof of his hold upon the popular imagination may be seen than what emerged one catastrophic week in March 1955, when New York WOR-TV programmed *Kong* for seven evenings in a row (a total of sixteen showings). Many a rival network vice-president must have scowled when surveys showed that *Kong*—the 1933 B-picture—had lured away fat segments of the viewing populace from such powerful competitors as Ed Sullivan, Groucho Marx and Bishop Sheen.

[3]But even television has failed to run *King Kong* into oblivion. Coffee-in-the-lobby cinemas still show the old hunk of hokum, with the apology that in its use of composite shots and animated models the film remains technically interesting. And no other monster in movie history has won so devoted a popular audience. None of the plodding mummies, the stultified draculas, the white-coated Lugosis with their shiny pinball-machine laboratories, none of the invisible stranglers, berserk robots, or menaces from Mars has ever enjoyed so many resurrections.

[4]Why does the American public refuse to let King Kong rest in peace? It is true, I'll admit, that *Kong* outdid every monster movie before or since in sheer carnage. Producers Cooper and Schoedsack crammed into it dinosaurs, headhunters, riots, aerial battles, bullets, bombs, bloodletting. Heroine Fay Wray, whose function is mainly to scream, shuts her mouth for hardly one uninterrupted minute from first reel to last. It is also true that *Kong* is larded with good healthy sadism, for those whose joy it is to see the frantic girl dangled from cliffs and harried by pterodactyls. But it seems to me that the abiding appeal of the giant ape rests on other foundations.

⁵Kong has, first of all, the attraction of being manlike. His simian nature gives him one huge advantage over giant ants and walking vegetables in that an audience may conceivably identify with him. Kong's appeal has the quality that established the Tarzan series as American myth—for what man doesn't secretly image himself a huge hairy howler against whom no other monster has a chance? If Tarzan recalls the ape in us, then Kong may well appeal to that great-granddaddy primordial brute from whose tribe we have all deteriorated.

⁶Intentionally or not, the producers of *King Kong* encourage this identification by etching the character of Kong with keen sympathy. For the ape is a figure in a tradition familiar to moviegoers: the tradition of the pitiable monster. We think of Lon Chaney in the role of Quasimodo, of Karloff in the original *Frankenstein*. As we watch the Frankenstein monster's fumbling and disastrous attempts to befriend a flower-picking child, our sympathies are enlisted with the monster in his impenetrable loneliness. And so with Kong. As he roars in his chains, while barkers sell tickets to boobs who gape at him, we perhaps feel something more deep than pathos. We begin to sense something of the problem that engaged Eugene O'Neill in *The Hairy Ape*: the dilemma of a displaced animal spirit forced to live in a jungle built by machines.

⁷*King Kong*, it is true, had special relevance in 1933. Landscapes of the depression are glimpsed early in the film when an impresario, seeking some desperate pretty girl to play the lead in a jungle movie, visits soup lines and a Woman's Home Mission. In Fay Wray—who's been caught snitching an apple from a fruitstand—his search is ended. When he gives her a big feed and a movie contract, the girl is magic-carpeted out of the world of the National Recovery Act. And when, in the film's climax, Kong smashes that very Third Avenue landscape in which Fay had wandered hungry, audiences of 1933 may well have felt a personal satisfaction.

⁸What is curious is that audiences of today remain hooked. For in the heart of urban man, one suspects, lurks the impulse to fling a bomb. Though machines speed him to the scene of his daily grind, though IBM comptometers ("freeing the human mind from drudgery") enable him to drudge more efficiently once he arrives, there comes a moment when he wishes to turn upon his machines and kick the hell out of them. He wants to hurl his combination radio-alarm clock out the bedroom window and listen to its smash. What subway commuter wouldn't love—just for once—to see the downtown express smack head-on into the uptown local? Such a wish is gratified in that memorable scene in *Kong* that opens with a wideangle shot: interior of a railway car on the Third Avenue El. Straphangers are nodding, the literate refold their newspapers. Unknown to them, Kong has torn away a section of trestle toward which the train now speeds. The

motorman spies Kong up ahead, jams on the brakes. Passengers hurtle together like so many peas in a pail. In a window of the car appear Kong's bloodshot eyes. Women shriek. Kong picks up the railway car as if it were a rat, flips it to the street and ties knots in it, or something. To any commuter the scene must appear one of the most satisfactory pieces of celluloid ever exposed.

[9]Yet however violent his acts, Kong remains a gentleman. Remarkable is his sense of chivalry. Whenever a fresh boa constrictor threatens Fay, Kong first sees that the lady is safely parked, then manfully thrashes her attacker. (And she, the ingrate, runs away every time his back is turned.) Atop the Empire State Building, ignoring his pursuers, Kong places Fay on a ledge as tenderly as if she were a dozen eggs. He fondles her, then turns to face . . . the Army Air Force. And Kong is perhaps the most disinterested lover since Cyrano: his attentions to the lady are utterly without hope of reward. After all, between a five-foot blonde and a fifty-foot ape, love can hardly be more than an intellectual flirtation. In his simian way King Kong is the hopelessly yearning lover of Petrarchan convention. His forced exit from his jungle, in chains, results directly from his single-minded pursuit of Fay. He smashes a Broadway theater when the notion enters his dull brain that the flashbulbs of photographers somehow endanger the lady. His perilous shinnying up a skyscraper to pluck Fay from her boudoir is an act of the kindliest of hearts. He's impossible to discourage even though the love of his life can't lay eyes on him without shrieking murder.

[10]The tragedy of King Kong, then, is to be the beast who at the end of the fable fails to turn into the handsome prince. This is the conviction that the scriptwriters would leave with us in the film's closing line. As Kong's corpse lies blocking traffic in the street, the entrepreneur who brought Kong to New York turns to the assembled reporters and proclaims: "That's your story, boys—it was Beauty killed the Beast!" But greater forces than those of the screaming Lady have combined to lay Kong low, if you ask me. Kong lives for a time as one of those persecuted near-animal souls bewildered in the middle of an industrial order, whose simple desires are thwarted at every turn. He climbs the Empire State Building because in all New York it's the closest thing he can find to the clifftop of his jungle isle. He dies, a pitiful dolt, and the army brass and publicity-men cackle over him. His death is the only possible outcome to as neat a tragic dilemma as you can ask for. The machine-guns do him in, while the manicured human hero (a nice clean Dartmouth boy) carries away Kong's sweetheart to the altar. O, the misery of it all. There's far more truth about upper-middle-class American life in *King Kong* than in the last seven dozen novels of John P. Marquand.

[11]A black friend from Atlanta tells me that in movie houses in black neighborhoods throughout the South, *Kong* does a constant business. They show the thing in Atlanta at least every year, presumably to the

same audiences. Perhaps this popularity may simply be due to the fact that Kong is one of the most watchable movies ever constructed, but I wonder whether Negro audiences may not find some archetypical appeal in this serio-comic tale of a huge black powerful free spirit whom all the hardworking white policemen are out to kill.

[12]Every day in the week on a screen somewhere in the world, King Kong relives his agony. Again and again he expires on the Empire State Building, as audiences of the devout assist his sacrifice. We watch him die, and by extension kill the ape within our bones, but these little deaths of ours occur in prosaic surroundings. We do not die on a tower, New York before our feet, nor do we give our lives to smash a few flying machines. It is not for us to bring to a momentary standstill the civilization in which we move. King Kong does this for us. And so we kill him again and again, in much-spliced celluloid, while the ape in us expires from day to day, obscure in desperation.

part

THREE

LANGUAGE
AND STYLE

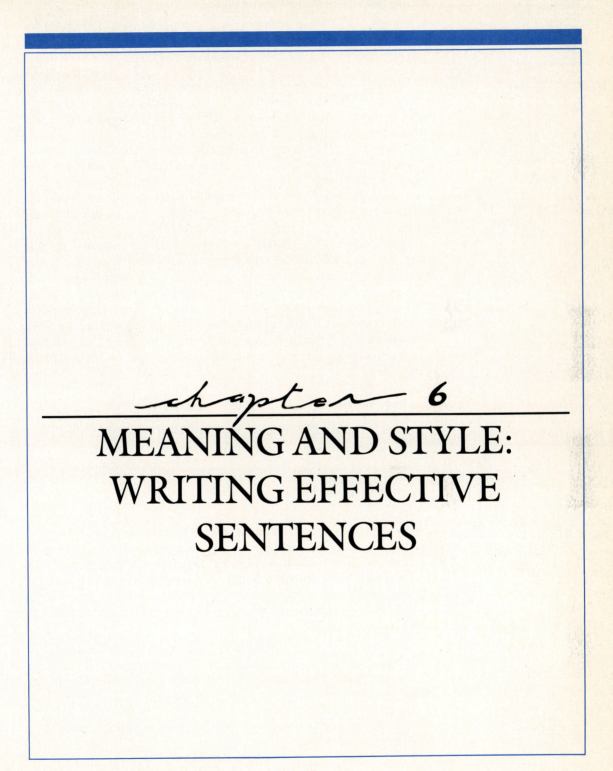

chapter **6**

MEANING AND STYLE: WRITING EFFECTIVE SENTENCES

THE BASIC
ENGLISH
SENTENCE

Peter's car rammed into the dilapidated Ford pick-up.
The dilapidated Ford pick-up rammed into Peter's car.

There is a world of difference between these two sentences. Although they contain precisely the same words, their meanings are opposite: In the first, it's Peter who'll pay the damages, and in the second, the pick-up driver is the culprit.

This pair of sentences demonstrates the reliance of the English sentence on *word order* to convey meaning. In fact, these sentences follow a primary rule of English: The subject of the verb precedes it in most cases. Because of this rule, the reader easily distinguishes who hit whom—"car rammed" and "pick-up rammed" mean two different things.

The "subject first, then verb" word order is considered normal order. For our purposes, we will define the *basic English sentence* as one that expresses a complete thought while following normal order. You must master this basic sentence in order to express your meaning effectively and clearly to your reader. Also, in order to polish and improve your style of writing, you need a strong command of the basic sentence pattern. Then you can expand, refine, and vary the pattern.

The following sentences are all basic (subjects are underlined once, verbs twice):

I left town.

Two men and a woman were responsible.

He fell.

Karen received five scholarship offers.

He gave me the box.

Each sentence has a subject and a verb, which together form the core of the meaning. To be grammatically correct, any sentence must possess at least one subject-verb combination that expresses a whole thought. In the Handbook we'll discuss the more technical grammatical aspects of subjects, verbs, and sentence structure. For now, keep in mind that a great many of the sentences you write will maintain the normal order of subject first, then verb.

Exercise

To test your skill at finding subjects and verbs, determine which of the following sentences are written in normal order.

1. At first the brothers could not get along in their business venture.
2. They argued constantly.

3. There seemed to be no end to the problems between them.
4. One would attract a promising new client.
5. The other would manage somehow to insult the prospect.
6. Out went the deal.
7. Finally, the two decided to discuss their differences.
8. Each realized greater cooperation was necessary for the business to succeed.
9. Both vowed to act in a more professional manner and to leave personal differences at home.
10. Twenty years went by with no further problems.

BUILDING ON THE BASIC PATTERN

You will write most of your sentences using the normal word order. But usually you will not write only sentences composed of sparse subject-verb combinations, such as the group of five sentences we examined on page 196. Although those sentences are grammatically correct, they are not stylistically effective. If you wrote only short simple sentences, your essays would read like grade-school primers and would not accurately reflect the level of your thinking. Rather, to be effective, you will embellish your core ideas with additional information—as much as you need to convey your intended meanings to your readers.

Adding Words and Phrases

You can add information to your subject-verb core by using either single words, or groups of words acting as units, or a combination of both. Let's take another look at the series of five sentences:

1. I left town.
2. Two men and a woman were responsible.
3. He fell.
4. Karen received five scholarship offers.
5. He gave me the box.

Each of these gives the reader only minimal information. If you, as the writer, wish to add more, you could simply add single words, like this:

1. I *immediately* left town.
2. Two *young* men and an *elderly* woman were responsible.
3. He fell *hard*.
4. Karen received five *excellent* scholarship offers *today*.
5. He gave me the *heavy* box *quickly*.

Or, you can add *phrases*, groups of words that act as units but contain no subject-verb cores:

1. I left town *for a few weeks.*
2. Two men and a woman were responsible *for perpetrating the fraud.*
3. *Tripping suddenly,* he fell *on his own sidewalk.*
4. Karen received five scholarship offers *to top-flight colleges.*
5. He gave me the box *with the green wrapper.*

More often, our ideas are sufficiently complex that we need to add *combinations* of both single words and phrases to express our thoughts completely:

1. I *immediately* left town *for a few weeks.*
2. Two *young* men and an *elderly* woman were responsible *for perpetrating the fraud.*
3. *Tripping suddenly,* he fell *hard on his own sidewalk.*
4. Karen received five *excellent* scholarship offers *to top flight colleges today.*
5. He *quickly* gave me the *heavy* box *with the green wrapper.*

Notice that adding all these words and phrases makes the ideas more precise. Saying "I left town" expresses a complete thought; grammatically speaking, the sentence specifies a subject, its verb, and the verb's object. Adding "immediately" and "for a few weeks" does not, then, make the sentence more *correct*, but it does give the reader a more precise, more specific meaning. "Immediately" answers the question "When?" and "for a few weeks" answers "For how long?"

Words or phrases that answer such questions as "When?" "How many?" "How?" "What kind?" and so on, are called *modifiers*. Depending on the type of information given, the modifier will either be an *adjective* or an *adverb* (see pp. 441–444 of the Handbook). Adjectives and adverbs flesh out the ideas we have. In so doing, they help us reduce the chance that our readers will misunderstand what we say—by making our ideas more specific, modifiers allow fewer alternative meanings for the sentences we create.

For example, take another look at this sentence:

Two men and a woman were responsible.

To how many different situations could this sentence refer? The men and the woman could be responsible for many things:

The success (or failure) of a project
The robbing of a bank
The saving of a life
The writing of a letter

Similarly, the characteristics of the individuals could be specified in many combinations:

Two old men and a young woman
Two bald-headed men and a dark-haired woman
Two men, one young and one old, and a middle-aged woman
Two men, both strangers to me, and a woman, a friend of mine

The information in this basic sentence could be expanded to fit a seemingly infinite number of situations. But if we word the idea more specifically, then those nearly limitless possibilities are narrowed considerably:

Two young men and an elderly woman were responsible for perpetrating the fraud.

We don't know anything about the fraud, nor do we know much about the people responsible, but we do have far fewer options for misunderstanding because the added words and phrases qualify the intended meaning.

Exercise

To each of the sentences below, add words and/or phrases that will help make the meaning more specific.

1. The plants looked feeble.
2. The mall was jammed.
3. Cars stalled everywhere.
4. The pass was incomplete.
5. He organized the rally.
6. She looked away.
7. Sports attract people.
8. The stapler jammed.
9. Phones rang.
10. Three hours passed.

Adding Clauses: Using Compound and Complex Sentences

A *clause* is a group of words containing a subject and a verb. The basic sentences we have been examining are all examples of clauses. They are also *independent* (or *main*) *clauses* because they express complete thoughts.

Another way to expand the basic sentence pattern to express your meanings more precisely is to combine two or more independent clauses into a single sentence called a *compound sentence* (see pp. 471–72 of the Handbook for a detailed discussion of the compound sentence). The clauses are commonly joined by words called *coordinating conjunctions* (*conjunction* means "joining"). Some of the most frequently used conjunctions are these:

and	for
but	so
or	yet
nor	

Here is an example of a compound sentence:

I left town, and two men and a woman were responsible.

Notice that *and* separates the sentence into two parts, each of which could be used as an independent, complete sentence. Note, too, that the two parts contain equally important ideas, closely related by cause and effect. Omit one or the other and a significant part of the writer's message is gone. A compound sentence is ideally suited for expressing in one sentence ideas of equal importance.

Exercise

Finish each of these sentences by adding one or more independent clauses, thus creating a compound sentence.

1. I had intended to take a long vacation, but . . .
2. The children swam playfully around, and . . .
3. Picnics can be fun, or . . .
4. Negotiating the slippery roads was a hazardous business, but . . .
5. For many years they enjoyed travelling abroad, yet . . .
6. The phone rang noisily and frequently, so . . .
7. Saks Fifth Avenue's annual sale is eagerly awaited, but . . .
8. Inviting and warm, the beach was a great place to be, and . . .
9. After the operation I was happy to be alive, for . . .
10. Our car wouldn't start yesterday morning, so . . .

Sometimes the ideas we add on to the basic sentence are not whole sentences by themselves, even though they contain subject-verb combinations. Consider these examples:

Whenever I have the time

Although the car stalled several times

Which belonged to Harry [*not* a question]

Notice that each of these clauses is *not* a sentence because it does not express a complete thought. Groups of words that contain a subject and a verb but do not contain complete thoughts are called *subordinate* (or *dependent) clauses*, and the sentences in which they occur are called *complex sentences*. A complex sentence may contain one or more dependent clauses, as well as at least one independent clause (see also pp. 472–74 of the Handbook).

Subordination (the use of subordinate clauses) is helpful for expressing a particular relationship between ideas. Examine these sentences:

I enjoy skiing. I have the time.

The implication is that the writer enjoys skiing *and* has the time to do it. But notice what happens when we add *whenever*:

I enjoy skiing *whenever* I have the time.

The meaning has changed; now the writer clearly does *not* always have time available for skiing. Here are other possibilities:

I enjoy skiing *because* I have the time.
I enjoy skiing *if* I have the time.

Both *because* and *if* pinpoint a certain relationship between the two ideas and help the writer convey a specific meaning. These *subordinating conjunctions* ensure that the reader understands the logical relationships among the ideas the writer expresses. (See p. 447 of the Handbook for a list of subordinating conjunctions.)

Subordination can also aid the writer in focusing the reader's attention on one idea or another. Generally, the more important idea in the sentence is placed within the independent clause (the one that expresses a complete idea); the less important one is placed within the subordinate clause. For example, which of these ideas is more important?

It was raining. I wrote my letter of resignation.

In most circumstances, the idea in the second sentence is more important than that in the first. And so we could write the sentences:

While it was raining, I wrote my letter of resignation.

This construction focuses the reader's attention on the second, more important idea.

But what if we wanted to stress the apparently less important fact that it was raining—perhaps to suggest a correspondence between the depressing weather and the depressed state of mind brought on by the resignation? Then we might write:

It was raining while I wrote my letter of resignation.

Or what if the rain was the more important element to the story? Such might be the case if the sentences appeared in a tale about a flood:

While I wrote my letter of resignation, it was raining. Suddenly the dam burst.

In this case, the letter of resignation is not the important element, and subordination helps convey the true picture.

Using compound and complex sentences can thus make your style—*how* you say something—reinforce your meaning—*what* you say. Remember these techniques and employ them when appropriate.

Exercise

Following are pairs of independent clauses. Rewrite each pair as a single sentence by subordinating one clause to the other.

1. The professor checked the calendar. She called the hotel to make reservations.
2. Only the good die young. The rival will live to a ripe old age.
3. They arrived at the Coliseum. It was already packed.
4. Unseasonably warm weather descended on the area in early February. The crocuses began to bloom.
5. Ocean liners were at one time the principal means of travel between England and America. They are no longer used on the transatlantic run.
6. I brought my umbrella along. It is raining.
7. Every morning the clown put on her make-up. She had her coffee.
8. We were about to give up and start walking. The bus came in sight.
9. Dr. Jones is the best cardiovascular surgeon at General Hospital. He could be replaced if necessary.
10. I can drink my tea without lemon. I prefer not to do so.

Left-branching, Right-branching, and Embedding

We have said that sentences composed of single, unadorned subject-verb cores are generally not sufficient to express complex ideas. And we have examined ways in which writers can add words, phrases, and clauses to elaborate and refine their meanings. But where should this additional material be placed?

Basically, there are three positions for such information: *before* the subject, *after* the verb, and *between* the subject and verb. Sentences having most of their added information before the subject are called *left-branching*, and those with more information after the verb are called *right-branching*. Placing groups of words between the subject and the verb is called *embedding*.

Here is a left-branching sentence:

      _____ + S + V
While it was raining,   I wrote my letter of resignation.

And here are examples of right-branching sentences:

      S + V + _____
Each realized greater cooperation was necessary for the business to

succeed.

      S + V +_____
Both vowed to act in a more professional manner and to leave personal

differences at home.

A sentence that makes use of embedding is the one you're reading.

      S + _____+ V
A sentence that makes use of embedding is the one you're reading.

A few points remain. First, *combinations* of branchings and embeddings are useful and occur frequently. For instance, the example of embedding that we examined is also a right-branching sentence:

      S + _____+ V +_____
A sentence that makes use of embedding is   the one you're reading.

Here are examples of other possible combinations:

Left-branching and right branching _____ + S+V +_____
After I heard the news , I felt terrible, although goodness knows he

deserved what he got.

Left-branching, embedding, and _____ S + ____
right-branching Being basically optimistic and decidedly carefree, the youngster, who
_____ + V +_____
should have known better, climbed the rickety snow fence bordering

the interstate.

A writer does have to exercise caution in using the various combinations. Otherwise, the result can be a sentence of gargantuan proportions, one that confuses even the sharpest of readers:

Whenever I have both the time and the inclination, a circumstance arising none too often these days, by the way, I, whom most people consider a very unathletic type indeed, like to jump rope, which I find to be not only relaxing but also essential in helping me to keep my weight under control.

This sentence, which combines left-branching, right-branching, and embedding, is grammatically correct. Yet the reader may forget the main idea before reaching the end. In general, any sentence that seems overly long should be considered for possible division into shorter sentences.

Another point: We are using the terms *left-branching*, *right-branching*, and *embedding* to refer to sentences with substantial information added in the given positions. Most of the examples we've examined contain clauses or long phrases amplifying the sentence's basic meaning and coming before, after, or between the subject-verb core. Take another look at the example of left-branching:

While it was raining, I wrote my letter of resignation.

At first, you might identify the sentence as right-branching because "my letter of resignation" follows the verb. But although the phrase "of resignation" refines the basic meaning of the sentence, it is so brief that we can classify the sentence as without significant right-branching elements.

As you work at refining and elaborating the meaning of your sentences, employ left-branching, right-branching, and embedding— the three important alternatives in constructing sentences.

Exercise

1. Examine the sentences you wrote for the Exercise on page 202. Label each as left- or right-branching. Did you use embedding in any of them?

2. Reconsider this sentence:

   Whenever I have both the time and the inclination, a circumstance arising none too often these days, by the way, I, whom most people consider a very unathletic type indeed, like to jump rope, which I find to be not only relaxing but also essential in helping me to keep my weight under control.

Revise it by dividing it into two sentences. Note whether the new sentences are left- or right-branching and/or whether they have any embedded elements.

ACHIEVING SENTENCE MATURITY

Sentence maturity refers to the level of complexity of sentence structure. The maturity of your sentences should be appropriate for the complexity of your thinking. As a college student, you would not do well to write all of your thoughts in simple sentences. (On the other hand, you should avoid needlessly complicating sentences just for the sake of making them seem "mature" or making your ideas sound sophisticated.) Let's discuss some ways to work toward achieving sentence maturity.

Sentence Combining

Sentence combining is a technique that helps beginning writers achieve a more mature style. Practicing sentence combining also helps a writer see the many correct alternatives possible for expressing an idea. And the technique can be used as a revision strategy, as we explore later in this chapter.

A sentence-combining exercise looks like this:

1. It was a holiday.
2. The mall was crowded.
3. The mall was in the suburbs.
4. Everyone was looking.
5. The looking was for bargains.

The exercise consists of a group of basic sentences called *kernels*, each having a subject-verb core and little, if any, modification. The idea is to combine the kernels into one grammatically correct sentence. No one answer is *the* right solution, for in most cases many correct options exist. The only stipulations are that the combined sentence be grammatically correct and that it preserve the intended meaning of the kernel sentences. In combining the kernels, subordination, coordination, or embedding can be helpful. For example, the five kernels above can be combined in these ways:

> Because it was a holiday, the suburban mall was crowded, and everyone was looking for bargains. (subordination and coordination)
> It was a holiday, and the suburban mall was crowded, with everyone looking for bargains. (coordination only)

Both versions are grammatically correct and both preserve the meanings of the original group of kernel sentences. All details have been included. Choosing between the two becomes largely a matter of personal choice: The one that sounds better to you is the one to use.

By combining groups of kernel sentences, you can gain a clearer knowledge of the various types of possible structures, and, according to some studies, you will likely apply this knowledge to your own writing. You will be able to create more varied and sophisticated sentences of your own.

When approaching a sentence-combining exercise, the first thing to look for is repetition of some sentence elements. In the five kernels above, for instance, the repetitions of *mall* and *looking* are clues that these elements will figure in the combination. As another example, consider this group of kernel sentences:

1. The office telephone rang.
2. The ringing was noisy.
3. The ringing was intrusive.
4. Catherine was annoyed by it.

Because *rang* and *ringing* are part of each of the first three sentences, you know that sentence combining will focus on those elements. Possibilities include:

> The office telephone rang noisily and intrusively, and Catherine was annoyed by it.
> Ringing noisily and intrusively, the office telephone annoyed Catherine.
> Because the office telephone rang noisily and intrusively, it annoyed Catherine.

All three versions involve taking the common element—*ringing*—from the first three kernels and moving the modifiers (*noisy* and *intrusive*) near it. Because each version uses *ring* as a verb, the adverbial forms of *noisy* and *intrusive* (*noisily* and *intrusively*) must be used. Sentence combining often involves such shifting of modifiers, whether they be words or phrases. Placing *suburban* in front of *mall* in the preceding group of kernels is another example. *Suburban* replaces "in the suburbs," because the phrase "the in-the-suburbs mall" is awkward.

A word of caution: The aim of sentence combining is not to force you to write only long sentences. A short sentence can often be both effective and necessary (see pp. 215-17). Rather, sentence combining encourages you to discover various alternative structures and to write sentences with appropriately mature structures. Use these structures *when you need them*—not necessarily all the time.

Sentence combining also encourages economy of style, in that combining the kernels nearly always reduces repetition. In the example on the preceding page, the three combined versions contain thirteen, nine, and eleven words respectively, compared to a total of seventeen words in the original four kernels. Thus, although each combined sentence is longer than any of the separate kernels, each expresses the idea of all the kernels in fewer total words, a desirable stylistic feature.

Exercise   Work through each of the following sentence-combining exercises. Read the kernels aloud. Then write out at least two versions of each exercise. Read your combinations aloud, too, and be certain that your combinations are grammatically correct and preserve the original meanings. Occasionally, to vary the lengths of your sentences or to add special emphasis, you may choose not to combine all the kernels in a group.

THE MALL

A.   1.   It was a holiday.
    2.   The mall was crowded.
    3.   The mall was in the suburbs.
    4.   Everyone was looking.
    5.   The looking was for bargains.

    6.   It was difficult.
    7.   The difficulty lay in walking through the mall area.
    8.   The mall area was jammed.
    9.   It got worse.

 *10.   The stores were also crowded.
  11.   Lines formed at the registers.
  12.   The lines were long.

  13.   The lines contained people.
  14.   The people were young.
  15.   The people were old.
  16.   The people were in-between.
  17.   The people were hot.

  18.   Sarah stood in a line.
  19.   Sarah wondered something.
  20.   The something was why she had bothered to come.

    *Sentences 10 through 17 can be combined into one sentence.

THE BIG MATCH

B.   1.   Even the observer could see something.
    2.   The something was the concentration on her brow.
    3.   The observer was casual.
    4.   The concentration was intense.

    5.   The two players were old rivals.
    6.   They had met many times before.
    7.   They were equally matched.

    8.   The atmosphere was electric.
    9.   The atmosphere was charged with tension.

10. The sun glared down.
11. The glaring was merciless.
12. Not a breeze disturbed the air.
13. The humidity was high.
14. The humidity was oppressive.

15. Beads formed on her brow.
16. Beads formed on her arms.
17. The beads were of sweat.
18. She traded shots with her opponent.
19. The shots were low.
20. The shots were long.
21. The shots were hard.

22. She was determined.
23. She would win this time.
24. She smashed her serve.
25. The ball skidded as it hit the service line.

26. The crowd applauded.
27. The applause was noisy.
28. The applause was enthusiastic.

29. The vendors did their business.
30. The business was brisk.
31. The heat parched everyone's throats.

32. She allowed herself something.
33. The something was a brief smile.
34. Her opponent's ball flew into the net.
35. The match was hers.

Suggestion for Writing

Write a paper in which you describe being in a place or at an event that is memorable to you. Try to make the place or the event as real to your reader as it is to you. Pay special attention to sentence structure, using the techniques we have described to structure or improve your sentences.

Using Parallelism

Parallelism refers to a similarity or correspondence in the form of two or more closely related sentence elements, whether at the level of word, phrase, clause, or sentence. In some cases, parallelism is essential for grammatical correctness. For instance, in the following sentence, the italicized words *must* be held parallel to each other in order to preserve proper grammar:

The four-year-old struggled to put on her own *shoes* and *socks*.

Shoes and socks are said to be parallel to each other in this case because both are nouns and both serve the same grammatical function. Failure to preserve parallelism in this case would result in bad grammar—and confused meaning:

> The four-year-old struggled to put on her own *shoes* and *quickly*.

In this example, *shoes*, a noun, and *quickly*, an adverb, do not serve the same function and so are not parallel.

Similarly, consider the following example:

> During my visit to Lake Placid, I enjoyed *skiing*, *skating*, and *to sled*.

Here *skiing* and *skating* are parallel to each other, but the third item, *to sled*, is not parallel with the other two. In this case, the nonparallel item is the right part of speech, a verb form (or verbal). But although *to sled* is a verb form like *skiing* and *skating*, it is not the *same* verb form: *skiing* and *skating* are present participles and *to sled* is an infinitive. To correct the grammar, *to sled* should be changed to *sledding*.

Using the same type of phrase is another way of achieving parallelism. Let's examine the following sentence:

> The server tossed the ball *with great care, with accuracy,* and *quickly*.

Here two prepositional phrases used as adverbs are joined to a one-word adverb, and so the three are not parallel. Changing *quickly* to *with some speed* produces this:

> The server tossed the ball *with great care, with unerring accuracy,* and *with some speed*.

Note, too, that *with* could be deleted to produce a parallel series of nouns modified by one-word adjectives:

> The server tossed the ball with *great care, unerring accuracy,* and *some speed*.

Or, simply, three one-word adverbs could be used:

> The server tossed the ball *carefully, accurately,* and *quickly*.

Achieving sentence maturity requires using parallelism correctly and so avoiding such ungrammatical structures (see p. 493 of the Handbook for more on parallelism and grammar). But, when applied to larger structures, parallelism can also refine and clarify meaning and improve style.

As you compose, look for related ideas that can be more efficiently grouped and ordered through parallel structure. For instance, here are two acceptable sentences:

> The taxi driver was confused by the poor directions.
> There were no road signs to help him, either.

By using parallelism, you can collapse the two into one, more compact sentence:

> The taxi driver was confused *by the poor directions*
>   and *by the lack of helpful road signs.*

The first version adequately conveys the meaning, but the second version is an improvement. By placing the idea of the second sentence parallel to an important idea in the first sentence, the second version refines the meaning for the reader. It makes clearer and more definite the relationship between the poor directions and the lack of road signs. They are now seen as two *equally important* factors contributing to the taxi driver's confusion. The writer of the second version has more clearly ordered the facts for the reader and has set up a pattern to express them more effectively.

Stylistically, too, the second version is better. Instead of presenting the content in two rather undistinguished sentences, it expresses it in one graceful and balanced sentence. Parallelism lends a pleasing balance and sophistication to writing. Picture an old-fashioned scale or balance. On the left side, we put the first phrase, "by the poor directions" (Figure 6.1). The phrase causes the left side of the scale to sink. So, to balance off this phrase, we put the parallel phrase, "by the lack of helpful road signs," on the right side (Figure 6.2). The conjunction *and* is the pivotal point on the balance. The patterning and balance achieved through parallelism are characteristics of sentence maturity.

Exercise

Rewrite the following, using parallelism to make each sentence clearer, balanced, and grammatically correct.

1. The woman's behavior clearly demonstrated that she is sensitive and her courage.
2. The Army wants you whether you are young or those who are old.
3. In my spare time I like to do macrame and restoring early American furniture.
4. The security guard asked the woman about the contents of her bag and what was her purpose in visiting. He also wanted to know how long she would stay.

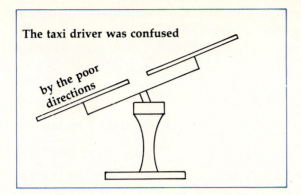

The taxi driver was confused

by the poor directions

Figure 6.1

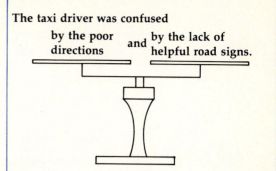

The taxi driver was confused

by the poor directions   and   by the lack of helpful road signs.

Figure 6.2

5. Notre Dame's fullback is both large and has a lot of power. He has excellent reflexes in addition.
6. To the weary sales representative, the cushions certainly did look soft. They were inviting.
7. The mechanic's hands were covered with sludge. There was also rusty, scaly dirt all over them.
8. If I can avoid careless mistakes, I will be able to answer most of the questions correctly. My grade will be at least a *B*. My parents will be thrilled.
9. Baseball has been called "a game of inches," but so has football. Basketball and hockey have been called that, too.
10. A recent study on the effects of TV violence indicates that watching violent cartoons encourages moderately aggressive behavior in some children. Truly violent behavior was found to result in the case of other children.

Parallelism can also occur between two or more separate sentences. Consider this example:

> If his clothing were within easy reach, my son would dress himself. If cereal or fruit were to be found, he would feed himself. If the other children's toys were scattered about, he would pick them up.

These three sentences are not only very similar in form, but also in word usage; there is a strong element of repetition from sentence to sentence. Such repetition is intended and desirable (unlike unneeded repetition of the type discussed on pp. 213–15). This parallel repetition gives the content or meaning greater emphasis and force than it would otherwise have. By using parallelism as a stylistic device, the writer piles up evidence to support the idea that her son is extremely self-reliant and responsible.

Many writers find that parallelism helps them attain elegance in their style. By using parallelism within or between sentences, or both, a writer can achieve a very sophisticated effect. Consider the following paragraph, for example:

At the base of boxing, there is something *so great* and *so grotesque, so pure* and *so corrupt,* it stirs you and makes you shudder. It is *undefinable as a passion* and *indefensible as a sport.* The *only way boxing can be discussed* is in the context of a caveman's sport, and the *only way it can be understood* is if you love this sport, God help you. ("Boxing Shadows: The Bittersweet Science," *Time*)

The arrows trace three instances of parallelism within these sentences. In the first sentence, there are four predicate adjectives, each modified by the adverb *so*, in a parallel series. Sentence two features two predicate adjectives (*undefinable, indefensible*), each followed by a prepositional phrase, linked by *and* to form a parallel series. Finally, the third sentence is composed of two independent clauses, the subjects of which are parallel to each other in form: "The only way [that] boxing can be discussed ... . the only [that] it can be understood. ..." (See also Chapter 3, pp. 96–98, which discusses parallelism as a means of achieving coherence within a paragraph.)

Exercise

Rewrite each of the following to achieve correct parallelism.

1. The jockey pulled sharply back on the reins, and "whoa" was shouted by her.
2. After a lengthy search, the Coast Guard announced that the diver was officially missing. They said he was presumed dead.
3. She appeared in a number of Broadway plays before she landed a major role. Through that role she achieved stardom.
4. When the air traffic controller saw a collision was about to occur, he took action. He averted a disaster.
5. When I worked at City Hospital, I witnessed many frightening instances of clerical mix-ups. Because of clerical mix-ups, emergency room patients were often left unattended for hours. Because of clerical mix-ups, necessary patient transfers were often delayed. Patients often were not given their medicine because their records were mislaid. Doctors even operated on the wrong people or performed the wrong operations on the right people because charts were misfiled.

ACHIEVING VARIETY

Sentence variety adds life and flair to writing—and is therefore a hallmark of good style. And variety is not difficult to achieve. Whether you concentrate on varying your sentences as you initially compose them, or whether you work for variety during revision—or both—you always do so by varying sentence openers, sentence length, and word order. We will focus on each of these methods singly, although all three are usually used together in achieving variety.

Varying Sentence Openers

A sentence opener may consist of only one word:

Green is my favorite color.

two words:

Each student brought something for show and tell.

or many words:

The majority of the senators voted against the bill.

The sentence opener in each of these examples is also the subject of the sentence. But a sentence opener need not be the subject:

After the show we wandered through the business district.

Most often the sentence opener is a word or a phrase, as in all of the above examples. But in a complex sentence, sometimes a whole clause is the sentence opener:

When the lightning struck, we were hiding in the cellar.

Achieving variety in sentence openers is important to good style. In fact, sentences that otherwise have flair and variety can seem totally monotonous solely because of the sameness of their openers:

(1) The final inspector on an engine assembly line has a great deal of responsibility. (2) For example, in certain cases the inspector must know by sight alone which items can pass and which need further testing. (3) This requires years of experience and a trained eye. (4) This is one of the things supervisors value most, along with the ability of the inspector to use precision instruments. (5) This can include micrometers, gauges and specialized machinery. (6) This job is so important because if it is not done right, the efforts of all the plant's other employees could be wasted.

This paragraph is not so poorly written, except that its style becomes monotonous. The openers in the first three sentences are fine ("The final inspector . . .," "For example . . .," and "This requires . . ."), but sentence 4 begins the pattern of monotony by repeating the opener used in sentence 3: "This . . . ." Thereafter, every sentence opens with the same word. (Notice the distinction between *unwanted* repetition like this and *intentional* repetition to achieve parallelism, discussed earlier in the chapter.) Simply by changing some of the problem openers we can improve the paragraph:

> (1) The final inspector on an engine assembly line has a great deal of responsibility. (2) For example, in certain cases the inspector must know by sight alone which items can pass and which need further testing. (3) This requires years of experience and a trained eye, qualities which supervisors value most, along with the ability of the inspector to use precision instruments. (4) Inspection tools that must be mastered can include micrometers, gauges, and specialized machinery. (5) The inspector's job is so important because if it is not done right, the efforts of all the plant's other employees could be wasted.

By combining sentences 3 and 4 and substituting new words for the repetitive *this* in sentences 5 and 6 of the original version, we eliminate the monotony and achieve variety in the sentence openers.

We can also improve sentences that have repetitive openers by pulling a phrase or clause out of a sentence and moving it to the opening position. Consider this sequence:

> (1) On my first visit to the clinic the doctor discovered that I had diabetes. (2) He explained to me that my case was not severe. (3) He said that new medications have been developed in recent years, making the outlook for diabetes patients much brighter. (4) He told me I wouldn't need to take daily insulin shots like my aunt has done for most of her life. (5) He cautioned me, however, that this was no reason to take my condition lightly.

As in the paragraph on engine inspectors, the sentences in this paragraph are not poorly written except that their openers are much too similar. Sentences 2 through 5 all begin with *he*. Moreover, each *he* is followed directly by a simple past tense verb (*explained, told, said, cautioned*). It is good that each of the past tense verbs is different—if they were all *said*, the monotony would be much greater. But the fact that their form is similar contributes to the repetitive effect created by the series of "*He* . . ." openers: "He explained . . . He said . . . He told . . . He continued."

We can eliminate the monotony by reaching into alternating sentences and moving a phrase or word to the beginning of the sentence:

(1) On my first visit to the clinic the doctor discovered that I had diabetes. (2) He explained to me that my case was fortunately not severe. (3) *In recent years*, he said, new medications have been developed, making the outlook for diabetes patients much brighter. (4) He told me I wouldn't need to take daily insulin shots like my aunt has done for most of her life. (5) *However*, he cautioned me that this was no reason to take my condition lightly.

Only two minor changes were made to rectify the problem of repetitive openers in four consecutive sentences: The phrase "in recent years" was made the opener of sentence 3, and "however" was moved to the beginning of sentence 5. In these two paragraphs, then, we have changed monotonous sentence openers by (1) combining the sentence with the sentence that precedes it; (2) changing the repetitive opening word itself to a different word; and (3) moving a word or phrase from the middle or end of the sentence into opening position. Remember these techniques and use them as you write and revise.

Exercise

The openers in each of these groups of sentences may or may not need to be varied. Decide whether the openers lack variety and suggest appropriate changes for the ones that do.

1. The hogs are first loaded onto the ramp. The hogs are then given a cold shower. The hogs are sent into a holding pen after they are dried off.
2. Since it began in the mid-sixties, New Journalism has grown in popularity. At first only colorful figures like Tom Wolfe and Truman Capote practiced it. Now practically every small town daily in America has at least one New Journalist on its staff.
3. I first saw *King Kong* when I was seven years old. I have seen it probably a hundred times since then. I am still greatly moved by the death of the great ape.
4. The car plowed through the giant puddle. The car sent murky water in all directions.
5. After the dance they stopped at the Rathskeller. After that they had a nightcap at the Tap House. After that they called it an evening.

Varying Sentence Length

We've seen that when the openers of two consecutive sentences are repetitive, it is not necessary to change both of them to achieve variety—changing one or the other will do. Variety is a relative quality stemming from a difference between or among sentences. To achieve variety in sentence length, you can occasionally include sentences that are shorter or longer than most of the others. What is *short* and what is *long* is determined, in part, by the length of your *average* or normal sentence. Examine this paragraph from F. Scott Fitzgerald's *The Great Gatsby*, in which the narrator attempts to analyze Gatsby's feelings on being reunited with Daisy:

> (1) As I went over to say good-by I saw that the expression of bewilderment had come back into Gatsby's face, as though a faint doubt had occurred to him as to the quality of his present happiness. (2) Almost five years! (3) There must have been moments even that afternoon when Daisy tumbled short of his dreams—not through her own fault, but because of the colossal vitality of his illusion. (4) It had gone beyond her, beyond everything. (5) He had thrown himself into it with a creative passion, adding to it all the time, decking it out with every bright feather that drifted his way. (6) No amount of fire or freshness can challenge what a man will store up in his ghostly heart.

This passage begins with a long complex sentence of 37 words and a short, emphatic fragment of only 3 words. The third sentence is quite long (29 words), whereas sentence 4 is very short (7 words). The paragraph concludes with another long-short combination, 27 words in sentence 5 and 18 words in sentence 6.

In this excerpt from *A Farewell to Arms*, Ernest Hemingway, a contemporary of Fitzgerald, also uses a variety of sentence lengths. Here the character Frederic Henry nervously passes the time at a café while awaiting word from the hospital about the condition of his lover:

> (1) I drank another beer. (2) There was quite a pile of saucers now on the table in front of me. (3) The man opposite me had taken off his spectacles, put them away in his pocket and now sat holding his liquor glass and looking out at the room. (4) Suddenly I knew I had to get back. (5) I called the waiter, paid the reckoning, got into my coat, put on my hat and started out the door. (6) I walked through the rain up to the hospital.

Note that although Hemingway's sentences are on the average shorter than Fitzgerald's (the average length is 15 words per sentence as compared to 20 words per sentence in the Fitzgerald paragraph), he still builds variety into the length of his sentences:

SENTENCE	NUMBER OF WORDS
1	4
2	15
3	37
4	8
5	20
6	9

In general, you should use longer-than-average sentences to express rather complicated thoughts or to join together a series of thoughts. All such sentences require that you use one or more of the devices we have discussed earlier in this chapter; you will take the basic sentence and add some combination of words, phrases, and clauses, and you will likely make use of left-branching, right-branching, and embedding—singly or in combination. And you will usually use shorter sentences to create emphasis or make an impact, as in Fitzgerald's "Almost five years!" Ordinarily, your shorter-than-average sentences will follow the basic, unelaborated pattern discussed at the beginning of this chapter, a pattern used in the final sentence of the following sequence:

> Both authors write about people attempting to relive a past which they instinctively know to be gone. Unfortunately, the characters in both stories must go to a lot of trouble to learn the hard way that the old days cannot be recovered. *The past is dead.*

Here the main point is given extra impact through a short, basic sentence.

_____

Exercise   For each of the following, decide whether sentence variety would best be achieved by adding a short sentence or a long sentence, and then add that sentence.

1. Most people realize that a hobby is useful for relieving the stress generated by daily confrontations in today's high-pressure society. However, finding a hobby to take up when you are not really interested in anything can be a problem. Why try fishing if you really don't like the outdoors, or stamp collecting if you find that concentrating on all that small print gives you a headache? _____ _____.

2. Practice makes perfect. That's what my German teacher always said. However, he said it in German, a language I could never master. I tried to practice. Then came test time. _____.

3. When I was younger I was sure that all people were good at heart and that, if you only gave them the chance, they would prove their goodness. _____. I have since become a good deal more worldly and cynical on the subject of human nature.

_____

Varying Word Order   Earlier we examined the basic sentence and the idea of normal word order (the "subject first, then verb" pattern). We also outlined some ways of refining and elaborating upon this pattern. But even when you refine and expand the basic sentence in desirable ways (by left-branching, coordinating, and so on), you must take care that the finished sentences in any given paragraph do not resemble each other too closely in form. Consider the following student paragraph, for example. Although the writer has elaborated on the basic pattern in all sentences, there is still a problem—the sentences lack variety because they are all right-branching:

> (1) The Oberlin Conservatory of Music is a beautiful, well designed edifice conducive to the creation of music. (2) Its corridors are filled with every variety of instrumental sound. (3) Practice room windows reveal enclosed gardens, as well as musicians working in other rooms. (4) One is taken by the feeling of unity with both nature and peers. (5) The lounges are places to discuss future productions of great musical works. (6) Each person experiences anticipation and excitement in displaying a love of music. (7) The Oberlin Conservatory provides a perfect atmosphere for the development of musicians and the performance of great music.

In each sentence, an opening subject-verb core is followed by a right-branching series of added phrases. In fact, except for sentences 4 and 7, each sentence adds precisely two phrases to the base sentence. The result is a feeling of sameness as we read from sentence to sentence.

Because all of the sentences develop with right branching, the form of the sentence openers also repeats. Each sentence looks roughly like this:

subject + verb + (object) + phrase group

Every sentence starts with its subject-verb core. To achieve variety in the paragraph, the writer could make some sentences left-branching instead of right-branching. Doing this would break up the right-branching monotony while simultaneously bringing variety to the sentence openers. For example, sentences 6 and 7 currently have this repetitive form:

subject	+	verb	+	object	+
(6) Each person		experiences		anticipation and excitement	in

phrase group		subject	+
displaying a love of music.	(7) The Oberlin Conservatory		pro-

verb +	object	+	phrase group
vides	a perfect atmosphere		for the development of musicians

and the performance of great music.

They could be rewritten as follows:

$$\text{phrase group} \quad + \quad \text{subject} \quad + \quad \text{verb}$$

(6) ⌐In displaying a love of music,¬ ⌐each person¬ ⌐experiences¬

$$+ \quad \text{object} \quad\quad\quad \text{subject} \quad\quad + \quad \text{verb}$$

⌐anticipation and excitement.¬ (7)⌐The Oberlin Conservatory¬ ⌐provides¬

$$+ \quad \text{object} \quad\quad + \quad\quad\quad \text{phrase group}$$

⌐a perfect atmosphere¬ ⌐for the development of musicians and the

performance of great music.¬

Now these sentences differ not only in that one is left-branching and the other is right branching, but also in that the form of their openers varies.

Another technique for achieving sentence variety is the inversion of normal subject-verb word order:

$$\text{V} \quad + \quad\quad \text{S}$$
Out <u>went</u> the <u>deal</u>.

Normal word order is used most often because it works so well in so many situations. Inverting the order too often can make you feel like you're standing on your head:

Out <u>went</u> the <u>deal</u>. <u>Angry</u> was the <u>client</u>. <u>Drove</u> home and <u>soaked</u> in a hot tub <u>I</u>. Then <u>wrote</u> a new résumé <u>I</u>.

But an occasional inversion of normal subject-verb order can give variety and interest to your sentences. For instance, we can rewrite sentence 3 of the student paragraph above like this:

$$\quad\quad\quad\quad\quad\quad\quad\quad\quad\quad \text{V} \quad + \quad\quad\quad \text{S}$$
Through the practice room windows <u>can be seen</u> enclosed <u>gardens</u> and
$$\quad \text{S}$$
<u>musicians</u> working in other rooms.

Using verb-then-subject order adds variety to the style.

Exercise   In each of the following, comment on sameness or lack of variety in sentence patterning and then make suggestions for achieving variety.

1. The rat had to wait for the proper signal. He would then push the button in the prescribed manner. A pellet of food would appear within thirty seconds. The signal would soon reappear to start the next test.

2. At the last dance class of the winter season, he confessed his love. Amid the coats and umbrellas in the cloakroom he took her aside. In the romantic atmosphere of the evening, she agreed to be his. With the orchestra playing "Anniversary Waltz" over and over, they danced the night away.

3. The little boy had always wanted a hat like his father's. He had finally persuaded his father to buy him one only a week earlier. The rising wind had now caught him unprepared with his arms full of packages. The hat blew away, rolling along on its brim and turning over and over.

REVISING SENTENCES

In most of this chapter, we have been discussing how to revise sentences: Achieving sentence maturity and achieving sentence variety obviously involve revising ineffective sentences into more effective ones. But let's examine revision more closely.

We have stressed that revision is an integral, ongoing part of the writing process, not an optional, detachable feature. Whether you revise as you compose, after you have finished a rough draft, or both, view your revision attempt seriously; revision is as time consuming as it is necessary. It is not a sign of weakness or a form of punishment, but rather a fact of the writer's life.

Sentence Revision: Style and Meaning

In considering how to shape effective sentences, we have discussed making improvements in the areas of meaning and style. Yet many people consider a distinction between meaning (what is being said) and style (how it is being said) to be artificial and invalid. They maintain that the style of a written utterance is inextricably linked to the meaning produced, and that changing the style in some way (however slightly) changes the meaning. Consider, for instance, these sentences:

> I returned to college on the train, and I resolved to seek admission to the new computer science program.
>
> Returning to college on the train, I resolved to seek admission to the new computer science program.

At first glance, these sentences seem to mean the same thing. But using the participle *returning* to modify *I*, instead of retaining the form "I returned . . . and . . . I resolved," leads to a somewhat different meaning. In the second sentence the resolution to apply to the computer science program was almost certainly formed on the train. In the first sentence, returning and resolving were discrete actions, and the resolution was more likely formed once the student was back on campus.

On the other hand, many authorities, while conceding some truth to the inseparability of style and meaning, believe it is possible to choose different words or phrases that for all practical purposes say the same thing. For instance, is there any difference in meaning between the following two sentences?

I like to read.
I like reading.

The purist who insists that style and meaning are inseparable might argue that there is a difference: The second sentence could refer to liking reading as a concept, as a subject area, as an area of human activity. The first sentence, however, could only refer to liking reading as a personal process. But in most cases, the second utterance would also be used to refer to liking reading as a personal process, and so, for all practical purposes, the two utterances do mean the same thing.

Of course, in your revisions you will often purposely change wording to refine meaning. But you will also find that revising to improve your sentence style alone without significantly altering meaning is often both possible and desirable.

Exercise

Explain any differences in meaning in the following pairs of sentences.

1. The man who came to dinner happened to be my father.
   My father happened to come to dinner.
2. The music of the fifties holds a lot of special memories for me.
   I remember the music of the fifties fondly.
3. That I could still lose all my winnings on the last horse race was not a happy thought.
   I was in despair at the possibility of losing all my winnings on the last horse race.
4. Going home to New England for Thanksgiving is a family tradition.
   The members of my family always return to New England for Thanksgiving.
5. The U.S. hockey team's performance in the 1980 Olympics was incredible.
   The U.S. hockey team played magnificently in the 1980 Olympics.

Sentence Combining Earlier, we used sentence combining as an exercise in writing longer and
in Revision more complicated sentences. Sentence-combining techniques can also
be used in revision. As you reread your work, get into the habit of
looking for sentences that can be combined. For instance, two sentences
in a row that begin with the same subject should usually be combined:

> She composed the speech quickly. She refined her thoughts as she
> wrote.

Revised She composed the speech quickly, refining her thoughts as she
wrote.
Composing the speech quickly, she refined her thoughts as she wrote.

Notice that the revisions result in a smoother, more sophisticated style
without significantly altering the meaning.

Similarly, a series of simple sentences with the same subject can be
combined into one simple sentence with a compound verb:

> Last summer on the farm I cleaned the stalls. I helped with the
> milking. I also fed the pigs.

Revised Last summer on the farm I cleaned the stalls, helped with the milking,
and fed the pigs.

Consecutive sentences can also be combined when the first sentence
ends with the subject of the second sentence:

> The award was given to the young lifeguard. She saved the swimmer's
> life at great risk to her own.

Revised The award was given to the young lifeguard who saved the swimmer's
life at great risk to her own.

Combining by using the relative pronoun *who* reduces the choppiness of
the original sentences.

Coordination and subordination, discussed earlier as means of
refining and elaborating the basic sentence (pp. 199–202), are also useful
revision techniques. Frequently, two rather short, simple sentences will
read more effectively as a single compound sentence:

> The chair has two removable cushions. The armrests are thickly
> padded.

Revised The chair has two removable cushions, and the armrests are thickly
padded.

Even though the grammatical subjects of the sentences were different
(*chair* and *armrests*), both short sentences were about the chair, and by
combining them the idea is expressed more efficiently.

Similarly, combining through subordination will generally make clearer a relationship between short sentences, a relationship that perhaps you have taken for granted:

> I was born in 1958. My dad sold our Oldsmobile in 1961. I must have been three years old.

Revised Since I was born in 1958, I must have been three years old when my dad sold our Oldsmobile in 1961.

Here, three simple sentences are combined into one complex sentence by using two subordinating conjunctions, *since* and *when*, and again the stylistic effect of the revision is more pleasing.

Exercise Revise each of the following by combining the separate sentences into one.

1. In her bestselling novel, she writes about social unrest. She tries to shed light on its causes.
2. Turning the corner, I saw that my path was blocked by a tall fence. The fence stretched from one end of the complex to the other.
3. Air fares were raised last June. Traffic is down about 12 percent.
4. The boxer glared at his opponent. He refused to shake hands. He turned his back.
5. The girl insisted that she was hungry for a hamburger. She begged her father to stop at the next fast-food restaurant.

Editing Strategies and Techniques Although revision in general is an ongoing process that cuts across all stages of the writing process, editing for style and correctness usually occurs after you have written a draft of a paper. You may do some editing as you actually compose. But usually that editing is not enough because it lacks one ingredient vital to the editing process: distance from the material. When we are too close to something, we are unable to judge it objectively, to see it as others would. Effective editing requires distance. You can use these three techniques to gain distance:

1. Let the draft sit before editing it.

2. Pretend you are someone else when you edit.

3. Edit for correctness by reading from the last sentence in the paper toward the first sentence.

Letting the draft sit before editing it allows you to gain distance *in time* from your sentences. Most writers, when they have just finished a piece, have a sense of pride in it. And at this point the natural tendency is to reread the paper uncritically because it seems to be an extension of the writer's self. Crossing out a sentence amounts to criticizing oneself. By letting your draft sit before editing it, however, you begin to forget what you said and how you said it. And then when you come back to it, you can approach the editing of your prose more objectively. The writing will appear somewhat new and strange, more like something written by someone else. But this approach takes time. Ideally, you should allow a day or two to pass before returning to your draft to edit it.

The second strategy calls for you to pretend that you are someone else when reading your draft. Instead of creating distance in time, this approach tries to create a distance *in attitude* immediately. You can avoid the time delay of the first technique by using this method. But you must pretend that you are a skeptical reader, thereby allowing yourself to cut through the obstacle of self-pride. (For a fuller discussion of this technique, see pp. 176–78.)

These two editing strategies will help you gain the distance needed to revise sentences for meaning and style. The third strategy, reading from the last sentence to the first, can help you edit for correctness in sentence constructions. Reading your sentences in reverse order spotlights the grammar of each sentence by distancing you from the overall meaning of your piece. Reading the draft in normal order gives a sense of forward-moving meaning, which may distract you from grammatical problems. Consider this example:

> It is hard to decide whether to buy an American car or a foreign car. At first it seems an easy choice because the foreign cars are better made and more maneuverable. Whereas the American cars are shoddily made and awkward to handle. Still, I like the American cars because they are more comfortable and cheaper to maintain. There used to be a big difference in initial cost, but now the prices are about the same.

You may have failed to notice that the third sentence is a fragment. But reading from the last sentence to the first helps isolate the grammar by deemphasizing overall meaning:

> There used to be a big difference in initial cost, but now the prices are about the same. Still, I like the American cars because they are more comfortable and cheaper to maintain. Whereas the American cars are shoddily made and awkward to handle. At first it seems an easy choice because the foreign cars are better made and more maneuverable. It is hard to decide whether to buy an American car or a foreign car.

Now the grammar of each sentence stands out more clearly. It is easier to see that "Whereas the American cars . . ." is a fragment when the sentence that precedes it ("At first it seems . . .") is not there to give it a meaningful context.

Exercise

Describe your approach to editing in as much detail as you can. What do you do first? What next? How do you decide whether a specific sentence needs revising or editing? Interview one other person (a friend, instructor, roommate, relative) to find out how he or she edits and describe that person's approach, using the same format you used in writing about your own.

Suggestions for Writing

Write an essay in which you focus on one thing you have learned since beginning college. You might discuss something you have learned about yourself, a friend, human relationships, or an academic subject. If you feel that you have not learned anything important, then write an essay explaining why you haven't.

During invention, be sure to determine not only your ideas but also your purposes in writing, and to analyze your readers' needs or expectations. You might want to use the patterns discussed in Chapter 4 to aid you in generating and structuring your ideas.

Once you have produced a rough draft, put it aside for a few days. Then reexamine it, paying special attention to the sentences you have composed and employing the revision techniques we have suggested. Turn in to your instructor examples of sentence-level revisions you have made, along with the finished paper.

chapter 7

USING WORDS
EFFECTIVELY

In the last chapter we discussed the sentence as a whole unit. Next we will examine the words and phrases that make up the sentence. As in Chapter 6, many of the topics we will discuss in this chapter are examined in more detail in the Handbook.

BASIC DICTION: Good writing is economical and concise, expressing an idea in the fewest
ACHIEVING possible words. Consider this sentence from a government document:
ECONOMY

> At this stage, the guidance counselor will help the student in making application for admission to the colleges that the student and the counselor believe are well suited to the student in terms of the student's needs, abilities, and goals.

The vocabulary of this sentence is not unusual—every word is a familiar one. But the sentence is not economical. First, it uses a long phrase where a shorter one will do:

> help the student ~~in making application for admission~~ to the colleges

Second, the sentence includes unnecessary words—words that contain no new information:

> well suited to ~~the student in terms of~~ the student's needs

By dropping the unnecessary words and by changing the long phrase to a shorter one, we can produce a revised version:

> At this stage, the guidance counselor will help the student apply to the colleges that the student and the counselor believe are well suited to the student's needs, abilities, and goals.

This sentence is clearer, and we have sacrificed none of its content.

But we can revise even further. We already know that guidance counselors help students by talking with them and determining their "needs, abilities, and goals," and so the long relative clause beginning with *that* is unnecessary. By deleting the entire relative clause and inserting the words *most suitable* before *colleges*, we can reduce the original to:

> At this stage, the guidance counselor will help the student apply to the most suitable colleges.

This final version is even clearer and more direct.

To write economically and concisely, you must be sure that each of your sentences makes a clear and definite point. Reexamine this sentence from Chapter 1:

The inspiring likelihood that beings of superior intellect are flourishing on celestial bodies other than earth has been made gloriously manifest to this author.

One problem with this sentence is that it is very wordy. Here is an improved version:

It is likely that intelligent life exists elsewhere in the universe.

This sentence is preferable because it makes its statement directly.

If you have a tendency to write wordy sentences, you can economize by reducing each sentence (usually as you revise and edit) to its basic subject-verb core form. For every sentence, ask yourself, "What is the simplest form of the statement I'm making here?" For instance, consider the following sentence, taken from an announcement of a job opening:

The duties falling to the incumbent mathematics instructor will include assisting the Dean in designating and implementing procedures for ascertaining effectiveness of the program of mathematics studies.

We can reduce it to its simplest form like this:

The new instructor will help the Dean evaluate the mathematics program.

Here's the point: When you reduce a wordy sentence to its simplest form, you will realize just how wordy it is, and you will see how to make it clearer and more concise.

Exercise

Review the following sentences for wordiness and write more economical versions. You may wish to use the technique of reducing the sentence to its simplest form.

1. I learned immediately from the grocery store manager about her expectations in terms of my satisfactory discharging of obligations on the job.
2. Referring to the job description, she observed that the employee in all cases must avoid any activities that might lead to any failure to continue the competent performance of duties.
3. The job description further noted that clerks engaged in the handling and display of stock merchandise during high-traffic periods must have shelves replenished in a timely manner.
4. Those clerks designated as responsible for transfer of stock items to grocery bags at check stations must comport themselves as courteous-

ly as deemed possible, regardless of negative attitudes on the part of the customer.

5. Clerks charged with transporting customer orders to automobiles are expressly forbidden any acceptance of gratuities.

6. The mayor now regards as unwise his decision to accept campaign funds not allowed by law.

7. The mayor's acceptance of illegal campaign funds will likely impact negatively upon his plans to pursue a seat in the Senate.

8. In all probability the school bus did not make its stop at the scheduled time due to the unanticipated failure of essential mechanical components.

9. Because the school bus failed to arrive at the appointed time, instruction could not proceed at the hour prescribed by regulations.

10. Although the majority of the teachers were perturbed by the delay of classes, most of their youthful charges welcomed this variation in their daily routine.

USING PLAIN LANGUAGE

Another way to streamline your sentences is to use plain language. Reducing wordy sentences to their basic subject-verb core is much easier when you use plain, everyday words in constructing your simplest forms.

To understand better the idea of plain language, consider this sentence again:

> The inspiring likelihood that beings of superior intellect are flourishing on celestial bodies other than earth has been made gloriously manifest to this author.

Not only is this sentence wordy, as we have noted, but it is also filled with ornate—and inappropriate—language. "Inspiring likelihood . . . beings of superior intellect . . . flourishing . . . celestial bodies other than earth . . . gloriously manifest . . ."—all these fancy words and phrases get in the way of the meaning. By using plain language, we can revise the sentence to read:

> It is likely that intelligent life exists elsewhere in the universe.

Or, even more clearly:

> I believe that human life exists on other planets.

What exactly is "plain language"? In large part, it consists of basic, everyday words that all English speakers could use in all situations. It is not the same as overly informal or slang usage, and it is not learned or specialized language. Here are some typical plain words:

VERBS	NOUNS
buy	bed
come	car
go	food
take	home
talk	job
try	sky
walk	thought

These words would be appropriate in either a scholarly treatise or a streetcorner conversation. Obviously you cannot write a whole paper using only such plain, basic words. But you can use these words in place of longer, fancier ones when you are trying to pare down a wordy sentence. For instance, when you are striving for economy by reducing sentences to their simplest forms, remember that it is better to "buy" something than to "acquire" it; better to "try" than to "make the attempt"; better to "talk" than to "vocalize"; better to "take" than to "appropriate"; and better to "walk" or "go" than to "peregrinate." Likewise, it is better to talk about a "car" than a "vehicle" or "conveyance"; better to discuss "food" than "nourishment"; and better to refer to one's "home," than to one's "residence."

We don't intend to belittle specialized or learned vocabulary; such a vocabulary has many legitimate uses. But we do want to note that plain language is nearly always appropriate and useful and economical. For instance, using *purchase* instead of *buy* is altogether acceptable and would not by itself lead you away from economical writing. But don't underestimate the value of *buy*. In many cases it's just as good, even if not quite as fancy.

The use of plain language also involves the question of *tone*—that is, the attitudes and level of formality expressed in your writing. For instance, using *purchase* makes a sentence only slightly more formal in tone than using *buy*. But using *peregrinate* instead of *walk* radically changes the tone.

Exercise

Replace each of the following words or phrases with a single plain word.

1. utilize   *USE*
2. bestow upon   *GIVE*
3. contemplate   *FINISH*
4. consume   *EAT*
5. render inoperative   *BREAK*
6. illumination device   *FLASHLIGHT*
7. conflagration   *FIRE*

8. vestibule *Room*
9. chronometer *CLOCK*
10. remuneration *to NUMBER*

USING DENOTATION AND CONNOTATION

She was too cheap to take a vacation.
She was too frugal to take a vacation.

Both of these sentences comment on a person's tendency to watch carefully how she spends her money. And yet, the writer of each has a different perspective, and each sentence is intended to stimulate a different response in the reader. The writer of the first sentence, by choosing to use the word *cheap*, criticizes the person, while the writer of the second, by calling the person "frugal," praises her. Both writers hope the reader will recognize not only the dictionary meanings of *cheap* and *frugal* but also their respective negative and positive associations.

Dictionary meanings of words are called *denotations*; all the attitudes and feelings, positive and negative, that constitute a reader's reaction to a word are its *connotations*. Ideally, connotations act together with denotations to help ensure that the writer's intended meaning will be transmitted to the reader. In our examples above, *cheap* and *frugal* have similar denotations, but the connotations are quite different, as we have seen. Connotations are particularly important when you compose papers that are meant to be persuasive, since you can select words with positive connotations to argue for something and those with negative connotations to argue against something.

But even when your paper is not directly persuasive (in the sense of arguing one side of an issue), you do want your readers to react favorably to whatever you write. Using denotation and connotation correctly and effectively can help ensure that.

Let's examine denotation more closely. Be sure that the words you use in fact denote what you think they do. Memorable characters from Mrs. Malaprop to Jimmy Durante to Archie Bunker have misapplied words quite comically: "I looked into their windows through high-powered *spectaculars*," says Archie. But you're not in college to write comic scripts, and so you must be certain that you understand the dictionary meanings of the words you use.

Furthermore, by misusing denotations, you not only confuse and mislead your reader, but also undermine your credibility. Use a few words incorrectly and the reader may decide that the content of your paper is as weak as your use of the language; your reader will not accept your ideas or argument. In general, then, do not use a word if you're unsure of its denotations and cannot determine its dictionary meaning.

Sometimes a problem with denotation occurs because two words that have different meanings sound or are spelled very much alike—for example, *effect* and *affect*, or *accept* and *except*. The Glossary (pp. 520–37) contains other commonly confused pairs of words and their definitions. Memorize as many of these as you can, and you will avoid such problems with denotation.

Using connotations to your advantage is more difficult. The connotations of a word will vary somewhat from person to person because they are partly determined by a person's background, nationality, education, age, and other characteristics. Thus the same word may have positive connotations for one person and negative ones for another. For example, suppose you broke your leg the first time you went skiing. That painful experience convinced you to stay off skis forever. For you, *ski* has unpleasant connotations. But for a person who is an excellent skier and who never had a serious injury while skiing, the word *ski* is all delight.

If you wrote, "The only thing worse than skiing is writing a term paper," that ski buff would not understand what you mean. You would have to choose another word to be sure your meaning was clearly expressed. Likewise, when you are using a word that is part of an emotionally-charged issue, be sure you know your readers well enough to predict correctly the connotations such words hold for them.

Fortunately, a large body of words carry fairly predictable, built-in connotations that hold true for most people. For instance, consider the differences in connotations between the italicized pairs of words in these sentences:

The officer *peered intently* at the troops and *issued* a command.
The officer *glared* at the troops and *barked* a command.

Although *peered intently* and *glared* both denote that the officer looked at the troops, the connotations of these words are different. *Peered intently* conveys to us that the officer's action was businesslike, while *glared* suggests an emotional and hostile look. Similarly, although *issued* and *barked* both denote that the officer *spoke*, they have widely differing connotations. *Issued* suggests a calm, direct approach, whereas *barked* suggests hostility and even savagery.

Although the associations of words may vary from person to person, you can often predict connotations accurately with only a minimal knowledge of your reader. For instance, for most people reared in capitalist countries the word *communist* has negative connotations and for most communists *capitalist* has negative connotations. Many Americans enjoy some type of sports; consequently, *sports* has generally positive connotations. The word *homicide* has negative connotations; but note the shift in meaning in the phrase "justifiable homicide": The reader's positive response toward the first word overrides a negative response toward the second.

As we have already noted, connotations are particularly important in persuasive communications. They are an excellent tool for adding impact to what you say without adding additional words.

You can use connotations to your advantage in constructing an argument in at least two ways. First, you can use words that you are fairly certain have particular associations for nearly everyone—words like *homicide* and the others we mentioned above. Choose those whose connotations—positive or negative—reinforce the side of the issue you are arguing. Second, choose words whose associations for your audience you *predict* will match your argument. This is more risky because you must know your readers in order to guess correctly, but it is a risk you must take. Lessen it by learning as much as you can about your readers first.

As an example of what we've just said, let's assume you're writing an essay supporting your country's involvement in a war. In arguing for the involvement, you can appeal to certain values that possess positive connotations for your readers. You can say, for instance, that *honor* or *integrity* is at stake. You can argue that *security* must be maintained. These values have nearly universally positive associations and thereby will reinforce your argument. Your hope is that invoking them will influence even those readers who disagree with your position.

To a large extent, then, word meanings reside in the individuals using them. Consider only the denotations of words and you're not using them as effectively as you could. There is a world of difference between *slim* and *skinny*, even though their denotations are similar. To write effectively, consider what a dictionary tells you and also be sensitive to how those around you react to words.

Exercise

1. Prepare a list of ten or more words that have strong connotations, positive or negative, for you. Be ready to explain how you formed your reactions to each word. Compare your list with those of classmates.

2. Read through the following list of words. Do any of them have fairly predictable connotations? Why? Can the connotation of others vary somewhat? What types of audiences would perceive those in a given way?

   a. advertising
   b. baby
   c. book
   d. freedom
   e. poverty

f. security
g. politician
h. television
i. equality
j. housewife
k. rain
l. blonde
m. sensitive
n. redneck
o. homemade

Suggestion for Writing

Assume that enrollments at your college have been declining and so the school has hired a public relations firm to produce a new brochure. Anyone asking about admission to the college will receive this brochure. The public relations firm has decided that a good way to sell the college is to ask current students to write about their positive experiences. You are the first student selected, and so you can choose to write about any of these four areas: (1) the attractiveness and/or convenience of the campus and its buildings; (2) the strength and/or diversity of the curriculum; (3) the variety and/or quality of extracurricular activities; or (4) the resourcefulness and/or helpfulness of the people (faculty, students, administrators). You can write your statement in either an essay or letter format. Because your task is to encourage your audience to apply to your school, be especially aware of the connotations of the words you choose.

USING ABSTRACT WORDS AND CONCRETE WORDS

Another way to use language effectively is to employ abstract words and concrete words appropriately. Abstract words refer to intangible qualities or actions, concepts that cannot be perceived by the five senses:

NOUNS

fear
glory
honor
love
morality

ADJECTIVES

glorious
honorable
noble
sinful

VERBS

(to) appreciate
(to) desire
(to) repent
(to) respect

ADVERBS

impressively
honorably
hatefully
lovingly

Concrete words refer to tangible things—objects, qualities, or actions that are physically evident:

NOUNS	ADJECTIVES
bed	cloudy
easy chair	costly
crystal goblet	loud
lamp	red
living room	sharp
smile	tearful
station wagon	wet

VERBS	ADVERBS
(to) cry	loudly
(to) grab	laughingly
(to) hit	quietly
(to) jump	lazily
(to) laugh	noisily
(to) pour	sleepily
(to) shoot	softly

In one sense, the notions *abstract* and *concrete* may seem to be *absolute*—something is either tangible or intangible, physically perceptible or imperceptible. In reality, however, there are degress of abstraction and concreteness. For instance, *chair* is a concrete term. But the chair in the first sentence below is not as concrete as the chair in the second:

A *chair* is a piece of furniture that comes in many different shapes and sizes.

I collapsed on the *red easy chair in my living room.*

Similarly, a concrete term such as *children* can be very concrete—"I laughed loudly as *my children* ran up and started tickling me"—or barely concrete—"*Children* should be seen and not heard." In the latter case, the word is used so generally that it is practically an abstraction—that is, it makes no reference to any *particular* children.

Abstract words also vary in the degree of their abstractness. In the sentence "*Love* conquers all," the word *love* is highly abstract. Yet in the sentence "At the dance David's *love* for Mary was apparent to all," the love is not quite so abstract; it is somehow perceptible to those watching the couple on the dance floor. Notice that as statements get more *specific,* the words they contain (whether these words are abstract or concrete to begin with) tend to become more *concrete,* and as statements get more *general,* the words they contain tend to become more *abstract.*

Exercise

1. Label the following words as either abstract or concrete.

ant	nose
bleach (noun)	outrageous
consideration	cunningly
deliberate (adj.)	pardonable
essential	qualified (adj.)
football	recreation
harshly	sit
gripe (verb)	think
hotel	ugly
implicit	happily
jazz	valid
kite	water
lemonade	xerox (verb)
manageable	youthful
warmly	zest

2. Some of the following sentences are more general than the others. Pick out the words that change in their degree of abstraction or concreteness depending on how general the sentence is.

   a. Out-of-town conventions are usually enjoyable, but with today's prices it's a hardship to pay for your own travel, lodging and food.
   b. At the National Science Fiction Society Convention held last November in Dallas, the hotel room cost me $75 a night.
   c. Coffee shops are no longer inexpensive places to get a quick snack.
   d. My first lunch at the hotel coffee shop was a shocker: $18.35 for a "Burger Supreme" with french fries, coffee, and dessert.
   e. Because of my tight schedule and my ignorance of the Dallas area, I decided to return to the coffee shop for dinner.

Experienced writers use a combination of general and specific statements. In this way they ensure that their language is neither too abstract nor too concrete. Beginning college writers, however, often use language that is too general and thus too abstract. Instead of writing about their own experiences and observations directly, they take those experiences and abstract or generalize them. Of course, abstractions and generalizations are sometimes needed to convey important concepts and ideas. But notice what can happen when a beginning writer uses mostly abstractions and general statements:

Academic success is a very hard thing to define. For me, it is having knowledge of all aspects of life: a broad-based education. I see academic success as an ideal and one that always remains in the distance, never to be reached. But this ideal inspires constant growth. Intelligence is something everyone has. It is basically common sense. Some people learn faster than others, but I don't think that means those people have any more of that mysterious thing called intelligence. Too often, academic success is defined for us in terms of intelligence. We must overcome these set definitions and create our own. So, according to my definitions, we all have intelligence and we all can strive for academic success. Yet in addition to this intelligence it is necessary to have motivation to seek knowledge with a never-ending interest. Armed with this we all can begin to achieve our success.

You may have to read this paragraph several times to follow exactly what the writer is saying. The paragraph moves from idea to idea instead of sticking to one point; it goes from academic success to intelligence to motivation. And much of the language is abstract and general—the paragraph uses no concrete words or specific statements. Phrases like "knowledge of all aspects of life," "inspires constant growth," and "motivation to seek knowledge" all have meaning, but without specific or concrete language to illustrate, clarify, and support them, they remain vague. We may have some understanding of what is being said in this paragraph, but the words don't create a sharp or vivid picture in our minds.

By adding specific and concrete details, we can give the language more impact:

For me, academic success is having knowledge of all aspects of life: knowing how to solve a trigonometry problem as well as how to analyze a Shakespearean sonnet; knowing how to relate to people from my own community as well as people from exotic cultures; knowing what Marxist economists say about our economic system as well as what free market economists say about communism; knowing how to appreciate a Mozart sonata as well as how to program a computer to run the elevators in a large office building.

Including specifics and concretes not only clarifies what exactly is meant by "knowledge of all aspects of life," it also gives a *voice*—that is, life and personality—to the writing. Because abstractions and generalities apply to less tangible things and to a broader range of experiences, they often don't convey much personality. When we read the phrase "knowledge of all aspects of life," for instance, we don't get the sense of a unique individual speaking. But concretes and specifics, because they refer to more tangible things and to particular experiences, seem to belong solely to the people who write them. Although anyone could have written "knowledge of all aspects of life," only one person would ever come up with the exact phrase "knowing how to appreciate a Mozart sonata as well as how to program a computer to run the elevators in a large office building."

At the same time, it is important not to get carried away with concretes and specifics. If you use only or mainly concretes and specifics, you will run two risks. First, because abstractions and generalizations are needed to express concepts and ideas, writing that avoids them is likely to lack ideas or interpretation. A reader looking at a specific story or a series of concrete incidents without any abstractions and generalizations will probably ask "So what? What does it all *mean*?" Second, if you use too many concretes and specifics and not enough abstractions and generalizations, you may carry the notion of voice too far. That is, you may go beyond the point of sounding like a unique, interesting personality and start to sound scatterbrained, eccentric, or out of control, like a longwinded storyteller whom everyone tries to avoid at a party. In other words, *excessive* use of specifics and concretes can damage your credibility as a serious writer and thinker.

As we said earlier, good writers constantly try to blend abstract-general language with concrete-specific language. In your attempts to achieve that blend, remember to use abstract-general language when you want to make thoughtful or philosophical points; that is, generalizations and abstractions are essential in making analytic or interpretive points. Likewise, you will need to use concrete-specific language to support and detail the more thoughtful sections, and to give personality to the writing.

Exercise

Read the following student paragraphs and decide in each case whether the writing contains a good blend of abstract-general language and concrete-specific language or whether one type is lacking. If one type of language is lacking, suggest how the author could achieve a better blending.

1.   One spring day a couple of years ago, Bob Morris, a couple of other guys, and I decided to go on a hike to the Vermilion River. As we started off we could tell it wasn't that far into spring. It was a very cold day, and the sun stayed behind the clouds. The walk was fairly long, so we brought a couple of guns with us. As we walked we started to hunt for rabbits, but our luck wasn't that good so we decided to quit hunting. Then we decided to see who was the best shot. We picked smaller and smaller targets and whoever kept hitting them won. By the time we did all this, we were already at the river bank. So we decided to add another factor of difficulty into our targets. We would throw an object into the water and see who could hit it on the move.

After a couple of hours we ran out of bullets, and started looking for something else to do. We saw this tree that hung out over the river, and a couple of guys had the idea of climbing out on to its branches and playing "King on the Mountain." Since it was so cold out, and such a long walk back, Bob decided he wasn't going to do it. He also convinced me that I shouldn't do it either, because I had an important track meet the next week and I could get a really bad cold if I fell in. So Bob and I sat on the river bank and watched the rest of them play "King on the Mountain." After their clothes started to freeze, they decided it was time to walk back. On the way back they started to get frostbite, so Bob and I started giving them some of our dry clothes. And by the time we got back they were all cold as ice cubes.

2.   Psychological experiments were conducted several years ago by a researcher named Stanley Milgram in New Haven, Connecticut, to test human obedience to authority. The procedure involved an authority figure (the experimenter, dressed in a white coat to appear more legitimate), giving orders to people who had volunteered to participate in the experiment but were unaware of its real purpose. The participants were told that the experiment was to test the effects of punishment (electrical shocks) on learning behavior. They were to administer the shocks to another person (a "plant" who sat in another room and was not really being shocked) each time he or she answered a question incorrectly. For every wrong answer the voltage was to be increased. Before the experiment took place it was predicted that a very low percentage of individuals would listen to the authority figure and shock the learners beyond a low voltage. However, the astonishing results showed that over 50 percent of the subjects were willing to administer electrical shocks to other people to a dosage that would have been lethal.

3.   Some towns may be small in size but large in quality. In a large city, the people are apt to be concerned about themselves and about business that relates to them only. However, in a small town a stranger is likely to get the impression that the people are friendly, helpful, and sincere. And while small towns may look inadequate when compared to larger cities, many are well equipped with the necessities of life.

BUILDING VOCABULARY

Building your vocabulary has some obvious benefits. First of all, the more words you know, the more able you will be to select ones that express your ideas precisely, thus making your writing tasks easier. In addition, as you mature, and especially as you become better educated, others expect you to become more articulate. You don't, of course, want to sound phony or artificial, but you do want to sound like the educated person you are. In this section we will suggest practical ways to increase your vocabulary.

Reading, Writing, and Vocabulary

Reading, writing, and vocabulary are closely related. The more widely you read, the more you will be exposed to a broad range of words. Further, you will perceive these words in context, which is the best way of determining and remembering their meanings. And the more you write, the more opportunities you will have for using the new words you learn.

Let's examine more closely the relationship between vocabulary building and reading. Reading exposes you to a wide variety of words, especially if you read a range of materials—your favorite hobby magazine, for example, and the Sunday *Times*, and the novels of John Irving, and *Business Week*. This reading gives you an opportunity to learn new words as well as other meanings for words you already know.

Our first suggestion for improving your vocabulary, then, is to get into the habit of jotting down, *as you read*, words with which you are unfamiliar. Look up the definitions and write them down, too. Keep your lists in a special folder or notebook for handy reference. You can also list words that you have read previously but whose meanings you still do not know. Probably you can think of several such words right now: words that you have read on several occasions without stopping to consider what they actually mean. Take the time to learn them; they will probably appear in your reading again and then you'll understand them immediately.

When you jot a word down, also record the sentence in which it appeared. Depending on how a writer uses it, a word can have different meanings. Write down both the context and the dictionary meaning, and then you'll know the proper denotation should you read that word again.

One more point: Whenever you can, avoid using the dictionary alone to determine the meaning of a word. See if you can first figure out the meaning through the context. You may even have to look at sentences coming before and after the one that contains the unfamiliar word. Learning the word through a specific context can help ensure that you'll select the meaning appropriate for the material you've been reading.

A second way to build your vocabulary is to *use* the new vocabulary you develop. Using the words as often as you can places them firmly in your mind. You may wish to use the words first in speaking so that you can get comfortable with them, and then use them in your writing. Keep in mind that some of the vocabulary words you learn may be more formal than those you normally employ in conversation; these words can become part of your writing vocabulary, but you may use them in speaking only occasionally.

Exercise

1. During the next week, follow the above suggestions whenever you read a word you know you've read before but never stopped to learn. Share and discuss your list with other people in your class.

2. Following is a list of words and their contexts. Check each word to determine whether (a) you know its meanings; (b) the word is totally unfamiliar; or (c) the word is familiar but you are unsure of its meaning. Write down the meaning of each word as it is used in the example.

   a. *affluent*
   Thus we are left with one alternative; by busing children and putting the *affluent* with the poor, we will get what we want. . . .

   b. *burnish*
   The sun shines only to *burnish* her skin and gild her hair. . . .

   c. *congruent*
   As more of an outside observer, Stringer could not provide first-hand tidbits as Calmon did, but he was able to evaluate equally all interpretations . . . and form them all into one *congruent* picture.

   d. *debilitating*
   Or, since success in medicine is generally measured by longevity, he may recommend painful, *debilitating* therapy.

   e. *defoliated, decimated*
   We *defoliated* and destroyed the landscape and *decimated* the population of a country whose affairs were not ours to interfere with.

   f. *denizens*
   Perhaps the biggest benefactors of Winfield's windfall will be the other *denizens* of George Steinbrenner's Bronx zoo.

   g. *eccentricities*
   Any mention of his name begets "What did he do this time?" And there is always plenty to talk about, because my Uncle George, my father's brother, has many *eccentricities*.

h. *ideologies*
    Peaceful coexistence without chauvinistic *ideologies* seems virtually impossible.

i. *inveighed, posthumous*
    Somerset Maugham asked his friends to destroy his letters; both Willa Cather and Ernest Hemingway *inveighed* against *posthumous* publication of theirs.

j. *prestigious*
    Immediately I had grand visions of working in a very *prestigious* position where I would be taught about the market.

k. *resonance*
    He explained that the string that holds the bars on the instrument creates a modal point having very little *resonance*.

l. *scrutinize*
    The ambitious Steven proceeds to *scrutinize* the many hundreds of green peas. . . .

Another way to build vocabulary is to learn prefixes and suffixes whose meanings are relatively consistent. You can use these prefixes and suffixes in conjunction with context to determine the meaning of words formed with them. Here are some common prefixes and suffixes:

PREFIX	MEANING	EXAMPLE
a-, an-	not; without	apolitical
anti-, ant-	against	antagonist
bi-, bin,	two	binary
cardi-, cardio-	referring to the heart	cardiac
centi-, cent-	one hundredth	centimeter
centro-, centr-	center	centrifugal
contra-	against; contrary	contraband
de-	reversal; undoing	dethrone
dis-	negation; lack	distrust
eu-	well; beneficial	eulogy
ex-	former; out	exhale
inter-	between, among	intercept
intra-	within	intramural
iso-	equal; similar to	isotope
kilo-	one thousand	kilometer
macro-, macr-	largeness; longness	macroscopic
mal-	bad; badly or wrongly	maladjusted

micro-	the smaller or more detailed of two objects	microcosm
multi-	many	multifaceted
neo-	new form, type, or development	neonatal
para-	near; resembling	paramedic
poly-	many	polygon
pre-	before; earlier	premature
re-	return; repeat; again	renew
retro-	back; backward	retrograde
sub-	under	submarine
sur-	over; beyond	surcharge
syn-, sym-	together; same	synonym
til-, tele-	distance	teleport, television
theo-, the-	god or gods	theology
trans-	across; beyond	transport
un-	not	uninvited
uni-	being single; only one	unilateral

SUFFIX	*MEANING*	*EXAMPLE*
-able	able to be	believable
-gen, -gene	that which produces	carcinogen
-graph	apparatus that writes or records; that which is recorded	telegraph
-ize	to cause to be or become	materialize
-kinesis	movement; division	telekinesis
-less	free of; without	wireless
-logy	science or study of	geology
-mania	indicates an exaggerated desire for or pathological interest in something	egomania
-meter	indicates a measuring device	chronometer
-ness	state; quality	freshness
-ous	possessing; having	beauteous
-phobia	fear of	acrophobia

Exercise

Check your list of familiar words with unknown meanings. Could a knowledge of prefixes and suffixes such as those listed above have helped you discover any of their meanings? Jot down other prefixes and suffixes you run across and note their meanings for future reference.

Thesaurus: Friend and Foe

A thesaurus is a reference book set up much like a dictionary, except that instead of defining the words it lists, it gives synonyms for them. The thesaurus is a double-edged tool. Used correctly, it can help you achieve necessary variety in your word choice. But used unwisely, it can make your writing unclear, confusing, or even unintentionally humorous.

Often a thesaurus is very helpful. Instead of repeating a word again and again, a writer can consult a thesaurus for possible synonyms. For instance, examine the word choices Kate made in this paragraph:

> Refinishing antique furniture has been a hobby of mine for some time, a hobby that I can recommend to everyone. It's a hobby that can accommodate every schedule, since you can invest as much or as little time as you want, depending on how soon you want the finished product. It's also a very satisfying hobby. You have something to show off when you're done, and, especially if you've taken "before" photos, you can take great pride in your accomplishment. Refinishing can be an expensive hobby, but only if you choose to work with large or rare pieces. When working with small pieces such as stools or magazine racks, it is a relatively inexpensive hobby. In general, I feel refinishing is a very worthwhile hobby.

After reading this rough draft, Kate decided that she had used *hobby* too often, and began thinking of ways to reduce the repetition. She wanted to keep the emphasis gained by repeating the word in sentence 1, and decided that "It's a hobby that . . ." (in sentence 2) could be changed to "It can accommodate . . .," since the antecedent of *it* is clearly *hobby*. But the use of *hobby* in sentence 3 had to go. Kate had trouble thinking of synonyms so she consulted a thesaurus and found *pastime*, a word appropriate in denotation, connotation, and level of language for her paragraph. "It's a very satisfying pastime" retains her intended meaning and eliminates the repetition. Sentence 5, she decided, could be revised by replacing *an expensive hobby* with *expensive*. The final sentence could then use *hobby* and still be effective.

Here is Kate's revised paragraph:

> Refinishing antique furniture has been a hobby of mine for some time, a hobby that I can recommend to everyone. It can accommodate

every schedule, since you can invest as much or as little time as you want, depending on how soon you want the finished product. It's also a very satisfying pastime. You have something to show off when you're done, and, especially if you've taken "before" photos, you can take great pride in your accomplishment. Refinishing can be expensive, but only if you choose to work with large or rare pieces. When working with small pieces such as stools or magazine racks, it is relatively inexpensive. In general, I feel refinishing is a very worthwhile hobby.

This paragraph reads more smoothly than the original because it eliminates needless repetition. The writer handled most of the unnecessary repetition by making structural changes within sentences, but she found in one instance that a synonym was what she needed. *Pastime* was better than anything she had thought of herself and, she felt, was very appropriate for what she wanted to say.

If a thesaurus can provide you with an appropriate synonym, then it is doing the job you want it to do. For Kate, it reminded her of a word she knew but would not have remembered on her own. But look at other words the thesaurus listed under *hobby*:

> avocation, sideline, side interest, diversion, recreation, relaxation, divertissement, entertainment, amusement, fun, play, sport, game
> *Inf.* cup of tea
> *Sl.* thing, bag

Many of these are clearly inappropriate and unacceptable for Kate's paragraph. Try reading some of these possibilities:

> Refinishing antique furniture has been an *avocation* of mine for some time. . . .
> It's also a very satisfying *divertissement*.
> In general, I feel it is a very worthwhile *amusement*.

Or, how about this:

> Refinishing antique furniture has been my *bag* for some time. . . .

Avocation sounds a bit stuffy, while *divertissement* and *amusement* sound frivolous. *My bag* is not a good choice either; slang terms are generally inappropriate for college writing assignments.

Obviously, you must use a thesaurus with care. For example, *rekindle* is listed in one thesaurus as synonymous with *revive*. Suppose your original sentence was "The lifeguard tried desperately to revive the victim." In this case, substituting *rekindle* for *revive* would not work: "The lifeguard tried desperately to rekindle the victim."

Because the thesaurus presents only a list of alternatives without indicating their suitability for your particular piece of writing, you can unknowingly wind up with an unsatisfactory synonym. It's best, then, to avoid plucking a totally unfamiliar word from the list. If a word looks unusual or is particularly long, choose another, more familiar word. If you see a word listed that you've read before and think is suitable, you might look it up in a dictionary to double-check its meaning. But remember that a dictionary does not present connotations—another reason to avoid choosing unfamiliar words from a list the thesaurus gives.

Exercise

1. Assume you are writing a brochure promoting a given city. In part of it you discuss transportation available to the tourist. You mention cabs (*"Cab* service is excellent"), wish to say more about them, and feel you need a synonym. Checking a thesaurus provides the following list:

   taxi, taxicab; carriage, cabriolet, brougham, hansom, hack, hackney, four-wheeler, fiacre, droshky, coach, vehicle, conveyance

   Would any of these be suitable for your purposes? Why or why not?

2. You are writing a memo discussing a change in policy ("This policy has been *revised*") and wish to avoid overusing *revise*. Here is a list of synonyms:

   rewrite, redraft; rework, update, bring up to date; edit, emend, emendate; retouch, revamp, overhaul, doctor, repair

   What ones might be used in your memo?

3. *Soar, sail, zoom, cruise, coast, sweep, skim*—All of these are given as possible synonyms for *fly* (used as a verb). What are some differences in meaning between them? With what types of motion do you associate each? What object, animal, or type of person could you picture doing each?

4. *Archetype* and *paradigm* are given as substitutes for *mold* (used as a noun). How would you have to be using the word *mold* for one or the other to be an appropriate synonym?

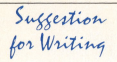

Suggestion for Writing

Assume you are a contributing writer of a brochure promoting your hometown or a large city you know well. You can write any one of the following sections of the brochure: (1) transportation and hotel or tourist accommodations; (2) restaurants; (3) things to do. Choose and write a section. Whichever section you write, you probably will need to use synonyms for such terms as *cab, bus, room, restaurant, meal,* and so on. You may consult a thesaurus if you wish.

USING ACTIVE AND PASSIVE VOICE

Examine the following sentences:

The batter slugged the ball as hard as she could.
The ball was slugged as hard as the batter could do it.

They have the same meaning in the sense that both refer to the same action. Structurally, however, they are different.

In the first sentence, the subject of the main clause ("The batter slugged") is *batter*, the person who is doing the action expressed by the verb (*slugged*). In the second sentence, the subject of the main clause ("the ball was slugged") is *ball*, and the verb form ("was slugged") tells the reader the action was done by something or someone *other* than the ball.

Sentences written so that the subject carries out the action expressed by the verb are in what is called *active voice*. Sentences written so that the subject of a verb does not perform the action expressed by the verb are in what is called *passive voice*.

Here are some examples, with subjects underlined once and verbs twice:

Active voice   Experts no longer consider turtles desirable pets. They may carry diseases such as salmonella.

Passive voice   Turtles are no longer considered desirable pets by experts. Diseases such as salmonella may be carried by them.

Sentences written in passive voice usually follow this pattern:

Subject	+	some form of *to be*	+	Verb form	+	(by)		
Turtles	+	are	+	considered	+	by	+	experts.
Diseases	+	may be	+	carried	+	by	+	them.

The person or object doing the action of the verb (*experts* and *them*) follows the word *by*, which is optional.

The terms *active* and *passive* reveal which construction is generally preferable—*active* implies liveliness, whereas *passive* implies a lack of vigor. Sentences written in active voice make your writing livelier and usually add greater forcefulness to your ideas. Therefore, try to use active voice as much as you can. If you are consciously trying to impart a sense of immobility, then use passive constructions to reinforce your idea. You can also use passive voice if your purpose is to highlight the receiver of action rather than the doer, as in "Begonias were sold by the florist." Here you are emphasizing that *begonias* are available, not that the florist sells them.

Exercise

1. Rewrite the following sentences to create active constructions:

   a. The child was temporarily blinded by the suddenness of the light.
   b. Forty-eight cartons of milk are being spilled by the delivery person.
   c. All of the banks in the small town were robbed by the same gang of aging criminals.
   d. My heart was left in San Francisco.
   e. Markers of every hue imaginable had been purchased by the elementary school teacher.
   f. Bicycles were given away as prizes in the drawing held by the famous charity.
   g. Never had the audience heard the songs sung with such enthusiasm by the performers.
   h. Five pounds of chocolate candy were eaten by the hapless German Shepherd.
   i. All the candles on the cake had been blown out by the birthday celebrant.
   j. None of the tasks will be done by a competent person.

2. Think of some ideas you feel might be appropriately expressed in passive voice. Then compose the sentences, following the pattern suggested above.

EMPLOYING DESCRIPTIVE AND FIGURATIVE LANGUAGE

Beyond the shadow of the ship,
I watched the water snakes:
They moved in tracks of shining white,
And when they reared, the elfish light
Fell off in hoary flakes.

Within the shadow of the ship
I watched their rich attire:

> Blue, glossy green, and velvet black,
> They coiled and swam; and every track
> Was a flash of golden fire.
>
> (Samuel Taylor Coleridge,
> "The Rime of the Ancient Mariner")

Highly descriptive and figurative language is common in fiction, particularly in poetry. Note, for instance, how detailed a picture Coleridge presents of the water snakes that the ancient mariner sees. He uses many visual images: of color ("shining white," "glossy green") and of movement ("reared" and "coiled"). He expresses the mariner's sudden appreciation of the beauty and the fantasy of the scene: The snakes have "rich" attire, and the "flakes" of light they throw are "golden" and "elfish." In addition, he uses personification ("attire") and metaphor ("every track was a flash of golden fire") to stress the beauty of the scene.

Writers use figurative language because figures of speech are more evocative than is ordinary language. A poet can thus appeal to the reader on many levels, making an intellectual point while involving the reader's senses through imagery.

In much of your writing, using figurative language will probably not be essential. Business and technical writing especially tend to avoid figures of speech altogether. On the other hand, knowing how to use major figures of speech can help you when you want to make your writing more vivid, descriptive, and imaginative. Let's examine some examples of descriptive and figurative language more closely.

Imagery

A Brazilian musical? The words evoke memories of Carmen Miranda, *teeth gleaming, hips undulating, r's trilling, balancing a headdress of tropical fruit heavy enough to give the strongest Rio dock worker a hernia.* (Richard Corliss, *Time*)

A writer conveys vivid descriptions to a reader largely through imagery. *Imagery* depicts, through words or phrases, sensory experiences. It can appeal to any of the senses, but since much of our sensory input comes to us through our eyes, writers frequently rely on visual imagery. Notice how many of the images used above are visual:

> teeth gleaming
> hips undulating
> balancing a headdress of tropical fruit heavy enough to give the strongest Rio dock worker a hernia

The phrase "heavy enough to give the strongest Rio dock worker a hernia" not only helps you to picture the headdress better, but also invites another image, that of the "strongest" dock worker failing to lift it. And one of the images appeals to the reader's sense of hearing: "r's trilling." The writer wants to give you a vivid description, one that includes hearing as well as seeing. Even if you've never heard of Carmen Miranda, this description is so striking that you would probably recognize her immediately should she walk into your life.

The description that follows (from the student essay on pages 172–73) also shows how writers use imagery to make their descriptions vivid:

> This torso, about fourteen inches high, is a Roman copy of the Greek original. Unfortunately, it is poorly preserved. The *once whitish marble* has turned a *light yellowish color with occasional brown spots throughout*. Similarly, the *surface is scarred* and therefore *roughened by chips*, also an indication of bad exposure. The *hips are worn*, minimizing somewhat the fuller natural curve, and at the same time *exposing the original color*.

This student writer included a photograph of the statue with the paper he turned in to his instructor. But he still needed imagery to reveal details of color and texture that the photo alone would not reveal. His main idea, that the statue "is poorly preserved," is supported by those images; without them, his point would not be convincing.

Whenever you are trying to help your readers picture (or taste, touch, hear, or smell) the scene, object, or person you are describing, you will want to employ imagery.

Exercise

Identify the images in the following examples and note the senses to which they appeal:

1. . . . tall, pudgy, bearlike (he still has his winter beard), toothy and even dark, but not sinister. In sneakers and a black leather motorcycle jacket, he exudes a let's-get-this-sword-out-of-the-stone earnestness. (from a description of novelist Stephen King, author of *Carrie* and *The Shining*, by William Wilson, *New York Times Magazine*)

2. . . . the Plaza is a 55-acre, 15-square-block district of classy stores, bars, and restaurants laid out in tasteful exercises in Spanish architecture, featuring tile roofs, mosaic walls, inlaid floors, towers, turrets, and fountains. (*Ebony*)

3. The scion is a length of vigorous stem with at least two buds on it from last year's growth (for best results). The thickness of the wood should be about the diameter of a pencil. (*Organic Gardening*)

4. Mel has the amazing ability to team a pretty but cheap 99-cents-a-yard piece of fabric with a smartly designed pattern and come up with a

smashing party dress. Sometimes by lunging right in with a pair of dull scissors, without a pattern or training in pattern drafting, she will come up with a suit that looks like a Paris original. Her most notable example of this is the white wool Chanel-type jacket and skirt she whipped up last year.

5. The trees weren't budding yet, there were still snow patches on the ground, and the temperature wasn't far above freezing. Out he went, his blue and ivory feet crushing the wet salad of the lawn. (Kurt Vonnegut, *Slaughterhouse-Five*)

Metaphor and Simile

Although *imagery*, *metaphor*, and *simile* refer to different aspects of language, the terms are related. Using imagery doesn't necessarily involve using metaphors and similes, but using metaphors and similes *always* requires using imagery. Imagery can be *literal*:

> Looking down the tracks he was momentarily blinded by a *huge locomotive headlight.*

But metaphors and similes use imagery in a *figurative*, not a literal, way:

> He was wearing a belt buckle the size of a *locomotive headlight.* (*Time*)

The image of the locomotive headlight is not presented for its own sake, but to say something about the belt buckle, to suggest how huge and dominant it is.

Metaphors and similes are figurative comparisons. A literal comparison lines up two essentially similar terms to gain tangible, realistic information about them:

> *My brother* is much stronger than *I* am.

But metaphors and similes line up two *essentially dissimilar* things, usually one literal term and one figurative term, to convey an impression or subjective truth (and not any factual information) about the literal subject:

> When my brother was forced into a fight, *his fists* became *uncontrolled punch presses.*

Here the literal term, "his fists," and the figurative term, "uncontrolled punch presses," are the essentially dissimilar things being compared. The purpose is not to comment on the punch presses, but to suggest something about the brother's fists.

The fists are like punch presses in a figurative way, for they have enormous power and speed. In every metaphor and simile the literal and figurative terms will have *shared qualities* (power and speed in this one). Although in essence the terms will be radically different, they will have some point or points of similarity. And the writer relies on the reader to recognize the point of similarity.

Metaphors and similes are different in one important way: Metaphors are *direct* comparisons, whereas similes are *indirect* comparisons. Metaphors state directly that one item *is* (or *was* or *becomes*) another. Similes state that one item is *like* another, thus making the comparison indirect. Metaphors will usually contain some form of the verb *to be* or *to become*, while similes will contain *like* or *as*.

The figurative comparisons we've examined so far are all metaphors; they could easily be turned into similes:

Metaphor his fists *became* uncontrolled punch presses

Simile his fists were *like* uncontrolled punch presses

Similarly, consider this example:

Metaphor Against the dark winter sky, the trees *were* skeletons whose bones rattled in the wind.

Simile Against the dark winter sky, the trees were *like* skeletons whose bones rattled in the wind.

Sometimes, metaphors do not use *to be*, but they nonetheless directly compare two unlike things. Note this example from the Exercise on imagery (p. 252):

Out he went, his blue and ivory feet crushing *the wet salad of the lawn*.

In deciding whether to use a metaphor or a simile, consider how directly you wish to state your comparison. Metaphors make stronger statements in the sense that they figuratively equate one object with another. In their indirectness, similes set up a more subtle image.

Why do writers use metaphors and similes? They do so to give freshness and color to their writing and to gain shades of meaning that could not be achieved with ordinary, literal statements. What a lackluster substitute this version is for the earlier sentence above:

When my brother was forced into a fight, his fists were *very quick* and *powerful*.

Although you probably won't use figurative comparisons often in scholarly kinds of writing, you will find them valuable in writing informal essays, personal experience papers, and letters.

The examples of figurative comparisons we've shown so far include both the literal and the figurative terms of the comparisons:

LITERAL TERM	FIGURATIVE TERM
belt buckle	locomotive headlight
fists	punch presses
trees	skeletons
lawn	wet salad

At times, though, the literal terms of the comparisons may be omitted altogether:

> Ominous clouds of inferiority began to form in her little mental sky. (Martin Luther King, "Letter From Birmingham Jail")

King does not state directly what literally corresponds to the "little mental sky," but from the context the reader knows he means his daughter's perspective or outlook on life.

Besides adding lively description to your writing, metaphors and similes can also add persuasiveness. For instance, King's use of "little mental sky" adds a sense of the girl's vulnerability, and thus gives greater force to what he says. When members of the New York Yankees baseball team are referred to as "denizens of George Steinbrenner's Bronx Zoo," a range of qualities—ferocity, crudity, strength—comes to mind. By adding this range of meanings the writer expresses the concepts more persuasively.

Figurative comparisons thus can significantly enrich language. However, when they have been used so much that they have become clichés, they accomplish the opposite: The language becomes dull and trite. When we speak, for instance, of someone's "jumping on the bandwagon" or "riding a hobby horse," the triteness of these metaphors strips them of any effectiveness they may once have had. As George Orwell said (speaking metaphorically himself), clichés are nevertheless "a continuous temptation, a packet of aspirin always at one's elbow." Remember that the metaphorical expression that comes quickly to your mind probably comes to everyone else's as well. If you cannot come up with a fresh metaphor or simile, it is usually better to state the idea literally than to use a cliché. For instance, instead of writing "In his speech on foreign aid, the president rode his hobby horse," you could write "In his speech on foreign aid, the president enthusiastically outlined his favorite plan."

1. Explain the metaphor being used in the following cartoon. Would you consider this metaphor a cliché? Why or why not?

"The seasons fly by so fast, don't they?"

Drawing by Modell; © 1981. The New Yorker Magazine, Inc.

2. Each of the following sentences contains a clichéd metaphor or simile. Substitute for each (a) your own metaphor or simile,

preserving the original meaning, and (b) a literal phrase or statement.

a. She was the apple of her father's eye.
b. He arose from his nap fresh as a daisy.
c. The police officer wondered from under what rock the criminal had crawled.
d. Upon hearing his son's lies, the father went up in a mushroom cloud.
e. The supervisor later regretted her hasty dismissal of a secretary who might have had some potential. Oh well, she thought, no sense crying over spilled milk.
f. For this particular tennis pro, acing her opponent was like falling off a log.
g. The child had had it drummed into his head not to talk to strangers.
h. The giant fund-raiser helped the mayor get the ball rolling for the campaign.
i. At first the doctor refused to prescribe the new miracle drug, feeling it was insufficiently tested. However, now she, too, jumped on the bandwagon.
j. When I turned over the examination and saw my grade, I was as mad as a hornet.
k. When I turned over the examination and saw my grade, I was happy as a clam.
l. After stealing the ring, the girl acknowledged she felt the heavy yoke of conscience.

Suggestion for Writing

Write an essay in which you focus on something you did in your younger days that you now consider foolish or immature. As part of your process of invention, read the following student essay on the same topic. Pay attention not only to its content and structure but also to its use of language. Is the diction basic and economical? Are abstract and concrete words well blended? Is imagery used? Are there any figures of speech, and are they effective or ineffective?

NATURAL FOLLY

[1]For as long as I can remember, I have spent at least two weeks of every summer in the mountains of the Lincoln National Forest in Ruidoso, New Mexico. In the summer of 1977, when I was a curious fourteen year old, I experienced an adventure with nature I will never forget. In this stage of budding adolescence, feeling invincible and independent, I set out on a journey I had often dreamed about.

[2]It all started one morning in July. Sitting against a rock, glaring into the campfire with a cup of coffee in my hand, I was planning the events of the day. I really did not want to go fishing with my father. My mother wanted to go for a walk, but I turned that down too. Instead, I wanted to sit and think about the majestic mountain that stood before the campground. I stared at it with fascination and imagined myself standing at the top, looking down on the world. I let my mind go wild. Actually believing I could climb the mountain, I jumped to my feet and ran toward it.

[3]I gave no thought to preparing for the climb; all I could think about was getting to the top. In my hiking boots and Levi jacket, I began. On my own natural high, I was moving pretty fast. As I was getting higher, it finally struck me that I had not left a note at camp as to where I was going. It was all right, though, because I would be back soon. How mistaken I was. The mountain seemed to be getting larger and higher the more I climbed. Not even halfway up, I got really tired and took a breather. It was at this point I realized this venture would not be as easy as I thought.

[4]After my break, I got on my feet and started walking again, but for some reason it was harder to climb. I had lost momentum, and the recognition of what this mountain actually was dampened my motivations. My fast pace had diminished, and I convinced myself that a slower one would be better because I could get to see nature, forest plants, and animals I had not seen before.

[5]Walking slower gave me the chance not only to witness nature, but to consider how foolish I had been in not preparing for the climb. I started to feel the lack of food, proper climbing supplies, and warm clothing. However, I was so taken in by the mystery of the mountain and my own curiosity that I could not have cared less. I kept reassuring myself how strong and capable I was, and how I would climb to the top no matter what it took.

[6]As I got higher up, the trees started getting closer and closer together. I could not see anything in front of me but the trunks of tall pine. It was a true awakening to nature's simplicity. The sun's rays came through the trees at certain spots to blend with the leaves and ground, creating a beautiful contrast of color. Sitting by a tree for another rest, I was further impressed with the enormity of sounds that made me feel puny and insignificant in this untouched land. I could hear the trickling of water and the song of the bluebird as the trees rustled with the steady blowing of the wind. The smell of pine and clean air drove me further into an elated state of self-oblivion. I could have sat there forever, close to the gifts of nature we take for granted so often.

[7]All of this was a wonderful experience with nature, but I had originally intended to get to the top of the mountain. God knows how long I spent sitting at that tree contemplating the surroundings. I must

have dozed off or lost my sense of time because I suddenly realized that the sun had moved some distance in the sky. It was a bit colder, and I was getting hungry; I figured it was noon. I could have very easily walked down the mountain to get my stomach filled and my body warmer, but I figured that if I turned back I wouldn't want to go up anymore. Once again, my ignorance drove me further up the mountain. As the slope of the mountain got steeper, my legs began giving out. By this time, I was feeling the wind against my goose-pimpled skin, and my stomach was roaring.

[8]All of a sudden, the density of the trees cleared, and I was looking at the top of the mountain for the first time. The only thing that separated me from my destination was a clearing of rocks where a stream once ran through. Hesitant about going on, I sat down to think about a path to follow. It looked fairly easy, but I was drained of energy and I was really cold now. Well, I couldn't turn back, so I started up the rocky road.

[9]Traveling up the slope of rocks, I fell down several times, scraping my knee and ripping my pants. I was frustrated with myself and cursed the mountain. I was at the point of giving up the climb. It seemed as though hours had passed since I had stepped on this final rocky path, and I wasn't in a cheerful state, as one could expect. I debated whether or not to go on. Cursing the mountain one more time, I headed back down, short of my goal.

[10]If anything about this adventure was really miserable, it was coming back down. Walking down the rock clearing, I fell down again and tore my Levi jacket at the elbow. But I was too tired to get mad; I simply got up and started walking again. Finally, I came to the trees where I had spent so much time earlier that day. Breathing heavily, I sat down and closed my eyes. I heard the same sounds I had before, but the sun was going down and the color was gone. Just then, I opened my eyes and saw a giant snake a few feet away from me. I was scared out of my pants, and my first reaction was to get out of there. I got up and ran down the mountain as fast as my tired legs would go. Once again, I lost my balance, fell down, and this time landed on poison ivy.

[11]As the sun set behind the mountain, I was scared in the darkness, hungry, itching, and bleeding from my reopened knee. This strong boy had lost his battle with the wild. All I wanted was to get back to camp and never to see this mountain for as long as I lived. Not knowing where I was going, I kept trying to reassure and calm myself down. I was lost, but I knew that if nature brought me up, then it must bring me down. Remembering the sound of the trickling water, I listened and heard it not far away. I knew I would be back home soon.

[12]All of a sudden, I heard people calling my name. The voices did not sound familiar so I did not answer, but I was running in their direction. As I got closer to the lighted campgrounds, it clicked in my

head that the voices were those of the Forest Rangers. I yelled out, and before I knew it, there was a bright flashlight on my face. I was so happy, but the Ranger had a scowl on his face. I smiled innocently, and he said, "Boy, where the hell have you been?" I told him my story, and received the lecture I had expected. He took me to the camp where my mother and father had the gloomiest faces I have ever seen. They ran to me and hugged me so hard I almost fainted.

[13]After I changed to some warm clothes and was sitting by the fire with a cup of coffee and a sweet roll, my father gave the third-degree scolding I deserved. I could only say that I was sorry and would never do such a thing again.

part

FOUR

SPECIAL
ASSIGNMENTS

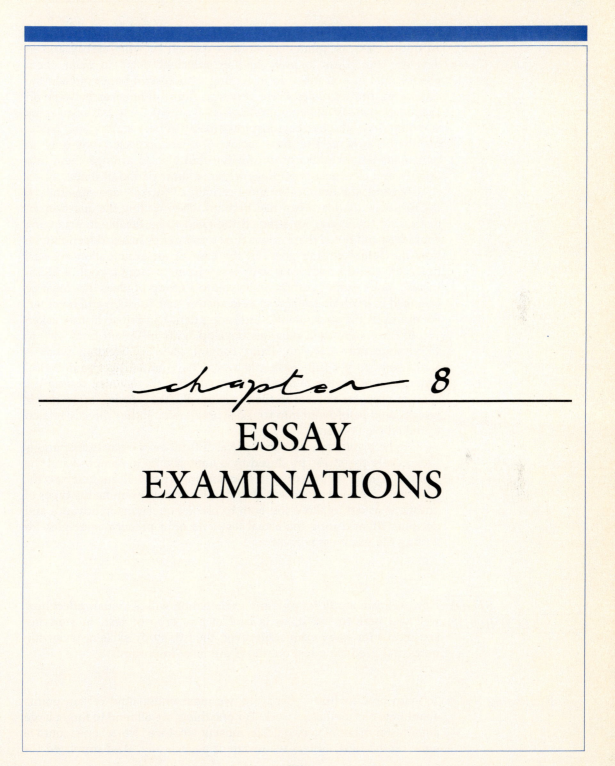

chapter 8

ESSAY
EXAMINATIONS

Writing an essay for an examination is similar to writing an essay for an out-of-class assignment. You are expected to write clearly and to develop your ideas logically and in sufficient detail to make them precise, just as you must do in writing a successful paper outside the classroom. But there are a few very significant differences between an examination essay and an out-of-class assignment. First, the exam essay is written in a situation that inspires anxiety at best or, at worst, panic, mainly because of the time factor. You are expected not only to remember large chunks of information but also to arrange them into orderly and clear pieces of prose within a short period of time.

Second, the exam essay must contain a "correct" answer—that is, the response the instructor had in mind when writing the question. In discussing the essay, we stressed the need to be flexible in arranging your ideas and noted that various final forms are possible, depending on how the actual writing goes. In the case of an examination answer, however, you do not create your essay from so large a pool of ideas. Instead, each exam question limits you to a group of ideas that must be arranged in a certain fashion so as to answer that question and no other. For example, if a question on a final examination in British history asked you to trace significant religious developments in Britain from 1400 to 1558, your only decision about content may be deciding what is significant. To get full credit you would have to list, in chronological order, events having religious significance for the country during the span of years mentioned in the question. Political, social, or economic issues could be brought into your discussion only if they directly related to the religious events.

To help you cope with the special difficulties of essay examinations —especially the stress produced by a limited time to compose and the relative rigidity imposed by test questions—we will suggest specific guidelines for you to follow in studying for exams; examine the types of questions asked to allow you both to predict questions in advance and decipher them during the actual test; and offer practical strategies for writing the exam essay itself.

STUDY TECHNIQUES

How well you study for an essay examination will obviously affect how well you perform on it, as is true of any type of test. In studying specifically for essay exams, however, the two study skills of reviewing notes and predicting test questions are most important.

Reviewing Notes

To learn how to study effectively, we must understand certain points about how our memories work. For one thing, we all tend to forget large amounts of material very quickly; most of what we "learn" one month is gone by the next, unless we review it periodically. And unrelated (or apparently unrelated) information is forgotten more quickly than ideas we perceive as unified in some way. Another point: Large chunks of new information presented within relatively short periods of time are harder to assimilate initially and are also forgotten more easily than smaller bits of more familiar material. Finally, new learning works to confuse, or even erase from our memories altogether, old learning. And unfortunately, old learning also interferes with our recalling the new. Thus we are doubly disadvantaged.

Reviewing the notes you take during lectures and class discussions and while reading is the primary way to counteract these negative factors and to build in your memory the storehouse of materials on which to base your essay answers. Review sessions are also opportunities for you to make new observations about the connections between the material in your notes.

When reviewing your notes, keep these guidelines in mind:

1. Review your notes as often as you can, preferably once a week. If possible, reread your notes immediately following the lecture or the reading you've done. Many college courses demand that you learn a lot of brand-new material in a fairly short period of time. Going over your notes helps make the material clearer.

2. As you review, work at seeing how the concepts you are studying are related. Sometimes an important issue creates many side issues, not always obviously related, and it is far easier to recall these ideas later if you first realize and then keep in mind that they are unified through their relationship with the larger concern. Be especially alert in recognizing ideas or issues that arise near the end of the term and that point back to concepts discussed earlier in the semester. Frequently, essay examination questions involve recognizing such relationships even though they have not been specifically noted in lectures or discussed in class. Anticipating such questions obviously makes you far better prepared to answer them.

3. Test whether you have learned the ideas contained in your notes by looking away from your notes and attempting to recite significant ideas, issues, or events in your own words. Generally speaking, if you can paraphrase an idea, preserving the author's intent and meaning, you understand that idea. For example, looking away from your notes on *Great Expectations*, see if you can recite Charles Dickens' major thematic concerns in the novel, and then cite ways in which those concerns are similar to or different from the issues discussed by other Victorian novelists. It may strike you as odd to be repeating to yourself what you think you've just learned, but such verbalization can imprint that learning more solidly on your memory than reading alone can do. Moreover, you will be rehearsing material that could likely be in your answer to a test question.

Of course, to use these guidelines, you must keep up with your reading assignments. Get behind on your reading and you'll get behind on note-taking; time for review may then be out of the question. Taking notes that reflect the major ideas in your texts and enough minor points to support those ideas is also crucial; otherwise your reviewing will suffer. If you feel your study skills need additional refining, check whether your college or university offers a study skills course. Knowing the proper strategies in studying can make a tremendous difference in your academic performance.

Following the guidelines on reviewing notes should help you recall ideas for an exam. You will have ideas well in mind that will provide material for your response to the test questions.

Predicting Questions

Probably the most anxiety-producing aspect of taking any exam is the unknown quantity it represents; after all, only a small number of ideas covered in the course will actually appear on the examination. The critical question then becomes "*Which* ideas will appear?"

Being sensitive to verbal cues given by the instructor can help you determine which issues may show up on an exam. Very often, the ideas or concepts a college professor describes as "important," "significant," or "major" also will appear on a test. For instance, when the instructor opens a lecture by commenting, "These ideas are among the most significant current theories in retail merchandising," that lecture is a good source for potential exam materials. And note which concepts the instructor stresses through repetition; these, too, are likely to be on an exam.

Being sensitive to cues also works well in reviewing your notes. Working from your notes, be alert for ongoing issues that appear to relate separate incidents, ideas, or theories. Keep in mind that essay questions requiring relatively lengthy answers are necessarily broad in scope, covering large portions of the semester's work. Professors commonly compose such questions by focusing on relationships among ideas. And remember that recognizing how concepts are related can also improve your recall of those concepts; issues we perceive as interrelated are much easier to remember than unrelated bits.

As you review, then, deliberately consider which concepts the professor has stressed and which appear to interrelate; this knowledge can aid you in predicting what the questions on your exam will be like. Also, be wary of units in a course that seem isolated from or unrelated to what is generally being studied. You may be asked to supply that missing connection during a test. Similarly, an assigned outside reading selection that was never discussed in class is likely to pop up in an exam question. Try to predict questions that relate these kinds of materials to the major points of the course.

Once you have pinpointed key items and have begun to formulate hypothetical questions, list those questions following each weekly review session. Look over questions from the previous weeks as well, reciting possible answers whenever you have the time. Even if the questions on the exam are not exactly the same as those you have made up, your practice will give you a solid base for answering the questions that do appear.

Exercise

Choose one course you are currently taking in which you will be writing an essay examination. After thoroughly reviewing your notes for the course, predict at least one question you might be asked from each week's material. Also predict at least two questions that interconnect separate units studied in the course.

TYPES OF QUESTIONS ASKED

Even though you have studied thoroughly and followed the suggestions we have made for predicting questions, you will sometimes find, when actually facing the test, that some of the questions don't immediately suggest an answer—"What does he mean by *that*?" "Where did she get *this*?" "How am I supposed to know *that*? We *never* studied it." Or you may think you know what a question requires of you, only to discover differently halfway through your answer. Let's examine the types of essay questions an instructor might ask on an examination. Knowing the available types will help you to predict questions you might be asked and to decipher confusing or unclear questions while you are taking the test. If, as you read an exam question, the answer instantly leaps to mind, you don't need to be concerned about what type of question it is. But if you are uncertain about what the instructor is asking you to do, being able to identify the type of question will give you a place to begin. Becoming familiar with these types can increase your confidence as a writer of essay exams, for you will have more insight into the instructor's mysterious "bag of tricks." After all, there are only a limited number of ways to ask a question, and knowing the ways can benefit you.

Type 1: Recitation of Facts and Information

    a. Cover the characteristics, the types, the causes, the major influences . . .
    b. Trace the events or steps . . .

The question that asks you to recite facts and information is probably the easiest and most straightforward type of question to answer. You are required to recall information from your reading or from class lectures and to present it as it was presented to you. A typical Type 1a question might ask, "What were the most important factors contributing to the assimilation of the French language by the English language following the Norman Conquest of 1066?" or "What are the chief characteristics of Gothic architecture?" Your instructor and/or the textbook will have answered these questions at some point, and your task is to recall the material and recreate it in a clear and orderly fashion. Type 1b is similar, except that you must recall and present an exact sequence of events or steps. Typical questions might be, "Detail the events that led to the signing of the peace of Westphalia" or "Describe the process of bone cell division."

In "trace" questions—and, in fact, in nearly all types of questions —the language used by the instructor can make it difficult to recognize what you are actually being asked to do. Notice that in the last two examples the words *detail* and *describe* could both be replaced with the word *trace*, resulting in a somewhat clearer question. Or, in the following example, the use of *discuss* might lead you to think the instructor wanted you to do more than simply trace a series of steps: "Discuss the acquisition of language as a function of the development of motor skills." A simpler and clearer way of phrasing the question would be "Trace the interrelated development of motor skills and language acquisition."

In studying all eight types of questions you should recognize that the basic terms and phrases for giving directions might sometimes be used casually by an instructor. Therefore, when you come across an instruction such as *discuss*, ask yourself whether you can translate it into clearer terms. Are you to "discuss" in the sense of showing relationships (as in Type 5) or in the sense of "trace" (as in the example just given) or in some other sense (as in the extension of knowledge, Type 3)?

Type 2: Comparison/Contrast

Besides being a basic mode of thought and a common pattern used in organizing college papers, comparison/contrast is also a popular type of essay question. Generally, comparison/contrast questions are more difficult than recitation questions: Whereas reciting requires only the understanding, recollection, and replay of information, comparing two items requires you to make a comparative *point* about them. And so you must have a clear thesis statement to guide and control a comparison/ contrast answer. Without such a controlling idea you will probably fall into the "descriptive trap"—that is, you will describe A and then describe B without actually stating how they compare or what the comparison reveals. For this reason we recommend conducting a point-by-point comparison on an essay test (*A/B-A/B-A/B* rather than *A, then B*). With that organization you are more likely to structure your answer as a series of comparative statements rather than as a descrip-

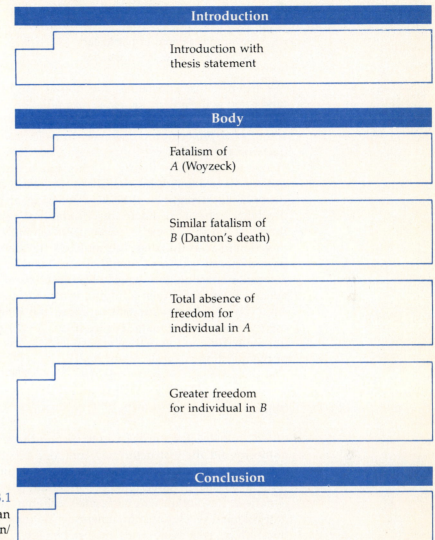

Introduction

Introduction with
thesis statement

Body

Fatalism of
A (Woyzeck)

Similar fatalism of
B (Danton's death)

Total absence of
freedom for
individual in *A*

Greater freedom
for individual in *B*

Conclusion

Figure 8.1
The structure of an
answer to a comparison/
contrast essay question

tion. Here is a typical comparison/contrast question from an upper-level German literature course: "Compare and contrast Buchner's philosophy of fatalism in *Woyzeck* and *Danton's Death*." In answering this question, you would *not* want simply to describe the fatalistic philosophy in the first play and then the philosophy in the second play; rather you would want to compose a comparative thesis statement, such as "While both *Woyzeck* and *Danton's Death* exhibit a similar fatalism, the plays differ in that *Danton's Death* allows the individual at least a small degree of control over his or her fate." You could then structure your answer as shown in Figure 8.1 above.

Type 3: Extension of Knowledge

    a. From general to particular
    b. From particular to general

The extension of knowledge question is one of the most challenging kinds you will face in an essay examination. This type of question requires you to take something you have learned and apply it to a new situation or project it imaginatively to its logical conclusion. A Type 3a question (general to particular) from a psychology course might read, "How would *XYZ*'s theory of the ego account for the behavioral differences exhibited by the identical twins in the following case history?" Or it might be phrased, "Construct an imaginary case history involving behavioral differences in identical twins to illustrate *XYZ*'s theory of the ego." Type 3b (particular to general) asks you to reverse the direction of your thinking: "Formulate a theory of aesthetics to encompass the early works of Stendhal and Flaubert." With both types of extension question, it is usually best to respond by first laying out the general theory and then applying it to a series of particular features. And you should not hesitate to admit the limitations of the general theory where appropriate. For instance, *XYZ*'s theory of the ego may not apply fully to the particular case history, even though the wording of the question suggests that it does.

Type 4: Evaluation of a Claim or Argument

Often an instructor will ask you to respond to a statement made by an authority. Or the instructor may compose a statement and ask you to agree or disagree with it. Here is an example of this type of question from a course in government. "Professor *ABC* observes that 'The American Revolution was completely different in nature from modern anti-colonial revolutions in emerging nations of the Third World.' Support or take issue with this statement." A good procedure for dealing with this type of question is to think of arguments on both sides and then to organize your essay based on those arguments. Most often you will be able to find arguments on both sides of the issue, and your essay should—if this is so—take account of that fact. In other words, even if you ultimately decide to make a strong case for one side of an argument, you should show some understanding of the opposing evidence. Moreover, you should not rule out the possibility of an answer that only partially supports or refutes the statement. When evidence exists on both sides, you can answer the question by saying that the statement is only partially accurate.

Type 5: Discussion—Tie Together Information to Show Relationships

The discussion question is one of the most elusive and difficult types to answer. As with the extension question (Type 3), you are required to do a good bit of imaginative manipulation; the path to your answer will likely be less straightforward than with some other cases. What you must do in a true discussion question (remember that the term *discuss* is sometimes loosely applied) is to pick out a number of relevant points or instances and show how they relate to or revolve around a central point. But unlike the case of the recitation question (Type 1), you must work from your own perceptions and form your own conclusions, rather than merely repeating what you have taken in. Here is a specific example: "In *The Great Gatsby*, is Nick Carraway as honest and reliable a narrator as he would like us to believe he is?" In answering this question you would first identify the theme or point around which your supporting points will center. Here you would choose "honesty and reliability" and then catalogue in your mind the various instances in the book in which you recall Nick's acting—or not acting—reliably and honestly. Generally, questions that begin with *Why* are discussion questions. Answering the following question would require you to pick out a number of facts and ideas and to structure them around the central characteristics of the Gilded Age: "Why is the period from 1870 to 1885 often termed the 'Gilded Age'?" This question might be phrased more clearly as "Discuss the reasons and factors that have led historians to call the period from 1870 to 1885 the 'Gilded Age.'"

Type 6: Combinations

Sometimes a single question will incorporate two or more types: trace and extend, evaluate and contrast, and so on. For example, you might be asked to recite a theory and then extend or apply it to a particular situation. Or a question might require you to trace a sequence of events and then discuss the larger significance of the sequence. We include combinations as a separate type of question to alert you that sometimes no single category will be adequate for classifying a question.

Type 7: The Creative Question

Perhaps the most difficult part of handling a creative question is recognizing that it is not as hard as it seems at first. Creative questions are actually concealed variations of the basic types (compare, evaluate, extend). Consider this example: "Imagine a meeting between Hemingway's Jake Barnes (*The Sun Also Rises*) and James' Christopher Newman (*The American*) and invent a dialogue between the two." Rather than being stunned by this unusual request, you should identify it as a creative question. Recognize that the instructor basically is asking for a comparison/contrast of the two characters, and, by extension, a comparison/contrast of the themes of the two novels as well. You are to concoct a meeting between the central characters of the two books and have them speak and react to each other in a way that reveals their personalities and compares the basic themes of the books. Also, recognize that you should devote some energy to making the *creative* part of the answer lively and entertaining: Each speaker could use some of his own characteristic expressions, for example. In answering this type of essay question, then, you should make an imaginative attempt to create a situation into which you build a solid answer to one of the standard types of questions discussed earlier.

Type 8: The Deleted Premise

Like the combination question and the creative question, Type 8 is a variation on the five basic types of questions. The deleted premise question is particularly challenging because it may fool you into thinking that it is based totally on material that you have not studied and therefore cannot talk about. This impression is created because the phrasing of the question leaves out an important link or key term that would relate the question to something you have studied. For example, recall one of the questions used to illustrate Type 3a, extension of knowledge from general to particular: "How would *XYZ*'s theory of the ego account for the behavioral differences exhibited by the identical twins in the following case history?" This question would be a deleted premise type if it simply read, "Comment on the behavioral differences exhibited by the identical twins in the following case history." Without any direct mention of the key term "*XYZ*'s theory of the ego" (which probably had been studied at length in the course), this question might strike the test taker as coming out of nowhere. The case history by itself might seem totally unfamiliar unless the needed link to the theory could be seen. If you find yourself facing a question of this type, you should not panic and assume that the teacher is asking an unfair question. Rather, you should calmly sort through the most important concepts, theories, principles, and figures covered in the course, searching for the link. Remember, the link *is* there. No instructor will ask you a question that is not directly based on something you have studied (except, perhaps, in the case of an extra credit question).

Exercise

1. Classify the following sample essay examination questions according to type.

a. Discuss the emergence of the local-color novelists and their significance to the realistic movement of the late nineteenth century.

b. In light of recent theories about the social and biological foundations of language, consider the following: To what extent could a child who had spent his or her first five years isolated from all exposure to language acquire the ability to speak?

c. Erich Fromm has said that "Our whole culture is based on the appetite for buying, on the idea of a mutually favorable exchange." Support or refute his belief.

d. Why, in your opinion, have most archaeologists hesitated to date the following artifacts?

e. As the assistant editor of an anthology you must decide whether to include an article which maintains that Andrew Johnson was impeached because he abused executive power or one which asserts that his impeachment stemmed from disagreements with Congress over Reconstruction. Write a statement explaining your decision to the senior editor.

f. The philosophy behind a liberal arts education is that breadth of study and training in critical thinking and problem solving are the best preparation for life and a career. The philosophy behind a specialized education (such as engineering or accounting) is that in-depth training in a specific area is the best preparation. Write an essay supporting one system or the other, being certain to base your argument on a careful assessment of the relative strengths and shortcomings of each system.

g. Discuss the major developments in federal civil rights legislation between the landmark Supreme Court case of *Brown* vs. *Board of Education* and the end of Lyndon Johnson's tenure as president.

h. Write an essay in which you challenge the wisdom of an established saying, such as "Absence makes the heart grow fonder" or "Out of sight, out of mind."

i. Which of the terms used by Abraham Maslow in discussing his idea of "self-actualization" would be most useful in explaining the experiences of the Vietnam war veterans highlighted in Smith's longitudinal study?

j. Explain what Joan Didion means when, in "On Keeping a Notebook," she says that "we are well advised to keep on nodding terms with the people we used to be, whether we find them attractive company or not."

2. Review the list of questions you predicted for the Exercise on page 267. Classify those questions according to type. Did your list include at least one question of each type? If not, formulate one question of each type not represented on your list.

TAKING THE TEST: PREVIEWING AND BUDGETING

Once the test begins, you should devote the first five or so minutes to reading *all* the questions and allotting a certain amount of time for each. As you preview, consider several things:

1. Do all the questions appear to be equally difficult?

2. Are all the questions worth roughly the same number of points?

3. Is the test composed entirely of essay questions, or are there short-answer questions, too?

If the answer to both 1 and 2 is *yes*, then you can proceed to budget equal time for each question and to answer the questions in the order in which they are presented in the test. However, if all the questions are not equally difficult, then you should consider answering the easier questions first, to make sure that you will have the time to respond to them with essays deserving of full credit. If you attempt to answer the most difficult questions first, you may never get to the easier ones. Don't fall victim to the fallacy that because the more difficult questions are the most challenging, they should be dealt with first. For one thing, the more difficult questions may not, in fact, be more difficult in the eyes of the instructor. They may simply seem more difficult to you because you are not as familiar with the material they cover. Although essay tests can be valuable learning experiences, never forget that one of your primary objectives in test-taking is to score points. Thus, in addition to answering significantly easier essay questions first, you should also consider filling in the short answers you know early in the test, even if they are presented last on the test sheet.

Similarly, if all questions are not worth the same number of points, you may want to change the order of approach presented in the exam sheet. If, for instance, the first four questions are all worth ten points each and question five is worth sixty points, you will certainly want to budget most of the test period for answering question five. And if the answer to the fifth question seems as though it will be longer but perhaps no more difficult than the answers to questions one through four, you may want to tackle question five first.

If you decide to write the answers to your exam in an order different from the one the instructor gives, it's a good idea to leave the first page blank. Then go ahead and complete the exam in the order you wish, numbering the pages as you write. After you have completed the exam, set up a table of contents on the first page for your instructor to use. In this way, you not only give yourself valuable flexibility, but also avoid inconveniencing or confusing your grader. Particularly in an exam for a large class, you run the risk of losing credit altogether for certain questions if the grader doesn't understand that you changed the order of your responses.

Exercise

Examine the questions asked on any essay examinations you have taken previously. Try to remember how you responded when you were first handed the test. Did you preview the questions and budget your time? If not, try doing so now. For each examination, determine a workable budget and order of approach. ♪

TAKING THE TEST: WRITING THE ESSAY

Invention plays a somewhat limited role in the writing of examination essays. The bulk of invention occurs during reviewing notes and predicting questions before the test. Aside from using an awareness of the types of questions as a probe to get your memory working, however, you will devote minimal time during the exam to generating ideas. Freewriting in order to find your direction, for instance, is pretty much out of the question. Only as a last resort should you start writing an essay answer without a definite sense of your thesis and its support.

Whenever possible, first answer the question in one concise sentence. Such a sentence can serve both as your thesis statement and as a guide to organizing the essay that elaborates on the thesis. For example, let's say that you were being tested on some of the contents of this book. Here is the question:

> What are the chief benefits of using specific details in expository essays?

Recognizing this as a recitation question, you might give the following concise, one-sentence answer:

> Using specific details can give clarity, support, and a sense of personality to expository writing.

This sentence would constitute your thesis statement, and it would allow you to sketch (preferably in the margins of your exam book) the following outline (each roman numeral represents one paragraph):

I. Introduction and thesis statement
II. Specific details and clarity
III. Specific details and support
IV. Specific details and personality
V. Conclusion

You would then write the essay accordingly, elaborating in each body paragraph on the ways specific details contribute to the particular quality mentioned.

Now let's look at some actual student examination essays. The first sample was written for a final examination in an education course. Here is the question:

> Describe and then discuss three instances from your experience in which there was conflict between the expectations of a teacher or school and your personal needs.

The student's first impulse was simply to choose three random instances and then discuss them in terms of the conflicts that existed. However, the more he thought about what episodes he would describe, the more he came to realize that this was a Type 3 question: extension of knowledge from general to particular. The general principle involved was that of conflict between role expectations and actual behavior in the classroom. Thus the student would have to use this general principle as a guide in choosing his three experiences. His task is like that in the sample question under Type 3a: "Construct an imaginary case history involving behavioral differences in identical twins in order to illustrate XYZ's theory of the ego." In this instance, however, he was to draw the case histories from personal experience, not construct them through imagination, and he was to cite three of them, not one. And because the directions asked the student to "describe and then discuss" the experiences, he knew that the order in which he presented them would be specific to general, or experience to observation about experience. Here is the essay he wrote:

The opening sentence concisely states what is to come, using the wording in the question itself. Since the question did not lend itself to a thesis statement, the writer instead supplies a statement of purpose. In the second sentence, the student further explains his strategy: He will choose episodes from the whole spectrum of education.

In the first body paragraph the writer describes the first experience. Because exam essays are written extemporaneously, the description contains some irrelevant material ("most of my

[1]I will describe and discuss three instances from my own experience in which there was conflict between the expectations of a teacher or school and my own personal needs. I will cite one incident from elementary school, one from high school, and one from college to achieve a wide representation of the nature of such conflicts.

[2]When I was a third-grader, I developed an enthusiastic gregariousness with respect to my classmates. Actually, I had been rather shy up until then, and I was just really beginning to make friends. Most of my friends were boys, and I enjoyed talking with them during class time. We would often whisper to each other, as well as giggle and draw each other pictures. Needless to say the teacher didn't like this. She was middle-aged and seemed to fit the "stern teacher" stereotype. She repeatedly warned me and my friends to be quiet. I was afraid of her, and so I tried to abstain from talking, but my need for overt signs of friendship was so great that I couldn't. Eventually, she gave me "check marks" (demerits), and told me she would call my mother.

friends were boys"). Readers of
*exam essays are usually more
lenient in criticizing such lack of
polish than are readers of regular
essays.*

*Here is the "discuss" section for
the elementary school experience.
Note how the writer explains the
conflict in terms of the role
expectations theory that he has
already decided is the key theory he
is expected to apply.*

*In the next example the student,
feeling more comfortable with the
task, keeps extraneous details to a
minimum by beginning to discuss
the significance of the episode while
still describing what happened.*

*Paragraph 5 analyzes the second
experience in terms of role
expectations.*

*Here is the third and final
experience. By this point the
student is ready to discuss role
theory at the start of the example.*

*The student analyzes the last
experience and uses it to lead into
an overall conclusion.*

After this, I shut up. But whenever I thought I could get away with it, I slipped notes back and forth with my friends.

[3]In looking at the teacher's behavior, it seems that she was trying to live up to her role as disciplinarian by squelching my desire for comradeship. Perhaps her transgression was that she didn't tell me *why* I should be quiet. She only told me that I must. This made me view her as an ogre. She must have viewed me as a nasty little pagan. But I knew nothing of role restraints at the time.

[4]The next incident occurred during my senior year in high school. The group of kids I kept company with decided to have a "dress-down" day. Feeling the need to conform, I came to school in very raggedy clothes. My homeroom teacher bawled us all out for a while. He told us how immature and irresponsible we were. This was, I suppose, expected of him as "guardian of American youth." But his expectation of us as mature citizens conflicted with our desires to conform in nonconformity. We felt rebellious. Rebelliousness was not to be tolerated in a student. The teacher sent us to the principal, who backed him up 100 percent and sent us home to change clothes.

[5]In this instance, the teacher was conforming to the administration's expectations of his role, certainly not to the students' expectations of his role. We, the students, were yielding to our own needs, not conforming to the teacher's expectations of us.

[6]The last instance occurred at college. Here in college, we see that the teacher's role is somewhat different: He no longer is expected to be a disciplinarian. But his expectations of students are different from an elementary or high school teacher's, too. I was scheduled to make a five-minute speech one day in Public Speaking. Unfortunately, I had two midterm tests on the same day, and I felt the need to devote my time to these, in order to get good marks. Consequently, I didn't have time to prepare the speech. The professor, like many professors, seemed to feel that his course should be my sole concern in life. I explained to him about my tests, but he was rather hard on me.

[7]The expectations of the college teacher are different than those of the elementary or high school teacher. The college teacher has academic rather than disciplinary expectations of the student. But regardless of the type of teacher, expectations *do* exist, and they often clash with students' needs, thereby creating conflict.

To gain a better understanding of why this essay was successful, study the following example, written in response to the same question. This essay did not fare so well.

*The writer starts off by choosing
an instance from his school
experience; note that he fails to*

[1]The first instance I want to talk about happened my sophomore year in high school, when I got in trouble for going along with my peers. It was in my seventh period geometry class. No one respected

provide a separate introductory paragraph.

The writer is a good storyteller and his narrative seems to be progressing satisfactorily here, although he becomes too concerned with the small details. The reader hopes he will get to the point.

The writer concludes the episode, but fails to discuss its significance in light of the theory of role conflict. He has simply told us what happened and how he felt. Having told this story quickly, he should present an analysis of the episode—but he doesn't.

In the last paragraph, the writer does make a point. Unfortunately, it is not a point about violation of role expectations. Note also that, although the question asked for three instances, he has supplied only two.

the teacher, and I can't say that I blamed them. She was past retirement age and was, quite frankly, getting senile. She would forget our names, present the wrong solutions to proofs, and even lose our test papers. As if that weren't bad enough, she tried to be a stern disciplinarian, and she freely handed out demerits for talking—often to people who weren't even talking.

[2]Well, one day the leaders in our class got together at lunch and decided that they would get even with her. The plan was to pelt her with fruit peels while she was at the blackboard with her back turned to us. So we pooled the peels from our lunches that day—mostly from oranges and bananas—and hid them in our pockets. The plan worked almost too well. Every time she turned her back to write the next step in a proof, one of us would jump up and let her have it. But when she turned around, everyone disclaimed any knowledge, and she was too senile to catch anyone in the act. The episode ended with her going to the principal in tears. Though we all laughed heartily at our revenge, I really felt sorry for her.

[3]My freshman year I also had a conflict with the school, but it was over something more trivial: which entrance door to use. At my school, freshmen and sophomores were required to use the back door, whereas juniors and seniors were privileged to use the front. Well, it so happens that one day I overslept and had to run nearly all the way to school. Since my route normally took me by the front door first, I decided to risk using that door to avoid being late. Of course the assistant principal spotted me, and I wound up having detention for the next week. It seems that a rule was a rule, regardless of the circumstances.

[4]I was a straight-A student and didn't usually have trouble with the teachers or administrators, but these couple of instances show that even good students can run afoul of our very rigid school systems.

In this case, the writer tells an engaging story, but he totally misses the point of the question he has been asked. Instead of analyzing the episodes in terms of role theory, he simply narrates them. He then concludes with a thoughtful point—but, for the purposes of this exam, it is the wrong point. His failure to recognize that he is faced with a Type 3 question, and to respond appropriately, cost him a good grade.

The next sample essay we will examine was written for a literature examination. Here is the question:

The plays *Everyman* and *Dr. Faustus* both offer examples of characters who understand that their lives are a preparation for some kind of future life. Contrast the moral lessons presented to the audience by the deaths of these two figures. Concentrate on the final scenes in each play.

In this case the student considered the question and decided that it was a Type 2 question—compare/contrast. On her copy of the test sheet, she underlined the words *contrast the moral lessons* and *concentrate on the final scenes*. She quickly devised a concise answer: *Everyman* provides assurance about the afterlife while *Dr. Faustus* frightens the audience with a vision of awful damnation. Here is the outline she sketched:

I.   Introduction and thesis statement
II. The ending of *Everyman*
   a.   Some cause for alarm
   b.   Yet a reassuring message
III. The ending of *Dr. Faustus*—shock and a vision of hell
IV. Conclusion: Both Christian, but very different

Following is the actual essay. We have not provided any commentary so that you can make your own observations on the strategies and structure employed by the student.

   [1]The moral lessons presented in *Everyman* and *Dr. Faustus* are indeed different. *Everyman* instructs the audience by revealing how peaceful death may be, by assuring them that having faith, not fear, is the proper way to meet Death. *Dr. Faustus*, on the other hand, reveals to the audience how horrible death is when the soul is assured of eternal damnation. The earlier play contains instruction of a calmer sort, and reassures the audience that death is easy for the good Christian, while the later work presents the audience with the horrifying prospect of everlasting hellfire.

   [2]In the last scenes of *Everyman*, Everyman learns the qualities that he values most highly on earth will be of no use to him when he dies. Strength, Discretion, Beauty, and Five Wits all leave him. As he learns the unhappy truth, the lesson is also clear to the audience—they must not depend on qualities of earthly value and transience. Yet the lesson is not as horrifying as it could be, for Everyman learns another, more important one almost immediately. He finds that Good Deeds will descend into the grave with him, and, moreover, will speak for him when the Judgment comes. So Everyman is gladdened, as is the audience. The lesson is clear and reassuring—if man leads a life filled with Charity he need not fear the vengeance of the Lord. Everyman descends into the grave willingly and hopefully: "Into thy hands, Lord, my soul I commend." The viewer of the play is induced to see death as a reunion of the soul with God, not as something to be feared. Despite the fact that the Doctor, who has the last comments concerning the action, warns that divine retribution will follow a lack of Charity, the force of the lesson is still hopeful, assuring the good Christian of a happy death.

³The situation, however, is very different in *Dr. Faustus*. Faustus, too, learns a lesson, but its result is meant to shock the audience into remembering the moral teaching that concludes the play.

⁴*Everyman* learns in time to save his soul, but Faustus finds out much too late that his aspirations have damned him. In the final scene, Lucifer, Beelzebub, and Mephistopheles all enter the stage to make this completely clear to the audience. Again, their purpose is more or less to terrify the audience into submission. *Everyman* holds out the prospect of divine reward to the virtuous, while *Dr. Faustus* emphasizes the damnation of the evil.

⁵The death scene of Faustus especially contrasts with that of Everyman. Whereas the latter gladly commends his soul to God, Faustus sees in the Lord only "ireful brows" and "heavy wrath." He seeks in vain to escape that wrath and finally, amid "fearful shrieks and cries," is torn to bits by the devils. Surely this is instruction through intimidation. The play presents a warning not to attempt to surpass the bonds of mortality and uses as inducement the grisly torment of Faustus.

⁶The moral lessons of both plays involve the Christian feelings about Death and the afterlife, but while *Everyman* presents an essentially positive outlook, that of *Dr. Faustus* is totally negative. The passing of Everyman echoes Donne: "As virtuous men pass mildly away," but the death of Faustus remains a grim warning.

In discussing the first sample examination we noted that instructors reading test essays may be more lenient in criticizing a lack of polish because they are aware of the difficulties in writing extemporaneously. As you consider your teacher-audience, recall all that we said about the college audience in Chapter 1. Moreover, you should understand that, in the case of most essay examinations, the instructor will have to read a massive stack of papers in a very short period of time—perhaps thirty or forty booklets in one or two evenings. Because of this, the instructor is likely to respond positively to lively writing. That is, don't hesitate to use humor and imagination in your essays or to give some of your original opinions if the question has asked you to give your opinion. If you can introduce a bright spot into an otherwise long and serious evening of reading, your instructor will look fondly on your writing.

Suggestions for Writing

The following questions are designed to give you practice in writing essay examinations. In each case you should read the questions in advance and study the material until you are satisfied that you are familiar with it. The actual exam will be open-book, with a 45-minute time limit per question.

1. Carefully examine the automobile advertisements reproduced on the following pages. Write an essay in which you compare and contrast the two in terms of the audiences to which you feel they are addressed. Be certain to cite specific evidence from the advertisements to support your claims.

2. Reread the student essay on the changing image of Mary, page 134. In your own words briefly trace the development of Mary's religious significance as described by this student writer.

3. Discuss the process of invention as described in Chapter 1 and 2, being certain to show how at least two of the invention techniques examined could be applied to specific writing tasks of your choice.

* **$7,990.** Mfr's sugg. retail price includes a 12-month <u>unlimited</u> mileage, limited warranty. Transp., tax, license, dealer prep add'l.

They're going fast.

0 to 50 mph in just 7.2 seconds. Sales that have accelerated even quicker. That's how fast the VW Rabbit GTI is moving.

And no wonder.

It's been universally acclaimed by the motoring press as an extraordinary performance car.

With its eager 1.8 litre fuel-injected engine. Its crisp 5-speed transmission. And the very precise way its suspension contends with a road.

But that same motoring press has also hailed the German engineered, German designed Rabbit GTI as an extraordinary bargain. Just $7,990.*

Now there's only one way to catch a Rabbit that goes as fast as this one. You have to sneak up on it. At your VW dealer, of course.

Seatbelts save lives

Nothing else is a Volkswagen.

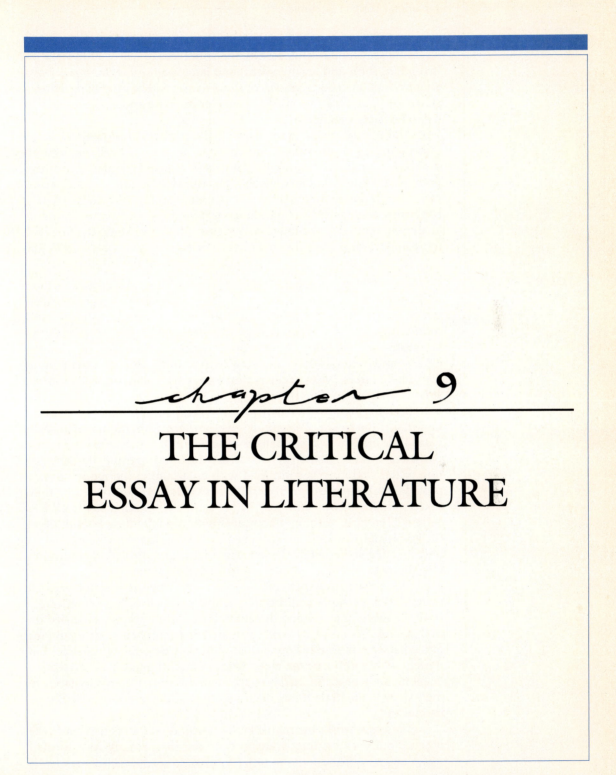

chapter 9

THE CRITICAL
ESSAY IN LITERATURE

In many respects, critical essays about literature are similar to other kinds of essays. Like other essays, the critical essay will require work on invention, form and arrangement, and language and style. It will have an introduction, a body, and a conclusion, and will be guided by a thesis statement. You will also need to consider purpose and audience and to make revision a central aspect of composing.

The special challenge in writing the critical essay lies mainly in understanding your subject matter—the literature—well enough to discuss it effectively. Because literature is so rich and complex (Northrop Frye, a well-known literary scholar, has called it "a human apocalypse, man's revelation to man"), it requires careful reading and study. We will begin this chapter with suggestions on how to read, understand, and analyze literature. In writing a critical essay, these make up the first and most important part of the invention process.

UNDERSTANDING AND ANALYZING LITERATURE

By *literature* we generally mean imaginative writing that creates its own fictional world. Typically, literature is divided into three categories called *genres*: poetry, narrative fiction (including novels and short stories), and drama. While other types and genres of writing may be considered literature—for instance, nonfictional narratives, biographies, travelogues, and letters—they are usually not the focus of attention in literature courses. Most of the critical essays you will write will examine serious imaginative literature.

Serious literature is that which attempts to convey something important about life. Perhaps it gives insight into human nature in general or into the ways of fate or of society. Or it may shed light on a particular kind of character or a certain historical period. By contrast, nonserious literature is concerned with entertaining the reader: it may provide temporary escape from the real world, but offer the reader little understanding about life. *Jaws* is nonserious literature; *Moby Dick* is serious literature. Although both deal with the relentless pursuit of an incredibly powerful and menacing aquatic beast, the former emphasizes only escapist action while the latter provides not only action but insight into the nature of human aspirations and obsessions.

One reason literature offers such a challenge is that the ideas it conveys are presented indirectly. In this sense it differs significantly from the more practical and direct kinds of writing we have focused on in this book. As an essay writer you are careful to state your main idea immediately and to develop and support it as directly as possible. But writers of literature never make their points in such a cut-and-dried fashion. A novelist, for instance, advances his or her points by fabricating a story to illustrate them. Such a story would imply rather than state its meanings.

Literature works by indirection not because authors are trying to be obscure but because they want to do more than simply convey their views or ideas. They write in order to provide readers with a complete experience, not just a set of points or insights. Thus the best approach for understanding and analyzing literature is to begin by immersing oneself in the work and experiencing it on its own terms. That is, when you read, you should allow yourself to get caught up in the story, the language, and the emotions of the piece—that is why it was written. If you allow yourself to be moved by the work, you will then find it easier to go back for a second or third reading in which you concentrate more actively on identifying the major ideas being conveyed.

You should, then, respond to literature by first respecting its indirect nature. On the other hand, if you intend to write in a direct way about literature, you must also come to understand it in more direct terms. Since the author does not tell you directly what he or she means, you will find the technique of analysis, discussed in Chapter 4 (pp. 139–47), to be helpful. Analysis involves going beneath surfaces to find meanings that are not immediately apparent, and so it is ideally suited to describing the ideas contained in a work of literature.

Approaches to Analyzing Literature

There is no single right way to analyze a literary work but rather a number of valid approaches. For example, you might discuss a work as a reflection of the person who wrote it, or of the society which produced that author, making use of biography or history. You might focus on the moral value of the work, or on the lessons it teaches. Some critics prefer to emphasize the uniqueness of each reader's responses to a work. Probably the most common approach is to focus on the text itself, identifying its literary features and explaining their relationship to the work's meaning.

In order to practice this kind of text-centered analysis (often referred to as New Criticism), you should be familiar with a number of specific aspects that may comprise a serious work of literature. Let's discuss some of these features.

Plot Plot refers to the basic events that constitute the action or development of the story. A poem may or may not have a plot. If it is a narrative poem (see "Mr. Flood's Party," pp. 304–306) it will tell a story, but poetry that makes general observations about life or nature will probably be plotless. Narrative fiction and drama are nearly always plotted.

In one sense, the plot gives rise to everything else in a work. Yet critics seldom concentrate on plot because discussing a storyline generally doesn't require much analytic thinking. In your own critical essays you should avoid summarizing the plot, being careful to retell parts of the story only when they are clearly essential as evidence to support a point you are making about the work. Even then, be careful to condense the summary and to state it immediately after, not before, the generalization it supports.

Theme   The *theme* of a literary work is the central insight, or main idea, that the writer conveys. Writers express their themes in a variety of ways—through the plots, characters, symbols, or other aspects of the fiction they create. A complex work may have more than one theme, though often one idea will predominate.

In determining a work's theme, it is often helpful to differentiate it from the work's plot or its subject matter. The subject matter is what the work is specifically about. For instance, a novel may be about a World War I Army officer, John O'Reilly, and his struggles to survive during battle. The theme, however, would be a more general statement, such as "War is hell; there is nothing glorious about it." Note that the theme is a statement about some aspect of life in general; it is not about John O'Reilly and World War I, even though his story illustrates and develops the theme.

Because the theme of a work is seldom stated directly, your role as a reader is to make inferences about the theme and to try to formulate a direct statement of it. While readers may agree in general about the theme of a work, there is really no single correct statement. For instance, another reader of the novel about John O'Reilly might formulate this statement of theme: "War is not the heroic business that society has led us to believe it is." This formulation would be just as acceptable as the one stated earlier, provided that the reader could give evidence to support the idea that the values of society were being criticized in the novel.

Structure   The term *structure* is used in two closely related ways. First, it refers to the component parts or units (structural elements) of a literary work. Second, it refers to the order or arrangement of structural elements within the work. A poem, for example, may be structured as a series of three-line stanzas, as in Shelley's "Ode to the West Wind":

> O wild West Wind, Thou breath of Autumn's being,
> Thou, from whose unseen presence the leaves dead
> Are driven, like ghosts from an enchanter fleeing,
>
> Yellow, and black, and pale, and hectic red,
> Pestilence-stricken multitudes: O Thou,   5
> Who chariotest to their dark wintry bed
>
> The winged seeds. . . .

In this case, the poem also has a larger structure: it is divided into five sections, each of which is comprised of four of the three-line stanzas and a concluding couplet (two-line stanza).

Similarly, dramatists make use of structure by dividing their works into acts and scenes. Shakespeare's plays, for example, have five acts, each of which generally contains several scenes. Sometimes the structural elements in a play are less obvious. The well made play of the late nineteenth century, for instance, embodied several less rigid, but nonetheless formal, divisions or stages. The play would begin with a section of exposition, in which the situation and the circumstances necessary to understanding the action were given. The second stage was one of complication and rising action, leading to the third stage, the climax or high point. The fourth stage was the denouement, or falling action, and the last stage was the conclusion.

The most obvious use of structure in narrative fiction is in the division of novels in chapters. Attempts to structure a work are also evident in a fiction writer's use of time sequences. Writers may tell their stories chronologically, or they may use mixed chronology. Joseph Conrad's *Lord Jim*, for example, uses flashbacks to fill in the details of Jim's life. Moreover, the presence of Marlowe as narrator indicates another kind of fictional structure. The story of Marlowe's interest in Jim's career frames Jim's own story, which is really a story within a story. The principles of selection and positioning are also important in studying the structure of a work. For example, each of the first three chapters of F. Scott Fitzgerald's *The Great Gatsby* focuses on a different social gathering. Chapter 1 presents the Buchanans' dinner party, Chapter 2 depicts Myrtle Wilson's apartment party, and Chapter 3 describes Gatsby's extravagant house party. By selecting these events and positioning them side-by-side, Fitzgerald uses structure to encourage us to compare and contrast the parties.

In studying the structure of a work, regardless of the genre, you should relate points about structure to points about meaning. From the discussion above, for example, we see that structure is a way of creating emphasis and achieving balance, as well as a device for shaping the development of the plot and controlling the time frame of a story. In addition to noting the existence of various structures and structural elements, then, you should try to understand and explain what effects they help the author create. Observing that each section of "Ode to the West Wind" contains four *terza rima* stanzas followed by a couplet may be a good place to begin your observations about the poem's structure; however, if you make no attempt to explain the relationship of this structure to the poem's meaning, you will have done little to increase your understanding.

Point of View   *Point of view* refers to the way in which a literary work is narrated. In the case of novels, short stories, and narrative poetry, it refers to who relates the events that take place. In the case of non-narrative poetry and conventional drama, the point of view is said to be *objective*. That is, while it is assumed there is an author who created the work, no narrator presents the events to the readers (or viewers).

Authors may select from a variety of points of view:

Omniscient
Limited omniscient
   Major character
   Minor character
First-person
   Major character
   Minor character
Objective

Stories told from the *omniscient* point of view are those in which the author may reveal to the readers all happenings in the story and all ideas and emotions of all the characters. As the events unfold, the readers see and hear everything the various characters see and hear, and the readers are privy to the characters' thoughts as well.

Limited omniscient point of view means that the story is told from the perspective of one person, though not in that person's own words. The readers know everything which happens to that one person and everything which that person thinks and feels, but they are limited in their knowledge of other characters. The readers know only as much as does the character from whose point of view the story is told. The character may be central to the story or may be a minor character.

First-person point of view is a story told in the words of one of the characters, either major or minor.

Objective point of view, used rarely in fiction, is also called *dramatic* point of view. Here the readers are presented with the words of the characters and view their actions, but there is little or no authorial commentary. Conventional dramas are written using this point of view.

Authors select their points of view depending largely on what they wish to accomplish in their works, since each point of view has advantages and disadvantages. Omniscient point of view, for instance, gives the readers a lot of information but is basically unrealistic, since no one in real life can know the thoughts, feelings, and actions of everyone else. Limited omniscient is more realistic in that only one person's mind is entered, but then that person must be carefully chosen to ensure that readers get the information they need to understand the story. First-person point of view gives a sense of immediacy and may appear more realistic. Here, though, the readers must be cautious. The tendency is to believe everything the narrator says. At times, however, the narrator may not be expressing the ideas or share the values esteemed by the author. Thus, for instance, when the narrator in Edgar Allan Poe's "The Tell-Tale Heart" says he is "nervous," not "mad," Poe expects his readers to make the opposite judgment. The danger, then, is that first-person point of view can lead to confusion regarding the author's intent. Sometimes that intent is itself hard to determine. Scholars for years have been arguing over the stability of the narrator, a governess, in Henry James' "The Turn of the Screw." Determining whether she is a narrator whom the reader can trust is a crucial decision in this case. If she is insane, the story is not a mere ghost story but a psychologically terrifying tale of her illness destroying children.

Character   *Character* is the nature of an individual. It includes all the personality traits which make that person unique. The term is also used to refer to fictional creations—the *characters* are the actors in the fictional work.

Depending on the writer's purpose, delineating character may be of greater or lesser importance. If the delineation of character is the primary purpose a writer has in creating a work, then the story is called a *character sketch* and that work exists mainly to depict a central character in action.

Character as a strategy to use in writing a critical essay is discussed in detail on pages 302–309.

Imagery   *Imagery* is the depiction in words of sensory experiences, including sight, hearing, taste, touch, and smell. In an earlier section of this text (pp. 250–54), we discuss imagery in nonfiction writing. Fiction writers use it for some of the same reasons: Images make writing more vivid, more descriptive, and more imaginative.

In addition, for writers of fiction, imagery is one of the major tools used to add richness to their works. By using images, fiction writers engage their readers' minds on several levels, stimulating them intellectually, of course, but also appealing to their senses. Thus, for instance, readers can *know* what an experience was like for characters in a story and can also *feel* what it was like, because of the images.

Poets in particular make use of imagery, since it enables them to make multiple appeals to their readers in few words. In poetry, every word is important. If a poet, in a given number of words, can allow a reader to *feel* or *smell* or *hear*, as well as to understand, what's happening, then the impact may be greater. Imagery was extremely important to the poet John Keats. In the following lines, from the "Ode to a Nightingale," he describes the suffering he sees in the world:

> The weariness, the fever, and the fret
>   Here, where men sit and hear each other
>   groan;
> Where palsy shakes a few, sad, last gray hairs,
>   Where youth grows pale, and spectre-thin,
>   and dies. . . .

How many images can you find in these lines? To which senses do they refer?

Metaphors and Similes   Closely related to images are *metaphors* and *similes*, both of which are comparisons of essentially dissimilar things.

Because they invoke at least two images, the literal and figurative terms, metaphors and similes are especially powerful and economical devices. By using them, writers can increase the impact of their works. In general, the more innovative and imaginative the metaphors and similes are, the more memorable, appealing, or even shocking they will be.

Symbol   A *symbol* is anything that represents more than what it literally is. A country's flag, for example, is a symbol of the country itself. Symbols are plentifully used in literature. In F. Scott Fitzgerald's novel *The Great Gatsby*, Daisy Buchanan, the woman Gatsby loves, becomes for him a symbol. He pursues her over so many years that she comes to symbolize the very wealth and power that he must achieve before he can win her. In John Keats' "Ode to a Nightingale," the nightingale symbolizes a world of peace and happiness that contrasts with the world of suffering in which the poet lives.

Actions, as well as people and objects, may also function as symbols. For example, at the start of *Great Expectations*, when the convict Magwitch grabs the young Pip and turns him upside-down, the action symbolizes the various reversals of fortunes and values that take place throughout the novel.

When analyzing a literary work to identify symbolism, keep in mind that your interpretation of the symbol must be supported by the meaning of the work as a whole. For instance, in *The Great Gatsby* Fitzgerald comments throughout on the American dream; interpreting Daisy Buchanan as a symbol of its realization fits within the commentary of the novel as a whole. At times inexperienced readers tend to find too many symbols, deciding that every gnarled oak represents an old woman or every cloudy day the state of mind of the character. Be cautious in looking for symbols, and use the themes of the work to guide you. In addition, in longer works symbols often recur, so you can look for objects or actions that are repeated and seem important for the central meanings of the story or poem as you determine whether symbolism is being used.

Irony   *Irony* is saying (or doing) one thing and meaning the opposite. It may involve sarcasm, as it would if you walked into a room and said to your napping friend, "My, aren't you working hard today!" What you mean, of course, is that your friend is not working at all—the opposite of what you said. Irony also refers to words, actions, or situations that are the opposite of what you would *expect* to be true. Thus it is *ironic* when a lifeguard drowns or a police officer commits a crime.

Fiction writers use irony often. Sometimes the characters in the work consciously make ironic comments, just as we all do in real life. More often, however, the irony in literature is unintended and unrecognized by the characters themselves, though the readers do recognize it—or at least the writer intends they should. Thus in *Death of a Salesman*, when Willy Loman tells his wife that he misses her when he travels and that he hates being alone so much, the viewer is supposed to see his words as ironic, since Willy has love affairs while traveling. Willy, of course, does not intend that Linda recognize the irony of what he says; he wants her to think he is sincere. This type of irony, in which the readers understand the difference between what is said (or done) and what is true (or expected) is called *dramatic irony*—probably the most important type to understand in interpreting literature. It is up to the reader to recognize dramatic irony. Otherwise, the opposite meaning is received. Like Linda Loman, the reader will be misled.

WRITING THE CRITICAL ESSAY

In the first section of this chapter, we have presented a brief overview of the various elements which may be present in literary works, and have also suggested the indirect, complex nature of literature. Here we will discuss various approaches and techniques that are used in composing essays about literature.

Approaches to Critical Essays

There are several different ways to approach writing about literature. You can choose one of the features of literature that we have just examined and write your paper on *how well* the author uses it. Thus, for example, you might choose to discuss how effectively Fitzgerald uses symbolism in *The Great Gatsby* or Keats uses imagery in "Ode to a Nightingale." To write such a paper, which evaluates an author's technique, you must have a good command both of the work and of the specific element. Or, you can focus on one element and discuss how that feature is used to support the themes of the work. This common approach is explained in detail on pages 307–309, where character is the feature being analyzed.

You can also approach the work by discussing what about it makes it uniquely that author's work. By learning about the author's life you may reveal ways in which the work reflects or in other ways comments on it. Then your approach in your paper is to discuss those ideas. Or, if you've read other works by the same writer, you can discuss how this one relates to the rest. Tackling more than one novel, story, or play is probably more suitable for a longer paper, perhaps one supplemented by research on the author's style of writing. In an introductory course it is likely not to be appropriate.

Another approach to literary analysis is to examine the ways in which a story or poem comments on or reflects the attitudes, values, and conditions of the historical period during which it was written. Social criticism, for instance, is a major theme of many authors, and a good paper may be written analyzing an author's commentary. Of course, to take this approach, you must know about or research the relevant historical period.

In an introductory course you will likely be asked to focus on the work itself and to discuss the central insights its writer is trying to impart. Always be certain that you do *analyze* the literature. Avoid merely retelling the story or paraphrasing the ideas. After all, you are writing about a work that your instructor has likely read and studied. Mere repeating of content should be kept to a minimum. Rather, focus on the author's insights, thus enabling your instructor to evaluate your responses to the work. If you are writing about narrative fiction, keep plot summary to a minimum, also. Refer to events to demonstrate the truth of your analysis of the story or poem.

Exercise

Read the following poem carefully. Then read the two essays based on it. Note the differences between them, particularly in the amount of analysis each writer undertakes. Be prepared to discuss and evaluate them in class.

THEME FOR ENGLISH B

The instructor said,

> *Go home and write*
> *a page tonight.*
> *And let that page come out of you—*
> *Then, it will be true.*   5

I wonder if it's that simple?
I am twenty-two, colored, born in Winston-Salem.
I went to school there, then Durham, then here
to this college on the hill above Harlem.
I am the only colored student in my class.   10
The steps from the hill lead down into Harlem,
through a park, then I cross St. Nicholas,
Eighth Avenue, Seventh, and I come to the Y,
the Harlem Branch Y, where I take the elevator
up to my room, sit down, and write this page: 15

It's not easy to know what is true for you or me
at twenty-two, my age. But I guess I'm what
I feel and see and hear, Harlem, I hear you:
hear you, hear me—we two—you, me, talk on this page.
(I hear New York, too.) Me—who?   20

Well, I like to eat, sleep, drink, and be in love.
I like to work, read, learn, and understand life.
I like a pipe for a Christmas present,
or records—Bessie, bop, or Bach.
I guess being colored doesn't make me *not* like   25
the same things other folks like who are other races.
So will my page be colored that I write?

Being me, it will not be white.
But it will be
a part of you, instructor.   30
You are white—
yet a part of me, as I am a part of you.
That's American,
Sometimes perhaps you don't want to be a part of me.
Nor do I often want to be a part of you.   35
But we are, that's true!

As I learn from you,
I guess you learn from me—
although you're older—and white—
and somewhat more free.   40

This is my page for English B.

(Langston Hughes)

1.   [1]After being given an assignment by his teacher, Hughes contemplates exactly what he should write about.
            [2]Since the theme was to come out of him and his experiences, Hughes' truths, inhibitions, etc., were to be expressed in his paper. He begins by giving a physical description of himself and he feels this in itself makes him different from the instructor and the other members of his class. He also feels very strange about being the only black student in the class.
            [3]Every day after leaving the college campus, which is probably located in a clean and uncluttered section of New York, he must walk through the ghetto areas to reach his little room in the Y.
            [4]Hughes then goes on to state that even though he is black and is literally at the bottom rung of the social ladder, he still does normal things like eat and sleep. Also, he likes to work, read and write— things that some white people during that era did not think blacks could do. In essence, his blackness does not mean he does not want a piece of the American dream.
            [5]The concluding lines of Hughes' poem state that even though we may not like it, both black and white people are a part of each other.

2.   [1]Langston Hughes' poetry in "Theme for English B" is not intense or complicated, but rather simple and precise. Hughes writes in a

conversational manner to give the reader a better understanding of his themes, which in much of his poetry center around the struggles and hardships of black people. In "Theme for English B," the speaker, a black man, expresses his feelings about himself and the white man, and we see that the struggle of this poem has to do with his identity.

²From the start, the speaker is aware that he is different. Being the only "colored student" in his class and living across the park along St. Nicholas and Seventh Avenue creates a distinction between himself and the white man. Although he likes the things white folks like, he makes it clear that "Being me . . . will not be white" (line 28). The character in the poem feels a certain pride in being different and unique. As a black, he doesn't "often want to be a part of you [the white instructor]" (38).

³Yet the speaker also seems to be insecure. For one thing, he is still young: "It's not easy to know what is true for you or me/ at twenty-two . . . " (16–17). For another, although he is proud and sure of his blackness, he seems to be confused about his identity. The instructor has said "*let that page come out of you*" (4), but the speaker says "I wonder if it's that simple?" (6) On the one hand, he is Harlem: the poverty, the misfortunes and the struggles. "Harlem, I hear you" (18), he says. On the other hand, he also hears New York. The lines "hear you, hear me—we two—you, me, talk on this page/ . . . Me—who?" (19–20) express his confusion.

⁴He seems confused by the fact that in certain ways, he is like the white man (white New York and his college "on the hill above Harlem"—[9]). He is alike in his education and in some of his interests: "I like to work, read, learn. . . . /I like . . . Bach" (22, 24). And yet he is the black man struggling and living in an environment that is not receptive to people of his race. He emphasizes this by stressing his isolation as he walks home to his room in "the Y, / the Harlem Branch Y" (13–14).

⁵The character's uncertainty about his identity is also evident in his view of the instructor. He says: "You are . . . / a part of me, as I am a part of you / . . . You don't want to be a part of me. / Nor do I often want to be a Part of you" (31–32, 34–35). He seems to prefer a separation between himself and the white man. Yet he stresses there is a learning relationship in which both contribute equally. Both are equal in this sense: "But we are, that's true!" (36). And yet the speaker remains confused because the instructor is "white— / and somewhat more free" (39–40).

Techniques in Writing Critical Essays

As we noted at the start of this chapter, you will employ many of the same techniques in writing critical essays that you do in writing effective essays generally. You will develop, then support, a thesis, keeping in mind your reader's expectations and demands. And you will certainly revise your writing, possibly inventing new ideas as you write. Beyond all this, however, there are a few techniques especially useful for writing essays about literature.

First, let's consider prewriting (remembering that you may continue to think of ideas throughout the composing process). You can use brainstorming to get started. Thoughtfully consider what you've read and how you've responded to it. Jot down ideas about characterization, images, themes, and so on, as they come to you. Look over what you've written and see if any of the approaches suggested above are appropriate for your ideas. Work toward focusing on one of them and composing a thesis statement.

You may also be able to use personal experience as a source of inventing ideas. Perhaps you have read other works by or about the same author, or about the period of time during which the author wrote. In that case, you can recall what you've read or look up some of the material to reread it in order to stimulate your thinking.

In composing papers about literature, you'll also need to reread, or skim, at least parts of the work you're writing about. You'll want to refresh your memory to be sure that the ideas you're generating accurately reflect the work.

As you consider your ideas, remember the various patterns of thought we've discussed. It may be that your thoughts will lend themselves to the appearance versus reality essay structure or some other type of essay structure.

When you arrange your ideas, use an arrangement appropriate for your thinking, one that will emphasize your major points. If your paper is on narrative fiction and discusses an idea or theme that develops as the work progresses, you can use chronological order as you point to incidents supporting your statements. If you discuss an aspect of the work that is not related to the progression of the story's events, then a topical arrangement is probably best. For comparison/contrast and the other patterns, try using one of the arrangements we discussed in Chapter 4.

One special technique you will have to master in writing papers about literature is that of effectively using quotations from a work. It is, after all, mainly through direct quotations and paraphrases (your wording of the author's ideas) that you will support your observations. Pointing to an excerpt from the text is invaluable; even though your readers are familiar with the literature, they still need to reread the passage that supports what you are saying and to read your analysis of its details. Thus you should use at least one quotation from the text each time you make a significant point in your critical essay. And sometimes you may want to cite more than one passage to illustrate or support your point.

Quotations from the literature not only "prove" the points you are making, but also add a flavor of the literature to your work. By skillfully interweaving quotations from the text with your own words, you will show your familiarity with the work and also enhance your style. Consider this example from an essay on Hamlet:

> Ophelia, "blasted with ecstasy," emerges as a particularly pathetic victim of Hamlet's revenge.

By using the quotation "blasted with ecstasy" (meaning "rendered insane"), the writer is making Shakespeare's more colorful language his own. Moreover, since that phrase was originally uttered by Ophelia herself when she feared Hamlet had lost *his* sanity, the writer is subtly and efficiently indicating his awareness of an irony in the play's action: that it is Ophelia and not Hamlet who goes mad.

When supplying quotations (especially long ones) to support a point, first use a lead-in sentence or two in which you state precisely what the quotation illustrates or why it is important. Then quote the passage itself. Some beginning writers assume that the quotation speaks for itself. But to make your point most effectively you should elaborate further. You might follow a quotation with several sentences in which you show more specifically, by commenting upon the meaning or by pointing to specific details, *exactly how* the quotation illustrates what you say it does. Or you might follow up by explaining how the meaning of the quotation relates to another point you have discussed or you are about to discuss.

Consider the following example from a paper on "The Rime of the Ancient Mariner" in which the writer first places the quotation in context and then interprets, in a few sentences, its importance:

> The Mariner's tale has had such an emotional impact on the Wedding Guest that the guest can no longer join in the celebration. Further, his ignorance of any harrowing spiritual experience such as the Mariner has had and his naive joy have vanished:
>
> A sadder and a wiser man,
> He rose the morrow morn.

Sadder he must be, since he has lost what must have been a limited understanding of life, and, actually, has become more like the Mariner in spirit. The knowledge of what can happen to the human soul, though a valuable insight, darkens his outlook considerably. Wiser he must also be, since the impact of the Mariner's tale leaves no doubt that he has learned his lesson well.

On the other hand, be careful not to overuse quotations, especially when, because of space limitations, including them means excluding your own observations. When quoted passages are so numerous that they threaten to overshadow your discussion, prune some of them out and develop your own comments further. Even when accompanied by commentary, an overabundance of quotations can damage your paper by fragmenting its style, making it seem like a patchwork quilt rather than a tightly woven fabric.

When you are revising a critical essay, consider each point on this checklist:

1. Are the statements I make supported by the work as a whole? Be wary of ideas that seem to apply only to a limited extent when viewed in the context of the total work.

2. Have I used enough quotations or paraphrases? As we have suggested, strike a balance here, and be sure that you find specific examples to support your statements.

3. Does my thesis reflect my response to the work? Use ideas to which you are committed, ones that grow from your own experience with the literary work.

4. Do I interpret and comment, as appropriate, on the events of the story, without retelling it needlessly? Remember that your reader is thoroughly familiar, in most cases, with the work you analyze. Don't waste time saying what is already known.

5. Have I double-checked research information and do I credit my sources? Review other materials as needed and be certain to cite the authors and works whose ideas you use in your paper. To do otherwise is *plagiarism*, a serious offense. See Chapter 11 for a discussion of proper documentation.

6. Overall, is my paper analytic? Do I try to interpret, not just paraphrase, the events or ideas to which I refer? Work to see that your ideas go beyond surface meanings that are readily apparent without your contribution.

Following is a good example of a student essay on literature. Read carefully first the poem and then the paper analyzing it:

> I look into my glass,
> And view my wasting skin,
> And say, "Would God it came to pass
> My heart had shrunk as thin!"
>
> For then, I undistrest   5
> By hearts grown cold to me,
> Could lonely wait my endless rest
> With equanimity.
>
> But Time, to make me grieve,
> Part steals, lets part abide;   10

And shakes this fragile frame at eve
With throbbings of noontide.

(Thomas Hardy)

A CRITICAL COMMENT: "I LOOK INTO MY GLASS"

The writer first presents his overall impression of what the poem communicates. Furthermore, he indicates what aspects of the poem—connotations and figurative language—he will concentrate on to prove his points.

[1]Thomas Hardy's poem, "I Look into My Glass," is a terse soliloquy in which the speaker's despondent, intensely personal reflections on being old, unloved, and yet still experiencing painfully intense feelings evoke a powerful response from the reader. More specifically, the connotative meanings of specific words and the figurative language in the poem add a great deal to the reader's understanding of the magnitude of the speaker's feelings of helplessness, dejection, and loneliness.

In this case the writer comments on the poem line by line and stanza by stanza, an effective way to analyze a short poem. He begins by noting the structure of the stanza, then narrows his focus to specific words and their importance for the poem's meaning.

[2]The overall structure of the poem is precise, comprised of three quatrains that present the speaker's thoughts in the form of a logical argument. The first stanza is a brief statement of the situation, followed by his hypothetical proposition. Line 1 is a key passage of the poem because the speaker immediately describes what he is doing. The connotative meaning of that line is of great importance to the reader's conception of the speaker's thoughts. The use of "look into" suggests he is not merely gazing at his reflection in the mirror; the reader senses that the haggard image he sees in the "glass," a hard-edged, brittle, utterly frank object, impels him to probe beyond his time-worn physical appearance and to assess his inner being, his state of mind.

[3]He presents his hypothetical proposition in line 3. His emphatic desire is that fate would have had his emotional side undergo as much deterioration as his physical being. The word "heart" is a conventional symbol which signifies the center of one's emotions, especially one's ability to love. The speaker's desire to have a heart that had "shrunk" is consistent with the imagery of his wrinkled, wasting skin in line 2. "Shrunk" suggests contraction, a dwindling, like a prune withering with age. Furthermore, "thin" heart is also consistent with the thinness and consequent translucency of the skin following the loss of subcutaneous fat. Thus, the more significant connotative meaning of line 4 is that he wishes he would not be able to love or experience similarly strong feelings.

Beginning by relating the second stanza to the first in terms of structure, the writer once again focuses on the poet's language. He analyzes how the connotations of various words contribute to the work's overall impact.

[4]In the second stanza, the speaker specifically states the consequences that would follow if the hypothetical condition were met. For example, line 5 begins with "For then," which implies that if condition *A* is met, then the consequence *B* will take place. The word "undistrest" means freedom from anxiety and suggests a numbness to strong feelings. In line 6, "hearts" takes on an additional symbolic association, referring to the people who, over a period of time (as suggested by "grown"), have become indifferent to him; they have no feelings for him. Whether these people were former lovers, friends, or

family members, the speaker must have had strong feelings for them. And he must still be experiencing some intense pain from his sensitivity.

[5]The speaker evokes the reader's sympathy; the reader can imagine the turmoil and anguish he is undergoing from his description in lines 7–8 of what he actually would be able to do if he was undisturbed by his feelings. The position of "lonely" before "wait" underscores the sense of desolate loneliness he is experiencing; furthermore, the use of "wait" conveys the sense of impotence, resignation, and passivity which is pervading the psyche of this old man. He has resigned himself to his fate—waiting for his "endless rest." In line 8 the word "equanimity" suggests he would wait for death with composure. "Equanimity" and "undistrest" have a similar meaning in reference to the speaker's desire—they refer to the quality of not being easily disturbed.

As the writer examines the third stanza, he emphasizes the importance of the personification of time and explains how this figure of speech functions in relation to the theme of the poem. The writer continues to interpret the connotative values of those words he feels are significant. Note that throughout the essay he quotes words and phrases, or refers to specific lines, in order to support his interpretations of what Hardy intends in his poem.

[6]In the third stanza, the speaker states the resolution, which for him is the harshness of his present situation. More specifically, line 9 begins with the word "but," which emphasizes the contrast between reality and his escapist desire. The dominant figure in the third stanza is the personification of time. The relatively abstract notion of time is made much more vivid and powerful by being described as a person. The personification of time is significant in that the speaker's somewhat passive attitude toward time and his life is manifested; he knows he can not change the past, and he views time as an antagonistic entity which painfully impinges on him. He asserts in line 9 that time purposely and consciously makes him suffer.

[7]Furthermore, he regards time as having control over his life. For example, in line 10 he mentions that time "Part steals," taking away part of his being. Man is comprised of a physical component (the body) and an emotional, intellectual component. The word "steals" suggests the unjustness of time having taken away the physical strength and vitality of his youth. Time is selective in how it affects him; it leaves other aspects—his mental and emotional qualities—unchanged.

[8]Line 11 offers further evidence of his perception of time as a powerful, adverse force which he cannot escape. He detachedly remarks that time "shakes this fragile frame at eve." The active verb "shakes" gives the reader an idea of the magnitude of the force with which time stirs his feelings. The connotations of "fragile frame" (frail, like a paper kite) also add to the reader's mental associations with the speaker's weak, easily broken bones—bones which can be shattered as easily as glass as his death grows near. The last line provides an understated, poignant, and powerful conclusion. The word "throb-bings" is evocative of the heart symbolism present in the preceding quatrains and underscores the intensity of the overwhelmingly strong feelings he is experiencing. The word "noontide," in the context of the poem, refers to the climax of his life, a climax which occurred when he was younger.

Suggestion for Writing

Read carefully the following short poem about death, guilt, ritual, and expiation. Formulate a precise statement of the poem's theme, and then write an essay in which you show how the poet's use of descriptive language and images helps to create or reinforce the theme.

JAYWALKER

His arm leaves a dent in my hood.

He lies on the pavement, smiling
to reassure me.
                         Weeks later
the leak in his brain begins.
I try to imagine his headaches,   5
the murmuring nurses, the priest.
By then he is dead.

                         *

Twenty-two years. I can't
remember his face or name.   10
He came from a farm across the river.
We tried to visit his father and mother.

Tonight it's as though
my brakes have failed
and I roll through the hushed sirens   15
past white faces, past
the weary Night Dispatcher, steering
my old, slow Mercury toward
the figure across the river,
the boy from the empty farmhouse   20
with his smile, his trick headaches.

I would like to light him a candle.
I would like to bring him a drink of
water.
I would like to yield the right of way.
I would like to call across the river.   25

"It's all right now?" I'd shout.

His head would bob in the wind.

(David Young)

CHARACTER AND THEME: A SPECIFIC STRATEGY

Briefly, character is the essence of a person's nature. It is comprised of his or her background, beliefs, motivations, general behavior traits, and specific actions. These factors can all be sources of information about a person's character; as you read, you should be aware of them.

Certainly not all literature is equally concerned with character. Some of the most famous poetry, for instance, is about life in general or about nature. But more often, authors write about people and their behavior. Even so, however, they are not always concerned with what students of literature call "character." Sometimes, for example, people appear in a work simply to help along the plot. Sometimes there is no real interest in them as complicated human beings with complex motivations and behavior, but rather a concern for their value as one-dimensional stereotypes. When the fictional creations seem to be stereotypes rather than real people, the author is probably more interested in some other aspect, such as plot or structure. Generally, you should avoid writing about character in a work if the people are either incidental to the plot or stereotypical, for beyond noting these facts about them, there would be very little to say.

Two key terms to keep in mind when assessing character are *qualities* and *traits* (which mean roughly the same thing). If you can translate information about a person's background, beliefs, motivations, and so on into one-word qualities or traits, you will be well on your way to analyzing that person's character. Qualities or traits may be expressed in either noun or adjective form:

NOUN	ADJECTIVE
arrogance	arrogant
compassion	compassionate
determination	determined
enthusiasm	enthusiastic
greed	greedy
honesty	honest
insecurity	insecure
loneliness	lonely
selfishness	selfish

Information about character in a work of literature generally comes to the reader through one or more of these four possible forms:

1. Through direct statement by the narrative voice:

   His measured, springless walk was the walk of the skilled countryman as distinct from the desultory shamble of the general labourer; while in the turn and plant of each foot there was, further, a dogged and cynical indifference personal to himself, showing its presence even in the regularly interchanging fustian folds, now in the left leg, now in the right, as he paced along. (Thomas Hardy, *The Mayor of Casterbridge*)

2. Indirectly, through actions performed by the character:

   "I order you to halt," I called. They went a little faster. I opened my holster, took the pistol, aimed at the one who had talked the most, and fired. I missed and they both started to run. I shot three times and dropped one. The other went through the hedge and was out of sight. I fired at him through the hedge as he ran across the field. (Ernest Hemingway, *A Farewell to Arms*)

3. Through dialogue, monologue, or inner monologue (that is, a character's thoughts):

> BIFF: I stole myself out of every good job since high school!
> WILLY: And whose fault is that?
> BIFF: And I never got anywhere because you blew me so full of hot air I could never stand taking orders from anybody! That's whose fault it is! . . . I had to be boss big shot in two weeks, and I'm through with it! (Arthur Miller, *Death of a Salesman*)

4. Ironically, through methods 1, 2, or 3:

Consider Marc Antony's famous statement in Shakespeare's *Julius Caesar:* "Brutus is an honorable man." In this case, the speaker is being ironic: He means the opposite of what he says. If we share his point of view, we will conclude that Brutus is deceitful and contemptible. Ironic methods of revealing character don't apply as readily to category 2, actions performed, as to categories 1 and 3, because a character's actions usually demonstrate rather directly his or her nature. Still, if the action was insincerely motivated or not truly representative of the person's character as demonstrated in the rest of the work, it, too, could be an ironic statement of character.

You will need to develop a sensitivity to the literature in order to spot evidences of character as you read. To some extent, this will be an intuitive process. But if you pay close attention to what the author is telling you about a person's nature through any or all of the four forms and attempt to translate that information into specific qualities or traits, you will be gaining insights into the person's character.

Exercise

Read the following poem carefully. How would you describe Eben Flood's character? What qualities or traits does he have? How do you know? Which of the four forms does the poet use to give us information about character?

MR. FLOOD'S PARTY

Old Eben Flood, climbing alone one night
Over the hill between the town below
And the forsaken upland hermitage
That held as much as he should ever know
On earth again of home, paused warily.   5

The road was his with not a native near;
And Eben, having leisure, said aloud,
For no man else in Tilbury Town to hear:

"Well, Mr. Flood, we have the harvest moon
Again, and we may not have many more;   10
The bird is on the wing, the poet says,
And you and I have said it here before.
Drink to the bird." He raised up to the light
The jug that he had gone so far to fill,
And answered huskily: "Well, Mr. Flood,   15
Since you propose it, I believe I will."

Alone, as if enduring to the end
A valiant armor of scarred hopes outworn,
He stood there in the middle of the road
Like Roland's ghost winding a silent horn.   20
Below him, in the town among the trees,
Where friends of other days had honored him,
A phantom salutation of the dead
Rang thinly till old Eben's eyes were dim.

Then, as a mother lays her sleeping child   25
Down tenderly, fearing it may awake,
He set the jug down slowly at his feet
With trembling care, knowing that most things break;
And only when assured that on firm earth
It stood, as the uncertain lives of men   30
Assuredly did not, he paced away,
And with his hand extended paused again:

"Well, Mr. Flood, we have not met like this
In a long time; and many a change has come
To both of us, I fear, since last it was   35
We had a drop together. Welcome home!"
Convivially returning with himself,
Again he raised the jug up to the light;
And with an acquiescent quaver said:
"Well, Mr. Flood, if you insist, I might.   40

"Only a very little, Mr. Flood—
For auld lang syne. No more, sir; that will do."
So, for the time, apparently it did,
And Eben evidently thought so too;
For soon amid the silver loneliness   45
Of night he lifted up his voice and sang,
Secure, with only two moons listening,
Until the whole harmonious landscape rang—

"For auld lang syne." The weary throat gave out,
The last word wavered, and the song was done.   50

He raised again the jug regretfully
And shook his head, and was again alone.
There was not much that was ahead of him,
And there was nothing in the town below—
Where strangers would have shut the many doors   55
That many friends had opened long ago.

(Edward Arlington Robinson)

Analyzing someone's character or explaining how an author develops someone's character may in themselves constitute adequate paper topics, depending upon the literature being discussed. Probably a more effective strategy, though, is to relate character to the theme of the work. For instance, suppose that a novel offers the theme that modern society is increasingly lacking in ethical or spiritual values. If, in developing the major figures, the author depicts some of them as lacking in ethics and/or spirituality, you could write a paper showing how the novelist's handling of character reveals the book's theme.

You will probably want to structure your paper around a series of qualities or character traits that you have identified for the character you are discussing. For each quality you should offer ample evidence from the text to support your assertion that the character does in fact have that quality. You could then discuss in detail the relationship of the character (and his or her qualities) to the theme. The following essay on Robert Browning's ''My Last Duchess'' uses this technique.

MY LAST DUCHESS

That's my last duchess painted on the wall,
Looking as if she were alive. I call
That piece a wonder, now: Frà Pandolf's hands
Worked busily a day, and there she stands.
Will't please you sit and look at her? I said   5
''Frà Pandolf'' by design, for never read
Strangers like you that pictured countenance,
The depth and passion of its earnest glance,
But to myself they turned (since none puts by
The curtain I have drawn for you, but I)   10
And seemed as they would ask me, if they durst,
How such a glance came there; so, not the first
Are you to turn and ask thus. Sir, 'twas not
Her husband's presence only, called that spot
Of joy into the Duchess' cheek: perhaps   15
Frà Pandolf chanced to say, ''Her mantle laps
Over my lady's wrist too much,'' or, ''Paint

Must never hope to reproduce the faint
Half-flush that dies along her throat": such stuff
Was courtesy, she thought, and cause enough   20
For calling up that spot of joy. She had
A heart—how shall I say?—too soon made glad,
Too easily impressed; she liked whate'er
She looked on, and her looks went everywhere.
Sir, 'twas all one! My favor at her breast,   25
The dropping of the daylight in the West,
The bough of cherries some officious fool
Broke in the orchard for her, the white mule
She rode with round the terrace—all and each
Would draw from her alike the approving speech,   30
Or blush, at least. She thanked men,—good! but thanked
Somehow—I know not how—as if she ranked
My gift of a nine-hundred-years-old name
With anybody's gift. Who'd stoop to blame
This sort of trifling? Even had you skill   35
In speech—which I have not—to make your will
Quite clear to such an one, and say, "Just this
Or that in you disgusts me; here you miss,
Or there exceed the mark"—and if she let
Herself be lessoned so, nor plainly set   40
Her wits to yours, forsooth, and made excuse,
—E'en then would be some stooping; and I choose
Never to stoop. Oh, sir, she smiled, no doubt,
Whene'er I passed her; but who passed without
Much the same smile? This grew; I gave commands;   45
Then all smiles stopped together. There she stands
As if alive. Will't please you rise? We'll meet
The company below, then. I repeat,
The Count your master's known munificence
Is ample warrant that no just pretense   50
Of mine for dowry will be disallowed;
Though his fair daughter's self, as I avowed
At starting, is my object. Nay, we'll go
Together down, sir. Notice Neptune, though,
Taming a sea-horse, thought a rarity,   55
Which Claus of Innsbruck cast in bronze for me!

(Robert Browning)

First, the writer states that the Duke's character illuminates more than just his individual personality. In several ways he will serve

[1]In Robert Browning's "My Last Duchess" the character of the Duke is not only fascinating in itself, but it serves as a vehicle for the poet to reveal social customs of the Duke's times, especially those relating to the status of women. Browning increases the poem's

effectiveness by writing it as a dramatic monologue, thereby allowing the Duke himself to "speak" and disclose his character indirectly. Readers hear only his version of the events described and make their judgments of his character based on what he says.

[2]Browning rapidly establishes the Duke as an autocratic, arrogant, status-conscious nobleman. That he has complete power over his household is suggested early, in lines nine and ten: ". . . none puts by/The curtain I have drawn for you, but I." The implication is that since he controls such a relatively trivial matter as opening a curtain covering a portrait, he must therefore control everything, or as close to everything, as he can.

[3]From this perspective, included in his control very clearly should be his wife, but beginning with line 13 ("Sir, twas not/Her husband's presence only . . .") it is obvious that she at first did not meet his expectations. He criticizes her severely for merely smiling; his main objection seems to be that she should smile *only* at him on cue, as it were. Instead, she found much to make her "glad" independent of the Duke: "the dropping of the daylight in the West,/The bough of cherries . . . broke . . . for her, the white mule/She rode with . . ." (lines 26–29). All of these have nothing to do with her husband; he does not provide her with them as he does with his "nine-hundred-years-old name" (line 33). Therefore, he ultimately does not permit her to smile at them: "I gave commands;/Then all smiles stopped together" (lines 45–46). Browning does not tell the readers whether the Duke in fact murdered his wife, but it is evident that such control of life and death is certainly consistent with the way in which he wishes to rule his household.

[4]The Duke is arrogant as well. He boasts not only of his family name, but also of his power, as when he makes a point of saying only he can draw aside the painting's cover. In addition, he explains how even reprimanding his wife is beneath him. She should *automatically* obey and respect him; he will "never . . . stoop" (line 43) to discussing the matter with her, as that might imply she is his equal, which "such an one" (line 37) could never be. Even when he is supposedly being humble, as in lines 35 and 36 ("Even had you skill/In speech—which I have not") it is clearly false modesty.

[5]His pride and arrogance feed his status-consciousness, which reveals itself most strikingly in his attitude toward the art objects he possesses. He obviously uses them to impress the Count's emissary. He is careful to mention the artists' names and even to point out the statue of Neptune lest his listener not notice it. The value of art for him is the way in which it increases his own stature. It is a symbol of his own wealth and glory.

[6]Finally, the Duke is a greedy man. As he plans to wed his *next* Duchess, the dowry concerns him more than does the woman in question. Note how the following lines are structured:

> . . . I repeat,
> The Count your master's known munificence
> Is ample warrant that no just pretense
> Of mine for dowry will be disallowed;
> Though his fair daughter's self, as I avowed
> At starting, is my object. . . . (lines 48–53)

The idea given greater prominence is the dowry; the "daughter's self" is added as an afterthought.

Having established that the Duke possesses the various traits the writer feels are significant, she now turns to the issue of what those traits reveal about the times in which the Duke lived.

[7]How does the Duke's character help to illuminate the customs of his times? Many of the traits he possesses help to give Browning's readers an idea of what the nobility was like, though certainly the Duke is not to be considered totally typical. After all, there is a strong implication that he is homicidal; the *last* Duchess may not even have been the *first* one, is definitely not the *final* one, and may be one in a string of murder victims.

The writer asserts that, primarily, the story of "My Last Duchess" reveals the status (or lack of status) of even women of noble birth in the Duke's time. She carefully qualifies her statement, pointing out that the Duke's behavior is in only some ways typical.

[8]The Duke's character does, nevertheless, reveal a lot about his society. His treatment of his wife is extreme in some ways, but in others reflects the social and legal status of women at the time. Dowries were the most important consideration in joining your "nine-hundred-years-old name" to that of another family. Marriages were political, social, and economic alliances forged by the male members of the family. The Duke may appear greedy in mentioning first the money, then the woman, but his expectations of financial gain in return for his marriage are appropriate to his society.

[9]In addition, the way in which he considers his wife part of his possessions (her having to get his permission even to enjoy her surroundings) is legitimate in view of the times. Women had no legal entities and were at the mercy of their fathers and then their husbands. The Duchess's beauty is a bonus for the Duke. She can add to his status because of it. She is thus not only a possession but a highly attractive one. Ultimately she literally, of course, becomes a beautiful possession, one whose smile the Duke finally can completely control, just by pulling a curtain. Again, the Duke's treatment of her is extreme, but women of the times, even those of noble birth, were expected to be subservient to their husbands and to do all they could to enhance their status.

In her last point, the writer notes that the Duke's attitude toward art also is typical, though from his self-centeredness comes some benefit.

[10]Also, the Duke is a reminder of the importance to the arts of the nobility. True, he uses art to increase his own stature, but his patronage and that of others like him provided a livelihood for the artists of the times and stimulated their enormous artistic achievements.

[11]In "My Last Duchess" Browning thus presents insights into the customs of the times as well as into the character of his narrator, and he does both indirectly, thereby making the poem more intriguing for its readers.

Write an essay in which you discuss the relationship of character to theme in the following work.

THE CITY

by John Updike

[1]His stomach began to hurt on the airplane, as the engines changed pitch to descend into the city. Carson at first blamed his pain upon the freeze-dried salted peanuts that had come in a little silver-foil packet with the Whiskey Sour he had let the stewardess bring him at ten o'clock that morning. Fifty, he did not think of himself as much of a drinker, but the younger men in kindred gray business suits who flanked him in the three-across row of seats had both ordered drinks, and it seemed a way of keeping status with the stewardess. Unusual for these days, she was young and pretty. So many stewardesses seemed, like Carson himself, on second careers, victims of middle-aged restlessness. A long-divorced former mathematics teacher, he worked as a sales representative for a New Jersey manufacturer of microcomputers and information-processing systems. Late in life, after twenty years of driving the same suburban streets from home to school and back again, he had become a connoisseur of cities—their reviving old downtowns and grassy industrial belts, their rusting railroad spurs and new glass buildings, their orange-carpeted hotels and bars imitating the interiors of English cottages. But always there was an individual accent, a style of local girl and historic district, an odd-shaped skyscraper or a museum holding a Cézanne or a medieval altarpiece that you could not see in any other city. Carson had never before visited the city into which he was now descending, and perhaps a nervous apprehension of the new contacts he must forge and the persuasions he must deliver formed the seed of the pain that had taken root in the center of his stomach, just above the navel.

[2]He kept blaming the peanuts. The tempting young stewardess, tanned from West Coast layovers, had given him not one but two packets in silver foil, and he had eaten both—the nuts tasting tartly of acid, the near engine of the 747 haloed by a rainbow of furious vapor in a backwash of sunlight from the east as the great plane droned west. This drone, too, had eaten into his stomach. Then there was the Whiskey Sour itself, and the time-squeeze of his departure, and the pressure of elbows on the armrests on both sides of him. He had arrived too late to get an aisle or window seat. Young men now, it seemed to him, were so corpulent and broad, with the mixture of exercise and beer the culture kept pushing. Both of these wore silk handkerchiefs in their breast pockets and modified bandit mustaches above their prim, pale, satisfied mouths. When you exchanged a few words with them, you heard voices that knew nothing, that were tinny. They were gods but without timbre. Carson put away the

papers on which he had been flow-charting a system—computer, terminals, daisy-wheel printer, dual-drive disks, optional but irresistible color-graphics generator with appropriate interfaces—for a prospering little manufacturer of electric reducing aids, and ran a final check on what could be ailing his own system. Peanuts. Whiskey. Being crowded. In addition to everything else, he was tired, he realized: tired of numbers, tired of travel, of food, of competing, even of shaving in the morning and putting himself into clothes and then, sixteen hours later, taking himself out of them. The pain slightly intensified, as if a chemical jot more had been added to its tarry compound. He pictured the pain as spherical, a hot bubble that would break if only he could focus upon it the laser of the right thought.

³In the taxi line, Carson felt more comfortable if he stood with a slight hunch. He must look sick, he was attracting the glances of his fellow-visitors to the city. The two young men whose shoulders had squeezed him for three hours had melted into the many similar others with their attaché cases and polished shoes. Carson gave the cab driver not the address of the manufacturer of reducing and exercise apparatus but that of the hotel where he had a reservation. A sudden transparent wave of nausea, like a dip in the flight of the 747, decided him. The cool autumnal air beat through his suit upon his skin. As he followed the maroon-clad bellhop down the orange-carpeted corridor, not only were the colors nauseating but the planes of wall and floor looked warped, as if the pain that would not break up were transposing him to a set of new coordinates, by the touch of someone's finger on a terminal keyboard. He telephoned the exercise company from the room, explaining his case to an answering female and making a new appointment for tomorrow morning, just before he was scheduled to see the head accountant of another booming little firm, makers of devices that produced "white noise" to shelter city sleep. The appointment-squeeze bothered Carson, but abstractly, for it would all be taken care of by quite another person—his recovered, risen self. The secretary he had talked to had been sympathetic, speaking in the strangely comforting accent of the region—languid in some syllables, quite clipped in others—and had recommended Maalox. In the motion pictures that had flooded Carson's childhood with images of the ideal life, people had "sent down" for such things, but during all the travelling of his recent years he had never come to believe that this could be done; he went down himself to the hotel pharmacy. A lobby mirror shocked him with the image of a thin-limbed man in shirtsleeves, with a pot belly and a colorless mouth tugged down on one side.

⁴The medicine tasted chalky and gritty and gave the pain, after a moment's hesitation, an extra edge, as of tiny sandy teeth. His hotel room also was orange-carpeted, with maroon drapes that Carson closed, after peeking out at a bare brown patch of park where amid the fallen leaves some boys were playing soccer; their shouts jarred his membranes. He turned on the television set, but it, too, jarred. Lying

on one of the room's double beds, studying the ceiling between trips to the bathroom, he let the afternoon burn down into evening and thought how misery itself becomes a kind of home. The ceiling had been plastered in overlapping loops, like the scales of a large white fish. For variation, Carson stretched himself out upon the cool bathroom floor, marvelling at the complex, thick-lipped undersides of the porcelain fixtures, at the distant bright lozenge of mirror. Repeated violent purgations had left the essential intruder, the hot tarry thing no longer simply spherical in shape but elongating, undissolved. When vomiting began, Carson had been hopeful. The hope faded like the light. In the room's shadowy spaces his pain had become a companion whom his constant interrogations left unmoved; from minute to minute it did not grow perceptibly worse, nor did it leave him. He reflected that his situation was a perfect one for prayer, but Carson had never been at all religious, and so could spare himself that additional torment.

⁵The day's light, in farewell, placed feathery gray rims upon all the curved surfaces of the room's furniture—the table legs, the lamp bowls. Carson imagined that if only the telephone would ring his condition would be shattered. Curled on his side, he fell asleep briefly; awakening to pain, he found the room dark, with but a sallow splinter of street light at the window. The soccer players had gone. He wondered who was out there beyond the dark whom he could call. His ex-wife had remarried; of his children, one, the boy, was travelling in Mexico and the other, the girl, had disowned her father. When he received her letter of repudiation Carson had telephoned and been told, by the young lawyer she had been living with, that she had moved out and joined a feminist commune.

⁶He called the hotel desk and asked for advice. The emergency clinic at the city hospital was suggested, by a male voice that to judge from its briskness had just come on duty. Shaking, lacing his shoes with difficulty, smiling to find himself the hero of a drama without an audience, Carson dressed and delicately took his sore body out into the air. A row of taxis waited beneath the corrosive yellow glare of a sodium-vapor street light. Neon advertisements, stacked cubes of fluorescent offices, red and green traffic lights scratched at the taxi windows, glimpses of the city that now, normally, with his day's business done, he would be roving, looking for a restaurant, a bar, a stray conversation, possibility of contact with one of the city's unofficial hostesses.

⁷The hospital was a surprising distance from the hotel. A vast and glowing pile with many increasingly modern additions, it waited at the end of a swerving drive through a dark park and a neighborhood of low houses. Carson expected to surrender the burden of his body utterly, but instead found himself obliged to carry it through a series of fresh efforts—forms to be filled out, proofs to be supplied of his financial fitness to be ill, a series of waits to be endured, on crowded benches and padded chairs, while his eye measured the distance to

the men's-room door and calculated the time it would take him to hobble across it, open the door to a stall, kneel, and heave vainly away at the angry visitor to his own insides.

[8]The first doctor he at last was permitted to see seemed to Carson as young and mild and elusive as his half-forgotten, travelling son. The doctor's wife, it somehow came out, was giving a dinner party, for which he was already late, in another sector of the city. Nevertheless the young man politely, circumspectly gave him time. Carson was, he confessed, something of a puzzle. His pain didn't seem localized enough for appendicitis, which furthermore was quite unusual in a man his age.

[9]"Maybe I'm a slow bloomer," Carson suggested, each syllable, in his agony, a soft, self-deprecatory grunt. There ensued a further miasma of postponement, livened with the stabs of blood tests and the banter of hardened nurses. He found himself undressing in front of a locker so that he could wait with a number of other men in threadbare, backwards hospital gowns to be X-rayed. The robust technician, with his standard bandit mustache, had the cheerful aura of a weight lifter and a great ladies' (or men's) man. "Chin here," he said. "Shoulders forward. Deep breath: hold it. Good boy." Slowly Carson dressed again, though the clothes looked, item by item, so shabby as to be hardly his. One could die, he saw, in the interstices of these procedures. All around him, on the benches and in the bright, bald holding areas of the hospital's innumerable floors, other suppliants, residents of the city and mostly black, served as models of stoic calm, which he tried to imitate, though it hurt to sit up straight and his throat ached with gagging. The results of his tests were trickling along through their channels. The young doctor must be at his party by now; Carson imagined the clash of silver, the candlelight, the bare-shouldered women—a festive domestic world from which he had long fallen.

[10]Toward midnight, he was permitted to undress himself again and to get into a bed, in a kind of emergency holding area. White curtains surrounded him, but not silence. On either side of him, from the flanking beds, two men, apparently with much in common, moaned and crooned a kind of blues, and when doctors visited them pleaded to get out, promised to be good henceforth. From one side came a sound of tidy retching, like that of a cat who has eaten a bird bones and all; on the other side, interns seemed to be cajoling a tube up through a man's nose. Carson was comforted by these evidences that at least he had penetrated into a circle of acknowledged ruin. He was inspected at wide intervals. Another young doctor, who reminded him less of his son than of the legal-aid lawyer who had lived with his daughter and whom Carson suspected of inspiring and even dictating the eerily formal letter she had mailed her father, shambled in and, after palpating of Carson's abdomen, sheepishly shrugged. Then a female doctor, dark-haired and fortyish, with a Slavic accent, came and gazed with sharp amusement down into Carson's face and said, "You don't protect enough."

[11]"Protect?" he croaked. He saw why slaves had taken to clowning.

[12]She thrust her thumb deep into his belly, in several places. "I shouldn't be able to do that," she said. "You should go through the ceiling." The idiom went strangely with her accent.

[13]"It did hurt," he told her.

[14]"Not enough," she said. She gazed sharply down into his eyes; her own eyes were green. "I think we shall take more blood tests."

[15]Yet Carson felt she was stalling. There was a sense, from beyond the white curtains, percolating through the voices of nurses and policemen and delirious kin in this emergency room, of something impending in his case, a significant visitation. He closed his eyes a second. When he opened them a new man was leaning above him—a tall tutorial man wearing a tweed jacket with elbow patches, a button-down shirt, and rimless glasses that seemed less attachments to his face than intensifications of a general benign radiance. His hair was combed and grayed exactly right, and cut in the high-parted and close-cropped style of the Camelot years. Unlike the previous doctors, he sat on the edge of Carson's narrow bed. His voice and touch were gentle; he explained, palpating, that some appendixes were retrocecal; that is, placed behind the large intestine, so that one could be quite inflamed without the surface sensitivity and protective reflex usual with appendicitis.

[16]Carson wondered what dinner party the doctor had arrived from, at this post-midnight hour, in his timeless jacket and tie. He wished to make social amends but was in a poor position to, flat on his back and nearly naked. With a slight smile, the doctor pondered his face, as if to unriddle it, and Carson stared back with pleading helpless hopefulness. He was as weary of pain and a state of emergency as he had been, twelve hours before, of his normal life. "I'd like to operate," the doctor said softly, as if putting a suggestion that Carson might reject.

[17]"Oh yes, *please*," Carson said. "Great. When, do you think?" He was very aware that, though the debauched hour and disreputable surrounds had become his own proper habitat, the doctor was healthy, and must have a home, a family, a routine to return to.

[18]"Why, right *now*" was the answer, in a tone of surprise, and this doctor stood and seemed to begin to take off his coat, as if to join Carson in some sudden, cheerfully concocted athletic event.

[19]Perhaps Carson merely imagined the surgeon's gesture. Things moved rapidly. The sheepish legal-aid look-alike returned, more comradely now that Carson had received a promotion in status, and asked him to turn on one side, and thrust a needle into his buttock. Then a biracial pair of orderlies coaxed his body from the bed to a long trolley on soft swift wheels; the white curtains were barrelled through; faces, lights, steel door lintels streamed by. Carson floated, feet first, into a room that he recognized, from having seen its blazing counterpart so often dramatized on film, as an operating room. A masked and youthful population was already there, making chatter, having a party. "There are so many of you!" Carson exclaimed; he was

immensely happy. His pain had already ceased. He was transferred from the trolley to a very narrow, high, padded table. His arms were spread out on wooden extensions and strapped tight to them. His wrists were pricked. Swollen rubber was pressed to his face as if to test the fit. He tried to say, to reassure the masked crew that he was not frightened and to impress them with what a "good guy" he was, that somebody should cancel his appointments for tomorrow.

²⁰At a point and place in the fog as it fitfully lifted, the surgeon himself appeared, no longer in a tweed jacket but in a pale-green hospital garment, and now jubilant, bending close. He held up the crooked little finger of one hand before Carson's eyes, which could not focus. "Fat as that," he called through a kind of wind.

²¹"What size should it have been?" Carson asked, knowing they were discussing his appendix.

²²"No thicker than a pencil," came the answer, tugged by the bright tides of contagious relief.

²³"But when did you sleep?" Carson asked and was not answered, having overstepped.

²⁴Earlier, he had found himself in an underground room full of stalactites. His name was being shouted by a big gruff youth. "Hey Bob come on Bob wake up give us a little Smile that's the boy Bob." There were others besides him stretched out in this catacomb, whose ceiling was festooned with drooping transparent tubes; these were the stalactites. Within an arm's length of him, another man was lying motionless as a limestone knight carved on a tomb. Carson realized that he had been squeezed through a tunnel—the arm straps, the swollen rubber—and had come out the other side. "Hey Bob, come on, give us a smile. *Thaaat's it.*" He had a tremendous need to urinate; liquid was being dripped into his arm.

²⁵Later, after the windy, glittering exchange with the surgeon, Carson awoke in an ordinary hospital room. In a bed next to him, a man with a short man's sour, pinched profile was lying and smoking and staring up at a television set. Though the picture flickered, no noise seemed to be coming from the box. "Hi," Carson said, feeling wary, as if in his sleep he had been married to this man.

²⁶"Hi," the other said, without taking his eyes from the television set and exhaling smoke with a loudness, simultaneously complacent and fed-up, that had been one of Carson's former wife's most irritating mannerisms.

²⁷When Carson awoke again, it was twilight, and he was in yet another room, a private room, alone, with a sore abdomen and a clearer head. A quarter-moon leaned small and cold in the sky above the glowing square windows of another wing of the hospital, and his position in the world and the universe seemed clear enough. His convalescence had begun.

²⁸In the five days that followed, he often wondered why he was so happy. Ever since childhood, after several of his classmates had been

whisked away to hospitals and returned to school with proud scars on their lower abdomens, Carson had been afraid of appendicitis. At last, in his sixth decade, the dread enemy had struck, and he had comported himself, he felt, with passable courage and calm. His scar was not the little lateral slit his classmates had boasted but a rather gory central incision from navel down; he had been opened up wide, it was explained to him, on the premise that at his age his malady might have been anything from ulcers to cancer. The depth of the gulf that he had, unconscious, floated above thrilled him. There had been, too, a certain unthinkable intimacy. His bowels had been "handled," the surgeon gently reminded him, in explaining a phase of his recuperation. Carson tried to picture the handling: clamps and white rubber gloves and something glistening and heavy and purplish that was his. His appendix indeed had been retrocecal—one of a mere ten per cent so favored. It had even begun, microscopic investigation revealed, to rupture. All of this retrospective clarification, reducing to facts the burning, undiscouragable demon he had carried, vindicated Carson. For the sick feel as shamed as the sinful, as fallen.

²⁹The surgeon, with his Ivy League bearing, receded from that moment of extreme closeness when he bent above Carson's agony and decided to handle his bowels. He dropped by in the course of his rounds only for brief tutorial sessions about eating and walking and going to the bathroom—all things that needed to be learned again. Others came forward. The slightly amused dark Slavic woman returned, in her white smock, to change his dressing, yanking the tapes with an, he felt, unnecessary sharpness. "You were too brave," she admonished him, blaming him for the night when she had wanted to inflict more blood tests upon him. The shambling young doctor of that same night returned, no longer in the slightest resembling the lawyer Carson's daughter had spurned in favor of her own sex, and there appeared a host of specialists in one department of Carson's anatomy or another, so that he felt huge, like Gulliver pegged down in Lilliput. All of them paid their calls so casually and pleasantly that Carson was amazed, months later, to find each visit listed by date and hour on the sheets of hospital services billed to him in computer printout—an Apple II Plus interfaced with an old Centronics 739 dot-matrix printer, from the look of it.

³⁰Hospital life itself, the details of it, made him happy. The taut white bed had hand controls that lifted and bent the mattress in a number of comforting ways. A television set had been mounted high on the wall opposite him and was obedient to a panel of buttons that nestled in his palm like an innocent, ethereal gun. Effortlessly he flicked his way back and forth among morning news shows, midmorning quiz shows, noon updates, and afternoon soap operas and talk shows and reruns of classics such as Carol Burnett and "Hogan's Heroes." At night, when the visitors left the halls and the hospital settled in upon itself, the television set became an even intenser and warmer companion, with its dancing colors and fluctuant glow. His

first evening in this precious room, while he was still groggy from anesthesia, Carson had watched a tiny white figure as if taking a sudden great stitch hit a high-arching home run into the second deck of Yankee Stadium; the penetration of the ball seemed delicious, and to be happening deep within the tiers of himself. He pressed the off button on the little control, used another button to adjust the tilt of his bed, and fell asleep as simply as a child.

[31]Normally, he liked lots of cover; here, a light blanket was enough. Normally, he could never sleep on his back; here, of necessity, he could sleep no other way, his body slightly turned to ease the vertical ache in his abdomen, his left arm at his side receiving all night long the nurturing liquids of the I.V. tube. Lights always burned; voices always murmured in the hall; this world no more rested than the world beyond the sides of an infant's crib. In the depths of the same night when the home run was struck, a touch on his upper right arm woke Carson. He opened his eyes and there, in the quadrant of space where the rectangle of the television had been, a queenly young black face smiled down upon him, a nurse taking his blood pressure. She had not switched on the overhead light in his room and so the oval of her face was illumined only indirectly, from afar, as had been the pieces of furniture in his hotel room. Without looking at the luminous dial of his wristwatch on the bedside table he knew this was one of those abysmal hours when despair visits men, when insomniacs writhe in an ocean of silence, when the jobless and the bankrupt want to scream in order to break their circular calculations, when spurned lovers roll from a soft dream onto cold sheets, and soldiers awake to the taste of coming battle. In this hour, she had awakened him with her touch. No more than a thin blanket covered his body in the warm dim room. She pumped up the balloon around his arm, relaxed it, pumped it up again. She put into Carson's mouth one of those rocket-shaped instruments of textured plastic that have come to replace glass thermometers, and while waiting for his temperature to register in electronic numbers on a gadget at her waist she hummed a little tune, as if humorously to disavow her beauty, that beauty which women have now come to regard as an enemy, a burden and cause for harassment placed upon them. He thought of his daughter.

[32]Though many nurses administered to him, and as he strengthened he came to develop small talk with them even at four in the morning, this particular one, her perfectly black and symmetrical face outlined in light like an eclipsed sun, never came again.

[33]"Walk," the surgeon urged Carson. "Get up and walk as soon as you can. Get that body moving. It turns out it wasn't the disease used to kill a lot of people in hospitals, it was lying in bed and letting the lungs fill up with fluid."

[34]Walking meant, at first, pushing the spindly, rattling I.V. pole along with him. There was a certain jaunty knack to it—easing the wheels over the raised metal sills here and there in the linoleum

corridor, placing the left hand at the balance point he thought of as the pole's waist, swinging "her" out of the way of another patient promenading with his own gangling chrome partner. From observing other patients Carson learned the trick of removing the I.V. bag and threading it through his bathrobe sleeve and rehanging it, so he could close his bathrobe neatly. His first steps, in the moss-green sponge slippers the hospital provided, were timid and brittle, but as the days passed the length of his walks increased: to the end of the corridor, where the windows of a waiting room overlooked the distant center of the city; around the corner past a rarely open snack bar and into an area of children's diseases; still further to an elevator bank and a carpeted lounge where pregnant women and young husbands drank Tab and held hands. The attendants at various desks in the halls came to know him, and to nod as he passed, with his lengthening stride and more erect posture, his handling of the I.V. pole soon so expert as to be comically debonair.

[35]His curiosity about the city revived. What he saw from the window of his own room was merely the wall of another wing of the hospital, with gift plants on the windowsills and here and there thoughtful bathrobed figures gazing outward toward the wall of which his own bathrobed figure was a part. From the windows of the waiting room, the heart of the city, with its clump of brown and blue skyscrapers and ribbonlike swirls of highway, seemed often to be in sunlight while clouds shadowed the hospital grounds and parking lots and the snarl of taxis always around the entrance. Carson was unable to spot the hotel where he had stayed, or the industrial district where he had hoped to sell his systems, or the art museum that contained, he remembered reading, some exemplary Renoirs and a priceless Hieronymus Bosch. He could see at the base of the blue-brown mass of far buildings a pale-green bridge, and imagined the dirty river it must cross, and the eighteenth-century fort that had been built here to hold the river against the Indians, and the nineteenth-century barge traffic that had fed the settlement and then its industries, which attracted immigrants, who thrust the grid of city streets deep into the surrounding farmland. This was still a region of farmland; thick, slow, patient, pious voices drawled and twanged around Carson as he stood there gazing outward and eavesdropping. Laconic phrases of resignation fell into place amid the standardized furniture and slippered feet and pieces of jigsaw puzzles half assembled on card tables here. Fat women in styleless print dresses and low-heeled shoes had been called in from their kitchens, and in from the fields men with cross-hatched necks and hands that had the lumpy rounded look of used tools.

[36]Sickness is a great democrat, and had achieved a colorful crosssection. Carson came to know by sight a lean man with regally dark Negro skin and taut Oriental features; his glossy shaved head had been split by a Y-shaped gash now held together by stitches. He sat in a luxurious light-brown, almost golden robe, his wounded head propped by a hand heavy with rings, in the room with the pregnant

women and the silver elevator doors. When Carson nodded once in cautious greeting, this apparition said loudly, "Hey, man," as if they shared a surprising secret. Through the open doorways of the rooms along the corridors, Carson glimpsed prodigies—men with beaks of white bandage and plastic tubing, like those drinking birds many fads ago; old ladies shrivelling to nothing in a forest of flowers and giant facetious get-well cards; an immensely plump mocha-colored woman wearing silk pantaloons and a scarlet Hindu dot in the center of her forehead. She entertained streams of visitors, thin dusky delicate men and great-eyed children; like Carson, she was an honorary member of the city, and she would acknowledge his passing with a languid lifting of her fat fingers, tapered as decidedly as cones.

³⁷On the third day, Carson was put on solid food and disconnected from the intravenous tubing. With his faithful, docile pole removed from the room, he was free to wave both arms and to climb stairs. His surgeon at his last appearance (dressed in lumberjack shirt and chinos, about to "take off," for it had become the weekend) had urged stair climbing upon his patient as the best possible exercise. There was, at the end of the corridor in the other direction from the waiting room, from whose windows the heart of the city could be viewed, an exit giving on a cement-and-steel staircase almost never used. Here, down four flights to the basement, then up six to the locked rooftop door, and back down two to his own floor, Carson obediently trod in his bathrobe and by now disintegrating green sponge slippers.

³⁸His happiness was most intense out here, in this deserted and echoing sector, where he was invisible and anonymous. In his room, the telephone had begun to ring. The head of his company back in New Jersey called repeatedly, at first to commiserate and then to engineer a way in which Carson's missed appointments could be patched without the expense of an additional trip. So Carson, sitting up in his adaptable mattress, placed calls to the appropriate personnel and gave an enfeebled version of his pitch; the white-noise company expressed keen interest in digital color-graphics imaging, and Carson mailed them his firm's shiny brochure on its newest system (resolutions to 640 pixels per line, 65,536 simultaneous colors, image memory up to 256K bytes). The secretary from the other company, who had sounded sympathetic on the phone so long ago, showed up in person; she turned out to be somewhat younger than her voice, and comely in a coarse way, with bleached frizzled hair, the remnant of a swimming-pool tan, and active legs she kept crossing and recrossing as she described her own divorce—the money, the children, the return to work after years of being a pampered suburbanite. "I could be one again, let me tell you. These women singing the joys of being in the work force, they can *have* it." This woman smoked a great deal, exhaling noisily and crushing each cerise-stained butt into a jar lid she had brought in her pocketbook, knowing the hospital discouraged smoking and provided no ashtrays. Carson had planned his afternoon in careful half-hour blocks—the staircase, thrice up and down; a visit

to the waiting room, where he had begun to work on one of the jigsaw puzzles; a visit to his bathroom if his handled bowels were willing; finally, a luxurious immersion in a week-old *Newsweek* and the late innings of this Saturday's playoff game. His visitor crushed these plans along with her many cigarettes. Then his own ex-wife telephoned, kittenish the way she had become, remarried yet something plaintive still shining through, and with a note of mockery in her voice, as if descending into a strange city with a bursting appendix was, like his leaving her and ceasing to teach mathematics, one more willful folly. His son called collect from Mexico the next day, sounding ominously close at hand, and spacey, as long awkward silences between father and son ate up the dollars. His daughter never called, which seemed considerate of her. She and Carson knew there was no disguising solitude.

[39]He found that after an hour in his room and bed he became homesick for the stairs. At first, all the flights had seemed identical, but now he had discovered subtle differences among them—old evidence of spilled paint on one set of treads, a set of numbers chalked by a workman on the wall of one landing, water stains and cracks affecting one stretch of rough yellow plaster and not another. At the bottom, there were plastic trash cans and a red door heavily marked with warnings to push the crash bar only in case of emergency; at the top, a plain steel door, without handle or window, defied penetration. The doors at the landings in between each gave on a strange outdoor space, a kind of platform hung outside the door leading into the hospital proper; pre-poured cement grids prevented leaping or falling or a clear outlook but admitted cool fresh air and allowed a fractional view of the city below. The neighborhood here was flat and plain—quarter-acre-lot tract houses built long enough ago for the bloom of newness to have wilted and dilapidation to be setting in. The hospital wall, extending beyond the projecting staircase, blocked all but a slice of downward vision containing some threadbare front yards, one of them with a tricycle on its side and another with a painted statue of the Virgin, and walls of pastel siding in need of repainting, and stretches of low-pitched composition-shingled roof—a shabby smalltown vista here evidently well within the city limits. He never saw a person walking on the broad sidewalks, and few cars moved along the street even at homecoming hour. Nearest and most vivid, a heap of worn planking and rusting scaffold pipes, and a dumpster coated with white dust and loaded with plaster and lathing, testified to a new phase of construction as the hospital continued to expand. Young men sometimes came and added to the rubbish, or loudly threw the planking around. These efforts seemed unorganized, and ceased on the weekend.

[40]Drab housing and assembled rubble, what he saw through the grid of the cement barrier that permitted no broad view nevertheless seemed to Carson brilliantly real, moist and deep-toned and full. When he had first come to this landing—still unable to climb stairs, the

I.V. pole at his side—just shoving open the door had been an effort, and the raw true outdoor air had raked though his still drugged system like a sweeping rough kick, early fall air mixing football and baseball, stiff with cold yet damp and not quite purged of growth. Once he heard the distant agitation of a lawnmower. Until the morning he was released, he would come here even in the dark and lean his forehead against the cement and breathe, trying to take again into himself the miracle of the world, programming himself, as it were, to live—the air cool on his bare ankles, his bowels resettling around the ache of their healing.

[41]The taxi took him straight to the airport; he saw nothing of the city but the silhouettes beside the highway and the highway's scarred center strip. For an instant from the air a kind of map spread itself underneath him, and was gone. Yet afterward, thinking back upon the farm voices, the far-off skyscrapers, the night visits of the nurses, the doctors with their unseen, unsullied homes, the dozens of faces risen like bubbles to the surface of his pain, it seemed he had come to know the city intimately; it was like, on other of his trips, those women who, encountered in bars and paid at the end, turned ceremony inside out, and bestowed themselves without his knowing their name.

chapter 10
BUSINESS WRITING

Most business writing is extremely practical: Usually, its purpose is to inform or to persuade. Because of its pragmatic nature, business writing has certain characteristics that distinguish it from writing in other disciplines.

First, business communications generally are of immediate use to their readers; they are written in response to specific needs that arise in the course of business activities. For example, a memorandum may contain information about the time, date, and place of a sales meeting; a business letter may notify a client that a copying machine has been back-ordered.

Moreover, business communications are often useful in helping readers make decisions. The supervisor who receives a report explaining the advantages and disadvantages of currently available word processors will base the decision to purchase a particular processor at least partially on that information. The customer who has requested an increase in a credit limit waits for a letter confirming it before making a major purchase. Thus the primary purpose of the business writer is to convey information clearly and accurately. When that aim is not achieved, the reader may make an unwise decision.

In addition, accurate information must be given directly and concisely. Heeding the cliché, "Time is money," business people want their correspondents to get to the point of the message. For instance, the busy decision-maker often reads only the summary section of a long document first. The reader then decides whether the entire document merits further attention. The wise business writer makes sure to summarize the important points of the message directly and concisely.

Because business writing conveys material of actual or potential usefulness, it is extremely reader-oriented. Writers must consider how the readers will use the information, and must anticipate the type and amount of data that readers will require. Besides presenting accurate and concise information, then, business writers must be sure their messages are timely and appropriate. For example, the department head wishing to hire a floor supervisor within two weeks needs the personnel office's recommendations quickly in order to use them effectively. If that supervisor wants to hire someone with experience, then the recommendations must include detailed information on the employment history of each applicant to be appropriate for the supervisor's needs.

Besides providing information, business writers often aim to persuade their readers of the worth of their ideas or proposals. Although sometimes their reports or letters are intended to be purely objective in presenting data, they are more often asked to interpret the data and to make recommendations accordingly. To be persuasive, the writing must be logically organized and the conclusions well supported—as is true of persuasive communication in any field.

Instructors of business courses make the same kinds of demands on the writer that business people do. Thus students writing for business courses should make sure that their writings are clear, concise, and appropriately informative or persuasive for the circumstances of the assignment. Very often those assignments will take a problem-solving approach, with the instructor setting up a hypothetical business situation (sometimes called a *case study*) and the student composing an appropriate response. Let's examine some specific types of business communication.

WRITING THE BUSINESS MEMORANDUM

The memorandum is the most common type of business correspondence. Within an organization, memos document procedures, meetings, and decisions traveling upward to higher levels of management, downward to subordinates, or laterally to other departments. The messages they transmit are generally short and quite specific. If the memo is being used to document a decision, sender and receiver are familiar with the content; the sender takes this into consideration when composing, and includes only the necessary details.

Most institutions have their own standardized memorandum form, which generally gives headings for the date, the person who will receive the message, the person sending the message, and the subject (see Figure 10.1). The body of the memo follows these headings. If copies are sent to others, then *cc:* (meaning "carbon copies"), followed by the individuals' names, is typed flush left three or four lines below the last line of the body.

DATE:

TO:

FROM:

SUBJECT:

Figure 10.1
A standard memorandum form

Figure 10.2 shows a typical memorandum. A meeting was held to establish procedures for handling large checks during the night shift at a large bank's operations center. The memo was then written to inform employees of the decisions.

INTER-OFFICE CORRESPONDENCE

TO: Carol Randall

FROM: Jack Evans

DATE: February 1, 1984

SUBJECT: Guidelines for charge-ins after the 4:00 a.m. deadline

The following guidelines have been instituted regarding large dollar checks to Item Processing after the 4:00 a.m. deadline:

1. Item Processing will accept checks only up to 4:30 a.m.

2. Only checks of 1 million dollars or more will be accepted.

3. No more than 5 checks will be accepted per night.

4. Only those checks with originating banks listed on the Due From Bank listing will be accepted. (Listing will be provided by Item Processing.)

5. Checks will be taken to the supervisor in Item Processing.

If you have any questions, please contact me.

cc: Bob Caldwell

Figure 10.2
A typical memorandum

This memo gets to the point immediately and lists specific guidelines; the guidelines are numbered and separated from each other by a line of space to make them more readable. Further, the five items are grammatically parallel: They are all complete sentences and all have verb phrases beginning with *will*. Using a parallel grammatical structure makes sentences clearer, and clarity is crucial here.

Note that procedures 2 through 5 are expressed in the passive voice. Most writing instructors advise students to use the *active* voice whenever possible. But in this case, the writer was following his institution's stated preference for passive constructions. Every organization has a preferred style of writing, and many companies provide style manuals so that usages can be standardized. Be sure to find out what is acceptable stylistically in your organization.

This particular memorandum was written to a supervisor to confirm that the guidelines had been created. It was also sent to all others who had attended the meeting. Because the memo documents what had been decided at the meeting, the writer was especially careful to be accurate, so that the memo would be satisfactory to all involved. Accuracy was doubly important, moreover, because employees would be following the stated procedures; the guidelines had to be stated clearly and precisely in order for the job to be done correctly. And because a copy of the memo was sent to the writer's supervisor, he wished it to be a positive reflection of his abilities and talents. Thus the writer took into account content, audience, and the uses to which the information would be put as he composed.

Suggestion for Writing

You are the new dean of students at your college or university, and your first order of business is to write a more lenient (or, if you wish, more rigid) policy on student attendance. Your audience is the faculty, with whom you have already met to help formulate your ideas. Write a memorandum to inform them of the procedures you are officially establishing. Ask yourself these questions as you compose:

1. Who needs and/or has requested the information?
2. What, precisely, do they need? (What, exactly, have they requested?)
3. To what use will my readers put the information? Do they need recommendations or directives from me in addition to information?
4. What form is most appropriate and most readable, given the above content and audience?

WRITING THE BUSINESS LETTER

Business letters, like memoranda, provide or document information. Unlike memos, however, they are generally sent to individuals outside the organization. As a result, business letters can reinforce (or detract from) the positive image of the company. Because, in most cases, sender and receiver never meet face-to-face, the business letter represents the firm in the same way that its employees do at meetings or conferences. If the letter is neat, clear, accurate, and professional, the receiver will likely perceive the company to be all those things as well. Thus, while your memos will reflect an image of yourself to supervisors, coworkers, and subordinates, your letters will reflect the image of the firm as a whole.

The Format

Business letters follow a fairly standard format. Figure 10.3 shows a letter typed in the *modified block style*. In the *block style*, the date, complimentary close, and signature are also typed flush left.

The date is typed in the upper right of the page, three lines below the letterhead.

Receiver's name and address are typed flush left, two lines below date.

The salutation is also typed flush left, followed by either a colon (in formal letters), a comma (in informal letters), or by no punctuation.

The body of the letter follows. Paragraphs are not indented, and a line of space is left between paragraphs.

The complimentary closing is centered and is followed by a comma or by no punctuation.

The typist's initials are typed in lowercase letters flush left, two lines below the last line of the signature.

BURWICK & CO.
"Dover's Finest"

November 10, 1983

John H. Campbell
35824 Lark Lane
Dover, NY 16034

Dear Preferred Customer:

We all know that gift shopping can dampen our holiday spirits by putting an unusual strain on the family budget. At Burwick & Co. we are offering a special financing plan to help our preferred charge-account customers take the pinch out of their holiday pocketbooks.

Here's how it works: Beginning November 28 you may charge purchases as usual and request that billing be deferred until February. Simply tell your salesperson that you wish to participate in "holiday deferred billing" at the time of your purchase.

We at Burwick & Co. value your patronage and wish you and your family a happy holiday season.

Sincerely,

BURWICK & CO.

Carole Adams

Carole Adams
Vice President
Marketing Division

jm

Figure 10.3 The modified block style

The Salutation and Closing

Salutations of letters sent to recipients whose sex is unknown should ideally be nonsexist; note the *Dear Preferred Customer* salutation above. If you find it impossible to think of a suitable term, use the format of the Administrative Management Society (AMS) and omit the salutation altogether. (If you use the AMS style and omit the salutation, omit the complimentary close as well.) If you use the traditional salutation *Dear*

Sir or *Gentlemen* in a letter to a group of receivers that includes even one woman, you may antagonize that group. Wherever possible, of course, use the receiver's name; use *Ms.* for women unless the woman has indicated a preference for *Miss* or *Mrs.*

Punctuation following the salutation and the closing is optional. If it is included (a colon following the salutation in formal letters, otherwise a comma; a comma following the closing), the style is called *mixed*. *Open* style means the opening colon (or comma) and the closing comma have been omitted.

Types of Business Letters

The Negative Message Letter Business organizations send out many different types of letters daily, depending on the nature of the firm. Because the image-building nature of letters is so important, the hardest type of letter to write is probably the "bad-news" letter. The writer of that letter must compose the message in such a way that receivers will continue to have positive attitudes toward the company.

An example of a "bad-news" letter is shown in Figure 10.4 (p. 330). We can discover several guidelines for writing the negative message business letter in that example. First, the writer begins on a polite, positive note. Even if what you have to say is far from positive from your reader's point of view, beginning your message in a positive way puts your reader into a better frame of mind (however temporarily) for what is to follow.

Also, the writer gives a rationale for the company's decision and stresses that the charity is worthy of serious attention. Bad news must be presented honestly, but in such a way that the decision is seen as logical rather than arbitrary and that the writer is perceived as sympathetic to the receiver, albeit unable to grant the request.

This letter also allows for the possibility of future contributions. Whenever possible, a bad-news letter should include some indication of what can be done in the future to improve the situation. For instance, a letter turning down a request for credit may explain that the company requires additional credit references and may suggest that when such references can be obtained, the applicant should try again. A letter informing a customer that an order cannot be filled on time may explain the unusual circumstances, set up a new delivery date, and stress the quality of the goods. Always, the writer must be honest but must also try to generate goodwill at a time when the receiver may not be inclined to feel it.

The Letter of Acknowledgment Another common type of business letter that is important for generating goodwill and increased patronage is the letter acknowledging an order (see Figure 10.5, p. 331). This is a "good news" letter—it politely and promptly acknowledges the custom-

---

NORMANDY PLUMBING SUPPLY
3803 East Avenue
Normandy, IN 30563

July 15, 1983

Ms. Roberta Hahn, Vice President
The Peters Foundation
884 Seventh Street
Normandy, IN 30563

Dear Ms. Hahn:

I was much interested in the materials you sent me about
the Peters Foundation. I have heard several people speak
highly of your activities in general. Reading your brochures
gave me an opportunity to learn more specifically of the good
your organization does for our community.

Unfortunately, at this time Normandy Plumbing Supply is unable
to make a contribution to your capital fund drive. Each
quarter, we have a limited amount of funds available for
charitable purposes, and at present such funds are exhausted.

Now that I know of your need, it may be possible to budget
some funds for a contribution next quarter, thus helping your
organization continue its fine efforts. Please contact me
again in a month or two, and I will reconsider your request.

Sincerely,

Christopher Walters

Christopher Walters
Executive Vice President

kab

Figure 10.4
A ''bad-news'' letter

er's order. It also affords the firm the opportunity to encourage additional patronage. In this case the writer capitalizes on the customer's interest
in gardening by informing him that Duffy Seed Co. also sells products
other than seeds and by sending him a catalog. As added encourage-
ment he mentions the 10 percent discount. The closing paragraph
reiterates the firm's thanks and notes that it backs its seeds with the offer
of a refund should the customer be dissatisfied. The letter primarily

DUFFY SEED CO.
1458 Coastline Road
Braemar, MA 06123

February 10, 1984

Mr. David Foster
3820 Dearborn Avenue
Lafayette, WI 60304

Dear Mr. Foster,

Thank you for your recent seed order. All items have been
shipped and should be delivered to your home by March 1, well
before planting time in your area.

The Duffy Seed Co. hopes you will enjoy our products, as many
satisfied customers have over the years. In addition to
ordering our seeds, you may also be interested in our line of
garden-related merchandise, including hand tools, insecticides,
tillers, and indoor gardening equipment. So that you may
examine what we have to offer, we have enclosed our new Spring
Catalog with your seed order. If you order from this catalog
prior to May 1, you will receive a discount of 10 percent on
every item.

We're sure that you will find our seeds to be the best you've
planted. Remember, though, that they are fully guaranteed.
Should a problem occur, simply write directly to us, and we
will refund your money.

Thank you again for your order, and happy gardening!

Sincerely,

DUFFY SEED CO.

Paul Koterna

Paul Koterna
Vice President

kb

Figure 10.5
A "good news" letter

aims to show how much the company appreciates the business; secondarily, this type of letter also serves as a marketing device.

Overall, business letters must show concern for the readers' needs
and attitudes. Even when the letter carries a negative message, the
writer must take care to present it diplomatically so as to avoid
alienating the receiver. The image of the company very often rises or
falls on the strengths or weaknesses of its correspondence.

Suggestions
for Writing

Compose letters or memoranda suitable for the following situations:

1. You, as Credit Manager, must compose a form letter to be sent to all those who owe your company money and are in danger of being referred to a collection agency. You must specify a deadline for receipt of the payment and explain the consequences of nonpayment. Invent whatever additional details you need.

2. Compose the letter to Normandy Plumbing Supply that prompted the reply on page 330.

3. An accountant in your department (you are the supervisor) has been chronically late. Although her work has been completed satisfactorily, other employees in the office are grumbling, and you feel she should arrive on time all the time, not just occasionally. You meet with her, discuss the situation, and resolve the problem. She begins to arrive at work on time, but you want to send her a memo documenting your agreement. Compose the memorandum, making up whatever other details are necessary.

4. A potential customer writes to inquire about ordering a certain type of sports equipment. Your firm does not carry the specific brand requested, but you decide to answer by explaining the advantages of the brands you do carry. Write the letter, choosing a specific type of equipment.

5. Write a letter acknowledging a first-time customer's order for a product of your choosing. In this case your primary aim will be to cultivate this customer for future patronage.

WRITING SHORT REPORTS

Like memos, reports circulate within organizations. Most often, they transmit information upward to those who have requested it. A report may be written to provide information that the writer does not interpret in any way. For example, a supervisor might request a report listing possible inventory control methods within a department, including advantages and disadvantages of each, with no recommendation from the writer regarding which one to adopt. On the other hand, a report may be written to justify a particular approach, a purchase, a change in procedures, or other decisions. Then its purpose is not only to present data but also to present it in such a way that the writer's conclusions and recommendations are accepted.

Let's consider a typical format for a short report requiring minimal research, usually in the form of in-house investigation. (Business reports requiring library research will be discussed in Chapter 11.)

Short reports often use a memorandum heading, listing the date, receiver, sender, and subject. In the body of the report, headings are used to separate sections. These headings serve several purposes:

1. By separating sections, they add white space and thus contribute to readability.

2. By telling in general what the section discusses, they serve as a preview to the reader, again increasing readability.

3. By previewing content for readers, headings draw the readers' attention to those sections that are most pertinent to them.

Within sections, short reports focus on ideas that are based on the writer's investigation of some aspect of the general topic. The writer must support those ideas, generally with data and observations. Supporting evidence listed in the form of tables or other graphics is placed in an appendix to avoid interrupting the narrative flow. However, the writer carefully quotes within the text the *most important* information from the tables or graphs so that the reader can understand the point without having to turn to the appendix. For example, the most important data may be figures that show how much money the company can save by adopting a certain procedure (or what the company is wasting following current procedures). In any case, report writers must be careful to distill the strongest evidence in support of their ideas and emphasize it in the text, not bury it in an appendix.

Report sections should follow some logical order, such as most important idea to least, or problem, alternatives, and solutions. Predicting your readers' reaction may help you decide on an arrangement for persuasive reports. If they are likely to react positively to your recommendations, you can use a direct approach, presenting your conclusions first and then supporting them. If you anticipate that your readers may resist your message, you might better follow an indirect arrangement: Carefully lay the groundwork for your conclusions by first presenting your evidence and then stating your recommendations. Moreover, in presenting your data and observations, try to answer potential objections. The more you can anticipate and answer your readers' objections, the more persuasive your report will be.

When you're unsure of your direction as you compose, confer with the person who requested the report. Be sure that you clearly understand what your purpose is and that you are doing the type of analysis the reader wants.

If you are asked to make recommendations, try to include alternatives to your own approach. Of course, you hope that your suggestion will be followed, but showing that you are aware of other ways of handling the problem, even though you feel they are inferior, adds to your credibility and persuasiveness. It demonstrates that you are a thorough investigator and that you have been objective in reaching your conclusions.

The short report in Figure 10.6 (pp. 334-38), which uses a memorandum format, justifies a particular course of action. In the opening paragraph of this report, the writer defines the problem by first

INTER-OFFICE CORRESPONDENCE

TO: Paul Jacobs

FROM: Donna Hill *D. Hill*

DATE: October 13, 1983

SUBJECT: Replacement of Bell & Howell Baum Folder

The Bell & Howell Baum Folder was purchased over ten years
ago and has generally been a reliable piece of equipment.
However, in 1979 erratic folds, machine jams, and feeding
problems became common, necessitating the refurbishing of
the machine in 1980. Thereafter, its operation was virtually
error-free until late 1982 when these same problems emerged
again (see Appendix I). Adjustments have failed to resolve
these persistent problems. This machine rarely makes precise
folds and usually produces folds that are crooked (see
Appendix II). Although no statistics are available on any
mailing delays caused exclusively by improper folds, statements
incorrectly folded do cause delays in the mailing process and
declines in customer service. Therefore, I recommend the
replacement of the unit.

FOLDER REQUIREMENTS: VOLUME AND ACCURACY

The machine is used to fold approximately 2.8 million checking
account statement pages per year. In addition, it folds
approximately 476,000 statement pages a year for Savings Control
(see Appendix III). Because of this volume, the Checking
Accounts department needs a folder that can withstand heavy
usage.

All statement pages must be accurately folded so that the bar
encoding (the symbols that indicate the number of pages and
checks for an account) can correctly be read by the Phillipsburg (the check inserting machine). If the bar encoding is
not read correctly, the Phillipsburg stops, causing a delay
in the mailing process. More importantly, customer service
declines.

Figure 10.6
A short report

- 2 -

October 13, 1983

ALTERNATIVES

Most of the folders available are of the table-top type,
costing approximately $2,000. They produce accurate folds
but are not designed to withstand the volumes processed in
Checking Accounts. Therefore, they would not be acceptable.

Another alternative, the Stahl Folder, manufactured by
Heidleberg Eastern, is a more complex machine and costs
approximately $10,000. Although this machine produces
accurate folds and is designed to process our volumes, such
expense is not warranted.

A third alternative, refurbishment of our present folder,
would cost approximately $2,600. This would not be a viable
solution, however, since the same operational problems would
likely recur in a couple of years.

Bell & Howell makes a folder called the Phillipsburg PF 1722,
which can accommodate all our needs and costs only $4,800.
It makes accurate, precise, and consistent folds. In addition,
this machine operates at a faster rate than our current folder.
Its speed will reduce labor costs by $4,258 per year, thus it
has a rapid pay-back period of a little more than one year
(see Appendix IV).

RECOMMENDATION

The present folder in Checking Accounts is not adequate to
serve our needs. Because the Bank must be able to rely on a
machine that produces accurate folds, I recommend that we
purchase the Phillipsburg PF 1722. I also recommend that we
purchase a limited service contract costing approximately
$320 (consisting of 4 PMIs), assuming few malfunctions will
occur on a new machine. The present folder should be traded
in or sold, generating as much salvage value as possible
(salvage value estimated at $500). Your prompt consideration
of this proposal is appreciated.

sc
Attachments

APPENDIX I

MAINTENANCE RECORD

Date	Reason	Cost
8/27/82	Not folding properly	N/C
9/09/82	Won't demand feed/crooked folds	N/C
9/23/82	Erratic folds	N/C
9/25/82	Not feeding straight/bad folds	N/C
11/13/82	Not counting/not folding/not diverting	N/C
11/14/82	Erratic folds	N/C
11/19/82	Not folding properly/jamming	N/C
1/05/83	Jamming	$ 78.
1/10/83	PMI	N/C
1/12/83	Not folding	$ 78.
1/13/83	Jamming in rollers	$126.
2/16/83	PMI	N/C
2/22/83	Paper feed wheeler/retard roller	$ 75.95
2/25/83	Jams at feeder	N/C

Although service calls have not been made recently, the folder
continues to provide crooked folds, which delays the mailing
process. Adjustments do not correct this problem.

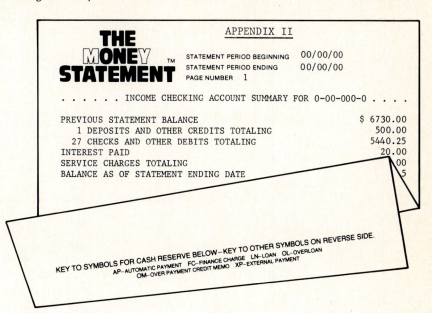

APPENDIX II

THE MONEY STATEMENT ™

STATEMENT PERIOD BEGINNING 00/00/00
STATEMENT PERIOD ENDING 00/00/00
PAGE NUMBER 1

. . . . INCOME CHECKING ACCOUNT SUMMARY FOR 0-00-000-0 . . . .

PREVIOUS STATEMENT BALANCE	$ 6730.00
1 DEPOSITS AND OTHER CREDITS TOTALING	500.00
27 CHECKS AND OTHER DEBITS TOTALING	5440.25
INTEREST PAID	20.00
SERVICE CHARGES TOTALING	.00
BALANCE AS OF STATEMENT ENDING DATE	5

KEY TO SYMBOLS FOR CASH RESERVE BELOW – KEY TO OTHER SYMBOLS ON REVERSE SIDE.
AP–AUTOMATIC PAYMENT FC–FINANCE CHARGE LN–LOAN OL–OVERLOAN
OM–OVER PAYMENT CREDIT MEMO XP–EXTERNAL PAYMENT

APPENDIX III

PAGES FOLDED

Type of Statement	Monthly Totals	*Month End Quarter Totals	Year Totals	
Checking Account	238,000	238,000	2,856,000	
Statement Savings	10,000	--	120,000	
Commercial Savings	3,000	3,000	36,000	}476,000
Savings Quarterly	--	80,000	320,000	
Total of Items Folded	251,000	321,000	3,332,000	

*Total pages folded for the months of January, April, July, and October when an additional 80,000 Statement Savings statements are folded.

APPENDIX IV

LABOR COST

STATISTICS USED TO DERIVE LABOR COST

1. Hourly labor rate: $8.00

2. Pages folded yearly: Checking Account   - 2,856,000
                          Statement Savings -   120,000
                          Commercial Savings -   36,000
                          Quarterly Savings   320,000
                                                3,332,000

3. Throughput rate: Present Machine   - 3,692/hour
                     Phillipsburg PF 1722   - 9,000/hour

4. Total hours needed for folding:
                     Present Machine   - 902.49/year
                     Phillipsburg PF 1722   - 370.22/year

TYPE OF STATEMENT	PRESENT FOLDER	PHILLIPSBURG PF 1722
Checking Account	$6,189.00	$2,539.00
Statement Savings	260.00	107.00
Commercial Savings	78.00	32.00
Quarterly Savings	693.00	284.00
Total Yearly Processing Cost	$7,220.00	$2,962.00

TOTAL COST SAVINGS PER YEAR: $4,258.00

explaining the repair record of the present check-folding machine. The last sentence directly states her recommendation.

The two sections, Folder Requirements and Alternatives, are logically arranged: The writer presents the specific needs before listing alternatives that may meet those needs. The recommended unit is discussed last, emphasizing that it is the only machine which meets the requirements and is financially feasible.

The writer emphasizes the machine's affordability, specifying the savings in labor and the subsequent pay-back period. All companies try to use the most cost-effective methods available, so appeals to financial benefits are sure to be attractive.

Appendices are well used in this report. Bottom-line figures are quoted within the narrative to support what the writer says, and if the readers wish to examine the derivations of those figures, they can check the appendices.

In the last section, the writer reiterates her recommendation. She makes it more detailed by also recommending a service contract. (Note that she carefully states her reason for recommending a limited contract.) She also includes an estimate of the salvage value of the Bell and Howell Baum Folder, demonstrating that she has done a thorough job and is interested in saving the company's dollars.

Suggestion for Writing

An organization to which you belong (or for which you work) is sponsoring a convention next year. Its site has been narrowed to two possibilities. Your task is to prepare a report in which you recommend to the group's executive committee (or to your supervisor) one of the cities as the convention site.

In doing this assignment you'll need to make up many of the details, including the following:

1. The names of the two cities;
2. The organization, be it a business or a club;
3. The type and number of people who will be attending;
4. Your title or office;
5. The make-up of the committee or the type of supervisor to whom you will be reporting.

As you argue in favor of the city of your choice, keep the needs of your group uppermost in your mind. Obviously, the city will have to have physical facilities to accommodate the conventioneers. If you decide that spouses (male and female) may attend, then you should also consider what the city has to offer them. Present the most persuasive information you can to prove the city's desirability.

WRITING THE JOB APPLICATION LETTER

Another type of business correspondence, one you will probably use very soon, is the job application (or cover) letter. In writing this letter, be sure to apply the various principles of effective business writing that we have already examined; the cover letter should be accurate, direct, concise, timely, and persuasive. And keep in mind the particular situation for which you are writing. This letter is the first impression a potential employer will have of you—make sure it is a good one.

How can you make a good impression through the job application letter? First, personalize each letter. Remember that the primary purpose of the cover letter is to get you an interview. By personalizing each cover letter you write, you will impress each employer with your ambition, initiative, and interest. Research the position, the department, the firm—even the supervisor, if possible—so that you can tailor your letter to the specific opening available. Be sure to highlight only those experiences and abilities which are specifically related to that job. Remember, the company is not interested in you, but in what you can bring to the company.

Second, be selective as to what you include in your letter. Normally, the job application letter accompanies a résumé, which contains all the pertinent information about your educational and employment history. So the cover letter should touch on only those items that relate directly to the position.

Third, structure your letter logically. A job application letter argues that you are the best person for the job, and sound logic is a key to good argumentation. Here's a simple and effective structure to employ:

Introduction Identify yourself, your present position, and how you learned of the position for which you are applying.

Body paragraphs Review your work experience, education, and other pertinent details, spending perhaps a paragraph on each.

Closing Emphasize your interest and abilities and state when you are available for an interview. Throughout, stress what you can accomplish for the firm, not what it can do for you.

Figure 10.7 shows a typical letter of application.

WRITING THE RÉSUMÉ

A résumé summarizes on one page an individual's career goals, professional and academic qualifications, and noteworthy accomplishments. It supplements the letter of application, detailing all the information that the brief letter cannot.

Typically, a résumé begins with personal data, including name, address, and phone number. Other personal information, such as

Figure 10.7
A letter of application

In the opening sentence, the writer immediately states his interest in the job, identifying the job by its title and naming the source in which it was advertised. He briefly introduces himself in the second sentence.

In paragraph 2, he discusses his pertinent work experience. Note that the writer gives specific information about his previous job duties. He indicates that he is familiar with his potential employer's product.

In paragraph 3, the writer focuses on his pertinent education and training. He also includes evidence of his expertise with computers by mentioning a special honor for which he has been chosen.

In the fourth paragraph, the writer states his availability for an interview. Since he is still a student, he suggests the possibility of future employment with the company as an incentive for Compurite to hire him.

---

981 Wendover Lane
Broxton, Ohio 44000
March 24, 1984

Mr. John Farnsleigh
Director of Personnel
Compurite Corporation
Shaker Tower, East
Cleveland, Ohio 44010

Dear Mr. Farnsleigh:

I would like to apply for the summer position of Stockroom Attendant II, which you advertised in the March 24 issue of The Plain Dealer. Currently, I am a junior at Forest City College, where I am working toward a Bachelor's degree in Business Administration with a major in systems analysis.

For the past two summers I have held a similar position with California-Pacific Computing Corporation in Palo Alto, California. I worked as the summer replacement in their stockroom, where I was responsible for monitoring the microchips inventory and filling in-house requisitions for all circuitry needed in assembling California-Pacific's model 9800 Wordprocessor. Since that unit is very similar to Compurite's 720 series, I believe I could work in your stockroom without a great deal of additional training.

At Forest City College, I have taken courses in mathematics through differential equations and have learned three computer languages: BASIC, FORTRAN, and COBOL. In addition, I have studied computer design and have done advanced work in systems analysis. Next month my major advisor is taking me and one other student to a national computing competition for college students. The team that designs the best new program will earn a four-year scholarship for the university they represent.

Except for the week of April 4-8, when I will be at the computer competition, I am available for an interview at your convenience. My career goal is to work in the computer industry, preferably in Northeast Ohio. I would therefore be eager to work for you this summer, and could consider a possible career with Compurite after graduation.

I look forward to hearing from you.

Sincerely,

James Turner

James Turner

marital status or age, is optional. Include it only if you feel it will enhance your chances for the position you seek. But beware of giving any information that might cause the employer to lose interest in you. For instance, do not list your health as "Fair"—the potential employer may interpret this as a potential liability for the company and so may reject you as a candidate for the position without even talking to you. Remember, you want to keep the employer focused on your abilities, talents, and training, not on your personal characteristics.

If you do not have much relevant work experience, you will list next your educational background and scholastic honors. Include the names and cities of colleges or universities attended, the degrees granted (including majors), and dates. If you're a recent graduate, you might want to list those courses that are relevant to the position you are seeking and your grade point average—if it is a good one. Showing a solid academic record can make you an appealing candidate to your potential employer and can help compensate for a lack of work experience.

After the academic information, list your work experience, with the most recent position given first. Any major projects accomplished should also be listed, particularly if they pertain directly to the position you are seeking.

At the end of the résumé, list the names of those individuals who have agreed to act as your references, giving enough information so that they can be reached easily. Or, instead of listing specific names, you can state that references will be sent on request. (College placement offices sometimes handle the sending of references for their students and alumni; see the résumé on p. 344.)

Examine the résumé used by James Turner, the student whose cover letter we examined earlier (the résumé is shown in Figure 10.8). In this résumé, James presents a clear and logical outline of his academic and work life. Although he has had no full-time work experience, his two part-time positions contribute to the image he wants to convey to his potential employer. The grocery clerk job has no relation to his career goals but does show stability, as he held it over a period of time going back to high school. The job at the computer firm has direct bearing on his future and should be attractive experience for the new employer. James also lists the technical courses he feels show a grasp of theory needed in the position, if not on-the-job applications. Under "References" he lists individuals from each of the three important areas—his college and his previous two jobs.

The overall goal of any résumé is to present an image of a hard-working, knowledgeable individual who would be an asset to the firm. In this case, a person with limited experience structures the résumé to present himself to his best advantage.

```
                         James Craig Turner
                         981 Wendover Lane
                        Broxton, Ohio 44000
                          (216) 881-6833




EDUCATION        Forest City College
                 Cleveland, Ohio
                    --Bachelor's degree expected, June 1986
                    --Major:  Systems Analysis
                 Northview High School
                    --Graduated June 1982


HONORS           Participant in national computing competition,
                    Spring 1984
                 High School Valedictorian


COURSES          BASIC, COBOL, and FORTRAN languages
TAKEN            Advanced Systems Analysis
                 Calculus I and II
                 Administrative Management
                 Business Decision Making
                 Applied Quantitative Techniques


EXPERIENCE       California-Pacific Computing Corporation
                 Palo Alto, California
                    --Stockroom, Summer 1983 and Summer 1982
                 Al's Bi-Well Market
                 Cleveland, Ohio
                    --Grocery Clerk, summers and other vacations,
                      1979-1981


REFERENCES       Ms. Sharon Caldecott
                 California-Pacific Computing Corporation
                 Palo Alto, California 90623

                 Mr. Alvin Freund
                 Al's Bi-Well Market
                 8503 East 187th Street
                 Cleveland, Ohio  44011

                 Professor John Todd
                 Computer Science Department
                 Forest City College
                 Cleveland, Ohio 44010

                 Professor Caroline Krinsky
                 Computer Science Department
                 Forest City College
                 Cleveland, Ohio 44010
```

Figure 10.8
A student's résumé

```
                    HELEN J. SAWYER
                    21385 North Avenue
                    Columbia, North Carolina   33000
                    (216) 834-6556


CAREER GOAL         Senior administrative position in the
                    health care industry

SUCCESSFUL          1982 to present
ADMINISTRATIVE      Assistant Administrator
EXPERIENCE          St. Clare's Hospital
                    Columbia, North Carolina   33000

                      --Supervise the Personnel, Admitting,
                        and Purchasing Departments at this
                        45-bed general hospital

                      --Designed and implemented a successful
                        system of employee performance reviews

                      --Designed a more efficient inventory
                        control system for the Purchasing
                        Department

                    1980 to 1982
                    Personnel Director
                    Clearview Medical Center
                    Clearview, North Carolina   33001

                      --Reviewed and monitored personnel
                        policies and procedures for 100
                        employees

                      --Maintained all personnel records

                    1977 to 1980
                    Employee Relations Specialist
                    Conover Industries
                    Clearview, North Carolina   33001

                      --Administered the union contract,
                        including monitoring grievances

RELATED             Master's Degree in Business Administration,
EDUCATIONAL            1979
BACKGROUND          Concentration in Health Services Management
                    University of North Carolina, Chapel Hill

                    Bachelor's Degree in Business Administration,
                       1977
                    Major in Management
                    University of North Carolina, Chapel Hill
                    Degree granted cum laude, with
                       departmental honors

REFERENCES          Are available upon request from:
                       The Placement Office
                       University of North Carolina
                       Chapel Hill, North Carolina   33020
```

Figure 10.9
A résumé detailing work
experience

Figure 10.9 (opposite) shows the résumé of an individual with considerably more experience. Notice that the basic organization remains the same. In this résumé, however, the work experience is full-time and responsibilities and accomplishments are detailed. Because potential employers will examine her employment record to determine whether she is qualified, the applicant has listed clearly and precisely the types of jobs she held and the successes she achieved while holding them.

Both of these examples are traditional one-page résumés. For individuals with a lot of experience, especially for those applying for senior positions of some responsibility, one page may not be enough to list the various positions held and projects completed.

Regardless of the length of your résumé or the amount of your work experience, be sure to emphasize, clearly and logically, your talents and abilities. The résumé should work with your letter of application to persuade the employer that you are the one for the job.

Suggestions for Writing

1. Research job opportunities in the field you wish to pursue. Then write a letter of application for one of the positions you find. You may wish to apply for an actual job, perhaps a part-time or summer position.

2. Construct the résumé to send with your letter.

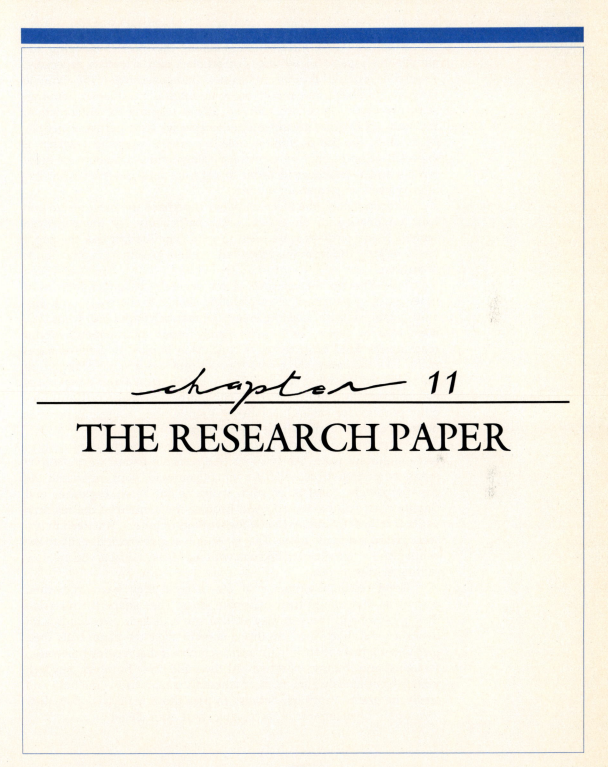

chapter 11

THE RESEARCH PAPER

Researching a topic in order to answer questions, solve problems, or simply gather useful information is among the most challenging and stimulating aspects of writing. For scholars and scientists especially, research is crucial. Likewise, in business and government, the ability to research problems and report one's findings is invaluable. Some research is *primary*, involving inquiry ..uch as scientific experimentation, the study of original documents, or interviews with pertinent people. More often for the beginning college student, *secondary* research is expected—that is, inquiry into the findings and conclusions of other writers and researchers in order to organize and interpret what has already been written about a topic.

Unfortunately, the research paper is perhaps the most feared and least understood of all assignments, particularly for inexperienced writers. Many of these fears seem to stem from the fact that the paper has to be long and from the belief that it differs greatly from other kinds of writing.

But although the research paper generally is longer than most other types of papers, it is surprisingly similar to the essays you are already familiar with. Like the essay, the research paper may focus on a main idea or thesis, or it may merely report information without reaching the kind of interpretive conclusion implied in a thesis statement. Like the essay, the research paper provides a vehicle for you, as the writer, to say what you perceive to be the truth about a topic. It is *not*, contrary to popular belief, a cut-and-paste collage of the things other people have said. Qualitatively, then, writing a research paper is no more difficult than writing any other paper.

However, the research paper does differ from the standard essay in some important ways. As you write the research paper, your *invention process* is guided strongly by the things you read; your input into the paper's content consists of your ability to interpret, organize, and classify what you have read. And because the content of the research paper is so heavily influenced by the writings of others, you need to use some *system of documentation*. That is, you must give credit directly to the people who originally supplied you with the ideas and facts you are now putting in your paper.

Good research writers treat the material they learn from their reading as they would treat their own ideas: They shape the material, they organize and focus it, they write about it in their own words with their own style and voice. All this is done to make the paper truly their own and not just a lifeless, haphazard scrapbook that records the words, thoughts, and findings of others. At the same time, however, research writers scrupulously keep track of where their materials come from and credit the original authors, because to pass those materials off as their own would be dishonest, unacceptable, and even illegal.

Unlike the essays you have written, then, the research paper always involves reading and documentation. Since invention in the research paper is so heavily influenced by reading, let's first discuss how to use the library.

USING THE LIBRARY

The average university or large public library presents you with a situation that is both advantageous and disadvantageous; namely, you will find too much, rather than too little, material available in researching most topics. Because you want your paper to be accurate and complete, having abundant information is obviously beneficial. But you may feel at a loss as to how to begin *finding* that information, much less writing about it. Fortunately, the library has many resources that can aid you in your search—provided that you know how to use them.

If you are visiting a particular library for the first time, ask the librarian or other staff member to explain its organization. Most libraries have informative brochures that will tell you what floor or room houses what discipline, but a librarian can supply even more details. Your ultimate goal is to be able to use the library as independently of librarians as possible, and learning basic information is a good first step. But do not hesitate to ask librarians to help you, especially when you are learning your way around. Helping users is one of their chief duties.

Once you have located the appropriate area for your research, keep in mind that, regardless of the specific discipline concerned, printed matter comes in two basic forms, each with its own set of resources and methods for use. The first form is books, and the path to the books you need is the card catalog.

The Card Catalog

For every book in the library, the card catalog contains three cards: a subject card, an author card, and a title card. So you can find a book if you know *either* its title *or* its author *or* its topic. When you are just beginning your research, check what books are available on a given subject by looking up that topic in the *subject* card catalog.

For instance, suppose you were researching how to use mathematics in business decision-making. Among the cards you'd find under the subject "Management" is the one shown in Figure 11.1 (see p. 350). If you looked under the author's name you'd find the card in Figure 11.2 (p. 351). And if you checked under the title, you'd find the card shown in Figure 11.3 (p. 351).

The number in the upper left corner of each card is the *call number* of the book which helps you locate it on the shelves. Any library uses either the Library of Congress system or the Dewey Decimal System. The Library of Congress classifies books by subject matter as follows:

A	General works	M	Music
B	Philosophy-Religion	N	Fine arts
C	History-Auxiliary sciences	P	Language and litera-
D	Foreign history and topography		ture
E-F	American history	Q	Science
G	Geography-Anthropology	R	Medicine
H	Social sciences	S	Agriculture
J	Political science	T	Technology
K	Law	U	Military science
L	Education	V	Naval science
		Z	Bibliography—
			Library science

In this system, the call number of a book on religion will contain a *B*. The Dewey system classifies books as follows:

000-099	General Works	500-599	Pure science
100-199	Philosophy	600-699	Useful arts
200-299	Religion	700-799	Fine arts
300-399	Social sciences	800-899	Literature
400-499	Philology	900-999	History

Get into the habit of writing down the call numbers of all promising books immediately. That way you can avoid checking the catalog again just to get a book's number. (If you go to find the book at another library, however, you should check its card catalog for the call number, since that library may not use the same clasification system or assign the same number to the book that the other library does.)

```
                    MANAGEMENT--MATHEMATICAL MODELS

            McLaughlin, Frank S.
    HD           Quantitative techniques for management
    30      decisions / Frank S. McLaughlin and Robert C.
    .M16    Pickhardt. - Boston, MA : Houghton Mifflin Co.,
    P96     1979.
    1979         xvii, 578p. : illus. ; 24 cm.

            Includes index.

            1. Operations research.  I. McLaughlin, Frank
    S. II. Pickhardt, Robert C., jt. author.
    III. Title.
```

Figure 11.1
A subject card

```
              McLaughlin, Frank S.
  HD               Quantitative techniques for management
  30          decisions / Frank S. McLaughlin and Robert C.
  .M16        Pickhardt. - Boston, MA : Houghton Mifflin Co.,
  P96         1979.
  1979             xvii, 578p. : illus. ; 24 cm.

              Includes index.

                   1. Management--Mathematical models.
              2. Operations research. I. Pickhardt, Robert C.,
              jt. author. II. Title.
```

Figure 11.2
An author card

```
              Quantitative techniques for management decisions
  HD          / Frank S. McLaughlin and Robert C. Pickhardt. -
  30          Boston, MA : Houghton Mifflin Co., 1979.
  .M16             xvii, 578p. : illus. ; 24 cm.
  P96
  1979             Includes index.

                   1.  Management--Mathematical models.
              2. Operations research. I. McLaughlin, Frank S.
              II. Pickhardt, Robert C., jt. author.
```

Figure 11.3
A title card

The Periodicals Index

A second major form of printed material is periodical literature, such as newspapers and magazines. Finding the information you need in periodicals is a different process from locating information found in books; the articles in most periodicals are listed, usually by subject, in indexes, not card catalogs. Some of these indexes are fairly general, such as *The Reader's Guide to Periodical Literature*, which lists articles in magazines as varied as *Woman's Day*, *Newsweek*, and *Popular Mechanics*. Indexes can also be more specialized; the *Education Index*, for example, lists only those periodicals published in the field of education. Most indexes are updated monthly.

When you're looking for the most current information available on your topic—or if you want to read what was written when a certain event took place—you will use a periodicals index, not the card catalog, to find that information. For instance, let's look at the *Business Periodicals Index*, the standard periodical index for the business field. Assume that you're researching computer crime. Looking in the January 1983 issue of the Index under *Computer crimes*, you find the listing displayed in Figure 11.4 (p. 352). This entry lists six recently published articles on computer crimes and provides the information necessary for locating them: the title of the article, the author (if given), the magazine (or journal), the pages on which the article is found, and the volume number and/or the date of the magazine. Note that the titles of the periodicals are abbreviated. *Data Management*, for example, is listed as *Data Manage*. All abbreviations and the full titles of the magazines and journals indexed in the *Business Periodicals Index* are listed at the front of the volume; the *B.P.I.* also provides the addresses of those periodicals

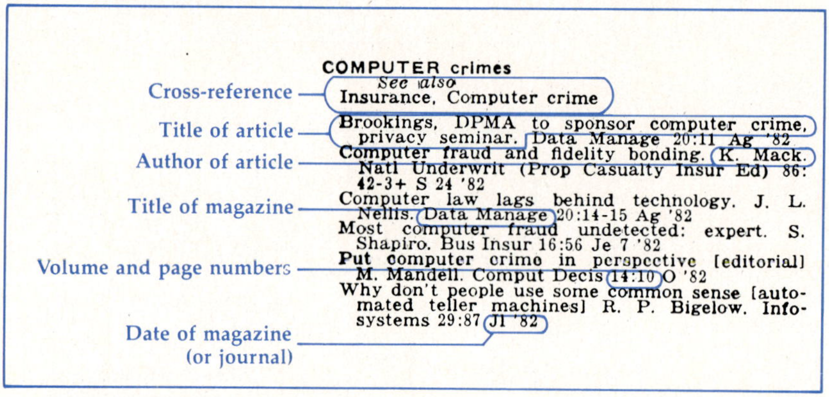

COMPUTER crimes
See also
Insurance, Computer crime
Brookings, DPMA to sponsor computer crime, privacy seminar. Data Manage 20:11 Ag '82
Computer fraud and fidelity bonding. K. Mack. Natl Underwrit (Prop Casualty Insur Ed) 86:42-3+ S 24 '82
Computer law lags behind technology. J. L. Nellis. Data Manage 20:14-15 Ag '82
Most computer fraud undetected: expert. S. Shapiro. Bus Insur 16:56 Je 7 '82
Put computer crimo in perspective [editorial] M. Mandell. Comput Decis 14:10 O '82
Why don't people use some common sense [automated teller machines] R. P. Bigelow. Infosystems 29:87 Jl '82

Figure 11.4
An entry in *Business Periodicals Index*

Other indexes of periodicals generally follow the format used in the *B.P.I.* The standard periodical indexes for other disciplines are these:

Education Index
Humanities Index
Social Sciences Index
MLA International Bibliography
(for both language and literature)

In addition, *The Reader's Guide to Periodical Literature* can be useful for a variety of topics. The *New York Times Index* and the *Wall Street Journal Index* provide references to articles in those publications; libraries in your area may have indexes of local newspapers as well.

Once you have the necessary information, you can look up the article in the journal, magazine, or newspaper. You can find the periodical yourself in libraries where the periodicals are shelved alphabetically in an accessible reference area. But stacks of periodicals are not always open to library users; in that case you will ask a librarian for the issues you need.

As you search, be aware that not every library subscribes to every one of the many periodicals listed in a periodical index. Before you begin to hunt for a particular newspaper or magazine on the shelves, check the library's list of periodical holdings to be sure it is available.

Let's go through a typical search for information. Assume that you have decided on a general topic. The first step in seeking information on that topic is to read about it in a good general reference encyclopedia like the Encyclopedia American. Encyclopedias will be shelved alphabetically in the reference section (which you should have found in acquainting yourself with the library). Located nearby will be specialized encyclopedias, such as the *International Encyclopedia of the Social Sciences* or the *Encyclopedia of Philosophy*. Such works may cover your topic in more detail, and you will want to use them if your topic is not covered, or is not covered sufficiently, in a general encyclopedia.

By reading an encyclopedia article, you will gain an overview of your subject and may thus discover a specific aspect of it that interests you. Also, at the end of the encyclopedia article you will find a bibliography that you can use in your search for additional information.

Armed with that bibliography, proceed to the card catalog to look up call numbers of any books that are listed. The bibliography from the encyclopedia article will likely also list journal articles, which you can look up in the appropriate reference area.

As you read through the sources you've found, you will see that most of them refer to other sources, which you can also use. Pay particular attention to those sources that are listed in several of the books and periodicals; most likely, they are the classic sources in the field.

In some disciplines, a citation index is published, which lists the number of times a work is cited within a given period of time. These indexes will also help you determine the standard sources for your topic. The *Social Science Citation Index* and the *Arts and Humanities Citation Index* are two you might find useful.

Note, too, that the footnotes and endnotes in articles you read may contain important, detailed information on your topic. Often the newest articles or books contain summaries of the most important earlier research done on the topic (whether in the footnotes or in the text). The findings of published researchers can provide you with a short-cut: You can save time by using those references as a guide in locating your materials.

Reference guides, abstracts, and handbooks can also help shorten your search. The American Library Association's *Guide to Reference Books* lists reference materials by subject, for example, and *Ulrich's International Periodicals Directory* lists available periodicals by subject. Both can help you locate sources on a given topic. Abstracts list summaries of articles published in books and magazines on various topics. For example, the abstract *Accounting Articles*, published every four years, lists summaries of articles by topic, such as Auditing, Cost Accounting, and Budgeting. Handbooks are another good source: *The Marketing Manager's Handbook*, for instance, is a miniature encyclopedia of articles pertaining to marketing. Check a reference guide to see whether a similar handbook exists in your field.

To bring your search up to date, you will want to check the card catalog and the appropriate periodical indexes for the most recently published books and articles on your topic. Keep in mind, however, that the nature of your subject will affect your search strategy. A fairly new topic—for example, computer crime—will probably be discussed often in certain magazines or journals, but will rate comments in few books. Issues that have been discussed or researched for years, on the other hand, are likely discussed in books as well as periodicals.

SEARCH STRATEGY: SCREENING SOURCES

Again, you will probably find more material during your search than you can use. Part of your search strategy, then, involves selecting the best sources from the many you will uncover. Remember that you can use a citation index to help you determine which sources are worthwhile. If there is not such an index for your subject area, keep a list of works that appear frequently in the various bibliographies and footnotes you find. Works that are cited often are usually among the most important sources on a topic.

Another way to screen potential sources is to read through annotated bibliographies, which provide summaries of all books and articles listed. Look in the subject card catalog under your topic for the available annotated bibliographies.

Texts you use in your courses can also help you narrow your list of sources. Check for bibliographies at the ends of chapters. The authors will likely list only the classic or most highly regarded sources of information. And sometimes these bibliographies are annotated. Just remember also to check the periodicals indexes for the most recent publications.

Exercise

How would you set up a search strategy for each of the following topics? Would all the topics require the same type of search? Identify any key factors that might influence and shape each search.

1. The most recent advances in the microcomputer industry
2. The uses of hypnotism in the treatment of medical and emotional disorders
3. Jean-Paul Sartre's views on free will and determinism
4. Symbolism in Nathaniel Hawthorne's *The Scarlet Letter*
5. The video game boom

INVENTION: DETERMINING PURPOSE AND CONTENT

In order to write a research paper, you must devote time to invention, just as you would in writing any paper. Most often, your general purpose will be shaped by the task assigned to you. For instance, in writing the business research report on pages 334–38, the writer's purpose was to recommend a course of action to her supervisor. The writer's boss asked her, in effect, to solve a problem: What should be done about this troublesome folding machine? To solve the problem, the writer researched the repair and maintenance history of the machine and then investigated available replacements. Based on her research, she concluded that the machine should be replaced, and she recommended a specific brand and model as best suited to the bank's needs and budget.

When you are writing a research paper for a course in a particular discipline, your purpose will often be guided by the instructor's assignment. Consider the social sciences evaluative essay, ''The Relationship of Birth Order to Intelligence and Academic Achievement,'' on pages 421–26. Because the instructor had assigned an essay that featured a review of important past and current research, this writer knew she would first have to find a topic—within the field of psychology—that was significant enough to have been studied by many professional researchers. After some general reading, she decided that the topic of birth order fit the requirement and was interesting to her. She knew that she must then read the existing articles on the topic and organize and discuss their findings, using her own judgment to evaluate the researchers' work.

Often, however, students must write research papers under less clear-cut circumstances. If you are assigned simply to write ''a research paper'' in a composition course, for instance, you may not have a strong sense of what your subject-matter ought to be or what your purpose should be in discussing it. But in such a case, an important purpose for writing the research paper may be to take part in a learning experience: to learn something about your topic and to learn how to research, compose, and document a paper. In writing this kind of research paper, you will usually proceed by choosing a general topic from a list (generally provided by the instructor) like the following:

Auto Industry (U.S.)
Busing for Desegregation
Collegiate Sports
Electoral College
Hypnotism
Jogging
Lobbying
Martial Arts
Mass Media
Mass Transit

New Journalism
Nuclear Energy
Organized Crime
Presidency (U.S.)
Radical Organizations
Religious Cults
Tax Laws
United Nations
Welfare Systems

If you are most interested in the United Nations, for instance, you would choose that as your general topic and then proceed to set up a search strategy.

Narrowing the Topic

Both the exact purpose and the content of your research paper on the United Nations would be shaped from a careful consideration of your reading on the subject. As you read, you should employ several techniques to help you define purpose and content. One of these is narrowing and focusing the topic.

Successful research paper writers generally stay away from overly broad topics. A subject such as the United Nations would probably be more suited to a series of volumes than to a research paper. "Conflict Resolution in the United Nations" would be a bit better, but it is still somewhat broad. A more workable topic for a good research paper would be "The Failure of the United Nations to Resolve the Iranian Hostage Crisis." By narrowing the topic to a specific case of conflict resolution, we have made it more manageable. The task of determining the paper's content will be much easier, and the resultant paper will more likely have unity and depth.

When you narrow a general topic, think of it as creating subcategories from one main general category, as we did with the "United Nations" topic. Put into outline form, what we did looks like this:

> United Nations
>> Conflict Resolutions
>>> Failure to Resolve Iranian Hostage Crisis

How do you create the subcategories? By putting more and more *limits* on the topic. These limits may be geographical or chronological, or they may relate to various aspects of the general topic. In moving from "Conflict Resolutions" to "Failure to Resolve Iranian Hostage Crisis," for instance, we added limits of time (twentieth century) and aspect (failures only).

Let's look at another example. Suppose you were interested in the topic "The auto industry." You could narrow it geographically and chronologically ("American auto manufacturing, 1970–1980"), then narrow it by aspects ("Most popular American autos manufactured, 1970–1980"), and perhaps then to "Preferences of Americans buying American-made automobiles, 1970–1980."

Limiting a topic geographically or chronologically is relatively easy. Limiting by considering various aspects is harder, especially if you don't know enough about the topic to subdivide it. To overcome this difficulty, you can look up your general subject in a periodicals index or abstract and see what kinds of articles have been published about it lately. From looking at the titles or summaries of articles you may find a more specific idea on which to write. You can also look up the topic in the subject card file to see what types of books have been written. This method of narrowing your topic also provides you with an immediate research lead on which to base additional work.

Writers also use several other techniques in invention. Many of the approaches we discussed earlier (on pages 50–55) also can be used in writing the research paper. For example, by using the cause/effect thinking pattern, we can generate at least two versions of "The Failure of the United Nations to Resolve the Iranian Hostage Crisis":

1. "Why the United Nations Failed to Resolve the Iranian Hostage Crisis" (focusing on causes)
2. "The Failure of the United Nations in the Iranian Hostage Crisis: Implications for Future Peacekeeping Efforts" (focusing on effects)

Besides using your reading to narrow and focus your topic, you should begin reading with an investigative spirit. From the start, be on the lookout for (1) a problem that needs solving, (2) a question that needs answering, or (3) a hypothesis that needs testing. In the early stages of research, actively seek a way into your subject. Once you have found that way, you will be able to read more efficiently, because you will be able to determine which readings are relevant to your paper.

In the middle stages of your reading, you will still be investigating, trying to find answers and solutions to the questions and problems you have posed for yourself. At a certain point you will feel that you have investigated your topic enough, that you understand as much about it as you are going to. Many of the new materials you read will yield little new information. After this point, any further reading you do will not be in the spirit of investigation, but in a practical frame of mind as you attempt to find additional evidence to bolster your argument.

INVENTION STRATEGIES: A SPECIFIC CASE

To illustrate the invention procedure for research writing, let's follow the path taken by Tim, who chose the United States auto industry as the general topic for his research paper. An avid reader of newspapers and news magazines, Tim already had some idea of how he wanted to narrow his topic. The decline of the auto industry, a subject much in the news at the time he wrote his paper, was his chief area of interest. After some preliminary reading on the subject, he decided to pose this question: What are the chief factors responsible for the decline of the auto industry in the United States? Continuing his reading, he focused mainly on sources that dealt with this subject. Before long, he discovered many apparent causes of the industry's woes: a declining economy in general, the world oil shortage, the rising popularity of imported cars, and increasingly high union wage demands.

But he felt that most of these causes were already well known, and so he decided to look deeper. Another, less obvious, cause began to suggest itself: The automakers' unwillingness to change in response to changing consumer demands—the automakers' inflexibility—was largely responsible for their difficulties. Quickly shaping this idea into a hypothesis, he checked it against the materials he had already read and began testing it against the new information he continued to uncover.

The more Tim read, the more he was convinced that the auto industry had declined because it had not been flexible enough to adapt to changing times and tastes. At this point, his invention process was nearly complete: He had developed a valid thesis idea and had gathered a good deal of evidence from books and articles.

Even after he began composing, however, he continued scanning new sources, looking for additional evidence. For example, after he had written a first draft, he came upon a useful quotation while glancing through a book about waste and mismanagement in the auto industry. The passage shed light on the mentality of Detroit's top decision makers, who seemed "to forget that a cloistered executive whose only social contacts are with similar executives who make $500,000 a year, and who has not really bought a car the way a customer has in years, has no basis to judge public tastes" (John Z. DeLorean, *On a Clear Day You Can See General Motors*). Tim realized that this quotation could help explain why auto executives are inflexible in meeting the changing demands of the consumer, and so he used it to bolster his case.

Taking Notes

Throughout the invention process, you will take notes from your readings. Whether you record those notes on three-by-five-inch or four-by-six-inch index cards (the preferred method because of ease of organization) or on sheets of notebook paper (a method used with success by many students), they are crucial to the success of your paper. They are the evidence you will later draw on as you compose the paper. Just as important, they are a developing written record of your efforts at invention. The moment you begin taking notes, you begin determining what you will write about—even though at first you may be quite uncertain about what to write down and what to let pass. Deciding to record something on your note cards helps you narrow your topic. And as you narrow your topic and get farther along in your readings, you will know what to take down in your notes.

As you take notes, you will have to decide what form to use: quotation, paraphrase, or summary. A *quotation* records the exact words used, as the card in Figure 11.5 illustrates. (The *ellipsis*—the three periods—at the beginning indicates that the quotation starts in mid-sentence.)

Figure 11.5
A notecard containing
a quotation

"... a cloistered executive whose only social contacts are with similar executives who make $500,000 a year, and who has not really bought a car the way a customer has in years, has no basis to judge public taste."

A *paraphrase* restates a passage in your own words, and does not use those of the original author. Paraphrases are generally about the same length as the passages from which they are derived. Because you use your own words, the number of possible paraphrase versions of any given passage is virtually limitless. Figure 11.6 shows a possible paraphrase for our quotation. Although the paraphrase does not borrow word-for-word from the original, it does express the same idea, and it is similar in length. Note that no quotation marks are used for paraphrases.

Figure 11.6
A notecard containing
a paraphrase

Since top-level executives socialize only with other extremely wealthy executives, and since they have had no recent experience buying cars like ordinary people do, they have lost touch with the buying public.

Like a paraphrase, a *summary* is written in your own words, but condenses the ideas into fewer words. Just as there are many ways to paraphrase a passage, so are there many ways to summarize one. A possible summary of the same passage is given in Figure 11.7. This summary captures most of the information of the original in only about half the length.

Figure 11.7
A notecard containing
a summary

Top executives have become so rich and isolated that they have no idea what the common person wants.

Whether you use quotation, paraphrase, or summary, you must give credit to the source from which you are taking the idea. We will discuss proper practices and forms for documentation in detail later in this chapter.

Each of the three forms of note-taking has its own uses. You will want to use quotations when the wording of the original is particularly effective. If you feel that you could not make the same point as impressively in your own language, then you should copy the passage word-for-word in your notes for later inclusion in your paper. Or, if the wording of the original is quite complex or tricky, you may want to record a quotation to insure complete accuracy when you write the paper. When your source is a recognized authority, you may also want to quote verbatim. But don't use quotations out of sheer laziness.

The paraphrase is probably the most generally useful form; it is the one you should plan to use most often. If you paraphrase well as you take notes, you will find that the actual writing of your paper will go quickly—because some of the work of putting ideas into your own words will already be done. In deciding whether to paraphrase or summarize, consider whether you will want to discuss the point in detail in your paper, or whether you will simply mention it in passing. In the latter case, a summary will suffice.

Regardless of the form you use in taking notes, consider adding your own comments or questions on the card. In this way, you force yourself to think about what you are reading as you read it. For instance, in taking notes on the isolation of auto executives, you might want to add a comment such as "might help explain industry's slow response to public's demand for fuel-efficient cars" or "typical of industry-wide attitudes?" Adding comments like these to your notes can help you analyze what you read as well as focus your investigation on your topic.

Exercise

For each of the following quotations, write a paraphrase version and a summary version.

1. "Fresh air is good for all plants and frequent airing of a room where plants are growing is always sensible. But be cautious about opening windows directly in front of plants. No plant should be in a draft. Some plants, such as poinsettias, will drop leaves if exposed to drafts."(Joan Lee Faust, *The New York Times Book of House Plants*)

2. "In our time, political speech and writing are largely the defense of the indefensible. Things like the continuance of British rule in India, the Russian purges and deportations, the dropping of the atom bombs on Japan, can indeed be defended, but only by arguments which are too

brutal for most people to face. . . .'' (George Orwell, ''Politics and the English Language'')

3. ''Indeed, the thought that the [Watergate] break-in might somehow be the work of the Republicans seemed implausible. On June 17, 1972, less than a month before the Democratic Convention, the President stood ahead of all announced Democratic candidates in the polls by no less than 19 points.'' (Carl Bernstein and Bob Woodward, *All the President's Men*)

4. ''African-Americans comprise only about five percent of the workforce in the electronics industry. Black students earn an even smaller percentage of the bachelor's and graduate degrees in electronics related fields. However, the contributions Black professionals and Black students are making in electronics far exceed their numerical representation.'' (''Blacks in Electronics,'' *The Black Collegian*)

5. ''Deadpan [newspaper] reporting of the contents of a report, speech or the like, even when the source is reputable, may be misleading in that it does not give readers the 'whole' or 'essential' truth . . . . It certainly is newsworthy when someone important in public life attacks another person. Such news often cannot be ignored. It can, however, be put in better perspective if there is simultaneous opportunity for reply by the otherwise injured party.'' (Curtis D. MacDougall, *Interpretative Reporting*)

DOCUMENTING YOUR PAPER

Documenting your paper means crediting your research sources. All ideas, facts, opinions, and statistics that are not your own must be documented through footnotes or endnotes and the bibliography.[1] We will examine and illustrate the most common of these forms; use them unless your instructor requires more specialized documentation. (Papers in the sciences and social sciences are usually documented somewhat differently. See pages 371–72 for a brief discussion of documenting scientific papers.) For a full treatment of footnote, endnote, and bibliography forms, we recommend the *MLA Handbook for Writers of Research Papers, Theses, and Dissertations*. (Note: The latest edition of the *MLA Handbook*, published in 1984, slightly modifies the documentation forms for several types of entries. On pages 394–95 we show entries in both the old and new MLA styles. Be sure to use the documentation style recommended by your instructor.)

---

[1]When a note appears at the bottom of the page, as does this one, it is called a *footnote*. When it appears in a list along with other notes at the end of a paper, it is called an *endnote* or simply a *note*. For talking about notes without regard to their placement, we will adopt the common practice of referring to them as *notes*.

Whenever you cite specific facts, ideas, or statistics from research sources, you must immediately credit those sources in either a footnote or endnote. Contained within the note will be all the information needed should a reader desire to consult the original source.

Traditionally, notes were placed at the bottom of the page containing the information to which they refer. This was convenient for the reader—and somewhat challenging for the typist. The trend now is to place all notes at the end of the paper (under the heading "Notes"). Be sure to follow your instructor's directions about where to place your notes.

In deciding whether material needs to be documented, remember that information not original with you must be credited to its source. Obviously, a direct quotation falls into this category. If a quotation takes up fewer than four typed lines, put it into quotation marks and include it within the body of the paper. For instance, in writing a research paper on pharmacy as a career for women, one writer used and documented some pertinent ideas and statistics like this:

```
Pharmacy is one field that has had a rising number of

female practitioners.  According to one study, "currently

about 17% of the approximately 143,000 registered pharmacists

in the U. S. are women, up from 10% in 1970."⁴  This stands

in contrast with many other professions, where the number

of women remains depressingly small.
```

All notes are numbered consecutively throughout a paper. Notice that the superior number follows the period and quotation mark. The note for this reference was:

```
    ⁴ Robert Brody, "Careers:  Pharmacy," Working Woman,

April 1982, p. 138.
```

If a quotation is longer than four lines, set it off from the body of the paper by a triple space and type it indented and doublespaced. No quotation marks are used around a block quotation:

Pharmacy is one field that has had a rising number of female practitioners. According to Robert Brody, writing for <u>Working Woman</u>,

> Pharmacy offers a good salary, security, and profes-sional prestige, and opportunities for women are better than ever. Currently about 17% of the approximately 143,000 registered pharmacists in the U.S. are women, up from 10% in 1970. Slightly more than 40% of all pharmacy-school graduates in 1981 were women -- a trend with long-term implications. In fact, last year women sophomores outnumbered male classmates in 21 of the 72 U.S. pharmacy schools.

The note for this reference is the same as for the single-sentence quotation above.

Even when you paraphrase or summarize the ideas of others, you must still give credit to them. For example, suppose the writer of the pharmacy paper paraphrased the last sentence of the block quotation like this:

> In 1981, in nearly a third of the U.S. pharmacy schools, there were more female sophomores than male.

This statement would have to be documented; the note would be identical to the one used for the direct quotation.

Failure to document sources amounts to *plagiarism*, an offense serious enough to warrant a failing grade or suspension at most colleges. Some students commit this offense unknowingly, thinking that because they have paraphrased ideas in their sources, they do not have to document them. Don't make this mistake.

However, one type of information does not have to be documented even though it is not your original thinking. Any idea that is part of what an average person might know needs no documentation. For instance, you would not have to credit a source for the statement (in your own words) that George Washington was the first U.S. president, or that an atomic bomb was dropped on Hiroshima—these ideas are part of what could be called a "public domain" of knowledge.

But unless you're sure that an idea "belongs" to everyone, give credit to your source. And always credit the source for a direct quotation, even if an idea in the quotation is common knowledge. For instance, suppose you are writing a paper on the French Revolution. You know that it began in the summer of 1789; this is common knowledge. And so you would not have to document a sentence in which you stated that fact:

The French Revolution began in the summer of 1789.

But if you borrow a phrase from a book to announce the same fact, you must document it:

The summer of 1789 precipitated that frightening and cacaphonous tumult called the French Revolution.[1]

Sample Reference Notes

Notes take different forms depending on the types of sources being documented. Here are sample notes for commonly used sources.

Books

For a book with one author:

[1] David Gootnick, <u>Getting a Better Job</u> (New York: McGraw-Hill, 1978), p. 155.

For a book with two authors:

[2] Eva L. Baker and W. James Popham, <u>Expanding Dimensions of Instructional Objectives</u> (Englewood Cliffs, N.J.: Prentice-Hall, 1973), p. 105.

For a book with more than three authors:

[3] Walter B. Meigs et al., <u>Advanced Accounting</u>. (New York: McGraw-Hill, Inc., 1966), p. 145.

For a book with an editor:

[4] Sterling M. McMurrin, ed., <u>Resources for Urban Schools</u> (New York: Committee for Economic Development, 1971), p. vii.

For an article in a collection:

[5] Samuel R. Levin, "The Conventions of Poetry," in <u>Literary Style: A Symposium</u>, ed. Seymour Chatman (New York: Oxford University Press, 1971), p. 180.

For a specific edition of a book:

[6] Norman B. Sigband, <u>Communication for Management and Business</u>, 3rd ed. (Glenview, Ill.: Scott, Foresman, 1982), p. 59.

Periodicals

For a signed article from a magazine:

[7] Susan Quinn, "The Competence of Babies," <u>The Atlantic</u>, Jan. 1982, p. 58.

For an unsigned magazine article:

[8] "The Readers' Revenge," <u>People</u>, 14 March 1983, p. 41.

For an article in a scholarly journal:

[9] Thomas M. Linehan, "Style and Individuality in E. E. Cummings' <u>The Enormous Room</u>," <u>Style</u>, 13 (1979), 48.

Note: If the volume number is not given, precede the page number(s) by *p.* for "page" or *pp.* for "pages."

For a newspaper article:

> 10 Joseph Lelyveld, "South African Flees His Trial for
> Treason," New York Times, 19 April 1983, Sec. 1, p. 3,
> col. 4.

Other Sources

For an interview (specify as "personal" or "telephone"):

> 11 Personal interview with Joy Peters, Personnel
> Director, Second Bank, 8 Oct. 1981.

Note: Give the person's title if it is important to lend credibility to your source.

For an encyclopedia article:

> 12 Joseph Chapman Andrews, "Magnets and Electromagnets,"
> Encyclopaedia Britannica: Macropaedia, 13, 1974.

Note: If the article is unsigned, begin with the title. You need not give the volume number if the encyclopedia is alphabetically arranged.

Subsequent References For subsequent references to sources, your note need not repeat all the information. Simply use the author's (or authors') last name followed by a comma, followed by the page number on which the material was found. Here is a second reference to the work cited in note 2 above:

> 13 Baker and Popham, p. 39.

If no author was given, use the title of the work. If you cite more than one work by the same author, subsequent references should list the author's name and an abbreviated title.

Content Notes Although notes are most often used to show indebtedness to other sources, they can also be used for other purposes. These types of notes make use of the writer's own commentary—that is, they contain content, just as the body of the paper does. They are not limited to citing the names of authors and the titles of works, as were all the notes we have presented so far.

Type 1 Use a note to indicate blanket or general indebtedness to several sources. This is useful for "semi-common" background knowledge, or material which is generally known to students of your subject but not to others.

14 The details of Erikson's early experiments are widely known. See Michael Jenkins, <u>Modern Chemistry</u> (Toronto: Eaton Press, 1968), pp. 98-103, and Martin Kirk, <u>Frontiers in Chemistry</u> (New York: Delta, 1971), pp. 52-61.

By using this note you are telling your reader that the discussion which follows the note is almost common knowledge, but that you consulted the two sources, *Modern Chemistry* and *Frontiers in Chemistry*, to verify the information, and that the reader may do so as well.

Type 2 Use a note to indicate indirect or partial indebtedness to a source that provides you with an idea that you have used as a point of departure in developing your own idea.

15 Roger Kearney mentions the emergence of this particular miner's union as a political force, but does not speculate on its probable role in prlonging the uprising of 1922. See <u>The Rise of Labour Unions in South Africa</u> (London: Alfred Press, 1948), p. 143.

In this case, you are informing your reader that Kearney's book led you to think about the miner's union in the first place, but that the idea about its role in the uprising (which appears in the body of your paper) was your own.

Type 3 Use a note to list additional sources in order to inform readers more fully of the relevant literature on a particular question and to demonstrate the breadth of your research. Particularly if the primary purpose of your paper is to persuade readers, such a demonstration is important. Further, citing divergent opinions will increase your credibility and dispel any notions that your research was one-sided.

¹⁶For a markedly different interpretation of measures

taken by the I.R.S., see Ronald Markowitz, "Tax Reform,"

Journal of Political Economy, 7 (1964), 22-26. Markowitz

contends, for example, that Title VI is unconstitutional.

In the body of your paper you suggest that Title VI is *not* unconstitutional.

Type 4 Use a note to discuss any useful point that supplements but does not strictly belong in the text.

¹⁷Keats may have used the imagery of sickness and

disease in this poem because of his own health problems.

Here, the idea is all yours: Because you are familiar with the poet's life, the point occurred to you as you were writing the paper. Thus the note is all content—it contains no references to any other sources. You think it is an important idea, yet you can see no graceful way of inserting it into the body of the paper. Hence, you decide to put it in a note. Although this type of note is useful, avoid relying on it too heavily. Your reader can quickly become annoyed by such interruptions.

Most of these notes are actually combinations of references and content. The content you add explains something about the references you used. For many writers the content note is an indispensable tool. To limit themselves to only straight reference notes would be to deny or ignore much of the complexity that arises in the research writing process. Content notes allow research writers to explain more precisely how they used their sources.

Bibliography The bibliography must list all the sources you have cited directly in your essay. Some instructors prefer that you also list all your reading for the paper in the bibliography. This would include sources that you have used directly as well as those that have provided background or more general inspiration. Ask your instructors for their guidelines.

Bibliography entries are arranged alphabetically according to the last name of the author. "Selected Bibliography" is the most versatile heading, but you could also use "List of Works Cited" or "List of Works Consulted," depending on the nature of the bibliography. The bibliography is the final section of a paper, appearing after all text and notes.

A bibliography entry contains much of the same information as a reference note, but in a slightly different form. A notable difference in content is that a reference note often includes a specific page number because it refers to one specific place within a work. By contrast, a bibliography entry refers to the whole work, and page numbers appear only when they are needed to refer to the specific pages of an article within a periodical or an anthology.

A reference note is punctuated as one sentence; a bibliography entry for most sources is punctuated as three. Also, whereas only the first line of a note is indented, the second and all subsequent lines of a bibliography entry are indented. Finally, the author's last name, not first name, is given first in a bibliography entry.

Here is the bibliography entry for the first sample note on page 364:

Gootnick, David. <u>Getting a Better Job</u>. New York: McGraw-

    Hill, 1978.

The spacing of the bibliography entry emphasizes authors' names. Additional examples of the bibliography entries for the sources listed in the notes on pages 364–66 are as follows:

Books

For a book with two authors:

Baker, Eva L. and W. James Popham. <u>Expanding Dimensions of</u>

    <u>Instructional Objectives</u>. Englewood Cliffs, N.J.:

    Prentice-Hall, 1973.

Note that only the *first* author's name is given in reverse order.

For a book with more than three authors:

Meigs, Walter B., et al. <u>Advanced Accounting</u>. New York:

    McGraw-Hill, Inc., 1966.

For a book with an editor:

McMurrin, Sterling M., ed. Resources for Urban Schools.

New York: Committee for Economic Development, 1971.

For an article in a collection:

Levin, Samuel R. "The Conventions of Poetry." In

Literary Style: A Symposium. Ed. Seymour Chatman.

New York: Oxford Univ. Press, 1971, pp. 177-98.

For a specific edition of a book:

Sigband, Norman B. Communication for Management and

Business. 3rd ed. Glenview, Ill.: Scott, Foresman,

1982.

Periodicals

For a signed article from a magazine:

Quinn, Susan. "The Competence of Babies." The Atlantic,

Jan. 1982, pp. 54-62.

For an unsigned magazine article:

"The Readers' Revenge." People, 14 March 1983, pp. 40-50.

For an article in a scholarly journal:

Linehan, Thomas M. "Style and Individuality in E. E.

Cummings' The Enormous Room." Style, 13 (1979), 45-59.

For a newspaper article:

Lelyveld, Joseph. "South African Flees His Trial for

Treason," New York Times, 19 April 1983, Sec. 1,

p. 3, col. 4.

Other Sources

For an interview (specify as "personal" or "telephone"):

```
Peters, Joy.  Personal interview.  8 Oct. 1981.
```

For an encyclopedia article:

```
Andrews, Joseph Chapman.  "Magnets and Electromagnets."

    Encyclopaedia Britannica:  Macropaedia.  1974 ed.
```

Specialized Documentation

In most cases the standard forms of documentation we have discussed will be all you need. However, many disciplines in the sciences and social sciences have devised somewhat different methods for referring to sources, and you may be asked to use "scientific-style" documentation, particularly in an upper-level science course.

Typically, instead of using notes at the bottom of the page or the end of the paper, scientific writers credit their sources through a parenthetical reference in the text itself. The most common technique is the author/year method:

> One characteristic of all viruses is that they have no metabolism of their own, but instead make use of the host cell's metabolism (Novikoff and Holtzman, 1970).

If the reference is to a specific fact or quotation taken from a specific page, the page number is indicated this way:

> . . . metabolism (Novikoff and Holtzman, 1970, 163).

To find more complete information on the source, the reader turns to the bibliography (which, in specialized documentation, is usually headed "Literature Cited" or "References" rather than "Bibliography"). For a paper in biology, the bibliography entry for the source just given would look like this (as recommended by the Council of Biology Editors):

```
Novikoff, A. and Eric Holtzman.  1970.  Cells and

    organelles.  Holt, Rinehart and Winston, New York,

    N.Y.
```

Notice that the entry differs in many respects from the standard bibliography form: the date is placed earlier in the entry, only the first word of the title is capitalized, the title is not underlined, and the positions of city and publishing company are reversed.

Here are several entries from the bibliography for the social sciences evaluative review essay, "The Relationship of Birth Order to Intelligence and Academic Achievement," which appears in Chapter 12 on pages 421–26. In that paper, the writer used the author/year method. The form of her bibliography follows that recommended by the American Psychological Association.

References

Bayer, Alan E. (1966) Birth order and college attendance. Journal of Marriage and the Family, 28, 480–484.

Cicirelli, Victor G. (1967) Sibling constellation, creativity, IQ, and academic achievement. Child Development, 38, 481–490.

Foster, John W. & Archer, Stanley J. (1979) Birth order and intelligence: An immunological interpretation. Perceptual and Motor Skills, 48, 79–93.

Nuttall, Ena Vasquez, et al. (1976) The effects of family size, birth order, sibling separation and crowding on the academic achievement of boys and girls. American Educational Research Journal, 13, 217–223.

Compare the forms used in this paper with the entry for the biology book on page 371 and you'll see some variations. Moreover, be aware that although the author/year method of citation is the most common, there are other methods as well. If you are asked to use specialized documentation in a paper, check with your instructor or a librarian to get additional recommendations for the exact forms to use.

PUTTING IT TOGETHER

After researching, reading about, and thinking about your topic, you're ready to put your paper together. If you have concentrated on invention, you will have a good idea of your paper's primary purpose and main ideas. The next step is to examine your note cards and group them according to the main ideas they explain or support. (One advantage of using cards is that you can group them easily.) You should also record on cards your own thoughts and reactions while doing your research.

In rearranging your notes you may find that you need to do more research in order to achieve your primary purpose. For instance, an idea that appears useful as evidence in support of your thesis may not have had that importance early in your research, and you may wish to take another look at that source for more detailed information. Or it may develop that you simply need more information altogether in order to prove your point or inform your reader adequately. You should allow enough time for the writing process so that you can spend some extra moments on further research.

Once you have grouped your notes according to the main ideas they support, you'll need to decide in what order you wish to discuss them. Keeping your primary purpose in mind, choose an arrangement that you feel will best help you achieve that purpose. You may wish to review the sections in Chapters 3 and 5 (pages 84–93 and 163–67) that discuss possibilities such as order of importance, likes with likes, and so on.

If your instructor requests an outline along with the research paper, find out whether you're expected to turn in a formal or a working outline. Even if you are not required to turn in an outline, have some strategy in mind *and* on paper for organizing your report. The sheer length of typical research papers makes remembering what you want to say and when you want to say it difficult unless you've jotted it down. (You may want to review the section on outlining, pages 158–61.)

If you are not required to submit a formal outline with your paper, you can try a different planning device, such as the informal outline (discussed on pages 154–58) or the block outline. The value of the block outline is that it lets you visualize your structure more concretely than does a formal outline. As an example, let's consider the opening sections of a block outline for a paper entitled "Understanding the Pilgrimage to Mecca." In a block outline, each paragraph is represented by a rectangular block, and the paragraphs are numbered consecutively (see Figure 11.11, p. 374.

Note that the writer of this block outline also included the appropriate source citations for each section. These citations, such as "Ciewinski, p. 65," correspond to the writer's notes. By including them in the outline she strengthens her understanding of exactly how and where she will use the materials collected during her research.

Remember, too, that most plans or outlines will need some alteration before you are done. Seldom does a writer predict the exact form of the finished paper. As you organize and reorganize your ideas, reshuffle your note cards accordingly. Writing a first draft will be easier because you'll always have a good idea of what you're going to say next. At the same time, try to stay flexible. As you write, you may decide to rearrange some ideas and to add or delete others. Don't hesitate to make

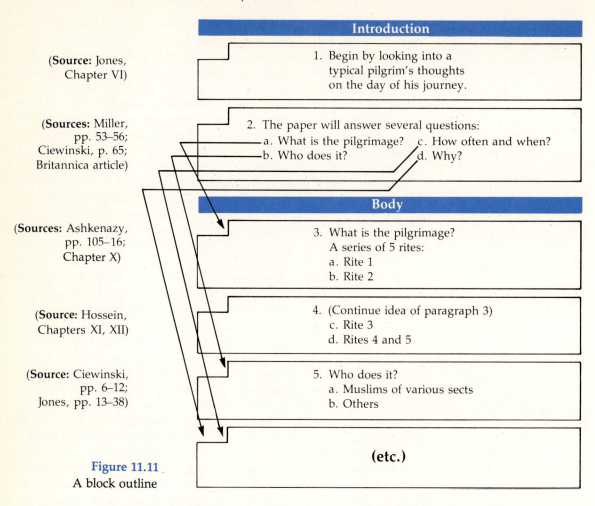

Introduction

(**Source:** Jones, Chapter VI)

1. Begin by looking into a typical pilgrim's thoughts on the day of his journey.

(**Sources:** Miller, pp. 53–56; Ciewinski, p. 65; Britannica article)

2. The paper will answer several questions:
   a. What is the pilgrimage?   c. How often and when?
   b. Who does it?   d. Why?

Body

(**Sources:** Ashkenazy, pp. 105–16; Chapter X)

3. What is the pilgrimage? A series of 5 rites:
   a. Rite 1
   b. Rite 2

(**Source:** Hossein, Chapters XI, XII)

4. (Continue idea of paragraph 3)
   c. Rite 3
   d. Rites 4 and 5

(**Source:** Ciewinski, pp. 6–12; Jones, pp. 13–38)

5. Who does it?
   a. Muslims of various sects
   b. Others

(etc.)

Figure 11.11
A block outline

changes that you feel will strengthen your work, even though such changes take time. Be especially flexible while creating the outline itself, since changing it involves merely reshuffling your cards or papers.

During the actual writing, remember to use paraphrase and summary of the ideas from your sources, rather than direct quotation, as your dominant techniques. Of course, do not hesitate to quote directly if the original wording is very effective or if you want to use the words of an authority. But overuse of quotations can give a fragmented feeling to your paper. As a rule of thumb, limit your use of direct quotations to an average of two per page, depending upon the length of the quotation and the nature of your subject.

Whether you quote, paraphrase, or summarize an idea, be sure to add commentary of your own. Most often your comments will take the form of explanations of the significance of the information you've just given. For instance, if, in a paper on the economy of Peru, you state that 720,000 tons of agricultural products were exported in 1982, you would want to add some comment on the importance of this fact to your paper. Does the fact show that Peru is a major exporter of foodstuffs? Or does it show that agricultural exports are not a crucial aspect of Peru's economy? Does the fact show that Peru no longer exports as much produce as it used to? Or does it show that exporting agricultural products is a growing business in Peru? Don't make the common mistake of believing that the facts and ideas will speak for themselves.

Finally, while you compose your first draft, remember to insert reference notes in your text as you go. You can always add more notes later, but don't let that fact lull you into ignoring the placement of notes while you initially compose your paper. Going back to put in all the notes once you've written a complete draft will be unpleasant and time-consuming.

Typing and Arranging the Finished Product

Most research papers have four parts: a title page, the body of the paper, the reference notes pages, and the bibliography pages, put together in that order. The title page contains, in addition to the title, the author's name, the course for which it was written, the instructor's name, and the date. Center all this information (see the title page of the sample research paper, p. 377). Including the instructor's name is good insurance in case the paper is lost or mislaid; the finder will probably be able to return it more easily to the instructor than to you.

The body of the paper is typed in paragraph form as a long essay would be. Maintain a one inch margin on each side. You can use a sheet of paper with the margins drawn on it in black marker under the sheet you're typing to help you keep all pages looking uniform. Double-space throughout, unless you're using on-page reference notes. Indent and double-space block quotations and separate them from the text with a triple-space; footnotes are also separated from the body of the paper with a triple space and are typed single-spaced.

Because your research paper will discuss ideas that are more complex than those in the shorter papers you write, you'll want to be especially careful in your opening paragraphs. There you should introduce your readers to the purpose of your paper and indicate how you're planning to achieve it. An average essay may need only an introductory sentence or two, but a research paper usually needs a paragraph or more of introduction. Similarly, in concluding your work, you may find you'll need more than a couple of sentences to end your paper.

After the body of the report, set up the "Notes" and "Bibliography" pages, following the forms we examined on pages 364–71 or those in a style manual.

Type the page numbers of your reports in the upper right-hand corner, with two exceptions. The title page and the first page of the body are not numbered at all.

SAMPLE RESEARCH PAPER Following is a sample research paper written for a bioethics course. As you read it, pay attention to how the student handles her research sources, particularly the way she blends them in with her own discussion. You can also use this sample paper to check details of format and presentation.

This student used upper and lowercase letters for the title, which is the standard practice. Your instructor may prefer all uppercase letters.

The writer includes her name, the course title, the name of the instructor, and the date of submission.

Genetic Engineering:

The University/Corporate Connection

by

Jennifer Sturr

Bioethics

Professor Keith Boone

April 7, 1984

The title is repeated at the top of page one. If you are required to submit an outline, place it between the title page and page one.

The writer gets the reader's attention through a colorful introduction. Her opening sentence sketches a futuristic scenario. Sentences 2 and 3 stress the importance of the general topic of microbiology research.

Paragraph 2 narrows the general topic to the emerging "biotechnology industry." Notes 2 and 3 indicate borrowing of direct quotations; note 1 documents a paraphrase.

Genetic Engineering:

The University/Corporate Connection

[1] Scarce human hormones suddenly available in abundance; plants that can produce their own nitrogen, thus eliminating the need for fertilizer; miracle drugs such as the compound interferon. . . . In the past twenty years, knowledge of gene-splicing methods and recombinant DNA technology have multiplied at an astounding rate. Microbiology research is probably the fastest growing area of scientific progress today.[1]

[2] Besides the excitement among scientists over recent findings, there has also been increasing excitement among business people over another aspect of genetic engineering: the biotechnology industry. According to Fortune magazine, small companies such as Genetech, Inc., Biogen, S.A., and half a dozen others have sprung up to realize the profit potential of the new techniques for drug manufacture: "With the gleam of big profits in their eyes, they are plotting ways of capturing a good share of the World's Market for novel drugs and chemicals."[2] With promises to faculty of money and facilities for research, and even shares in the company, "venture capitalists" are scouring the campuses for the brainpower needed to get into the business."[3]

2

Paragraphs 3, 4, and 5
announce the specific
purpose of the research
paper.

[3] These commercial sources are without a doubt a tremendous boost to universities suffering from cuts in federal
grant money. However, there are some serious problems
inherent in these new ties between university research and
the private sector. As the Fortune article puts it, many
scientists "fear that their commericially oriented colleagues will emphasize secrecy and fast payoff rather
than basic research."[4]

[4] In this paper I will present the problems that accom-
pany the commercialization of research, and will raise
some of the ethical questions facing universities engaged in agreements with corporations. My purpose is
perhaps best phrased by Dr. Jonathan King of MIT in
testimony before a congressional subcommittee. Responding to a statement that it is better to have the money
of industry than no money at all, Dr. King generally
agrees, but goes on to say:

Note the format used for
longer quotations (over
four lines). The passage is
introduced with a colon
and is indented five spaces.

> On the other hand, you have a situation where
> everybody is saying, "Wow, this new commerical
> genetic engineering is going to solve all the
> world's problems." I am sure you are going to
> get witnesses who will testify about this. . . .
> I think it is appropriate for a few voices to point
> out, "Look, you lose something this way, too. . . .

3

We are going to lose certain things, lose a certain

aspect of the integrity of the educational system.
"[5]
. . .

The introduction to this paper comprises five paragraphs. Research papers often have longer introductions than regular essays. However, you should avoid putting too much detail in the introduction; save the evidence for the body.

[5] The potential losses spoken of by King merit immediate attention. These new corporate/academic alliances in the field of microbiology will discourage communication within scientific circles, promote hastily achieved results at the expense of accuracy, and enable private interests to "skim the cream off the top" of publicly funded research.[6] Even more serious than all this, the contamination of the academic world by corporate powers threatens to alter the course of scientific inquiry, since the interest in profit will over-shadow the pursuit of knowledge for its own sake.

Here begins the body of the paper. The writer raises the first problem likely to come from the corporate/university partnership: the loss of open communication among scientists.

[6] One of the biggest losses incurred by the new corporate/ university association is that of communication, both inter-scholastic and interdepartmental. As any serious student of science knows, openness among scientists has always been a crucial element in the scientific process. Due to the openness of research, there exists within the scientific community a system of checks and balances whereby scientists are able "to influence each other's attitudes and actions and to check (disapprove or sanction) each other's behaviors . . . not as policemen but as team members."[7] Another check is provided by the practice of replication

4

of experimentation. Traditionally, any procedure performed
may be repeated at any time by anyone desiring to verify
or dispute results. This expectation is built into the
scientific process itself, as any student in a scientific
lab course knows. Students are taught to make lab reports
clear and detailed so that the work can be repeated. As
expressed by Patricia Woolf of Princeton University, there
are good reasons behind the tradition:

> The system of publication, the facilitation of
> replication, and citation of preceding research is
> designed to detect any results that cannot serve as
> adequate building blocks for the edifices of scien-
> tific knowledge. . . . . The anticipation of repli-
> cation induces more care in initial research.[8]

[7] Commercialization of gene-splicing technology could
pose a grave threat to the free exchange of ideas so vital
to the scientific process. Once we understand that a conflict of interests exists, we can speculate on the outcome.
Corporations financing researchers in return for patent
rights would be likely to pressure researchers to remain
silent about their progress and to guard against replication until patent rights are secured. Colleagues working
at the same institution but having a stake in competing
companies might cease to exchange ideas and results.

This paragraph contains no reference note numbers because the student did not draw the material from any particular source. Rather, she decided to "speculate on the outcome" of a conflict of interests. Taking what she knew about scientific research, standard corporate practices, and the nature of conflicts of interest, she sketched this scenario on her own.

5

Universities under financial obligation to separate companies would be unlikely to communicate, much less coop-
erate, on various projects. Scientists developing a
particular compound in hopes of attracting investors
would struggle for results, unaided by shared insights,
collaboration on methods, or comparison of results. The
promise of huge monetary returns on patented methods
would breed secrecy and impede the flow of information.

[8] These fears are not merely unfounded speculation.
There is in fact a growing trend toward secrecy evidenced
by recent incidents at scientific conventions. Dr. King
recalled several examples of such secrecy in his testimony. Particularly disturbing was his account of a patent
lawyer from Exxon informing an audience of scientists in
Dallas that:

> In the future when you come to scientific meetings
> and you are going to give a presentation, consider
> going to a notary public and have notarized this
> material you are going to say, . . . consider not
> telling them things because if they go run with what
> you told them, they are not in violation of any law.[9]

[9] This, then, is the first difficulty faced by individuals and institutions hoping to profit by teaming up with

Here the writer sums up
her first major point before
going on to her next point.

6

industry: Can we risk the loss of the communication so
important to the advancement of research?

Paragraph 10 launches the
second major point.

10 Some scientists and investors believe that corporate/
university partnerships will accelerate the rate at which
discoveries are made by "reducing that time lag between
advances made in the basic research laboratory and applications in human services."[10] However, the problem with
this viewpoint is that it presumes that the time lag is
a negative factor, that science would be better off if the
lag were reduced or eliminated. It is important to realize
that this is not necessarily true. Granted, there is often
a significant delay between the time a process is worked
out in the lab and the time it is actually applied and
available for commercial use, and this can be frustrating
and seem wasteful. However, this delay seems less likely
to stem from inactivity, incapability, or lack of incentive
than from the careful, deliberate approach of those performing the research. It is the time taken to test, retest,
verify, reject, and repeat the processes. It ensures
accurate results and prevents the chance of "science by
press conference, where incomplete results are sometimes
ballyhooed to attract investors."[11]

Quotations need not
always be formally
introduced. This quotation
is integrated into one of
the student's sentences.

11 Thus the acceleration of research in an effort to gain
ownership rights could actually result in a lower quality
of biotechnological output. Hastily prepared findings

7

announced prematurely in order to acquire a patent or
appeal to investors would eliminate most of the traditional
control mechanisms of science.

[12] Once again, these speculations are backed by fact.
In June of 1979, Charles Weissman, working for Biogen,
announced that the compound interferon had been produced
inside the bacterium E. coli.[12] The news was exciting because interferon is thought to be of great value in treat-
ing many diseases, including cancer. This announcement
is significant, however, because the interferon created
by Weissman was not what one might have thought; it was
not identical to human interferon because it lacked a
particular sugar chain. Though "probably usable," the
product was not complete.[13] In addition, the chemical was
produced by the bacterial cells at a rate one thousand times
less than that of human cells. Said a Biogen competitor:
"They went public quickly with a crude method to get the
jump, for commerical reasons, on other teams doing the same
work."[14]

[13] Besides the loss of communication, then, there is
this question: Do we really care to sacrifice accuracy,
safety, and quality in order to decrease the lab-to-
market delay?

[14] A third area of concern has to do with the nature of
genetic research: It is different from research in other

Notice how the writer introduces factual evidence to support an idea she has presented above. In paragraph 11 she says, "the acceleration of research . . . could actually result in a lower quality . . . ." Here she supplies evidence that it already has happened.

Paragraph 13 briefly summarizes the second problem.

Here is the third problem area.

8

Two subpoints explain the differences between genetic and other types of research. The first (in par. 14) is that discovery of knowledge and application of knowledge are nearly identical in genetic research. The second, discussed in paragraph 15, is that genetic research could have graver consequences than most other types of scientific research.

areas of science that business has subsidized, such as computers, electronics, and the space program. In most other areas of science, the work carried out on university campuses is primarily the basic research, and thus the knowledge itself is the product. The application of this knowledge is then most often carried out by private research centers and industry, who have an interest in the products of the knowledge. In the words of Rep. Doug Walgren:

> Traditionally, basic and applied sciences have been
> separated. Scientists in the two areas approach
> research from entirely different angles. Also,
> discoveries pass through stages: from the basic
> scientists to the applied scientists and then to
> industry.[15]

However, in the field of genetic engineering, there is less of a differentiation among these three stages. Universities are almost immediately able to apply the knowledge, to carry out the technical phase, as well as the intellectual. They are thus also able to reap the profits of the applications immediately. Vice President of DNA Science, Inc., Zsolt Harsanyi explains:

> Much of the research in biotechnology cannot
> clearly be categorized as "basic," as opposed to

9

"applied. . . ." The research on how the genetic

code determines the binding of a certain enzyme to

the DNA is about as basic as one can get. At the

same time, . . . this could be of significant

industrial value if it increases the efficiency

of production.[16]

Hence, the basic research in this area is nearly identical

to the applied research. This explains why the scientists

are so highly sought by industry.

[15] Aside from this point of technical difference between

microbiology and other fields of science, there is also a

more basic element of recombinant DNA technology that cannot

be ignored: Not only does it relate directly to human con-

cerns and medical concerns,[17] but the mechanisms of gene

splicing are "extraordinarily powerful tools. . . . Given

such potency and power, it seems almost inevitable that

their influence on human events will be great."[18]

[16] One of the supposed benefits of the university/corporate

connection is that it supplies badly needed funding for

research, yet in many cases private corporations may be

benefitting from research that is partially funded by the

federal government. For example, a recent agreement be-

tween Massachusetts General Hospital and the German cor-

Paragraph 16 introduces the fourth problem area. Two concerns are here: (1) that corporations, in exchange for their money, will profit from public monies already spent on similar projects; and (2) that corporations, in exchange for their money, will direct the research itself according to "misplaced priorities."

10

poration, Hoechst, is causing quite a furor. Hoechst gave
the hospital a $50 million grant to establish a new depart-
ment of molecular biology. In return, Hoechst receives
exclusive license to products of this department. Yet
Hoechst clearly stands to profit from the $26.1 million in
federal money that the hospital had already received.[19]
There seems to be good reason to fear that private investors will "skim the cream off the top" of research that
has been federally funded for years.

[17] Not only do the private companies in such situations
profit from public monies, they are also likely to have
undue control over the nature of the research, the pace of
the research, and the researchers themselves. They will
"be able to influence some of the best faculty and graduate
students in the country through the financial support
they choose to give, and that translates into a fair
measure of control over the direction of research. . . ."[20]

[18] Unfortunately, since the motive of most investors is
profit, they will most likely choose to develop what will
make the most money, not necessarily what is most needed by
society. An example of misplaced priorities was given by
Jonathan King, who feels that finding ways to prevent
diabetes would be more beneficial than finding new treatments for it:

11

. . . the most important long-term goal of biomedical

research is to discover the causes of disease in order

to prevent disease. Curing disease is what you do

when you don't know how to prevent it. . . . The focus

on cure often leads to a social policy of accepting

the idea that disease will strike, and focusing on

developing and selling people a cure. A recent example

has been the publicity over the production of insulin

through recombinant DNA technology. . . . The sale

of human insulin is going to do basically nothing for

diabetics [in terms of preventing the disease]. It

will make a bundle for Eli Lilly and the person who

holds the patent.[21]

A similar example could be the development of products that

are primarily of cosmetic value. These products will make

money for the patent holder, while taking money away from

research of more critical value to medicine.

[19] The expanding field of biotechnology is indeed exciting,

for it holds the promise of many valuable medical break-

throughs. On the positive side, the growing university/

corporate partnerships accompanying this new technology are

aiding scientists and universities with much needed funds

for research. Yet these seemingly advantageous alliances

between the academic world and industry need to be inves-

Note the use of ellipses in this quotation. The three periods (four when at the end of a sentence) indicate that some words have been omitted.

Also note the use of brackets around the phrase "in terms of *preventing* the disease." The brackets indicate that this phrase has been added by the student to clarify the passage.

The absence of a reference note numbers here again indicates that this idea is the student's and was not borrowed from any particular source.

The conclusion briefly and succinctly puts the whole issue into a thoughtful perspective. Note, too, that the work done for the conclusion is the student's own—she sums up the paper from her own view and hence uses no reference notes.

12

tigated more closely. Universities hoping to supplement

their resources and scientists hoping to profit individually

from research should thoroughly examine the ethical

questions and the long-term implications of combining

science and business.

13

Notes

Notes and Bibliography pages are numbered.

The Notes begin on a new page.

[1] Much has been written on the subject of recombinant DNA research, both about the techniques used and the controversial implications. See, for example, Bernard Davis, "Three Specters: Dangerous Powers, Products, or Ideas," in Genetics and the Law II, ed. Aubrey Milunsky and George J. Annas (New York: Plenum Publishing, 1980), pp. 3-8, and Key Dismukes, "Recombinant DNA: A Proposal for Regulation," in Bioethics, ed. Thomas A. Shannon (Ramsey, N.J.: Paulist Press, 1981), pp. 433-44.

The first note is a combination of content and reference.

[2] Gene Bylinsky, "DNA Can Build Companies, Too," Fortune, 16 June 1980, p. 145.

This is the form for a magazine reference.

[3] Bylinsky, p. 145.

[4] Bylinsky, p. 146.

Notes 3 and 4 are in the standard form for subsequent references to a source.

[5] U.S. Cong., Subcommittee on Investigation and Oversight, Hearings on Commercialization of Academic Biomedical Research, 8-9 June 1981 (Washington, D.C.: GPO, 1981), p. 75.

[6] U.S. Cong., Subcommittee on Investigation and Oversight, p. 2.

[7] U.S. Cong., Subcommittee on Investigation and Oversight and Subcommittee on Science, Research and Technology, Hear-

This is the form to use for U.S. government documents; GPO stands for Government Printing Office.

14

ings on Fraud in Biomedical Research, 31 March– 1 April 1981

(Washington, D.C.: GPO, 1981), p. 355.

[8] U.S. Cong., Subcommittee on Investigation and Oversight
and Subcommittee on Science, Research and Technology, p. 355.

[9] U.S. Cong., Subcommittee on Investigation and Oversight,
Hearings on Commercialization, p. 75.

[10] U.S. Cong., Subcommittee on Investigation and Oversight,
Hearings on Commercialization, p. 7.

[11] Bylinsky, p. 145.

[12] Bylinsky, p. 152.

[13] Bylinsky, p. 149.

[14] Bylinsky, p. 149.

[15] U.S. Cong., Subcommittee on Investigation and Oversight, Hearings on Commercialization, p. 4.

[16] U.S. Cong., Subcommittee on Investigation and Oversight, Hearings on Commercialization, p. 121.

[17] "Biotechnology No Longer Provokes Public Concern,"
New York Times, 15 Dec. 1981, Sec. C, p. 1, col. 1.

[18] Robert Reinhold, "Government Scrutinizes Link Between
Genetic Industry and Universities," New York Times, 16 June
1981, Sec. C, p. 1, col. 4.

[19] Reinhold, p. 1.

In this subsequent reference, an abbreviated title is used to avoid confusion with *Hearings on Fraud in Biomedical Research.*

This is the form for a reference to an unsigned newspaper article.

Here is the form for a signed newspaper article.

15

[20] Reinhold, p. 1.

[21] U.S. Cong., Subcommittee on Investigation and Oversight, <u>Hearings on Commercialization</u>, p. 78.

16

Bibliography

"Biotechnology No Longer Provokes Public Concern." <u>New York Times</u>, 15 Dec. 1981, Sec. C, p. 1, col. 1.

Bylinsky, Gene. "DNA Can Build Companies, Too." <u>Fortune</u>, 16 June 1980, pp. 144-52.

Davis, Bernard. "Three Specters: Dangerous Products, Powers, or Ideas." In <u>Genetics and the Law II</u>. Ed. Aubrey Milunsky and George J. Annas. New York: Plenum Publishing, 1980, pp. 3-8.

Dismukes, Key. "Recombinant DNA: A Proposal for Regulation." In <u>Bioethics</u>. Ed. Thomas A. Shannon. Ramsey, N.J.: Paulist Press, 1981, pp. 433-44.

Reinhold, Robert. "Government Scrutinizes Link Between Genetics Industry and Universities." <u>New York Times</u>, 16 June 1981, Sec. C, p. 1, col. 4.

U.S. Cong., Subcommittee on Investigation and Oversight. <u>Hearings on Commercialization of Academic Biomedical Research</u>, 8-9 June 1981. Washington, D.C.: GPO, 1981.

U.S. Cong., Subcommittee on Investigation and Oversight and Subcommittee on Science, Research and Technology. <u>Hearings on Fraud in Biomedical Research</u>, 31 March-1 April 1981. Washington, D.C.: GPO, 1981.

Always begin the Bibliography on a new page.

The student chose to include only those sources she had cited in her notes. Optionally, she could have included materials that served her as background reading.

CHANGES IN MLA STYLE OF DOCUMENTATION

The newest edition of the *MLA Handbook,* published in 1984, makes some changes in the documentation forms for several types of entries. For example, the old MLA style of a bibliography entry for a signed article in a magazine looks like this:

```
Quinn, Susan.  "The Competence of Babies."  The Atlantic,

     Jan. 1982, pp. 54-62.
```

The new MLA style does away with the *pp.* abbreviation, and so the entry looks like this:

```
Quinn, Susan.  "The Competence of Babies."  The Atlantic,

     Jan. 1982, 54-62.
```

Similarly, the old style for a signed newspaper article is this:

```
Talbott, Basil, Jr.  "Jackson Pushes for Britain's

     Poor, Aid for South African Blacks."  Chicago

     Sun-Times, 13 September 1983, p. 5.
```

In the new MLA style, the same bibliography entry is this:

```
Talbott, Basil, Jr.  "Jackson Pushes for Britain's

     Poor, Aid for South African Blacks."  Chicago

     Sun-Times, 13 September 1983, 5.
```

Other changes have been made in the bibliography entry for an article in a scholarly journal. Here is such an entry in the old style:

```
Linehan, Thomas M.  "Style and Individuality in

     E. E. Cummings' The Enormous Room."  Style,

     13 (1979), 45-59.
```

In the new MLA style, the entry would look like this:

```
Linehan, Thomas M.  "Style and Individuality in

     E. E. Cummings' The Enormous Room."  Style

     13 (1979): 45-59.
```

Notice that the comma after the journal title has been deleted and that a colon, rather than a comma, follows the date in parentheses.

A more substantial change is in the notation system used within the text of a research paper. Our research paper uses the old style—raised numerals indicate that a quotation or paraphrase is documented on the "Notes" page that follows the body of the paper:

Small companies such as Genetech, Inc., Biogen, S.A.,

and half a dozen others have sprung up to realize

the profit potential of the new techniques for

drug manufacture: "With the gleam of big profits

in their eyes, they are plotting ways of capturing

a good share of the World's Market for novel drugs

and chemicals."[2]

The new MLA style uses a parenthetical reference in the text itself, listing the author's last name and the page number of the work cited:

the profit potential of the new techniques for

drug manufacture: "With the gleam of big profits

in their eyes, they are plotting ways of capturing

a good share of the World's Market for novel drugs

and chemicals" (Bylinsky, 145).

Complete information on the source is given in the bibliography, which the new MLA style calls "Works Cited." Content notes are on the "Notes" page; no documentary notes are given there.

If your instructor requires that you use the new MLA style in your research paper, consult the 1984 edition of the *MLA Handbook* or the fourth edition of *Writing Research Papers* by James D. Lester (Scott, Foresman, 1984).

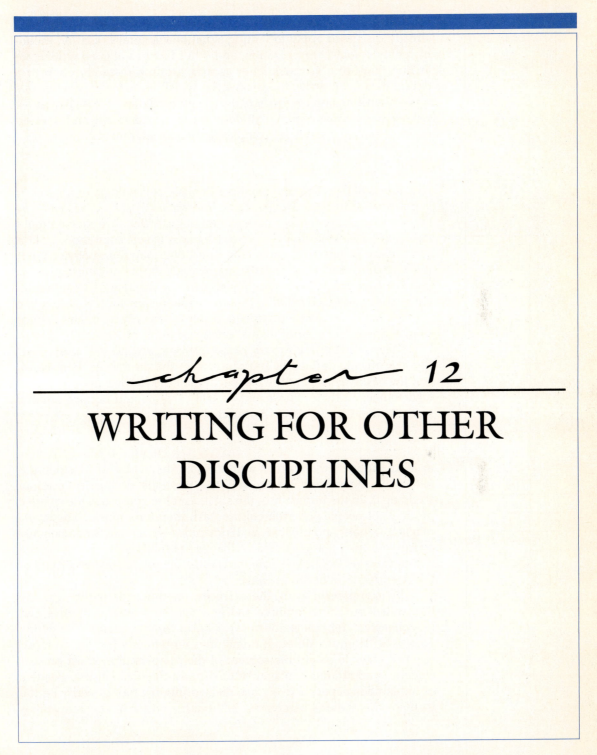

chapter 12

WRITING FOR OTHER DISCIPLINES

Most of the ideas and advice regarding effective writing that we have already discussed apply to writing situations generally. Clarity, economy of style, logical organization, and other features of good writing are as important in a business letter as they are in a research report or a critical essay. However, the *processes* by which writers compose various types of writing and the *products* that result do differ. In this chapter we will examine some common student writing assignments and develop some general strategies for completing those assignments.

TAKING THE CORRECT PERSPECTIVE

Regardless of the discipline, whether English, psychology, or physics, it is essential to treat your paper topic *from the major perspective implied by the discipline*. For instance, a paper for an English literature course should take a literary perspective on its topic, a paper in sociology should take a sociological perspective, and so on. This point may sound obvious, but it is amazing how often students, particularly at the introductory level, fail to recognize it. A beginning student in sociology, for example, having been assigned a "ten-page term paper on any topic related to the course" may mistakenly produce a paper on the effects of child abuse from a *psychological* rather than a *sociological* point of view.

What exactly is a *literary perspective* or a *psychological perspective*? These terms are defined by the concerns of the disciplines themselves, and the best way to learn the perspectives of the various disciplines is to take courses in them. However, we will examine and become familiar with the major perspectives in selected areas.

THE HUMANITIES: The Attitudes of the Humanities Writer

In all disciplines, the writer's attitudes are shaped by two factors: the nature of the subject matter and the methods of inquiry used in studying it. In the humanities, the subject matter comprises the creative products of people and their cultures: art, literature, music, languages, religious beliefs, and great ideas. Humanities writers are fundamentally concerned with things human—that is, with those activities which differentiate us from biological objects that act predictably according to the scientific laws of the universe.

By comparison with the sciences, methods of inquiry in the humanities are more intuitive and less rigorous, more subjective and less objective. Yet this is not to say that, in the humanities, "anything goes"—far from it. Although humanities writers rely heavily on intuitive processes to invent the content of their papers, they must present evidence and rational explanation to support their statements. Readers of humanities papers actively use their intuitions, too, in verifying the truth of the writer's assertions. Although writing in the humanities generally lacks the experimental purity of the scientific method, it is governed by its own style of intellectual rigor.

The intuitions humanities writers employ when they invent ideas vary with the individual; usually they involve analysis and interpretation. The specific devices these writers use to stimulate invention are those we have discussed in Part One: Personal Experience, Thinking It Over, and Using Common Patterns of Thinking in Writing. In arrangement and style, too, the techniques discussed in Chapters 3 through 7 apply to humanities papers.

Writing Interpretive Essays, Critiques, and Reviews

A standard assignment in humanities courses is to write an interpretive essay, a critique, or a review about someone's work. Your philosophy instructor might ask you to write an interpretive essay on a reading selection by Nietzsche; your English professor might assign an interpretive essay on a short story by Faulkner (for a fuller discussion of the critical essay in literature, see Chapter 9). In history class you might be asked to review a book about Theodore Roosevelt; in a religion course, to critique Martin Buber's *I and Thou*.

Many students who are familiar with doing interpretive essays panic when they are assigned a critique; those who are comfortable writing a critique may flounder when assigned a review. But the panic is unwarranted. All three types of assignments—interpretive essay, review, and critique—call for substantially the same end product.[1]

This is another version of the problem we discussed earlier: Students often aren't certain how to decipher the assignment when an instructor asks for "a paper." Even when instructors are more specific about the kind of paper they want, they often use terms rather loosely—"Write a paper *discussing* historian A's approach," "*Interpret* author B's message," "*Critique* philosopher C's views." And as we saw in Chapter 8, this problem becomes especially critical in writing essay examinations.

We will present a model approach for humanities papers that are called interpretive essays by some or critiques or reviews by others. We will then reproduce a short reading selection that might be studied in a course in the humanities and a student paper that could be called an interpretive essay, critique, or review of that selection. The following model is applicable to humanities writing in a general way but may need refinements for papers in specific disciplines.

---

[1]This is true for writing course papers, but may not be so for specialized kinds of writing. A review for a newspaper, for instance, may differ considerably from an interpretive essay on the same subject written for a college course.

Guide for Writing an Interpretive Essay/Critique/Review   The interpretive essay, critique, or review, written for an introductory level humanities course, should contain:

1. *A basic summary or description* of the main points or features of the work, and

2. *Your own input* on one or more of the points or features, usually in the form of further explanation and evaluation of the work.

The invention process for such a paper breaks down into two broad categories. You need to generate a summary of the contents, and then you need to generate some ideas *about* the content. Here are some questions that may help you:

Questions relevant mainly to summary/ description

1. What are the main points, ideas, or arguments of the work (book, article, play, treatise, and so on)?
2. How is the work organized?
3. What evidence/support does the author give? Is it direct or indirect?

Question relevant to summary/ description or your own input, depending upon whether the purpose is clearly stated within the work itself

4. What is the primary purpose of the work?

Questions relevant mainly to your own input

5. Can I supply further explanation to clarify or support any of the main points, ideas, arguments?
6. Does the work achieve its purpose? Fully or only partially? Why or why not?
7. Was the purpose worthwhile to begin with? Or was it too limited or trivial? Too broad? Too theoretical?
8. Are there any problems with weak or insufficient evidence to support the points? If so, where? If not, is the evidence/ support particularly impressive? Why?
9. Are there sections I still don't understand? If so, is this my fault or the writer's?
10. Could I have done without any sections? Or is anything lacking that might have contributed to the work?
11. Is the organization of the work an important factor? Does its organization help me understand it, hinder my understanding, or neither?
12. Is anything about language or style noteworthy?

Check back to the techniques for invention discussed on pages 41–55; these might also be helpful.

Arrangement of a two- to five-page paper can follow one of three patterns, as shown in these figures:

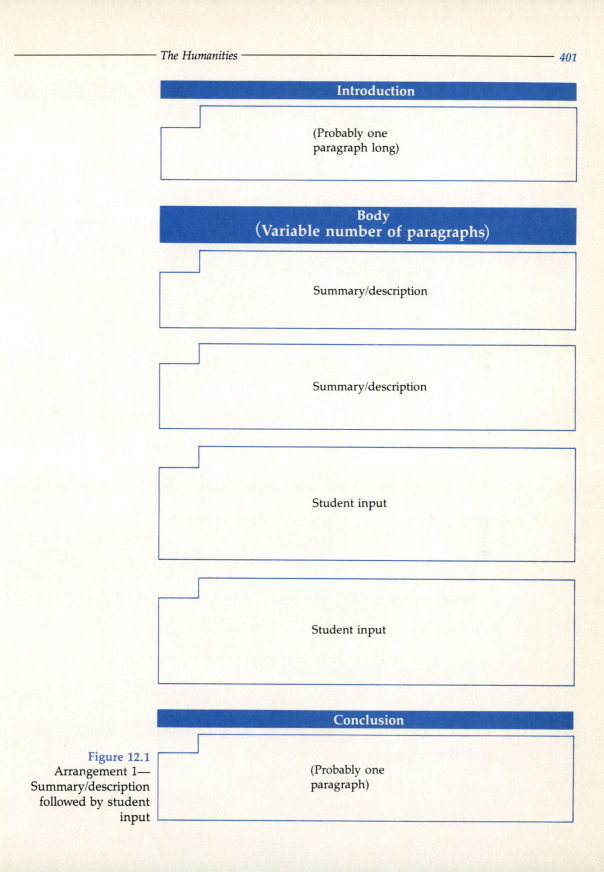

Introduction

(Probably one
paragraph long)

**Body
(Variable number of paragraphs)**

Summary/description

Summary/description

Student input

Student input

Conclusion

(Probably one
paragraph)

Figure 12.1
Arrangement 1—
Summary/description
followed by student
input

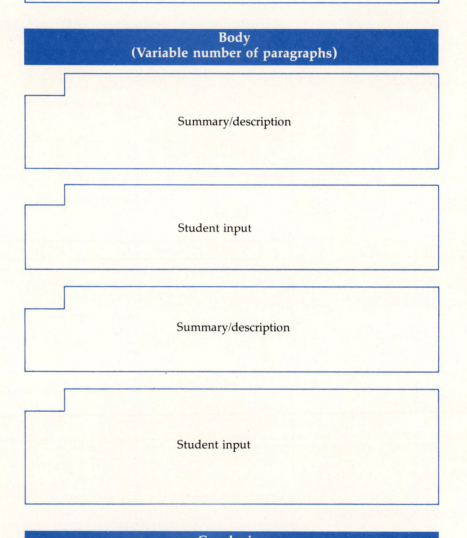

Introduction

(Probably one paragraph)

Body
(Variable number of paragraphs)

Summary/description

Student input

Summary/description

Student input

Conclusion

Probably one paragraph

Figure 12.2
Arrangement 2—
Alternating summary/
description with student
input

A variation of this arrangement features alternating or combining summary/description with student input *within* each paragraph of the body:

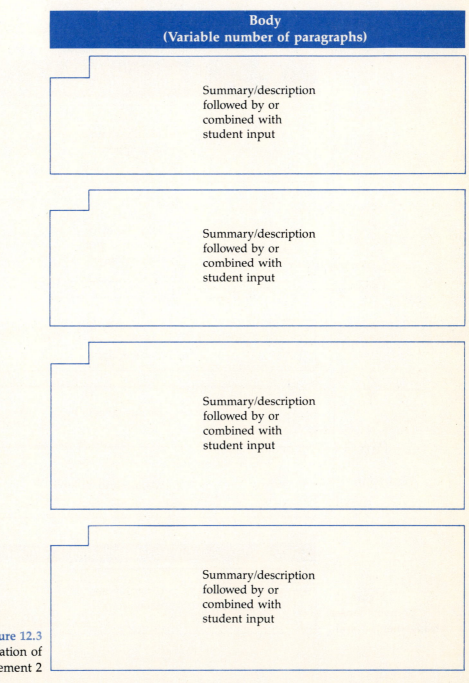

Figure 12.3
A variation of
Arrangement 2

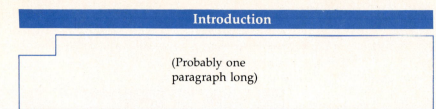

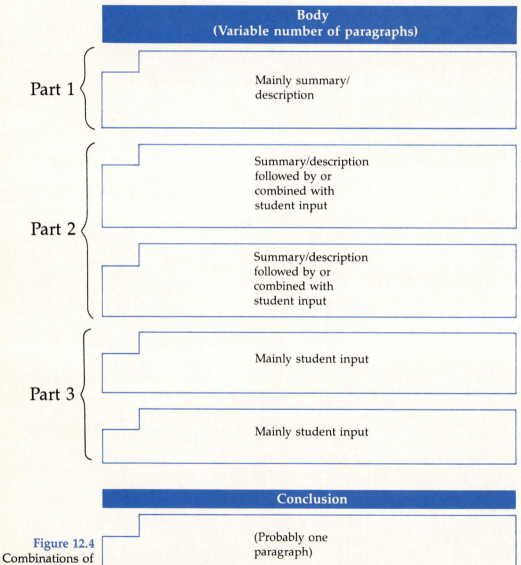

Introduction

(Probably one
paragraph long)

**Body
(Variable number of paragraphs)**

Part 1 { Mainly summary/
description

Part 2 {
Summary/description
followed by or
combined with
student input

Summary/description
followed by or
combined with
student input

Part 3 {
Mainly student input

Mainly student input

Conclusion

(Probably one
paragraph)

Figure 12.4
Combinations of
Arrangements 1 and 2

To gain a better understanding of the typical humanities writing assignment we have been discussing, read the following selection by Joan Didion and then read the interpretive essay a student wrote about it.

ON KEEPING A NOTEBOOK

[1] " 'That woman Estelle,' " the note reads, " 'is partly the reason why George Sharp and I are separated today,' *Dirty crepe-de-Chine wrapper, hotel bar, Wilmington RR, 9:45 a.m. August Monday morning.''*

[2] Since the note is in my notebook, it presumably has some meaning to me. I study it for a long while. At first I have only the most general notion of what I was doing on an August Monday morning in the bar of the hotel across from the Pennsylvania Railroad station in Wilmington, Delaware (waiting for a train? missing one? 1960? 1961? why Wilmington?), but I do remember being there. The woman in the dirty crepe-de-Chine wrapper had come down from her room for a beer, and the bartender had heard before the reason why George Sharp and she were separated today. "Sure," he said, and went on mopping the floor. "You told me." At the other end of the bar is a girl. She is talking, pointedly, not to the man beside her but to a cat lying in the triangle of sunlight cast through the open door. She is wearing a plaid silk dress from Peck & Peck, and the hem is coming down.

[3] Here is what it is: the girl has been on the Eastern Shore, and now she is going back to the city, leaving the man beside her, and all she can see ahead are the viscous summer sidewalks and the 3 A.M. long-distance calls that will make her lie awake and then sleep drugged through all the steaming mornings left in August (1960? 1961?). Because she must go directly from the train to lunch in New York, she wishes that she had a safety pin for the hem of the plaid silk dress, and she also wishes that she could forget about the hem and the lunch and stay in the cool bar that smells of disinfectant and malt and make friends with the woman in the crepe-de-Chine wrapper. She is afflicted by a little self-pity, and she wants to compare Estelles. That is what that was all about.

[4] Why did I write it down? In order to remember, of course, but exactly what was it I wanted to remember? How much of it actually happened? Did any of it? Why do I keep a notebook at all? It is easy to deceive oneself on all those scores. The impulse to write things down is a peculiarly compulsive one, inexplicable to those who do not share it, useful only accidentally, only secondarily, in the way that any compulsion tries to justify itself. I suppose that it begins or does not begin in the cradle. Although I have felt compelled to write things down since I was five years old, I doubt that my daughter ever will, for she is a singularly blessed and accepting child, delighted with life exactly as life presents itself to her, unafraid to go to sleep and

unafraid to wake. Keepers of private notebooks are a different breed altogether, lonely and resistant rearrangers of things, anxious malcontents, children afflicted apparently at birth with some presentiment of loss.

[5]My first notebook was a Big Five tablet, given to me by my mother with the sensible suggestion that I stop whining and learn to amuse myself by writing down my thoughts. She returned the tablet to me a few years ago; the first entry is an account of a woman who believed herself to be freezing to death in the Arctic night, only to find, when day broke, that she had stumbled onto the Sahara Desert, where she would die of the heat before lunch. I have no idea what turn of a five-year-old's mind could have prompted so insistently "ironic" and exotic a story, but it does reveal a certain predilection for the extreme which has dogged me into adult life; perhaps if I were analytically inclined I would find it a truer story than any I might have told about Donald Johnson's birthday party or the day my cousin Brenda put Kitty Litter in the aquarium.

[6]So the point of my keeping a notebook has never been, nor is it now, to have an accurate factual record of what I have been doing or thinking. That would be a different impulse entirely, an instinct for reality which I sometimes envy but do not possess. At no point have I ever been able successfully to keep a diary; my approach to daily life ranges from the grossly negligent to the merely absent, and on those few occasions when I have tried dutifully to record a day's events, boredom has so overcome me that the results are mysterious at best. What is this business about "shopping, typing piece, dinner with E, depressed"? Shopping for what? Typing what piece? Who is E? Was this "E" depressed, or was I depressed? Who cares?

[7]In fact I have abandoned altogether that kind of pointless entry; instead I tell what some would call lies. "That's simply not true," the members of my family frequently tell me when they come up against my memory of a shared event. "The party was *not* for you, the spider was *not* a black widow, *it wasn't that way at all.*" Very likely they are right, for not only have I always had trouble distinguishing between what happened and what merely might have happened, but I remain unconvinced that the distinction, for my purposes, matters. The cracked crab that I recall having for lunch the day my father came home from Detroit in 1945 must certainly be embroidery, worked into the day's pattern to lend verisimilitude; I was ten years old and would not now remember the cracked crab. The day's events did not turn on cracked crab. And yet it is precisely that fictitious crab that makes me see the afternoon all over again, a home movie run all too often, the father bearing gifts, the child weeping, an exercise in family love and guilt. Or that is what it was to me. Similarly, perhaps it never did snow that August in Vermont; perhaps there never were flurries in the

night wind, and maybe no one else felt the ground hardening and summer already dead even as we pretended to bask in it, but that was how it felt to me, and it might as well have snowed, could have snowed, did snow.

[8]*How it felt to me*: that is getting closer to the truth about a notebook. I sometimes delude myself about why I keep a notebook, imagine that some thrifty virtue derives from preserving everything observed. See enough and write it down, I tell myself, and then some morning when the world seems drained of wonder, some day when I am only going through the motions of doing what I am supposed to do, which is write—on that bankrupt morning I will simply open my notebook and there it will all be, a forgotten account with accumulated interest, paid passage back to a world out there: dialogue overheard in hotels and elevators and at the hat-check counter in Pavillon (one middle-aged man shows his hat check to another and says, "That's my old football number"); impressions of Bettina Aptheker and Benjamin Sonnenberg and Teddy ("Mr. Acapulco") Stauffer; careful *aperçus* about tennis bums and failed fashion models and Greek shipping heiresses, one of whom taught me a significant lesson (a lesson I could have learned from F. Scott Fitzgerald, but perhaps we all must meet the very rich for ourselves) by asking, when I arrived to interview her in her orchid-filled sitting room on the second day of a paralyzing New York blizzard, whether it was snowing outside.

[9]I imagine, in other words, that the notebook is about other people. But of course it is not. I have no real business with what one stranger said to another at the hat-check counter in Pavillon; in fact I suspect that the line "That's my old football number" touched not my own imagination at all, but merely some memory of something once read, probably "The Eighty-Yard Run." Nor is my concern with a woman in a dirty crep-de-Chine wrapper in a Wilmington bar. My stake is always, of course, in the unmentioned girl in the plaid silk dress. *Remember what it was to be me*: that is always the point.

[10]It is a difficult point to admit. We are brought up in the ethic that others, any others, all others, are by definition more interesting than ourselves; taught to be different, just this side of self-effacing. ("You're the least important person in the room and don't forget it," Jessica Mitford's governess would hiss in her ear on the advent of any social occasion; I copied that into my notebook because it is only recently that I have been able to enter a room without hearing some such phrase in my inner ear.) Only the very young and the very old may recount their dreams at breakfast, dwell upon self, interrupt with memories of beach picnics and favorite Liberty lawn dresses and the rainbow trout in a creek near Colorado Springs. The rest of us are expected, rightly, to affect absorption in other people's favorite dresses, other people's trout.

[11]And so we do. But our notebooks give us away, for however dutifully we record what we see around us, the common denominator of all we see is always, transparently, shamelessly, the implacable "I." We are not talking here about the kind of notebook that is patently for public consumption, a structural conceit for binding together a series of graceful *pensées*; we are talking about something private, about bits of the mind's string too short to use, an indiscriminate and erratic assemblage with meaning only for its maker.

[12]And sometimes even the maker has difficulty with the meaning. There does not seem to be, for example, any point in my knowing for the rest of my life that, during 1964, 720 tons of soot fell on every square mile of New York City, yet there it is in my notebook, labeled "FACT." Nor do I really need to remember that Ambrose Bierce liked to spell Leland Stanford's name "£eland $tanford" or that "smart women almost always wear black in Cuba," a fashion hint without much potential for practical application. And does not the relevance of these notes seem marginal at best?:

In the basement museum of the Inyo County Courthouse in Independence, California, sign pinned to a mandarin coat: "This MANDARIN COAT was often worn by Mrs. Minnie S. Brooks when giving lectures on her TEAPOT COLLECTION."

Redhead getting out of car in front of Beverly Wilshire Hotel, chinchilla stole, Vuitton bags with tags reading:

> MRS LOU FOX
> HOTEL SAHARA
> VEGAS

[13]Well, perhaps not entirely marginal. As a matter of fact, Mrs. Minnie S. Brooks and her MANDARIN COAT pull me back into my own childhood, for although I never knew Mrs. Brooks and did not visit Inyo County until I was thirty, I grew up in just such a world, in houses cluttered with Indian relics and bits of gold ore and ambergris and the souvenirs my Aunt Mercy Fransworth brought back from the Orient. It is a long way from that world to Mrs. Lou Fox's world, where we all live now, and is it not just as well to remember that? Might not Mrs. Minnie S. Brooks help me to remember what I am? Might not Mrs. Lou Fox help me to remember what I am not?

[14]But sometimes the point is harder to discern. What exactly did I have in mind when I noted down that it cost the father of someone I know $650 a month to light the place on the Hudson in which he lived before the Crash? What use was I planning to make of this line by Jimmy Hoffa: "I may have my faults, but being wrong ain't one of them"? And although I think it interesting to know where the girls

who travel with the Syndicate have their hair done when they find themselves on the West Coast, will I ever make suitable use of it? Might I not be better off just passing it on to John O'Hara? What is a recipe for sauerkraut doing in my notebook? What kind of magpie keeps this notebook? *"He was born the night the Titanic went down."* That seems a nice enough line, and I even recall who said it, but is it not really a better line in life than it could ever be in fiction?

¹⁵But of course that is exactly it: not that I should ever use the line, but that I should remember the woman who said it and the afternoon I heard it. We were on her terrace by the sea, and we were finishing the wine left from lunch, trying to get what sun there was, a California winter sun. The woman whose husband was born the night the *Titanic* went down wanted to rent her house, wanted to go back to her children in Paris. I remember wishing that I could afford the house, which cost $1,000 a month. "Someday you will," she said lazily. "Someday it all comes." There in the sun on her terrace it seemed easy to believe in someday, but later I had a low-grade afternoon hangover and ran over a black snake on the way to the supermarket and was flooded with inexplicable fear when I heard the checkout clerk explaining to the man ahead of me why she was finally divorcing her husband. "He left me no choice," she said over and over as she punched the register. "He has a little seven-month-old baby by her, he left me no choice." I would like to believe that my dread then was for the human condition, but of course it was for me, because I wanted a baby and did not then have one and because I wanted to own the house that cost $1,000 a month to rent and because I had a hangover.

¹⁶It all comes back. Perhaps it is difficult to see the value in having one's self back in that kind of mood, but I do see it; I think we are well advised to keep on nodding terms with the people we used to be, whether we find them attractive company or not. Otherwise they turn up unannounced and surprise us, come hammering on the mind's door at 4 A.M. of a bad night and demand to know who deserted them, who betrayed them, who is going to make amends. We forget all too soon the things we thought we could never forget. We forget the loves and the betrayals alike, forget what we whispered and what we screamed, forget who we were. I have already lost touch with a couple of people I used to be; one of them, a seventeen-year-old, presents little threat, although it would be of some interest to me to know what it feels like to sit on a river levee drinking vodka-and-orange juice and listening to Les Paul and Mary Ford and their echoes sing "How High the Moon" on the car radio. (You see I still have the scenes, but I no longer perceive myself among those present, no longer could even improvise the dialogue.) The other one, a twenty-three-year-old, bothers me more. She was always a good deal of trouble, and I suspect she will reappear when I least want to see her, skirts too long, shy to the point of aggravation, always the injured party, full of recrimina-

tions and little hurts and stories I do not want to hear again, at once saddening me and angering me with her vulnerability and ignorance, an apparition all the more insistent for being so long banished.

[17]It is a good idea, then, to keep in touch, and I suppose that keeping in touch is what notebooks are all about. And we are all on our own when it comes to keeping those lines open to ourselves: your notebook will never help me, nor mine you. *"So what's new in the whiskey business?"* What could that possibly mean to you? To me it means a blonde in a Pucci bathing suit sitting with a couple of fat men by the pool at the Beverly Hills Hotel. Another man approaches, and they all regard one another in silence for a while. "So what's new in the whiskey business?" one of the fat men finally says by way of welcome, and the blonde stands up, arches one foot and dips it in the pool, looking all the while at the cabana where Baby Pignatari is talking on the telephone. That is all there is to that, except that several years later I saw the blonde coming out of Saks Fifth Avenue in New York with her California complexion and a voluminous mink coat. In the harsh wind that day she looked old and irrevocably tired to me, and even the skins in the mink coat were not worked the way they were doing them that year, not the way she would have wanted them done, and there is the point of the story. For a while after that I did not like to look in the mirror, and my eyes would skim the newspapers and pick out only the deaths, the cancer victims, the premature coronaries, the suicides, and I stopped riding the Lexington Avenue IRT because I noticed for the first time that all the strangers I had seen for years—the man with the seeing-eye dog, the spinster who read the classified pages every day, the fat girl who always got off with me at Grand Central—looked older than they once had.

[18]It all comes back. Even that recipe for sauerkraut: even that brings it back. I was on Fire Island when I first made that sauerkraut, and it was raining, and we drank a lot of bourbon and ate the sauerkraut and went to bed at ten, and I listened to the rain and the Atlantic and felt safe. I made the sauerkraut again last night and it did not make me feel any safer, but that is, as they say, another story.

"HOW IT FELT TO ME": THE IMPORTANCE OF SELF IN "ON KEEPING A NOTEBOOK"

*Paragraph 1 summarizes Didion's main ideas. Note that through the modifiers **refreshing** and **inspiring** the student reveals her attitude toward Didion's essay.*

[1]In the refreshing essay, "On Keeping a Notebook," Joan Didion examines the reasons why she believes it is important to keep a special private notebook. She explores some of her opinions, citing excerpts from her journal, and concludes that the ultimate value of her notebook has been to keep her in touch with the numerous facets of her self. Her essay is inspiring, especially for an avid notebook keeper, because she defends the right to be engrossed in oneself, pointing out

that society, on the whole, condemns such behavior. "Only the very young and the very old may recount their dreams at breakfast, dwell upon self. . . . The rest of us are expected, rightly, to affect absorption in other people's favorite dresses, other people's trout." She follows this notion further by asserting that it is of utmost importance that we do not lose touch with our pasts—including our past experiences, feelings, and behaviors.

The student continues to summarize, taking one major idea and giving examples from the essay to clarify what she believes Didion means.

²One of Didion's main points hinges on the importance of the "emotive" ring a passage has. The importance of her notebook is not in providing a factual daily record of life's events. It is not a "notebook that is patently for public consumption," but one filled with words that evoke strong memories. Its importance lies in the fact that these memories can help her relive bygone days and experience parts of herself associated with those times, things she cherishes and learns from. For instance, one passage she wrote was _"He was born the night the Titanic went down."_ To anyone else this would appear as rather a trivial, idiotic piece of information, but to her it is significant. It serves as a rich link to the past—reminding her of a specific situation, a certain woman she had been talking to—and she is able to relive what her perceptions and feelings were at that point in her life. In this instance she recalls what a dreamer she had been, and how the world had seemed so vast, and how she had become overwhelmed with a sense of dread " . . . because I wanted a baby and did not then have one and because I wanted to own the house that cost $1,000 a month to rent and because I had a hangover."

In paragraph 3 the student begins by restating another major point from the essay and then, in the last two sentences, gives her own interpretation of the concept.

³Didion believes that ". . . we are well advised to keep on nodding terms with the people we used to be, whether we find them attractive company or not. Otherwise they turn up unannounced and surprise us . . . and demand to know who deserted them, who betrayed them, who is going to make amends." She feels that if we deny our past selves we will later be tortured by things we used to be, do, and say. If remembering our past is like eating sour grapes, then we should just keep eating them and force ourselves to endure the puckering. Basically, her point revolves around a widely accepted psychological theory that all of us need to be able to claim our own existence, our own lives, and take responsibility for all of our actions in order to strive toward personal integration. The essence of Joan Didion's essay seems to be that notebook keeping is at least one way to facilitate this vital process of integration.

The final paragraph emphasizes her feeling about the worth of what Didion has written. She disagrees partially with the essay, but affirms her basic respect for what Didion says.

⁴Though it is questionable that we _all_ are haunted by ghosts from our past or tormented by the "unfinished business" of our psyches, we all do need to feel a sense of our own identities and personalities—the richness and depth that we all possess. We must recognize the diverse sides that are a part of the total person, as Didion confesses the existence of her twenty-three-year-old who angers her with "her vulnerability and ignorance," as well as her seventeen-year-old who

Using examples from the essay, the student writer concludes by restating her own perspective. drinks vodka and orange juice while listening to Les Paul. "We forget all too soon the things we thought we could never forget. We forget the loves and the betrayals alike, forget what we whispered and what we screamed, forget who we were." Jotting down a seemingly nonsensical phrase like "smart women almost always wear black in Cuba" recaptures a bygone time and place, and a part of ourselves. The value is not in the factual elements but in our ability to gain, in retrospect, further insight into our present selves.

The student presents a competent interpretation of the Didion piece by including both summary statements and some of her own insights. Because of the literary nature of Didion's essay, summarizing that essay requires of the writer more judgment and creativity than if it were, say, a simple narrative or a description of a straightforward process. For instance, the student had to select the ideas on which to focus and the details and quotations appropriate for supporting them. She also had to decide the order in which to present them. A less complex selection would probably have lent itself to a more straightforward summary. Thus, although in a sense the essay relies more heavily on summary than on student input, the student has put far more of herself into it than might at first appear.

Suggestion for Writing

The Suggestion for Writing on page 187 in Chapter 5 asked you to read X. J. Kennedy's "Who Killed King Kong?" and to use it as a point of departure for an essay of your own. Your present assignment is to reread Kennedy's article and to write an interpretive essay, critique, or review of it. If you have seen the 1933 movie, you might wish to evaluate Kennedy's interpretation of it. If you have not seen the movie, you can still comment on the value of Kennedy's belief that humans are the victims of the very technologies that are supposed to liberate them and thus would like to see the fruits of those technologies destroyed.

Using Argument and Analysis in the Philosophy Paper

First and foremost, philosophers work with ideas. They are concerned not only with formulating valid ideas of their own, but also with recognizing strengths and weaknesses in the ideas of others. Although they share many attitudes with other humanities writers, philosophy writers differ mainly in their concern for expressing both sides of a position. Philosophy students do write papers guided by thesis statements, but they strive less to present a singleminded support of their thesis and more for a balanced awareness of the good and bad points of the ideas raised than do other humanities writers.

In philosophy, then, writers forge their major argument by analyzing the strengths and weaknesses of the smaller, component statements and arguments. You'll find a good example of this multiple-perspective approach to argument by examining the topic sentences of a student paper written for an introductory philosophy course. The first six paragraphs set up the paper's purpose and define numerous key terms. At the outset, the writer states that he will argue that the philosophical approach called "rule utilitarianism" is superior to another called "act utilitarianism." Here are the topic sentences, beginning with paragraph 7:

7. The good points of act utilitarianism are fairly straightforward.
8. However, act utilitarianism can lead to detrimental consequences.
9. Another problem with act utilitarianism is that it doesn't take into account *prima facie* obligation. . . .
10. The rule utilitarian, on the other hand, decides particular cases by following general rules dictated by society.
11. Act utilitarians argue that rule utilitarians are "rule worshippers," and that the system is too complicated for the ordinary person to follow.
12. There is some truth to the act utilitarians' charges.
13. An argument that tends to refute the act utilitarian's charges is that the rule utilitarian would in fact have some flexibility in his choice of rules.
14. Even though I favor rule utilitarianism, I should note that some people argue that there is not any clear distinction between act and rule utilitarianism, that these are really the same theory.
15. However I feel that there is a distinction between the two theories.
16. Thus I accept rule utilitarianism for two main reasons.

We can see that the writer did have a thesis in favor of rule utilitarianism, but that supporting it was not a straightforward matter of lining up the good points of that philosophical approach. Rather he acknowledged the weak points as well as the good points of act utilitarianism, even though he would eventually reject it. Topic sentences 11, 12, and 13 illustrate clearly the philosophy writer's tendency to give all sides their due. Sentence 11 recognizes the problems that opponents see with rule utilitarianism, sentence 12 acknowledges that those charges have some validity, and sentence 13 explores what the charges fail to take into account.

Within the field of philosophy writing, perhaps the most common type of introductory level essay involves the support (or refutation) of a claim or argument. Typically, an instructor will ask you to analyze the arguments of a well-known philosopher (Descartes, for instance) as they appear in a given treatise and to agree or disagree with the arguments. Or the instructor might present you with a claim (such as "Good and evil cannot be objectively defined") and ask you to support or refute it.

Although you probably will take a definite stand in the thesis statement, you will bring forth numerous arguments both for and against the claim as you establish your point.

The following student essay was written to support the claim made in its opening sentence. Note the extent to which the writer acknowledges and refutes opposing views that could damage the claim she is supporting.

Here is the claim being supported.

Two levels are examined; the first presents no difficulty for the claim, but the second does.

But the writer plans to refute the point of difficulty and support the claim.

[1]Everything an individual does is inevitably tied to self-gratification. That is to say, our actions result from a self-oriented need to gratify the desires lodged within us. On one level, few people would dispute such a statement, for many examples support it. People sleep because they are tired; they do not sleep because other people are tired. Therefore such an act is self-oriented: It is done to gratify wholly personal needs. But in less obvious need-gratification relationships, this selfish quality is slightly harder to trace. Because of this difficulty, many people support the notion of self*less*ness. I feel, however, that true selflessness does not exist and that our actions are always tied to the desire to enhance our self or preserve our self-image.

Here is an argument commonly made against the claim.

The writer examines it more carefully.

[2]Opponents of this "selfish" view argue the case of the charitable good-deed-doers. They question how such a generalized statement applies to people who spend time working solely for the sake of others. They point to volunteers, to people who donate to various charities, to teachers who spend extra time after school hours with students. In all of these cases I do not dispute the positive values of the actions. I wish merely to question the motives behind them. Why does the volunteer volunteer? Why does the donor donate? Why does the teacher spend the extra time with students? In each of these examples the answer is based in self-gratification.

She attempts to refute the volunteer/donor example.

But she recognizes that her own refutation has weaknesses.

[3]Consider the volunteer. Many people volunteer because they have too much time on their hands. Thus, by volunteering for some sort of service, their boredom is relieved. Such an explanation, however, does not account for why a volunteer may offer to do an unpleasant job, nor does it explain why those with too much to do often find themselves volunteering to take on more and more tasks. To understand these last two cases, the idea of self-image must be considered.

The student advances a major argument in support of the claim.

[4]In these cases it is primarily the self-image that benefits from doing the undesirable or thankless jobs. That is to say, when a person does things that he labels "selfless," he is gratifying his personal image of himself as a selfless person. Therefore the very person who denies that she is self-oriented proves herself wrong every time she does something supposedly non-self-oriented, by virtue of the fact that doing it is self-gratifying.

This section elaborates on the argument advanced in paragraph 4.

[5]The volunteer can say to himself, "I am good because I have done something purely for the good of others." The more unpleasant or difficult the task, the better he may allow himself to feel for having

The student adds a further qualification to her argument.

done it. If he did not perform the task, he would deny himself the illusion of being selfless. He would then have a low opinion of himself for not living up to his own standards and expectations.

⁶This reasoning is not part of a person's conscious thinking. People do what they do because they tell themselves that it is right. Deep inside, however, they act because they want to be responsible for having done a good thing. When the teacher stays late, she succeeds in meeting the desires of her students and therefore feels that she has done something worthwhile. She thus can feel good about herself as a person. The person who donates money to a charitable cause can sit

In paragraphs 6 and 7 the student sums up her case against those who would argue that doers of good deeds are selfless.

back and reflect upon what a beneficial thing he has done. He has created a situation in which he can feel a sense of self-worth. In all of these cases, by proving to themselves that they can be selfless, the people are developing feelings of self-worth that are self-gratifying and self-benefiting.

⁷This helps to explain why, following a brave rescue attempt, people say such things as, "I just couldn't have lived with myself if anything had happened to you." They "could not live" with themselves because their image of themselves would have been tarnished had their inaction allowed someone else to suffer. The ego-damaging consequences of inaction are thus the cause of action.

The writer discounts a possible, but incorrect, conclusion and restates her thesis.

⁸Preservation of self-image, which I have labeled *selfishness*, is not in these cases a greedy, negative trait. But the seemingly nonselfish person may in fact be just as self-oriented as the "greedy" selfish person, because all of an individual's acts are tied to self-gratification.

Like the student who wrote the essay on utilitarianism, this writer explores opposing perspectives and examines the strengths and weaknesses of the positions she is discussing. Even though her paper is quite short, she captures a sense of the complexities inherent in the initial claim. Moreover, she does all this in a positive, decisive style. Her awareness of complexities does not lead her to become wishy-washy or indecisive; rather, it permits her to be even more certain about the direction of her argument.

Suggestion for Writing

Write an essay in which you attempt to refute the claim supported by the student in the paper on page 414: "Everything an individual does is inevitably tied to self gratification." In doing so, be certain to advance both (1) arguments for your case against the claim and (2) arguments against the student writer's support for the claim.

THE SCIENCES In this section we will examine the attitudes and approaches of writers in both the social and the natural sciences. Because of the strong research orientation of these disciplines, some of the papers we will examine draw heavily from published studies and therefore contain much documentation. Because the mechanics of research and documentation are treated in Chapter 11, we will here concentrate mainly on invention, arrangement and style and not comment further on the mechanics of research and documentation.

The Attitudes of the Social Sciences Writer

While those in the humanities primarily explore the creative products and ideas of people, social scientists examine mainly the behavior of people and the workings of their institutions—social, cultural, economic, and political. Psychologists, for instance, concentrate on the workings of the mind and the resultant behavior of the individual. Sociologists study group behavior—behavior both within groups (for example, the family unit) and among groups (for example, interactions between blue-collar and white-collar workers). Economists analyze the workings of various systems for producing and distributing wealth and goods; political scientists examine governmental structures.

Although subjects in these disciplines are sometimes examined through subjective, humanistic methods of inquiry, writers in the social sciences have become increasingly conscious of the scientific nature of their work. Social scientists today draw many of their conclusions by conducting controlled experiments and surveys and by analyzing the results (or *data*) obtained. Not surprisingly, they value the objectivity of tone that accompanies rigorous inquiry. Thus most instructors in the social sciences will discourage you from using *I* in a paper, from citing direct personal experience as support for a point, and from using informal vocabulary or sentence constructions that might be acceptable to another instructor.

We will focus on two types of papers often assigned in the social sciences: (1) the application of a concept or principle to a new set of circumstances, and (2) the evaluative review of the literature on a subject. The first type represents the more subjective, less quantitative side of the social sciences, and the second reflects the experimental, data-oriented approach.

Writing the "Application of a Concept" Paper

Social sciences instructors often assign the "application of a concept" paper in introductory courses because that assignment is appropriate for beginning students. After all, such students are often limited in their ability to generate their own experimental data, and they may lack the skills needed to process statistical data collected by other researchers. During the time that they are learning these specialized techniques, applying a concept provides a way of exploring some basic principles of the discipline.

Whether the concept you choose is drawn from class lectures or from readings, the new circumstances to which you apply it should be determined by the nature of the discipline. In a government course, for instance, the concept might be applied to a different political structure; in psychology, it might be applied to a different personality type; in a sociology course, to a different group, social class, or organization.

Of course you must first thoroughly understand the concept itself before you can proceed. Most of your invention process will then be spent in deciding which aspects of the new circumstances to discuss and how the concept would apply to these.

Although such a paper resembles writing done in the humanities, note that your reader will be somewhat more exacting about the rationale and evidence for your own input. Whereas the humanities reader would likely accept observations based on generalized logic and intuition, readers in the social sciences will want to know that your ideas are in line with any available evidence and/or basic principles that apply to the discipline. In the sample student paper that follows, most of the writer's observations are based on her understanding of *role theory*, the notion that people present themselves differently depending on the situation and the nature of their audience. Pay particular attention to how the writer clearly relates her points about college students to such concepts as *the back stage* (the major concept being applied), *the performance, control strategies,* and *nonpersons.*

THE COLLEGE STUDENT AND THE BACK STAGE

Paragraph 1 clearly indicates the source of the concept and explicitly identifies both the concept (back stage) and the group to which it will be applied (college students). Here the writer summarizes some of Goffman's ideas. In particular she discusses interaction as a performance on a stage. The last sentence provides a transition to the main concept of back stage.

[1]In *The Presentation of Self in Everyday Life,* Erving Goffman focuses on social interactions as performances and individual people as performers. Particularly important in Goffman's discussion is his distinction between the front and back stage regions. Although Goffman doesn't discuss college students, his concept of front stage and back stage can shed light on the student as a performer.

[2]Goffman explains that a front stage region is "the place where the performance is given." It is there that one must strive to project an ideal image of himself through performance. In doing so the performer must pay close attention to both the impressions he gives and those he gives off, so as to control the performance and thus be the one to define the situation that he and other performers (who are simultaneously his audience) create. As Goffman points out, an effective showing is easily ruined by the slightest error. The performer must therefore remain constantly on guard to eliminate such errors. Because this demands energy and concentration, back stage regions have developed.

In paragraph 3 the writer defines the concept itself.

[3]The back stage region, as Goffman defines it, is "a place relative to a given performance where the impression fostered by the performance is knowingly contradicted." It is there, Goffman explains, that the performer may relax. For example, the performer who has projected a well- kept, tidy image of herself during a given performance may kick off her shoes and belch loudly back stage if she so desires.

[4]Goffman's definition needs further qualification: that of the importance of privacy. If a performer is truly to relax, she must be rid of *all* performing constraints. The presence of another individual prohibits this, for the performer must continue to peform. As long as others are present, role-playing must continue. Goffman does not emphasize any need for privacy in his definition and discussion of back stage. This can be seen in considering his example of a restaurant's kitchen as a typical example of back stage.

[5]The restaurant's kitchen, Goffman suggests, is a waitress' back stage. There, he says, she may drop the service facade that she maintains while performing before her customers. In my opinion, however, the kitchen is merely a less formal, perhaps less demanding, front stage region, for the waitress still remains before an audience: the cooks, the potwashers, and other staff. Goffman instead calls this audience the waitress' team because together they all perform for the customers. Although this seems accurate, there is a distinction between the true back stage of total privacy and the partial back stage of the team situation where others are still present.

[6]A true back stage region provides not only a place for relaxation, but a place for private reflection and contemplation as well. Because our performances are not consistent with each other (we act differently with our family than with our peers, colleagues, employers), our back stage regions become a place where we may gain a sense of who we really are by removing all of the many masks we wear during our various performances. However, unlike most people, the college student living in a dorm, usually with a roommate, is deprived of a true back stage region. This affects both the student himself and the nature of his interaction with his roommate.

[7]A student, like a professional, a merchant, or a service worker, spends her day performing upon numerous front stages. In turn, she wears the many masks needed to project the various impressions she wants to make. At the end of the day, however, she does not return to the private back stage region of a house or apartment but instead returns to a dorm. Most performers may go completely back stage in their homes by removing themselves from the rooms in which their spouse or relatives interact. The student's dorm, however, is a far cry from a house or apartment. Her living room is a well traveled lounge; her relatives are the 50 or 100 or 200 other students who also live in the dorm. In the company of relatives, most performers may enjoy a rather lax performance compared to the ones they must perform on the job.The student, on the other hand, surrounded by her dorm mates, finds herself engaged in perhaps some of her most strenuous performances. The impressions her peers infer from her performances are of the utmost concern to the college student. These peers judge her personal performance far more critically than the professors, class-mates, and college personnel for whom she has performed during the day. Even the student's room does not provide her with an escape.

Because the student's room is her most workable stage (that is, she is surrounded by many personal "props"), she is likely to encourage others to view her in this setting. And when her chosen audience leaves, she must often continue to perform because her roommate is present.

In paragraph 8, she begins to examine how the lack of a back stage influences the college student's social interactions.

[8]Because the student receives such little time back stage, she is less able to gain a sense of who she really is and of how her various performances tie together. When one considers that the average student attends college during some of the most critical years of her life (for she is now away from home and is in the process of formulating a strong independent image of herself), one may begin to understand the student's real need for a time of reflection. Because she is not provided with this time, she changes her behavior in an attempt to compensate. This is best illustrated by the nature of the relationship that evolves between the student and her assigned roommate.

The writer examines in closer detail some of the behavior that results. Note her reference to the "control strategies" as a type of social behavior arising from the lack of a true back stage.

[9]As college roommates perform for one another, many control strategies come into play. Each seeks to manipulate the other in such a way as to insure respect for her half of the room. A definite invisible line develops between the two sides. It is understood that this line is not to be crossed. An article of clothing that is mistakenly left on the other's side is likely to remain there for a very short time. The student who is more successful in defining her space is doubtless the one furthest from the door. Her half of the room is less infringed upon by the other for it need not be constantly passed through. Though a working relationship will form between the two students, rarely will a true friendship develop. This is because both students are overly exposed to the inconsistencies of the other's performances. They each see the other playing too many separate roles before the numerous other people who step into the room. Goffman points out that to believe in a performer's performance, one must believe in the performer's sincerity. Because there is usually a great discrepancy between the roles each roommate sees the other performing, sincerity is not established.

By referring to an accepted role theory—that "different audiences require different performances"—the writer explains an obstacle that arises in the roommates' relationship.

[10]As each student tries to imagine how the other thinks of her, she begins to feel all too aware of these discrepancies herself. Thus she tries to improve her act in an attempt to gain the other's respect and thereby her own. But it is impossible to escape the fact that different audiences require different performances. The ability to project an ideal image before the audience of the roommate who is ever-present in the theater thus becomes impossible.

Using another concept from Goffman's discussion, the student further defines the kind of relationship that develops between roommates in the absence of a back stage.

[11]For this reason roommates often try to become for each other what Goffman called nonpersons. While one is performing before a visiting audience, the other tries to seem as if she is not there. She avoids all conversation and attempts to go about her business as if oblivious to the performance being given. This is an attempt to alleviate pressure from the performing roommate's performance. It is understood that similar behavior will be awarded when the situation is reversed.

Roommates in this way exercise tact and discretion, but their strong awareness of each other still prevents either from enjoying a true back stage.

¹²Beyond the room, roommates continue to exercise discretion. Rarely do they engage in conversations with other dorm mates in an attempt to weaken their roommate's performances. While they each know many deep secrets about the other, it is understood that those secrets will be honored; both individuals are equally subject to the knowledge the other possesses. Because of this threat, most roommates remain on good terms with one another.

¹³Roommate interaction consumes much energy. When one considers that college students must face this demand following a long day of study and performance, one begins to realize why most desire a single room. A single would provide an escape from performance; a single would provide the true back stage region that every performer needs.

¹⁴Perhaps by viewing the student as an ever-performing performer, one may more easily understand her vulnerability to increases in work pressure and to her own poor performances. Considering that at most colleges there are thousands of performing students lacking a back stage region, it is not surprising that they often resort to unproductive or even destructive forms of release. The performer who lacks a back stage region is likely to become at times a rather unstable actor.

*This paragraph takes the discussion of the roommate's relationship a step further: to their attitudes toward each other **outside** the room setting.*

Here the writer emphasizes the stress put on the college student due to the lack of a back stage and notes a possible solution.

In her conclusion, the writer briefly considers the larger implications of the back stage concept as it applies to college students living in dormitories.

We can see that the writer applied the concept to a new set of circumstances. Having chosen college students as her group, she made every effort to show how social relationships were influenced by the concept of *back stage*. Each time she made observations of her own, she carefully connected them to the principles and concerns of the discipline she was working in—sociology.

Suggestion for Writing

Write an essay in which you apply the notion of "back stage" (as it is discussed in the paper beginning on page 417) to a new situation. (You may or may not accept the student's qualification of privacy.) For your new set of circumstances, choose a situation with which you have some experience—for example, "back stage and the grocery clerk," or "back stage and the telephone solicitor."

Writing an Evaluative Review of the Literature

The second type of paper we will examine reflects more closely the scientific attitude in the social sciences; in fact, it is also a major type of paper written in the natural sciences. An evaluative review of the literature requires you to research a topic and then summarize and evaluate the most important studies that have been published. To complete this assignment, you first need library and research skills (these are discussed in Chapter 11). Second, you need to be familiar with important topics in the discipline. Finally, you need to know how to interpret the findings of the researchers in the field and how to spot strengths and weaknesses in their research designs.

The student paper that follows was written for an intermediate level course in developmental psychology. Although many of the studies it reviews could also have sociological significance, its basic purpose is guided by a concern of psychology: the development of certain abilities *within the individual*.

In studying this student essay, pay particular attention to its systematic organization:

1. Introduction
2. General Review
3. The Confluence Model
4. Environmental Factors
5. Sex Differences
6. Biological Factors
7. Conclusion

Also note that the student's *evaluation* of the studies she reviews takes two forms. First, mainly within sections 3 through 6, she frequently uses the findings of some authors to contradict or to confirm the findings of others. Second, mainly in her conclusion, she draws on her knowledge of research designs in the social sciences to note flaws in the studies that currently constitute the literature on her topic.

THE RELATIONSHIP OF BIRTH ORDER TO INTELLECTUAL ABILITY AND ACADEMIC ACHIEVEMENT

Introduction

[1]Researchers and theorists in developmental psychology have attributed a variety of differences between siblings to the order of their birth in the family. Freud said, "A child's position in the sequence of brothers and sisters is of great significance for the course of his later life" (cited in Rosen, 1961). The characteristics said to be related to birth order are numerous and often conflicting. This paper will attempt to summarize and evaluate some of the research related to sibling differences in intellectual ability and academic achievement. Although much research has been done, the effects of birth order have yet to be satisfactorily explained.

General Review

This section gives a quick review of the major studies.

[2]Many studies have concluded that the first-born child in a family tends to be academically superior to his later-born siblings (Sayer, 1966; Cicirelli, 1976; Green, 1978; Oberlander, 1967; Schachter, 1963; White, 1979), do better on math and English skills tests (Marjoribanks,

It does not go into detail but establishes an overall picture.

The writer uses author/year documentation, a method explained in Chapter 11.

1976), and go to college more often (Bayer, 1966) than his younger siblings. According to Koch (cited in Rosen, 1961), first-borns are more competitive than their brothers and sisters, and Sampson (1962) concludes that they have a higher need for achievement. Some say first-borns are more self-reliant and adult-oriented (Rosen, 1961) than their siblings, but others state that they are more dependent (Bayer, 1966; Schooler, 1972) and less responsive to adult approval (Koch, 1956b). Some researchers even conclude that the oldest child is quite a bit more open to social pressures than later-borns.

[3]Younger siblings tend to have slightly lower levels of academic achievement and to do worse on standard verbal and numerical skills tests (Marjoribanks, 1976) than first-borns. Whereas first-borns do more work of "an abstract verbal nature," later-borns tend to do work related to their sensory perceptions, according to Cicirelli (1967).

[4]These differences in ability correlated with birth order could be caused by biological factors related to birth or could arise from a variety of environmental conditions. Parents may alter the home situation when a new child arrives, and increasing family size combined with economic factors could possibly change the environment for later siblings. The sex of the children also seems to play a crucial role in determining sibling difference in academic and other abilities.

The Confluence Model

Beginning with this section, and continuing through the section titled Biological Factors, the writer focuses on specific areas within the larger topic.

In each case, she begins with a summary, in her own words, of the researchers' findings

[5]R. B. Zajonc, Hazel Markus, and Gregory Markus (1979) have come up with one theory for explaining the "birth order puzzle." They claim that their confluence model can resolve any conflicts existing in the literature.

[6]Two basic notions form the foundation of this model. The first is that the intellectual level of a family unit is the sum of all the family members' individual levels divided by the number of people in the family. In other words, it is the average of the individual intellectual levels. When a new birth takes place, the intellectual environment is "diluted" because the existing total must be divided by one more person. As members of the family grow older, their individual levels increase, but if new people are often added to the family, the dilution may be greater than the increase in average family level.

[7]The second notion behind the confluence model is that older family members profit from acting as intellectual resources for younger members. This is the so-called teaching effect that only the youngest child never benefits from. When a new birth occurs, the older children experience a rise in their teaching effect and a drop in the family intellectual level. As he grows older, the first-born child experiences a rise in family intellectual level plus a rise in the teaching effect, but the youngest experiences the "last-born's handicap" in that he never gets to teach. This causes intellectual development as shown on the graph opposite, with the first-born ultimately achieving the levels of later-

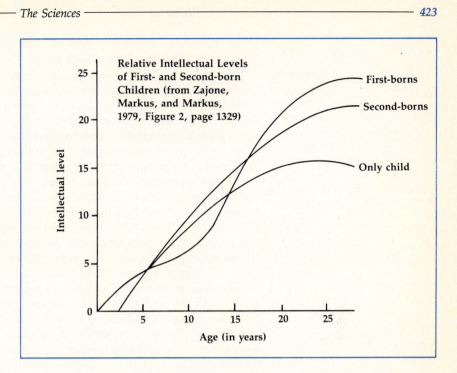

Relative Intellectual Levels of First- and Second-born Children (from Zajone, Markus, and Markus, 1979, Figure 2, page 1329)

borns in the 7 to 15 age range. The final levels of those born third, fourth, or fifth would be lower than that of the second-born, according to the confluence model.

[8]According to this model, first-borns should be intellectually superior in the preschool years. Data reported by White, Kaban, and Attanucci (1979) from the Preschool Project, a longitudinal study of preschoolers' intellectual development, tend to support this. They found that at age two to three, first-borns had slightly better language skills as well as better scores on the Bayley Mental Index.

[9]Marjoribanks' research (1976) on eleven-year-old Canadian boys also lends some support to the model. At this age the second- and later-born boys usually had better verbal abilities as the model would predict, but in the area of quantitative abilities first-borns were superior (Kaltsounis, 1978; Marjoribanks, 1976), contradicting the model. Cicirelli (1967) also studied children in late elementary school. He found that IQ measures relate not so much to the birth order of a child in his family as to the sex of the child and of his or her siblings. Another study of elementary school children conducted by Schoonever (1959) also found no differences between IQ and achievement of older and younger siblings, and a study of seventh- and eighth-graders in Chicago showed first-borns superior on IQ and academic achievement (Oberlander, 1976). The research overall does not lend much support to the prediction that first-borns' intellectual

Here the writer begins to evaluate the confluence model, to see its strengths and weaknesses as a tool for explaining the influence of birth order. She first notes data from another study that would confirm the model.

In paragraph 9 the student cites another study that confirms the model, but then points out that another aspect of the study, as well as numerous other studies, contradicts the model. She concludes the paragraph with a summary statement questioning this particular aspect of the model.

achievement will dip below that of their younger siblings in the elementary and junior high school years.

Taking another aspect of the model, the writer cites support from additional researchers, then concludes the paragraph by noting more contradictions. Note that throughout this evaluation she continues to use the technique of citing some authors to support or contradict the findings of others.

[10]By late high school or college age, the confluence model predicts that the first-born would again be superior intellectually. A study done by Morris Rosenberg in 1965 (cited in Green, 1978) with juniors and seniors in high school supports this prediction. He found that first-borns made higher grades on the average than later-borns. Altus' data (cited in Bayer, 1977) showed that as ordinal position increased, the likelihood of the person going to college decreased, even when family size was held constant. There are 12 percent more first-borns in college and 20 percent more in graduate school than later-borns. Studies of eminent researchers show that their ranks include an overabundance of first-borns (Visher, 1948; West, 1960/61). Another study, however, also looked at the performance of middle children and found their school achievement even lower than that of the last-born (Cicirelli, 1967), contrary to Zajonc, Markus, and Markus' confluence model.

[11]Because of the conflicting research results, especially with young adolescents, the confluence model does not seem to explain adequately the differences in academic achievement of siblings at different birth positions in a family. Not only is there much data contradicting the model, but the model fails to take into consideration many variables besides age that appear to influence the differences. These variables are discussed next.

Environmental Factors

In this section, the writer reviews other significant factors that have been investigated by researchers but were not accounted for by the confluence model. She states that these variables are important, but stresses in her summary the ultimate inconclusiveness of researchers' findings.

[12]Differing treatment of siblings resulting from their birth order could influence their academic achievement. Rossard's 1945 study showed that parents adjust their speech level to that of the oldest child in the family (cited in Green, 1978), which could possibly retard speech development in later-borns. Marjoribanks (1976), however, suggests that the higher verbal scores of second-born boys in his study of eleven-year-olds could be due to parents' increased skill in creating a stimulating environment for the later-born child. Most researchers lean the other way, though, hypothesizing that since mothers spend twice as much time with a first-born as with a later-born child, and since first-time parents tend to be more open-minded and less set in their ways (White, 1979), the first-born will be more adult-oriented, more sensitive to his parents' expectations, and more achievement-oriented (Rosen, 1961). Second-borns do not spend such a large proportion of their time with their parents, and the parents are often more permissive (Green, 1978) and over-indulgent with them, thereby lowering their achievement motivation in comparison with first-born children (Rosen, 1961). The second children seem to be more peer-oriented than adult-oriented (Rosen, 1961).

The student's summary of research on family size

[13]Another important variable in the study of sibling differences is family size. According to some researchers, mean IQ and achievement

continues to stress the contradictory evidence.

scores decrease as family size increases (Bayer, 1966; Green, 1978; Nuttall, 1976), but this could be due to the general trend toward larger families in lower socioeconomic classes or to the tendency for increased crowding in larger families (Nuttall, 1976). There is conflict on these issues, however. Altus' data (cited in Bayer, 1966) showed that even when family size is held constant, the likelihood of younger children going to college is less than that of their older siblings. But the data from Project Talent, a study of 88,000 high school seniors, showed that when family size and socioeconomic status are held constant, the middle children are the least likely to attend college. The first and last are equally likely to attend (Bayer, 1966). And according to Cicirelli (1967), "there is no statistically significant relation between family size and measures of ability and achievement in families ranging in size from one to eleven children."

The final factor examined in this section, spacing, shows promise, for there are no contradictory studies. In the last sentence, the student brings up a feature of the confluence model to help confirm the potential value of this variable.

[14]Yet another variable possibly affecting the birth order data is the spacing, or amount of time between births of siblings. The smaller the time span between births, the greater the effects of birth order, according to Chittenden (cited in Cicirelli, 1977). Cicirelli (1967) found that boys with a brother close in age and girls with a sister close in age scored higher on verbal creativity, reading, and arithmetic tests than those siblings spaced far apart. He also found that boys with a sister spaced closely tended to score higher than other boys. Possibly Zajonc, Markus, and Markus' teaching effect could have more influence on siblings close in age.

[The sections on Sex Differences and Biological Factors have been omitted because the writer's techniques in these sections are identical to those we have already examined.]

Conclusion

The writer begins her conclusion by discussing the problems with the designs of the studies she has reviewed and suggesting some directions for future studies.

[15]The studies mentioned in this paper have some serious flaws that could affect the conclusions drawn about sibling intellectual and academic differences. Nearly all of them draw their data from white, urban, middle-class American subjects from nuclear families. The results cannot be generalized to other cultures or other socioeconomic groups. In addition, some of the sex differences found in the studies may no longer be valid, considering the recent changes in the attitudes of our society toward females and the female role. It must be pointed out also that the differences found were often quite small, so that knowing only the birth position of a person tells little about him. Great improvements in our knowledge of sibling differences could be made by conducting longitudinal studies of children living in kibbutzim, tribal cultures, traditional Oriental "extended" families, and orphanages, to mention just a few possibilities. More research is also necessary on possible biological influences.

In her last paragraph the student states her own findings, reemphasizing the inconclusiveness of the research on the topic.

[16]Differences in academic achievement correlated with birth order have been explained in a variety of ways. Possibly they are caused by factors such as family size, socioeconomic status, age gaps between siblings, or differing parental attitudes. Most likely, all these variables are closely linked to sibling differences, but none can be properly considered unless in conjunction with the sex of the child and of his or her siblings. Clearly, despite the considerable research that has been done so far, siblings' intellectual differences are still inadequately explained in developmental psychology.

References

Bayer, Alan E. (1966) Birth order and college attendance. *Journal of Marriage and the Family*, 28, 480–484.

Cicirelli, Victor G. (1967) Sibling constellation, creativity, IQ, and academic achievement. *Child Development*, 38, 481–490.

Cicirelli, Victor G. (1976) Sibling structure and intellectual ability. *Developmental psychology*, 12, 369–370.

Cicirelli, Victor G. (1977) Children's school grades and sibling structure. *Psychological Reports*, 41, 1055–1058.

Foster, John W. & Archer, Stanley J. (1979) Birth order and intelligence: An immunological interpretation. *Perceptual and Motor Skills*, 48, 79–93.

Green, Ernest J. (1978) *Birth order, parental interest and academic achievement*. San Francisco: R & E Research Associates.

Kaltsounis, Bill (1978) Creative performance among siblings of various birth positions. *Psychological Reports*, 42, 915–918.

Koch, Helen L. (1955) The relation of certain family constellation characteristics and the attitudes of children toward adults. *Child Development*, 26, 13–40.

Koch, Helen L. (1956) Children's work attitudes and sibling characteristics. *Child Development*, 27, 289–310.

Marjoribanks, Kevin. (1976) Birth order, family environment, and mental abilities: A regression surface analysis. *Psychological Reports*, 39, 759–765.

Nuttall, Ena Vazquez, et al. (1976) The effects of family size, birth order, sibling separation and crowding on the academic achievement of boys and girls. *American Educational Research Journal*, 13, 217–223.

Oberlander, Mark & Jenkins, Noel. (1967) Birth order and academic achievement. *Journal of Individual Psychology*, 23, 103–110.

Rosel, Bernard C. (1961) Family structure and achievement motivation. *American Sociological Review*, 26, 574–585.

Sampson, Edward E. (1962) Birth order, need achievement, and conformity. *Journal of Abnormal and Social Psychology*, 64, 155–159.

Schachter, Stanley. (1963) Birth order, eminence and higher education. *American Sociological Review*, 28, 757–768.

Schooler, Carmi. (1962) Birth order effects: Not here, not now. *Psychological Bulletin*, 78, 161–175.

Schoonover, Sarah M. (1959) The relationship of intelligence and achievement to birth order, sex of sibling, and age interval. *The Journal of Educational Psychology*, 50, 143–146.

Sears, Robert R. (1950) Ordinal position in the family as a psychological variable. *American Sociological Review*, 15, 397–401.

Smelser, William T. & Stewart, Louis H. (1968) Where are the siblings? A re-evaluation of the relationship between birth order and college attendance. *Sociometry*, 31, 294–303.

Visher, Stephen Sargent. (1948) Environment backgrounds of leading American scientists. *American Sociological Review*, 13, 65–72.

West, S. Stewart. (1960/61) Sibling configurations of scientists. *The American Journal of Sociology*, 66, 268–274.

White, Burton L., Kaban, Barbara T. & Attanucci, Jane S. (1979) *The origins of human competence*. Lexington, Mass.: D.C. Heath.

Zajonc, R.B., Markus, Hazel & Markus, Gregory B. (1979) The birth order puzzle. *Journal of Personality and Social Psychology*, 37, 1325–1341.

We have seen two kinds of evaluative techniques used in this paper—playing researchers' findings off against each other and looking for design flaws. A third skill is also evident: organizing and categorizing. The literature on this student's topic exists in bits and pieces dispersed throughout various journals and books. Once she used her research skills to unearth her sources, she still faced a mass of unorganized material. Note how well she categorized and organized the once-scattered materials into a coherent scheme.

Exercise

1. The following is taken from the Biological Factors section of the student paper discussed above. Read the passage and comment on the evaluative technique used.

Some researchers have also considered nonenvironmental influences. Possibly ordinal sibling differences are caused by biological factors. John Foster and Stanley Archer (1979) proposed one biological theory to explain why first-borns have higher levels of academic performance on the average than later-born children. They studied the immune attack on the fetal brain by antibodies in the mother's blood serum and found that the number of antibodies increases with each birth. These antibodies may go through the placenta and damage the structure and learning capacity of the fetal brain (Foster, 1979). This hypothesis, however, fails to explain the sex differences related to ordinal position as well as the superiority of some last-borns over middle-born children (Bayer, 1966).

2. Working from knowledge gained in a social sciences course, prepare a list of possible topics that could serve as the focus for an evaluative review of the literature. ✑

The Attitudes of the Natural Sciences Writer

Unlike social scientists, who are concerned with human behavior, organizations, and institutions, natural scientists (chemists, physicists, biologists, geologists, and others) focus on the workings of nature and the physical universe. To aid them in their probings, natural scientists have developed the most rigorous method of inquiry among all the disciplines: the *scientific method*. This method ideally features an hypothesis, controlled experimentation, observation, and conclusion. Accordingly, a major concern of most writers in science is to convey accurately and clearly the phenomena they have observed during their inquiries. Scientific writing thus is often very technical and specialized, its tone objective, and its descriptions (of chemical compounds, of biological processes, of physical motion) intricate.

Despite these differences, an evaluative review essay for a science course is quite similar in structure to the evaluative review discussed in the social sciences section, and so we will not discuss it here. We will examine one of the most commonly assigned papers in science courses: the lab report.

Writing the Lab Report

The lab report is the only opportunity most students will have to write about a scientific inquiry of their own. It is not what scientists call a *primary* study because the experiments conducted in lab have been designed by someone else and performed many times by other students. Yet the lab report, like a primary study report, presents the writer's own findings based on first-hand experimentation.

Although the experiments you conduct are not original or primary, you should approach them as though they were. In conducting these experiments, which may have been done countless times before, your goal is to experience the spirit of scientific inquiry and to learn the methods and principles of research and experimentation in the discipline. In fact, the format you will use in lab reports is nearly identical to the format used by research scientists when they present their primary studies.

Most often, lab experiments will be carefully planned for you and explained in detail in a lab manual, on assignment sheets, by the instructor, or through a combination of all three. Although the details of format may vary somewhat from course to course, discipline to discipline, or school to school, the basic structure is similar. The model format we present in this section (from a biology lab) is quite elaborate and inclusive; most variations you would need to make for a specific course would involve omitting some of its features.

Report Format The first page of the lab report should contain your name, your lab partner's name (if applicable), your lab day, the instructor's name, the date and title of the experiment. The body of the report should be divided in these sections, each preceded by the proper section heading:

I. Introduction
    A. A description of the technique(s) used—that is, definition of the technique(s), the theoretical background involved, and the relevant mathematical formulae and chemical reactions.
    B. A discussion of the material(s) utilized. For example, if the exercise involves use of an enzyme, define *enzyme* and discuss the nature of enzymatic action.
    C. A hypothesis: A statement of the question being addressed in the experiment and the general results you expect to obtain based on your prior reading.

[Material helpful in writing the introduction can generally be found in lab handouts, lab lectures, course lectures, and the library. If you use outside readings, use the author/year style documentation to acknowledge your sources, as explained in Chapter 11.]

II. Materials and Methods
    If the procedure followed is exactly the same as indicated in the lab manual or assignment sheet, do not rewrite the procedure in this section. You may state that it was conducted according to instructions in the lab manual, or photocopy the relevant outline of the procedure and paste it in your report. Any deviations from the standard procedure—unanticipated errors or difficulties, optional dilutions, and so on—*must* be noted in this section.

III. Results
    A. All data derived from the experiment. Data are best expressed in table and graph form. Tables and graphs should have titles; both axes on graphs must be labeled, including the relevant units. (See the example in Figure 12.6, p. 430.)
    B. Calculations, including samples of all calculations done for the report.

IV. Discussion and Conclusions
    A. Explanation and comments on all data, referring specifically to the data expressed in tabular and graphic

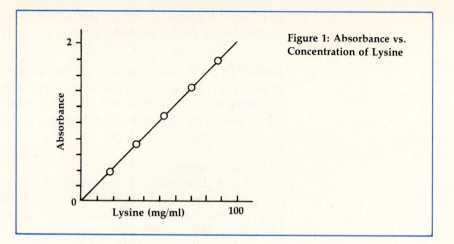

Figure 1: Absorbance vs.
Concentration of Lysine

form in Section III. To the extent possible, the significance
of all data listed should be addressed. If the results are
not consistent with your expectations, any and all sources
of error must be noted.
B. Conclusion(s) derived from the data.
C. Acceptance or rejection of the stated hypothesis, based on
all the data obtained and (if applicable) the integration of
your findings with those of previously published studies.

[Be careful not to make unsupported, blanket statements in your
discussion. Conclusions drawn must be supported by the data or by
evidence from documented scientific literature.]

V. References
Optional, depending upon whether the experiment calls for outside reading. List any sources cited in the report. Arrange in
alphabetical order by authors' last names. (See pp. 371–72 for
examples of proper bibliographic form.)

As you write the lab report itself, keep in mind that you should be
as complete and clear as possible in your discussions. Besides reading
your report to determine the accuracy of your results, many instructors
will judge your report by deciding whether other students would be able
to reproduce the experiment. Ideally, your lab report should be written
in enough detail so that others could conduct the experiment for
themselves and either achieve the same results you did or know why
they did not achieve those results.

Your style should be descriptive and straightforward. As much as
possible, use basic, everyday language to describe and discuss the

experiment. Because the report is directed at a scientific audience, you may also use the same degree of specialized vocabulary used in the lab manual or assignment sheet—but only if you understand and are comfortable with the terminology. As in any type of writing, some variety in sentence patterns and vocabulary will make the piece more readable. Thus, for instance, you should avoid needlessly monotonous accounts of the procedures you followed. Similarly, use synonyms to avoid repetition, but only if they are accurate. If you have been talking about bacteria cells reproducing, for instance, you can probably substitute *replicate* for *reproduce*. However, in some cases, repetition may be unavoidable. There is, for example, no synonym for *cell*. If you are doing an experiment in cellular biology, you may simply have to repeat the term cell more than you would like.

HANDBOOK
OF GRAMMAR
AND USAGE

INTRODUCTION This Handbook is a brief guide to the main points of English grammar and usage. It is divided into five sections:

> Parts of Speech
> Sentence Structure
> Common Usage Errors
> Punctuation and Mechanics
> Glossary of Usage

Edited English In the Handbook, certain usages are labeled *Faulty* and others *Acceptable* for the kind of writing situations encountered in college and in business and professional life. As college is a preparation for an active role in the world of affairs, a college course in writing should inform students of those language usages that will be unclear or irritating to readers accustomed to a certain variety of English. That variety of English is called "edited English" in this Handbook. Edited English means the American English usages found in most textbooks, scholarly publications (books and journals), and business and governmental reports. Edited English is the variety of English expected of professional people when they write in formal situations.

From a purely linguistic viewpoint, usages characterized as "faulty" in this Handbook are understandable as the product of dialectal differences or historical and linguistic processes at work in the language. However, from a rhetorical and social viewpoint, faulty usages are, nevertheless, to be avoided.

From the rhetorical viewpoint, certain of these usages simply send readers confusing signals. Suppose, for example, that the following construction was found in a piece of college writing:

> Which told me that he was not really serious.

The use of a capital *w* on *which* and a period after *serious* signals that this construction is a sentence. At the same time, the construction does not read like a sentence. (Compare "*She* told me that he was not really serious.") So the construction both does and does not seem like a sentence. Because it sends conflicting signals, this kind of construction, called a "sentence fragment," is labeled *faulty* and should be avoided in formal writing situations. Sentence fragments are not examples of edited English.

From a social viewpoint also, faulty usages are to be avoided. Suppose, for example, the following sentence fragment appeared in a letter of application for an accounting or engineering job:

> Especially since I have used your products for years.

An audience who spotted this usage might draw a picture of the writer as someone who is careless or uninformed about the basics of written communication—as someone who appears to have a less than professional approach to the business of finding a job. Such a picture of the writer's attitude or knowledge could detract from the persuasiveness of the letter of application.

If your teacher indicates that you need work on any of the usages discussed in this Handbook, take that observation seriously and learn to recognize your incorrect usages and correct them. By doing so, you will gain confidence that you can use edited English in a professionally acceptable manner to communicate clearly with audiences whose trust and respect you want to win.

Answers to Exercises Answers to odd-numbered items in each set of exercises are provided in the Answer Key on pages 541–52. Check your answers against the key after you complete each exercise set. If you've made any errors, look back over the relevant material.

PARTS OF SPEECH

English words have been divided according to form, function, and meaning into eight categories called **parts of speech**. These parts of speech are nouns, verbs, adjectives, adverbs, pronouns, prepositions, conjunctions, and interjections.

NOUNS Nouns (N) name persons (*George Washington, barber*), places (*Ohio, church*), things (*Statue of Liberty, table*), qualities (*love, beauty*), and ideas (*relationship, theory*). Nouns show possession by adding 's (*John's, dog's*). Most nouns also distinguish between plural and singular by a change in form—usually by adding an *-es* or *-s* (*dress/dresses, tent/tents*). Nouns can be preceded by words like *the, a/an, this, her,* or adjectives like *nice, pretty,* and *grim*. Nouns can function as

1. The subject of a verb:

    N
    The **boy** *ran* away.

2. The object of a transitive verb:

N
She ate the pie.

3. The indirect object of a transitive verb:

N
She told John to jump in.

4. The complement of a linking verb:

N
He is a teacher.

5. The object of a preposition:

N   N
along the Mississippi   in the car

6. An appositive:

N
Ginger, my orange cat, eats too much.

7. An attributive:

N
a country gentleman.

8. The modifier of a verb:

N
We work days.

Nouns can be classified according to their meaning. **Proper nouns** are the given names of particular persons, animals, places, and things (*Roosevelt, Benji, Utah, Rosetta Stone*). All other nouns that do not name particular persons, animals, places, or things (*waitress, lion, pond, rose*) are called **common nouns**. Nouns can be further classified as

1. Concrete:

bacon   wool   tree

2. Abstract:

    beauty   love   philosophy

3. Count:

    table   egg   book

4. Mass:

    coffee   copper   wheat

5. Collective:

    committee   nation   government

Noun equivalents are pronouns, gerunds, infinitives, and noun clauses that function like nouns. (See the entries under these headings for more details.)

Exercise

Using the above explanations about the form, function, and meaning of nouns, identify the nouns in the following sentences.

1. The Vikings were bold sailors and savage warriors.
2. John took a photograph of some flowers in a vase on his mother's table.
3. When mixed with hydrochloric acid, the mixture first turned black and then gray.
4. Brokers are interested in the future value of a stock.
5. Dwight D. Eisenhower, the 34th president of the United States, came into national prominence through his achievements during World War II.
6. Day and night, B-52 bombers and battleships bombarded the Vietnamese coast.
7. Shakespeare gave the English language many turns of phrase like "to be or not to be" and "the winter of our discontent."
8. In training cats, you must use great patience.
9. The Matterhorn is one of the most famous peaks in the Swiss Alps.
10. The loon, Minnesota's state bird, has a loud, harsh cry.

• Answers to odd-numbered exercises begin on page 541.

Verbs (V) designate an action or state of being or becoming.

> V
> Susan *slipped* the cake into the oven.

> V
> Susan *rolled* off the bed.

> V
> Susan *is* ill.

> V
> Susan *grows* stronger with each passing day.

They indicate differences in time (present and past) through changes in form: *roll/rolled; is/was; grow/grew*. Except for **modals** (see p. 439) and *be*, all verbs take these characteristic endings: *-s/-es* (*rolls, misses*) and *-ing* (*rolling, growing*). **Regular verbs** show past tense by adding one of three endings to the base of the word: *-ed* (*rolled, dented*), *-d* (*hoed*), or *-t* (*crept, left*). **Irregular verbs** show past tense by a change of vowel (*run/ran; sing/sang*).

In a clause (see p. 464), the **main verb** (MV) or finite verb is the form that signals tense. Nonfinite forms or **verbals** (Vb) cannot signal tense differences. Instead, verbals function as modifiers and nouns.

Verbals as Modifiers

> Vb   Vb   MV   Vb
> **Turning** sharply, the **drunken** driver *missed* the **startled** pedestrian.

> MV   Vb
> France *is* the best place **to see** cathedrals.

Verbals as Nouns

> MV *Vb*
> My hobby *is* **sewing**.

> Vb   MV
> **To meet** Joan again *would* give me a big lift.

Verbals are classified as **participles** (present—*turning*; past—*drunken, startled*), **gerunds** (*sewing*), and **infinitives** (*to see*). The *-ing* form of the verb is called a **present participle** when it acts as a modifier and a **gerund** when it functions as a noun.

-ing *Form as Present Participle*

      Vb
Watching the pitcher go through his windup, the runner inched away from first base.

        Vb
I saw him **stealing** candy from the counter.

-ing *Form as Gerund*

      Vb
Watching baseball on television is my favorite pastime.

       Vb
His **stealing** of candy will get him into trouble one day.

Verbals can also be used with **helping verbs** to form **verb phrases** (see pp. 460–62). There are two kinds of helping verbs: **auxiliary verbs** (*be, do, have*) and **modal verbs** (*can, could, may, might, ought, shall, should, will, would*).

Helping verbs enable us to express more distinctions in time than just present or past:

Progressive

She *is* sewing a dress.
She *was* sewing a dress.

Perfective

She *has* sewn dresses before.

Past Perfect

As a child, she *had* always sewn her own dresses.

Future

From now on, she *will* sew her own clothes.

Future Perfect

By the end of the year, she *will have* sewn 300 dresses.

Auxiliaries are also involved in forming negative statements:

> She *does* not know how to sew.

in forming questions:

> *Does* she know how to sew?

and in forming the passive voice:

> Her clothes *are* all sewn by her mother.

Finally, modal verbs enable us to form verb phrases that express permissibility, possibility, capability, obligation, and willingness:

> She *can* sew her own clothes.
> She *must* sew her own clothes.

Past participles of regular verbs are formed by adding one of three endings to the verb: *-ed*, (rolled, dented), *-d* (hoed), or *-t* (crept, left). Past participles of irregular verbs often take a different vowel from the present or past (past tense—*sang*; past participle—*sung*) and sometimes add an *-n* or *-en* (past tense—*drew*; past participle—*drawn*). Infinitives are simply the base form of the word (*roll; sing*) or the base form preceded by *to* (*to roll; to sing*).

Verbals may be used by themselves (*To love is to live*), or they may be used to form **verbal phrases**. Such phrases combine verbals and direct or indirect objects (*giving him a kiss*), complements (*becoming angry*), or modifiers (*turning sharply*). (See p. 462 for more about verbal phrases.)

Exercise

Identify the main verbs (V) and verbals (Vb) in the following sentences.

1. In times of rising inflation, accountants sometimes use the LIFO system of evaluating inventory.
2. Like other water fowl, pelicans must swallow their catch without chewing it.
3. If President Kennedy had not been killed, he would have been only 46 years old at the end of his first term of office.
4. Performing well in a judo contest requires participants to concentrate hard.
5. General Custer believed that the Indians would have only about 1,000 men in their camp.

6. When a car is in overdrive, its drive shaft may turn only four times for every three turns of the crankshaft.
7. When the tide is coming in, lifeguards must be especially careful not to allow swimmers to stray too far from shore.
8. Why did the president choose to veto the bill?
9. Three drivers did not see that the road had collapsed.
10. Having buried the dead child, the pioneers packed up their household goods and left.

ADJECTIVES

Adjectives (Adj) are words like *brilliant*, *tough*, and *proud* that modify nouns. They characteristically precede nouns and follow linking verbs like *is*, *seem*, and *appear*.

> Adj
> The *burly* priest knocked the robber down.

> Adj
> The robber had committed *terrible* crimes.

> Adj
> The robber was *clever*.

> Adj
> The priest seemed *gentle*.

Adjectives express comparative and superlative degree through the endings *-er* and *-est* or through the use of *more* or *most*.

> Adj
> The priest was *gentler* than the robber.

> Adj
> The priest was more *ethical* than the robber.

> Adj
> He was the *strongest* priest in his order.

> Adj
> He was the most *intelligent* priest I ever met.

Adjectives of one syllable and many adjectives of two syllables express comparative and superlative degree by adding *-er* and *-est* (*strong*,

● Answers to odd-numbered exercises begin on page 541.

stronger, strongest; stingy, stingier, stingiest). Adjectives of three or more syllables express differences in degree through the use of *more* and *most* (*sympathetic, more sympathetic, most sympathetic*).

The, a, and *an* belong to a special category of adjectives called **articles** (Art). When used with nouns, words like *this, that, some, any, many,* and *all* are also considered adjectives. Words like *his, her, my, your, our,* and *their* are called **possessive adjectives**.

> Art   Adj   Art Adj
> *The* priest is *gentler* than *a brutal* criminal.

> Adj Art   Adj   Art
> *All the* priests were *angry* with *the* robber.

> Adj   Adj
> *Some* robbers commit *terrible* crimes.

> Adj   Adj
> *This* robber was *clever*.

> Adj   Art Adj
> *Their* priest is *a former* boxer.

Exercise

Identify the adjectives (Adj) and articles (Art) in the following sentences.

1. Of all breeds of cat, the Abyssinian has the softest voice.
2. At night the desert wind can be cold.
3. The white pelican is larger than some other pelicans.
4. Ale is darker and heavier than most beers.
5. Persian rugs are known for their dark red color and their beautiful designs.
6. Professional jockeys are usually short, slender, and strong.
7. Symphonic music sounds beautiful when played by skillful musicians.
8. His beautiful voice rang out over the attentive audience.
9. On any day, this successful team can overwhelm an opponent.
10. While he was in the army, his most dangerous moment came when he had to land his airplane in an open field.

ADVERBS

Adverbs (Adv) are words like *well, quickly,* and *sadly* that modify verbs, adjectives, other adverbs, and even whole sentences.

>   Adv
> He *quickly* answered her.

Adv
Her husband is *very* handsome.

Adv   Adv
This piece is one of the *most* difficult she *ever* wrote.

Adv Adv
He answered her *quite quickly*.

Adv
Finally, preserving whales from extinction will express our best human impulses.

Adverbs answer the questions *how, why, when, where,* and *to what degree*. Adverbs also express affirmation (*surely, certainly*) and negation (*not*). Like adjectives, adverbs can express degree (*worse, worst; more profoundly, most profoundly*).

Adverbs that modify verbs or whole sentences can be placed in various positions in the sentence.

Slowly, he began lecturing the students on their responsibilities.
He *slowly* began lecturing the students. . . .
He began *slowly* lecturing the students. . . .
He began lecturing the students *slowly* . . .

Conjunctive adverbs are words like *therefore, thus, nevertheless,* and *however* that modify a clause or sentence so as to show how it relates to a preceding idea.

Adv
He lectured the students for fifteen minutes; *however*, they failed to listen to what he said.

Exercise   Identify the adverbs in the following sentences.

1. However, a slave uprising did not occur then.
2. The Surgeon General's report was immediately misinterpreted by some very uninformed reporters.
3. Three highly skilled marksmen were under orders to fire as soon as the general walked inside.
4. Shakespeare apparently wrote his plays very quickly.
5. After twenty-three hours in the water, the long-distance swimmer wearily waded ashore.

● Answers to odd-numbered exercises begin on page 541.

6. Nevertheless, medieval bishops frequently took part in battles.
7. Since being introduced into the United States, the starling certainly has adapted very well to its new home.
8. Ernest Hemingway worked harder to perfect his craft than most writers do.
9. The sales manager specifically asked her salespeople to prepare detailed reports of their activities.
10. In the battle of Agincourt, 13,000 Englishmen thoroughly beat a French force almost four times as large.

PRONOUNS

Pronouns (Pr) function like nouns in sentences and can stand for nouns. The nouns that are replaced by pronouns are called the **antecedents** of the pronouns.

After letting John hold the watch for a moment, Mary took *it* back.

The car's tires were flat, so I had to change *them*.

John held onto the watch *that* Mary had given *him*.

The audience enthusiastically applauded the dancer *who* had lost *her* shoe.

Pronouns are classified as

1. Personal:

    I   you   he   we   they

2. Possessive:

    mine   yours   his   ours   theirs

3. Demonstrative:

    this   that   these   those

4. Indefinite:

    each   all   everybody   some

5. Reflexive or intensive:

   myself   yourself   ourselves

6. Relative:

   who   which   that

7. Interrogative:

   who   which   what

Exercise

Identify the pronouns in the following sentences.

1. This system of inventory evaluation allows them to avoid paying unnecessary income taxes.
2. The pelicans that we were watching suddenly plunged into the water.
3. Although in his young manhood he had endured prolonged exposure to severe winter weather, exposure to the cold in his last year of life apparently brought on his fatal illness.
4. The Black Plague that swept across Europe in the fourteenth century must have psychologically damaged all of those who survived.
5. The Swiss pride themselves in their mountain-climbing and skiing abilities.
6. Inadvertently, they mixed certain chemicals into the cattle feed.
7. The Soviets' military tanks are probably still better than ours.
8. When she turned 51, Margot left the company to start her own firm.
9. Jefferson began his manifesto with the immortal words "We hold these truths to be self-evident."
10. What was this great writer's contribution to the development of our language?

PREPOSITIONS

Prepositions (Prep) are words like *after, in,* and *without* and phrases like *except for* and *instead of* that link nouns and noun equivalents to the rest of the sentence. The resulting **prepositional phrase** (Prep Phrase) functions as an adjective or adverb.

Prep Phrase   Prep Phrase

Prep   Prep

At midnight Cinderella ran *out of* the palace.

• Answers to odd-numbered exercises begin on page 541.

Prep Phrase

Prep

The good guys are the cowboys *in* white hats.

Prep Phrase

Prep

In baking cakes, you should be sure to use fresh eggs.

Prep Phrase

Prep

He hurried quickly *from* the young man's house

Prep Phrase

Prep

to the young woman's house.

At midnight and *out of the palace* modify the verb *ran*, telling when and where Cinderella ran. *In white hats* limits the meaning of the noun *cowboys*. *In baking cakes* modifies the verb phrase *should make*. *From the young man's house* and *to the young woman's house* modify the verb *hurried*.

CONJUNCTIONS

Conjunctions (Conj) are words like *and, but, since,* and *although* that join various sentence elements together. *And, or, but, for, neither, nor,* and *yet* are called **coordinating conjunctions**. Coordinating conjunctions join words, phrases, and clauses of equal importance.

Words Joined by Coordinating Conjunctions

Conj

Burr **and** *Hamilton* fought each other in a duel.

Conj

The artist used *paper, cloth,* **and** *wood* to make her collage.

Phrases Joined by Coordinating Conjunctions

Conj

He occupied his time in *writing poetry, composing music,* **and** *playing the piano.*

Conj

Washington was neither *America's greatest general* **nor** *its cleverest politician.*

Clauses Joined by Coordinating Conjunctions

Conj

Cinderella thought the prince had forgotten her, **but** *he hadn't.*

Conj

Washington was not America's greatest general, **nor** *was he its cleverest politician.*

Subordinating conjunctions (*since, although, if, when, where, whether, that*) join dependent clauses to independent clauses or integrate dependent clauses into independent clauses (see p. 464). **Subordinate clauses** act as noun equivalents or as modifiers (see pp. 465–66).

Subordinate Clauses as Noun Equivalents

Sub Clause

Conj

She asked **whether** *the livestock had been fed.*

Sub Clause

Conj

What *was in his mind was hard for him to express.*

Subordinate Clauses as Modifiers

Sub Clause

Conj

Things were quiet **until** *Tigger bounced onto the scene.*

Sub Clause

Conj

Washington's spirits sank **when** *the new recruits failed to arrive.*

INTERJECTIONS

Interjections (Int) are words like *oh, wow,* and *help* that express strong emotion and stand outside of the grammar of the sentence.

> Int
> *No,* you may not go.

> Int
> *Oh,* do you really think so?

> Int
> *Wow!*

Exercise

Identify the prepositions (Prep), conjunctions (Conj), and interjections (Int) in the following sentences.

1. Although at one time Paul had persecuted the Christians, ne later became a Christian leader with an influence rivaled only by that of Jesus.
2. If the English monks of the Anglo-Saxon period had been more careful, they would not have built important monasteries on islands or along the coast where marauding Vikings could easily attack them.
3. When Henry bought a few guppies, he had no idea the trouble that they would bring to his family.
4. The pilot completed her report and sent it to the airline.
5. Oh, did John ever want to hit a home run then!
6. Ship propellers do create a great deal of noise in the ocean, but whales are still able to hear each other over the noise.
7. Often when the United States has difficulties with foreign countries, our government uses the export of farm products for diplomatic purposes.
8. Until Washington made his moving statement about going blind in the service of his country, his officers had been thinking of resigning.
9. Evangelical religion was a powerful force on the American frontier, but alcohol was too.
10. The defenseman did not see the shot coming, nor did the goalie.

SENTENCE STRUCTURE

A sentence is a grammatically complete statement containing at least one independent clause called the **main clause** of the sentence. Each main clause is a group of related words containing a subject (S) and a predicate (P).

SUBJECT The subject of the main clause is the subject of the sentence. The subject consists of a noun and its modifiers.

S   P
Jane is a brilliant scientist.

S   P
Jane, having given the graduation address, left for the airport.

S   P
Jane, who is a brilliant scientist, addressed the students at graduation.

S   P
The star has exhausted all its hydrogen.

S   P
The red star has exhausted all its hydrogen.

S   P
The red star, which was discovered in 1596, has exhausted all its hydrogen.

The subject can also consist of noun substitutes—words, phrases, and clauses that can act as nouns—plus their modifiers and other related words.

S   P
He ran away from home.

S   P
Everybody went to look for him.

S   P
Everybody in the family went to look for him.

S   P
Everybody in the family who was in town went to look for him.

● Answers to odd-numbered exercises begin on page 541.

S   P
Jogging is happiness.

              S   P
Jogging on grass is happiness.

                        S
Jogging, a fast-growing sport in America, gives some people

        P
happiness and some people pain.

    S   P
To err is human.

                   S
To err in working geometry problems is a bad idea

    P
when taking a test.

               S   P
That she loves competition is quite obvious from her performance.

               S   P
What she wanted to say was not pleasing to her audience.

The subject names what the sentence is about—the person or thing whose action is described by the predicate, or the person or thing about which the predicate makes an assertion. (Who ran away? *He* did. What is happiness? *Jogging on grass.*)

Position of Subject in the Main Clause

In **declarative sentences** (ones that express statements rather than questions or commands), the subject normally comes *before* the predicate of the main clause.

Declarative Sentence—Normal Word Order

S | P
Maple leaves turn red in autumn.

S | P
To write good comedy requires a strong sense of timing.

S | P
Hunting seals in an open boat is dangerous.

S | P
What surprises me about the Vikings is their seamanship.

However, in some declarative sentences, the subject comes after the **main verb** (MV) of the predicate. In the usual subject position before the verb, such sentences have an **anticipatory subject** (AS) or an **expletive** (Ex).

Declarative Sentence—Inverted Word Order

AS MV | S
It **is thought** *that toothed whales have only one blowhole.*

AS MV | S
It **is** my opinion *that our national defense system is ineffective.*

AS MV | S
It **used to be** true *that we offered a full refund on returned goods.*

AS MV | S
It **is** foolish *to expect a simple answer.*

AS MV | S
It **was** my desire *to alert the accounting department of the error.*

AS MV | S
It **was** necessary *to cut down the whole tree.*

    Ex MV   S

There **are** *whiskers* on the jaws of some whales.

    Ex   MV   S

There **were** *many students who wanted financial aid*.

    Ex MV S

There **is** *a draft* in this room.

In questions, the subject is sometimes placed before the main verb, and sometimes after.

Question—Subject Before Main Verb

       S   MV

Which composer **wrote** "Pictures at·an Exhibition"?

   S   MV

Who **killed** Cock Robin?

    S MV

What **is** meant by "multitudinous seas incardine"?

Question—Subject After Main Verb

           MV S

Which composer **do** *you* like best?

       MV   S

Who **did** *Cock Robin* kill?

       MV   S

What **did** *Shakespeare* mean by "multitudinous seas incardine"?

In **imperative sentences**, the subject (an implied *you*) is usually left unexpressed.

Imperative—Subject (You) Left Unexpressed

   MV

Take out books, pencils, and paper.

MV
Come to the window.

MV
Study chapters four, five, and six for the test.

Exercise

A. Identify the subjects of the following sentences. Suggestions: Ask who or what is performing the action, or who or what the sentence is making an assertion about. Remember that subjects are composed of nouns or noun substitutes and related modifiers. Remember that subjects of declarative sentences normally come before the main verb.

1. The meeting will now come to order.
2. John Adams wrote many letters to his wife Abigail.
3. The author is an outstanding writer of science fiction.
4. The quarterback dropped back for a pass.
5. In August, the locusts began to sing.
6. Knitting is not as difficult as you might think.
7. The trees with the white trunks are birches.
8. To frighten someone with a gun is a punishable offense.
9. Playing the piano requires great manual dexterity.
10. That I got any chance to study is amazing.
11. The geologist, who believed in the theory of evolution, wrote a letter to the editor defending this theory.
12. Beethoven, a virtuoso pianist, often entertained audiences by improvising at the keyboard.
13. Inside the theater, a performance of *Macbeth* was being given.
14. What I admire in Washington is his determination.
15. Keeping pace with the ship, two dolphins surfaced off the starboard bow.

B. Identify the subjects of the sentences in this second set. Remember that in some declarative sentences and in some questions the subject of the sentence comes after the verb or helping verb.

1. There are several weak areas in our defensive strategy.
2. Do you recognize the name James Baldwin?
3. Who won the gold medal in the 1500-meter race?
4. When will the whale surface again?
5. Which of the trees will survive the winter?

● Answers to odd-numbered exercises begin on page 541.

6. Which of the trees will the lumberjacks cut down?
7. There is a terrible fight going on down in the cafeteria.
8. It is astounding that he can sing so many high notes.
9. It was hard to buy books in the bookstore.
10. In your anger, did you hit her?
11. Where the disease will strike next is our big worry.
12. Where will the disease strike next?
13. When making bread, how long must you allow it to rise?
14. It has been a long time since we met.
15. Through the most difficult times, it was Washington's determination to carry on that enabled our nation to survive.

PREDICATE

The predicate (P) of sentences includes verbs or verb phrases, direct and indirect objects, complements, and all related modifiers.

The basis of the predicate is a verb or verb phrase.

Predicate—Single Verb

        S   P
Rabbits *hop*.

        S   P
Bears *hibernate*.

                        S   P
Everyone who sees his performance *weeps*.

        S   P
The car *skidded* on the icy road.

Predicate—Verb Phrase

        S   P
The rabbits *are hopping*.

        S   P
Bears *must hibernate*.

       S   P

Everyone who sees his performance *has to weep.*

    S   P

The car *had skidded* on the icy road.

Whether the predicate will also include a direct object, an indirect object, or a complement depends on the nature of the verb. Intransitive verbs do not require additional words to complete their meaning while transitive verbs and linking verbs do.

Intransitive Verbs Verbs like *hop* and *hibernate* that do not require additional words to complete their meaning are called **intransitive verbs**. Intransitive verbs include—among others—verbs for moving (*come, go, walk, run, tremble*), verbs for making sounds (*whistle, sing, talk*), and verbs for bodily functions (*eat, drink, breathe, sleep*).

    S   P

The dog *trembled.*

    S   P

John *is sleeping.*

    S   P

Spring *has come.*

    S   P

You *must eat.*

In speaking and writing, of course, intransitive verbs are often used with modifiers (Mod)—words, phrases, and clauses that answer the questions *how, why, when, where,* and *to what degree.*

    S   P

         MV Mod   Mod

Robins *sing* merrily in the spring.

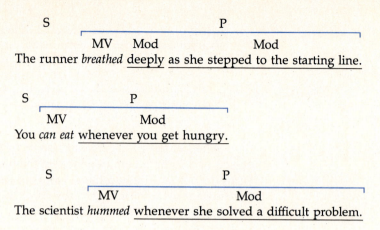

```
  S                                    P
        MV     Mod              Mod
The runner breathed deeply as she stepped to the starting line.
```

```
  S                    P
        MV         Mod
You can eat whenever you get hungry.
```

```
  S                              P
        MV            Mod
The scientist hummed whenever she solved a difficult problem.
```

Transitive Verbs Verbs like *grab, hit, stun,* and *caress* are called **transitive verbs.** Transitive verbs require **direct objects** (DO)—nouns, pronouns, phrases, or noun clauses—to complete their meaning.

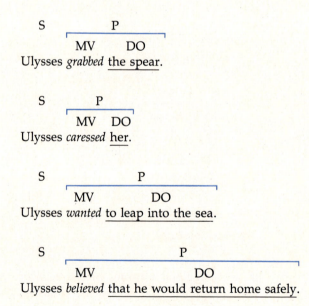

```
  S          P
        MV    DO
Ulysses grabbed the spear.
```

```
  S       P
        MV  DO
Ulysses caressed her.
```

```
  S            P
        MV        DO
Ulysses wanted to leap into the sea.
```

```
  S                        P
        MV            DO
Ulysses believed that he would return home safely.
```

Direct objects receive the action of transitive verbs. (What did Ulysses grab? The *spear.* Who did he caress? *Her.*)

In addition, some transitive verbs like *give, show,* and *tell* require **indirect objects** (IO) as well as direct objects to complete their meaning.

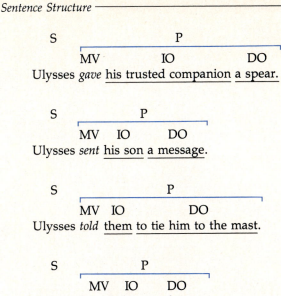

S   P
MV   IO   DO
Ulysses *gave* his trusted companion a spear.

S   P
MV   IO   DO
Ulysses *sent* his son a message.

S   P
MV   IO   DO
Ulysses *told* them to tie him to the mast.

S   P
MV   IO   DO
Ulysses *brought* her good news.

Indirect objects are nouns and pronouns that tell *to whom or what* or *for whom or what* an action is done. (What did Ulysses give? A *spear* [DO]. To whom? His trusted *companion* [IO].)

Some verbs like *eat, drink,* and *read* can be either intransitive or transitive, depending on the context.

Intransitive:

S   P
MV   Mod
Ulysses' men *ate* heartily.

S   P
MV   Mod
Ulysses' men *sailed* between the islands.

Transitive:

S   P
MV   DO   Mod
Ulysses' men *ate* the lotus plants heartily.

```
         S                              P
     ┌──────┐              ┌──────────────────────┐
          MV      DO              Mod
Ulysses' men sailed their ship between the islands.
```

Linking Verbs Linking verbs like *is*, *seem*, and *appear* require *complements*—nouns and adjectives plus modifiers—to complete their meaning.

```
      S     P
     ┌──┐
Ulysses was crafty.
```

```
      S        P
     ┌──────────┐
Ulysses seemed very sleepy.
```

```
      S           P
     ┌──────────────┐
Ulysses appeared ready for action.
```

```
      S                  P
     ┌───────────────────────┐
Ulysses felt torn between two equally strong desires.
```

```
      S       P
     ┌──────────┐
Ulysses was a skillful king.
```

Instead of receiving the action of a verb, a complement is related to the subject of the clause by the linking verb.

Some verbs like *look*, *feel*, *smell*, *taste*, and *sound* are linking verbs in some contexts but not in others.

Linking:

```
      S       P
     ┌──────┐
My father looked weary.
```

```
      S      P
     ┌─────┐
My father felt happy.
```

Intransitive:

```
      S          P
     ┌────────────┐
My father looked wearily at the book.
```

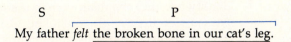

My father *felt* along the seat of the chair.

Transitive:

My father *felt* the broken bone in our cat's leg.

When *looked* and *felt* relate the adjectives *weary* and *happy* back to the subject *father*, they are called linking verbs. As intransitives, *looked* and *felt* do not relate modifiers back to the subject. As a transitive, *felt* takes *the broken bone* as a direct object.

The predicate of a sentence, then, describes the action performed by the subject or asserts something about the subject. In declarative sentences, the predicate usually follows the subject. The basic element in the predicate is the verb or verb phrase. Predicates may also include direct objects, indirect objects, and complements as well as all related modifiers.

Exercise

A. Identify the predicates of the following sentences. Suggestions: Ask what the subject of the sentence did or what the sentence asserts about the subject. Remember that the most important element of the predicate is the main verb. If you can find the main verb, you are well on your way to identifying the predicate of the sentence.

1. The singer opened her mouth.
2. Jonathan dived into the pool.
3. The blue whale is an enormous creature.
4. The team looked exhausted.
5. The Eskimo gave his dogs some meat.
6. Rain forests often contain a wide variety of plants and trees.
7. He told the captain to meet him on the other side of the river.
8. The injured player hoped that his team would win.
9. One of the tragic stories of nineteenth-century America is the expulsion of the Eastern Indians from their tribal territories.
10. With the approach of autumn, hornets begin to make a hive where the queen can lay her eggs.
11. When fishing in groups, white pelicans, which are among America's largest water birds, sometimes swim in a long line, beating the water with their wings to drive the fish before them.
12. What the minister seemed to hope was that the congregation would not make a lot of trouble for him.

● Answers to odd-numbered exercises begin on page 541.

13. To hurt everyone he knows seems to be John's great plan.
14. To hurt everyone he knows, John says the most sarcastic things.
15. Hurting everyone he knows by making sarcastic comments, the bright young man somehow remains able to keep his old friends.

B. Identify whether the main verb in the following sentences is transitive (T), intransitive (I), or linking (L). Remember that transitive verbs take direct (and sometimes indirect) objects, that linking verbs relate complements back to subjects, and that intransitive verbs do not require other words to complete their meanings.

1. His lectures are dull.
2. The mother carried her son into the emergency room of the hospital.
3. The mother carried on about her son until the hospital attendants were forced to subdue her.
4. My grandfather fell down the stairs.
5. My grandfather felled the robber with one punch.
6. Aunt Sophie was sleepy.
7. Aunt Sophie slept for three hours every afternoon.
8. The singer cracked three eggs on the edge of a bowl.
9. The singer's voice cracked on a high note.
10. *The Great Gatsby*, a novel by F. Scott Fitzgerald, reads quite easily.
11. Many years ago, I read F. Scott Fitzgerald's novel *The Great Gatsby*.
12. Professor Jones looked sick today.
13. Professor Jones looked over his class notes while still in his office.
14. Running on railroad ties is not a sport for the clumsy.
15. Running on railroad ties appears to be his only physical outlet.

PHRASES AND CLAUSES

A **phrase** (Ph) is a group of related words that act as a unit within a sentence, a clause or another phrase. A phrase differs from a clause in that a phrase lacks a subject, a predicate, or both. There are several types of phrases: noun phrase, verb phrase, verbal phrase, prepositional phrase.

A **noun phrase** (NPh) consists of a noun and its single-word modifiers.

      NPh   NPh
The choir sang *the anthem* beautifully.

NPh   NPh
The weary hiker took off *her heavy backpack.*

NPh
John Adams was *an energetic person.*

NPh   NPh
All the king's horses and *all the king's men* couldn't put Humpty together again.

NPh   NPh
Most football players are larger and heavier than *baseball players.*

NPh   NPh
The experienced hiker knew she could not wear *her friend's boots.*

A **verb phrase** (VPh) consists of an auxiliary verb or a modal verb plus infinitive(s), participle(s), and modifying adverbs.

Verb Phrase—Auxiliary Verb plus Infinitive

VPh
Did the teacher *understand* your question?

VPh
My dog *does not like* dry dog food.

VPh
But we *do understand* your problem.

Verb Phrase—Auxiliary Verb plus Participle

VPh
Blue jays *were screeching* from the treetops.

VPh
The solution *was heated* to the boiling point.

VPh
That day the soldiers *had marched* for 20 miles.

VPh
Both teams *have been playing hard* all afternoon.

Verb Phrase—Modal Verb plus Infinitive

> VPh
> The author *could not finish* the book on time.

> VPh
> Many diabetics *must take* daily insulin injections.

> Vph
> Our team *should have easily beaten* theirs.

> VPh
> I *would like to have found* a job in my hometown.

A **verbal phrase** (VbPh) consists of an infinitive, participle, or gerund plus related subjects, direct and indirect objects, complements, and modifiers.

Verbal Phrase with Infinitive

> VbPh
> It is difficult for me *to show her my love.*

> VbPh
> She has a long way *to go.*

> VbPh
> *To appear nonchalant,* she lit another cigarette.

Verbal Phrase with Participle

> VbPh
> *Turning quickly,* she departed.

> VbPh
> *Having completed Phase One,* we can now start on Phase Two.

> VbPh
> The pharmacist carefully locked up the store, *fearing that thieves might break in.*

Verbal Phrase with Gerund

> VbPh
> *Eating health food* is supposed to be good for you.

VbPh
She loved *painting portraits* of famous people.

VbPh
Running marathons gives him great satisfaction.

Infinitive phrases act as nouns, adjectives, and adverbs: "To show her my love" acts as the real subject of the first sentence above; "to go" modifies the noun *way*; "to appear nonchalant" modifies the verb *lit*. Participial phrases act as adjectives: "Turning quickly" and "Having completed Phase One" modify the subjects of their respective sentences. Gerund phrases act as nouns: "Eating health food" is the subject of its sentence; "painting portraits" is the direct object of the verb *loved*.

A **prepositional phrase** (PrPh) consists of a preposition and its object. A noun, noun phrase, or noun equivalent (pronoun, gerund or gerund phrase, or noun clause) can be the object of a preposition.

PrPh
The governor avoided questions *about economics.*

PrPh
The diver plunged *into the icy waters.*

PrPh
We have done all we could *for her.*

PrPh
For answering our questions, we will give you an attractive gift.

PrPh
There are many problems *with what you are trying to do.*

Prepositional phrases act as adjectives or adverbs: "About economics" modifies the noun *questions*; "into the icy waters" modifies the verb *plunged*.

Exercise

In the following sentences, identify the noun phrases (NPh), verb phrases (VPh), verbal phrases (VbPh), and prepositional phrases (PrPh). Consider noun phrases within verbal and prepositional phrases as part of the larger phrase.

• Answers to odd-numbered exercises begin on page 541.

1. Our cat loves to sleep on our comforter.
2. Strumming his guitar, John set the rhythm for the band.
3. The violinist now wants to play the piano.
4. Teachers should return papers quickly.
5. Whales must be able to withstand the cold of their environment.
6. The tree specialists came today to spray all the maple trees on our property.
7. After a hard day at work, my father would take a long nap before he ate dinner.
8. Requiring students to write papers seems to make some professors happy.
9. To set up a field goal possibility, the quarterback decided to throw a pass to the tight-end.
10. Fully expecting to be fired, Sue opened the door to her boss' office.
11. Having wanted for a long time to play racquetball with each other, the boys finally decided to telephone each other to make a date.
12. The concert choir would like to have been chosen to represent the United States in the international choral competition.
13. The students would have greatly preferred to have been allowed to have gone fishing.
14. Our Western capitalist economies have traditionally been subject to severe financial declines.
15. In bringing the news to the listening public, our all-news station must have news crews on the street twenty-four hours a day.

Both **independent clauses** (IC) and **dependent clauses** (DC) are groups of related words containing a subject *and* predicate. However, unlike an independent clause, a dependent clause can function as a noun, adjective, or adverb but cannot function as a complete sentence. Dependent clauses begin with a relative pronoun or subordinating conjunction (see pp. 445 and 447), words that are almost always expressed but can, under certain conditions, be implied. In the following examples, note how the use of a relative pronoun or subordinating conjunction turns an independent clause into a dependent clause.

IC

He had just broken the phonograph record.

DC

that he had just broken the phonograph record

DC

because he had just broken the phonograph record

DC
which he had just broken

As they stand, the last three clauses are incomplete and need to be used with an independent clause in order to make sense.

IC
DC
The disc jockey said *that he had just broken the phonograph record.*

IC
DC
That he had just broken the phonograph record made the disc jockey angry with himself.

IC   DC
The disc jockey was angry *because he had just broken the phonograph record.*

IC   DC
The caller requested the record *which he had just broken.*

Dependent clauses can take the place of nouns within an independent clause.

Dependent Clause as Noun Clause

DC
My hope was *that I would lose fifteen pounds in five days.*

Dependent clauses can act as adjectives and adverbs, modifying some element in another clause or modifying the entire clause.

Dependent Clause as Adjectival Clause

DC
Bull seals *that survive the winter* return to their mating grounds in early spring.

DC
I can remember a time *when milk was brought to the house in a horse-drawn wagon.*

These dependent clauses function like adjectives because they modify the nouns *seals* and *time.*

Dependent Clause as Adverbial Clause

DC
When I first came to the campus, I felt quite frightened.

DC
He will come to dinner *if you promise to bake a cake.*

These dependent clauses function like adverbs because they modify the verbs *felt* and *come.*

Most dependent clauses begin with a **subordinating conjunction** (*as, if, when, although, since, how, whether, that*) or a **relative pronoun** (*who, whose, whom, which, that*). However, the subordinating conjunction is sometimes omitted from noun clauses that are direct objects of verbs.

Noun Clause—Subordinating Conjunction Omitted

DC
The disc jockey said (. . .) *he had just broken the phonograph record.*

DC
She believed (. . .) *she could conquer the world.*

DC
He thought (. . .) *the world owed him a living.*

DC
The champion claimed (. . .) *she'd never play tennis again.*

Also, relative pronouns that are objects of verbs or prepositions are sometimes omitted from the sentence.

Adjective Clause—Relative Pronoun as Object Omitted

DC
The one nation (. . .) *he failed to conquer* was Russia.

DC

The thirsty hiker drank the water (. . .) *she found in an old rain barrel*.

DC

The only people (. . .) *she knows* are scientists.

Some words that act as subordinating conjunctions or relative pronouns can play other roles in sentences, too. The function these words fulfill in any given sentence, therefore, can only be determined through careful analysis. Certain words like *before, after, as, since,* and *until* can be both subordinating conjunctions and prepositions.

Subordinating Conjunction

After the party was over, Bill spent three hours cleaning up his apartment.

Preposition

After the party, Bill spent three hours cleaning up his apartment.

To recognize the function of a word like *after,* you need to check whether the unit it introduces does or does not contain a subject and predicate. *That* can be a subordinating conjunction or a relative pronoun.

Subordinating Conjunction—Signals Noun Clause

Jefferson believed *that all men were created equal*.

Relative Pronoun—Signals Adjective Clause

Jefferson believed in the idea *that all men are created equal*.

In the first of these sentences, *that* introduces a unit which stands as the object of *believed*. In the second, *that* introduces a unit that defines *idea*. *Who, whose, whom,* and *which* can function as relative pronouns and interrogative pronouns (words that signal a direct question).

Relative Pronoun

Jefferson, *who* owned many slaves, claimed that all men are created equal.

Interrogative Pronoun

Who wrote that all men are created equal?

Where, when, and *what* can function as subordinating conjunctions and interrogative pronouns.

Subordinating Conjunction

What I think is none of your business.

Interrogative Pronoun

What interest do you have in my business?

Exercise

A. Identify the dependent clauses in the following sentences. Suggestion: Look for a subordinating conjunction or a relative pronoun followed by a verb. (However, remember that the subordinating conjunction is sometimes omitted from noun clauses that function as direct objects, and that occasionally the subordinating conjunction of noun clauses or the relative pronoun of adjective clauses is omitted. In such instances, look for a group of related words containing a subject and predicate that functions as a noun or an adjective.)

1. My father, who did not go beyond the eighth grade in school, earned a good living as a carpenter.
2. I was told Japanese husbands and wives do not go out on dates together very often.
3. If Milton were living today, he might never have gone blind.
4. The class he spoke to seemed very receptive to him.
5. She changes into her jogging clothes as soon as she gets home from work.
6. Whether extraterrestrial life exists is not the question.
7. The teenagers returned to the pool where the monster lived.
8. Because I didn't know the answer, I had to guess.
9. My father must have been sick for years before he died.
10. If a creature from Mars landed on this campus today, what would it think of us?
11. Wishing he had gone into some other work, the opera singer, who had a sore throat, went onto the stage to sing his big aria.
12. The mother he left in a Denver nursing home said she still loved him.
13. He wondered what he thought he was doing when he painted his new car with a product he had never even tried.
14. Since the last time he had seen Ellen they had had a fight, he wondered how he would react when she came to the meeting.
15. The soldiers were about to open fire when the house they had surrounded exploded with a roar that was heard twenty miles away.

B.   Now that you have identified the dependent clauses in the sentences above, identify each clause as a noun, adjectival, or adverbial clause.   ✂

SENTENCE TYPES
Simple Sentences

The basis of a sentence is the independent clause. A clause is labeled **independent** if it is grammatically complete in itself. The following are independent clauses.

> The committee will meet tomorrow.
> Does the committee meet tomorrow?
> The cowboy stayed on the wild steer for thirty seconds.
> The price of soybeans has fallen.

As the punctuation indicates, these independent clauses are also sentences. Sentences that consist of a single independent clause are called **simple sentences**. Independent clauses can be simple sentences even if they have a **compound subject** or a **compound predicate**.

Simple Sentence with Compound Subject

S

The manager and her secretary went out to lunch.

S

The maples and birches swayed in the wind.

S

Jogging, swimming, and cycling are good aerobic activities.

S

My brothers and sisters, my mother and father, and all my cousins met at the farm for a family reunion.

Simple Sentence with Compound Predicate

S   P

The manager *hung up the telephone and lit a cigarette.*

● Answers to odd-numbered exercises begin on page 541.

S   P

The maples *pitched and tossed in the high wind.*

S   P

Jogging *strengthens the heart and lungs but is hard on the knees and*

ankles.

S   P

My cousins *met at the farm, changed into swimsuits, and went for a*

refreshing swim.

Simple Sentence with Compound Subject and Predicate

S   P

The manager and her secretary went to lunch at noon and returned at

1 p.m.

S   P

The maples and birches pitched and tossed in the high wind.

Subjects are compound if they contain at least two nouns (and/or noun substitutes) joined by a **coordinating conjunction** (*and, or, but, for, nor, yet*). Predicates are compound if they contain at least two verbs or verb phrases joined by a coordinating conjunction.

If a sentence contains a single independent clause, it is a simple sentence, no matter how many verbal phrases (see p. 460) it may contain.

Simple Sentence with Verbal Phrases

VbPh

After having been high for so long, gasoline prices have fallen, *declining*

VbPh

three cents through December and another three cents during January.

VbPh   VbPh   VbPh

Rushing over rocks, tumbling through the ravine, pouring off a cliff,

VbPh

and thundering down onto the stream bed below, the river made its way toward the ocean.

Compound Sentences

Compound sentences contain at least two independent clauses joined by a coordinating conjunction (see p. 446) or semicolon.

Independent Clauses Joined by a Coordinating Conjunction

IC

Busing may be a way to restore racial balance to the public schools, or

IC

it may be a way to accelerate middle class flight to the suburbs.

IC   IC

I like jogging, but *I like singing even more.*

When two independent clauses are joined by a coordinating conjunction, the conjunction is preceded by a comma.

Independent Clauses Joined by a Semicolon

IC   IC

Most land mammals have vocal cords; whales do not.

IC

For most of the year, my hometown is quite peaceful; however, *every April*

IC

its peace is broken by crowds of young people coming to town to see the state high school basketball tournament.

Words like *however, consequently, nevertheless, therefore,* and *thus* are called **conjunctive adverbs** because they simultaneously act like conjunctions and adverbs. Like coordinating conjunctions, they can join independent clauses to form a compound sentence. Like adverbs, they can be moved to a number of positions in a clause.

For most of the year, my hometown is quite peaceful; *however,* every April its peace is broken by crowds. . . .

For most of the year, my hometown is quite peaceful; every April, *however,* its peace is broken by crowds. . . .

For most of the year, my hometown is quite peaceful; every April its peace is broken, *however,* by crowds. . . .

Because they can be moved to various positions, conjunctive adverbs are used with semicolons to prevent misreadings. For example, suppose you wanted to join these two independent clauses with *however*:

My hometown is quite peaceful.
In the spring its peace is broken by crowds of young people.

If you separated the two clauses with a comma instead of a semicolon, the reader might initially interpret "in the spring" as belonging to the first independent clause. The slashes in the illustration below highlight this misreading:

My hometown is quite peaceful, however, in the spring // its peace is broken by crowds of young people.

With a semicolon before *however,* this misreading is prevented:

My hometown is quite peaceful; however, in the spring its peace is broken by crowds of young people.

Complex Sentences

Sentences are complex if they contain a dependent clause.

IC   DC

Whales have skin *that is quite smooth and thin.*

DC   IC

When I tell people about my fear of the devil, they usually laugh at me.

IC   DC

Like American men, Japanese men feel *that they must not talk about their feelings.*

A dependent clause is separated from the independent clause with a comma in these situations:

1. The dependent clause is an introductory adverbial clause:

DC

When I dive beneath the surface of the clear waters around Bermuda, I

IC

enter a beautiful and strange world.

2. An adverbial clause is only loosely connected with the independent clause it follows:

IC

A salesclerk is taught never to stop a shoplifter, *even if the clerk*

DC

is big enough to play tight end for the Dallas Cowboys.

3. An adverbial clause is placed between elements of the independent clause:

IC   DC

A salesclerk, *even if he is big enough to play tight end for the Dallas Cow-*

IC

boys, is taught never to stop a shoplifter.

4. An adjective clause is *nonrestrictive:*

IC   DC

Abigail Adams, *who spent many years separated from her husband,*

IC

became quite skillful at managing the family's business affairs.

IC   DC

Ulysses had himself tied to the mast of his ship, *which was about to*

sail past the coast of the Sirens.

Restrictive and Nonrestrictive Clauses   A **nonrestrictive clause** gives information that is not essential to the meaning of the sentence. Hence, commas are used to separate the clause from the rest of the sentence.

A **restrictive clause** gives essential information that limits or defines meanings. Hence, no commas separate the clause from the rest of the sentence.

Compare the sentence above about Abigail Adams with the following:

        IC   DC

Women *who spend years separated from their husbands* often become

                      IC

quite skillful at managing the family's business affairs.

In this sentence, the information in the dependent clause is essential; it limits the meaning of the sentence to one group of women rather than to all women. In the sentence about Abigail Adams, the clause gives relevant but nonessential information: The clause is not needed to identify the person who became skillful at managing family affairs since she is already identified by name.

Compound-Complex Sentences

Sentences are **compound-complex** if they contain at least two independent clauses and at least one dependent clause.

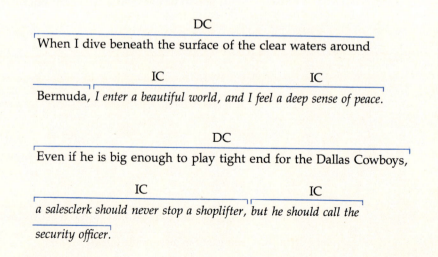

                     DC

When I dive beneath the surface of the clear waters around

           IC   IC

Bermuda, *I enter a beautiful world,* and *I feel a deep sense of peace.*

                     DC

Even if he is big enough to play tight end for the Dallas Cowboys,

           IC   IC

a salesclerk should never stop a shoplifter, but *he should call the*

security officer.

Exercise

A. Identify each of the following sentences as simple (S), compound (C), complex (CX), or compound-complex (C-CX).

1. George Washington wrote out his own military orders.
2. Israel is a tiny nation; however, it is a military giant in comparison to its neighbors.
3. Although Israel is a tiny nation, it is a military giant in comparison to its neighbors.
4. The wide receiver outran the defensive back, but the quarterback threw the ball over the receiver's head.
5. She knows what she wants.
6. The company has lost over $200 thousand this year; nevertheless, the president has decided to keep the entire work force on the payroll.
7. Italy and Greece were once the centers of great empires, but now they are fairly small and weak nations.
8. Italy and Greece were once the centers of great empires but are now fairly small and weak nations.
9. The left guard was followed closely by the tailback as they swept around the end of the line, avoided several tacklers, and plunged across the goal line.
10. The left guard, followed closely by the tailback, swept around the end of the line, avoided several tacklers, and plunged across the goal line.
11. Although the president knows that the company is not doing well and that the annual report will show substantial losses, he has refused to fire anyone.
12. If the president, who all along has refused to fire anyone, continues to maintain this position, he will be risking his job, but he will also be earning the respect of his employees.
13. Running the rapids, fishing in the deep pools, picnicking along the banks, sleeping in tents through the warm nights, Jill and Eve canoed along the river through the end of August and on into the beginning of September.
14. Running rapids that threatened to capsize their canoe and then drifting along stretches where the current was slow, Jill and Eve were sometimes frightened and sometimes bored.
15. Even though they had spent over a month together canoeing down the river, Jill and Eve felt they had not come to know each other well, but they were still happy they had use their vacation this way.

B. The following sentences have deliberately been printed without commas or semicolons to separate clauses. In which of these sentences should a comma or semicolon be used to separate clauses? Where should the mark of punctuation be placed?

1. As I was coming out of the anesthesia I could see two of everything.
2. The hostages who were killed will be buried tomorrow.
3. Our employees look forward to the time when the new parking ramp will be finished.
4. When the new parking ramp is completed our employees will find parking much more convenient.
5. George Washington who was one of the tallest men in the American Colonies made an impressive figure on horseback.
6. Adams and Jefferson were friends in their earlier years and toward the very end of their lives however for a time in their middle years their friendship waned.
7. Adams did want the President to be addressed with the deepest respect though it was not a major point of policy during his time in office.
8. Jones decided to take the matter to his boss who had often helped him put problems into perspective.
9. Benjamin Franklin never went to college yet he became one of the wisest men in the American Revolution.
10. John and Abigail Adams were separated for many years of their married life nevertheless their love for each other continued undiminished.
11. Adams recognized that Franklin was an excellent politician but felt uncomfortable about the manner Franklin adopted in pursuing the nation's business.
12. The new parking ramp will be completed in about six months after which time employees will once again be permitted to park on the company's premises.
13. Eve who had accompanied Jill on a long canoeing trip wondered whether they would ever become good friends or whether they would remain just acquaintances.
14. Evans threw the ball to Tinker who then threw to Chance even though Chance had been slow in getting up off the ground and running to first base.
15. If Tinker should ever learn to play his position correctly he and Evans will make a great combination but I doubt that he will ever improve.

COMMON USAGE ERRORS

The previous sections of this Handbook define and illustrate the basic elements of English—its parts of speech and sentence elements. The purpose of those sections is to improve your understanding of the basic grammar of the language and the terms used to describe that grammar. This section on common usage errors identifies deviations from edited English that can irritate and confuse your audience. The section also gives you practice in identifying and correcting such problems so as to strengthen your ability to edit them out of your own writing.

SENTENCE ERRORS
Comma Splice

cs

A comma splice is the use of a comma rather than a period or semicolon to separate independent clauses. This error frequently occurs when the two independent clauses are closely related in meaning or when the second begins with a conjunctive adverb (see p. 443).

Faulty: Our team could no longer lose any games, we had to win.
Faulty: Many Irishmen became policemen, hence we have the old stereotype of the Irish cop.
Faulty: People look with awe at the woman who is the president of a large corporation, they look down on the homemaker.
Faulty: The reason you practice is not to make yourself better, it is to help the team win.

A comma signals the separation between sentence elements that are less important than independent clauses. Hence, using a comma instead of a period or semicolon gives your reader a false clue to your meaning.

If you make this error, you will need to give extra attention to your use of commas as you edit your writing. Go through your paper one time looking at commas and nothing else. Be particularly on the lookout for commas that separate independent clauses. When you find such commas, you can change them to periods or semicolons, add a coordinating conjunction, or rewrite the entire sentence.

Acceptable: Our teams could no longer lose any games. We had to win.
Acceptable: Many Irishmen became policemen; hence, we have the old stereotype of the Irish cop.
Acceptable: People look with awe at the woman who is the president of a large corporation, but they look down on the homemaker.
Acceptable: You practice to help the team win rather than to make yourself a better player.

Exercise

The following sentences are either correctly punctuated, or they are examples of comma splices. Find and correct the errors.

1. Start the engine to warm the oil, then shut the engine off.

● Answers to odd-numbered exercises begin on page 541.

2. During peak hours, visitors find the parking ramp full, consequently, they have to find a parking place on the street.
3. The author intends his child characters to be more than just cute, they play an important role in expressing the theme of the story.
4. The typical pioneer businessman did not become discouraged, even when scheme after scheme resulted in failure.
5. Changing oil is a simple procedure, however, to change your oil you must be familiar with the location of the engine's crankcase.
6. Humiliated by the men who served under him, the president became a victim of situations over which he had very little control.
7. This part of the story does have value, it shows how Joe vents his anger toward his wife.
8. Whenever I heated the solution, it started to boil over, sending out pink vapors.
9. After she came back from her canoeing trip with Jill, Eve left home for Colorado, she just needed to get away by herself for a while.
10. My favorite Country and Western singer will be in town on Friday, he will appear at Bronco Billy's Bar.
11. The employees at our Joliet plant have gone on strike, protesting working conditions, they are concerned about the amount of asbestos in the air.
12. Lincoln was known as a kindly, good-natured man, his basic good humor came out in the many jokes he told.
13. Bald eagles used to be a fairly common type of American bird, they now are concentrated mostly in Alaska and Florida.
14. Lincoln's death shocked people into recognizing what a great man he was, what enduring qualities he had that would make him stand out among our nation's presidents.
15. Usually, the male red-winged blackbirds arrive in the area first, they come early to establish nesting territories. *fs*

Fused Sentence

A fused sentence lacks any mark of punctuation to show the separation between independent clauses.

Faulty: In high school you hated to lose in college you're afraid to lose.
Faulty: The judgment of players and spectators makes no difference to the referee his own judgment is all that matters.

Because the independent clauses are not properly separated, the sentences are very confusing.

When you find a fused sentence in editing your paper, you can correct the error by inserting a period, semicolon, or comma and coordinating conjunction at the appropriate place, or by rewriting the entire sentence.

Acceptable: In high school you hated to lose. In college you're afraid to lose.

Acceptable: In high school you hated to lose; in college you're afraid to lose.

Acceptable: The judgment of players and spectators makes no difference to the referee, for his own judgment is all that matters.

Acceptable: A referee must ignore spectators and players and rely entirely on his own judgment.

Exercise

The following sentences are either correctly punctuated, or they are examples of fused sentences. Find and correct the errors.

1. Fluorescent lights would cost a total of $360 I know that we would need an electrician to install new light fixtures.

2. The diamonds to be found in the field come in sizes ranging up to six carats and can be scooped up or picked up with any object that can be carried in one hand.

3. The white-footed mouse is one of the most common species of mice in the United States it is also a common winter prey of owls because it runs across the snow instead of tunneling under it.

4. The naturalist had walked for miles in search of someone with a tractor to pull his car out of the mud in the barnyard where it was stuck.

5. One of Lee's most important mistakes was believing in his own invincibility he had just had too much success in the South and believed that he could push out beyond his lines into the North.

6. One theory of the origin of comets is that they are produced from planets or their satellites another is that they were produced at the formation of our solar system.

7. After the defeats at Gettysburg and Vicksburg, a growing sense that defeat was inevitable began to grip the South, a sense that increasingly led Southerners to insist that their leaders sue for peace with the North.

8. Cost accountants try to measure the degree of sacrifice involved in certain activities to do so they may use data gathered on day-to-day activities.

9. The boll weevil is one of the 500 insect species that are harmful to cotton luckily the boll weevil can be controlled through the application of various insecticides.

10. The credit union in our plant has so outgrown its office that on payday the line of workers waiting to cash their checks goes down the hall about 100 feet.

11. On many of the Greek islands the natives use an unusual kind of windmill it has small triangles of cloth to catch the wind these are positioned at the ends of poles that swivel around a central axle.

12. Unlike baseball, cricket is played with eleven players another difference is that the cricket bat is flat like a paddle rather than cylindrical.

● Answers to odd-numbered exercises begin on page 541.

13. Crocodiles lie in wait for their prey with just their eyes and nostrils above the water when the prey comes to the stream to drink, the crocodile attacks.

14. A naval cruiser is larger than a destroyer but smaller than a battleship it has light armor and guns that are not as large as those of the battleship thus it has greater mobility than a battleship.

15. Since Cuba lies in the northern part of the tropical zone of the western hemisphere, the temperature on the island does not vary more than 40 degrees throughout the year, a fact which means that the seasons we know in the northern United States simply do not occur there.

Sentence Fragment

frag.

A sentence fragment is an incomplete construction that is punctuated as though it were a complete sentence. The sentence fragment may be a phrase or group of phrases or even a dependent clause. Very often sentence fragments are continuations of preceding sentences and should be punctuated accordingly. The following examples give both the preceding sentence and the sentence fragment (in italics).

Faulty: My history midterm was completely unfair. *Especially since it covered material that had not even been assigned or discussed in class.*

Faulty: Referees are always in demanding situations, constantly making split-second decisions. *Decisions that can make the difference in the outcome of the game.*

Faulty: People would sit and express their opinions on various topics or just tell jokes. *Like a doctor or a lawyer sitting at the bar of the local country club.*

To spot sentence fragments, read your paper sentence by sentence from the end backwards to the beginning, testing each sentence for completeness. When you spot a sentence fragment, incorporate it into the preceding sentence or rewrite it as a complete sentence.

Acceptable: My history midterm was completely unfair, especially since it covered material that had not even been assigned or discussed in class.

Acceptable: Referees are always in demanding situations, constantly making split-second decisions, decisions that can make the difference in the outcome of the game.

Acceptable: People would sit and express their opinions on various topics or just tell jokes. They seemed just like doctors or lawyers sitting at the bar of the local country club.

Exercise

A. The following sentences are either complete sentences or sentence fragments. Pick out the sentence fragments and make them complete sentences.

1. Whereas the competition at the Southland Mall is quite substantial.
2. While he was in his beloved South, Lee experienced great success, success that may have gone to his head and caused him to move his operations northward into Pennsylvania.
3. While the way to distinguish the turkey vulture from the eagle at a distance is to observe the way the bird holds its wings.
4. Although the two birds have similar wingspreads, the turkey vulture holds its wings in an upward *V* while the eagle holds its wings flat.
5. Which meant that, even though Lee had a well-fed army whose morale was tremendously high, he and his loyal forces suffered defeat at the hands of a Union force which should not have been any match for them.
6. Although Lincoln, despite the good feelings many people had for him, was often criticized by the press and by the abolitionists, who felt that he had delayed too long in freeing the slaves.
7. Who said that the sandhill crane's diet consists mostly of vegetable matter, even though it eats insects and crayfish as well?
8. Including drop cloths, putty knife, spackling compound, roller, pan, and a stepladder tall enough to allow you to reach the ceiling while standing on the second step from the top.
9. Yet is connected to a support post by a hollow plastic valve that allows a vacuum to build up inside when the entire chamber is rotated to a vertical position.
10. Running with his head held back and his arms pumping like windmills, the track star won the race by several meters, even though he had broken every rule of proper form.
11. Feet that screw up or down to adjust the instrument to the proper height so that the top of the instrument is perfectly level and so that the instrument can be conveniently used.
12. Despite our efforts to keep the nestlings alive, they all eventually died.
13. Who told the story of a Danish princess that lost her husband, son, and brother in a series of battles.
14. All of which makes me wonder about the character's morality and ask what it was that made her fall in love with a man whose wife was confined to a wheelchair.
15. Since she was truly still a kitten and was not yet used to our strange way of living.

B. The following paragraph contains comma splices, fused sentences, sentence fragments, and acceptable sentences. Rewrite the para-

● Answers to odd-numbered exercises begin on page 541.

graph, correcting the errors. (The sentences are numbered for your convenience in checking your answers in the Answer Guide.)

(1) When I think of Abraham Lincoln, I find my mind filled with certain pictures. (2) Some from childhood stories about "Honest Abe." (3) Some from his statue in the Lincoln Memorial. (4) Some from my reading of American history. (5) In one picture little Abe is doing his homework by the firelight in another Abe the shopkeeper is walking miles to give back a few pennies of change. (6) Or tirelessly splitting logs. (7) The Abe Lincoln in these mental pictures is physically strong, homely, gaunt, the Abe Lincoln of my mental pictures is also saintly and patient. (8) He has a sad but kindly face and powerful but gentle hands. (9) He does not have personal problems to worry him. (10) Only the problems of the nation. (11) He has no grief over a dead son, he has no wife who is on the verge of going crazy. (12) To add such personal difficulties to the stress of being president during the Civil War seems wrong no one could bear up under such double difficulties. (13) The Abe Lincoln of my mental pictures is a sixteen-foot-tall hero who single-handedly held the nation together through its time of trouble.

AGREEMENT AND REFERENCE ERRORS
Number Agreement —Subject and Verb

Edited English requires that verbs agree in number with their subject. Number agreement errors are especially frequent in the following constructions.

agr 1 **Subject Separated from Main Verb** The number agreement rule is particularly hard to observe when the subject is separated from the main verb by an intervening element. In the following examples of faulty number agreement, the number of the main verb is determined not by the subject (as it should be) but by the noun immediately before the verb.

Faulty: A major trend toward rising health care *costs have* affected local and national businesses.

Faulty: Dr. Smith's views on the emotional topic of *abortion is* very disturbing.

In the first sentence, *trend* is the subject; hence, the main verb should be *has*. In the second, *views* is the subject; hence, the main verb should be *are*.

Acceptable: A major *trend* toward rising health care costs *has* affected local and national businesses.

Acceptable: Dr. Smith's *views* on the emotional topic of abortion *are* very disturbing.

There Is/Are Because the subject comes after the verb in clauses beginning *there is/are*, it is easy to make number agreement errors when using this construction.

Faulty: There *is* too many *boys* who want to try out for the football team.
Faulty: There *is* several *rooms* that need to be painted.
Acceptable: There *are* too many *boys* who want to try out for the football team.
Acceptable: There *are* several *rooms* that need to be painted.

Compound Subjects Compound subjects sometimes take a singular, sometimes a plural verb. You can reduce any uncertainty you may have about whether to use a singular or a plural form by learning the rules for number agreement between compound subjects and main verbs:

1. Singular nouns joined by *and*—use a plural verb.

   The robin and the hermit thrush *belong* [not *belongs*] to the same family of birds.
   The pitcher and the catcher *are* [not *is*] the most important players on a baseball team.

2. Singular nouns joined by *or, nor,* or *but*—use a singular verb.

   A robin or a bluebird *is* [not *are*] sitting on the edge of the birdbath.
   Neither John nor Jean *writes* [not *write*] as well as I do.

3. Compound subject with a singular and a plural noun joined by *or, nor,* or *but*—make the verb agree in number with the noun nearest to it.

   Neither the father nor his three sons *play* [not *plays*] very well.
   Not only the three sons but also their father *plays* [not *play*] tennis at our country club.

Subject and Complement of to be *Differ in Number* The verb *to be* agrees with its subject even when the subject differs in number from the complement.

   Our love of freedom and the strength of our will *are* [not *is*] our best protection against our enemies.
   The outcome we should fear most *is* [not *are*] overpopulation and starvation.

Indefinite Pronouns The indefinite pronouns *anyone, each, everyone, everybody, no one, nobody, somebody,* and *something* take singular verb forms.

Each of his sisters *has* [not *have*] red hair.
Everybody in the class *warms up* [not *warm up*] before exercising.

Exercise

Some of the following sentences contain errors in number agreement between subject and verb. Find and correct these errors.

1. Each of the squirrels were busy hiding nuts in the garden.
2. There's twenty-five girls waiting to try out to be cheerleaders.
3. Anyone who buys his or her yearbook before November 12th will pay the discount price.
4. During the first eight measures of the piece, John and Tanya are going to stand up to play their instruments.
5. The results of the fiercely contested election, in which the outcome was uncertain even up to the last minute, has now been tabulated.
6. Neither the captain nor the rookies likes the new uniforms.
7. Many students living away from home for the first time finds it difficult to make friends.
8. There's too many books to read in Mr. Johnson's course.
9. In chess, the bishop, the queen, and the king moves on the diagonal.
10. Neither the bishops nor the queen jumps over other men.
11. The smart swimmer who wants to avoid allergic reactions to the chemicals used to purify the water in swimming pools wears protective goggles.
12. Neither the club members nor their adviser see the need for dues.
13. The differences between the two computers is the basis for my analysis.
14. Each of the cars and trucks being produced by our two assembly lines are undercoated with our special salt-resistant coating.
15. The suggestion you make in your report that placing an optical department in our pharmacy would severely reduce our profits come as a real surprise.

Number Agreement —Pronoun and Antecedent

agr 2

Pronouns agree in number with their antecedents, the nouns which they replace and to which they refer.

A *child* may feel awkward discussing family matters in front of *his* or *her* [not *their*] classmates.
Children may feel awkward discussing family matters in front of *their* classmates.

You may find yourself unsure whether to use a singular or a plural pronoun when the antecedent is an indefinite pronoun (see p. 444). Although usage on this point is changing, in situations calling for edited English you should use a singular pronoun. Contemporary usage avoids using just the masculine pronoun when both sexes are meant (not just *he*, but *he or she*, *he/she*).

> *Everybody* was minding *his* or *her* [not *their*] own business.
> *Each* of the players has *his* [not *their*] own cleats.
> If *anyone* finds a flaw in your material, *he* or *she* [not *they*] will criticize you severely.

You can avoid awkward *he or she* contructions by recasting the sentence in the plural.

> If *people* find flaws in your material, *they* will criticize you severely.

Exercise

Some of the following sentences contain number agreement errors between pronoun and antecedent. Find and correct these errors.

1. A person who wants to participate in the six-mile race on Sunday should send in their entry form by Thursday.
2. All the boys on the team were expected to bring their uniforms.
3. Every politician—no matter whether at the local, state, or federal level—likes to have their name in the newspaper.
4. A patient often feels awkward moving around the hospital dressed only in their hospital gown.
5. Medieval ladies and queens often had to rule the manor or the kingdom in their husband's absence.
6. Somebody who knows how to repair this computer will have to bring their special tools along on the job.
7. A police officer does not like to show fear or even indecision when being watched by their fellow officers.
8. People from the accounting and sales department take their coffee break at 10:45 A.M.
9. None of the men in the division who had seen the incident could believe their eyes.
10. One thousand Wings' supporters came out to meet their team when the chartered flight landed at 2 A.M. this morning at Hays Airfield.

• Answers to odd-numbered exercises begin on page 541.

Vague Reference

ref

Make sure that pronouns refer to specific noun or pronoun antecedents. Be especially careful about using *this* or *that* to refer to a whole sentence and *which* to refer to a whole clause.

Faulty: Friends and family put a lot of emphasis on the way you perform in the game, *which* made losing easier.

Faulty: Dr. Adler may feel that he is to blame for Wilhelm's failure. *This* could account for the doctor's actions throughout the story.

Acceptable: Friends and family put a lot of emphasis on the way you performed in the game. *Their emphasis on how well you played made losing a lot easier.*

Acceptable: Dr. Adler may feel that he is to blame for Wilhelm's failure. *The doctor's guilt* could account for his actions throughout the story.

Exercise

Some of the following sentences contain vague references to pronouns. Find the errors and correct them.

1. Our pilot has prepared a status report on our company's aircraft. It will give you a brief review of its past utilization, peformance, and capabilities.
2. The valley contains a tremendous number of bird species, which shows that it ought to be declared a bird sanctuary.
3. In 1979, the Transportation Department became a part of the Marketing and Distribution team, which enabled Transportation to be directly involved with the various Operating Divisions' goals and strategic plans.
4. We obtained the average balance for each center for 1980. This should provide some understanding of the distribution of charge sales. This should be as follows: Center #1—37.8% charge sales; Center #2—6.4% charge sales.
5. After John had fixed the typewriter, it worked for only a few hours before it again broke down.
6. The pan on the balance scale had become loose and tipped whenever materials were placed on it. This is the cause of the payment made to Jones Laboratory Equipment Company.
7. The farmer left some suet and bird seed for the robins and jays which had decided to winter over in the woods on his farm.
8. We find it difficult to estimate how much this equipment would be used or how much time it would save us. It could possibly be heavy for one long and involved report. Then it might not be used for several weeks.
9. We will pay the trucker directly, provided that, at the point of inspection on delivery, it is marked on the ticket with the amount to be deducted plus the trucker's name and address.

10. The school has lost one-third of its budget for equipment and supplies, which will probably make instruction more difficult.

MISPLACED MODIFIERS

Modifiers must be placed close to the sentence element they modify. Otherwise, you can confuse your reader or create an unintentionally humorous effect.

Faulty: *Leaping high out of the waves,* we watched a school of dolphins from the back of the boat.

Faulty: Juliet says that she wants the day to pass quickly *while standing on her balcony.*

Acceptable: From the back of the boat, we watched a school of dolphins *leaping high out of the waves.*

Acceptable: *While standing on her balcony,* Juliet says that she wants the day to pass quickly.

Be especially careful about sentences that end with more than one modifier. Make sure the order of the modifiers is not confusing.

Faulty: The quarterback, Jerry Gantner, dropped back *to throw a long pass behind the line.*

Faulty: The black stallion saves the boy *from drowning in the story.*

Acceptable: The quarterback, Jerry Gantner, dropped back *behind the line to throw a long pass.*

Acceptable: *In the story,* the black stallion saves the boy *from drowning.*

Also be careful about where you place such adverbs as *only, nearly, merely, even,* and *scarcely.* In speech, these limiting adverbs are often placed before the main verb even when they modify some other sentence element. However, in situations requiring you to use edited English, you should place them immediately before whatever element they modify.

Faulty: The soprano *only* sang for 15 minutes.

Faulty: Grandfather *merely* told her that Grandmother had died.

Acceptable: The soprano sang for *only* 15 minutes.

Acceptable: Grandfather told her *merely* that Grandmother had died.

• Answers to odd-numbered exercises begin on page 541.

A "squinting" modifier seems to be modifying two sentence elements at the same time.

Faulty: The girl who wanted her lover to come home *quickly* wrote a note to him.

Acceptable: The girl who wanted her lover *quickly* to come home wrote a note to him.

Acceptable: The girl who wanted her lover to come home wrote a note to him *quickly*.

In eliminating a squinting modifier, it is sometimes better to rephrase the entire sentence instead of merely moving the modifier.

Acceptable: The girl who couldn't wait to see her lover wrote him a note as soon as she heard he was safe.

Exercise

Some of the following sentences contain misplaced or squinting modifiers. Find and correct the errors.

1. The young man only remembered to put on his tie at the last minute.
2. I watched a bluejay chasing a squirrel from my hiding place under a bush.
3. The boy who wanted to triumph completely failed.
4. The umpire called the runner out at third base while standing behind home plate.
5. When I was a child, I was allowed to play only with the children on my own block.
6. I will discuss our sales for the quarter and the dates you are to submit your reports when we next meet.
7. All employees who are late for work occasionally will lose some pay.
8. My mother said when the pianist had finished playing we could leave.
9. The water only boiled for five minutes.
10. Lincoln was shot by John Wilkes Booth at Ford Theater as he was enjoying an evening's entertainment away from the pressures of the presidency while sitting in his box. ⌐

DANGLING MODIFIER

dm

Make sure that modifiers are sensibly related to the words they seem to modify. Dangling modifiers are those that do not make sense with the words they seem to modify. Many dangling modifiers are introductory verbal phrases.

Faulty: Having been a homemaker for eleven years, my new *goal* is to get a college degree.

Faulty: After working all day in the fields, the *bar* is crowded with tired and thirsty farmhands.

For introductory verbal phrases to fit smoothly into sentences, their implied subjects must be identical with the expressed subject of the main verb of the sentence. In the first faulty sentence, *I* is the implied subject of *having*, but *my new goal* is the subject of the main verb. In the second faulty sentence, *farmhands* is the implied subject of *working*, but *the bar* is the expressed subject of the main verb. To correct the dangling modifiers in these sentences, both implied and expressed subjects must be made identical.

Acceptable: Having been a homemaker for eleven years, *I* have made my new goal the completion of a college degree.

Acceptable: After working all day in the fields, *the tired and thirsty farmhands* crowd into the bar.

Exercise

Some of the following sentences contain dangling modifiers. Find the errors and correct them.

1. Charging up the hill, the Americans calmly waited for the British soldiers.
2. To survive the winter at Valley Forge, food and warm clothing were needed.
3. Totally frustrated by the situation, the students complained to the dean.
4. Diving hundreds of feet beneath the surface, the harpoon finally came loose.
5. Before attempting to swim the English Channel, swimmers coat their bodies with grease as a protection from the cold.
6. When thinking about my hometown, memories of a small neighborhood on the southwest side come to mind.
7. To get the experiment to work properly, I had to hold the blowtorch in my right hand while operating the controls with my left.
8. In preparing to run a marathon, shoes should be checked for signs of wear and for proper fit.
9. Having been denied jobs and good homes, the people's lives were quite miserable.
10. While driving through that part of the country, the roads seemed quite bad.

• Answers to odd-numbered exercises begin on page 541.

UNNECESSARY SHIFTS

There are three major kinds of unnecessary shifts to avoid in writing: shifts in verb tense and voice, shifts in pronoun form, and shifts in grammatical form between elements in a series. Let's examine each of these in turn.

Shift in Verb Tense and Voice

Unless you have good reason to change tenses, keep the same verb tense throughout a passage.

shift 1

Faulty: Three measures of sodium bisulphate and one of sodium chloride *are* placed in a dry test tube. This mixture *was* heated over a flame for two minutes.

Faulty: As we *were* walking along the top of the cliff, our leader suddenly *stops* and *tells* us that we *are* going over the side instead of taking the long way around.

Acceptable: Three measures of sodium bisulphate and one of sodium chloride *were* placed in a dry test tube.

Acceptable: As we *were* walking along the top of the cliff, our leader suddenly *stopped* and *told* us that we *were* going over the side instead of taking the long way around.

Writers are sometimes inconsistent in using verb tenses because they are uncertain about which tense is correct in certain situations. The following rules may help reduce this uncertainty.

1. When describing the contents of a piece of writing, use the present tense.

2. When describing your reactions to or your interpretations of a piece of writing, use the present tense.

Faulty: In the climactic scene of this drama, the husband *entered* the room and then *crossed* to his wife's bed to strangle her.

Faulty: In Marilyn French's novel *The Bleeding Heart*, Victor first *met* Dolores on a train bound for Oxford, England.

Faulty: The author *opened* his biography by telling how he bought the farm. In chapter two, he *described* his first walk around the place.

Acceptable: In the climactic scene of this drama, the husband *enters* the room and then *crosses* to his wife's bed to strangle her.

Acceptable: In Marilyn French's novel *The Bleeding Heart*, Victor first *meets* Dolores on a train bound for Oxford, England.

Acceptable: The author *opens* his biography by telling how he bought the farm. In chapter two he *describes* his first walk around the place.

In the last example, note how the past tense form *bought* is used to describe a real event that took place in the past, while the present tense forms *opens* and *describes* are used to tell what the book contains.

Faulty: The simplicity of the female character *acted* as a contrast to Seymour's complexity. To Seymour, she also *represented* innocence in an unjust world.

Faulty: The major conflict between Dolores and Victor *arose* from her insistence that a woman's way of thinking *was* better than a man's.

Acceptable: The simplicity of the female character *acts* as a contrast to Seymour's complexity. To Seymour, she also *represents* innocence in an unjust world.

Acceptable: The major conflict between Dolores and Victor *arises* from her insistence that a woman's way of thinking *is* better than a man's.

3. Usually, in telling what happened to you, use the past tense.

Faulty: We *are* walking past the back yard when suddenly a huge dog *appears* out of nowhere, *charges* to the fence, and *starts* snarling, growling, and barking at us.

Faulty: After I *jump* into the deep end of the pool, I *freeze* up with fear and *start* to sink.

Acceptable: We *were* walking past the back yard when suddenly a huge dog *appeared* out of nowhere, *charged* to the fence, and *started* snarling, growling, and barking at us.

Acceptable: After I *jumped* into the deep end of the pool, I *froze* with fear and *started* to sink.

Besides avoiding unnecessary shifts in tense, avoid abrupt shifts between active and passive voice.

Faulty: The reader *recalls* the conversation in the tearoom with Esme, and a new meaning for the conversation *is adopted*.

Faulty: We *totaled* up the cash sales, and then the credit sales *were entered* in the ledger.

Acceptable: The reader *recalls* the conversation in the tearoom with Esme and *perceives* a new meaning for the conversation.

Acceptable: We *totaled* up the cash sales and *entered* the credit sales in the ledger.

Exercise   Some of the following passages contain incorrect uses of verb tenses or shifts in verb tense or voice. Find the errors and correct them.

1. The rose motif carries over from the third to the fourth stanza. However, the mood changed in the fourth stanza.

2. One day as my friend Bill and I were walking home from school, a lady comes out of the house we were passing and starts threatening to call the police on us.

3. If an object is placed on the pan, the pan will go down and the pointer goes up.
4. The author organizes his book in the form of a diary.
5. The student mixed the solution, and then the solution was poured into the large beaker.
6. In the article, he compared the effectiveness of the lecture method and the self-study method.
7. The violinist first tuned her instrument; then the opening movement of the piece was played.
8. At halftime, the players came into the locker room. There they get suggestions from their coach about how they should change their plays during the second half.
9. Heading down the hill on our sled, we see a tree in our way and swerve to avoid it.
10. The bunsen burner is then lit, and the mixture was heated to the boiling point.

Shift in Pronoun Form

Be consistent in using *you* or *one* to refer to people in general. Also, don't switch from the third person (*salesclerk* in the second example below) to some other person (such as *you* in the example).

shift 2

Faulty: In playing high school sports, *one* can be more interested in *one's* own performance than in the team's won and lost record. But in playing college sports, *you* have to be more concerned with the team than with *yourself*.

Faulty: A *salesclerk* that works in the candy department has to have a lot of willpower. *You* just can't allow yourself to be tempted by all the delicious smells if *you* want to keep *your* figure.

Acceptable: In playing high school sports, *you* can be more interested in *your* own performance than in the team's won and lost record. But in playing college sports, *you* have to be more concerned with the team than with yourself.

Acceptable: *Salesclerks* that work in the candy department have to have a lot of willpower. They just can't allow *themselves* to be tempted by all the delicious smells if *they* want to keep *their* figure.

Acceptable: As a *salesclerk*, *I* found *I* had to use all *my* willpower when *I* worked in the candy department. Since *I* wanted to keep *my* figure, *I* just couldn't allow *myself* to be tempted by all the delicious smells.

Exercise

The following sentences illustrate shifts in pronoun form. Find and correct the errors.

1. The reason why marines go through such tough training is so that you'll be able to perform well in combat.

2. When one visits a foreign country, you have to try to see as much as you can.
3. When you first come to college, everything seems strange. It may take one several months before you get used to living away from home and not having parents around to make you study.
4. Some people never learn that to get to work on time you might have to get up earlier than you would like.
5. A hockey player should be strong and durable since you have to take many body checks and falls on the ice. ⟨ſ⟩

Faulty Parallelism
//

Make sure that elements in a series are parallel in grammatical form. Failing to maintain parallel structure sometimes results in a glaringly ungrammatical statement and always makes your style seem awkward and unpolished.

Faulty: The sharecroppers all meet at the store *so that they can relax* [clause] and *to forget about work* [phrase].

Faulty: Wilhelm's inability to cope with life can be illustrated by *his loss* [phrase] of a job, *the destruction* [phrase] of his marriage, and *that he failed to see Tony's untrustworthiness* [clause].

In the first sentence, two modifiers of different grammatical types—a clause and a phrase—are joined by *and.* In the second, three objects of the preposition *by*—two phrases and a clause—are written as a series. In each sentence, the writer should have used the same grammatical form for the elements joined by *and.*

Acceptable: The sharecroppers all meet at the store *to relax* and *to forget* about work.

Acceptable: Wilhelm's inability to cope with life can be illustrated by *his loss* of a job, *the destruction* of his marriage, and *his failure* to see Tony's untrustworthiness.

Exercise

Some of the sentences below contain faulty parallelisms. Some do not. Find and correct the errors.

1. Prepare yourself for your stretching routine by assuming the proper position, relaxing the calf, and assistance to increase the stretch.
2. The orchestra played Beethoven's Leonora Overture, Brahms' Fourth Symphony, and Mozart's Piano Concerto No. 3.
3. She wanted to improve her serve, how she handled lobs, and the strength of her backhand shot.

● Answers to odd-numbered exercises begin on page 541.

4. To be successful on the job, employees should remember three things: (1) the importance of being on time; (2) to work as hard as possible; (3) to look for opportunities to make improvements in the company's operation.

5. The fact that robins appeared in our backyard yesterday, the northward flight of geese, and seeing grackles overhead all tell me that spring is here.

6. In the workshop, you will learn how to erect a wall, proper wiring techniques, and how you should treat wood before painting.

7. On Friday nights, I get together with my three buddies to go swimming and then to go for a drink, but mostly so that we can just have some fun together.

8. When you have finished the first step, check for errors and especially that you have not forgotten to turn off the mixer.

9. What bothers me is that he sings off-key, his piano technique, and his absolute lack of rhythm.

10. He asked her to buy more paper for him and for some help in typing his report.

Mixed Constructions

mix

A mixed construction is a sentence or clause in which the beginning and end do not fit together grammatically. Many mixed constructions are the result of forgetting how sentences begin or being careless about sentence construction.

Faulty: In some of the symptoms are nausea, blurred vision, and fever.
Faulty: When the loons come back to the north country reminds me that spring is about to begin.

In the first sentence, the writer has forgotten that the sentence begins with a preposition which prevents *some* from acting as the subject of the sentence. In the second sentence, the writer has falsely assumed that "When the loons come back" can be the subject of a verb.

Acceptable: Some of the symptoms are nausea, blurred vision, and fever.
Acceptable: The return of the loons to the north country reminds me that spring is about to begin.

Exercise

Some of the following sentences contain mixed constructions. Find and correct the errors.

1. We feel rising health care costs are a major concern of businesses and is underrated by many authorities.

2. By belonging to Sunny Dale Country Club has improved my family's social position.

3. Because gypsum sand dissolves in water is why the sand in certain places had become as hard as cement.

4. A faculty with so many Ph.D.'s and yet the students don't know how to write a simple English sentence.

5. Since the winter has been so mild, the ice on the ponds in the city parks has not yet frozen solid enough for people to go ice skating.

6. After the proofs have been corrected is when you can start to relax.

7. The machine's use might be heavy for short periods of time and then not be used again for several weeks.

8. Check that the lever to be in the "Off" position.

9. Until you see her shoot from twenty and twenty-five feet away from the basket, you won't be able to understand why our coaches chose someone so short to play on our basketball team.

10. From the increase of sales has raised our hopes of breaking even this year. §

ERRORS IN WORD FORMS

Verb Forms

V 1 The -s Ending Some spoken dialects of American English do not always add the *-s* ending to verbs where it is expected in edited English. Speakers of such dialects may say "I roll" and "she roll," "I miss" and "she miss," and "I do" and "she do."

When writing in college and business, speakers of such dialects have the extra editorial job of putting in *-s* or *-es* endings they might have omitted through the influence of their spoken language.

Faulty: Susan roll out of bed at 9 a.m.
Faulty: She miss her bus.
Acceptable: Susan rolls out of bed at 9 a.m.
Acceptable: She misses her bus.

Exercise

In the following paragraph, some of the *-s* and *-es* verb endings have been omitted. Find and correct the errors. (The sentences are numbered for your convenience in checking your answers in the Answer Guide.)

(1) The mood of Robert Frost's poem "Stopping by Woods on a Snowy Evening" ranges from a feeling of being embarrassed to a longing to be able to stop forever. (2) The first stanza set the scene. (3) The narrator of the poem tells us that he know the owner of the

• Answers to odd-numbered exercises begin on page 541.

woods where he has stopped. (4) The reference to the owner tells us that, as he stop by the woods, the speaker is also aware of another world, that of the "village." (5) The speaker also seem to feel a little embarrassed about stopping in a snowstorm just to "watch the woods fill up with snow." (6) He say that the owner of the woods won't see him stopping like this, but we know that the speaker himself is the one who is worried about how he is acting. (7) In the second and third stanza, he project this worry into his horse's mind when he interpret the horse's movements. (8) To the speaker, the horse "gives his harness bells a shake // To ask if there is some mistake." (9) The third stanza also shows why the scene attract him. (10) The scene is beautiful and quiet. (11) The poet brings out this idea when he say, "The only other sound's the sweep of easy wind and downy flake." (12) This last line of the stanza look forward to stanza four where the poet tells more about why he like the woods.

v 2 Nonstandard Past and Past Participle Forms   Some spoken dialects of American English use past tense and past participle forms that differ from those used in edited English. For example, some Americans say, "He come up the walk" instead of "He came up the walk"; "I seen him do it" instead of "I saw him do it"; "She had went" instead of "She had gone."

If you are unsure whether a past tense or past participle form meets the expectations of a college or business audience, check your dictionary for the forms of the word used in edited English.

Exercise

Some of the following sentences contain past tense and past participle forms that are not found in edited English. Find and correct the errors. If you are in doubt, check the form in your dictionary.

1. Washington apparently had come to the decision some months earlier.
2. There he seen two soldiers patrolling around the oxen and the horses near the wagon train.
3. Above all, I want to compliment the staff for the way in which the project was ran.
4. After Aunt Polly fell asleep, Tom snuck out of the house by climbing down the trellis.
5. From the north of England, Harold and his weary army then went south through the whole of England to their fateful meeting with William at Hastings.
6. After a seven-hour hike through the August heat, we all drunk two quarts of water when we got back to camp.
7. Having brought the army through all those difficult years of revolution, Washington begun to long for a peaceful retirement on his plantation.

8. When stage coaches got stuck in the mud of the Black Swamp, they were drug back onto the corduroy road by teams of oxen.
9. After watching her mother, father, and brother all die within six months of each other, Julia felt that she had went through the worst period of her life.
10. Eight o'clock come and went, and we just set there waiting for the show to begin.

Pronoun Forms

Pr 1 Case Forms The forms of most personal pronouns and of the relative/interrogative *who* change according to function,

He told the children to be quiet.
The principal told *him* to be quiet.
It doesn't matter *who* sent the letter.
It doesn't matter *to whom* the letter was sent.

Edited English is more precise about matching pronoun form to function than is spoken English. Matching form and function can be especially troublesome in certain constructions.

Direct Object in Coordinate Phrase

Mary gave the watch to John and *me*. (not *I*: *me* is the direct object of *to*)
My mother kissed my sister and *me*. (not *I*: *me* is the direct object of *kissed*)

Pronoun Following Than

No one can run faster than *she*. (not *her*: *she* is the subject of an implied *can*)

Who/Whom at the Beginning of a Clause

John Adams, for *whom* I am named, was often vain and temperamental. (not *who*: *whom* is the direct object of *for*)
The jury found guilty a man *whom* defense witnesses had called "hopelessly insane." (not *who*: *whom* is the direct object of *called*)

Exercise

Some of the following sentences contain incorrect pronoun forms. Find and correct the errors.

1. The coach told he and I to go for a fast break on our next possession.
2. No one could have been angrier than him when he discovered that

• Answers to odd-numbered exercises begin on page 541.

Arnold had betrayed the cause for which Washington had given so much of his life.

3. John André, who Arnold had abandoned, was captured by three Americans and subsequently hanged.

4. My brother and me had just skated out onto the rink when the coach blew the whistle for the tryouts to end.

5. Despite his heavy schedule, Dr. Smith gave Sally and me his undivided attention.

6. Alexander Hamilton, who had never been a rich man, left his wife and family deeply in debt when he died of a gunshot wound.

7. Few of the athletes who had tried out were more disappointed than him and me over the poor condition of the track.

8. When we were younger, she and I were among our school's best athletes, excelling in track, field hockey, and basketball.

9. That is the end of the story of a man who Washington had once considered one of his most capable generals.

10. Few artists I know get more excited than she and I just before a performance.

Pr 2 Spelling of Possessive Pronouns   Spelling certain possessive pronouns correctly can be difficult. Possessive pronouns are not spelled with apostrophes even if they end in *-s.*

That cart is *ours.*
Victory was *theirs* that day.

You need to be particularly alert when you use *whose/who's* and *its/it's.* Use the form without the apostrophe when the word is a possessive.

Whose side are you on anyway?
Mary taught our dog all *its* tricks.

Keep in mind that *who's* means "who is/has" and *it's* means "it is/has."

Exercise   Some of the following sentences contain misspellings of possessive pronouns. Find and correct the errors.

1. In a huge colony of sea birds where hundreds and hundreds of the same species may nest on the same cliff, it is amazing that parent birds know which nest is theirs'.

2. When Cinderella realized that now the prince was hers, she was extremely happy.

3. The Senate committee wanted to know whose fault it was that the project was three million dollars over budget.

4. The committee wanted it's own research assistant to examine and evaluate the evidence.

5. Now that we have looked over her's, we realize how bad a job we did on our report.

6. The Westland Mall trade area has a clientele who's image of your planned store will have to be improved if you are to be successful.

7. Feeling that nothing in life is truly their's, many young women try to starve themselves so that at least they can control how much they weigh.

8. When it's nest is disturbed, the white-footed mouse often shows a great deal of courage, patiently waiting for its offspring to climb onto its back before it scurries for cover.

9. Their team has been so much better than ours' throughout the season that everyone thinks we will lose.

10. When a bird loses its' primary wing feathers, it not only can grow new ones, but it also continues to fly without any loss of speed and power.

Pr 3 Subjects of Gerunds

Subjects of gerunds are expressed as possessives (*his stealing; Sandra's flirting*). Subjects of gerunds are to be carefully distinguished from other pronouns that may be modified by present participles. Compare the following:

Gerund

He means no harm by *his flirting*.
His gambling will destroy him financially.

Participle

I saw *him flirting* with Sandra.
Can you imagine *him gambling* away his fortune?

Using object forms of pronouns as subjects of gerunds is considered faulty usage in edited English.

Faulty: I couldn't object to *John writing* to Eve so long as they did not become lovers.

Faulty: The salesclerk was annoyed at *him* continually *winking* at her.

Acceptable: I couldn't object to *John's writing* to Eve so long as they did not become lovers.

Acceptable: The salesclerk was annoyed at *his* continually *winking* at her.

• Answers to odd-numbered exercises begin on page 541.

Exercise   In some of the following sentences, object forms of pronouns are used as subjects of gerunds. Find and correct the errors.

1. The duelist ducked when he saw his opponent aiming a gun at him.
2. What bothered us most was him drinking all our wine and then refusing to chip in when we wanted to buy a six-pack.
3. The soldiers became tired of him fishing for compliments.
4. For hours we watched the hawk soaring effortlessly on thermal updrafts.
5. Their girlfriends' fathers objected to them keeping the girls out past one o'clock.
6. My mother claims that she could hear her father's snoring all the way down in the basement.
7. They cannot bear Jan running away.
8. He was really devastated by them moving to Virginia.
9. Our teachers really like our editing of the magazine.
10. We do not want him passing out again.

PUNCTUATION AND MECHANICS

END PUNCTUATION

. ! ?

Periods signal the end of all sentences except questions and exclamations. This rule includes sentences that incorporate an indirect question:

> She asked what assignment the teacher had given.

as well as courtesy questions:

> Won't you please send in your registration soon.

> **Question marks** signal the end of direct questions:

> What assignment did Mrs. Murphy give?

and indicate doubt about the accuracy of a date or a number:

> Shakespeare was born on April 23 (?), 1564.

> **Exclamation points** punctuate the end of interjections and emphatic commands.

> Wow!
> Stop that!

Never use more than one exclamation point at a time. Do not use exclamation points to make readers feel an excitement beyond that conveyed by the words themselves.

Faulty: The gray whale surfaced only fifty yards away!!!
Acceptable: The gray whale surfaced only fifty yards away.

Exercise

Supply the appropriate end punctuation for the following sentences. If you are in doubt about where to put end punctuation in sentences with quotation marks, see pp. 509–511.

1. Glaring at her audience sitting so quietly in their pews, the stern preacher asked, "If you will not act, then who *will* feed the starving and help the needy"
2. "He swings, and there's a high fly to right," said the announcer "It's deep And it's long gone It's a home run for Johnny Dreyfuss, the two hundred eighty-fifth of his long career"
3. The accountants all wondered how the new computer system would work once it was installed
4. When you receive this memorandum, would you please read it and pass it along to the next person on the distribution list
5. All the workers wanted to know when the contract would be signed
6. "Well, then, if you haven't been able to complete the job in a month, when do you think it will be done?" asked the angry customer
7. In this last year, our store exceeded its sales quota by a whopping 300 percent
8. "All right, then, if that's how you want it, I'm going to march you right to the principal's office and see that you are all suspended for your behavior toward me today"
9. In filling out these forms, would you make sure that you print clearly and carefully
10. Don't delay Send in your box top with twenty-five cents to receive your secret encoder

COMMAS Commas have a number of specific uses within sentences.

1. Place a comma before a coordinating conjunction that joins two long independent clauses.

I wish I could have gone to that meeting with you, but I got involved with an experiment and lost track of the time.

● Answers to odd-numbered exercises begin on page 541.

2. Place a comma after introductory elements, especially after transitional phrases and words (other than coordinating conjunctions), long introductory phrases, and dependent clauses.

> However, the hawk missed its prey.
> Despite the power and speed of its dive, the hawk missed its prey.
> Although the hawk dived rapidly, it missed its prey.

3. Set off nonrestrictive elements with commas. (Nonrestrictive elements give information that does not define or limit a term. In the following examples the nonrestrictive element is in italics.)

> Our school is named for President McKinley, *who was assassinated while in office.*
> John Wilkes Booth, *having assassinated Lincoln,* jumped from Lincoln's box to the stage of the Ford Theater.
> John Wilkes Booth, *Lincoln's assassin,* believed that he had acted to save his country from a great tyrant.

Compare the following sentences, each of which contains a **restrictive element**. Note that the restrictive elements (in italics) are not set off by commas.

> Our school is named for one of the presidents *who was assassinated while in office.*
> The man *coming toward us* has a fatal disease.
> The movie star *Marilyn Monroe* was once married to the former baseball player *Joe DiMaggio.*

4. Set off parenthetical expressions with commas.

> My own father, for example, earned a good living as a carpenter.

5. Separate elements in a series (words, phrases, or clauses) with commas; place commas between coordinate adjectives not linked by coordinating conjunctions.

> A good referee has knowledge of the game, good judgment, and self-confidence.
> Knowledgeable, self-confident referees are essential to every sport.

6. Use commas to separate direct quotations from words telling who wrote or said these words.

> Thomas Jefferson wrote, "All men are created equal."
> "All men," wrote Thomas Jefferson, "are created equal."

7. Use commas to prevent misreadings.

Faulty: For many sick people are to be avoided.
Acceptable: For many, sick people are to be avoided.

8. Avoid overusing or misusing commas. Commas should not ordinarily be used to separate important sentence elements (subject, verb, and direct object or complement; adjective and noun; preposition and object).

Faulty: The results of an investigation that involved interviews with hundreds of people, were still inconclusive.
Faulty: The winter birds ate, the cracked corn and suet that we have put out for them.
Acceptable: The results of an investigation that involved interviews with hundreds of people were still inconclusive.
Acceptable: The winter birds ate the cracked corn and suet that we have put out for them.

Exercise

Some of the following sentences contain commas where none should be used or where some other mark of punctuation should be used; some lack necessary commas; some are correctly punctuated. Find the errors in comma usage and correct them.

1. The king who ruled England during the Revolutionary War was George III.
2. King George III who ruled England during the Revolutionary War is sometimes referred to as "mad King George."
3. In describing his eighty-two day run across America James Shapiro speaks in great detail of the mental struggle, involved in an ultra-distance run.
4. James Shapiro an ultradistance runner had to rely on his willpower in running from California to New York City.
5. When in the middle of the siege upon his castle Macbeth learns of his wife's death he utters a very moving speech.
6. The news of his wife's death we can be sure, contributes greatly to Macbeth's mounting sense of despair.
7. Juliet says to Romeo "Thy lips are warm," then she dies from the poison she has drunk.
8. The poet was brilliant witty and completely mad.
9. I'm talking about the poet, who went mad and shot himself.
10. I will never forget the evening, when I found my mother out cold on the floor of our kitchen.

● Answers to odd-numbered exercises begin on page 541.

11. Shapiro reports that all across America he found roadsides littered with trash, on his run he even saw soiled paper diapers that had been tossed out of car windows.
12. I know a lot about joggers running every day as I do.
13. A short, slender, cute teenager shot past me at the eighteen-mile mark.
14. The teenager who shot past me at the eighteen-mile mark, never completed the race.
15. But, I still feel sorry for Macbeth when Fate seems to have turned against him at the end of the play.

SEMICOLONS

A semicolon (;) is a stronger mark of internal punctuation than a comma. It is used only to separate coordinate elements, never elements of different levels of importance such as a dependent and an independent clause.

1. Use semicolons to separate independent clauses with and without conjunctive adverbs.

   The old bridge has been condemned; however, people still use it.
   All around us lay orange and yellow leaves; autumn had come again to the maple grove.

2. Use semicolons to separate independent clauses linked by a coordinating conjunction only if the clauses are long and themselves contain commas.

   The blackbirds arrived that evening, chattering and squawking, weary from their long flight; and when they arrived, we all ran out on the front lawn and waved and shouted our greetings to them, delighted that spring was here again.

3. Use semicolons to separate items in a series when one or more of the items contain a comma.

   In the evening stillness, we could hear grackles, their "rusty-gate" squawk harsh upon our ears; robins, their merry "Cheerylio" punctuated by sharp warning calls; and from far off, several crows, their "caw-caw-caw" muted by the distance.

4. Do *not* use semicolons to introduce lists, summaries, and long quotations.

   Faulty: You will need the following tools; a hammer, a saw, a drill, and a plane.

Faulty: He brought along a number of provisions, including; flour, sugar, dried milk, raisins, and tea.

Acceptable: You will need the following tools: a hammer, a saw, a drill, and a plane.

Acceptable: He brought along a number of provisions, including flour, sugar, dried milk, raisins, and tea.

Exercise

In some of the following sentences, the semicolons are used correctly. In some, the semicolons are misused. In some, semicolons need to be introduced, or commas need to be replaced by semicolons. Find and correct the errors.

1. Whooping cranes moved away from us across the marsh; stepping regally and sedately through the muddy water.

2. The Confederate soldiers charged up the long incline, shouting war whoops, firing their rifles, falling over dead comrades, staggering to their feet again, firing, and continuing to charge, the Union army answered with volley after volley of cannon and rifle fire, staying behind their protective shelter, choosing their targets carefully, holding their ground with difficulty.

3. Furious with her, her father gave her four alternatives; leave home, stay but find a full-time job, stay but get a part-time job and go to school, get married and go live with her husband.

4. In the powerful desert wind, the tumbleweed plant held in the ground where it was rooted; until finally its stem snapped and it went bounding off in its characteristic fashion.

5. For many months, Bob and Eve did not see each other and rarely even communicated; however, when by chance they met one evening in the mall, all their powerful love returned in a rush.

6. The best known Australian marsupials are the kangaroo and the wombat in the United States the only marsupial is the opossum.

7. Because his car battery was dead when he tried to start the car after work, Sam was two hours late for dinner, however, his mother kept the soup simmering so that it would be hot for him when he arrived.

8. Before every performance, the opera singer ate one large, raw onion, cutting it into quarters and putting an entire quarter into his mouth at once, drank half a bottle of cream sherry, pouring it into a special mug he kept in his dressing room and gulping it down without even taking a single breath, and then did a series of yoga exercises, finishing up by standing on his head for twenty minutes.

9. Bodies of dead Confederate soldiers were strewn across the field; bodies of dead Union soldiers lay behind their fortifications.

10. At first, the new accounting system confused us, nevertheless, in time we grew used to it and came to appreciate its advantages.

• Answers to odd-numbered exercises begin on page 541.

COLONS

Colons (:) introduce summaries, explanations, lists, and long quotations.

> You will need the following equipment: a number 2 pencil, an 18-inch ruler, a black magic marker, masking tape, and cellophane tape.
>
> Thomas Jefferson wrote: "We hold these truths to be self-evident, that all men are created equal, that they are endowed by their Creator with certain unalienable Rights, that among these are Life, Liberty and the pursuit of Happiness."
>
> My interpretation must be correct: the maid was the only person to see the victim shortly before he died; she knew where he kept his heart medicine; she had given him the heart medicine on another occasion when she correctly decided that he was having a heart attack; and she had a grudge against him because he laughed at the advances she had made toward him.

In edited English, it is considered faulty usage to place a colon after only part of a sentence.

Faulty: Please bring: your permission slip, your money, warm clothing, and your ski equipment.

Acceptable: Please bring your permission slip, your money, warm clothing, and your ski equipment.

Acceptable: Please bring the following items: your permission slip, your money, warm clothing, and your ski equipment.

Exercise

In some of the following sentences, a colon must be inserted or deleted, or it must be used in place of some other mark of punctuation. In some, the colon is properly used. Find and correct the errors.

1. The advantages of my plan are: low cost, speed and ease of implementation, and the need for no new training.

2. In his immortal Gettysburg Address, President Lincoln wrote the following words; "Four score and seven years ago our fathers brought forth upon this continent a new nation, conceived in liberty, and dedicated to the proposition that all men are created equal."

3. Here, then, is the main thought I want to convey: if any of you wants a summer job that will give you both an interesting experience and good pay, consider participating in our special summer program.

4. In this lovely valley, there are many unusual types of birds, including: the kiskadee or Derby flycatcher, the chachalaca, green jays, golden-fronted woodpeckers, red-billed pigeons, and white-fronted doves.

5. Many factors influenced my decision to enroll in the college of pharmacy, my desire to work with people, my interest in science, my

fascination with the way the body works, and the influence of my mother and aunt, both of whom are pharmacists.

6. The Twenty-third Psalm contains the following statement: "Yea, though I walk through the valley of the shadow of death, I will fear no evil."

7. In my day, children were more physically active than they are now: Since they did not have anything like television to keep them in the house, they had to go out and play just to entertain themselves.

8. I'd like to put several things on my wish list someone to love, the chance to complete my education, and a job that will allow me to learn more about my field.

9. This stunning defeat was brought on by three factors; fatigue due to overpractice, a lack of interest in the outcome, and the sickness of our star player.

10. The patient had the following classical symptoms of diabetes: excessive urination coupled with extreme thirst, rapid weight loss, dilated eyes, and pain in the abdomen.

DASHES

Dashes (—) mark abrupt changes in thought, set off parenthetical remarks, and separate final summarizing or illustrating statements from the initial part of a sentence.

> Determination, patience, attentiveness to detail, and courage—more than great military genius—these are the qualities that made George Washington an outstanding leader of our nation.
>
> The best thing you could do—believe me—is to relocate to another place far away from here where you can make a fresh start.
>
> Three ingredients go into a successful career—skill, determination, and hard work.

As a mark of punctuation introducing a final summary or list, a dash is slightly less formal than a colon.

Exercise

Insert dashes in the following sentences wherever they would be appropriate.

1. Jefferson, Adams, Washington these three giants of American history took actions that affect our lives today.

2. Henry James poor man carried the burden of being a junior to his famous father and the younger brother of the famous psychologist William James.

● Answers to odd-numbered exercises begin on page 541.

3. It is surprising indeed, it is incredible that a mother suffering from cancer would have had the courage to watch her children being placed in adoptive homes before she died.

4. To eat one of my wife's gourmet dinners you need three things will power, a head cold, and bicarbonate of soda.

5. Monarch butterflies hundreds and hundreds of them came to the point of land and without hesitating continued on across the lake.

PARENTHESES AND BRACKETS

(/) [/]

Parentheses ( ) enclose explanatory remarks and other comments regarded as unessential to the main ideas of the sentence. Parentheses also enclose examples and the numbers used in enumerating points.

A large hawk (a redtail, I think) swung lazily on an updraft.

John Keats (1795–1821) was one of several British poets of the Romantic period who died at a young age (in Keats' case, at the age of twenty-six).

There are three important points to keep in mind: (1) land values have declined 25 percent in our state over the past four years; (2) farm prices have risen less rapidly than prices for other things, notably energy; (3) the cost of farm equipment has kept pace with the general rate of inflation.

Brackets [ ] enclose words inserted into a quotation.

"We have begged them [on the basis of] our blood ties to stop injuring us."

"Prisoners keep in touch with their parole officers for six [sic] to eighty days after they start working."

Sic, a Latin word, is placed between square brackets to show that the error in the quotation was in the original and is not your fault.

Exercise

Insert parentheses and brackets wherever appropriate in the following sentences.

1. One person's idea not mine, you may be sure was to cancel the show completely.

2. Percy Bysshe Shelley 1792–1822, another Romantic poet, lived for only twenty-nine years.

3. To paint the walls of a room, you need several things: 1 spackling compound, 2 putty knife, 3 paint, 4 paint tray, 5 roller, 6 step ladder, and 7 drop cloths.

4. During the Middle English period 1100–1500 the English language underwent rapid and important changes in vocabulary, pronunciation, morphology, and syntax.
5. "Along the Ouisconsin sic River, Robert Pratt has built a sawmill."

QUOTATION MARKS
Uses of Quotation Marks

Quotation marks (" ") set off quoted speech and words quoted from written sources.

"Mary, come away from that window," said John.
"No," said Mary.
The Revised Standard Version of the Bible uses the phrase "noisy gong" in place of the King James Version's "sounding brass."
Carson McCullers effectively describes a small, sleepy Southern town when she writes, "Not much is there except the cotton mill, the two-room houses where the workers live, a few peach trees, a church with two colored windows, and a miserable main street only a hundred yards long."

When passages quoted from sources run longer than four typed lines, they are set off by being indented.

```
Carson McCullers effectively describes a small, sleepy

Southern town when she writes:


    Not much is there except the cotton mill, the two-

    room houses where the workers live, a few peach

    trees, a church with two colored windows, and a

    miserable main street only a hundred yards long.

    On Saturdays the tenants from the near-by farms

    come in for a day of talk and trade.  Otherwise the

    town is lonesome, sad, and like a place that is far

    off and estranged from all other places in the world.
```

● Answers to odd-numbered exercises begin on page 541.

Sometimes a short passage you want to quote will already contain words enclosed within quotation marks. In such cases, place *double* quotation marks around the entire passage and *single* quotation marks around those words already quoted in the original passage.

Recalling the first time she saw Hitler in person, Gitta Sereny writes, "And then, when he arrived and the shout began: 'Sieg Heil, Sieg Heil' . . . I suddenly felt myself shouting with them—and so did my English friend, who spoke no German."

Place quotation marks around the titles of such short works as journal and newspaper articles, individual poems in a collection, short stories, essays, and individual episodes from a radio or television series.

Gitta Sereny's "Germany: The 'Rediscovery' of Hitler" describes her personal response to a Hitler rally.
One of America's most beloved poems is "Stopping by Woods on a Snowy Evening."

Use quotation marks around words used in a special sense. Quotation marks or italics are used to set off words used as examples. Choose one form and use it consistently throughout a particular piece of writing.

George Romney probably lost his bid for the Republican party's nomination for President by using the word "brainwashed" to describe his state of mind.
I must say his definition of "love" is a strange one.

Placement of Quotation Marks

Place endquotes *after* commas and periods.

Jesus' command, "Love thy neighbor as thyself," is a hard one to follow.
I used to be haunted by the Bible verse, "Many are called, but few are chosen."

Place endquotes *before* colons and semicolons.

Robert Frost is the author of "Stopping by Woods on a Snowy Evening"; it was Edward Arlington Robinson who wrote "Richard Cory."

Place endquotes *after* question marks, exclamation points, and dashes if the mark of punctuation is part of the quotation. Otherwise, place endquotes *before* these punctuation marks.

When the giant Goliath sees the boy David coming to fight him with a mere slingshot, he calls out, "Am I a dog, that you come to me with sticks?"

Was it Robert Frost or Edward Arlington Robinson who wrote "Richard Cory"?

Exercise

In some of the following sentences, quotation marks are improperly used or need to be inserted. Find and correct the errors.

1. "Silas Marner" is one of George Eliot's greatest novels.
2. "I'm very sorry to tell you this", my girlfriend said, "but I've fallen in love with Tom".
3. In her article "Whatever Happened to Iran's Treasures?" Jane Johansen details the way the shah's money and jewels were transported outside the country before the collapse of the government.
4. This famous psalm begins with the comforting words, The Lord is my shepherd. I shall not want.
5. Such common English words as table, honor, courtesy, and diverse originally were borrowed into the language from French.
6. One of the really memorable lines from Louis MacNeice's poem Eclogue by a Five-Barred Gate is all you do is shear your sheep to stop your ears.
7. Was it Emily Dickinson who used the expression "the nerves sit ceremonious like tombs?"
8. That, said the sobbing student, is when the teacher started to call me Nervous Prostration. That's the very expression she used, asked the principal, Nervous Prostration?
9. Her article, Black Holes: Their Origin and Role, appeared in the leading scientific journal in her field.
10. Can you really call our relationship one of "friendship" when all we do is argue with each other?

ELLIPSES

/.../

Ellipses (. . .) show that one or more words have been omitted from a quotation.

"Baltimore Oriole First Baseman Eddie Murray . . . has already hit 111 home runs, driven in 398 runs and averaged .291, yet he earned just $150,000 last season." (B.J. Phillips, *Time*)

If the ellipsis comes at the end of a sentence, place a period right after the last quoted word to signal the end of the sentence; place the three ellipsis marks after this period.

- Answers to odd-numbered exercises begin on page 541.

"If you want to communicate with your pet, first make sure you understand what it is trying to say to *you*. This is an ongoing process. . . ." (Jean Burden, "What Is Your Pet Telling You?")

To indicate that a whole paragraph or more has been omitted from a prose quotation or that one or more lines of poetry have been omitted from a quoted passage of poetry, insert a whole line of ellipses.

Finally, ellipses are also used in writing dialogue to show a pause or an unfinished sentence.

"John, I. . . . You've. . . ."
"Yes," said John, completing her thought. "You don't know what to say because I've taken you completely by surprise."

Exercise

Demonstrate your understanding of how to use ellipsis marks by inserting ellipses for the words in italics in the following sentences.

1. *"According to experienced bird watchers,* winter birds will come to a feeder even during a snowstorm."
2. "Washington, *who had seen the one love of his life married off to another man,* developed a stoical patience that served him and our country well during the Revolutionary War."
3. "The existence of an army gave colonists a visible symbol of their unity in opposing the British, *a symbol that was preserved largely by Washington's determination."*

APOSTROPHE

An apostrophe (') is used with nouns and indefinite pronouns to show possession.

Mary's dad took her to a rock concert last night.
Esme is everyone's cat.

In plural nouns and other nouns ending in -s, possession is shown by adding just the apostrophe.

horses' hooves   Chris' term paper

Apostrophes are *not* used with possessive pronouns (*its, his, hers, ours, yours, theirs*) nor with plural nouns not being used as possessives.

Use an apostrophe in contractions to show that one or more letters have been omitted.

can't   won't   mustn't   shouldn't

Exercise — In some of the following sentences, apostrophes are used correctly. In some, they are not. In some, apostrophes must be inserted. Find and correct the errors.

1. The purchasing agent could not believe that the machines actual power was as great as its' advertisements claimed.
2. This year, twenty-five of our supermarkets' either lost money or barely broke even.
3. Trucks brakes screeched as the convoy rounded the bend to find the road washed away.
4. A football players greatest reward is a kind word from his coaches'.
5. I know that the envelopes' seal was broken and that, when I opened the envelope, I found nothing inside.
6. The bald eagles range is now limited almost exclusively to two states—Florida and Alaska.
7. Green jays' calls echoed through the forest.
8. The great goal of all the boys' on our block was to be able to outrun Patsy Kelly, the prettiest girl on the street.
9. Be careful that, when you remove the old finish from your antique chair, you dont scratch or make marks in the wood.
10. Washington's graceful poise directly contrasts with Lincoln's awkwardness.

HYPHENS

/-/

Hyphens (-) are used to separate parts of words or to join words together to form a compound.

anti-intellectual   forget-me-not

If you cannot remember whether a particular word contains a hyphen, consult a recently published dictionary.

You may join words with a hyphen when they act as a single word modifier before a noun or when a hyphen will prevent a misreading.

total-commitment attitude
buck-the-establishment philosophy
get-lost look
antique-auto manufacturer; antique auto-manufacturer
broken-tape container; broken tape-container

Hyphens are also used to divide words at the ends of lines. If a word will not fit onto the line and if t͵ ͻing the whole word on the next line will create a noticeable unevennes͓ in your right margin, divide the word at an appropriate syllable break, using a hyphen. However, it is better to leave the margin uneven than to leave a single letter at the end

• Answers to odd-numbered exercises begin on page 541.

of the line as a result of dividing the word with a hyphen. Already hyphenated words are divided at the hyphen.

Faulty: Although Eve went to New York to study psych-
iatry, she went into theater instead and now
does lighting for off-Broadway shows.

Faulty: Many new students are afraid to give their o-
pinion about anything lest they irritate the
professor.

Faulty: Now that spring has come, I want to plant forget-me-nots in our garden.

Acceptable: Although Eve went to New York to study psy-
chiatry, she went into theater instead and now
does lighting for off-Broadway shows.

Acceptable: Many new students are afraid to give their
opinion about anything lest they irritate the
professor.

Acceptable: Now that spring has come, I want to plant forget-
me-nots in our garden.

Acceptable: Now that spring has come, I want to plant
forget-me-nots in our garden.

Exercise

1. Write out the following words and phrases so that they are spelled correctly. In some examples, you will have to write two words as one. In some, you will have to use a hyphen. In some, you will have to copy the words as they are printed here. Check your dictionary if in doubt.

large sand bar
wild life
hand knitted sweater
ring billed gull
hand me down garments
intraabdominal
ready made clothing
far off places
self analysis
wild whooping cranes
new executive suite
pre Napoleonic era
bird watching
200 horsepower engine
back country farmers
loose fitting clothing

forty five
ground hog
terrible mix up
built in heating system
ground hugging chassis
ex wife
old car thief
electron tube
high pitched instrument
Kentucky blue grass
anti American sentiment
white tailed hawks
hundred mile trip
granny knot
immature bald eagle
middle class

2. Find and correct the errors in syllable division and the use of hyphens at the ends of the lines in the following paragraph. (Lines are numbered for easy reference as you do the exercise.)

When we first entered our psychiatrist's office, I noticed that his little cocker spaniel trotted in with us. Wh-
en I asked the doctor whether the dog had to be in
such a small room with the four members of our family, he said th-
5   at the dog would have to stay. As the weeks of therapy rolled
by, I began to see the wisdom in his choice. Often, when one of
the family was feeling too emotional to say anything, the little dog would instinctively jump up on that person's lap and begin to lick them in the face. Also, when the children had not-
10   hing to say, they could cover over the silences by grabbing the
dog and rolling around on the floor with her.

ITALICS

ital

In printed materials, words and titles in italics appear in a slanted type-face like *this*. When you want to indicate italics in a handwritten or typed paper, you simply underline the part to be italicized.

1. Italicize titles of books, plays, films, newspapers, and magazines.

> *Great Expectations*
> *Othello*
> *The Wall Street Journal*
> *Time*

2. Italicize foreign words.

> In distinguishing between two kinds of love, Paul Tillich, the great twentieth-century theologian, uses the Greek words *eros* and *agape*. In Buddhism, one of the words meaning "emptiness" or "the void" is *sunyata*.

3. Words used as examples are italicized or placed between quotation marks. Choose either form and use it consistently throughout a particular piece of writing.

> Three verbs that illustrate this sound change are *sleep, creep,* and *leap*. *Run, brook,* and *branch* are three words for a small stream that are important in the study of American regional dialects.

● Answers to odd-numbered exercises begin on page 541.

4. You can italicize words for emphasis. But you should not use this device too frequently.

Faulty: I never *dreamed* it would be *unsafe* to go out on the lake since the weather forecast mentioned *only* the *possibility* of thunderstorms.

Acceptable: I never dreamed it would be unsafe to go out on the lake since the weather forecast mentioned only the *possibility* of thunderstorms.

Exercise   Insert or delete italics wherever necessary in the following sentences.

1. One of the best-known poems from Robert Frost's Mountain Interval is "The Road Not Taken."
2. I think *you* ought to *go out* there and *tell* her what you *really* think.
3. The Old French word daunger meant something like "aloofness."
4. The words I constantly misspell are accommodation, receive, and appearance.
5. I'm afraid you got the message all wrong. I did not want you to take the truck on your run.

CAPITALS Capital letters are used in writing:

cap
1. The first word in a sentence.
2. The first and last words in a title plus all other words except for articles, conjunctions, and prepositions of four letters or less.

The Nation Comes of Age
Meditations from the Breakdown Lane: Running Across America

3. Proper names, including names of the days of the week and the months of the year.

Wednesday, April 25, 1985
Judaism
United States
Abraham Lincoln
English

4. The pronoun *I*.

Be careful not to capitalize words like *university, father, spring, west, history, mathematics* unless they are proper names or parts of proper names or titles. All of the following are acceptable:

I have to travel two miles south each day to get to the university.

We travelled far into the Old South to visit the University of Mississippi.

"Father, Mary's dad is here to see you," I called.

In the spring term, I'm taking English, French, history, and mathematics.

Exercise

In the following sentences, change lowercase letters to capitals and capitals to lowercase letters wherever necessary.

1. The meeting will be held next wednesday.
2. My Professor is coming to town in October to lecture at the University.
3. We drove South along the Mississippi.
4. Our Department has been working hard for weeks to prepare our Annual Review of Achievements for the top Executives of our Company.
5. Last Spring, we moved to the Southwest.

ABBREVIATIONS

Although ordinarily you should use abbreviations sparingly, some abbreviations are acceptable in all writing situations.

ab

1. Common abbreviations for titles used with proper names.

   Dr. Richard Summers
   Richard Summers, Ph.D.
   Richard Summers, Jr.

   Other abbreviated titles used before names are *Mr., Ms., Mrs., St.* (or *Ste.* for female saints), *Rev.* Other abbreviated titles used after names are *M.D., M.A., S.J.*

2. Commonly abbreviated names of companies and organizations. (Some of these abbreviations appear without periods. Check your dictionary if in doubt about whether or not to use periods.)

   UN
   UNICEF
   IBM
   OSHA
   HEW
   CBS

● Answers to odd-numbered exercises begin on page 541.

3. Common abbreviations for time and date when used with a numeral.

    10 a.m.
    8 p.m.
    25 B.C.
    A.D. 1945

4. Commonly abbreviated Latin terms.

    etc.
    e.g.
    i.e.
    viz.

You step outside the conventions of edited English when you use abbreviations as in the following sentences:

Faulty: I picked her up in the a.m. and took her to see the Dr.
Faulty: Our Rev. is a real st.
Acceptable: I picked her up at 9 a.m. and took her to see Dr. Peoples.
Acceptable: Rev. John Phillips is a real saint.

Exercise

In the following sentences, correct all misuses of abbreviations. Also, abbreviate those expressions that normally are abbreviated.

1. By October 21, all three projects must be finished so that the EDP dept. can complete its phase by the end of the year.
2. On p. 42 of ch. 3, the author creates a quiet scene of the family eating a picnic lunch on the lawn of their house.
3. We have hired Lancelot Thompson, Doctor of Medicine, to head up the new infirmary in our plant.
4. The Washington Co. coroner pronounced Mister Daly dead on arrival at Mercy Hosp.
5. One of the most beautiful parts of N.Y. state is the Adirondack Mts.

NUMBERS
num

In nontechnical writing, write out all numbers that can be expressed in one or two words.

Two hundred enemy troops were kept at bay by five snipers armed with automatic rifles.
Twenty-five hundred salmon pass this point every spawning season.

Write out numbers at the beginning of sentences.

Faulty: 25 sailors went ashore.
Acceptable: Twenty-five sailors went ashore.

Even in nontechnical writing, however, there are certain situations in which numbers are presented as figures.

Use figures for numbers requiring three or more words; for specific sums of money (not round numbers); for numbers containing decimals or expressing percentages; for dates (except when the day of the month is not followed by the year: May 1st or May first) and time (except when used with *o'clock*); for temperature; for pages and chapters, acts and scenes, and line numbers; for statistics; for addresses.

The recall involves 175,000 [or 175 thousand] new automobiles.
The carpet is on sale for $925.25. (Compare: A five-cent candy bar now costs thirty cents.)
The results of the survey showed that 25.9 percent of the respondents preferred the lighter color.
On Wednesday, November 15th, a town meeting will be held at 7:30 p.m. in Salem Baptist Church. (Compare: The church service begins at eleven o'clock.)
At 5 a.m. the temperature was only 25° F.
Act III, scene ii begins on page 375 of your textbook.
The mean score of the control group was 11.2, and the mean score of the experimental group was 25.3, a difference that was statistically significant at the .05 level of probability.
The police followed the suspect to 1212 Chandler Street.

Exercise

Find and correct all errors in the use of numbers in the following sentences.

1. 45 members of the home team trotted onto the field to receive the cheers of the crowd.
2. Homecoming brought one hundred twenty-five thousand two hundred and nine people to the stadium to see Statler College whip Eastern University.
3. In the last three months, our firm has lost twelve thousand forty– two dollars and ninety–five cents.
4. Only twenty-five percent of all respondents thought that the new product was superior to competing products.
5. For five years now, I have wanted to be able to lift more than three hundred twenty-five pounds, and now I'm happy to say that I can.

● Answers to odd-numbered exercises begin on page 541.

GLOSSARY OF USAGE

This glossary is an alphabetical listing of words commonly confused with each other and usages that might irritate or distract readers.

a, an

In writing, use *an* before words beginning with vowels (*a, e, i, o, u*): *an apple, an egg, an idea, an opening, an understanding.* Use *a* before words beginning with a consonant.

accept/except

Use the *ex-* spelling (*except*) for the preposition meaning "excluding or but" and for the verb meaning "to exclude or leave out."

> Our cat is loved by everyone *except* the mice in our basement.
> John should be *excepted* from those who are going to receive prizes.

Use the *ac-* spelling (*accept*) for the verb meaning "to receive willingly" or "agree to."

> I *accepted* the award for my dead brother.

access/excess

Use the *ex-* spelling (*excess*) for the noun meaning "superabundance" or "a going beyond reasonable limits." Use the *ac-* spelling (*access*) for the noun meaning "admission" or "approach."

> This year Midwest farmers have produced an *excess* of all grains.
> Someone gained *access* to our house by cutting a screen and climbing through an open window.

advice/advise

Use the *-c-* spelling (*advice*) for the noun and the *-s-* spelling (*advise*) for the verb. (Just remember that *noun* comes before *verb* in an alphabetical list as *-c-* comes before *-s-*.)

Noun: Abigail Adams gave her husband John sound political *advice*.
Verb: My doctor *advised* me to substitute swimming for jogging.

affect/effect

Use the *e-* spelling (*effect*) for the noun meaning "result" or "consequence." (Note that *result* also has an *-e-*.) Use the *a-* spelling (*affect*) for the verb meaning "to influence" or "to move emotionally."

Noun: The *effect* of this rule was to encourage young people to cross the state line to buy beer.
Verb: Nothing I do seems to *affect* her opinion of me.

The most common error is to spell the noun meaning "result" with an *a-*.

    (There is also a verb spelled *effect* that means "to bring about" and a noun spelled *affect* that means "something that tends to arouse emotion.")

all right/alright

Alright has not yet been accepted in edited English. Use *all right*.

allusion/illusion

Use the *a-* spelling (*allusion*) for the noun meaning "an indirect or casual reference." Use the *i-* spelling (*illusion*) for the noun meaning "a false idea or impression; a misleading appearance."

My English professor drives me crazy with his frequent *allusions* to literary works I haven't read.
His *allusions* to a wide range of literature create an *illusion* of great learning.

a lot/alot

Alot is not yet an accepted spelling in edited English. Separate the two words: *a lot*.

already/all ready

Use the single-word spelling (*already*) for the adverb meaning "before a particular time."

The reporter was *already* on the scene.

Use the two-word spelling (*all ready*) for the phrase meaning "entirely prepared."

The reporter on the scene was *all ready* to broadcast her observations.

altogether/all together

Use the single-word spelling (*altogether*) for the adverb meaning "entirely, completely."

> Othello is *altogether* blind not to sense Iago's treachery and Desdemona's trustworthiness.

Use the two-word spelling (*all together*) for the phrase meaning "together in one place."

> Your books are *all together* on your desk.

among/between

Traditionally, *among* is used with three or more items, *between* with only two.

> The three young men should have shared the gold *among* themselves. She had a hard time deciding *between* mechanical and electrical engineering.

However, this tradition is breaking down, and *between* is used more and more frequently with more than two items, especially when the items are regarded individually rather than as an undifferentiated group.

> She soon will have to decide *between* mechanical, electrical, and industrial engineering.

Compare this sentence to the following:

> *Among* the many nations with an overabundance of people, Bangladesh is the most pathetic.

amount/number

Traditionally, *amount* is used with mass nouns like *wheat, coal, work, territory,* and *effort. Number* is used with count nouns like *table, computer, letter,* and *book.*

> This year farmers have produced a record *amount* of corn.
> John Hooper has pitched a record *number* of shutouts for Jones High.

and/or

In writing about general topics, avoid *and/or.* Some people object to this expression in papers on general topics because it is associated with the language of legal and commercial writing.

anyways/anywheres/nowheres/somewheres

Though sometimes heard in casual speech, *anyways, anywheres, nowheres,* and *somewheres* are not acceptable in writing. Use *anyway, anywhere, nowhere,* or *somewhere.*

as

See *like/as.*

at

It makes for unnecessary wordiness to use *at* in sentences like *Where do you live at?* and *Where are you at?*

bad/badly

Bad is an adjective, *badly* an adverb. Use the adjective *bad* after linking verbs. Just as you would not say, "You are badly," so you should not say,

Faulty: She looks *badly.*

Remember that *feel, appear, seem, smell* are or can be linking verbs.

Acceptable: She looks *bad.*
Acceptable: The banana smells *bad.*
Acceptable: She feels *bad.*

In situations requiring edited English, you will be expected to use *badly* where the word functions as an adverb.

Faulty: The tenor sang *bad.*
Faulty: The team played *bad.*
Acceptable: The tenor sang *badly.*
Acceptable: The team played *badly.*

being(s) as/being that

In situations requiring edited English, you will be expected to write *because* or *since* rather than *being(s) as* or *being that.*

beside/besides

Use the *-s* spelling (*besides*) when you mean "in addition to" or "over and above."

Faulty: There is no one *beside* my father who can make a really good fried-egg sandwich.

Acceptable: There is no one *besides* my father who can make a really good fried-egg sandwich.

Use *beside* when you mean "next to."

There is a mouse nest *beside* the old stone fence.

between

See *among/between.*

can/may

In writing, especially formal writing, observe the traditional distinction between *can*, implying capability, and *may*, implying permission.

The American auto industry *can* produce efficient, durable automobiles.
Our employees *may* have an increase in pay if they demonstrate a corresponding increase in productivity.

can't hardly/can't scarcely

In situations requiring edited English, avoid *can't hardly* and *can't scarcely*. (These expressions are considered examples of double negatives.) Instead, use *can hardly* and *can scarcely*.

center on/center around

Center around will bother some readers because the phrase seems self-contradictory. (How can something be simultaneously at the center and "around"?) Use *center on* instead.

cite/sight/site

Cite is a verb meaning "to quote" or "to refer to."

In proving his point, the author *cites* the opinion of three outdated authorities.

Sight is a noun meaning "view" or "the ability to see" and a verb meaning "to aim" or "to see."

It is a great *sight* to watch Old Faithful spout in Yellowstone National Park.
On October 12, 1492, one of the sailors in Columbus' group *sighted* land.

Site is a noun meaning "location."

> In the eighteenth and nineteenth centuries, the rapids marked the *site* of a large Indian camp.

compare/contrast

Compare means "to examine similarities or differences"; *contrast* means "to examine differences." However, in examination instructions, *compare* is commonly used in the restricted sense of "to examine similarities." *Compare* is followed by *to* or *with*; *contrast* is followed by *with*.

> *Compared to* our opponents, our players are quite small.
> The sportswriter *contrasted* our team *with* theirs.

complected/complexioned

In situations requiring edited English, avoid *complected* (as in *dark-complected*). Use *complexioned* (*dark-complexioned*) or reword the expression (*she has dark hair and eyes*).

complement/compliment

Use the -*e*- spelling (*complement*) when talking about completion. (Note that *complement* and *completion* contain -*e*- in their spelling.) Use the -*i*- spelling (*compliment*) when talking about praise. (Note that *praise* and *compliment* have -*i*- in their spellings.)

> A soda *complements* a cheeseburger perfectly.
> Our regional manager has sent us a memo *complimenting* us for our excellent work on the PL-1 project.

could of, must of, should of, would of

The *of* in *could of, must of, should of,* and *would of* is an incorrect spelling of the contraction *'ve* (*could've, must've, should've, would've*). When writing this contraction, keep alert to how you're spelling it.

council/counsel

Use the -*cil* spelling (*council*) for the meaning "assembly or deliberative group": *student council, President's Council of Economic Advisers.* Use the -*sel* spelling (*counsel*) for the noun meaning "advice" or "legal adviser" and for the verb meaning "to advise": *good counsel; Mr. Thompson counseled me to sell my stocks.*

criterion/criteria

Use the spelling with *-ion* (*criterion*) for the singular (*my one criterion*). Use the spelling with *-ia* (*criteria*) for the plural (*four criteria*).

data

In scientific writing, treat *data* as a plural (*the data show*). In nonscientific writing, treat *data* as a singular (*the data shows*). The original Latin singular, *datum*, is rarely used.

different from/different than

Before a noun or pronoun, a noun phrase, or a noun clause, write *different from*.

> My idea is *different from* yours.
> In the Revolutionary War, the American style of fighting was *different from* what British soldiers had previously experienced.

Different than is more apt to be acceptable to readers when *than* marks the beginning of a clause, especially a clause in which one or more major elements are left unexpressed and especially in a case where using *from* would be wordy.

> Wagner had a profoundly *different* conception of operatic music *than* any of his contemporaries had.

disinterested/uninterested

In situations requiring edited English, don't use *disinterested* to mean "uninterested."

Faulty: I find myself *disinterested* in accounting.
Acceptable: I find myself *uninterested* in accounting.

Reserve *disinterested* for the meaning "impartial."

> Janet tried to be a *disinterested* observer in the fight between Al and Joe.

don't

He/she/it doesn't is the acceptable usage in edited English.

Faulty: Othello *don't* see that Iago hates him.
Acceptable: Othello *doesn't* see that Iago hates him.

double negative

A double negative is the use of two negative words in a single construction where edited English requires only one.

Faulty: A mother whale *doesn't* have to teach her calf *nothing* about swimming.
Acceptable: A mother whale *doesn't* have to teach her calf anything about swimming.
Acceptable: A mother whale has to teach her calf *nothing* about swimming.

effect

See *affect/effect*.

elicit, illicit

Use the *el-* spelling (*elicit*) for the verb meaning "to draw out." Use the *ill-* spelling (*illicit*) for the adjective meaning "not permitted" or "unlawful."

President Thompson's speech *elicited* an angry editorial from the school newspaper.
A senior on the basketball team was arrested for selling *illicit* drugs.

except

See *accept/except*.

excess

See *access/excess*.

farther/further

Use either word when talking about distance.

Acceptable: Last week I ran twenty miles *farther* than I had ever run before.
Acceptable: If we had just traveled a little *further*, we would have found the road into the park.

Use *further* when you mean "more" or "in addition."

Acceptable: Dr. Rowland accepted my paper without asking for *further* revisions.

fewer/less

Fewer is used with items that can be individually counted. *Less* is used with abstract and collective ideas.

Our team won because we made *fewer* mistakes than our opponents.
Mother and Dad expressed *less* opposition to our getting married than
I thought they would.

good/well

In situations requiring edited English, don't use *good* as an adverb. Use
well instead.

Faulty: I was playing *good* until the coach put me on the defensive squad.
Acceptable: I was playing *well* until the coach put me on the defensive squad.

In sentences like "Brahms' First Symphony sounds surprisingly good in
the four-hand piano version," *good* is an adjective. (Remember that *feel,
seem, taste,* and *sound* are or can be used as linking verbs.)
    A distinction is made between *to feel good* and *to feel well. To feel good*
means "to be happy or contented." *To feel well* means "to feel healthy."

hanged/hung

Use *hanged* when talking about executions and *hung* when talking about
pictures, shelves, and the like.

The lynch mob *hanged* the captured slave.
My father proudly *hung* my diploma over the mantel.

he or she/his or her

Traditionally, the masculine pronouns *he/his/him* have been used to refer
to *person* or indefinite pronouns like *one, everyone,* and *everybody.* In an
attempt to avoid sexism in language, many writers are searching for
more inclusive alternatives. However, the phrases *he or she* and *his or her*
are alternatives that seem clumsy to many readers. Sometimes you can
avoid the whole problem by using the plural or avoiding pronouns
altogether.

Clumsy: Each student must pay *his or her* graduation fee before *he or she* can
    receive *his or her* diploma.
Acceptable: Students must pay *a* graduation fee before *they* can receive *their*
    diplomas.

hisself/himself; theirselves/themselves

Hisself and *theirselves* are not used in edited English. Use *himself* and
themselves instead.

Faulty: At the end of the play, Othello stabs *hisself.*
Acceptable: At the end of the play, Othello stabs *himself.*

illicit

See *elicit/illicit*.

illusion

See *allusion/illusion*.

imply/infer

Use *imply* to mean "express indirectly" or "hint." Use *infer* to mean "draw a conclusion."

> His words *imply* that he thinks women are inferior to men.
> From his words, I *infer* that he is a male chauvinist.

irregardless

Use *regardless* in situations requiring edited English.

kind of/sort of

Kind of a and *sort of a* are considered too informal for college and business writing.

Too informal: Dr. Schafer is the *kind of a* teacher I would someday like to be.
Acceptable: Dr. Schafer is the *kind of* teacher I would someday like to be.

Kind of and *sort of* are used with *this/that* and singular verbs.

> *This sort of* feeling haunts me during every graduation ceremony I attend.

If you are thinking about several *kinds* or *sorts*, use *these/those* and plural verbs.

> *These sorts of* feelings *are* typical of the first stage of grief.

Do not combine *these/those* with *kind/sort*.

Faulty: *These sort* of feelings are typical of the first stage of grief.

lay/lie

Similarity of form and meaning make these words easy to confuse. As a transitive verb, *lay* ("to put" or "to place") requires a direct object to complete its meaning.

> He *lays* flooring like an expert.

The Lone Ranger *laid* his revolver on the table.
I had just *laid* my pen down when Mike burst into the room.

In casual conversation, the forms of *lay* are commonly used with the meaning of *lie*, "to recline." In situations requiring edited English, use only the forms of *lie* to mean "to recline."

Faulty: Before she *lays* down on her bed, Desdemona sings the "Willow Song."
Acceptable: Before she *lies* down on her bed, Desdemona sings the "Willow Song."
Faulty: Captain O'Hara *laid* there huddling against a rock while bullets passed overhead.
Acceptable: Captain O'Hara *lay* there huddling against a rock while bullets passed overhead.

leave/let

In casual conversation, *leave* has come to be synonymous with *let* in the sense of "allow." However, in writing *leave* is used strictly in the meaning "to depart."

Faulty: Ms. Johnson promised that she would *leave* our group do all the planning for the fall advertising campaign.
Acceptable: Ms. Johnson promised that she would *let* our group do all the planning for the fall advertising campaign.

(The only exception to this rule is the expression *leave alone*, which is equal in acceptability to *let alone*.)

less

See *fewer/less*.

lie

See *lay/lie*.

like/as

In formal usage situations, do not use *like* as a conjunction. Use *as* instead.

Too informal: When Macbeth sees Banquo's ghost, he acts *like* you would expect him to.
Formal: When Macbeth sees Banquo's ghost, he acts *as* you would expect him to.

lose/loose

Use the *-o-* spelling (*lose*) for the verb meaning "to misplace." Use the *-oo-* spelling (*loose*) for the adjective meaning "not tight."

Faulty: The narrator fears that he will *loose* his mind.
Acceptable: The narrator fears that he will *lose* his mind.

moral/morale

Use the *-ale* spelling (*morale*) when talking about people's spirits. Use the other spelling (*moral*) when talking about ethics.

Faulty: Employee *moral* is quite high.
Acceptable: Employee *morale* is quite high.

must of

See *could of/must of/should of/would of.*

nowheres

See *anyways/anywheres/nowheres/somewheres.*

number

See *amount.*

personal/personnel

Use the *-nal* spelling (*personal*) for the adjective meaning "relating to a person." Use the *-nnel* spelling (*personnel*) for the noun meaning "people employed in a particular service."

Faulty: We must give our *personal* additional training.
Acceptable: We must give our *personnel* additional training.

plus

Plus should not be used as a conjunction in writing.

Too informal: We collected water samples from fifteen locations in the lake, *plus* we gathered twenty-five specimens of lake fish.
Acceptable: We collected water samples from fifteen locations in the lake, *and* we gathered twenty-five specimens of lake fish.

precede/proceed

Use the spelling *precede* for the meaning "to come before in time or rank." Use the spelling *proceed* for the meaning "to go forward or onward."

Acceptable: A comedian will *precede* the main attraction on the program.

Acceptable: After the interruption, the judge instructed the witness to *proceed* with her testimony.

principal/principle

Use the *-pal* spelling (*principal*) for the noun and adjective with the meaning "chief": *school principal; principal objection. Principal* also means "a capital sum of money" as in the phrase *principal of a loan.*

Use the *-ple* spelling (*principle*) for the noun meaning "rule" or "general truth."

Faulty: The patient's low blood count is the *principle* bit of evidence for the doctor's diagnosis.

Acceptable: The patient's low blood count is the *principal* bit of evidence for the doctor's diagnosis.

Acceptable: The philosopher shot himself rather than act against his *principles.*

proved/proven

Both *proved* and *proven* are acceptable as past participles in edited English.

Acceptable: The lawyer had *proved* [or *proven*] his point to the jury's satisfaction.

quite/quiet

Use the *-ite* spelling (*quite*) for the adverb meaning "completely." Use the *-iet* spelling (*quiet*) for the adjective and noun referring to the idea "opposite of loud."

Faulty: At night the farm was too *quite* for me.

Acceptable: At night the farm was too *quiet* for me.

quote/quotation

In formal writing situations, *quote* will seem excessively informal when used as a noun. Use *quotation* instead.

Too informal: These *quotes* from Abigail Adams' letters demonstrate how in John's absence she had come to rely on her own judgment in business transactions.

Acceptable: These *quotations* from Abigail Adams' letters demonstrate how in John's absence she had come to rely on her own judgment in business transactions.

real/really

In formal writing situations, *real* will seem excessively informal when used as an adverb. Use *really* or *very* instead.

Too informal: Several times during the Revolutionary War, American generals found it *real* difficult to keep the militiamen from deserting.
Acceptable: Several times during the Revolutionary War, American generals found it *very* difficult to keep the militiamen from deserting.

reason is because/reason is that

In formal writing situations, write *reason is that* instead of *reason is because*.

Faulty: The *reason* whales have so much fat *is because* they need to be insulated from the cold temperatures of the surrounding water.
Acceptable: The *reason* whales have so much fat *is that* they need to be insulated from the cold temperatures of the surrounding water.

Sometimes it is even better to reword the entire sentence.

Whales have so much fat because they need to be insulatated from the cold temperatures of the surrounding waters.

sensual/sensuous

Use the *-al* spelling (*sensual*) for the negative meaning "appealing to the gratification of base appetites" or "suggesting a voluptuous intent or temperament." Use the *-ous* spelling (*sensuous*) for the positive meaning "pertaining to the senses."

After being inflamed by Salomi's *sensual* dance, Herod was ready to grant her anything she wanted, even the decapitated head of John the Baptist.
The references to cold and warmth and to colors and textures give Keats' "Eve of St. Agnes" great *sensuous* appeal.

set/sit

In writing, do not use *set* with the meaning of *sit*.

Faulty: Leonardo da Vinci's famous painting "The Last Supper" depicts Jesus *setting* at a long table with his disciples.

Acceptable: Leonardo da Vinci's famous painting "The Last Supper" depicts Jesus *sitting* at a long table with his disciples.

sight/site

See *cite/sight/site*.

sort of

See *kind of/sort of*.

split infinitives

Despite the traditional prohibition against splitting infinitives, writers do use split infinitives when it seems natural to separate *to* and the verb with a modifier.

Acceptable: Our researchers want to carefully examine the data sent back from the space satellite.

Of course, you should avoid separating *to* from the verb with any word or phrase that seems awkward or misleading.

Faulty: John tried to meaningfully write about his war experiences.
Acceptable: John tried to write meaningfully about his war experiences.

stationary/stationery

Use the *-ary* spelling for the adjective meaning "fixed in position." Use the *-ery* spelling for the noun meaning "writing materials."

In this maneuver, the flag bearers remain *stationary* while the trumpet and trombone sections pivot around them.
Even the type of *stationery* you use for your cover letter will affect the way a recruiter regards your job application.

supposed to/used to

Suppose to and *use to* are common misspellings for *supposed to* and *used to*.

than/then

Remember to use the *-an* spelling (*than*) in comparative constructions and the *-en* spelling (*then*) when talking about time.

Faulty: No American general of the Revolutionary War impresses me more *then* Nathaniel Greene.

Acceptable: No American general of the Revolutionary War impresses me more *than* Nathaniel Greene.

their/there/they're

Whenever you write *their, there,* or *they're,* check to make sure you are using the appropriate spelling. *Their* is the possessive pronoun or adjective meaning "of them." *There* is the adverb meaning "at or in that place"; *there* is often used in place of the subject before the verb *to be* (*there are many reasons why I must refuse*). *They're* is the contracted form of *they are.*

theirselves

See *hisself/himself; theirselves/themselves.*

though

Though is frequently used as a synonym for *however* and *nevertheless* in casual conversation and informal writing. When using a formal style, use *however* or *nevertheless* instead.

Informal: According to another historian, *though,* the beginnings of the women's rights movement cannot be separated from the movement to abolish slavery.
Formal: According to another historian, *however,* the beginnings of the women's rights movement cannot be separated from the movement to abolish slavery.

When using *though* as a synonym for *however* and *nevertheless,* place *though* in the middle or at the end of the clause—never at the beginning.

Faulty: *Though,* according to another historian, the beginnings of the women's rights movement cannot be separated from the movement to abolish slavery.

to/too/two

Whenever you write *to, too, two,* check to make sure you have used the appropriate spelling. Use *to* for the preposition, *too* for the adverb meaning "also" and "excessively," and *two* for the number.

Faulty: Our test instrument gave respondents *to* many answers to choose from.
Acceptable: Our test instrument gave respondents *too* many answers to choose from.

thusly

Thusly is not an acceptable variant for *thus* in writing.

try and/try to

Though frequently heard in casual conversation, *try and* will sound excessively informal in writing. Use *try to* instead.

Too informal: Our staff has promised to *try and* finish phase one of the project before Christmas.
Acceptable: Our staff has promised to *try to* finish phase one of the project before Christmas.

type

In writing and formal speech situations, *type* should not be used as a synonym for *type of*. Use *type of* instead. (Compare *kind of* and *sort of*.)

Faulty: This *type* copier tends to produce overly dark copies.
Acceptable: This *type of* copier tends to produce overly dark copies.

uninterested

See *disinterested/uninterested*.

weather/whether

Use the *wea-* spelling (*weather*) for the noun meaning "atmospheric conditions." Use the *whe-* spelling (*whether*) for the conjunction.

Faulty: I doubt *weather* our team could have made the playoffs without John at quarterback.
Acceptable: I doubt *whether* our team could have made the playoffs without John at quarterback.

who/which/that

In writing and formal speech situations, do not use *which* to refer to persons. Use *who* or *that* instead.

Faulty: Our staff has only three people *which* have passed the security check.
Acceptable: Our staff has only three people *who* have passed the security check.

who/whom

In formal writing, use *who* as the subject form and *whom* as the object form.

> *Faulty:*   Benedict Arnold, *who* Washington had always relied on, became a notorious traitor.
>
> *Acceptable:*   Benedict Arnold, *whom* Washington had always relied on, became a notorious traitor.
>
> *Faulty:*   Benedict Arnold, *whom* betrayed Washington's trust, became a brigadier general in the British army.
>
> *Acceptable:*   Benedict Arnold, *who* betrayed Washington's trust, became a brigadier general in the British army.

To distinguish between *who* and *whom*, pay careful attention to the function of the word in the clause it introduces.

-wise

Because the tendency to attach *-wise* to words is associated with business jargon, new word formations with *-wise* will seem inappropriate to the topics of most college papers. Words like *taxwise, saleswise,* and *jobwise* should therefore be avoided in college writing. Such words may also seem awkward and irritating in business writing.

your/you're

Use *your* as the spelling for the possessive adjective (*your pencil*) and *you're* for the contraction of *you are*. Whenever you use either form, check to make sure you have used the appropriate spelling.

APPENDIX

ARGUMENTATIVE FALLACIES

COMMON FALLACIES Elsewhere in this text we mention specific strategies for composing and revising writing that has as its primary purpose argumentation. This section defines and illustrates flaws in reasoning that you should *avoid* when writing. You should also be on the alert for them when reading or listening to the arguments of others.

Substituting Personal Attacks for Evidence Sometimes, in order to persuade their audiences, speakers or writers resort to using personal attacks on their opponents rather than using logical evidence. In this way they deflect the audience's attention from the issues at hand and focus it on personalities instead. Instead of directly criticizing an opponent's stand on nuclear disarmament, for example, a politician may hint at problems in the person's background, hoping in this way to persuade people to lose confidence in that individual and to vote the opposite way. This tactic may, of course, backfire if the audience recognizes it for what it is.

In your own writing, *focus on your topic*, supporting it with as much evidence as you can. Don't avoid the issues by commenting needlessly on the personality, background, or other qualities of the people who present opposing views.

Confusing Correlation with Causation It is often tempting to think that because an event occurs at the same time as (or *correlates* with) another event, one causes the other. But such a conclusion must be carefully verified before it is accepted as truth. For example, for many years it was thought that malaria was caused by the night air. After all, people who became ill invariably did so after having been out at dusk; the evening air correlated perfectly with the disease. Eventually, however, doctors learned that parasites carried by mosquitoes caused the disease. In assuming the air to be at fault, people overlooked another correlation, one that happened to be the real cause.

When discussing a cause-effect relationship, then, investigate the causes and effects thoroughly to be sure that one does indeed cause the other to happen.

Failing to Look Beneath the Surface Just as it's tempting to equate correlation with causation, it's tempting to consider only the surface appearances in reaching conclusions. For example, if we see a man running down the street being followed by a man yelling, "Stop, thief!" we assume the first man stole something from the second. Although we may be correct, it is wiser to refrain from making an assumption based on what appears to be true. In this case the conclusion could be tested, perhaps by speaking to an eyewitness or by viewing a news report that evening.

In any event, offer as conclusions ideas you have thoroughly thought through or researched. Avoid presenting as facts ideas based on casual observations or hasty readings. When reading the arguments of others, read critically, examining their conclusions carefully to determine whether they are based on a thorough investigation of the situation at hand.

Employing Faulty Syllogisms A *syllogism* is a type of logical argument that presents two statements (or *premises*) which lead to a conclusion. Here is an example of a syllogism:

> I hate all fruits.
> Peaches are fruits.
> Therefore, I hate peaches.

Note that the third statement follows as a logical consequence of the two premises. Problems with syllogisms may occur, however, if either (or both) of the premises is untrue. Note the following:

> I hate all fruits.
> Carrots are fruits.
> Therefore, I hate carrots.

The third statment, like the third one in the first example, follows logically from the stated premises. But the syllogism is faulty because the second premise is not true.

When arguing an idea by constructing a syllogism, be sure that the premises from which you work are true. Likewise, when reviewing other people's conclusions, check to see that the foundations are accurate.

Using Limited Evidence to Support a Conclusion Often we are tempted to argue that what is true in one instance is true in general. In fact, what is true in one or two situations may not be true for all similar situations. For example, suppose you know of one or two cases of cheating on exams at your school. It would be risky to conclude on the basis of such limited evidence that students in general cannot be trusted to maintain an honor code. Chances are that a great many more students *can* be trusted. The only safe conclusion that could be reached from the above evidence is that *some* students cannot be trusted.

Sometimes writers make the mistake of using too little evidence to support a conclusion that may in fact be true. For example, in composing a critical essay you might assert that a character in a novel is rash and impulsive, but then offer only one action or episode from the book for support. Even if the character is genuinely rash and impulsive, an argument based on such limited evidence would generally be unacceptable. You should either offer additional evidence to support the point or abandon the point.

Creating False Dilemmas

Sometimes writers, in their zeal to persuade, reduce complex issues to an "either-or" situation that may not exist. They phrase their arguments so that their solutions appear to be the only acceptable alternative. For example, the slogan "If you're not part of the solution, you're part of the problem" forces a choice that appears to be the only one available: No one wants to be a problem; therefore the only other logical alternative is to embrace whatever solution is being offered. In this way the reader's attention is deflected from the issues at hand to making a choice that may not have to be made at all.

Argumentative fallacies such as these are used frequently and may in fact be persuasive. Responsible writers should avoid them in favor of more logical and substantial approaches.

ANSWER KEY

PARTS OF SPEECH **Exercise (p. 437)** on identifying nouns.

1. Vikings, sailors, warriors
3. acid, mixture
5. Dwight D. Eisenhower, president, United States, prominence, achievements, World War II
7. Shakespeare, language, turns, phrase, winter, discontent
9. Matterhorn, peaks, Alps

Exercise (p. 440) on identifying main verbs and verbals. (Main verbs are in italics.)

1. rising, *use*, evaluating
3. *had*, been, killed, *would*, have, been
5. *believed*, *would*, have
7. *is*, coming, *must*, be, allow, stray
9. *did*, see, *had*, collapsed

Exercise (p. 442) on identifying adjectives and articles. The numbers in parentheses indicate the number of times an article is used in the sentence.

1. all, the (2), softest
3. the (1), white, larger, some, other
5. Persian, their, dark, red, their, beautiful
7. symphonic, beautiful, skillful
9. any, this, successful, an (1)

Exercise (p. 443) on identifying adverbs.

1. however, not, then
3. highly, as, soon, inside (The second *as* is a conjunction introducing the clause *the general walked inside*.)
5. wearily, ashore
7. certainly, very, well
9. specifically

Exercise (p. 445) on identifying pronouns.

1. them (*This* is used as an adjective.)
3. he (*His* is used as an adjective.)
5. themselves
7. ours
9. we (*His* and *these* are used as adjectives in this sentence.)

Exercise (p. 448) on identifying prepositions, conjunctions, and interjections.

1. *Conjunction:* although *Prepositions:* at, with, by, of
3. *Conjunction:* when *Preposition:* to
5. *Interjection:* oh
7. *Conjunction:* when *Prepositions:* with, of, for
9. *Conjunction:* but *Preposition:* on

SENTENCE STRUCTURE

Exercise A (p. 453) on identifying the subjects of sentences.

1. the meeting
3. the author
5. the locusts
7. the trees with the white trunks
9. playing the piano
11. the geologist, who believed in the theory of evolution
13. a performance of *Macbeth*
15. two dolphins

Exercise B (p. 453) on identifying the subjects of sentences.

1. several weak areas
3. who
5. which of the trees
7. a terrible fight
9. to buy books in the bookstore
11. where the disease will strike next
13. you
15. Washington's determination to carry on

Exercise A (p. 459) on identifying the predicates of sentences.

1. opened her mouth
3. is an enormous creature
5. gave his dogs some meat
7. told the captain to meet him on the other side of the river
9. is the expulsion of the Eastern Indians from their tribal territories
11. when fishing in groups, . . . sometimes swim in a long line (*Beating the water with their wings to drive the fish before them* modifies the subject, *white pelicans,* even though it comes after the main verb.)
13. seems to be John's great plan
15. somehow remains able to keep his old friends

Exercise B (p. 460) on identifying whether the main verb is transitive (T), intransitive (I), or linking (L).

1. are (L)
3. carried on (I)
5. felled (T)
7. slept (I)
9. cracked (I)
11. read (T)
13. looked over (T)
15. appears (L)

Exercise (p. 463) on identifying noun phrases (NPh), verb phrases (VPh), verbal phrases (VbPh), and prepositional phrases (PrPh).

1. *NPh*—our cat *VbPh*—to sleep on our comforter *PrPh*—on our comforter
3. *NPh*—the violinist *VbPh*—to play the piano
5. *VPh*—must be able *VbPh*—to withstand the cold of their environment *PrPh*—of their environment
7. *NPh*—my father; a long nap *VPh*—would take *PrPh*—after a hard day; at work
9. *NPh*—the quarterback *VbPh*—to set up a field goal possibility; to throw a pass to the tight-end *PrPh*—to the tight-end
11. *NPh*—the boys *VbPh*—having wanted for a long time to play with each other; to play with each other; to telephone each other; to make a date *PrPh*—for a long time; with each other
13. *NPh*—the students *VPh*—would have greatly preferred *VbPh*—to have been allowed to have gone fishing; to have gone fishing
15. *NPh*—our all-news station; news crews; twenty-four hours; a day *VPh*—must have *VbPh*—bringing the news *PrPh*—in bringing the news; to the listening public; on the street

Exercises A and B (pp. 468–69) on identifying dependent clauses and their function.

1. who . . . school (adjectival)
3. if . . . today (adverbial)
5. as she . . . work (adverbial)
7. where . . . lived (adjectival)
9. before he died (adverbial)
11. he . . . work (noun); who . . . throat (adjectival)
13. what he thought (noun); he was doing (noun); when he . . . car (adverbial); he . . . tried (adjectival)
15. when the house . . . exploded with a roar (adverbial); they had surrounded (adjectival); that . . . away (adjectival)

Exercise A (p. 475) on identifying sentences as simple, compound, complex, or compound-complex.

1. simple
3. complex
5. complex
7. compound
9. complex
11. complex
13. simple
15. compound-complex

Exercise B (p. 475) on inserting commas and semicolons to separate clauses.

1. As I was coming out of the anesthesia, I could see two of everything.
3. Our employees look forward to the time when the new parking ramp will be finished.
5. George Washington, who was one of the tallest men in the American Colonies, made an impressive figure on horseback.
7. Adams did want the President to be addressed with the deepest respect, though it was not a major point of policy during his time in office.
9. Benjamin Franklin never went to college, yet he became one of the wisest men in the American Revolution.
11. Adams recognized that Franklin was an excellent politician but felt uncomfortable about the manner Franklin adopted in pursuing the nation's business.
13. Eve, who had accompanied Jill on a long canoeing trip, wondered whether they would ever become good friends or whether they would remain just acquaintances.
15. If Tinker should ever learn to play his position correctly, he and Evans will make a great combination, but I doubt that he will ever improve.

COMMON USAGE ERRORS

Exercise (p. 477) on correcting comma splices.

1. Start the engine to warm the oil; then shut the engine off. (The clauses could also be punctuated as two sentences.)
3. The author intends his child characters to be more than just cute. They play an important role in expressing the theme of the story.
5. Changing oil is a simple procedure; however, to change your oil. . . .
7. This part of the story does have value. It shows. . . .
9. After she came back from her canoeing trip with Jill, Eve left home for Colorado. She just needed. . . .
11. The employees . . . protesting working conditions. They are concerned. . . .

13. Bald eagles used to be a fairly common type of American bird, but they now are concentrated mostly in Alaska and Florida. (Alternative: Although bald eagles . . . bird, they now are concentrated. . . .)

15. Usually, the male red-winged blackbirds arrive in the area first. They come early to establish nesting territories.

Exercise (p. 479) on correcting fused sentences.

1. Fluorescent lights would cost a total of $360. I know. . . .
3. The white-footed mouse . . . United States. It is also. . . .
5. One of Lee's . . . invincibility. He had. . . .
7. Correctly punctuated
9. The boll weevil . . . cotton. Luckily, the boll weevil. . . .
11. On many of the Greek islands . . . windmill. It has. . . . These are positioned. . . . (Alternative: . . . *windmill which has small triangles of cloth . . . wind. These are. . . .*)
13. Crocodiles . . . water. When the prey . . . attacks.
15. Correctly punctuated

Exercise A (p. 480) on sentence fragments. (The proposed corrections represent just one way that the fragments can be eliminated.)

1. Fragment. *Correction*—Drop *whereas* and start the sentence with *the: The competition.* . . .
3. Fragment. *Correction*—Drop *while* and start the sentence with *the: The way to distinguish.* . . .
5. Fragment. *Correction*—Drop *which* and start the sentence with *This development.* . . .
7. Correctly punctuated
9. Fragment. *Correction*—Supply a subject for *is: Yet, the chamber is connected.* . . .
11. Fragment. *Correction*—Insert a subject and main verb: *The instrument has feet that screw up or down . . . used.*
13. Fragment. *Correction*—Substitute *he* for *who* to give the sentence an appropriate subject: *He told the story.* . . .
15. Fragment. *Correction*—Drop *since* and start the sentence with *she: She was truly still a kitten.* . . .

Exercise B (p. 481) on eliminating comma splices, fused sentences, and sentence fragments from a paragraph.

1. Correctly punctuated
3. Fragment
5. Fused sentence
7. Comma splice
9. Correctly punctuated
11. Comma splice
13. Correctly punctuated

Possible Rewrite

When I think of Abraham Lincoln, I find my mind filled with certain pictures—some from childhood stories about "Honest Abe," some from his statue in the Lincoln Memorial, and some from my reading of American history. In one picture, little Abe is doing his homework by the firelight. In another, Abe the shopkeeper is walking miles to give back a few pennies of change or is tirelessly splitting logs. The Abe Lincoln in these mental pictures is physically strong, homely, gaunt. The Abe Lincoln of my mental pictures is also saintly and patient. He has a sad but kindly face and powerful but gentle hands. He does not have personal problems to worry him, only the problems of the nation. He has no grief over a dead son. He has no wife who is on the verge of going crazy. To add such personal difficulties to the stress of being president during the Civil War seems wrong. No one could bear up under such double difficulties. The Abe Lincoln of my mental pictures is a sixteen-foot-tall hero who single-handedly held the nation together through its time of trouble.

Exercise (p. 484) on correcting errors in number agreement.

1. Each. . . . *was* busy. . . .
3. Correct: Anyone who *buys*. . . .
5. The results . . . *have*. . . .
7. Many students . . . *find*. . . .
9. In chess, the bishop, the queen, *and* the king *move*. . . .
11. Correct: The smart swimmer . . . *wears*. . . .
13. The differences . . . *are* the basis. . . . (Less awkward: "The basis for my analysis *is* the differences. . . .")
15. The suggestion . . . *comes*. . . .

Exercise (p. 485) on correcting number agreement errors between pronoun and antecedent.

1. *Persons* who *want* . . . should send in *their* entry form. . . .
3. *All politicians* . . . like to have *their* name. . . .
5. Correct
7. Drop *their* or use *his*: *A police officer does not like . . . when being watched by fellow officers. A police officer does not like . . . when being watched by his fellow officers.*
9. None of the men . . . could believe *his* eyes.

Exercise (p. 486) on correcting vague references.

1. In the second sentence, the first *it* means "the report"; the second *it* means "the aircraft." *Correction*—Substitute *the report* for the first *it* and *the aircraft* for the second.

3. *Which* has no clear antecedent. *Correction*—Break the sentence into two sentences at *team*; start the second sentence with *this change: In 1979, the Transportation Department . . . team. This change enabled Transportation. . . .*

5. Acceptable. In both cases, *it* clearly refers to *typewriter*.

7. Acceptable. *Which* clearly refers to *robins* and *jays*.

9. *It* has no clear antecedent. *Correction*—Make *the amount to be deducted plus the trucker's name and address* the subject of *is marked: We will pay the trucker directly, provided that, at the point of inspection on delivery, the amount to be deducted plus the trucker's name and address is marked on the ticket. Alternative correction*—Changing *plus* to *and* would make a plural subject and a smoother, less awkward construction: *. . . the amount to be deducted and the trucker's name and address are marked on the ticket.*

Exercise (p. 488) on correcting misplaced or squinting modifiers.

1. Move *only* to just before *at the last minute: . . . remembered to put on his tie only at the last minute.*

3. Depending on the meaning, move *completely* to the end of the sentence, or move it before *to triumph: The boy . . . failed completely. The boy who wanted completely to triumph failed.*

5. Acceptable

7. Depending on the meaning, move *occasionally* before *late* or after *will: All employees who are occasionally late for work will lose some pay. All employees who are late for work will occasionally lose some pay.*

9. Move *only* before *five: The water boiled for only five minutes.*

Exercise (p. 489) on correcting dangling modifiers.

1. Turn *charging up the hill* into a relative clause and move it to the end of the sentence: *The Americans calmly waited for the British soldiers who were charging up the hill.*

3. Acceptable

5. Acceptable

7. Acceptable

9. Make *the people* the subject of the main verb: *Having been denied jobs and good homes, the people were quite miserable.*

Exercise (p. 491) on verb tenses and shifts in tense and voice.

1. *Changed* should be in the present tense like *carries: However, the mood changes. . . .*

3. *Goes* should be in the future tense like *will go: . . . the pan will go down and the pointer will go up.*

5. Both clauses should be in the active or the passive voice: *Active—The student mixed the solution and then poured it. . . . Passive—The solution was mixed and then poured into the large beaker.*

7. The second clause should be in the active voice like the first: *The violinist first tuned her instrument; then she played the opening movement of the piece.*

9. *See* and *swerve* should be in the past tense since it is usually more appropriate to report personal experiences in the past tense than in the present: . . . *we saw a tree and swerved to avoid it.*

Exercise (p. 492) on shifts in pronoun form.

1. Change *you'll* to *they'll*: *The reason why marines go through such tough training is so that they'll be able to perform well in combat.*

3. Acceptable

5. Change *you* to *he*: *A hockey player . . . since he has to take many body checks.* . . . Alternative correction—*Hockey players . . . since they have to take many body checks.* . . .

Exercise (p. 493) on faulty parallelism.

1. *Assuming* and *relaxing* are verb forms; *assistance* is a noun. Insert *getting* before *assistance* to complete the parallelism: . . . *by assuming the proper position, relaxing the calf, and getting assistance to increase the stretch.*

3. *Her serve* and *the strength* are noun phrases; *how she handled lobs* is a clause which must be made parallel with the noun phrases: . . . *to improve her serve, her handling of lobs, and the strength.* . . .

5. *The fact* and *the northward flight* are noun phrases; *seeing grackles* is a verbal phrase which must be made parallel with the noun phrases: *The fact that robins . . . , the northward flight of geese, and the sight of grackles.* . . .

7. *To go* is an infinitive; *so that we can just have some fun together* is a clause which must be made parallel with *to go*: . . . *to go swimming and then to go for a drink, but mostly just to have fun together.*

9. *His piano technique* and *his absolute lack* are noun phrases; *that he sings off-key* is a clause which must be made parallel with the noun phrases: *What bothers me is his off-key singing, his piano technique, and his absolute lack of rhythm.*

Exercise (p. 494) on mixed constructions.

1. *We* is the subject of *feel* but not of *is*. Correction—Substitute *a concern that* for *and*: . . . *are a major concern of businesses, a concern that is underrated.* . . .

3. An adverbial clause like the *because* clause cannot be the subject of a verb. Correction—Start the sentence with *the sand*: *The sand in certain places had become as hard as cement because gypsum sand dissolves in water.*

5. Acceptable
7. *Then not be used* implies that *the machine* is the subject of the first main verb; however, *the machine's use* is the actual subject of that verb. *Correction*—Insert *the machine might* after *and then: The machine's use might be heavy . . . , and then the machine might not be used again. . . .*
9. Acceptable

Exercise (p. 495) on *-s* and *-es* verb endings. The verb forms that lack necessary *-s* endings are listed below alongside the number of the sentence in which they appear.

2. sets
3. knows
4. stops
5. seems
6. says
7. projects, interprets
9. attracts
11. says
12. looks, likes

Exercise (p. 496) on past tense and past participle forms not found in edited English.

1. Acceptable
3. Faulty—*ran.* Substitute *run.*
5. Acceptable
7. Faulty—*begun.* Substitute *began.*
9. Faulty—*went.* Substitute *gone.*

Exercise (p. 497) on incorrect pronoun forms.

1. Faulty—*he, I.* Substitute *him, me.*
3. Faulty—*who.* Substitute *whom.*
5. Acceptable
7. Faulty—*him, me.* Substitute *he, I.*
9. Faulty—*who.* Substitute *whom.*

Exercise (p. 498) on misspellings of possessive pronouns.

1. Faulty—*theirs'.* Acceptable—*theirs.*
3. Acceptable—*whose.*
5. Faulty—*her's.* Acceptable—*hers.*
7. Faulty—*their's.* Acceptable—*theirs.*
9. Faulty—*ours'.* Acceptable—*ours.*

Exercise (p. 500) on use of correct pronoun forms as the subjects of gerunds.

1. Acceptable—*his opponent aiming.*
3. Faulty—*him fishing.* Acceptable—*his fishing.*
5. Faulty—*them keeping.* Acceptable—*their keeping.*
7. Faulty—*Jan running.* Acceptable—*Jan's running.*
9. Acceptable—*our editing.*

PUNCTUATION AND MECHANICS

Exercise (p. 501) on end punctuation.

1. "... needy?"
3. ... installed.
5. ... signed.
7. ... 300 percent.
9. ... carefully.

Exercise (p. 503) on errors in comma usage.

1. Acceptable
3. ... across America, James ... struggle involved. ...
5. ... death, he utters. ...
7. ... Romeo, "Thy ... warm. Then. ..."
9. ... poet who. ...
11. ... with trash. On. ...
13. Acceptable
15. Acceptable

Exercise (p. 505) on errors in comma usage.

1. ... across the marsh, stepping. ...
3. ... gave her four alternatives: leave home; stay but find a full-time job; stay but get a part-time job and go to school; get married. ...
5. Acceptable
7. ... dinner; however, his mother. ...
9. Acceptable

Exercise (p. 506) on using colons.

1. The advantages of my plan are low cost. ... (No colon.)
3. Acceptable
5. ... of pharmacy: my desire. ...
7. Acceptable. (The sentence after the colon explains the sentence before the colon.)
9. ... factors: fatigue due to ...

Exercise (p. 507) on using dashes.

1. . . . Washington—these three giants. . . .
3. . . . surprising—indeed, it is incredible—that a mother. . . .
5. Monarch butterflies—hundreds and hundreds of them—came to the point of land. . . .

Exercise (p. 508) on using parentheses and brackets.

1. One person's idea (not mine, you may be sure) was to cancel. . . .
3. . . . you need several things: (1) spackling compound, (2) putty knife, (3) paint, (4) paint tray, (5) roller, (6) stepladder, and (7) drop cloths.
5. "Along the Ouisconsin [sic] river. . . ."

Exercise (p. 511) on using quotation marks.

1. *Silas Marner* is one. . . .
3. Acceptable
5. . . . as "table," "honor," "courtesy," and "diverse" originally were borrowed. . . .
7. ". . . ceremonious like tombs"?
9. Her article, "Black Holes: Their Origin and Role," appeared. . . .

Exercise (p. 512) on using ellipsis marks.

1. ". . . winter birds will come to a feeder even during a snowstorm."
3. "The existence of an army gave colonists a visible symbol of their unity in opposing the British. . . ."

Exercise (p. 513) on using apostrophes.

1. Faulty—*machines, its'*. Acceptable—*machine's, its*.
3. Faulty—*trucks*. Acceptable—*trucks'*. (*Trucks'* is a plural possessive and therefore requires an apostrophe.)
5. Faulty—*envelopes'*. Acceptable—*envelope's*.
7. Acceptable
9. Faulty—*dont*. Acceptable—*don't*.

Exercise (p. 514) on using hyphens in spelling words. The correct spellings of the words and phrases in the first column are as follows:

large sand bar
wildlife
hand-knitted sweater
ring-billed gull
hand-me-down garments
intra-abdominal

> ready-made clothing
> far-off places
> self-analysis
> wild whooping cranes
> new executive-suite
> pre-Napoleonic era
> bird-watching
> 200-horsepower engine
> back-country farmers
> loose-fitting clothing

Exercise (p. 515) on syllable division at the ends of lines. The correct syllable divisions at the ends of lines are as follows:

> Line 1—*no-* or *noticed*
> Line 2—*when*
> Line 4—*that*
> Line 7—*lit-* or *little*
> Line 8—*be-* or *begin*
> Line 9—*no-* or *nothing*

Exercise (p. 516) on the proper use of italics.

1. *Mountain Interval*
3. *daunger*
5. *not*

Exercise (p. 517) on the proper use of capitals and lowercase letters.

1. Wednesday
3. south, Mississippi
5. spring, Southwest

Exercise (p. 518) on using abbreviations.

1. department
3. M.D. (instead of "Doctor of Medicine")
5. New York, Adirondack Mountains

Exercise (p. 519) on using numbers.

1. Forty-five
3. $12,042.95
5. 325 pounds

Acknowledgments

Beavers—From "Rediscovery of the Underground Railroad" by Herman Beavers and Richard Littlejohn in *The Black Collegian*, April/May 1980. Copyright © 1980 by Black Collegiate Services, Inc. Reprinted by permission.   Black—From "Blacks in Electronics" in *The Black Collegian*, September 1981. Copyright © 1981 by Black Collegiate Services, Inc. Reprinted by permission.   Bodo—Peter Bodo, "Guillermo Vilas: How He's Found a New Tennis Life." *Tennis*, October 1982, p. 32.   Boles—From "Court Curves" by Doralice Donkewoet Boles in *Interiors*, February 1982. Copyright © 1982 by Billboard Publications, Inc. Reprinted by permission of Interiors Magazine.   Brody—From "Careers: Pharmacy" by Robert Brody. Reprinted with permission from *Working Woman*, April 1982. Copyright © 1982 by HAL Publications, Inc.   Business—"Computer Crimes" from *Business Periodicals Index*. Copyright © 1983 by The H. W. Wilson Company. Reprinted by permission.   Callahan—From "Boxing Shadows" by Tom Callahan in *Time*, November 29, 1982. Copyright © 1982 by Time Inc. All rights reserved. Reprinted by permission from *Time*.   Conrad—From *Letters from Joseph Conrad 1895–1924*, edited by Edward Garnett. Copyright 1928 by the Bobbs-Merrill Company, Inc. Used with permission of the publisher.   Corliss—From "Iced Coffee" by Richard Corliss in *Time*, November 24, 1980. Copyright © 1980 by Time Inc. All rights reserved. Reprinted by permission from *Time*.   Cover—Letter to the editor by Niceta Cover from *People*, July 6, 1981. Reprinted by permission of Neceta Cover.   "Why I'm Still Living at Home" by Ellen Darion in *McCall's*, October 1982. Reprinted by permission.   Didion—"On Keeping a Notebook" from *Slouching Towards Bethlehem* by Joan Didion. Copyright © 1966, 1968 by Joan Didion. Reprinted by permission of Farrar, Straus and Giroux, Inc.   Fischer—David H. Fischer, *Growing Old in America*. New York: Oxford University Press, 1977, pp. 90–91.   Halberstam—David Halberstam, "The Fire to Come in South Africa." *Atlantic*, May 1980, pp. 88–89.   Hardy—Thomas Hardy, "I Look into My Glass" in *Complete Poems*. New York: Macmillan Publishing Co., Inc., 1978.   Harris—From "Kansas City: It Calls Itself One of the Few Livable Cities" by Ronald Harris in *Ebony*, November 1980. Copyright © 1980 by Johnson Publishing Company, Inc. Reprinted by permission from *Ebony* Magazine.   Hellerstein—From "Cures that Kill" by David Hellerstein in *Harper's*, December 1980. Copyright © 1980 by Harper's Magazine. All rights reserved. Reprinted by special permission.   Inter-office memo to Paul Jacobs from Donna Hill of the National City Bank of Cleveland. Reprinted by permission.   Hillman—Letter to the editor by Ty Hillman from *Esquire*, July 1981. Reprinted by permission of Ty Hillman.   Hughes—"Theme for English B" from *Montage of a Dream Deferred* by Langston Hughes. Copyright 1951 by Langston Hughes. Copyright renewed 1979 by George Houston Bass. Reprinted by permission of Harold Ober Associates Incorporated.   Huston—From "The Meaningless Mean" by James A. Huston in *Chronicle of Higher Education*, January 19, 1983. Copyright © 1983 by the Chronicle of Higher Education. Reprinted by permission.   Hyde—H. Montgomery Hyde, *Oscar Wilde: A Biography*. New York: Farrar, Straus and Giroux, 1975, p. 13.   Kaplan—Letter to the editor by Stephen Kaplan from *Esquire*, July 1981. Reprinted by permission of Stephen Kaplan. Kennedy—"Who Killed King Kong?" by X. J. Kennedy in *Dissent*, Spring 1960. Copyright © 1960 by the Dissent Publishing Corporation. Reprinted by permission.   King—From pages 83–84 in "Letter from Birmingham Jail—April 16, 1963" from *Why We Can't Wait* by Martin Luther King, Jr. Copyright © 1963 by Martin Luther King, Jr. Reprinted by permission of Harper & Row, Publishers, Inc.   Kurle—From "The Whip-and-Tongue Graft" by Robert Kurle. Reprinted from *Organic Gardening*, Emmaus, PA 18049, January, 1978, with the permission of Rodale Press, Inc., Copyright © 1978.   Kwitny—Jonathan Kwitny, "Afghanistan: Crossroads of Conflict." *Atlantic*, May 1980, pp. 24, 26.   Laragh—From "Giving Salt a Fair Shake" by John H. Laragh in *Health*, February 1983. Copyright © 1983 by Family Media, Inc. Reprinted by special permission. All rights reserved. McCullers—Carson McCullers, "The Ballad of the Sad Cafe" in *The Ballad of the Sad Cafe and Other Stories*. New York: Houghton Mifflin Company, 1951.   Miller—From *Death of a*

Salesman by Arthur Miller. Copyright 1949, renewed 1977 by Arthur Miller. Reprinted by permission of Viking Penguin Inc.   Morrow—"The Great Bicycle Wars" by Lance Morrow in *Time*, November 24, 1980. Copyright © 1980 by Time Inc. All rights reserved. Reprinted by permission from *Time*.   Newton—Letter to the editor by P. Carter Newton from *Chicago Magazine*, August 1983. Reprinted by permission of P. Carter Newton.

Oney—From "The Last Roundup" by Steve Oney in *California*, November 1982. Copyright © 1982 by California Magazine, Inc. Reprinted by permission.   Orwell— George Orwell, "Politics and the English Language" in *Shooting an Elephant and Other Essays*. New York: Harcourt Brace Jovanovich, 1950.   Phillips—"Baseball's $20 Million Man" by B. J. Phillips in *Time*, December 29, 1980. Copyright © 1980 by Time Inc. All rights reserved. Reprinted by permission from *Time*.   Ramsey—Judith Ramsey, "How Tough Should Parents Be?" *Ladies' Home Journal*, September 1980, p. 42.   Robinson—"Mr. Flood's Party." Reprinted with permission of Macmillan Publishing Company from *Collected Poems* by Edwin Arlington Robinson. Copyright 1921 by Edwin Arlington Robinson, renewed 1949 by Ruth Nivison.   Sereny—From "Germany: The Rediscovery of Hitler" by Gitta Sereny in *Atlantic*, August 1978. Copyright © 1978 by Gitta Sereny. Reprinted by permission of the author.   Simon—Julian L. Simon, "The Scarcity of Raw Materials." *Atlantic*, June 1981, p. 33.   Simon—"Workers and Bums" by Roger Simon. Copyright © 1982 by Los Angeles Time Syndicate. Reprinted with permission.   Slavin —From "Winning Is Everything . . . Or Is It?" by Maeve Slavin in *House and Garden*, June 1979. Copyright © 1979 by The Conde Nast Publications Inc. Reprinted courtesy of House and Garden.   Smith—From "Raiding Grandma's Cabinet" by William E. Smith in *Time*, September 28, 1981. Copyright © 1981 by Time Inc. All rights reserved. Reprinted by permission from *Time*.   Time—From "Biography Comes of Age" in *Time*, July 2, 1979. Copyright © 1979 by Time Inc. All rights reserved. Reprinted by permission from *Time*.   Time—From "Life Along the Death Strip" in *Time*, September 15, 1980. Copyright © 1980 by Time Inc. All rights reserved. Reprinted by permission from *Time*.   Time —From "The Jolly Roger Still Flies" in *Time*, July 31, 1978. Copyright © 1978 by Time Inc. All rights reserved. Reprinted by permission from *Time*.   Updike—"The City" by John Updike in *The New Yorker*, November 16, 1981. Copyright © 1981 by John Updike. Reprinted by permission.   Whipple—A. B. C. Whipple, "The Raccoon Life in Darkest Suburbia." *Smithsonian*, August 1979, p. 86.   Yarrow—From "Starting a Day Care Center in Your Own Home" by Leah Yarrow in *Parents*, August 1980. Copyright © 1980 by Parents Magazine Enterprises. Reprinted by permission.   Young—"Jaywalker" from *The Names of a Hare in English* by David Young. Copyright © 1979 by David Young. Reprinted by permission.

INDEX

structure. *See* form

style, and active voice, 249; and parallel structure, 210, 212; and passive voice, 249; revision of, 220–21; and variety in sentences, 213–20. *See also* diction, sentences, words

subjects, 449–54; anticipatory, 451; in basic English sentence, 196–97; compound, 469, 483; expletive as, 451; nouns as, 449; noun substitutes as, 449; positioning of, 450–51

subordinate ideas, 38

subordination, 201–202; as revision strategy, 223; of clauses, 447. *See also* clauses

suffixes, 243–45

summary, 359–60

synonyms, choosing accurately, 245–48

tense, unnecessary shifts in, 490–91

term papers. *See* research papers

theme, 228; related to character, 306–310

thesaurus, 245–48

thesis statement, 106

thinking, patterns for invention, 50–55; steps in invention, 47–49

topical order, in analytic essays, 139–40; in essays of definition, 136; in paragraphs, 91–92

topic sentence, and direct support,

77; as guide to unity, 62; being specific, 65–66; construction of, 68; defined, 61, 62; final placement, 74–75; implied, 71; and indirect support, 77–78; initial placement, 69–70; in middle of paragraph, 72; and invention, 63–64; and level of generality, 64; and main idea, 62; placement of, 69–75; similarity to thesis statement, 106; refining through writing, 64; revision of, 68–69; split pattern, 71–72

transitions, 70, 119; in essays, 171–76; in paragraphs, 93–95; words and phrases, 93–95

transitive verbs, 456–57

unity, in essays, 107; in paragraphs, 60. *See also* main idea

usage, acceptable, 434–35; common errors in, 476, 500; faulty, 434–35; glossary of, 520–37

variety, in sentence length, 215–17; in sentence openers, 213–17; in word order, 217–20

verbals, 438–40; gerunds, 438–39; infinitives, 438; participles, 438–39; phrases, 462–63, 470

verbs, 438–40; auxiliary, 439–40; in basic English sentence, 196–97; intransitive, 455–56; irregular, 438;

linking, 458–59; main, 438, 451; modal, 439–40; phrases, 439, 454, 461–62; regular, 438; transitive, 456–57; unnesessary shifts in tense, 490–91; verbals, 438–40. *See also* predicate

vocabulary, strategies for improving, 240–48

voice, unnecessary shifts in, 491–92

wordiness, 228–31

word order, importance of, 196; inverted, 451; normal, 196, 450–51

words, abstract, 235–40; commonly confused, 520–37; concrete, 235–40; denotation and connotation, 232–35; errors in forms of, 495–500; plain language, 230–31; used to expand sentences, 197–99. *See also* diction, parts of speech, vocabulary

writing, application-of-concept papers, 416–20; in business, 324–25; for different disciplines, 398; as discovery, 2–4; evaluative reviews, 420–27; about the humanities, 398–415; lab reports, 428–31; about literature, 286–310; process of. *See* writing process; about the sciences, 415–31

writing process, 2–10; circularity of, 2–10, 178; models of, 3–4; in paragraphs, 98–100; and revision, 3–4, 8–9; steps of, 6–10

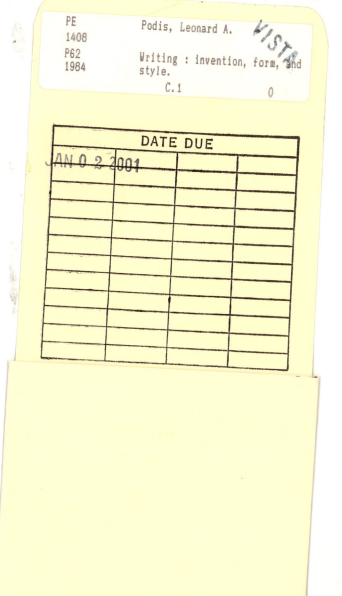

COMMON USAGE ERRORS